Bilingual Education and Bilingualism 1
Series Editors: Colin Baker and Nancy Hornberger

Foundations of Bilingual Education and Bilingualism

Second Edition

COLIN BAKER

Academic Consultant:
PROFESSOR OFELIA GARCÍA
School of Education, City College of New York

Multilingual Matters Ltd
Clevedon • Philadelphia • Adelaide

Library of Congress Cataloging in Publication Data

Baker, Colin, 1949-
Foundations of Bilingual Education and Bilingualism/Colin Baker, 2nd edn.
Bilingual Education and Bilingualism: 1.
Includes bibliographical references.
1. Education, Bilingual. 2. Education, Bilingual–Great Britain. 3. Bilingualism.
4. Bilingualism–Great Britain. I. Title. II. Series.
LC3715.B35
371.97–dc20   95-26506

British Library Cataloguing in Publication Data

A CIP catalogue record for this book is available from the British Library.

ISBN 1-85359-358-3 (hbk)
ISBN 1-85359-357-5 (pbk)

Multilingual Matters Ltd

UK: Frankfurt Lodge, Clevedon Hall, Victoria Road, Clevedon, Avon BS21 7SJ.
USA: 1900 Frost Road, Suite 101, Bristol, PA 19007, USA.
Australia: P.O. Box 6025, 83 Gilles Street, Adelaide, SA 5000, Australia.

Printed and bound in Great Britain by the Bath Press.

Foundations of
Bilingual Education and Bilingualism

BILINGUAL EDUCATION AND BILINGUALISM

Series Editors

Professor Colin Baker, *University of Wales, Bangor*
and Nancy Hornberger, *University of Pennsylvania*

Other Books in the Series

Becoming Bilingual: Language Acquisition in a Bilingual Community
  JEAN LYON
Building Bridges: Multilingual Resources for Children
  MULTILINGUAL RESOURCES FOR CHILDREN PROJECT
Curriculum Related Assessment, Cummins and Bilingual Children
  TONY CLINE and NORAH FREDERICKSON (eds)
Language Minority Students in the Mainstream Classroom
  ANGELA L. CARRASQUILLO and VIVIAN RODRIGUEZ
A Parents' and Teachers' Guide to Bilingualism
  COLIN BAKER
Policy and Practice in Bilingual Education
  O. GARCÍA and C. BAKER (eds)
Multicultural Child Care
  P. VEDDER, E. BOUWER and T. PELS
Teaching Science to Language Minority Students
  JUDITH W. ROSENTHAL
Working with Bilingual Children
  M.K. VERMA, K.P. CORRIGAN and S. FIRTH (eds)

Please contact us for the latest book information:
Multilingual Matters Ltd, Frankfurt Lodge, Clevedon Hall,
Victoria Road, Clevedon, Avon BS21 7SJ, England

Contents

Foreword

Through time, the task given to most teachers has been to educate children from their own communities, children with whom they were deeply familiar as they shared a common language and ethnicity. Decisions about the education of these children centered mostly on socio-pedagogical issues, having to do with the content of the curriculum and the appropriate educational methodology used to communicate that content.

But in the last thirty years, as the world has become increasingly inter-dependent, as ethnolinguistic diversity has become more recognized, and as the right to an education has been extended to more minority groups, teachers have been sternly challenged. The challenge comes from the new ethnolinguistic complexity that is increasingly reflected in their classrooms.

For some teachers, the change has to do with students who are now different linguistically, culturally, and perhaps racially from the children of their families and immediate communities. For others, the change hinges on their need to develop in children the ability to communicate with, and be mindful of, those who are different. For yet others, the change involves helping children whose ethnolinguistic identity is itself being transformed. In some cases, the teacher is faced with majority children for whom bilingualism is becoming a defining feature of their culture; in other cases, with children for whom the minority language has become the principal focus of cultural identity.

The greatest failure of contemporary education has been precisely its inability to help teachers understand the ethnolinguistic complexity of children, classrooms, speech communities, and society, in such a way as to enable them to make informed decisions about language and culture in the classroom. The success of Colin Baker's first edition of *Foundations of Bilingual Education and Bilingualism* confirms the need in all contemporary educational circles for information about the sociolinguistic and psycholinguistic issues that surround bilingualism and bilingual education.

This second edition keeps the features that made Baker's text so valuable; yet, it makes significant changes and additions. Baker has spent the last two years talking to students, educators, and scholars who have used the first edition. This second edition has benefited from the advice derived from these conversations with the international academic community.

As in the first edition, the book continues to offer a treatment of psychological and sociological questions that enables educators to take a more active role in defining what it is that they want to do in a classroom. The book seldom presents educators with a closed position. Rather, it gives theoretical and practical information from a variety of societal contexts, making it possible for teachers to see possibilities beyond the constraints of their particular classroom. Baker's is a liberating view of bilingual education because it follows neither a simple governmental definition nor a single societal perspective; and because it empowers teachers to make decisions about their chosen role in either developing or destroying their children's bilingualism. Thus the book performs the valuable function of raising the consciousness of the bilingual educator in her role as language planner.

Another aspect that has made Baker's book extremely popular, and that is preserved in this second edition, is its inter-disciplinary approach. Linguistic aspects are intertwined throughout the discussion of psychological, sociological, pedagogical and political issues. But at all times the teacher remains the focus, presenting the knowledge necessary to observe children, individuals, and speech communities; the knowledge necessary to decide on the socio-educational goals that would meet the needs observed; the knowledge necessary to design and develop programs, models and practices that would fit those goals.

While taking into account the plurality of societal contexts and of bilingual education models and strategies that characterizes the field, this second edition responds to many of the particular needs of bilingual educators, especially those in the United States. For example, although this edition continues to make no mention of the familiar labels used in the United States to limit the possibilities of bilingual education, it does present a history of language policy in the United States. This makes it easier for bilingual educators, whether in the United States or elsewhere, to understand their present role within a historical and sociological perspective.

Other important additions are the sections on Biliteracy and on Language Use in the bilingual classroom. Biliteracy is, after all, one of the most distinguishing characteristics of bilingual schooling, and one that teachers in particular are responsible for. A most important issue of bilingual schooling is how the two languages are allocated in the curriculum. Baker gives a full treatment of the topic, again offering a range of possibilities according to the different socio-educational needs of the many societies and language groups herein included.

As a keen observer of the European Union, Baker has included in this second edition a section on Bilingualism and the Economy, a topic that Baker himself feels has been neglected, and that is becoming extremely important in today's interdependent world.

Although the first edition of Baker's book covered the entire globe, it did not include a very important language minority population, the Deaf Community. This edition gives the Deaf the appropriate place they deserve within the field of bilingualism and bilingual education.

Finally, another topic in bilingual education that has become very important is the education of language minorities with special needs. This second edition also includes a section on Bilingual Special Education.

Baker introduces bilingualism on page one of his text by reminding us that whereas binoculars are for two eyes, bilingualism is simply not about two languages. Indeed, the lenses through which bilingualism and bilingual education are examined in this book extend and, at the same time, deepen our definitions and knowledge. Baker provides us not simply with binoculars, but with powerful lenses through which the multiple visions of bilingualism and bilingual education are reflected.

As a US bilingual educator, first a classroom practitioner and then an instructor of other bilingual teachers, I am poignantly aware of how important it is to bring Baker's multiple vision to classroom teachers; for teachers are often caught between administrative policies, parental requests, children's needs, and their own abilities and attitudes. The image of their classroom then becomes the only reality they see through their limited lens. Baker's book allows them to see their reality reflected and altered in different societal contexts, with other bilingual individuals, and other educational programs. It allows them to find the cracks in their static vision, and to see the possibility of transformation and change in their own educational practices and in their society.

My own vision has been expanded through the constant interaction I have had with Colin Baker while he prepared the first and second editions of this book. Our almost daily e-mail exchanges have become a most important way to check positions derived from seeing only the local bilingual reality. I contributed to the multiplicity of the vision contained in the first edition only because Baker is a good listener. But this second edition has gone beyond our own vision, including now all the many comments, suggestions, reflections and criticisms that have been passed on by students and educators. In this second edition, Baker's talent becomes apparent in his ability to connect more closely with the multiple readers of the first edition, bringing the focus closer to home, while at the same time pushing the readers to see realities beyond the ones that confront them.

Professor Ofelia García
School of Education, City College of New York

Acknowledgements

The idea of this introductory text derived from a fellow Essex gentleman, Mike Grover. He wrote one simple sentence that has affected my academic life ever since: 'Consider writing THE textbook on Bilingual Education'. My thanks to Mike of Multilingual Matters for not only risking me with this responsibility, but also for his continual encouragement and friendly, facilitative style. No publisher can be so gratifying to work with than Mike Grover.

In the first edition, I recorded my grateful thanks to those who helped in the construction of that edition. I wish to repeat my sincere gratitude to: Iolo Williams, Andrew Cohen, Edward David, Viv Edwards, Peter Garrett, Sharon Lapkin, Hilaire Lemoine, Bernard Spolsky, Merrill Swain, Ann Illsley and Dilys Parry. Choosing to write on bilingualism has always been inspired by my Welsh wife, Anwen, and three bilingual children who daily teach me the beauty of bilingualism. Their loving support is eternally appreciated. *Diolch yn fawr iawn am bopeth.*

Multilingual Matters perceptively appointed Ofelia García of the City College of New York as Academic Consultant for the first and second edition. I have always received detailed, sensitive, wise and judicious advice on each draft chapter. Achilles' heels have been quickly spotted, detailed polishing recommended, and cultural assumptions gently revealed. A great debt is owed for her generous amounts of time and patience, both in scores of e-mail responses and when visiting New York. The ideas shared, and her deep empathy for language minorities has been a true learning experience.

Pocos lectores hay que sean tan comprensivos, entusiastas, perspicaces, y conocedores tanto de la escuela como de la calle, y tan capaces de saber criticar y al mismo tiempo saber apoyar. Generosa y entregada a sus estudiantes tanto como a su investigación, la Profesora Ofelia García supo enseñarme, de hecho y de palabra, por correo electrónico y por su ejemplo personal, como se puede combinar en una misma persona el elevado logro académico y el alto altruísmo personal.

Professor García was first introduced to me in a letter from the publishers. The letter simply said: 'I have been in contact with one of the present top-rate people in the States'. So have I, and I totally agree.

The help and support given me has been extremely generous and far more than is deserved. However, the responsibility for all that is not as fair or just as it should be, is totally mine.

COLIN BAKER

An Introduction to the Second Edition

When the first edition of *Foundations* was written and published, a substantial sigh of relief reverberated around. Like a ferret, I had collected the available literature on bilingualism and bilingual education. Like a squirrel, I had carefully accumulated, then read and reviewed it all. The eighteen original chapters were written, rewritten, repetitively edited, passed for initial comment, then sent to learned experts in Europe and the United States. The book was revamped and revised. By September 30th 1992, the task allocated to me by the Multilingual Matters was complete. And forever. I could revert to what comes more naturally: researching and writing on specialist academic topics with increasing myopicity.

The only predictable part of life is unpredictability. I certainly didn't predict the first edition of this book would sell so many copies in so many different areas of the world. The reviews of the first edition were kind and understood the need for a book that attempted to be comprehensive and readable. However, the continuing sales of the book made me feel increasingly uncomfortable. Written between 1990 and 1992, the datedness of some sections, the movement of new ideas in bilingual education, the thrill of reading submitted manuscripts and proposals as a Series Editor for Multilingual Matters, and obtaining some important feedback from lectures in the United States and Britain, all made it important to up-date the book. The ferret and squirrel habits remained, even though administration and committee obligations tried, and failed, to change those habits.

These were the initial stimuli for producing a second edition. There were also critical bull's-eyes in reviews of the first edition that required a rethinking of the contents. Professors Nancy Dorian, Viv Edwards and John Eggleston were particularly instrumental here. Each made highly perceptive remarks in their reviews of the first edition that became embedded in my own critical view of the first edition. I am particularly grateful to Viv Edwards for an important observation about literacy that led to major changes in the second edition. The second edition will hopefully reveal that the subject matter of bilingualism and particularly bilingual education is not static. It is still developing and evolving. Such movements are represented in the new edition, particularly in chapters four, and eleven to twenty.

Instructors, in particular, will wish to know what are the specific changes in the second edition. First, there are many minor changes. For example, references have been updated, research findings added, study questions added, corrections made and more commentary added. Second, and importantly, there are new sections and chapters. The **additions** include: Literacy and Biliteracy (new chapters); the History of Bilingual Education in the United States; Assessment and Bilingualism; Bilingual Special Education; the Dual Coding Model of the Brain; Economics and Bilingualism; the Deaf and Bilingualism, and Language Boundaries in Classrooms.

The second edition does not go into great detail on classroom methodology. There are important reasons why this is so. Professor Ofelia García, City College New York, and the present author compiled a **Reader** to accompany this book. Areas that are important, but were only very briefly covered in the first edition of *Foundations*, are a major part of this reader entitled: *Policy and Practice in Bilingual Education: Extending the Foundations* (1995) and published by Multilingual Matters Ltd. This Reader contains a selection of the most important and influential recent contributions on bilingualism and bilingual education. Each has become a 'classic' or a pivotal paper. The Reader provides an introduction to recent fundamental and formative ideas on Bilingualism and Bilingual Education in four sections: Section 1, Policy and Legislation on Bilingualism in Schools and Bilingual Education; Section 2, Implementation of Bilingual Policy in Schools: Structuring Schools; Section 3, Using Bilingualism in Instruction: Structuring Classrooms; Section 4, Using the Bilingualism of the School Community: Teachers and Parents.

Discussions with students and instructors about the first edition led to attempting the following: to balance a North American and European perspective while increasingly revealing the global interest in bilingualism and bilingual education; to attempt to marry language minority perspectives with those of relatively advantaged bilinguals (e.g. speakers of French and English) and by doing so, to celebrate both for a common good; to write in straightforward English while doing justice to the depth of ideas; to write for undergraduates, postgraduates and in-service and pre-service teachers; to provide a balanced, fair and constructive introduction while adding analysis, interpretation and discussion; and to provide a synthesis of relevant material on bilingualism and bilingual education while adding a critical commentary.

Some instructors wanted a version that was only for Europe or only for the US. Other instructors indicated that the subject is international and transcontinental and wanted to retain a book that was universal. This is my bias; that any geographical limiting would do a disservice to one basis of the book: language minorities gain strength from association, and lose if isolated. Also, there are so many common features of bilingualism and bilingual education throughout the world that a universal perspective is liberating and empowering. Any nationally insular or introspective 'Foundations of Bilingualism' would be a self-contradiction and parochialize an authentically global subject.

In compiling the second edition, I have been superbly supported by Professor Ofelia García (City College of New York), Dr Sylvia Prys Jones (University of Wales, Bangor), Mike and Marjukka Grover (Multilingual Matters Ltd), Jim Kyle (Centre for Deaf Studies, University of Bristol), Professor Viv Edwards (University of Reading) and Professor Nancy Hornberger, University of Pennsylvania. In producing a Japanese translation of *Foundations*, Professor Hideo Oka's meticulousness and concern for accuracy of detail enabled some rough edges to be made smooth. To each, I offer my great gratitude for their time, generosity, patience and care. I am solely responsible for imperfections that remain in the text.

The hope is that the second edition will have retained the strengths of the first edition, eradicated perceived weaknesses of the first edition, and added new text to provide a comprehensive, international introduction to this increasingly important area of study.

Introduction to the Book

This book is intended as an introduction to bilingual education and bilingualism. Written from a cross-disciplinary perspective, the book covers a wide range of topics: individual and societal concepts in minority and majority languages; childhood developmental perspectives; general bilingual education issues, bilingual and second language classrooms, and political and multicultural perspectives.

In writing this introductory textbook, tough decisions had to be made as to what to include and exclude, what to present in detail and what to summarize, what assumptions to explore and what to take 'as read'. There was a debate as to what level to pitch the analysis and prose to avoid being simplistic and patronizing but also to avoid mystifying complexity. Another compromise surrounded developing a clear structure when there are myriads of inter-connections between the parts. I have often been asked about a variety of chapters: 'Why don't you put Chapter X earlier?' I agree, everything should be earlier. The introductions to the two sections explain the order of the book.

An attempt is made to balance the psychological and the sociological, the macro education issues and the micro classroom issues, the linguistic and the sociopolitical, and to balance discussion at individual and societal levels. The book is designed for a new generation of bilingual students. Therefore, an attempt is made to be inclusive of the major concerns in bilingualism and bilingual education with a future perspective. Faced with the social and political problems that surround bilinguals, students will find in this book an attempt to face constructively those problems and recognize the positive values and virtues in a future bilingual and multicultural world.

In a wide ranging, foundational textbook, the order and structure of the contents is important. For the novice, the structure may influence the accommodation of future reading and experience. This book starts with wide, macro issues, and then funnels down to specific, micro issues. Definitional, sociological and psychological issues provide the foundation. Discussions of bilingual education and bilingual classrooms are built on that essential foundation. However, the book is more than a cross-disciplinary foundation with a series of education layers built on top. Within the boundaries of clarity in writing style and readable structuring, explicit inter-connections are made between chapters. A simple

map of these inter-connections is given in Appendix 4. This conceptual map will, for most, only make sense after reading the whole book. The map also provides the instructor with a simplified but integrated plan of the book. It is an attempt to avoid the compartmentalization that sometimes results from reading discrete chapters, to show how themes link together into an integrated whole.

In writing the book, a constant challenge has been 'From whose perspective?' There are majority mainstream viewpoints, relatively advantaged minority language viewpoints and various disadvantaged minority language viewpoints. There are left wing and right wing politics, activist and constructivist ideas. The book attempts to represent a variety of viewpoints and beliefs. Where possible, multiple perspectives are shared. Readers and reviewers have kindly pointed out some of the hidden and implicit assumptions made, and kindly provided alternative viewpoints that I have tried to represent faithfully in the text. Where there are conclusions and dominating perspectives, I alone stand responsible.

Another problem has concerned generalization and contextualization. The book was written for an international audience to reflect ideas that transcend national boundaries. The book attempts to locate issues of international generalizability. Unfortunately, space limits discussion of a variety of regional and national language situations. There are other writings that will provide necessary contextualization. A list of these is presented after the last chapter. Where particular situations have been discussed (e.g. Canadian Immersion or US Language Minority debates), it is usually because of the thoroughness of documentation and the depth of analysis in the surrounding literature. Where bilingual situations are discussed, by inference this will usually include multilingual situations. In this book, multilinguals are implied in the use of the term 'bilinguals'.

In an attempt to make the contents of this book relevant to a variety of contexts and regions, various chapters focus on **integrating theories**. From one individual research study, it is usually impossible to generalize. A study from Canada may say little about Catalans. Results on six year olds may say nothing about sixteen or sixty year olds. Research on middle-class children in a French and English, dual majority language environment (e.g. Canada) may say little or nothing about children from a lower social class in a 'subtractive' bilingual environment (where the second language is likely to replace the first language). Therefore, an overview and integration of major areas of bilingual research is required. From a gray mass of research (e.g. on second language acquisition) and sometimes from a paucity of research (e.g. on cognition and bilingualism), a theoretical framework will attempt to outline the crucial parameters and processes. Thus a theoretical framework on a particular area of bilingualism may attempt to do one or more of the following: attempt to explain phenomena; integrate a diversity of (apparently contradictory) findings; locate the key parameters and interactions operating; be able to predict outcomes and patterns of bilingual behavior; be capable of testing for falsification or refinement; express the various conditions that will allow the theory to be appropriate in a variety of contexts.

ORGANIZATION OF THE BOOK

The book is divided into two sections: **The Individual and Social Nature of Bilingualism**, and **Bilingual Education Policies and Classroom Practices**.

Section A: The Individual and Social Nature of Bilingualism

The starting point of the book is an introduction to the language used in discussing bilingual education and bilingualism. Not only are important terms introduced, but also key concepts, distinctions and debates which underpin later chapters are presented. There are important dualisms and paradoxes throughout the study of bilingualism: the individual bilingual person as different from groups and societies where bilinguals live; the linguistic view compared with the sociocultural view; preservation and revivalist viewpoints; language skills and language competences; subtractive and additive forms of bilingualism. These are introduced in the first section which presents foundational issues that precede and influence discussions about bilingual education. Bilingual education is a component in a wider whole and directly relates to underlying macro issues. Before we can sensibly talk about bilingual education we need to tackle questions such as:

• Who are bilinguals?
• How does bilingual education fit into minority language maintenance, language decay and language revival?
• How does a child become bilingual?
• What effect does the home and the neighborhood play in developing bilingualism?
• Does bilingualism have a positive or negative effect on thinking?

Section B: Bilingual Education Policies and Classroom Practices

Having contextualized bilingual education inside more universal issues, the second section focuses on the many aspects of bilingual education. The section commences with a broad discussion of different types of bilingual education, followed by an examination of the effectiveness of those types. After a focus on systems of bilingual education, the section proceeds to examine bilingual classrooms. Situations where bilingualism is fostered through preserving the minority language, and situations involving the learning or acquisition of a second language are discussed. The underlying questions are:

• What forms of bilingual education are more successful?
• What are the aims and outcomes of different types of bilingual education?
• What are the essential features and approaches of a classroom fostering bilingualism?
• What are the key problems and issues of bilingual classrooms?
• How is a second language best learnt in a classroom setting?

The second section continues by looking at the political and cultural dimensions that surround bilingualism in society (and bilingual education in particular). Different views of the overall value and purpose of bilingualism join together many of the threads of the book, and culminate in a consideration of the nature of multiculturalism in society, in school and the classroom. The finale of the book responds to integrating and concluding issues such as:

- Why are there different viewpoints about language minorities and bilingual education?
- Why do some people prefer the assimilation of language minorities and others prefer linguistic diversity?
- Can schools play a role in a more multicultural and less racist society?

Study Questions and Study Activities

Study questions and study activities are placed at the end of each chapter. These are designed for revision purposes and for students wishing to extend their learning by engaging in various practical activities. Such activities are flexible and adaptable. Instructors and students will be able to vary them according to local circumstances. Many more study activities are found in the Reader that accompanies this text.

To end the beginning. The motivating force behind the book is to introduce students to a positive world of bilingualism and bilingual education. The book has been written for minority language students seeking to understand and preserve, and for majority language students seeking to become more sensitized. The book is an attempt to contribute to the conservation of a colorful world in which bilinguals and multiculturals are increasingly important language preservationists and diplomats between cultures. Bilinguals help preserve the variety and the beauty of the language garden of the world. Bilinguals are environmentally friendly people.

SECTION A

The Individual and Social Nature of Bilingualism

Section A of the book engages four foundational areas of bilingualism. Each area aims to provide a vocabulary and a framework for understanding bilingual education and bilingual classrooms which are considered in Chapters 10 and 20. These four areas are:

THE TERMINOLOGY OF BILINGUALISM

Most social science topics have a particular vocabulary used to refine discussion. Bilingualism and bilingual education is no exception. Along with the introduction of vocabulary go important definitions and distinctions which are examined mainly in Chapter 1, but also in Chapters 2, 3 and 4. The aim is to introduce not just terminology but concepts and constructs needed to understand more deeply bilingual people and situations.

Terms and concepts raise issues about 'measurement'. For example, 'to what extent' someone is bilingual suggests that measurement (quantitative and qualitative) may sometimes be required. Chapter 2 examines the measurement of bilingualism. Such measurement is not important in itself but aids conceptual clarification and is shown in Chapter 2 to have direct curriculum relevance.

THE SOCIAL NATURE OF BILINGUALISM

Chapters 3 and 4 move on from an 'individual person' consideration (which underlies Chapters 1 and 2) to a focus on groups and communities of language speakers. Language speakers live in language communities. Such language communities often change in their use of two languages. Therefore Chapters 3 and 4 consider key societal topics such as language planning, language shift, language maintenance, language death, language vitality, language revival and language reversal. The presupposition is that bilingual education is part of a wider social and political movement. Education is used to effect

1

language change; it is also affected by language shift. The social and political nature of two languages in contact is returned to as a finale to the book.

THE INDIVIDUAL DEVELOPMENT OF BILINGUALISM

Chapters 5 and 6 consider various routes in infancy, childhood and adulthood to achieving bilingualism. The role of parents, community and society as well as individual differences in development are discussed. Through presenting whole models and theories of bilingual development, the accent is on showing how social factors join individual factors in dual language acquisition. The developmental path to bilingualism is not simple. Single factors such as age of learning and aptitude in languages cannot be considered in isolation. Thus Chapter 6 provides holistic, interactive and integrated frameworks from different authors. The aim is to portray simply the complexity of bilingual development through comprehensive major models and theories. Instead of integrating and collapsing these theories, their original integrity as 'stand-alone' theories has been maintained.

THINKING AND BILINGUALISM

Section A of the book concludes by tackling the question of whether bilingualism affects thinking. Are there advantages, disadvantages or no effects for being bilingual when considering thinking skills and processes? Does bilingualism affect a person's 'intelligence'? Do bilinguals think more creatively if they have dual vocabularies and grammars? Are there differences between bilinguals and monolinguals inside the operating system of the brain? These questions are tackled in Chapter 7 ('intelligence') and 8 (thinking products and processes). Chapter 9 draws together parts of Chapters 5 to 8 by examining a theory that has evolved to explain research on the development of languages and thinking. This theory is shown to have direct relevance to the classroom.

CHAPTER 1

Bilingualism: Definitions and Distinctions

CHAPTER 1

Bilingualism:
Definitions and Distinctions

INTRODUCTION

Since a bicycle has two wheels and binoculars are for two eyes, it would seem that bilingualism is simply about two languages. The aim of this chapter is to show that the ownership of two languages is not so simple as having two wheels or two eyes. Ask someone if they are bilingual. While some may answer 'yes' or 'no', others would wish to qualify their answer. Is someone bilingual if they are fluent in one language but less than fluent in their other language? Is someone bilingual if they rarely or never use one of their languages? Such basic questions need addressing before other topics in this book can be sensibly discussed.

Before examining these questions, it is important to make an **initial distinction between bilingualism as an individual phenomenon and bilingualism as a group or societal possession**. Bilingualism and multilingualism can be examined as the possession of the individual. Various themes in this book start with bilingualism as experienced by individual people. For example, a discussion of whether or not bilingualism affects thinking requires research on individual monolinguals and bilinguals. From sociology, sociolinguistics, politics, geography, education and social psychology comes a different perspective. Bilinguals and multilinguals are usually found in groups. Such groups may be located in a particular region (e.g. Catalans in Spain), or may be scattered across communities (e.g. Chinese in the US). Bilinguals may form a distinct language group as a majority or a minority. Bilinguals and multilinguals within a country may be analyzed as a distinct group. For example, linguists study how the vocabulary of bilingual groups change across time. Geographers plot the density of bilinguals in a country. Educationists examine bilingual educational policy and provision for minority language groups.

The first distinction is therefore between bilingualism as an individual possession and as a group possession. This is usually termed **individual bilingualism and societal**

bilingualism. Like most distinctions, there are important links between the two parts. For example, the attitudes of individuals towards a particular language may affect language maintenance, language restoration, language shift or language death in society. In order to understand the term 'bilingualism', some important further distinctions at the **individual** level are discussed in this chapter. An introduction to bilingualism as a group possession (societal bilingualism) is provided in Chapter 3.

TERMINOLOGY

If a person is asked whether he or she speaks two languages, the question is ambiguous. A person may be **able** to speak two languages, but tends to speak only one language in practice. Alternatively, the individual may regularly speak two languages, but competence in one language may be limited. Another person will use one language for conversation and another for writing and reading. The essential distinction is therefore between **ability** and **use**. This is sometimes referred to as the difference between **degree** and **function**. This chapter continues by examining bilinguals' language abilities. Language use is discussed later.

Before discussing the nature of language abilities, a note about **terminology**. Entry into the many areas of bilingualism and bilingual education is helped by understanding often used terms and distinctions. There exists a range of terms in this area: language ability, language achievement, language competence, language performance, language proficiency and language skills. Do they all refer to the same entity, or are there subtle distinctions between the terms? To add to the problem, different authors and researchers sometimes tend to adopt their own specific meanings and distinctions. There is no standardized use of these terms (Stern, 1992).

Language **skills** tend to refer to highly specific, observable, clearly definable components such as handwriting. In contrast, **language competence** is a broad and general term, used particularly to describe an inner, mental representation of language, something latent rather than overt. Such competence refers usually to an underlying system inferred from language performance. **Language performance** hence becomes the outward evidence for language competence. By observing general language comprehension and production, language competence may be presumed. **Language ability** and **language proficiency** tend to be used more as 'umbrella' terms and therefore used somewhat ambiguously. For some, language ability is a general, latent disposition, a determinant of eventual language success. For others, it tends to be used as an outcome, similar but less specific than language skills, providing an indication of current language level. Similarly, language proficiency is sometimes used synonymously with language competence (e.g. Ellis, 1985); other times as a specific, measurable outcome from language testing. However, both language proficiency and language ability are distinct from **language achievement** (attainment). Language achievement is usually seen as the outcome of formal instruction. Language proficiency and language ability are, in contrast, viewed as the product of a variety of mechanisms: formal learning, informal uncontrived language acquisition (e.g. on the street) and of individual characteristics such as 'intelligence'.

BILINGUAL ABILITY

The Four Language Abilities

If we confine the question 'Are you bilingual?' to ability in two languages, the issue becomes 'what ability'? There are four basic language abilities: **listening, speaking, reading and writing**. These four abilities fit into two dimensions: receptive and productive skills; oracy and literacy. The following table illustrates:

	Oracy	Literacy
Receptive skills	Listening	Reading
Productive skills	Speaking	Writing

The table suggests avoiding a simple classification of who is, or is not, bilingual. Some speak a language, but do not read or write in a language. Some listen with understanding and read a language (passive bilingualism) but do not speak or write that language. Some understand a spoken language but do not themselves speak that language. To classify people as either bilinguals or monolinguals is too simplistic. Or, to return to the opening analogies, the two wheels of bilingualism exist in different sizes and styles. The two lenses of bilingualism will vary in strength and size.

The four basic language abilities do not exist in black and white terms. Between black and white are not only many shades of gray; there also exist a wide variety of colors. The multi-colored landscape of bilingual abilities is now portrayed. Each language ability can be more or less developed. Reading ability can be simple and basic to fluent and accomplished. Someone may listen with understanding in one context (e.g. shops) but not in another context (e.g. an academic lecture). This suggests that the four basic abilities can be further refined into sub-scales and dimensions. There are **skills within skills**. The main abilities have traditionally been listed as: pronunciation, extent of vocabulary, correctness of grammar, the ability to convey exact meanings in different situations and variations in style.

The range and type of sub-skills that can be measured is large and debated (Lado, 1961; Mackey, 1965; Macnamara, 1969; Oller, 1979; Carroll, 1980; Baetens Beardsmore, 1986). Language abilities such as speaking or reading can be divided into increasingly microscopic parts. Numerous colors are needed to paint an accurate picture. What in practice is tested and measured to portray an individual's bilingual performance is considered later in the book. What has emerged so far is that a person's ability in two languages will tend to evade simple categorization. Language abilities are multidimensional.

If language abilities are multicolored, and if bilinguals have a range of colors in both languages, then positive terms are needed to portray the variety. Calling bilinguals ESL (English Second Language) students in Canada and Britain, LEP (Limited English Proficiency) students in the US is negative and pejorative. Such labels stress children's perceived deficiency rather than their proficiencies, children's perceived 'deprivation' rather than their accomplishments, their lower, marginalized, minority status through majority eyes rather than their bilingual potentiality. Such labels stress past and present performance rather than potentialities and the possibility of full bilingualism.

A Fifth Language Competence

The four basic language abilities are commonly regarded as speaking, listening, reading and writing. However, there are times when a person is not speaking, listening, reading or writing but still using language. As Skutnabb-Kangas (1981) proposes, the language used for **thinking** may be a fifth area of language competence. This may be simply termed inner speech and placed under the umbrella title of 'speaking'. It may alternatively be worth differentiating from actual speaking as it raises the dimension of the ability of bilinguals to use both languages as thinking tools. Cummins (1984b) expresses this notion as cognitive competence in a language. That is, the ability to use one or both languages for reasoning and deliberation.

Minimal and Maximal Bilingualism

So far, it has been argued that deciding who is or is not bilingual is difficult. Simple categorization is arbitrary and requires a value judgment about the minimal competence needed to achieve a label of 'bilingual'. Therefore, a classic definition of bilingualism such as 'the native-like control of two or more languages' (Bloomfield, 1933) appears too extreme and maximalist ('native like'). The definition is also ambiguous (what is meant by 'control' and who forms the 'native' reference group?). At the other end is a minimalist definition, as in Diebold's (1964) concept of *incipient bilingualism*. (See the end of chapter for further terms and distinctions in bilingualism.) The term *incipient bilingualism* allows people with minimal competence in a second language to squeeze into the bilingual category. Tourists with a few phrases and business people with a few greetings in a second language would be incipient bilinguals. The danger of being too exclusive is not overcome by being too inclusive. Trawling with too wide a fishing net will catch too much variety and therefore make discussion about bilinguals ambiguous and imprecise. Trawling with narrow criteria may be too insensitive and restrictive.

Who is categorized as a bilingual or not will depend on the purpose of the categorization. At different times, governments, for example, may wish to include or exclude language minorities. Where a single indigenous language exists (e.g. in Ireland and Wales), a government may wish to maximize its count of bilinguals. A high count may indicate government success in its indigenous language policy. In comparison, in a suppressive, assimilationist approach, minority languages and bilinguals may be minimized (e.g. England).

Is there a middle ground in-between maximal and minimal definitions? The danger is in making arbitrary cut-off points about who is bilingual or not along the competence dimensions. Differences in classification will exist in terms of what language abilities make someone bilingual, and in terms of how much ability someone must possess to be labeled as bilingual.

One alternative is to move away from the multi-colored canvas of proficiency levels to a portrait of everyday use of the two languages. Categorization of bilinguals by their use of language is considered later in the chapter. Before such consideration, important labels and distinctions in terms of language ability are discussed.

Balanced Bilinguals

The literature on bilingualism frequently spotlights one particular group of bilinguals whose competences in both languages are well developed. Someone who is approximately equally fluent in two languages across various contexts may be termed an equilingual or ambilingual or, more commonly, **a balanced bilingual**. As will be considered in Chapter 8, balanced bilinguals are important when discussing the possible cognitive advantages of bilingualism.

Balanced bilingualism is sometimes used as an idealized concept. Fishman (1971) has argued that rarely will anyone be equally competent across all situations. Most bilinguals will use their two languages for different purposes and functions. For example, a person may use one language at work; the other language at home and in the local community.

Balanced bilingualism is also a problematic concept for other reasons. The balance may exist at a low level of competence in the two languages. Someone may have two relatively undeveloped languages which are nevertheless approximately equal in proficiency. While this is within the literal interpretation of 'balanced' bilingual, it is not the sense employed by many researchers on bilingualism. The implicit idea of balanced bilingualism has often been of 'reasonable' or 'good' competence in both languages. A child who can understand the delivery of the curriculum in school in either language, and operate in classroom activity in either language would be an example of a balanced bilingual.

Should we conclude that balanced bilingualism is of no use as a term? While it has limitations of definition and measurement, it has proved to be of value in research and discussion (see Chapter 8). However, categorizing individuals into such groups raises the issue of comparisons.

What is judged normal, proficient, skilled, fluent or competent? Who judges? The danger may be in using monolinguals as the point of reference. Grosjean (1985) argues that comparing bilinguals and monolinguals does not compare like with like. Can we fairly judge a 100 meter sprinter against a decathlete? Can we justly compare someone who only uses the breast stroke with a medley swimmer? Is it inappropriate to compare monolingual proficiency and dual language proficiency? Should bilinguals only be measured and categorized by reference to other bilinguals? When, for example, someone learns English as a second language, should that competency in English be measured against monolingual English speakers or against 'balanced' bilinguals?

'Semilingualism'/'Double Semilingualism'

Bilinguals will tend to be dominant in one of their languages in all or some of their language abilities. This may vary with context and change over time. Dominance in one language may change over time with geographical or social mobility. For others, the dominance may be relatively stable across time and place. The topic of dominance will be considered later (Chapter 2) when tests are discussed. For the present, there is a group that has been proposed as distinct from balanced and dominant bilinguals. Sometimes termed pejoratively as semilinguals or double semilinguals, the group is regarded as not having 'sufficient' competence in either language.

Hansegård (1975; see Skutnabb-Kangas, 1981) described semilingualism in terms of deficits in six language competences:

- Size of vocabulary
- Correctness of language
- Unconscious processing of language (automatism)
- Language creation (neologization)
- Mastery of the functions of language (e.g. emotive, cognitive)
- Meanings and imagery

Thus a semilingual is seen as someone with quantitative and qualitative deficiencies in both their languages when compared with monolinguals.

A **'semilingual'** is considered to exhibit the following profile in both their languages: displays a small vocabulary and incorrect grammar, consciously thinks about language production, is stilted and uncreative with each language, and finds it difficult to think and express emotions in either language.

The notion of semilingualism, or **double semilingualism**, has received criticism (e.g. Skutnabb-Kangas, 1981). There are **six major problems**. **First**, the term has taken on disparaging and belittling overtones, particularly in Scandinavia and with **in-migrant** groups in the US. [The term in-migrant is used throughout the book to avoid the negative connotations of the term 'immigrant' and to avoid the imprecise and loaded distinctions between migrant workers, guest workers, short stay, long stay and relatively permanent in-migrants]. Semilingualism may be used as a negative label which invokes expectations of underachievement which may evoke a self-fulfilling prophecy. **Second**, if languages are relatively undeveloped, the origins may not be in bilingualism *per se*, but in the economic, political and social conditions that evoke under-development. This is a theme considered in detail in later chapters. The danger of the term semilingualism is that it locates the origins of under-development in the internal, individual possession of bilingualism, rather than in external, societal factors that co-exist with bilingualism. Thus the term may be a political rather than a linguistic concept. **Third**, many bilinguals use their two languages for different purposes and events. Language may be specific to a context. A person may be competent in some contexts but not in others.

Fourth, the educational tests that are most often used to measure language proficiencies and differentiate between people may be insensitive to the qualitative aspects of languages and to the great range of language competences. Language tests may measure a small, unrepresentative sample of a person's total language behavior. This is considered in detail in the next chapter.

Fifth, there is dispute regarding the frequency of double semilingualism, for example among Finnish–Swedish speakers. How many or how few fit clearly into a semilingual category will be disputed. Establishing a cut-off point for who is and is not a double semilingual will be arbitrary and value laden. Is the term an empty concept lacking in meaning? There is a lack of sound objective empirical evidence on such a categorization.

Sixth, the comparison with monolinguals may not be fair. It is important to distinguish if bilinguals are 'naturally' qualitatively and quantitatively different from monolinguals in their use of their two languages (as a function of being bilingual). An apparent deficiency may be due to unfair comparisons with monolinguals.

The criticisms raise serious doubts about the value of the term 'semilingualism'. However, this does not detract from there being many language abilities on which people do differ, with some people at the earlier stages of development. Being at an early stage may not be a result of being bilingual. Economic and social factors or educational provision may, for example, be the cause of under-development in language. Rather than highlight the apparent 'deficit' in language development, the more positive approach is to emphasize that, when suitable conditions are provided, languages are easily capable of evolution beyond the 'semi' state.

Conversational Fluency and Academic Language Competence

So far, the chapter has centered on the variety of language abilities and the danger of categorization using a small or biased selection of language sub-skills. The question is whether the variety of sub-skills can be reduced to a small number of important dimensions. Hernández-Chávez *et al.* (1978), for example, suggest there are 64 separate components to language proficiency. In comparison, tests abound which purport to measure reading ability as a single entity. Many reading tests tacitly assume that reading can be reduced to one dimension (Levy & Goldstein, 1984).

Is it the case that children who perform well on a spelling test also do well on an oral comprehension test? Oller's (1982) research suggested that different language skills do tend to correlate moderately well. If a variety of measures of speaking, reading and writing are analyzed, the claim was of one underlying dimension. The individual test scores could be collapsed into one global score. The overlap was sufficient for Oller & Perkins (1980) to suggest that there exists a single factor of **global language proficiency**. This global factor is seen as co-existing with other specific language factors. However, such specific factors are seen as measuring relatively minor language skills.

The idea of a global language factor is contentious as Oller (1982) admits. 'The evidence now shows that there are both global and componential aspects of language proficiencies. The perfect theory of the right mix of general and specific components, however, has not been found — and probably will never be agreed on' (Oller, 1982: 710). Oller's (1982) idea of a global language factor is based on quantitative testing. As will be considered later in the book, such tests leave qualitative differences between people unexplored.

Oller's (1982) much disputed claim for one global language factor provides a starting point for a distinction between two different language abilities. Oller's (1982) language proficiency factor has been allied to the language abilities needed to cope in the classroom. Most (but not all) language tests are closely linked to the cognitive, academic language skills of the classroom. Reading and writing tests are obvious examples. The notion of a curriculum based language competence led various authors to make an important distinction. Apart from **academically related language competence**, it has been proposed that there is a conceptually distinct category of **conversational competence**. Skutnabb-Kangas & Toukomaa (1976) proposed a difference between **surface fluency** and **academically related aspects of language competence**. Surface fluency would include the ability to hold a simple conversation in the shop or street and may be acquired fairly quickly (e.g. in two or three years) by second language learning. To cope in the curriculum, conversational language competence may not be enough. Academically related language competence in a second language may take from five to seven years or longer to acquire. This theme is considered in detail later in the book when a distinction is made between basic interpersonal communicative skills and cognitive/academic language proficiency. Such a distinction between two levels of language competence is important as it involves disputing Oller's (1982) 'single factor' language skill.

The chapter now moves to focusing on language use rather than language ability.

AN INDIVIDUAL'S USE OF BILINGUALISM

In discussing an individual's language competence, it has become evident that language cannot be divorced from context. Language is not produced in a vacuum; it is enacted in changing dramas. As props and scenery, co-actors and actresses, the play and the part played change, so does language. A pure linguistic or psychological approach to two language competences is not sufficient. Communication includes not only the structure of language (e.g. grammar, vocabulary) but also who is saying what, to whom, in which circumstances. One person may have limited linguistic skills but, in certain situations, be successful in communication. Another person may have relative linguistic mastery, but through undeveloped social interaction skills, be relatively unsuccessful in communication. The social environment where the two languages function is crucial to understanding bilingual usage. This section considers the **use** and **function** of an individual's two languages.

An individual's **use** of their bilingual ability (**functional bilingualism**) moves away from the complex, unresolvable arguments about language proficiency that tend to be based around school success and academic performance. Functional bilingualism moves into language production across an encyclopedia of everyday events. Functional bilingualism concerns when, where, and with whom people use their two languages (Fishman, 1965).

To categorize when, where, and with whom a person uses either language will vary from culture to culture. The nature and range of social events vary from region to region, sub-culture to sub-culture. The table below provides examples of the different targets (people) and contexts (domains) where functional bilingualism is enacted.

Examples of Language Targets	Examples of Language Contexts (Domains)
1. Nuclear Family	1. Shopping
2. Extended Family	2. Visual and Auditory Media (e.g. TV, Radio, Records, Cassettes, CDs, Video)
3. Work Colleagues	3. Printed Media (e.g. Newspapers, Books)
4. Friends	4. Cinema/Discos/Theater/Concerts
5. Neighbors	5. Work
6. Religious Leaders	6. Correspondence/Telephone/Official Communication
7. Teachers	7. Clubs, Societies, Organizations, Sporting Activities
8. Presidents, Principals, Other Leaders	8. Leisure & Hobbies
9. Bureaucrats	9. Religious Meetings
10. Local Community	10. Information Technology (e.g. computers)

A distinction needs to be made between functional bilingualism and language background. (Baker & Hinde, 1984; Baker, 1985). Language background is a wider concept, referring to both participative and non-participative experience of language. Non-participative language background is indirect, bystander experience, and measured by questions such as 'What language does your mother speak to your father when you are present?'. Functional bilingualism is a narrower concept, concerning direct involvement in a language domain. Functional bilingualism is therefore restricted to the personal production and reception of language (i.e. speaking, writing, reading and direct listening in various domains). Functional bilingualism requires the study of five actions.

(1) Who is the subject? (i.e. who is the speaker?)
(2) Who is the language target ? (i.e. who is the listener(s)?)
(3) What is the situation? (e.g. in the factory, classroom, mosque)
(4) What is the topic of conversation? (e.g. sport, work, food)
(5) For what purpose? To what effect?

As one or more of these five factors changes, so may the language used. This suggests that language choice can be the result of a large and complex set of factors. In trying to predict 'who will speak what language, when and to whom' (Fishman, 1965), an individual's decision may be intricate. Sankoff (1972) uses a decision tree to give a taste of the complexity of choice.

The illustration below (adapted from Appel & Muysken, 1987) illustrates the choice of an adult Berber-speaking Moroccan in the Netherlands. The table commences with a Moroccan speaker and ends with a decision about which of five languages to speak. The decision will be based on who is the target person in the conversation and whether the situation is formal or informal. Romaine (1995: 32) gives a more complex example.

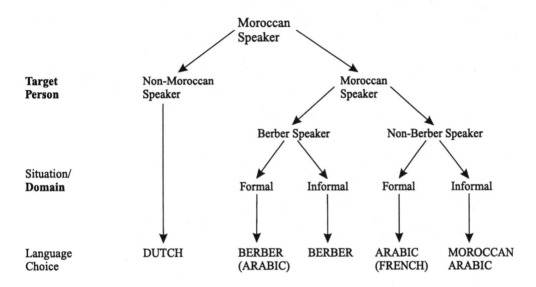

Inevitably, a decision tree oversimplifies and abbreviates a complex choice. It suggests the decision is logical, consistent across time and place, and is predictable. The reality is often less simply patterned and predetermined. Psychological factors are important. For example, someone may decide to use the language perceived as being more socially desirable or prestigious, or as more accommodating to the listener.

Sometimes a speaker may mix and switch between languages, (e.g. to explain an idea more exactly, to include other listeners, to tell a story). Often, bilinguals use their two languages in different domains (e.g. work compared with home; grandparents compared with offspring).

A consideration of distinctions and classifications about bilingual ability and function often moves to measurement. To what extent can we measure someone's performance in their two languages? How can we portray when, where and with whom people use their two languages? What are the problems and dangers in measuring bilinguals? These questions provide the themes for the next chapter.

CONCLUSION

Defining who is or is not bilingual is essentially elusive and ultimately impossible. Some categorization is often necessary and helpful to make sense of the world. Therefore categorizations and approximations may be required. Definitions in a few sentences (e.g.

Bloomfield's (1933) 'native-like control of two languages' are of little help. Intrinsically arbitrary and ambiguous in nature, they can be easily criticized and are difficult to defend.

A more helpful approach may be to locate important distinctions and dimensions surrounding the term 'bilingualism'. These should help to refine thinking about bilingualism. The foundational distinction is between bilingual ability and bilingual usage. Some bilinguals may be fluent in two languages but rarely use both. Others may be much less fluent but use their two languages regularly in different contexts. Many other patterns are possible. This distinction leads naturally into dimensions. In terms of proficiency in two languages, the four basic dimensions are listening, speaking, reading and writing. Thinking in those languages may be a fifth language proficiency. With each of these proficiency dimensions, it is possible to fragment into more and more microscopic and detailed dimensions (e.g. pronunciation, vocabulary, grammar, meaning and style). Those sub-dimensions can subsequently be further dissected and divided.

Creating a multidimensional, elaborate structure of bilingual proficiency may make for sensitivity and precision. However, ease of conceptualization requires simplicity rather than complexity. Therefore simple categorization is the paradoxical partner of complex amplification. This chapter has focused on the categories of balanced bilingualism, semilingualism, and one-factor ideas of language ability. These categories have received some depth of discussion and critical response. As will be revealed in later chapters, these categories also relate to central research on bilingualism and bilingual education.

Separate from bilingual ability is a person's use of their two languages. That is, what use is made of two languages by the individual; when, where and with whom? This highlights the importance of considering domain or context. As a bilingual moves from one situation to another, so may the language being used in terms of type (e.g. Spanish or English), content (e.g. vocabulary) and style. Over time and place, an individual's two languages are never static but ever changing and evolving.

SUGGESTED FURTHER READING

BAETENS BEARDSMORE, H., 1986, *Bilingualism: Basic Principles*. Clevedon: Multilingual Matters.
HOFFMANN, C., 1991, *An Introduction to Bilingualism*. London: Longman.
SKUTNABB-KANGAS, T., 1981, *Bilingualism or Not: The Education of Minorities*. Clevedon: Multilingual Matters.

REVIEW AND STUDY QUESTIONS

(1) Write short revision notes on the following:
    (i) The differences and overlaps in the following terms: language skills, language competence, language performance, language ability, language proficiency and language achievement.
    (ii) Balanced bilinguals and the notion and criticisms of 'double semilingualism'.

(iii)   The difference between conversational fluency and academic language competence.

(iv)   The different domains/contexts where languages are used.

(2)   What are the main differences between language ability and language use? In words or in a table, locate differences between these terms. Provide examples to illustrate the major differences.

(3)   In your language context, how valid and how useful do you find the terms 'balanced bilingual' and 'semilingualism'? What problems do you see in using these terms to describe children and adults?

(4)   What labels are used in your region to describe bilinguals? What problems and potential do you find in the use of these terms? Are there preferable terms?

STUDY ACTIVITIES

(1)   Do you consider yourself and/or people known to you as 'bilingual'? Would you describe yourself, or someone known to you, as 'balanced' in their languages? Which language or languages do you think in? Does this change in different contexts? In which language or languages do you dream?

(2)   This activity can be based on self-reflection or you may wish to interview someone who is bilingual. Make a table or diagram to illustrate how one person's dual or multilingual ability and language usage has changed and developed since birth. Write down how different contexts have affected that change and development. The diagram or table should illustrate the life history of someone's bilingualism indicating changes over time and over different contexts.

APPENDIX: FURTHER DISTINCTIONS & DESCRIPTIONS

- *Achieved Bilingualism*: acquisition of bilingualism later than childhood. Also termed *Successive Bilingualism*. See Chapter 6.
- *Ascribed Bilingualism*: acquisition of bilingualism early in childhood. Related terms are *Infant Bilingualism, Consecutive Bilingualism* and *Simultaneous Bilingualism.* See Chapter 6
- *Biliteracy*: reading and writing in two languages. Biliteracy is less common than bilingualism due to the increased complexity of skills (Hornberger, 1989). See Chapters 15 and 16.
- *Compound Bilingualism*: one language learnt distinctly later than the other often in separate contexts (Weinreich, 1970). See Chapter 6.
- *Co-ordinate Bilingualism*: two languages learnt during childhood in a fused context (Weinreich, 1970). See Chapter 6.
- *Diagonal Bilingualism*: situations where a 'non standard' language or a dialect co-exists with an unrelated 'standard' language (Pohl, 1965).
- *Dominant Language*: the language with the greater proficiency and/or usage.
- *First Language*: sometimes used to refer to the first language learnt; sometimes to the language most used; sometimes to the stronger language. *Second Language* is similarly ambiguous, being used variously to indicate a weaker language, a learnt

language (as in secondary bilingualism), the chronology in acquisition, or the 'less-used' language.

- *Horizontal Bilingualism*: situations where two languages have similar or equal status (Pohl, 1965).
- *Incipient Bilingualism*: the early stages of bilingualism where one language is not strongly developed (Diebold, 1964).
- *Mother Tongue*: the term is used ambiguously. It variously means (a) the language learnt from the mother (b) the first language learnt, irrespective of 'from whom' (c) the stronger language at any time of life (d) the 'mother tongue' of the area or country (e.g. Irish in Ireland) (e) the language most used by a person (f) the language to which a person has the more positive attitude and affection (see Skutnabb-Kangas & Phillipson, 1989).
- *Preferred Language*: self assessment of the more proficient language (Dodson, 1981).
- *Primary Bilingualism*: where two languages have been learnt 'naturally' (not via school teaching) (Houston, 1972). See Chapter 6.
- *Productive Bilingualism*: speaking and writing in the second language as well as listening and reading.
- *Receptive Bilingualism*: understanding and reading a second language without speaking or writing in that second language.
- *Secondary Bilingualism*: where the second language has been formally learnt. (Houston, 1972). See Chapter 14.
- *Vertical Bilingualism*: situations where two related languages (or a language and a dialect) co-exist, particularly within the individual (Pohl, 1965).

See also the **Glossary** in GARCÍA, O. and BAKER, C., 1995, *Policy and Practice in Bilingual Education*. Clevedon: Multilingual Matters.

CHAPTER 2

The Measurement of Bilingualism

Introduction

The Purposes of the Measurement of Bilinguals

Examples of the Measurement of Bilinguals
Language Background Scales
Self Rating on Proficiency
Language Balance and Dominance Measures
Communicative Language Testing
Criterion Referenced Language Tests

The Structure of Language Competence
Canale and Swain's Model of Language Competence
Bachman's Model of Language Competence

Conclusion

CHAPTER 2

The Measurement of Bilingualism

INTRODUCTION

Having discussed definitions, dimensions and distinctions, the topic of measuring bilinguals both elaborates and illuminates that discussion. Problems of categorizing 'bilinguals' makes further sense when we attempt to measure and categorize. We start by returning to the paradox of the last chapter. It is natural and meaningful to try to categorize the complexity of individual differences in bilingualism. We make sense of our world by continual classification. People are constantly compared and contrasted. Yet the simplification of categorization often hides the subtle complexity of reality. Sorting often simplifies unsympathetically. Individual differences are reduced to similarities. Yet over-complexity can be frustrating and confusing. Complications can confound those needing order and pattern. The measurement of bilinguals attempts to locate similarities, order and pattern.

THE PURPOSES OF THE MEASUREMENT OF BILINGUALS

Measurement of bilinguals can take place for a variety of purposes, and it is important initially to differentiate between some of these overlapping aims.

Distribution

An example of the measurement of bilinguals is found in Census questions, requesting information about ability or usage in two or more languages (e.g. in US, Canada, Ireland, Israel). Such Census data allows a researcher to estimate the size and distribution of bilinguals in a particular area. For example, geographers map the proportion and location of minority language groups within a state or region.

Selection

Bilinguals may be distinguished as a 'separate' group for selection purposes. For example, a school may wish to allocate children to classes or groups based on their degree of bilingual proficiency or language background. A different example is measuring bilinguals at the outset of research. An investigation may require the initial formation of two or more groups (e.g. 'balanced' bilinguals, 'partial' bilinguals and monolinguals).

Summative

When measuring the current performance level of a person, a wide variety of language proficiency and achievement tests are available (e.g. reading comprehension, reading vocabulary, spelling, grammar). Such tests may be used in schools to measure the four basic language abilities. In a minority language context, emphasis is often on measuring proficiency in both the minority language and the majority language. In the United States, emphasis on minority language groups becoming proficient in English has been a dominant issue in the testing of bilinguals. **Summing up** someone's language proficiency may occur at the end of a semester or a school year.

With proficiency testing, the measurement of bilinguals becomes fused with second language testing and the general area of language testing. Apart from general language tests, there are measures of the relative dominance of a person's two languages and the mixing of a person's two languages (sometimes pejoratively termed 'interference' — see Chapters 5 & 6). Such tests spotlight the particular characteristics of bilinguals as different from second language learners and first language development. Examples are provided later in this chapter.

Formative

Language proficiency tests are often used for summative judgments. In comparison, a test or assessment device that gives feedback during learning, and to aid further development is **formative assessment**. A student may be profiled on a precise breakdown of language skills to provide facilitative feedback to the teacher that directly leads to action. This is the notion of formative testing. If the test reveals areas where a child's language needs developing, there can be immediate intervention and remedial help. A diagnosis of a problem in language may lead to the formation of a plan to effect a remedy. The assessment of bilinguals is considered in Chapter 13.

EXAMPLES OF THE MEASUREMENT OF BILINGUALS

A full inventory of bilingual measurement devices would be immense and is not provided. The examples given below help to make essential points.

Language Background Scales

Language background or functional bilingualism scales are self rating scales. They endeavor to measure actual **use** of two languages as opposed to proficiency.

An example for schoolchildren is now presented (adapted from Baker, 1992):

Here are some questions about the language in which you talk to different people, and the language in which certain people speak to you. Please answer as honestly as possible. There are no right or wrong answers. Leave an empty space if a question does not fit your position.

In which language do YOU speak to the following people? Choose one of these answers

	Always in Spanish	In Spanish more often than English	In Spanish and English equally	In English more often than Spanish	Always in English
Father					
Mother					
Brothers/Sisters					
Friends in the Classroom					
Friends on the Playground					
Teachers					
Neighbors					
Grandparents					
Other relatives					
Friends outside School					

In which language do the following people speak TO YOU?

	Always in Spanish	In Spanish more often than English	In Spanish and English equally	In English more often than Spanish	Always in English
Father					
Mother					
Brothers/Sisters					
Friends in the Classroom					
Friends on the Playground					
Teachers					
Neighbors					
Grandparents					
Other relatives					
Friends outside School					

Which language do YOU use with the following?					
	Always in Spanish	In Spanish more often than English	In Spanish and English equally	In English more often than Spanish	Always in English
Watching TV/Videos					
Religion					
Newspapers/Comics					
Records/Cassettes/CDs					
Listening to Radio					
Shopping					
Playing Sport					
On the Telephone					
Reading Books					
Earning Money					
Clubs/Societies					
Other Leisure Activities					

This scale has **limitations** besides the problems of ambiguity and 'social desirability' considered later. It is not exhaustive of targets (people) or of domains (contexts). Language activity with uncles and aunts, discos, correspondence, organizations, clubs, societies, leisure, hobbies and travel are not included, for example. The choice of items included in such a scale is somewhere between an all-inclusive scale and a more narrow sample of major domains. At first glance, it may appear the more inclusive a scale the better. There is a problem, illustrated by Baker & Hinde (1984: 46):

> 'A person who says she speaks Welsh to her father (mostly away at sea), her grandparents (seen once a year), her friends (but tends to be an isolate), reads Welsh books and newspapers (only occasionally), attends Welsh Chapel (marriages and funerals only) but spends most of her time with an English speaking mother and in an English speaking school might gain a fairly high "Welsh" score.'

The example suggests that the 'to whom' question is insufficient. Frequency of usage in such contexts and with certain targets needs adding. Besides 'to whom and where', a 'how often' question is necessary. Further problems of language background and functional bilingualism scales are discussed by Baker & Hinde (1984) and Baker (1985).

Self Rating on Proficiency

Two examples of self rating on language proficiency are provided: the first from **Census questions**; the second from survey research. In a Census, questions are sometimes included about speaking a minority language. For example, a Census may ambiguously ask 'Does the person speak Welsh' (Baker, 1985). This question reveals a failure to discriminate between language ability and language use. Some can but don't. Others do but with difficulty. In the US, Census questions have been phrased as 'Does this person speak a language other than English at home? [If yes] What is the language? How well does this person speak English? *Very well/Well/Not well/Not at all.* This US Census question concerns non-English language **usage** rather than ability through specifying production at home. However, restricting the context to home ignores the wide variety of other contexts where languages may be used. The US Census question on bilingualism then switches to **ability** in English. Bilingualism is thus implicitly portrayed as **use** of a language other than English, and (in contrast) **ability** in English.

In the 1986 Canadian Census, one of the three language questions was 'Can you speak English or French well enough to conduct a conversation? This again reveals the ambiguity of Census questions. The terms 'speak', 'well enough' and 'conversation' may be interpreted in different ways by different people. What one person considers 'well enough' may be at a different level of fluency to another. A brief conversation in the shop can be at a different level from a conversation in the classroom or in the President's office.

A current movement in education is to involve students in their own assessment. While this will only form a small part of the assessment of language in school, it may help students to understand 'why' and 'how' their work is assessed, aiding motivation and interest. Students may assess their language strengths and weaknesses, review progress made in a semester, and set future learning targets. This may give students an increased awareness of the context, structure and evolution of classroom language activity as it affects them personally. While open to abuse and inaccuracy, **self assessment** in partnership with teacher assessment can be a powerful tool of teacher–student collaboration, and of increased student responsibility for their work.

The second example of self rating on language proficiency comes from a survey by the Linguistic Minorities Project (1985: 349). Children in London were asked to rate themselves on the four basic dimensions of language competency (see opposite).

Limitations in Measurement

The self rating covers the basic four language abilities across two languages (e.g. Spanish and English). The answers are possibly too broad (e.g. there are many graduations possible in between 'yes', 'quite well' and 'only a little'. Apart from this problem of scaling, there are other problems frequently encountered with measuring language competence. These may be listed as:

(1) **Ambiguity.** Words such as 'speak', 'understand', 'read' and 'write' include a wide variety of levels of proficiency. The range is from those with minimal proficiency to Bloomfield's (1933) maximum notion of 'native-like control of two languages'.

Tick one box for each question for each language

	One Language		Another Language
Can you **understand** this language if it is spoken to you now?	☐	Yes, quite well	☐
	☐	Only a little	☐
	☐	No, not now	☐
Can you **speak** this language now?	☐	Yes, quite well	☐
	☐	Only a little	☐
	☐	No, not now	☐
Can you **read** this language now?	☐	Yes, quite well	☐
	☐	Only a little	☐
	☐	No, not now	☐
	☐	Never could	☐
Can you **write** this language now?	☐	Yes, quite well	☐
	☐	Only a little	☐
	☐	No, not now	☐
	☐	Never could	☐

Allowing a range from learner to expert casts a very wide net without separating the catch into different varieties.

(2) **Context.** A bilingual may be able to understand a language in one context (e.g. a shop) and not in another context (e.g. academic lecture). Another bilingual may be able to read newspapers but not textbooks. Proficiency and usage will vary with changing environments. A response summated across contexts is required. This may not be sensitive to different levels of proficiency across different contexts.

(3) **Social desirability.** Respondents may consciously or unconsciously give a 'halo' version of themselves. Self ratings are vulnerable to exaggeration or understatement. People may say they are fluent in a second language (when in reality they are not) for self esteem or status reasons. Others may indicate they do not speak a language when they can. This may occur, for example, in a low prestige, 'subtractive' minority language environment where the introduction of the second language may replace the first language. Questions about proficiency can be interpreted as political referendum or attitudinal questions (Baker, 1985; Baetens Beardsmore, 1986).

(4) **Acquiescent response.** There is a slight tendency of respondents to answer 'yes' rather than 'no' in self-rating questions. It appears preferable to be positive rather than negative (Kline, 1983). This also tends to hold with a preference for 'Agree' rather than 'Disagree' and 'Like Me' rather than 'Not Like Me'.

(5) **Self awareness.** A self rating depends on accuracy of knowledge about oneself. This entails a knowledgeable frame of reference. For one person, the frame of reference may be other neighborhood children who are not so fluent. When compared to children in another community, apparent fluency may be less. What is competent in one environment may seem less competent in another. The age, nature and location of the reference group may cause self assessment not to be strictly comparable across a representative sample of people. A child may also self rate on surface fluency and not be aware of much less fluency in cognitively demanding language tasks (Skutnabb-Kangas, 1981).

(6) **Point of reference.** There is a danger of using monolingual proficiency and performance as the point of comparison.

(7) **Test aura.** Another danger is of raising language measurement to the level of scientific measurement with an accompanying exaggerated mystique. More 'natural' forms of language sampling may be given lower status (e.g. recording natural conversation) as they rarely carry the mystique of educational and psychological (psychometric) measurement.

(8) **Narrow sampling of dimensions of language.** Language measurement may unwittingly be perceived as something tangible and concrete (as when measuring height and weight). Rather, language tests mostly contain a specification of language skills that is hypothetical and debated. Such tests often contain only a small and unrepresentative sample of the totality of language proficiencies.

(9) **Insensitivity to change.** It is customary and seen as good practice to produce measurement which is reliable over time and across occasions (give consistent scores for the same individual over weeks or months). However the paradox is that such measurement may be insensitive to change within individuals. Test scores need an expiry date (e.g. not valid after two years).

(10) **Labeling.** Test scores are apt to create labels for individuals (e.g. someone is seen as having low performance) which create expectations (e.g. of further underachievement) that may lead to a self fulfilling prophecy.

Language Balance and Dominance Measures

Various tests have been devised to gauge the relative dominance or balance of a bilingual's two languages. While such measures have been used in research, they have also been important in US education. Because in many US states instruction for language minority children was mandated to take place in the child's dominant language, some measure of language dominance was needed. This may be through, for example, English language and Spanish language proficiency tests.

Five examples of psychometric tests are given below:

- **Speed of reaction in a word association task.** This seeks to measure whether a bilingual can give an association to stimulus words more quickly in one language than the other. No particular difference would seem to indicate a balanced bilingual. An example is presenting a word such as 'house', then measuring the time taken to produce an association (e.g. window). When a person is consistently quicker in giving associations in one language than another, the likelihood is that one language is dominant. However, dominance is different from competence. A person may be competent in two or more languages while being dominant in one. Similarly, there could be equal dominance and a low level of competence in both languages.
- **Quantity of reactions to a word association task.** Bilinguals are measured for the number of associations given within one minute when a stimulus word (e.g. 'color') is presented. An approximately equal number of responses might indicate a balance between the two languages.
- **Detection of words using both languages.** Words in both languages are to be extracted from a nonsense word such as DANSONODEND. The letters in the nonsense words must be equally representative of both languages. This is not easily achievable, and depends on relatively similar alphabets and scripts.
- **Time taken to read** a set of words in the respondent's two languages.
- **Amount of mixing** the two languages, the borrowing ('interference') and switching from one language to another.

A major **problem** with such balance and dominance tests lies in the representativeness of the measure of language proficiency and performance. In this respect, such tests would appear to tap only a small part of a much larger and more complex whole (language ability or language use). The tests cover a small sample of language sub-skills that might be tested. What can be tested is also only a small sample of a wide definition of language attributes of individuals. Dominance will vary by domain and across time, being a constantly shifting personal characteristic. It is possible to be approximately equally proficient in two languages, yet one may be dominant. Speed of processing may provide evidence about balance but not about dominance in actual language use, in different sociocultural contexts and over time (Valdés & Figueroa, 1994).

Communicative Language Testing

In attempting to assess a bilingual's competence in two languages, there is a danger of using a simple paper and pencil test believing the test will provide a faithful estimation of everyday language life. Multiple choice language tests, dictation, reading comprehension tests and spelling tests are all well worn paths in the testing of language skills. Reducing everyday language competence to tests of specific skills is like measuring Michelangelo's art solely by its range of colors. A radical alternative is seeing how bilinguals perform in both languages in a range of **real communicative situations**. Observing a bilingual in a shop, at home, at work and during leisure activity might seem the ideal way of measuring bilingual competence. This idea is impractical in terms of time and may be biased by who is the tester. Such an observation situation is unnatural because of the presence of the tester and being a 'test' situation, intrusive into individual privacy and unrepresentative across time and place. In short, real life observation is likely to be imperfect in terms of reliability and validity.

In order to collect data that is *realistic and representative*, we need to know how situations (domains) relate to one another. We also need to know the sample of language performance that relates adequately to all round language competence and what examples of test performance relate strongly to language competence. This demands an overall model or theory of language competence, a subject considered later in the chapter.

A particular emphasis in language testing is on **communicative competence** (Hart, Lapkin & Swain, 1987). While tests of spelling, grammar, written comprehension and reading abound, the importance of using languages in realistic, everyday settings is reflected in current testing movements. The ideal is expressed by Skehan (1988).

> 'Genuine communication is interaction-based, with more than one participant; unpredictable and creative, i.e. genuine communication may take the participants in unforeseen directions; is situated in a context which is both linguistic/discoursal and also sociocultural; has a purpose, in that participants will be trying to achieve something by use of language, e.g. to persuade, to deceive, etc.; uses authentic stimulus materials, and avoids contrived, specially produced materials; is based on real psychological conditions, such as time pressure; and is outcome evaluated, in that successful performance is judged in terms of whether communicative purposes have been achieved.' (p. 215)

A test of language proficiency which meets Skehan's (1988) criteria is probably impossible to achieve. A test that truly measures purposeful communication across sufficient contexts without tester effects is improbable. For some, the answer is simply not to test. For others, a best approximation is accepted. A test may therefore be used that measures the more limited notion of performance rather than the wider idea of competence.

A test that attempts to approximate the conditions outlined by Skehan (1988) is the **oral interview**. An example is the US Foreign Service oral interview which is in four stages (Lowe, 1983; Shohamy, 1983). Following a warm-up period, there is a check on the level of language proficiency, a deeper probe of that level, finishing with a wind-down period. The interview takes about half an hour. The two middle stages check that a person can perform consistently at a level across varying themes and in various language functions. The session is jointly conducted by two interviewers.

By training, the interviewers avoid narrow, predetermined checklists and attempt to make the interview sensitive to the candidate. The interviewers judge and score using prescribed criterion. A person is assigned to a level ranging from 0 (no competence) to 5 (Educated Native Speaker competence). This assumes a distinction between educated native speakers and other native speakers in their language competence. The levels 1 to 5 also have the possibility of a '+' rating, thus giving an eleven point rating scale.

Such interview procedures may not reflect reality. Does genuine communication take place between strangers, in a contrived, artificial context? Is the language repertoire of a person truly elicited? Is 'interview language' representative of a person's everyday language functioning? Can we generalize from oral communicative tests based on a single type of test, given on a single occasion, based on a test interview which is not a typical event in real life? There are doubts about whether such interview procedures can validly imitate and investigate real communicative competence. At the same time, they are a compromise between artificial pencil and paper tests and the impracticality of the detailed observation of individuals.

Criterion Referenced Language Tests: A Curriculum Approach to Language Testing

A recent shift in testing has been away from norm referenced tests to criterion referenced tests (UNESCO, World Education Report, 1991). This is partly due to the movement in language education towards communicative skills, curriculum objectives and mastery learning. What is the distinction between norm referenced and criterion referenced tests?

Language proficiency tests are usually classified into Norm Referenced and Criterion Referenced tests; the former usually being summative tests, the latter mostly being formative tests. Standardized norm referenced tests essentially compare one individual with others, as in an IQ test. A norm referenced test of reading ability, for example, may enable the teacher to compare one student with a national or regional average (norm). The student can then be exactly placed in an ordered list (e.g. in the top 16%). A **criterion referenced test** moves away from comparing one person with another. Instead it profiles an individual child on a particular language skill. The profile will test what a child can and cannot do on a precise breakdown of language skills. The parallel is with a car driving test. There are a variety of components to driving (e.g. backing around a corner, three-point turn, starting on a steep hill). Proficiency in driving often requires being able to satisfy an examiner on these sub-skills. Comparisons with other drivers are unimportant. An individual's mastery of specific tasks is the criterion for passing or failing.

Specifying driving criteria is easier than identifying language criteria, hence the analogy is not exact. The sub-components of language proficiency will be contested, and may not be easily definable or measurable. Apart from language skills, there are the qualitative aspects of language which are not simply reducible for testing (e.g. the emotive and poetic functions of languages).

One advantage for bilinguals of criterion referenced testing over norm referenced testing is the point of comparison. Norm referenced testing may compare bilinguals with monolinguals. Various authors (e.g. Grosjean, 1985) regard such comparison as unfair and invalid. Can the sprinter be fairly compared with the decathlete? In criterion referenced testing the bilingual will be profiled on specific language skills. In theory, **unfair comparisons** between bilingual and monolingual may then be avoided. In practice, however, criterion referenced tests *can* be used to create comparisons between children, between groups of children and between schools. An advantage of criterion referenced language tests is that they may facilitate feedback to the teacher that directly

Listening Objectives	Speaking Objectives
1. Sound discrimination	1. Pronunciation
2. Listening vocabulary	2. Speaking vocabulary
3. General comprehension of speech	3. Fluency of oral description
4. Understanding morphology of verbs	4. Control of morphology of verbs
5. Understanding morphology of prepositions	5. Control of morphology of prepositions
6. Understanding morphology of qualifiers	6. Control of morphology of qualifiers
7. Understanding morphology of nouns	7. Control of morphology of nouns
8. Understanding syntax of statements	8. Control of syntax of statements
9. Understanding syntax of questions	9. Control of syntax of questions

leads to action. This is the notion of formative testing. If the test reveals areas where a child's language needs developing, further action can be taken.

One illustration of testing language proficiency by criterion referenced tests is given by Harris (1984). Focusing on the attainment of Irish listening and speaking objectives, the above table specifies the test items.

The number of items to measure each objective ranged from three (control of syntax of questions) to 25 items (general comprehension of speech). Fourth grade children were assessed for their mastery of 140 separate items. Harris' (1984) language tests are based on linguistic theory. The next example is based on a communicative approach to language testing.

A broad set of language goals, for which assessment **tasks** were developed, was part of the National Curriculum in England and Wales from 1990 to 1995. The basic premise was that teaching and testing should not be separate but integrated. The National Curriculum specified the curriculum areas on which students will be assessed. Examples of requirements (language goals) for speaking in Welsh is given below as an illustration of language testing directly related to the curriculum (Department of Education and Science and The Welsh Office,1990). An example indicates the general kind of criterion referenced **tasks** that could be created to indicate an individual's level of attainment. This approach to language minority teaching and learning is explored in detail in Chapter 12.

Such test tasks are important because they tend to accent what a child can do, rather than typical classroom tests which focus on what cannot be done. Communicative skills, knowledge and understanding are profiled rather than marks, percentages or grades. **Competence** is highlighted rather than errors and deficiencies. Such tasks compare the child with a scheme of language development, rather than comparing the child with other

LEVEL ONE (Approximate Age 5)	
Example of a Language Goal:	Participate as a speaker and listener in group activities including imaginative play.
Example of Assessment Task:	Play the role of shopkeeper or a customer in a classroom shop. The teacher observes and records speaking proficiency with provided guidelines.
LEVEL TWO (Approximate Age 7)	
Example of a Language Goal:	Respond appropriately to complex instructions by the teacher, and give simple instructions.
Example of Assessment Task:	Follow three consecutive actions such as: list three places where a flower will grow best in the classroom; find out the views of others in the classroom, and reach a consensus viewpoint.
LEVEL THREE (Approximate Age 9)	
Example of a Language Goal:	Give, receive and follow accurately precise instructions when pursuing a task as an individual or as a member of a group.
Example of Assessment Task:	Plan a wall display or arrange an outing together in a group.
LEVEL FOUR (Approximate Age 11)	
Example of a Language Goal:	Give a detailed oral account of an event or explain with reasons why a particular course of action has been taken.
Example of Assessment Task:	Report orally on a scientific investigation.

children. Such tests are formative, giving direct feedback and 'feedforward' to enable curriculum decisions about individual children.

Criterion referenced language tests should provide direct feedback into (Baker, 1995b):

- teaching decisions (e.g. diagnosis of curriculum areas not mastered by an individual student);
- reporting to, and discussing achievement with parents;
- locating children needing special support and the type of curriculum support they need;
- identifying children for accelerated learning;
- informing about standards in the class in terms of curriculum development through a subject.

The chapter now continues by looking at various language structure theories. Theories about the structure of language competence provide an integrating consideration of the themes of the definition and measurement of bilingualism.

THE STRUCTURE OF LANGUAGE COMPETENCE

The language theories of the 1960s (e.g. Lado, 1961; Carroll, 1968) tended to center on language skills and components. The skills comprise listening, speaking, reading and writing and the components of knowledge comprise grammar, vocabulary, phonology and graphology. These earlier models did not indicate how skills and knowledge were integrated (Bachman, 1990). For example, how does listening differ from speaking? How does reading differ from writing? It has also been suggested that such skill and knowledge models tend to ignore the sociocultural and sociolinguistic context of language (Hymes, 1972a, 1972b). Earlier models fail to probe the competence of 'other' people in a conversation. In a conversation, there is negotiation of meaning between two or more people. Real communication involves anticipating a listener's response, understandings and misunderstandings, sometimes clarifying one's own language to ensure joint understanding (Paulston, 1992a).

Following the critique of Oller's (1979) proposal of one underlying competence for language behavior, various descriptive and empirical models of language competence have been developed. Two major examples will be briefly outlined; both have implications for the definition and measurement of bilingual proficiency, and both illustrate relatively comprehensive considerations of language competence.

Canale & Swain's Model of Language Competence

Canale & Swain (1980) and Canale (1983, 1984) suggest that language competence has four components: a **linguistic** component (e.g. syntax and vocabulary); a **sociolinguistic** component (e.g. use of appropriate language in different situations); a **discourse** component (e.g. ability to initiate and participate in sustained conversations and read sizable written texts), and a **strategic** component (e.g. improvisation with language when there is difficulty in communication).

Just as Oller's (1979) 'one factor' proposal has been criticized for not recognizing specific language areas, so Canale & Swain (1980) have been criticized for not showing whether or how the four components are inter-related, even if they can be subsumed into one overall global factor. Also, the description of a structure for language competence does not always relate easily to tests. Testing sociolinguistic and strategic competence is, of essence, likely to be difficult, contested and elusive, although not impossible, as Bachman (1990) reveals.

Bachman's Model of Language Competence

A second major model of language competence has been proposed by Bachman (1990). Bachman's model is valuable in that it considers both **language competence and language performance**. The model includes not only grammatical knowledge but also knowledge of how to use language in a particular communicative context. 'Communicative Language Ability can be described as consisting of both knowledge, or competence, and the capacity for implementing, or executing that competence in appropriate, contextualized communicative language use' (Bachman, 1990: 84).

To fully define, refine and enable the testing of communicative competence, Bachman (1990) has proposed a detailed model that is summarized in the following table.

Language Competence

(1) Organizational Competence
  (i)   Grammatical (e.g. Syntax, Vocabulary)
  (ii) Textual (e.g. Written and oral cohesion)
(2) Pragmatic Competence
  (i)   Illocutionary Competence (e.g. speech strategies, language functions)
  (ii) Sociolinguistic Competence (e.g. sensitivity to register, dialect, cultural figures of speech)

To explain the table: for Bachman (1990), communicative competence is composed of two major components: organizational competence and pragmatic competence. **Organizational competence** is broken down into two parts, grammatical competence and textual competence. Grammatical competence comprises knowledge of vocabulary, syntax, morphology and phonology/graphology. For example, a person needs to arrange words in a correct order in a sentence with appropriate endings (e.g. high, high**er**, high**est**).

Textual competence involves 'the knowledge of the conventions for joining utterances together to form a text, which is essentially a unit of language — *spoken or written* — consisting of two or more utterances or sentences' (Bachman, 1990: 88).

Pragmatic competence is composed of two sub-parts: illocutionary competence and sociolinguistic competence. Following Halliday (1973), Bachman (1990) lists four language functions as part of illocutionary competence: ideational (the way we convey meanings and experiences), manipulative (using language in an instrumental way to achieve ends), heuristic (the use of language to discover new things about our world and solving problems), and the imaginative function (using language beyond the 'here and now' (e.g. for humor or fantasy). The second part of pragmatic competence is sociolinguistic competence. Sociolinguistic competence is sensitivity to the context where language is used, ensuring that language is appropriate to the person or the situation. This may entail sensitivity to differences in local geographical dialect, sensitivity to differences in register (e.g. the register of boardroom, baseball, bar and bedroom). Sociolinguistic competence also refers to sensitivity to speaking in a native-like or natural way. This will include cultural variations in grammar and vocabulary (e.g. Black English). Another part of sociolinguistic competence is the ability to interpret cultural references and figures of speech. Sometimes, to understand a particular conversation, one needs inner cultural understanding of a specific language. A Welsh figure of speech such as 'to go round the Orme' (meaning 'to be long-winded') is only fully understandable within local northern Welsh cultural idioms.

In order to represent language as a dynamic process, Bachman (1990) argues that the listed components given in the table above interact with each other. He therefore adds to the model the notion of **strategic competence** where individuals constantly plan, execute and assess their communication strategies and delivery.

Since competence in a language is viewed as an integral part of language performance and not abstracted from it, tests of language competence cannot just use pencil and paper tests, but also need to investigate the language of genuine communication. Instead of tests that are artificial and stilted (e.g. language dictation tests), communicative performance testing involves creative, unpredictable, contextualized conversation.

This suggests that it will be difficult to measure communicative proficiency in an unbiased, comprehensive, valid and reliable way. Simple classroom tests are likely to be but a partial measure of the bilinguals' everyday performance. In testing communicative competence, Bachman (1990) adds a list of features that influence measured communicative competence. Such external influences are likely to affect the language competence profile of the person tested, often in a negative way. This list includes:

(1) Test Environment (e.g. effect of the tester; the scheduling and place of the test).
(2) Test Rubric (e.g. lay-out of the test, time allocation, language of the instructions, details as to what constitutes an appropriate response).
(3) Format of the Test (e.g. written, 'taped', 'live' testing).
(4) Nature of the Test Language (e.g. chosen topic, context embedded or context reduced communication).
(5) Nature of the Test Response (e.g. multiple choice or self created; written or spoken; concrete or abstract; allowing non-verbal communication or not).

CONCLUSION

The topic of measurement often follows from a discussion of definitions, distinctions, dimensions and categorizations. Just as dimensions and categorizations can never capture the full flavor of the global nature of bilingualism, so measurement usually fails to capture fully various conceptual dimensions and categorizations. Just as the statistics of a football or an ice hockey game do not convey the richness of the event, so language tests and measurements are unlikely to fully represent an idea or theoretical concept. Complex and rich descriptions are the indispensable partner of measurement and testing. The stark statistics of the football or ice hockey game and the colorful commentary are complementary, not incompatible.

Language background scales to measure language usage and a plethora of tests to measure language proficiency exist. The latter includes norm and criterion referenced language tests, self rating scales and language dominance tests. Particular attention in this chapter has been given to criterion referenced tests measuring mastery of specific language objectives. Suitable for both first and second languages, sometimes based on theoretical principles, sometimes eclectic, such tests tend to relate directly to the process of teaching and learning.

The chapter considered theories of the structure of language competence. Such theories join the first two chapters, integrating issues of definition with ideas about measurement.

In particular, the focus has been on linking a linguistic view of language competence with a communicative view. Language can be decomposed into its linguistic constituents (e.g. grammar, vocabulary). It is also important to consider language as a means of making relationships and communicating information. This important dualism will follow us through the book: ability and use; the linguistic and the social; competence and communication.

SUGGESTED FURTHER READING

BACHMAN, L.F., 1990, *Fundamental Considerations in Language Testing*. Oxford: Oxford University Press.

BAETENS BEARDSMORE, H., 1986, *Bilingualism: Basic Principles*. Clevedon: Multilingual Matters.

SKUTNABB-KANGAS, T., 1981, *Bilingualism or Not: The Education of Minorities*. Clevedon: Multilingual Matters.

VALDÉS, G. and FIGUEROA, R.A., 1994, *Bilingualism and Testing: A Special Case of Bias*. Norwood, NJ: Ablex.

REVIEW AND STUDY QUESTIONS

(1) Write short revision notes on the following:
    (i)   The different purposes of measuring bilinguals.
    (ii)   Styles of self rating on language proficiency and its problems.
    (iii)   The nature of communicative language testing, criterion referenced tests.
    (iv)   The structure of language competence.

(2) Consider the different reasons why minority and majority languages are 'measured'? What problems may be met in such measurement?

(3) Find out more about the distinction between norm referenced and criterion referenced testing. (Also read the section on assessment in Chapter 13.) What outcomes may derive from these two different forms of testing on language minority children? Does criterion referenced testing have similar or different potential outcomes to norm referenced testing for language minority children?

STUDY ACTIVITIES

(1) Use the Language Background Scale (modified to suit your context) on yourself or someone you know. This may also be used with a class of students. Examine the answers given and sum up in words or in numbers the balance and use of languages. If used with a group of students, are there groups or clusters of students? Are there those dominant in one language, those dominant in another language and those with a balance between the two?

(2) Using a local school(s), find out what tests are used to measure language achievement in the classroom. These may be listening, speaking, reading, writing or language development tests. Find out whether these are norm referenced or criterion referenced tests. For what purposes are these tests being used? How fair are these to bilingual children?

CHAPTER 3

Languages in Society

Introduction

Diglossia

The Language Garden: Language Planning

Language Shift and Language Maintenance

Language Decline and Death

Conclusion

CHAPTER 3

Languages in Society

INTRODUCTION

Bilingual individuals do not exist as separated islands. Rather, people who speak two or more languages usually exist in groups, in communities and sometimes in regions. People who speak a minority language within a majority language context may be said to form a speech community or **language community**. Bilingualism at the individual level is half the story. The other essential half is to analyze how **groups** of language speakers behave and change. Such an examination particularly focuses on the movement and change of a language across decades. A language minority is rarely stable in its size, strength or safety. It also entails examining the politics and power situation in which minority languages are situated.

This chapter focuses on the idea that there is no language without a language community. Since language communities do not usually exist in isolation of other communities, it becomes important to examine the **contact** between different language communities. In a world of mass communication, easy travel across continents and the movement towards a global village, language communities are rarely isolated from other language communities. The rapid growth of information and inter-continental travel has meant that language communities are rarely if ever stable. With every minority language and majority language there is constant change and movement. Some languages become stronger; other languages tending to decline, even die. Some languages thought to be dead, may occasionally be revived (e.g. Cornish). This chapter therefore seeks to examine language communities, language contact, language change and language conflict. It will be shown how decisions about bilingual education are a part of a much wider whole. That is, bilingual education can only be properly understood by examining the circumstances of language communities in which such education is placed.

This chapter takes a **sociolinguistic perspective** of language in society, examining central concepts such as diglossia, language shift, language maintenance, language death and language spread. There is also a linguistic view of these topics (e.g. change in syntax, semantics and lexicon) that is not covered in this or the following chapter on language revival (see Aitchison, 1991; McMahon, 1994 and Romaine, 1995 for a linguistic discussion of these topics). The sociolinguistic perspective begins by examining a central idea in sociolinguistics, that of diglossia.

DIGLOSSIA

The term bilingualism is typically used to describe the two languages of an individual. When the focus changes to two languages in society, the term often used is **diglossia** (Ferguson, 1959; Fishman, 1972, 1980). While the term **diglossia** has in the last twenty years become broadened and more refined, it was originally a Greek word for two languages. In practice, a language community is unlikely to use both languages for the same purpose. A language community is more likely to use one language in certain situations and for certain functions, the other language in different circumstances and for different functions. For example, a language community may use its heritage, minority language in the home, for religious purposes and in social activity. This language community may use the majority language at work, in education and when experiencing the mass media.

Ferguson (1959) first described **diglossia** in terms of two varieties of the same language (dialects). Fishman (1972, 1980) extended the idea of diglossia to two languages existing side by side within a geographical area. Ferguson's (1959) original description distinguishes between a high language variety (called H) and a low variety (called L). This distinction can also be between a majority (H) and minority (L) language within a country, which is a rather non-neutral and discriminatory distinction. In both situations, different languages or varieties may be used for different purposes as the table below illustrates.

Context	Majority Language (H)	Minority Language (L)
1. The home and family		✔
2. Schooling	✔	
3. Mass media	✔	
4. Business and commerce	✔	
5. Social & cultural activity in the community		✔
6. Correspondence with relations and friends		✔
7. Correspondence with government departments	✔	

The example shows that languages may be used in different situations, with the low variety more likely to be used in informal, personal situations; the high or majority language being more used in formal, official communication contexts. To use the low variety of language in a situation where the high variety is expected, is likely to be embarrassing, even ridiculed.

The table suggests that the different language contexts usually make one language more **prestigious** than the other. The majority language may sometimes be perceived as more superior, more elegant and educative a language. The high variety may be seen as the door to both educational and economic success.

The concept of diglossia can be usefully examined alongside the concept of bilingualism. Bilingualism, argued Fishman (1972), is the subject for psychologists and linguists. Bilingualism refers to an individual's ability to use more than one language. Diglossia, he argued, was a concept for sociologists and sociolinguists to study. Fishman (1980) combines the terms **bilingualism** and **diglossia** to portray four language situations where bilingualism and diglossia may exist with or without each other. The following table, based on Fishman (1980; see Glyn Williams, 1992, for a critique) portrays this relationship between bilingualism and diglossia.

		DIGLOSSIA	
		+	–
INDIVIDUAL BILINGUALISM	+	1. Diglossia and Bilingualism together	3. Bilingualism without Diglossia
	–	2. Diglossia without Bilingualism	4. Neither Bilingualism nor Diglossia

The **first** situation is a language community containing **both individual bilingualism and diglossia**. In such a community, almost everyone will be able to use both the high language (or variety) and the low language (or variety). The high language is used for one set of functions, the low language for a separate set of functions. Fishman (1972) cites Paraguay as the example. Guaraní and Spanish are spoken by almost all inhabitants. The former is the Low variety, Spanish is the High language.

The **second** situation outlined by Fishman (1972, 1980) is **diglossia without bilingualism**. In such a context there will be two languages within a particular geographical area. One group of inhabitants will speak one language, another group a different language. One example is Switzerland where, to a large extent, different language groups (German, French, Italian, Romansch) are located in different areas. The official status of the different languages may be theoretically equal. Fluent bilingual speakers of both languages may be the exception rather than the rule (Andres, 1990).

In some cases, the ruling power group will typically speak the high language, with the larger less powerful group speaking only the low language. For example, in a colonial situation, English or French was spoken by the ruling elite, with the indigenous language spoken by the masses.

The **third** situation is **bilingualism without diglossia**. In this situation, most people will be bilingual and will not restrict one language to a specific set of purposes. Either language may be used for almost any function. Fishman (1972, 1980) regards such communities as unstable and in a state of change. Where bilingualism exists without diglossia, the expectation may be that one language will, in the future, become more powerful and have more purposes. The other language may decrease in its functions and decay in status and usage.

The **fourth** situation is where there is **neither bilingualism nor diglossia**. One example is where a linguistically diverse society has been forcibly changed to a relatively monolingual society. In Cuba and the Dominican Republic, the native languages have been exterminated. A different example would be a small speech community using its minority language for all functions and insisting on having no relationship with the neighboring majority language.

Fishman (1980) argues that diglossia with and without bilingualism tends to provide a relatively stable, enduring language arrangement. Yet such stability may be increasingly rare. With increasing ease of travel and communication, increased social and vocational mobility, a more global economy and more urbanization, there tends to be more contact between language communities. As we shall see later in this chapter, language shift tends to be more typical than language stability. Changes in the fate and fortune of a minority language occur because the separate purposes of the two languages tend to change across generations. The **boundaries** that separate one language from another are never permanent. Neither a minority language community nor the uses that community makes of its low/minority language can be permanently compartmentalized. Even with the **territorial principle** (one language being given official status in one geographical area, the second language being given status within a separate geographical area), the political and power base of the two languages changes over time. However, keeping boundaries between the languages and compartmentalizing their use in society may be necessary for the weaker or lower variety to survive.

Where the **territorial principle** exists (e.g. in Wales, Switzerland), geography is used to define language boundaries, with inhabitants of a region classified as a distinct language group. The argument for the survival, maintenance and spread of the language is based on its historic existence within a defined boundary. As the indigenous language of the region, language rights may be enshrined in law. Welsh speakers have certain language rights in Wales (e.g. using Welsh in courts of law) but not when they cross the border into England. The territorial principle benefits the Welsh but has unfortunate implications for other 'in-migrant' language minorities in Britain (Stubbs, 1991). The danger and discriminatory nature of the territorial principle is revealed in a set of questions. If Welsh is the language of Wales, is English to be seen as the only rightful language of England? Do languages belong to regions and territories and not to the speakers of those languages or to groups of those languages wherever they may be found? Do Panjabi, Urdu, Bengali, Hindi, Greek and Turkish only belong in the home country? Do such languages have no home in Britain?

Under the **territorial principle**, should language minorities either speak the language of the territory or return to the home country? The territorial principle thus has benefits for some (e.g. the Welsh). For others, it is unacceptable and unfair. In Europe, there are many indigenous (or autochthonous) languages that are seeking preservation status in the European Community. But what status is accorded the in-migrant languages of Europe (e.g. the various Asian languages such as Panjabi, Urdu, Bengali, Hindi and Gujerati)?

The term **personality principle** is particularly helpful to describe minority groups who cannot claim a language territory principle. The 'personality' of each language is the sum of its more or less distinctive attributes (e.g. as revealed in its uses and functions, customs and rituals, culture and meanings, communication styles and literature; see Allardt, 1979). One example of the use of the personality principle is the Pennsylvania Amish who decided to ensure the continuity of their heritage language by reserving an exclusive place for that language at home, and reserving English for school and for contacts with the outside secular world. One language is reserved for particular societal functions; another language for distinctly separate functions. This compartmentalization exists in a relatively stable arrangement. Such separation of identity for each language exists within the psyche of each group member. There cannot be diglossia without bilingualism if diglossia is based on the personality principle. In contrast, there can be diglossia without bilingualism where the territorial principle exists.

The **personality principle** can be an attribute of those claiming territorial principle. However, the personality principle is an especially supportive concept for in-migrant groups (e.g. Asian languages in Europe and the many in-migrant language minorities in Canada and the US). Those who cannot claim territorial rights for their language can assert that their heritage language has a 'personality' and is used for particular functions that need safeguarding and separating from uses of the majority language. Such language groups can argue that their right to use their minority language is fully portable across national borders and boundaries because it has its own 'personality' of uses.

An attempted merging of the territorial and personality principles when applied to language rights has been termed the '**asymmetrical principle**' or 'asymmetrical bilingualism' (Reid, 1993). As conceived by its Canadian advocates (e.g. in Quebec), the principle gives full rights to minority language speakers and less rights to the speakers of a majority language. This is a form of positive discrimination, seeking to discriminate in favor of those who are usually discriminated against. Some of the functions of a minority language may be legislated for, so as to preserve that language in a proactive manner. The question of language rights is returned to in Chapter 19.

In language communities, the functions and boundaries of the two languages will both affect and be reflected in bilingual education policy and practice. In a diglossic situation, is the high or low variety of language used in the different stages of schooling, from kindergarten to University? If the low variety is used in the school, in which curriculum areas does it function? Is the low variety just used for oral communication or is biliteracy encouraged in the school? Are science, technology and computing taught in the high or low variety? Is the low variety just allowed for a year or two in the elementary school with the higher variety taking over thereafter? Does the school deliberately exclude the low variety as a medium for classroom learning? The purposes and functions of each language in a diglossic situation are both symbolized and enacted in the school situation. This links with Chapter 10 where different forms of bilingual education are examined.

THE LANGUAGE GARDEN: LANGUAGE PLANNING

Ofelia García (1992b), uses a powerful analogy to portray language planning. Her **Language Garden Analogy** commences with the idea that if we traveled through the countries of the world and found field after field, garden after garden of the same, one-color flower, how dull and boring our world would be. If a single color flower was found throughout the world without variety of shape, size or color, how tedious and impoverished the world would be.

Fortunately, there is a wide variety of flowers throughout the world of all shapes and sizes, all tints and textures, all hues and shades. A garden full of different colored flowers enhances the beauty of that garden and enriches our visual and aesthetic experience.

The same argument can be made about the language garden of the world. If there were just one language in the garden, it would be easy to administer, easy to tend. If one of the majority languages of the world (e.g. English) solely existed, how dull and uninteresting it would be. Rather, we have a language garden full of variety and color. For example, in London alone, there are said to be around 184 different languages being spoken. The initial conclusion is simply that language diversity in the garden of the world makes for a richer, more interesting and more colorful world.

However, language diversity makes the garden more difficult to tend. In a garden, some flowers and shrubs spread alarmingly quickly. Some majority languages, particularly English, have expanded considerably during this century. When the garden is neglected, one species of flower may take over, and small minority flowers may be in danger of extinction. Therefore some flowers need extra care and protection. This leads to the second part of García's (1992b) analogy. A free language economy allowing some flowers to dominate gardens is less preferred than careful **language planning** (Rubin, 1977; Eastman, 1983; Cooper, 1989). When a gardener wishes to create a beautiful garden, there will be both careful planning and continued care and protection. Sometimes radical action may be taken to preserve and protect. The analogy suggests that language diversity requires planning and care. Four examples follow:

(1) **Adding flowers to the garden.** The analogy suggests that, where the majority language is a person's first language, it may be enriching to add a second, even a third and fourth language. For example, in Canada, English speakers learning French may ensure that the colorful diversity of the Canadian multilingual situation is maintained. In mainland Europe, speakers of French, German, Spanish or Italian, for example, often learn a second or third language. In much of the United States, Australasia and Britain, a monochrome language garden seems relatively more common.

(2) **Protecting rare flowers.** In the diglossic situation of many countries throughout the world, the minority or indigenous language may be under threat from the quickly

spreading majority languages. Just as environmentalists in the twentieth century have awoken to the need to preserve the variety of flora and fauna, so in the language garden, it is environmentally friendly to protect rare language flowers. Through education and legislation, through pressure groups and planning, protection of language species in danger of extinction may be attempted.

(3) **Augmenting the numbers of those flowers that are in danger of extinction**. Where a language species is in danger of extinction, stronger action may be needed than protection. Special efforts to revive a threatened language may be needed through intervention. For example, positive economic discrimination towards the Irish language in certain defined heartland areas has attempted to preserve the indigenous language in its traditional strongholds.

(4) **Controlling flowers that spread quickly and naturally.** Flowers that spread rapidly and take the space of other flowers also need supervision and planning. While majority languages for international communication are an irreplaceable part of the Information Society, language planning may seek to allow spread without replacing and killing endangered species.

It is clear from using the language garden analogy that a *laissez-faire* situation is less desirable than deliberate, rational language planning. Gardeners are needed (e.g. teachers in schools) to plant, water, fertilize and reseed the different minority language flowers in the garden to ensure an enriching world language garden. While there are gardeners (e.g. teachers) tending the language garden, there are landscape engineers who tend to plan and control the overall shape of the language garden. The view of language landscape engineers (e.g. politicians, policy makers) is often to regard the language garden as just one part of a wider control of the environment. The dominant power groups who determine the social, economic and cultural environment may see language as just one element in an overall landscape design. For example, the type of bilingual education program that is allowed in a region (submersion, transitional, immersion or supportive of the minority community language — see Chapter 10) is but part of a design for the total landscape in which the languages are located.

A language landscape engineer who is concerned only for majority language flowers, will regard protecting rare flowers to be expensive and unnecessary, and will wish to standardize the variety of language in the country. A landscape engineer who wishes to protect rare flowers and increase flowers in danger of extinction may encourage the growth of such flowers alongside majority language flowers within bilingual education. In the US, for example, many politicians prefer monolingualism rather than bilingualism. The preference is for the assimilation of minority language communities into a more standardized, monochrome garden. The dominant ruling group in US society is monolingual, with little perceived need to know or speak the minority languages existing in the country. Thus their view of bilingual education is determined by their wider ideology.

It is important to note **variations in attitude** to the language environment. Williams (1991a) sums up differing 'environmental' attitudes to the survival and spread of minority languages. First, the **evolutionist** will tend to follow Darwin's idea of the survival of the fittest. Those languages that are strong will survive. The weaker languages will either have to adapt themselves to their environment, or die. A different way of expressing this is in terms of a free, *laissez-faire* language economy. Languages must survive on their own merits without the support of language planning.

However, survival of the fittest is too simplistic a view of evolution. It only accents the negative side of evolution: killing, exploitation and suppression. A more positive view of evolution is **interdependence** rather than constant competition. Cooperation for mutually beneficial outcomes can be as possible as exploitation (Williams, 1991a). An evolutionist argument about language shift also fails to realize that it is not a simple, spontaneous or impulsive process. Rather, the fate of languages is often related to the manipulated politics and power bases of different groups in society. **Language shift** (in terms of numbers of speakers and uses) occurs through deliberate decisions that directly or indirectly affect languages and reflects economic, political, cultural, social and technological change. It is therefore possible to analyze and determine what causes language shift rather than simply believing language shift occurs by accident. Thus, those who support an evolutionary perspective on languages may be supporting the spread of majority languages and the replacement of minority languages. Evolutionists who argue for an economic, cost-benefit approach to languages, with the domination of a few majority languages for international communication, hold a myopic view of the function of languages. Languages are not purely for economic communication. They are also concerned with human culture, human heritage, the value of a garden full of different colored flowers rather than the one variety.

The second approach to languages is that of **conservationists** (Williams, 1991a). Conservationists will argue for the maintenance of variety in the language garden. For conservationists, language planning must care for and cherish minority languages.

Just as certain animal species are now deliberately preserved within particular territorial areas, so conservationists will argue that threatened languages should receive special status in heartland regions of that language. Catalan in Spain, native Indian languages in North America, the Celtic languages in Britain and France, have invoked the conservationist argument. In Ireland, certain areas called Gaeltachta are officially designated for Irish conservation.

The third attitude to languages is that of **preservationists** (Williams, 1991a). Preservationists are different from conservationists by being more conservative and seeking to maintain the status quo rather than develop the language. Preservationists are concerned that any change, not just language change, will damage the chances of survival of their language. Such a group are therefore traditionalists, anti-modern in outlook. Whereas conservationists may think global and act local, preservationists will tend to think local and act local.

One example of language preservation may be when language is closely tied in with religion. The historical survival of Pennsylvania German within the **Amish** community in the US has been a classic illustration of a preservationist approach to language. The

Pennsylvania Germans, sometimes called the Pennsylvania Dutch, came to the US from Germany in the early eighteenth century. They originally settled in farm communities in southeastern and central Pennsylvania. The language is a German dialect related to that spoken in the German Palatinate along the river Rhine. Distinctive in dress, these Protestant Old Order Amish and Old Order Mennonite sectarians have spoken Pennsylvania German (a German dialect) at home and in the community. English is learnt at school since English is the language of instruction. English is also spoken with outsiders — increasingly so (Huffines, 1991). Archaic forms of German are used in Protestant religious worship. The language of the community has thus been preserved within the established boundaries of that community. However, particularly among the non-sectarian Pennsylvania Germans, the language is dying (Huffines, 1991). As English replaces the High German used in religious worship, the *raison d'être* for the use of Pennsylvania German in the home and community disappears. Religion has preserved the language. As religious practices change, preservation changes to transformation.

LANGUAGE SHIFT AND LANGUAGE MAINTENANCE

No garden of flowers is stable and unchanging. With changes of season and weather comes growth and death, blossoming and weakening. Minority language communities are similarly in a constant state of change. Such language shift may be fast or slow, upwards or downwards, but shift is as likely as is garden growth.

Generally, **language shift** is used in the literature to refer to a downwards language movement. That is, there is a lessening of the number of speakers of a language, a decreasing saturation of language speakers in the population, a loss in language proficiency, or a decreasing use of that language in different domains. The last stages of language shift are called language death. **Language maintenance** usually refers to relative language stability in its number and distribution of speakers, its proficient usage in children and adults, and to retaining the use of the language in specific domains (e.g. home, school, religion). **Language spread** concerns the increase, numerically, geographically or functionally in language users, networks and use (Cooper, 1989).

However, there is a **danger** in the ways these terms are used. First, the terms are ambiguous and may refer to the numerical size of the language minority, their saturation in a region, their proficiency in the language, or the use of the language in different domains. Second, these are predominantly sociolinguistic concepts. Linguists have their own use of these terms (e.g. referring to changes in grammar and vocabulary over time — see Aitchison, 1991; McMahon, 1994; Romaine, 1995). Third, languages do not lose or acquire speakers. Rather, speakers acquire or lose languages.

A variety of factors create **language shift**. For example, out-migration from a region may be vital to secure employment, a higher salary or promotion. In-migration can be forced (e.g. the capture of slaves) or may be more of free will (e.g. guest workers). Sometimes there is also forced or voluntary movement of minority language groups within a particular geographical area. Within a country, marriage may also cause shifting bilingualism. For example, a bilingual person from a minority language community may marry a majority language monolingual. The result may be majority language monolingual children. Increasing industrialization and urbanization in the twentieth century has led to increased movement of labor. With the growth of mass communications, information technology, tourism, road, sea and air links, minority languages seem more at risk. Bilingual education, or its absence, will also be a factor in the ebb and flow of minority and majority languages.

A relatively comprehensive list of factors that may create **language maintenance and shift** is given by Conklin & Lourie (1983) (see also Gaarder, 1977: 141 and following). This list essentially refers to in-migrants rather than indigenous minorities, but many factors are common to both groups. What is missing from this list is the power dimension (such as being in subordinate status — e.g. the Puerto Ricans in New York City — see Zentella, 1988).

FACTORS ENCOURAGING LANGUAGE MAINTENANCE	FACTORS ENCOURAGING LANGUAGE LOSS
A. Political, Social and Demographic Factors	
1. Large number of speakers living closely together.	Small number of speakers well dispersed.
2. Recent and/or continuing in-migration.	Long and stable residence.
3. Close proximity to the homeland and ease of travel to homeland.	Homeland remote or inaccessible.
4. Preference to return to homeland with many actually returning.	Low rate of return to homeland and/or little intention to return and/or impossible to return.
5. Homeland language community intact.	Homeland language community decaying in vitality.
6. Stability in occupation.	Occupational shift, especially from rural to urban areas.
7. Employment available where home language is spoken daily.	Employment requires use of the majority language.
8. Low social and economic mobility in main occupations.	High social and economic mobility in main occupations.
9. Low level of education to restrict social and economic mobility, but educated and articulate community leaders loyal to their language community.	High levels of education giving social and economic mobility. Potential community leaders are alienated from their language community by education.
10. Ethnic group identity rather than identity with majority language community via nativism, racism and ethnic discrimination.	Ethnic identity is denied to achieve social and vocational mobility; this is forced by nativism, racism and ethnic discrimination.

FACTORS ENCOURAGING LANGUAGE MAINTENANCE	FACTORS ENCOURAGING LANGUAGE LOSS
B. Cultural Factors	
1. Mother-tongue institutions (e.g. schools, community organizations, mass media, leisure activities).	Lack of mother-tongue institutions.
2. Cultural and religious ceremonies in the home language.	Cultural and religious activity in the majority language.
3. Ethnic identity strongly tied to home language.	Ethnic identity defined by factors other than language.
4. Nationalistic aspirations as a language group.	Few nationalistic aspirations.
5. Mother tongue the homeland national language.	Mother tongue not the only homeland national language, or mother tongue spans several nations
6. Emotional attachment to mother tongue giving self-identity and ethnicity.	Self-identity derived from factors other than shared home language.
7. Emphasis on family ties and community cohesion.	Low emphasis on family and community ties. High emphasis on individual achievement.
8. Emphasis on education in mother tongue schools to enhance ethnic awareness.	Emphasis on education in mother tongue.
9. Low emphasis on education if in majority language.	Acceptance of majority language education.
10. Culture unlike majority language culture.	Culture and religion similar to that of the majority language.

This concludes the initial consideration of the factors in language shift. It has been shown that such shift is particularly related to economic and social change, to politics and power, to the availability of local social networks of communication between minority language speakers and to the legislative and institutional support supplied for the conservation of a minority language. While such factors help clarify what affects language shift, the relative importance of factors is debated and unclear. There are various levels of establishing **causes** of language shift, levels such as the political, the economic, the psychological (e.g. at the individual or home level) and at the sociolinguistic level. A list of the relative importance of these factors is simplistic because the factors interact and intermingle in a complicated equation. Such a list does not prioritize more or less

FACTORS ENCOURAGING LANGUAGE MAINTENANCE	FACTORS ENCOURAGING LANGUAGE LOSS
C. Linguistic Factors	
1. Mother tongue is standardized and exists in a written form.	Mother tongue is non-standard and/or not in written form.
2. Use of an alphabet which makes printing and literacy relatively easy.	Use of writing system which is expensive to reproduce and relatively difficult to learn.
3. Home language has international status.	Home language of little or no international importance.
4. Home language literacy used in community and with homeland.	Illiteracy (or aliteracy) in the home language.
5. Flexibility in the development of the home language (e.g. limited use of new terms from the majority language).	No tolerance of new terms from majority language; or too much tolerance of loan words leading to mixing and eventual language loss.

(Adapted from Conklin & Lourie, 1983).

important factors in language shift. Nor does it reveal the processes and mechanisms of language shift.

It is difficult to predict which minority languages are in more or less danger of declining, and which languages are more or less likely to be revived. A frequent, if generalized, **scenario for in-migrants** is given by García & Diaz (1992):

> 'Most US immigrant groups have experienced a language shift to English as a consequence of assimilation into American life. The first generation immigrants sustain their native or first language while learning English. The second generation, intent upon assimilation into a largely English-speaking community, begin the shift towards English by using the native language with first generation speakers (parents, grandparents, others) and English in more formal settings. By slow degrees, English is used in contexts once reserved for the first language. Encroachment of English into the domain of the first language serves to destabilize the native language.
>
> Eventually, third generation speakers discontinue the use of the native language entirely. The shift completes when most of the third generation are monolingual English speakers' (p. 14).

However, a '**three generation shift**' is not the only possible pattern. Paulston (1994) cites the Greeks in Pittsburgh as experiencing a four generation shift. She attributes this slower shift to: use of a standardized, prestigious written language; access to an institution teaching Greek language and literacy (i.e. Greek churches in Pittsburgh), and arranged marriages with one partner being a monolingual Greek speaker from Greece. In contrast, the three generation shift among Italians in Pittsburgh is attributed to their speaking a non-standard, non-written dialect of Italian with no prestige; no religious institutional support as they shared English language Roman Catholic services with, for example, Irish priests, nuns and laity, and marriage to Roman Catholics with religious compatibility more important than language compatibility.

Amongst Panjabi, Italian, Gaelic and Welsh communities in Britain, there are occasional 'fourth generation' individuals who sometimes wish to revive the language of their ethnic origins. For some, assimilation into the majority language and culture does not give self-fulfillment. Rather, such revivalists seek a return to their roots by recovering the language and culture of their ethnic heritage. In Europe, with a pressure towards a European identity rapidly increasing, language minority members seem increasingly aware of the benefits of a more distinctive and intimate local identity. The pressure to become part of a larger whole seems to result in a counter-balancing need to have secure roots within a smaller and more domestic community. A local language is valuable in this more particular identity. Bilingualism provides the means to be international and local.

LANGUAGE DECLINE AND DEATH

Another way of identifying the causes of language shift is to examine a dying language within a particular region (e.g. Dorian, 1989).

Susan Gal (1979) studied in detail the replacement of Hungarian by German in the town of Oberwart in eastern Austria. After 400 years of relatively stable Hungarian–German bilingualism, economic, social and family life became more German language based. Using an anthropological style, Gal (1979) studied the process of language decline. For Gal (1979) the issue was not the correlates of language shift, but the process. For example, while industrialization was related to language decline in Oberwart, the crucial question became:

> 'By what intervening processes does industrialization, or any other social change, effect changes in the uses to which speakers put their languages in everyday interactions?' (p. 3)

Gal (1979) showed how **social changes** (e.g. through industrialization and urbanization) change social networks, relationships between people, and patterns in language use in communities. As new environments arise with new speakers, languages take on new forms, new meanings and create new patterns of social interaction.

Another celebrated study is by Nancy Dorian (1981). Dorian carried out a detailed case study of the decline of Gaelic in east Sutherland, a region in the north-east Highlands of Scotland. In the history of the region, English and Gaelic co-existed with English generally being the ruling language and the 'civilized' language. Gaelic was regarded as more of the 'savage' language of lower prestige. In this region of east Sutherland, the last two groups to speak Gaelic were the 'crofters' (farmers of a small amount of land) and the fishing community. Dorian (1981) studied the fishing community who had become a separate and distinct group of people in a small geographical area. Surrounded by English speaking communities, these fisher-people originally spoke only Gaelic and later became bilingual in English and Gaelic. The fisher-folk thought of themselves, and were thought of by their neighbors, as of lower social status. They tended to marry within their own group. When the fishing industry began to decline, the Gaelic speaking fishing-folk began to find other jobs. The **boundaries** between the Gaelic speakers and the English speakers began to crumble. Inter-marriage replaced in-group marriage, and 'outside' people migrated to the east Sutherland area. Over time, the community gave up its fisher identity and the Gaelic language tended to decline with it:

> 'Since Gaelic had become one of the behaviors which allowed the labeling of individuals as fishers there was a tendency to abandon Gaelic along with other "fisher" behaviors.' (Dorian, 1981: 67)

Across generations in the twentieth century, Gaelic in east Sutherland declined. Whereas grandparents talked, and were talked to, only in Gaelic, parents would speak Gaelic to other people but use English with their children and expect their children to speak English in reply. The children were able to understand Gaelic from hearing their parents speak it, but were not used to speaking it themselves:

> 'The home is the last bastion of a subordinate language in competition with a dominant official language of wider currency … speakers have failed to transmit the language to their children so that no replacement generation is available when the parent generation dies away.' (Dorian, 1981: 105)

A different and controversial perspective is given by John Edwards (1985). When languages die, Edwards asks, are they murdered or do they commit suicide? In the histories of the native Indian languages of Canada and the United States, and particularly in the histories of the African languages of those who became slaves, there is evidence of murder. In histories of the Irish, Gaelic and the Welsh language it is typically argued that the language has been murdered by English and England's dominant rule over the peripheries of Britain. Are monolingual English schools part of a language murder machine? It is debated whether the 'destruction' of Celtic languages has been deliberate and conscious, or unconscious and through indifference.

When minority language speakers become bilingual and prefer the majority language, the penalty for the minority language may be decline, even death. Yet, where people are determined to keep a language alive, it may be impossible to destroy a language. Language activists, pressure groups, affirmative action and language conservationists may fight for the survival of the threatened language. In Puerto Rico, the government has introduced English into schools to attempt bilingualization of the island. Over three-quarters of the population remain functionally monolingual in Spanish. Resnick (1993) has shown that nationalism, political uncertainty and the relationship between language and identity have made many Puerto Ricans resistant to language change and the use of English.

For Edwards (1985), **language shift** often reflects a pragmatic desire for social and vocational mobility, an improved standard of living. This provides a different slant on the language garden analogy. The answer to the environmentalist who wishes to preserve a garden of great beauty is that, when the priority is food in the stomach and clothes upon the back, 'you can't eat the view'. Sometimes, there may be a gap between the rhetoric of language preservation and harsh reality. This is illustrated in a story from Bernard Spolsky (1989b):

> 'A Navajo student of mine once put the problem quite starkly: if I have to choose, she said, between living in a hogan a mile from the nearest water where my son will grow up speaking Navajo or moving to a house in the city with indoor plumbing where he will speak English with the neighbors, I'll pick English and a bathroom!' (p. 451)

However, where there are oppressed language minorities who are forced to live in segregated societies, there is often little choice of where to live and work. In the quote, the Navajo may have had the choice. In actuality, many language minorities have little or no real choice. Thus, electing for language suicide is misleading. Attribution of suicide is a way of 'blaming the victim' and diverting a focus on the determination of real causes of language shift. Freedom of choice is more apparent than real. There is often no viable choice among language minority speakers.

CONCLUSION

This chapter has focused on languages at the group, social and community level. Two languages within a region is termed diglossia. Majority and minority languages are frequently in contact, sometimes in conflict. The relationship between the two languages tends to shift constantly as a consequence of a variety of changeable cultural, economic, linguistic, social, demographic and political factors.

The argument for preserving language minority communities sometimes relates to existing as an indigenous language in a defined territory. Also, language minorities may lay claim to the personality principle; their having unifying ethnic characteristics and identity. One 'preservationist' argument uses a gardening analogy. There is a need to maintain the colorful diversity in the language garden of the world. Language planning by adding and protecting, controlling and propagating is required to avoid monochrome gardens of majority-only languages. Conscious language planning to conserve and preserve may be preferred to the narrow view of evolutionists. Language planning may seek to create language vitality by attending to the economic, social and symbolic status, geographical distribution and institutional support accorded to a minority language. Not to plan for language maintenance and spread may be to court language death. Preserving a multicolored language garden requires the optimism of resurrection rather than the pessimism of decline and death. It is to a positive accent of construction rather than destruction that we turn in the next chapter.

SUGGESTED FURTHER READING

EDWARDS, J., 1985, *Language, Society and Identity*. Oxford: Blackwell.
EDWARDS, J., 1994, *Multilingualism*. London: Routlege.
FISHMAN, J.A., 1989, *Language and Ethnicity in Minority Sociolinguistic Perspective*.
    Clevedon: Multilingual Matters.
PAULSTON, C.B., 1994, *Linguistic Minorities in Multilingual Settings*. Amsterdam/
    Philadelphia: John Benjamins.
PAULSTON, C.B. (ed.) 1988, *International Handbook of Bilingualism and Bilingual
    Education*. New York: Greenwood.
SKUTNABB-KANGAS, T., 1981, *Bilingualism or Not: The Education of Minorities*.
    Clevedon: Multilingual Matters.

REVIEW AND STUDY QUESTIONS

(1) Write short revision notes on the following:
    (i) The meaning of the following terms: diglossia, the territorial principle, the person-
       ality principle, language shift, language maintenance, language loss, language death.
    (ii) The differences between an evolutionist, conservationist and preservationist
        attitude to languages.
(2) How does diglossia differ from bilingualism? Make a list of the differences.
(3) What is the distinction between the territorial principle and the personality principle?
    Contrast two societal contexts known to you (or from your reading) and explain how
    they are examples of the territorial and/or personality principle.
(4) What are the major factors in language retention and language loss? What factors
    are important in language minority maintenance and spread?

STUDY ACTIVITIES

(1) As a group activity or with a partner, make an abbreviated list of the factors of
    language shift from Conklin & Lourie (1983). On a 5 point scale (5 = very important,
    4 = fairly important, 3 = neither important or unimportant, 2 = fairly unimportant, 1
    = unimportant), rate your perception of the strength of these factors in language shift.
(2) Using the list of factors in language shift from Conklin & Lourie (1983), compare
    the prospects for maintenance or shift in two different language communities.
(3) Create a poster or a chart using the language garden analogy. This may be a chart to
    convey a large amount of information about the language garden. Alternatively it
    may be a simple poster advertising the importance of language variety in the world.
(4) Find out how many different languages are spoken in your area (local or regional). List
    the names of these languages and in which regions they are spoken as an indigenous
    language. Through interviews with language minority members, or through a library
    search, provide a brief example of that language (on paper or on tape).
    Are the languages in your list 'native' or 'in-migrant' languages in your area? Are
    they spoken by different generations or more by older generations? Is there preser-
    vation and maintenance of the language, or is the language declining?

CHAPTER 4

Language Revival
and Reversal

CHAPTER 4

Language Revival and Reversal

INTRODUCTION

The recent history of Hebrew and Welsh, of Catalan and Bahasa Melayu (the indigenous language of Malaysia) provide a more optimistic lyric than the lament of language decline and death. Just as rain forests and whales have become the subject of environmental protection, so languages may be protected and promoted to effect revival and reversal. This chapter focuses on the possibilities of language maintenance, and on optimistic attempts to encourage the growth of a minority language. To achieve this, major theoretical contributions are considered in detail. The first contribution seeks to answer the question 'How is language **vitality** achieved? Building on one part of this theory, the chapter examines the importance of economics in the maintenance and revitalization of a minority language. The next contribution considers 'How can a language be revived and reversed? We start with Giles, Bourhis & Taylor's (1977) consideration of language vitality.

A MODEL OF LANGUAGE SHIFT AND VITALITY

In an attempt to create a model rather than a list of the many factors involved in **language vitality**, Giles, Bourhis & Taylor (1977) propose a three factor model: status factors, demographic factors and institutional support factors, which combine to give more or less minority **language vitality**. Consideration of this model gives some explanatory flesh to the framework of Conklin & Lourie (1983), presented in the last chapter.

Status Factors

A key issue in language status is whether the language minority is in the ascendancy (superordinate) or is subordinate. The survival of Swedish in Finland is partly explained by the superior status of Swedish speakers in Finland. Language minorities are more often in subordinate status to a language majority (e.g. Asian languages in Canada and England; Spanish in the US). However, a more refined analysis requires a breakdown into different types of language status.

The **economic status** of a minority language is likely to be a key element in language vitality. Where, for example, a minority language community experiences considerable unemployment or widespread low income, the pressure may be to shift towards the majority language. A minority language may be sacrificed on the altar of economic progress. A language of the poor and of the peasant is not the language of prosperity and power. Guest workers, in-migrants and refugees looking for social and vocational mobility may place a high value on education in the majority language. After a consideration of Giles, Bourhis & Taylor's (1977) three factor model, the importance of an economic dimension to a minority language will be explored in detail as it is such a key element in language vitality and revival.

The **social status** of a language — its prestige value — will be closely related to economic status of a language and is also a powerful factor in language vitality. When a majority language is seen as giving higher social status and more political power, a shift towards the majority language may occur. Where language minorities exist, there is often a preponderance of lower socio-economic class families. Where a minority language is seen to co-exist with unemployment, poverty, social deprivation and few amenities, the social status of the language may be negatively affected.

A language's **symbolic status** is also important in language vitality. A heritage language may be an important symbol of ethnic identity, of roots in 'the glorious past'. The symbolic importance of a language is exemplified in the Celtic countries. In Ireland, for example, the Irish language is sometimes regarded as a mark of nationhood, a symbol of cultural heritage and identity. There tend to exist positive public attitudes to Irish, Scottish Gaelic and Welsh, but private skepticism. There exists interest in the survival of the minority language, but not in personal involvement in that language. As a symbol of ethnic history, of heritage and national culture, the Celtic languages are sometimes valued by the public. As a tool of widespread personal communication, as a medium of mass education, the languages are less valued. When the personal balance sheet includes employment, educational and vocational success and interpersonal communication, the credit of positive attitudes towards language as a cultural and ethnic symbol is diminished by the costs of perceived prior needs and motives. Goodwill towards the language stops when the personal pay-off is not great.

Is there a paradox beginning to emerge in the relationship between majority and minority languages? Majority languages such as English have high status as languages of international communication. At the same time, internationalism (e.g. the increasing Europeanization of the late 1990s) appears to awaken a basic need for rootedness, for an anchor in a local language and a local cultural community. Becoming European can revive and reawaken the need to belong to one's local heritage and historical groups. In becoming part of a larger whole, a **local identity is essential and foundational**. The push to become a member of the global village seems to lead to a strong pull towards primary roots.

Demographic Factors

The second of Giles, Bourhis & Taylor's (1977) factors concerns the **geographical distribution** of a language minority group. One part of this is the territorial principle;

two languages having their own rights in different areas within a country. Or, in Ireland, there being designated heartland areas where some protection and maintenance of the Irish language is encouraged (the Gaeltachta). A second part of this factor is the **number of speakers** of a certain language and their saturation within a particular area.

Research in Wales, using Census data, indicates that saturation of speakers within a particular area is important in language maintenance (Baker, 1985). For example, in communities where over 70% of people speak Welsh, there appears to be more chance of the language surviving. Also important in a language maintenance equation is the demographics of biliteracy. Analysis of the Welsh language Census data shows that where bilingualism exists without biliteracy, there is an increased likelihood of language decay. When someone can speak a minority language and not write in that language, the number of functions and uses of that language is diminished. Bilingualism without biliteracy also means a decrease in the status of that language, and less chances of a linguistically stable language.

At the same time, it is possible for a small language minority to survive when surrounded by the majority language. Three examples will illustrate that small numbers of minority language speakers can still provide a lively language community, even when surrounded by a majority language community. **First**, in a large city or in border areas, a small number of minority language speakers may be socially and culturally active in their minority language. Such speakers may interact regularly and create a strong language cell. The language of children in the home and street may be important for continuation over time. **Second**, when some language groups have strong religious beliefs, they may prefer not to interact with majority language speakers. Such is the case of the Old Order Amish, Pennsylvania Germans. They continued to speak Pennsylvania German at home and in the community. Such a minority has historically created strong boundaries in their language usage. **Third**, when minority language speakers can travel easily between the homeland and their current area of residence, the minority language may be invigorated and strengthened (e.g. Puerto Ricans in New York and Mexicans in Texas and California).

The idea of demographic factors relates to mixed, **inter-language marriages**. In such marriages, the higher status language will usually have the best chance of survival as the home language. With inter-language marriages specifically, and with language minority communities in general, there is likely to be movement across generations. For example, in-migrants may lose their heritage language by the second or third or fourth generation. This highlights the key importance of languages in the home as a major direct cause in the decline, revival or maintenance of a minority language. Language reproduction in the young is an important part of language vitality.

As a generalization, a minority language is more likely to be preserved in a **rural** than an **urban** area. Once migration of rural people to urban areas occurs, there is an increased chance of the minority language losing its work function. In the office and in the factory, the dominant language is likely to be the majority language with a minority language depreciated. In rural areas, the language of work and of cultural activity is relatively more likely to be the historical language of that area. The language of the farm or of the fishing boat, of religion and of rustic culture is more likely to be the minority language. There will be important exceptions (e.g. where an urban ethnic group generates its own industries, or is sited in a particular part of a city, or congregates regularly for religious purposes).

Institutional Support Factors

Language vitality is affected by the extent and nature of a minority language's use in a wide variety of institutions in a region. Such institutions will include national, regional and local government, religious and cultural organizations, mass media, commerce and industry, and not least education. The absence or presence of a minority language in the **mass media** (television, radio, newspapers, magazines, tapes and computer software) at the very least affects the prestige of a language. The use of a minority language in books and magazines, for example, is also important for biliteracy. Language may be given the status of a modern, twentieth century language when it is used in the media. The perceived quality of television programs (compared to majority language programs) will be important (Baetens Beardsmore & van Beeck, 1984). However, it is possible to exaggerate the importance of television and radio in its effect on the communicative use of a minority language. Television and radio provide only a passive medium for language. Research from Wales (see Baker, 1985, 1992) suggests that it is majority language mass media that is the destroyer of a minority language and culture, rather than minority language television and radio being the salvation of the language. The glossy, high quality of TV English language programs provides fierce competition for minority languages. Media attractiveness has resulted in the invasion of Hollywood productions in countries where English is not prevalent. Active participation in a minority language is required for language survival; an event that mass media by its receptive nature does not provide.

Religion can be a strong and important vehicle for the maintenance of a majority and a minority language. The use of classical Arabic in Islam, Hebrew in Judaism, and German among the Protestant Old Order Amish in Pennsylvania each illustrates that religion has been a preserver of language. It is said in Wales that the language would not have survived into the twentieth century had it not been for its dominant position in Welsh chapels and in Welsh religious life inside the home (e.g. the family reading the Bible in Welsh). Religion may help standardize a language. Through its holy books, tracts and pamphlets, traveling missionaries and teachers, a relatively standard form of a language may evolve.

Providing **administrative services** in a minority language also serves to give status to that language. It also increases the usefulness of that minority language for communication. The use of languages within educational institutions is probably an essential but not sufficient condition for language maintenance. Where **schooling** in a minority language does not exist, the chances of the long-term survival of that language in a modern society may be severely diminished. Where the minority language is used in the school situation, the chances of survival are greatly increased but not guaranteed. Nancy Hornberger's (1988) acclaimed anthropological study of language planning, language shift and bilingual education in the Quechua speaking highlands of southern Peru suggested that:

'Schools cannot be agents for language maintenance if their communities, for whatever reason, do not want them to be.' (p. 229)

Community support for bilingual education in the minority language and culture outside school are important. Education by itself cannot enable a minority language to survive. Other supports are essential, particularly regeneration of languages within the family and an economic basis for a language. The importance of the family in language maintenance is considered in the next chapter. After a brief critical comment on the concept of ethnolinguistic vitality, this chapter continues by a deeper consideration of the major importance of the economy in language reversal and maintenance.

Giles, Bourhis & Taylor's (1977) theory of language vitality has been **criticized** by Husband & Khan (1982). **First**, they suggest that the dimensions and factors are not separate and independent of each other. In reality, these elements interact, inter-relate and are often mutually dependent on each other. While presented as comprehensive and wide-ranging, a critique that the factors are 'something of an untheorised *pot pourri*' (p. 195), relates to a consensus rather than a conflict perspective (see Chapter 19), with no means of 'sifting and weighing the many variables that are listed' (p. 195). These authors doubt whether the listing of variables that constitute language vitality is any greater than the sum of its parts or creates an integrated whole.

Second, different contexts have widely differing processes and recipes that lead to more or less language vitality. The historical, social, economic, cultural and political processes that operate in any language community vary considerably. We need a historical and sociological perspective, for example, to help explain patterns of interaction that relate to language vitality. Change and variability across time is seemingly not catered for in this theory. **Third**, the theory is not easy to operationalize in research. Many of the factors may not be easily or unambiguously measured. Thus the theory is difficult to test.

This completes the consideration of Giles, Bourhis & Taylor's (1977) theory of language vitality. When the economic status of a language was introduced earlier in this chapter, it was suggested that economics is a key element in language loss, shift, vitality and revival. Therefore, this chapter now proceeds to give a more detailed examination of the importance of the economic dimension to language shift and vitality. However, it needs remembering that (1) the economic dimension is only one dimension in the status of a language — there are social and symbolic status factors as well; (2) the economic dimension interacts with other vitality factors, and is not a separate entity.

BILINGUALISM AND THE ECONOMY

There is sometimes a danger that writing and speeches about minority languages become romantic and cloistered. The love of a language and the need to preserve all that is valuable from the past is important. But life is often about finding a job, getting enough money to buy food, find shelter and own a TV, avoiding unemployment and poverty. For others, life is much about increasing salaries, affording a bigger house in a more pleasant neighborhood, affording vacations and cars, extras for the children and economic advantages over others.

Bilingual education is devalued unless it connects with the economy. Students want jobs, money and increasing affluence after leaving school. When a school fosters a form of bilingualism that connects with a local, national or international economy, the higher the value of that bilingual education. Thus, one premise of this section is that the future of language minorities is centrally related to individual, home and community economies. Because of this central relationship, the section will widen the discussion beyond language vitality.

This section explores a paradox among bilinguals. Among language minority groups, there is often unemployment, poverty and low wages. Yet bilinguals have linguistic capital. Bilinguals often have marketable language skills and intercultural knowledge. Bilinguals are often economically impoverished yet linguistically accomplished.

Bilingualism as an Economic Advantage

In an increasingly bilingual and multilingual world, with trade barriers being broken, with single markets in areas such as Europe growing, and with economic competition rapidly developing on a global scale, **competence in languages is increasingly important**. Those who have multilinguistic capital may be in a position to increase their economic capital.

This immediately raises the question of which languages may be useful for economic advancement? In many countries of the world, it is **English** as a second or foreign language that has visible economic value. As Coulmas (1992) suggests,

> 'no Japanese businessman ever tries to operate on the American market without a sufficient command of English, whereas the reverse case, of American business people who expect to be able to do business in Japan without being proficient in Japanese, is not at all rare. On the one hand, this is a reflection of the arrogance of power, but on the other hand, it testifies to the fact that the opportunities for realizing the functional potential of English on the Japanese market are far better than those of realizing the functional potential of Japanese on the American market.' (pp. 66 & 67)

Nevertheless **Japanese** has increasingly become a desirable modern foreign language, as people realize that to sell to the Japanese requires a knowledge of the Japanese language and culture. As Helmut Schmidt, former chancellor of the old Federal Republic of Germany once said: 'If you wish to buy fromus, you can talk any language you like, for we shall try to understand you. If you want to sell to us, then you must speak our language'.

Alongside the English language, the Japanese, German, French, Spanish and Portuguese languages have historically been regarded as important **trading languages**. However, in the future, this list of modern languages for marketing and trading purposes is likely to grow significantly. For example, Bahasa Melayu, Mandarin and Cantonese, Panjabi and Hindi, Arabic and Korean may each become increasingly valuable. This reflects the important half-truth of Coulmas (1992) who suggests that 'in spite of the non-economic values attached to language, what prevails in matters of language is often that which is profitable' (p. 152). The other half of the half-truth is that language is also related to less tangible, measurable and affective characteristics such as the social, cultural and particularly religious value in some language communities for a particular language. The half-truth also hides the tension that can often exist between economic development and cultural reproduction. The economic value of a language may at times clash with preserving that language to reflect heritage, home values and historical traditions. Nevertheless, the economic value of language relates strongly to the prestige of that language and hence its chances of maintenance and reproduction.

If languages are increasingly important in international trading, are they equally important in small and medium-sized businesses as in **multinational corporations**? In large businesses, as García & Otheguy (1994) reveal, we should be cautious in assuming that a modern foreign language is needed in top executives and top managers. In multinational corporations, for example, the tendency may not be to send executives with modern language qualifications abroad. Rather there will be local nationals within a country, working for that corporation, who are bilingual in both the regional or national language and an international language such as English. United State corporations who run their operations abroad, and multi-national organizations, may prefer locally based executives because of their native-like fluency in the national languages, their thorough understanding of the cultures of that region, and their ability to communicate with customers and the work force as well as with international colleagues. Local nationals are often paid a lower salary than executives sent from, for example, the United States.

This indicates that large corporations and multinational companies are increasingly aware that international business requires the use of regional and national languages. The imposition, for example of the English language, will not help to sell products abroad. To sell in Germany, Latin America, Japan, the Pacific Basin increasingly requires business people whose language and culture is congruent with that of the buyer. A **congruent language** is valuable for communication. Sometimes, there may be no other way to conduct trade (e.g. if the buyer does not speak English). Speaking the buyer's language also signals favorable attitudes to the buyer's ethnicity and culture. A competent understanding of the buyer's culture also signals respect for the buyer and their way of doing business.

García & Otheguy (1994) found in their research, **smaller and medium sized businesses** often require executives and managers who are capable of speaking in languages other than English or another majority language. To have the edge over competitors, the language of business is important, and where it is congruent with the language of the area for business, a competitive edge is added. Those who insist that English should be the international medium of business may be selling themselves short, economically, socially and personally.

This reflects a paradox. While **English** is often accepted as the international language in multinational companies and international trade, the massive spread of English during this century has led to a reaction, rather like adjusting a balance, with national and regional groups wishing to assert their local identity through a retention of their heritage language and culture. This has occurred in France and England, for example, and in many other European countries. An increased accent on national and regional languages in the face of international trade, has led to buying from those who are willing to speak the language and culture of the region rather than imposing their own language on the buyer. Nevertheless, the competitive edge has often more to do with prices, lowest quotations, and the lowest bid rather than language preference.

Minority Languages

In suggesting that bilingualism has economic advantages, the only languages to be highlighted so far in this section have been majority languages. English, German, French and Arabic, for example, are relatively prestigious majority languages. What is the **place of minority languages in the economy**? Will bilinguals from language minorities have no economic advantage, no valuable trading language in their minority language, no chance due to their bilingualism of getting out of the poverty trap that many experience?

In Europe, for example, the move from regional and state economies to a single European market policy, interlocking business structures in different European countries, encouraging mobility in businesses across European countries, may leave a distinction between **core and periphery**, between those in important urban business areas and those in rural peripheries (e.g. rural areas in Ireland, Wales and Scotland). Since many indigenous minority languages in Europe are found in regions that are relatively sparsely populated, economically under-developed, with poorer rural road and transport systems, there is a danger that there will growing inequality between core and periphery.

In the **economic restructuring** that has occurred in the last 60 years, increased competition has led to the need for more efficiency to maintain profit. Industries and services have frequently had to 'automate, emigrate or evaporate'. Emigration of industries has been to countries such as Taiwan, Mexico, Brazil and Singapore, where wages, and therefore production costs, are relatively low. Such outside investment may sometimes offer work and wages to language minority members. Such outside investment also has negative consequences for language minorities. Such consequences now need to be discussed.

One negative consequence is that the investment may not reach a language minority. For example, where such minorities live in **rural areas** (e.g. Irish and Welsh speakers), economic growth may be in the urban 'core' rather than the rural periphery. Alternatively, the higher grade jobs may be in relatively affluent city areas, and the lower grade, poorly paid work in the more remote areas.

A different scenario is when a peripheral area attracts inward investment (e.g. factories are located in remoter areas). The tendency is for the local language minorities to provide relatively cheap workers, while the better paid (language majority) **managers** either to operate from their far-away city headquarters or move into the periphery language community. In both cases (given below), the managers may have a negative effect on language maintenance:

(1) By working from city headquarters, there is a geographical separation of majority language manager and minority language worker that represents a status, and a social, cultural, economic and power division. Such a division has prestige consequences for the majority and minority language. Each language is identified with greater or lesser affluence, higher and lower status, more or less power.

(2) By living in the language minority community, a manager who does not learn the local language evokes a class distinction. The manager speaks the majority language; the workers the minority language. One is a higher socio-economic class; the other a lower socio-economic class. There is a social class division, and a separation or fracture within the social class structure of the community (Morris, 1992). Social tensions may result that lead to divisions along both social class and language dimensions. As Morris (1992) found in her research, one solution is language minority managers who are able to operate across social classes inside their language group. Being bilingual, such managers can also operate (e.g. for export purposes) in language majority and core regions.

For **language minorities**, it seems essential that, through entrepreneurial activity, enterprise and risk-taking, they develop networked small and medium sized businesses. Such businesses, often located in rural areas, sometimes producing goods for export, other times using ease of communications (e.g. via computers) to deliver services, are essential for local languages to be preserved. Language minority businesses need to be networked where possible, within a region and increasingly internationally.

The absence of community based, ethnically based businesses, increases the risk of the emigration of more able, more skilled and more entrepreneurial people away from the area, hence leaving the language itself in peril. A language community without **economic activity** is in danger of starving the language of one essential support mechanism. An economically wealthy language has a higher probability of being a healthy language. An economically impoverished language places that language at risk.

While language communities are not necessarily internally integrated, (having their own inner power and status struggles, differences and divisions), such language communities need to generate their own local economies and to able to market their products and services beyond the region. In Gwynedd, North Wales, for example, there are two examples of **economic language planning**. First, new businesses located in language minority communities are initially subsidized, professionally advised and developed. Second, many jobs now demand bilingual applicants. The ability to use Welsh and English is regarded as essential for employment in teaching, many administrative jobs, local authority services, secretarial and clerical posts. Thus the Welsh language is given a vital economic foundation.

Some **minority language businesses** (e.g. local radio and television stations) create language-related economic activity that, in itself, spawns secondary economic activity to support such businesses (e.g. catering services, translation services, music and drama activities).

In many countries of the world, there are examples of **language communities** who are immigrant rather than indigenous who, through fast food (e.g. the Chinese restaurants) and the clothes trade (e.g. various Asian groups) maintain their language via ethnic industries. The language is supported by businesses where factory workers, shop workers and managers work partly or mainly through their heritage language.

This raises an issue about those language minorities who are often located in inner city, **urban**, in-migrant communities. As already expressed at the start of this section, such families and language communities are often surrounded by poverty, deprivation, unemployment and inequality of opportunity to acquire wealth. García & Otheguy (1994) provide an analysis of the economic possibilities of such urban language communities, particularly in the United States. The ability to speak a minority language can be crucial in gaining access to such an ethnic business. If everyone else in the organization speaks Spanish or Cantonese, to gain employment requires knowledge of that language.

A minority language may also be valuable at the **customer** interface. García & Otheguy (1994) relate an example:

> 'As the burgers and fries popped over the counter at the usual speed on the line with the Spanish-speaking employee, the line with the English-speaking employee was moving slowly, creating inefficiencies caused by her difficulty in communicating with the Spanish-speaking customers.' (p. 110)

The problem with many **ethnic businesses** is the level of status, salary and conditions that such businesses provide for their employees. Often the jobs available are of a lower status with a relatively lower salary, and with advancement not always easy or possible. García & Otheguy (1994) found that in United States businesses, the demand for bilingual workers was not usually at the top executive levels. Rather, the need for bilinguals was for the lower and middle ranges of occupation. For example, US businesses required bilingual secretaries, clerks, shop floor assistants, rather than bilingual managers and executives. Waldman's (1994) US research found that the five most needed language abilities required were: telephone; customer contact or relations; translation and interpretation; word processing and correspondence. Spanish was the language most required by companies, followed by German, French and Japanese.

However, **smaller companies** indicated that language skills are of value in their higher positions. In small companies, the language of the whole workforce may be the minority language. Thus cohesion and an integrated purpose is attained when managers speak the same language as those whom they manage.

With the Spanish speaking population of the United States rapidly growing, and with **Spanish** an important trading language in Latin America and elsewhere, there is a possibility that Spanish may be of increasing economic value inside the United States and for marketing abroad. Therefore, it seems economically valuable in the next century to be bilingual. For some individuals, this is to gain employment and try to avoid poverty. For others, bilingualism may be of value to work locally for international and multinational corporations. For yet others, who wish to travel abroad to do their trade, languages also become increasingly important. The concept that speaking English is all one needs, whether in Europe or the United States, seems to only contain a part of the truth.

There is no guarantee that those who become linguistically assimilated (e.g. speak English only) in countries like the United States will gain **employment**. The evidence from García & Otheguy (1994) and Morales & Bonilla (1993) confirms that the ability to speak English does not give equal access to jobs and wealth. Linguistic assimilation does not mean incorporation into the economic structure of the country. If there is a growth of ethnic businesses (e.g. in urban areas), and a development of language minority businesses in peripheral, rural areas, then bilingualism rather than English monolingualism may become more economically valuable.

As important as is the economy of a language minority, this is only one factor in **language maintenance and language revival**. Therefore, this chapter moves on to examine a more global consideration of the factors and processes of language revival. Before examining the important contribution of Joshua Fishman, a short consideration of terminology is required.

Paulston, Chen & Connerty (1993) offer a non-exclusive **distinction** between language revival, language revitalization and language reversal which can be subsumed under the term 'language regenesis'. **Language revival** is reserved for the giving of new life to a dead language. An example is the revival of Hebrew — bringing a dead language alive. Maori and Welsh would not be included as there has been a continuous use of the language over many centuries. **Language revitalization** is the imparting of new vigor to an existing language, often by increasing the domains where the language is used (e.g. Finnish and Welsh). **Language reversal** refers to the turning around of current (downward) trends in a language. For Paulston, Chen & Connerty (1993), language reversal often focuses on a more prominent use of a language *vis-à-vis* its relation to other state language(s). This may be in legal terms (e.g. the gaining of official status for Catalan in 1978); a renaissance in use (e.g. Maori); or non-native language being accepted after a period of rejection for economic and international communication purposes (e.g. English in Singapore and Malaysia).

LANGUAGE REVIVAL AND REVERSAL

A major contribution to the theory of attempting the reversal of language shift is by Joshua **Fishman** (1991, 1993). Fishman (1991) notes a changing perspective in the topic of language shift. The premise has been that minority languages, like patients in a hospital or doctor's surgery, will ultimately die. Therefore all one can do is to understand the causes of death and illness, and attempt to overcome those causes for as long as possible. Instead, Fishman (1991) argues that language shift needs to take the jump of modern medicine by attempting 'not only to combat illness, but to cultivate "wellness"' (p. xii).

Fishman (1991) seeks to answer the question 'what are the priorities in planning language shift?' For example, what is the point of pouring money into minority language mass media and bilingual bureaucracy when home, family, neighborhood and face-to-face community use of the minority language is lacking? It is like blowing air into a punctured balloon. Blowing minority language air in through the mass media and legislation doesn't make a usable balloon, because of the unmended hole.

Fishman (1991) provides a list of **priorities** to halt language decline and attempt to reverse language shift. This plan also shows why many efforts to reverse minority language situations have often resulted in failure rather than success. Before we examine this plan, Fishman (1991) provides a basic philosophy and set of assumptions that are required before establishing priorities in reversing language shift .

Assumptions of Reversing Language Shift

First, when a society or community is losing its language and culture, it is likely to feel pain. This hurt may be symptomatic of the social injustice towards that community. Although it may not be a cancer but more like a toothache, to those who experience it, there is real rather than imaginary suffering. Such suffering needs remedying. **Second**, the basis of reversing language shift is that a more global village, a world more unified by mass communication and speedy travel, a more integrated eastern and western Europe, does not bury the need for local language and local culture. Indeed, a more centrally organized and uniform world may increase rather than decrease the need for language and cultural identity at a local level. Having local cultural and linguistic roots may be a necessary precondition before integrating into a global village. **Third**, and most importantly for Fishman (1991), the political basis of the plan is to support **cultural pluralism and cultural self-determination**. The destruction of minority languages is the destruction of intimacy, family and community, often involving oppression of the weak by the strong, subjugating the unique and traditional by the uniform and central. Thus, Fishman (1991) argues for 'greater sociocultural self-sufficiency, self-help, self-regulation and initiative' (p. 4) among linguistic communities.

Fourth, an ethnic or culture group that has lost its language is different from that group with their minority language. Fishman (1991) cites the case of Jews who, not speaking Hebrew, tend to have a different daily life-pattern, a different kind of sub-culture. Language shift accompanies cultural change. This suggests that language shift is not just about language; it is about the attendant culture as well. The argument for language restoration and resurrection must therefore involve a call for cultural change and greater cultural self-determination. Fishman (1991) warns of the danger of language as the sole focus for shift. The danger is that minority language activists will:

> 'become so accustomed to speaking only to each other that they forget how to speak effectively to others. What activists no longer need to explain to each other they often no longer know how to explain to others. They often need to remind themselves and to make themselves more conscious of their own RLS [Reversing Language Shift] 'basic principles', so that they can then make others more conscious of these principles as well.' (pp. 18/19)

A different warning is given to those who believe that reversing language shift is purely about the accumulation of **power and money** (e.g. as has been said about the use of Hebrew and Welsh). Believing that language minorities who are attempting language reversal and resurrection are concerned with achieving power and increasing wealth, is simplistic and misguided. Fishman (1991) argues that human values, feelings, loyalties and basic life-philosophies are present in the complex reasons for language change. Language activists often have ideals, commitments, even altruism that makes their motives more than just power and money. Minority languages and cultures, in their desire for a healthy existence, may be sometimes irrational or super-rational. This is similar to religion, love, art and music where there are personal elements that transcend conscious rationality, and transcend self-interest in power and money.

Fifth, to help understand language shift, Fishman (1991) clarifies the relationship between language and culture in terms of three links:

(1) **A language indexes its culture.** A language and its attendant culture will have grown up together over a long period of history, and be in harmony with each other. Thus the language that has grown up round a culture best expresses that culture. Its vocabulary, idioms, metaphors are the ones that best explain at a cognitive and emotive level that culture.

(2) **A language symbolizes its culture.** To speak German in the US, during World War 1 and France and Britain during World War 2 was not appropriate nor acceptable. Not that the allies were at war with the German language. Rather, the German language symbolized the enemy. Therefore, that language was inappropriate in allied countries. A language tends to symbolize the status of that language. For example, to speak English in Kuwait following the victory against Saddam Hussein of Iraq was to be symbolically associated with status, power and victory. Speaking English often symbolizes money and modernity, affluence and achievement. English may also symbolize colonial subjugation. A language that is apparently dying may symbolize low status and low income. In certain parts of Ireland and Wales, the indigenous language is sometimes perceived as a symbol of the past rather than the present, of disadvantage rather than advantage.

(3) **Culture is partly created from its language.** Much of a culture is enacted and transmitted verbally. The songs, hymns, prayers of a culture, its folk tales and shrewd sayings, its appropriate forms of greeting and leaving, its history, wisdom and ideals are all wrapped up in its language. The taste and flavor of a culture is given through its language; its memories and traditions are stored in its language. An example is a saying or a figure of speech in a minority language that requires a long explanation in another language. Even then that pithy saying may sacrifice some of its meaning and feeling in translation. At the same time, culture is derived from many more sources than language. For example, there are many different cultures which all use the Spanish language.

Sixth, Fishman (1991) makes an argument for **language planning**. Just as there is economic planning, educational planning and family planning, so there can and should be language planning. Such planning has as its base 're-establishing local options, local control, local hope, and local meaning to life. It reveals a humanistic and positive outlook *vis-à-vis* intergroup life, rather than a mechanistic and fatalistic one. It espouses the right and the ability of small cultures to live and to inform life for their own members as well as to contribute thereby to the enrichment of human kind as a whole' (p. 35).

Language planning, also called language engineering, refers to 'deliberate efforts to influence the behavior of others with respect to the acquisition, structure, or functional allocation of their language codes' (Cooper, 1989: 45). Such language planning involves **status planning** (raising the status of a language within society), **corpus planning** (concerning the vocabulary, spelling, grammar and standardization of the minority language) and **acquisition planning** (creating language spread by increasing the number of speakers and uses (via empowerment) by, for example, language teaching).

Cooper (1989: 98) provides a scheme for understanding language planning by asking a series of key questions:

- **Which actors** (e.g. elites, influential people, counter-elites, non-elite policy implementers)
- **attempt to influence which behaviors** (e.g. the purposes or functions for which the language is to be used)
- **of which people** (e.g. of which individuals or organizations)
- **for what ends** (e.g. overt (language-related behaviors) or latent (non-language-related behaviors, the satisfaction of interests)
- **under what conditions** (e.g. political, economic, social, demographic, ecological, cultural)
- **by what means** (e.g. authority, force, promotion, persuasion)
- **through what decision-making processes and means**
- **with what effect or outcome?**

This relatively comprehensive set of questions makes some important points. First, language planning may be generated by different groups. For example, poets, linguists, lexicographers, missionaries, soldiers as well as administrators, legislators and politicians may become involved in language planning. Cooper (1989) argues, however, that language planning is more likely to succeed when it is embraced or promoted by elite groups or counter-elites. Such **elites** tend to work primarily from their own self-interests. Language planning is motivated by efforts to secure or reinforce the interests of particular people. However, language planning may positively affect the masses by adding to their self identity, self-esteem, social connectedness and links with their heritage and future.

A consideration of language planning runs the danger of over-emphasizing its importance in overall political planning. **First,** there is often piecemeal pragmatism rather than planning. The revival of Hebrew is often quoted as one triumphant and successful example of language planning. Yet the rapid advance of Hebrew in Israel appears to have occurred by improvisation and diverse ventures rather than by carefully structured, systematic and sequenced language planning. **Second,** as Heath (1986) has shown, political and economic decisions usually govern language decisions. Language decisions are subsidiary and minor concerns of those in power, whose pervading interests are more frequently about power and purse. Language is usually an outcome from other decisions rather than a determinant of social, political or economic policies. Yet, as the European Commission has increasingly stressed, language minority issues and the need for bilingualism and multilingualism in a future Europe are relevant to European cultural and economic development. Bilingualism is one part of an interconnected whole in Europeanization.

Language status and corpus planning require full consideration of bilingualism and not just planning for the minority language. Where minority languages exist, there is usually the need to be bilingual if not multilingual. Minority language monolingualism is usually impracticable. To create blockades and barricades between languages is almost impossible in the twentieth century. Cross-cultural communication is the reality; a bunker approach to a minority language and culture may be tantamount to language death. This returns us to the concept of diglossia, highlighting the importance of different functions for the minority and majority language. Where different languages have different functions, then an **additive** rather than a **subtractive** bilingual situation may exist.

An **additive** bilingual situation is where the addition of a second language and culture is unlikely to replace or displace the first language and culture (Lambert, 1980). For example, English-speaking North Americans who learn a second language (e.g. French, Spanish) will not lose their English but gain another language and parts of its attendant culture. The 'value added' benefits may not only be linguistic and cultural, but social and economic as well. Positive attitudes to diglossia and bilingualism may also result. In contrast, the learning of a majority second language may undermine a person's minority first language and culture, thus creating a **subtractive** situation. For example, an in-migrant may find pressure to use the dominant language and feel embarrassment in using the home language.

When the second language is prestigious and powerful, exclusively used in education and in the jobs market, and when the minority language is perceived as of low status and value, stable diglossia and bilingualism may be threatened. Instead of addition, there is subtraction; division instead of multiplication. Additive and subtractive bilingualism is further discussed in the next chapter.

Steps in Reversing Language Shift

Fishman's (1990, 1991, 1993) Graded Intergenerational Disruption Scale (GIDS) is an aid to language planning and attempted **language reversal**. Just as the Richter scale measures intensity of earthquakes, so Fishman's scale gives a guide to how far a minority language is threatened and disrupted. The higher the number on the scale, the more a language is threatened. The idea of stages is that it is little good attempting later stages if earlier stages are not at least partly achieved. Various foundations are needed before building the upper levels. The value of the scale is not just in its eight sequenced steps or

> **Fishman's (1990, 1991) Graded Intergenerational Disruption Scale for Threatened Languages**
>
> Stage 8   Social isolation of the few remaining speakers of the minority language. Need to record the language for later possible reconstruction.
>
> Stage 7   Minority language used by older and not younger generation. Need to multiply the language in the younger generation.
>
> Stage 6   Minority language is passed on from generation to generation and used in the community. Need to support the family in intergenerational continuity (e.g. provision of minority language nursery schools).
>
> Stage 5   Literacy in the minority language. Need to support literacy movements in the minority language, particularly when there is no government support.
>
> Stage 4   Formal, compulsory education available in the minority language. May need to be financially supported by the minority language community.
>
> Stage 3   Use of the minority language in less specialized work areas involving interaction with majority language speakers.
>
> Stage 2   Lower government services and mass media available in the minority language.
>
> Stage 1   Some use of minority language available in higher education, central government and national media.

stages. Rather it provides a plan for action for reversing languages in decline and a set of priorities. The eight stages are briefly summarized, and then considered one by one.

Stage 8

Stage 8 represents the 'worst case' for a language. A few of the older generation will still be able to speak the language but probably not to each other because they are socially isolated. The few remaining speakers of a language are so scattered that minority language interaction is rarely possible. At this stage it is seen as important that folklorists and linguists collect as much information as they can from these few survivors of the language community. The folk-tales and sayings, grammar and vocabulary, need to be collected on tape and paper as a permanent record of that language. Since the language building is in ruins and the foundations have crumbled, can anything be done to save the language? The one ray of hope is that the records of the language can be used by a younger generation to revive the language. With Australian Aboriginal languages and Cornish in England, this has been attempted. Thus the remnants of the foundations can be reused to start to reconstruct the language.

Stage 7

A language in Stage 7 will be used on a daily communication basis, but by more mature-age speakers beyond child-bearing. A language used by the older rather than the younger generation is likely to die as that older generation disappears. The language is unlikely to be reproduced in the younger generation as mothers and fathers speak the majority language with their children. While the aim of Stage 8 is to reassemble the language, the aim of Stage 7 is to spread the language amongst the young. Mothers and fathers are encouraged to bring up their children in the minority language. It is essential to reproduce that dying language in children who may later bring up their children in that language to ensure language continuity.

Fishman (1991) is clear about well-intentioned but, in the long term future of a language, less important events. The danger of Stage 7 includes positive attitudes towards the language without positive action: 'the road to societal language death is paved with the good intentions called "positive attitudes"' (p. 91). The danger also is in exaggerating the value of symbolic events in the minority language, on the stage and the written page, in the gathering of the clans and at ceremonies. These events are relatively unimportant in the long term salvation of the language compared with the raising of children in that minority language. However, this is not to argue that such language events are valueless. Their value ultimately lies in indirectly encouraging language life at the daily participative level.

When a language is passed on from generation to generation through child rearing practices, then a language has some chance of long term success. In child development and particularly in the teenage years, using rather losing a minority language becomes crucial. When the popular majority language culture becomes attractive to teenagers, minority language youth activities with youth participating and interacting in their minority language becomes critical (Baker, 1992).

The importance of ensuring that a minority language is passed from one generation to another is summed up by Fishman (1991):

> 'The road to societal death is paved by language activity that is not focused on intergenerational continuity, i.e. that is diverted into efforts that do not involve and influence the socialization behaviors of families of child-bearing age.' (p. 91)

Performances and publications, ceremonies and cultural meetings need to be seen as a means to an end, and not as an end in themselves. Such formal language events, however carefully arranged, do not intrinsically lead to the passing of a language from generation to generation. Such events are valuable to the extent they foster the passing of a language across generations. Such events must not just be for the elite, the firm disciples or the converts, but have missionary aims to secure the language in the younger generation. Such events are important to the extent to which they encourage everyday activity, at family and community level, in that language. One-off events (e.g. eisteddfodau in Wales), may produce the feeling of a strong language and an emotional lift for the individual.

Fishman's (1991) argument is that unless such events link into usual, daily, family socialization, the language in the long term is not being promoted.

Stage 6

Stage 6 is seen as the crucial, pivotal stage for the survival of a language. In Stage 6, a language will be passed to the next generation. At this sixth stage, the minority language will be used between grandparents, parents and children. This is regarded as quintessential in the fate of a language. If the minority language is used in the family, it may also be used in the street, in shops, with neighbors and friends. The language will more probably be spoken in the neighborhood and in community life, in religious and cultural events, in leisure and local informal commercial activity. At Stage 6, there will be a language community of a greater or lesser proportion.

This stage essentially concerns the informal use of a language in the home and the community. As such, the language may be supported and encouraged, but it may be outside the realms of formal language planning. The focus of this stage is the family, and the family within its community. As an institution, the family creates and maintains boundaries from the outside that may prevent the majority language from over-intrusion. However, Fishman (1991) points out that the more urbanized twentieth century family does not live in a strong enough castle to prevent considerable outside influence from other languages. With the increase in one parent families and both parents going out to work, the idea of mother and father as sole transmitters of the minority language is less strong. The alternative is that agencies and institutions supporting the home also create a minority language and minority cultural environment (e.g. the availability of minority language nursery schools). What is crucial is that early childhood and teenage socialization is enacted in the minority language and culture. The danger is in believing that other institutions such as the school, the mass media, the economy and government legislation will reverse language shift in themselves. Rather, language reversal is pivotal on Stage 6. Fishman (1991) argues that Stage 6 cannot be dispensed with.

Unless a language is transmitted across the generations, other activity may have short term success and long term failure:

> 'If this stage is not satisfied, all else can amount to little more than biding time ... Attaining Stage 6 is a necessary, even if not a sufficient, desideratum of RLS [Reversing Language Shift].' (p. 399)

Stage 5

Stage 5 occurs when a minority language in the home, school and community goes beyond oracy to literacy. First, literacy in the minority language is seen to be important because it facilitates alternative means of communication, especially across distance and time. Second, the image and status of a minority language is raised when it is present in print. Such status is not merely symbolic. Literacy in the minority language means that a person is not just subject to majority language print media. Majority language media will contain dominant and powerful viewpoints, the attitudes of the center, the values and the beliefs of the majority language. Minority language literacy allows the possibility of minority language culture, political and ideological viewpoints to be presented. Third, literacy ensures a much wider variety of functions for a language. Such literacy may open more doors to employment, increase the chance of social and vocational mobility. However, at Stage 5, literacy in the majority language or biliteracy may be more important than literacy purely in the minority language if such mobility is desired.

Where education is through the majority language, then literacy in the minority language may be achieved through local community effort. Via Saturday and Sunday schools, in evening classes and through religious institutions, a literacy program in the minority language may be established. While such local efforts may be costly in money, they have the advantage of giving control in such literacy education to the community rather than to the central majority language government. With such control, local institutions can determine the appropriate means of literacy and cultural acquisition. While creating a financial burden, such activities may give a language community a focus, a shared commitment and a further *raison d'être*. While self-sacrifice is often hard and unfair, it can result in vitality, commitment, enthusiasm and a sense of unifying purpose.

For Fishman (1991), Stages 8 to 5 constitute the minimum basis of reversing language shift. The activities at these stages rely solely on the efforts of the language community itself. Such stages reflect a diglossic situation where the minority language has separate functions from the majority language. Given that bilingualism rather than minority language monolingualism will exist, such a minority language group may not be disadvantaged. They will usually have access to mainstream education from elementary to University levels. The full range of government services also will be available, including educational and welfare services. After Stage 5 comes the attempt to capture the formal functions so far reserved for the majority language (e.g. mass media, compulsory education, political self-determination). It is at this point that the minority language may come out of its enclave and seek to challenge majority language castles.

Stage 4

One of the first approaches into the majority language castle may be through education. Schools may be created and supported by the minority language community itself, not funded by the central purse. Such private schools may be outside the budgets of many relatively poor minority language communities. Therefore, minority language medium education paid for by central government may be sought. Central government will often still require some control over the curriculum of such schools. That is, minority language medium education may only partly be under the control of the local minority language community. Such schools may need to prove that they are as effective and as successful as neighboring majority language schools; those attending them not being at a disadvantage but an advantage.

Stage 3

In previous stages, some people will use their minority language in a place of work at the 'lower work' (local and less specialized work) level. In previous stages, a few such workers will function economically in a relatively isolated way in the local neighborhood or as a self-contained group. Few bridges will exist with the majority language community. At Stage 3, creating a wider economic base for the minority language becomes important.

Such economic activity will involve the establishment of minority language staffed enterprises and services, not just for the local market but for national and international markets as well. Such minority language enterprise will, at times, require communication in the majority language. However, the on-the-floor activity and in-house communication may all be through the minority language.

However, success by language minority enterprise in international and national economic activity may not be without danger to the minority language. The economic value of majority languages, and the arrival of in-migrants should there be economic success, are just two possible after-effects. As economic independence and self-regulation evolve, the temptation may be to increase profit by switching to international majority languages.

Such minority language economic activity nevertheless opens doors to increasing affluence, vocational mobility and social status. Young minority language speakers may be more willing to stay in an area rather than migrate to majority language pastures when there is economic opportunity. When there are jobs and money in the local community, the minority language has firmer roots and resources.

Stage 2

The penultimate stage is extending lower government services and mass media into the minority language. Local government institutions may offer their services through the minority language; health and postal services, courts and the police service for example. Telephone and banking services, energy providing bodies and supermarkets may also become willing to use the minority language in their service and communication with the public.

Central government may wish to control its services to language minority regions to influence attitudes and opinions, information and ideology. The more the decision making processes (educational, economic and political) are released to such regions, the more power that local language has to capture the minds of the minority. In Stage 2, national radio and television may be asked to provide a set number of hours in the minority language.

Alternatively, as in Wales, a particular channel may be mostly dedicated to minority language use. Not only does the use of minority language television and radio help to disseminate the attendant culture. It will also provide primary and secondary employment for minority language speakers.

The particular dangers of this stage may be in creaming off the most able and ambitious professionals into majority language positions. Minority language media also face severe viewing competition from Anglo-American, high-budget programs. The mass media provide status for a minority language, a channel for the minority cultural message, but no salvation for the language in and by itself.

Stage 1

In this final stage, the pinnacle of achievement in language shift, the minority language will be used at University level and will be strongly represented in mass media output, governmental services and throughout occupations. Alongside some degree of economic autonomy will also be cultural autonomy. At this stage the language will be officially recognized in central government legislation or a Language Act.

Throughout the four latter stages, Fishman (1991) is keen to point out that Stage 6 is still pre-eminent. When mass communications, economic rewards and vocational opportunities exist through the minority language, it is still the family, the neighborhood and community language life that is vital in the long term success of the language. All the trappings of language status (e.g. mass media), all the power of legislation, all the success in economic self-determination does not assure the future of a language. Important as are Stages 4 to 1, a language is ultimately lost and won inside the minds and hearts of individuals. While such individuals will doubtless be affected by economic, political and media factors, there is a personal cost-benefit analysis that ultimately determines whether one language is passed on to the next generation or not.

Limits and Critics

While Fishman (1991) is careful to point out that one stage is not necessarily dependent on a previous stage, there are priorities. The more advanced stages cannot usually be secured unless more foundational stages are either first built or repaired. The danger increases in advancing on all fronts. Attempting to win individual battles without having a strategy for the whole war does not champion success. There is also a danger in working solely for tangible, newsworthy, easily recognized victories (Fishman, 1993). Changing the language of road signs, tax forms and gaining minority language presence on television are battles that have been fought and won in some minority language regions. It is more difficult, but more important, to support and encourage the minority language for communication in daily family and community life. For Fishman (1991, 1993), it is the informal and intimate spoken language **reproduced across generations** that is the ultimate pivot of language shift.

Initial activity to reverse language shift will usually derive solely from the minority language community. The language community needs to be awoken and **mobilized** to support its language, especially at a family and community participative level. However, there may come a time when the majority language government will support that community's efforts to survive. Through the provision of bilingual education, government services and a minority language television service, the central government may come to support its minority languages.

Fishman (1991) is particularly guarded about how much **bilingual education** can achieve in reversing language shift. There is sometimes the belief that, where families do not transmit the minority language, the school is there to do it instead. Where parents do not bring up their children in the minority language, the school is expected to be the substitute minority language parent. The school may initiate second language acquisition in the minority language. But few rather than many may use the school-learnt language throughout life, particularly in parenting their children. Even when a child successfully learns minority language oracy and literacy skills in school, unless there is considerable support in the community and the economy outside school, that language may wither and die. A classroom-learnt second language may become a school-only language.

For that language to survive inside the individual, a person needs to become bonded in the **language community** while at school, and particularly after leaving school. There needs to be preschool, out-of-school and after-school support and reward systems for using the minority language. The minority language needs to be embedded in the family–neighborhood–community experience and in the economics of the family. Unless this happens, it is unlikely that bilingually educated children will pass on the minority language to the next generation. Thus, for Fishman (1991, 1993), each stage needs examining for how it can be used to feed into Stage 6 — the inter-generation transmission of the minority language.

Fishman's (1991) eight stages must be seen as overlapping and interacting. In language revival, it is not the case of going one step or stage at a time. The myriad of factors in language reversal link together in complex patterns. A language at Stage 2 may still be securing elements of previous stages. A language at Stage 6 may be engaged in long-term planning to secure higher stages. Also, different communities and different geographical areas may be at different stages within the same nation. One area may have secured bilingual education provision, a neighboring area may have undeveloped bilingual education provision. Minority language literacy may be strong in some communities, weak in others. The use of the minority language in business and the local economy may vary considerably from rural to urban areas, and according to closeness of access to airports, roads, railways and sea links. In some villages, language death may be close. In other villages within the same region, most community life may be in the minority language.

Glyn Williams (1992), in a **critique** of Fishman, has argued that the presupposition is that change is gradual, mechanical, evolutionary and cumulative. Williams (1992) suggests that the viewpoint of Fishman tends to be of a consensus nature, concerned with integration, equilibrium, order and cohesion. Williams (1992) regards the work of Fishman as politically conservative with a consequent limited discussion of deviance, power, struggle and conflict. The preference is to play down the conflict while ignoring power, thereby not expressing the anger, discrimination and frustration felt by language minority groups and their members. This theme is returned to when considering Paulston's (1980) equilibrium and conflict paradigm's in Chapter 19.

The theories of Fishman may be isolated from the world as viewed by language minority actors and actresses themselves. The explanations ethnic minority participants themselves provide can be an alternative basis for the explanation and understanding of language revival and reversal (a phenomenological perspective).

Typologies and graded scales are helpful in organizing thinking and create a general guide rather than a comprehensive map. They represent, in outline form, a highly complex interaction of a variety of phenomena. The GIDS scale is a valuable attempt at sequencing and prioritizing.

CONCLUSION

This chapter has focused on language vitality and language reversal. Languages do not just exist inside individuals; they exist inside groups varying in size and strength. Sometimes such language groups shift to insignificance even death. Other times they attempt to spread and not just survive. One argument for the survival of languages has been that as languages die, so does part of the totality of human history and culture. Just as species of animals and plants are threatened, so are many minority languages. In the twentieth century, preservation of the environment has become a dominant issue. Maintaining the diversity of nature has developed as part of twentieth century thinking. Preserving language diversity may also be environmentally friendly.

SUGGESTED FURTHER READING

FISHMAN, J.A., 1991, *Reversing Language Shift*. Clevedon: Multilingual Matters.
GILES, H. and COUPLAND, N., 1991, *Language: Contexts and Consequences*. Milton Keynes: Open University Press.
PAULSTON, C.B., 1994, *Linguistic Minorities in Multilingual Settings*. Philadelphia: John Benjamins.

REVIEW AND STUDY QUESTIONS

(1) Write short revision notes on the following:
    (i) The components of Language Vitality (economic status, social status, symbolic status, demographic and institutional support factors).
    (ii) The 'assumptions of reversing language shift'.
    (iii) The difference between status planning and corpus planning.
    (iv) The difference between additive and subtractive bilingual situations.
(2) What are the economic advantages of bilingualism? Discuss the place of minority languages in the economy.
(3) List the eight stages of language shift by Fishman. Which stages seem more crucial in language death and in language reversal? What overlaps might exist between the stages? What criticisms are there of the GIDS scale.

STUDY ACTIVITIES

(1) Draw a diagram, chart or poster of Fishman's eight RLS (Reversing Language Shift) stages. This may be a simple poster with an immediate effect or a chart giving the crucial factors in each stage.
(2) Using language minority groups or communities known to you, where do you think they may be placed on Fishman's RLS scale? Do you find any difficulties in placement of groups on that scale?

CHAPTER 5

The Development of Bilingualism

CHAPTER 5

The Development of Bilingualism

INTRODUCTION

This chapter looks at the various ways in which children and adults become bilingual. There are various routes to bilingualism. Such **routes** include: learning two languages early on in the home; acquiring a second language in the street, in the wider community, in the nursery school, elementary or high school; and, after childhood, learning a second or foreign language by adult language classes and courses. This chapter outlines different major routes to becoming bilingual and examines some of the central issues involved in traveling along these routes.

As the previous chapters of this book illustrated, a discussion of bilingualism has to take in psychological, linguistic, social and educational factors. While psychologists and linguists have studied the development of children's two languages, it is important to examine simultaneously the **social context** in which children acquire their languages. Macro social contexts such as being a member of an in-migrant community, an elite group, a counter-elite or a majority or minority language group are important influences in the acquisition or attrition of bilingualism. There are also micro social contexts of the street, the nursery, the school, and the local community that similarly foster functional bilingualism. Such contexts tend to make bilingualism a constantly shifting, rather than a stable phenomenon.

The variety of individual differences and social contexts makes simple generalizations about the development of bilingualism difficult and dangerous. The chapter therefore commences with a simple typology of the development of childhood bilingualism.

TYPES OF CHILDHOOD BILINGUALISM

An important initial distinction is between **simultaneous and sequential childhood bilingualism**. Simultaneous childhood bilingualism refers to a child acquiring two languages at the same time early in life. For example, where one parent speaks one language to the child, and the other parent speaks a different language, the child may learn both languages simultaneously. Sequential childhood bilingualism is when the child learns one language first, and then a second language later in life. An example would be where a child learns the language of the home, then goes to a nursery or elementary school and learns a second language. An approximate boundary between simultaneous and sequential childhood bilingualism is the age of three (McLaughlin, 1984, 1985). When a child acquires two languages before the age of three, Swain (1972) calls it 'bilingualism as the first language'. Before the age of three, the acquisition of two languages is likely to be natural, informal and untutored. After the age of three, there is an increased likelihood of the second language being acquired by formal instruction.

Some types of nursery provision and bilingual education encourage a child to acquire a second language without formal instruction in that language (Sharpe, 1994). In contrast, second language classes for children and adults foster bilingualism through direct instruction. This provides a distinction between informal **language acquisition** and more formal **language learning** (Krashen, 1977, 1981, 1982, 1985). However, the boundary between acquisition and learning is not distinct and separate (e.g. informal language acquisition can occur in a second language class). As has been indicated in Chapter 1, there is a movement towards making second language acquisition more naturalistic in an educational setting, developing communicative competence in a less formal way. Thus, the distinction between naturally becoming bilingual and being taught to become bilingual may have cloudy borders.

THE SIMULTANEOUS ACQUISITION OF BILINGUALISM

There are four basic dimensions along which the simultaneous acquisition of bilingualism in childhood varies. These four dimensions may be translated into four questions.

(1) **What language(s) is each parent ABLE to speak?** In some family situations, the parents or guardians may both be bilingual. That is, both parents may be able to speak both the languages of the particular society. For example in the US, the parents may both be able to speak English and Spanish fluently. Alternatively, both parents may be monolingual with the child acquiring the second language from relations, neighbors and the local community. In other families, one parent may be more or less bilingual, the other monolingual. It is important when asking the question of what language or languages each parent is able to speak, that consideration is made of whether those languages are minority or majority languages. Does the context concern additive or subtractive bilingualism?

(2) **What language(s) does each parent speak to the child IN PRACTICE?** While parents have the ability to speak both languages to their children, there is often a conscious decision or a latent understanding about which language to use with the child from birth upwards. A bilingual parent may choose to use both the languages with the child. A mother, for example, may use both English and Spanish with the child. A different situation is when one parent speaks one language to the child, the other parent speaks a different language. For example, the mother may speak Spanish to the child and the father will speak English only. A third circumstance is when

bilingual parents both speak the minority language to their children, leaving the child to learn the majority language outside the home.

(3) **What language(s) do other family members speak to the child?** There are families where both parents use the same language in speaking to their children, but where the children speak to each other in the 'outside' language. For example, with 'later generation' in-migrants, the parents speak the heritage language; the children speak to each other in the language of the street, school and television. Playing with neighborhood children, making friends in and out of school with majority language speakers and use of mass-media may create bilingualism in the child. An alternative scenario is when the grandparents and other relations use a different language with the child than the home language. For example, Chinese children in the US may speak English at home and at school, but acquire at least a passive understanding of Cantonese Chinese through regular visits to extended family members.

(4) **What language(s) does the child experience in the community?** Even before the age of three, the language experience with neighbors, local community and the nursery school may be a particularly important part of becoming bilingual (Cummins, 1991b). Sometimes a child may experience both the languages of home in the outside world. Alternatively, the child raised monolingually might pick up a second language outside the home. For example, children whose parents speak Spanish to them in the home, may attend an English medium nursery school and become bilingual in that way. The chapter continues by focusing on the more typical and better documented routes to childhood bilingualism.

Case Studies of Simultaneous Childhood Bilingual Acquisition

Some of the earliest research on bilingualism concerns detailed case studies of children becoming bilingual. For example, Ronjat (1913) described a case of the mother speaking German and the father speaking French in a French community. Ronjat's (1913) case study introduced the principle of '**one person, one language**'. That is, the case study announced the idea that a most effective method of raising children bilingually was for each parent to speak a separate language to the child.

While there have been a number of case studies of children growing up bilingually since Ronjat's first study, the most detailed case study is still Leopold's (1939 to 1949). Leopold's classic study of his daughter Hildegard was based on the father speaking German only in the home and the mother speaking only English.

Leopold was a phonetician by training and made a comprehensive record of the development of Hildegard's speech. The results were published in four books which Hakuta (1986) describes as 'a masterpiece of devotion to detailed description' (p. 48). Leopold analyzed the development of vocabulary, the sound system, word combinations and sentences. In the first two years of her life, Hildegard did not separate out her languages. During the first two years, German and English vocabulary was often mixed. It was not until she was three that Hildegard started to use the two languages separately. At the age of three she spoke German to her father, English to her mother and engaged in simple translations between the two languages. A few words of German were still used in English sentences, and vice versa. However Leopold suggested that this was not due to interference between the languages but to the child systematically simplifying the production of language. Efficient communication from the child's perspective naturally involved some language mixing.

One interesting aspect of Leopold's studies is the **shifting balance** of the two languages in childhood. When Hildegard went to Germany, her German became stronger. When back in the United States and attending school, Hildegard's English became the dominant language. This seems to reflect the reality of many bilingual situations where, at an individual level (and not just at a societal level), the languages shift in dominance. Hildegard, for example was reluctant to speak German during her mid-teens, with German becoming the weaker language. Leopold's second daughter understood German but spoke very little German to her father. In childhood, the second daughter, Karla, was a passive bilingual. Yet at the age of 19, Karla visited Germany where she was able to change from receptive German to productive German, managing to converse relatively fluently in German. Another example of shifting bilingualism in childhood is given by Fantini (1985) who details a child's shift between English, Italian and Spanish from birth to the age of 10.

The **problem** with case studies such as Leopold's is that the cases may be atypical. The children studied often tend to be relatively precocious children or the offspring of the linguists who are conducting the research. That is, the case studies may be of exceptional rather than ordinary children.

Apart from the 'one person, one language' method of raising bilingually, there are other case studies of **different patterns** (see Schinke-Llano, 1989; Romaine, 1995). Romaine (1995) provides a six-fold typology of early childhood bilingualism in terms of the language spoken by mother and father, the language of the community and the strategy of the parents. Each of the six patterns reveal different approaches that can be successful in bringing up children bilingually. We have mentioned two of these approaches: the parents speaking a different language to the child; and parents speaking a minority language to the child who acquires a second language in the community or extended family. Two further approaches must also be mentioned.

First, there is the case where both parents (and the community) are bilingual and constantly **mix** their languages. Romaine (1995) considers this 'a more common category than it might seem on the basis of its representation in the literature' (p. 186). For example, Maltese and English may be mixed together by both parents with little demarcation. The child grows up mirroring the language mixing of the parents. This, at times, may be both stable, frequent and totally acceptable within the language community. The Puerto-Ricans of New York mixing Spanish and English is a particularly strong example of this.

Second, a notable case study of simultaneous bilingualism is given by Saunders (1988) who raised his sons in English and German in Australia. Even though Saunders was not a native speaker of German, and there was little support for German speakers in the community, he raised his sons Frank and Thomas bilingually. From birth, the mother spoke to the children in English while the father used German. The parents spoke English to each other as did the two boys when speaking to each other.

Saunders (1988) observed that his children went through a three stage developmental sequence in becoming bilingual. While the notion of discrete stages (and allocation of ages) is contested and debated, the general developmental pattern follows. The **first** stage lasts until the child is approximately two years of age. During this time the child does not differentiate between the two languages. Vocabulary, for example, is treated as part of one global language system. During the **second** stage, the child may still be mixing the two languages on occasions. However there will be increasing differentiation between the two languages. For example, the vocabulary will be separated, the child will know what language to speak to which person, and what language to speak in which situations. Saunders (1988) also suggests that during this second stage, the child sometimes says both words for the same thing.

This may be to ensure the meaning is clear, or it may ensure that the parents attend to the child. The age at which a child maximally differentiates the two language systems and rarely mixes the two (**Stage 3**) will differ considerably from child to child. A variety of factors may affect the point at which a child separates the two languages: exposure to the two languages in different domains, the attitudes of parents to the two languages and to mixing the languages, the language abilities of the child, personality, peers and exposure to different forms of language education.

Studies of the acquisition of simultaneous bilingualism in childhood make two other key points. **First**, Swain (1972) found that the simultaneous acquisition of two languages did not differ in development order or process from the acquisition of one language. Children appear to learn two languages as if they were learning one. **Second**, and related, it seems possible to conclude that bilingualism can be the first language. This includes the idea that there may be a single language system underlying both the languages of the bilingual child. The two languages may be fused and integrated inside the linguistic–cognitive system of the bilingual. This is a theme examined in Chapter 9.

Language Loss in Children

Before considering the sequential acquisition of bilingualism, it is important to mention **language loss** in bilingual children. In particular, children from language minorities (indigenous and particularly in-migrant children) are often at risk of losing their minority language. With a higher status majority language ever present on the screen, in the street, at school and in shops, children quickly learn which language has prestige, power and preference. They quickly learn that they are different in language, behavior, ethnicity and culture, and may come to perceive their language and cultural differences as undesirable. Young children quickly perceive what helps them belong and get accepted in mainstream society. As Wong Fillmore (1991a) relates about US language minority children, they soon 'discover that one of the things that stands between them and easy participation in their world is language. They can tell by the way people interact with them that the only language that counts for much is English... If they want to be accepted, they have to learn English, because the others are not going to learn their language' (p. 342).

Research by Hakuta & D'Andrea (1992) and Wong Fillmore (1991a) suggests that the younger the US language minority child is in **acquiring English**, the greater chance that the minority language will be replaced. The later the age of learning to speak English, the greater the chance of retaining the minority language and becoming bilingual. Hakuta & D'Andrea (1992) propose that early exposure to English (e.g. in the home) not only may mean a shift from Spanish to English. It may also decrease the chances of placement in a bilingual education program where Spanish is used and possibly maintained.

When **English** is introduced early into a US language minority child's life, the minority language may be insufficiently stable and developed not to be affected by the majority language. A loss of the minority language may have consequences for the child: social, emotional, cognitive and educational, as later chapters will examine. As Wong Fillmore (1991a: 343) argues: 'What is lost is no less than the means by which parents socialize their children: When parents are unable to talk to their children, they cannot easily convey to them their values, beliefs, understandings, or wisdom about how to cope with their experiences'.

Thus minority language loss is an issue not just of regions and language communities but also of individual children, particularly when they are very young. The problem is not the majority language, but the **timing** of the introduction of the minority language. Young children need to build competence in the minority language before the powerful and almost inevitable encounter with the majority language begins.

THE SEQUENTIAL ACQUISITION OF BILINGUALISM

Sequential acquisition of bilingualism refers to the situation where a child acquires a first language, and later becomes proficient in the second language. McLaughlin (1984) recommends that the age of three is used as an arbitrary demarcation line between simultaneous and sequential acquisition of bilingualism. Sequential acquisition of bilingualism takes us into the field of **second language acquisition**. Such acquisition may be through formal or informal means; informally through street, nursery school and community, or formally through school, adult classes and language courses. There is no single 'best' route by which learners above the age of three become competent in a second language. There are a variety of informal and formal educational means of acquiring competency in a second language.

Background Issues

The evidence of the case studies is that children can become competent bilinguals through the process of simultaneous bilingualism. The evidence of bilingualism through second language acquisition or learning is not always so positive. In the US and Britain, despite the extensive second language and foreign language learning in school (and the extensive research on second language acquisition), only a small proportion of children learning a second language become functionally and fluently bilingual. In the US, less than 1 in 20 children become bilingual following second language instruction. There are several popular reasons for such **failure**: the emphasis on reading and writing rather than on authentic communication; having low ability or aptitude to learn a second language; a lack of motivation and interest, and a lack of opportunity to practice second language skills. Another popular explanation is attempting to learn a language too late; that is, believing that it is easier to learn a language when someone is younger rather than older. The issue of age in learning a language is considered later.

In certain European countries (e.g. Netherlands, Finland, Sweden, Belgium) and eastern countries (e.g. Israel, Singapore), second language learning has been relatively more successful. Such international comparisons highlight the need to bring political, cultural and economic factors into second language learning discussions. No language learner is an island. Surrounding the shores of the individual psychology of effective second language acquisition, lie the seas of social, cultural and political context. Any map of sequential bilingualism needs to include all these features.

Informal Second Language Learning

Bilingualism is often achieved through the informal acquisition processes of the street and screen, neighborhood and newspaper. A child sometimes rapidly acquires a language in addition to that of the home without planning or intent by parents. Peers in the street, cartoons and shows on television are two examples of language influences that may informally lead to bilingualism in the child and teenager. Little researched, the almost incidental addition of a second or third language via the street and screen may be as influential as formal education, and sometimes more potent than language classes. This particularly tends to be the case with acquiring the majority language of the neighborhood or nation.

Formal Second Language Learning

Where a second language cannot be acquired in the community (natural second language acquisition), **the school** has been the major institution expected to produce second language learning. Through second language and foreign language lessons, via language laboratories and computer aided language learning, drill and practice routines, immersion classes, drama and dance, the initial stages of monolingualism to bilingualism may occur. The role of the school in formal second language learning is considered in detail in the second half of this book.

The routes to bilingualism are not solely in early childhood and in formal education. Community provided, **voluntary language classes** sometimes exist for school-age children. In England and Canada, for example, evening classes, Saturday schools and Sunday schools are organized by various communities for children to learn the heritage language of their parents and grandparents. For example, children of second, third or fourth generation in-migrants may have learnt English as their first or dominant language. If parents have chosen to speak English to their children, even if their own first language is not English, the heritage language may be learnt in voluntary classes. Alternatively, where English is the dominant language of the community and the only language of the school, such voluntary classes may be important in attaining bilingualism rather than moving children towards majority language monolingualism (Linguistic Minorities Project, 1985; Ghuman, 1993, 1994).

Such voluntary provision may be for religious, cultural, social, integrative and ethnic minority vitality reasons. Thus the providers are often religious groups such as Synagogues, Mosques, Temples and Orthodox churches. In other communities, the providers are groups of enthusiastic parents and local community organizations who rent premises such as schools and halls to teach a heritage language. Tansley & Craft (1984) located at least 28 different languages being taught in over 500 **community and supplementary schools** in England. Asian languages such as Urdu, Panjabi, Bengali, Hindi and Gujerati were frequently taught. Also, European languages such as Greek, Italian, Spanish and Portuguese were supported by such voluntary provision.

Apart from voluntary classes for children, another well traveled route to second language acquisition is **adult provision** (see Baker & Prys Jones, 1997). Such provision takes varying forms in different geographical areas:

- **Evening classes**. Sometimes called night schools or classes, a second or foreign language is taught on a once or twice a week basis for several months to several years. Such classes have often traditionally aimed at securing formal qualifications in the language (e.g. passing exams in a second majority language), or at gaining proficiency in the majority language One example is 'English as a Second Language' classes established for in-migrants into the US and England. Recently, the growth has also been in acquiring communicative competence in a heritage language (e.g. Hebrew, Welsh).
- **Ulpan courses**. Ulpan courses originated in Israel in the 1970s and are more intensive than evening classes. Such courses are often for three to five mornings or three to five evenings every week, lasting from several months to a year or more. Intensive and saturated, there is evidence from Israel and Wales of their success. This success is partly due to the warm and encouraging environment created in an Ulpan as well as the language teaching.
- **Short term and long term residential courses**. Weekend, week-long and up to three month residential courses for minority language learning (taken in vacation time or via sponsorship from an organization) are other forms of intensive language learning. For example, in North Wales, a deserted village by the sea (Nant Gwrtheyrn) has been converted into an 'isolated' language learning center. The whole day's activity is varied, but is centrally focused on learning Welsh as a second language.
- **Distance learning methods**. A variety of media-based courses for learning a second language are often available to adults. Radio and television series, cassette tapes, records, compact discs, videos, video discs magazines and self-teach books, computer programs (Computer Assisted Language Learning) and correspondence courses are all well tried approaches in second language acquisition. Evaluation studies of the relative effectiveness of these different approaches tend to be lacking.

In early childhood, becoming bilingual is often an unconscious event, as natural as learning to walk and to ride a bicycle. In a school situation, a child is not usually the one who has made a decision about the language(s) of the classroom. Second language acquisition at school is often imposed by parents, teachers and a regional educational policy. For migrant workers, refugees and in-migrants, adult language learning also may be far less voluntary. In adulthood, second language acquisition sometimes becomes more voluntary, more open to choice.

The Age Factor

A much debated theme in second language acquisition is the relationship of **age in learning a second language** and success in gaining language proficiency (Harley, 1986). One set of proponents suggest that the younger the age a second language is learnt, the greater the long term proficiency gained in that language. According to this viewpoint, young children learn a language more easily and successfully. Others tend to argue that older children and young adults learn a language more efficiently and quickly than do young children. For example, a 14 year old learning Spanish as a second language has superior intellectual processing skills than the five year old learning Spanish. Therefore, less time is required in the teenage years to learn a second language than in the younger years.

A comprehensive and balanced review of this area is provided by Singleton (1989). Singleton's careful analysis may be briefly summarized as follows:

(1) Younger second language learners are neither globally more nor less efficient and successful than older learners in second language acquisition. There are many factors that intervene and make simple statements about age and language learning simplistic and untenable.

(2) Children who learn a second language in childhood do tend to achieve higher levels of proficiency than those who begin after childhood. Such a finding does not contradict the idea that someone can become proficient in learning a second language after childhood. This tendency may be related to social contexts in which language is acquired and maintained or lost, as well as to the psychology of individual learning. Younger children appear to pick up the sound systems and grammar of a new language more easily than adults.

(3) Broadly speaking, there are no age related differences in the process of language learning. Younger and older second language learners tend to show a similar developmental sequence and order.

(4) In a formal classroom language learning situation, older learners tend initially to learn quicker than younger learners. However, the length of exposure (e.g. the number of years of second language instruction) is an important factor in second language success. Those children who begin to learn a second language in the elementary school and continue throughout schooling, tend to show higher proficiency than those who start to learn the second language later in their schooling. In absolute rather than comparative terms, this still includes the possibility of late learners becoming highly proficient, particularly when they are highly motivated.

(5) Where the second language is used in schools as the medium of instruction, and where that second language is a majority language replacing the home minority language, early use of the second language may have negative educational and linguistic effects.

(6) Support for second language instruction at an early age in school needs to find its rationale and support from areas other than second language research. For example, teaching a second language early in the elementary school needs to be defended in terms of general intellectual stimulation, the general curriculum value of teaching a modern language, the benefits of biculturalism and the benefits of learning a language for as long as possible rather than as quickly and as efficiently as possible. Second language instruction in the elementary school rests on the suitable provision of language teachers, suitable materials and resources, favorable attitudes of the teachers and parents, and the need to make the learning experience enjoyable for such children.

(7) There are no critical periods in a child's development in childhood or adolescence when a second language should or should not be introduced in the school. As Singleton (1989) notes, the whole issue of age and second language learning is 'that the various age-related phenomena isolated by language acquisition research probably result from the interaction of a multiplicity of causes and that different phenomena may have different combinations of causes' (p. 266).

How **successful** have adults been in becoming bilingual? There is distinction between answering this question in an absolute and a relative manner. The 'absolute' answer simply is that adults do learn a second language to varying degrees of fluency. Some fall by the wayside, others reach a basic, simple level of communication, yet others become functionally bilingual. In Israel and Wales, New Zealand and Canada, the US and many parts of Asia, the adult route to bilingualism has many success stories.

The 'relative' answer involves comparing children and adults of varying ages. In this sense, the question becomes 'Who is more likely to master a second language, children or adults?' A specific example of adult success provides an illustration of a typical pattern. This example focuses on language usage rather than acquisition.

In-migrants into Israel during this century have often learnt Hebrew in a central attempt to revive the ethnic, religious language. From Israeli Census data, it is possible to examine whether older or younger adults become functional in Hebrew. For example, do young in-migrants become more or less functional in Hebrew as a second language compared with older in-migrants? The results follow a clear pattern (Bachi, 1956; Braine, 1987). As the figure on the following page illustrates (based on Bachi, 1956), the extent of the everyday use of Hebrew varies with age of in-migration. The younger the child, the more likely he or she will be to use Hebrew. Between 30 and 40 years of age, a notable drop occurs. Is this due to a loss of learning ability, less exposure to Hebrew, less motivation or decreasing social pressure? From age 40 onwards, the likelihood of being functional in Hebrew falls again.

One issue that frequently occurs for parents and teachers of children of differing ages is when one language is mixed with another. Terms such as Spanglish (mixed Spanish and English), Wenglish (mixed Welsh and English) are invented to describe such mixing. This will now be considered from a sociolinguistic perspective. Those interested in a purely linguistic perspective can consult Romaine (1995).

Codeswitching

One issue in language processing in bilingual children has been the extent to which such children **mix** and **switch** their languages. Code mixing has tended to be the term used to describe changes at the word level (e.g. a few words in a sentence). **Codeswitching** is when an individual (more or less deliberately) alternates between two or more languages. Such alternation can range from one word mixing, to switching in mid-sentence, to switching in larger speech blocks (Hoffmann, 1991). Language **borrowing** is the inclusion of foreign loan words into a language (e.g. '*le weekend*' in French).

Codeswitching tends to be used to describe changes which are relatively deliberate and with a purpose. This may be a switch in a particular phrase within a sentence or in different sentences. '*Leo un magazine*' (I read a magazine) would be mixing; 'Come to the table. *Bwyd yn barod*' (Food is ready) would be switching. However the distinction easily becomes blurred. For example is 'I wanted to fight her *con los punos*, OK! Is this a mix or a switch?

As Eastman (1992) suggests: 'efforts to distinguish codeswitching, codemixing and borrowing are doomed' (p. 1). Particularly in research in multilingual urban settings, where people of diverse linguistic backgrounds regularly interact, 'in normal everyday conversation, material from many languages may be embedded in a matrix language regularly and unremarkably' Eastman (1992: 1). Where codeswitching is regularly used, this is called an **unmarked** choice of language. In contrast, where people more deliberately use codeswitching for social, political, economic purposes, this is termed a **marked** choice of language (Myers Scotton, 1983, 1991).

Codeswitches have a variety of purposes and aims. Codeswitching will vary according to who is in the conversation, what is the topic, and in what kind of context the conversation occurs. The languages used may be negotiated and may change with the topic of conversation. Thirteen over-lapping **purposes of codeswitching** will now be considered.

(1) Codeswitches may be used to **emphasize** a particular point in a conversation. If one word needs stressing or is central in part of a conversation, a switch may be made.

(2) If a person does not know a word or a phrase in a language, they may **substitute** a word in another language. This often happens because bilinguals use different languages in different domains. A young person may, for instance, switch from the home language to the language used in school to talk about a subject such as mathematics or computers. For example, a university student in Kenya may switch from Kikuyu to English to discuss Geometry with his younger brother. 'Atiriri *angle* niati *has* ina *degree eighty*; nayo *this one* ina mirongo itatu'. Similarly, an adult may codeswitch when talking about work, because the technical terms associated with work are only known in that language.

(3) Words or phrases in two languages may not correspond exactly and the bilingual may switch to one language **to express a concept that has no equivalent** in the culture of the other language. For example, a French–English bilingual living in Britain may use words like 'pub', 'bingo hall' 'underground', when speaking French, because there are no French equivalents for these words. When such words or phrases from one language become established and in frequent use in the conversation of speakers of the other language, they are often called 'loans' or 'borrowings'. However, there is no clear line of demarcation between a codeswitch and a borrowing.

(4) Code switching may be used to **reinforce** a request. For example, a teacher may repeat a command to accent and underline it. (e.g. *Taisez-vous les enfants!* Be quiet, children!) In a majority/minority language situation, the majority language may be used to underline authority. Hoffmann(1981) found that Puerto Rican mothers in Jersey City tended to use English with their children for short commands like ' Stop it! Don't do that!' and then switch back into Spanish. Research in Wales found that language minority nurses repeat or amplify commands to Welsh speaking patients in English to emphasize their authority. Roberts (1994: 66) relates the following observation of a patient in hospital who is quickly becoming unpopular with nurses for continuously ringing the call button. The patient, on this occasion, rings twice. The nurse arrives at the bed:
> *Ganoch chi'r gloch DWY WAITH! Peidiwch byth a'i ganu e dwywaith —*
> *emergency ydy hynny. Dim on UNWAITH sydd angen.* Only ring it ONCE!'
> [You rang the bell TWICE! Don't ever ring it twice — that's an emergency. ONCE is enough. Only ring it ONCE!]

(5) Repetition may also be used to **clarify** a point. Some teachers in classrooms explain a concept in one language, and then explain it again in another language believing that repetition adds reinforcement and completeness of understanding.

(6) Codeswitching may be used to **communicate friendship**. For example, moving from the common majority language to the home language or minority language both the listener and speaker understand well, may communicate friendship and common identity. Similarly, a person may deliberately use codeswitching to indicate the need to be accepted by a peer group. Someone with a rudimentary knowledge of a language may inject words of that new language into sentences to indicate a desire to identify and affiliate. The use of the listener's stronger language in part of the conversation may indicate deference, wanting to belong or to be accepted.

(7) In **relating a conversation** held previously, the person may report the conversation in the language or languages used. For example, two people may be speaking Spanish together. When one reports a previous conversation with an English monolingual, that conversation is reported authentically — in English — as it occurred.

(8) Codeswitching is sometimes used as a way of **interjecting** into a conversation. A person attempting to break into a conversation politely may introduce a different language. Interrupting a conversation may be signaled by changing language. The message to the speakers from the listener is that 'I would like to become involved in this conversation'.

(9) Codeswitching may be used to **ease tension and inject humor** into a conversation. If discussions are becoming tense in a committee, the use of a second language may signal a change in the tune being played. Just as in an orchestra, different instruments may be brought in during a composition to signal a change of mood and pace, so a switch in language may indicate a need to change mood within the conversation.

(10) Codeswitching often relates to **social distance**. For example, when two people meet, they may use the common majority language (e.g. Swahili or English in Kenya). As the conversation proceeds and roles, status and tribal identity are revealed, a change to a regional language may indicate that boundaries are being broken down. A codeswitch signals there is less social distance, with expressions of solidarity and growing rapport indicated by the switch. A study of Italian in-migrants into the United States at the turn of the century (Di Pietro, 1977) showed that the in-migrants would tell a joke in English and give the punch line in Italian, not only because it was better expressed in that language, but also to emphasize the shared values and experiences of the minority group. Conversely, a **change** from a minority language or dialect to a majority language may indicate the speaker's wish to elevate their own status, or create a distance between themselves and the listener. Myers Scotton & Ury (1977) describe a conversation between a Kenyan shop keeper and his sister, who had come in to buy some salt. After exchanging greetings in their own Luyia dialect, the brother switches to Swahili in front of the other customers and says: *Dada, sasa leo unahitaji nini?* (Sister, what do you need today?) For the rest of the conversation the brother speaks in Swahili and the sister in the Luyia dialect. The brother's code switch to Swahili, the business language of Kenya, indicates to his sister that she cannot expect to receive anything for free.

(11) Codeswitching can also be used to **exclude** people from a conversation. For example, when traveling on the Metro (subway, underground), two people having been speaking English may switch to their minority language to talk about private matters,

thus excluding others from the conversation. Bilingual parents may use one language together to exclude their monolingual children from a private discussion. A doctor at a hospital may make a brief aside to a colleague in a language not understood by the patient.

(12) Codeswitching may be used to indicate a **change of attitude** during the conversation. For example, greetings may be expressed in the home, minority language. But when one person asks to borrow money or asks a favor of the other, the moneylender may change to the majority language. To indicate a change of relationship and a change of attitude, codeswitching occurs. Greetings in the native language; business in the majority language. At the end of the business conversation, farewells may revert to the native language. A change in relationship, on a temporary basis, is indicated by codeswitching.

(13) In some bilingual situations, codeswitching occurs regularly when certain topics are introduced (e.g. money). Spanish–English bilinguals in the South West United States regularly switch to English to discuss money. For example, a person may say 'La consulta era (the visit costs) *ten dollars and 50 cents*'. This reflects that English is the language of commerce, and also the language of education.

Familiarity, projected status, the ethos of the context and the perceived linguistic skills of the listeners affect the nature and process of code switching. Thus codeswitching has more than linguistic properties (Hoffmann, 1991). These thirteen purposes of codeswitching demonstrate that there are important social and power aspects of switching between languages, as there are between switching between dialects and registers.

A variety of **factors** may affect the extent to which children and adults switch between their languages (Romaine, 1995). The perceived status of the listeners, familiarity with those persons, atmosphere of the setting and perceived linguistic skills of the listeners are examples of variables that may foster or prevent code-switching. Such factors operate as young as two years of age. Whereas two-year-old's mixing of language has tended to be seen as 'interference' or a lack of differentiation between languages, Lanza (1992) has shown from one case study that codeswitching by two-year-olds can be context-sensitive (e.g. according to which parent is being addressed).

One situation where bilinguals mix the two language systems is sometimes found where both parents speak both languages to the children. Various investigators have argued that the 'one person, one language' or 'one language, one context' is the optimal method of rearing a child bilingually. This may help to avoid mixing two languages. For example, where both the father and mother speak French and German to the child, the child may have temporary difficulty in separating out the two languages. This used to be called 'interference'. This term reveals a negative stance from the listener's viewpoint. In contrast, a child mixing two languages may be conveying thoughts and ideas in the most personally efficient manner, and in a way that is understood by listeners. Such 'interference' may be termed **'transfer'** and is thus part of a natural bilingual developmental sequence. That is, mixing words often changes as children grow older. With increasing years there usually develops increasing separation of languages (Arnberg &

Arnberg, 1992). Such 'interference' is often reduced as language experience increases. Thus Fantini (1985) argues for a gradual evolutionary process of separation of, and transfer between, a child's two languages rather than the more static idea of 'interference'. However, some bilingual communities (e.g. Puerto Ricans born in New York) do not show increased separation as their children grow older. There can be continuous mixing throughout life, and this need not create a transitional state but a relatively stable language community (Zentella, 1988; Eastman, 1992).

The chapter concludes by examining a topic related to codeswitching: children acting as interpreters for their parents and others. Bilingual children (and adults) are frequently expected to act as go-betweens by interpreting from one language to another. Such an interpreter's role also illustrates how bilingual development impacts on other aspects of child development such as personality and family relationships.

Children as Interpreters

In language minority families, children often act as **interpreters** for their parents. For example, in first and second generation in-migrant families, parents may have a little or no competency in the majority language. Therefore, their children act as interpreters in a variety of contexts. When there are visitors to the house, such as sellers and traders, religious persuasionists and local officials, a parent may call a child to the door to help translate what is being said. The child interprets for both parties (e.g. the parent and the caller). Similarly, at hospitals, the doctor's, dentist's, optician's, school and many other places where parents visit, the child may be taken to help interpret. Interpretation may be needed in more informal places: on the street, when a parent is watching the television or listening to the radio, reading a local newspaper or working on the computer.

Pressure is placed on children in interpreting: linguistic, emotional, social and attitudinal pressure. First, children may find an exact translation difficult to achieve as their language is still developing. Second, children may be hearing information (e.g. medical troubles, financial problems, arguments and conflicts) that is the preserve of adults rather than children. Third, children may be expected to be adult-like when interpreting and child-like at all other times; to mix with adults when interpreting and 'be seen and not heard' with adults on other occasions. Fourth, seeing their parents in an inferior position may lead to children despising their minority language. Children may quickly realize when interpreting that the language of power, prestige and purse is the majority language. Negative attitudes to the minority language may result. Fifth, not all bilinguals are good interpreters (Malakoff, 1992). Proficiency in two or more languages is not enough. Some reflection on language (in Chapter 8 discussed as metalinguistic awareness), an awareness of the linguistic nature of the message, reflecting on the structural features of languages is also required (Malakoff, 1992). However, many bilinguals appear to be ahead of monolinguals on such metalinguistic awareness (see Chapter 8 for a review).

Interpreting also has many **positive outcomes**. **First**, it can bring parental praise, reward and status within the family for playing a valuable role. The research of Malakoff (1992) found that this ability is widely distributed among bilingual children who are quite expert as early as the third or fourth grade. Such ability may gain both esteem from others and raise self-esteem. **Second**, the child learns adult information quickly and learns to act with some authority and trust. Early maturity has its own rewards in the teenage peer group. **Third**, Kaur & Mills (1993) found that children accustomed to acting as interpreters learned to take the initiative. For example, a child may give the answer to a question rather than relaying the question to the parent. This puts children in a position of some power, even of language censorship.

Fourth, when parents become dependent on their children for interpretation, it may make the family more close and integrated. Such interpretation is a lifeline for the many parents who have to hand over much power to their children. Yet it may make parents aware of their own language inadequacies, feeling frustration and resentment, particularly in language minority cultures where children are expected to stay in a subordinate position for a long time.

Fifth, the cognitive outcomes for child interpreters may be valuable. Children who are regular interpreters for their parents may realize early on the problems and possibilities of translation of words, figures of speech and ideas. For example, such children may learn early on that one language never fully parallels another, and that it is hard to translate exactly the inner meaning of words and metaphors. This may lead such children to be more introspective about their languages. This is termed metalinguistic awareness and is considered in Chapter 8. Thus, interpretation may both require and stimulate metalinguistic awareness.

Sixth, another advantage for the child interpreter is in character formation, for example, possibly gaining more empathy. The children are negotiating between two different social and cultural worlds, trying to understand both, and provide bridges between these two worlds. This handling of dialogue may lead to increased maturity, astuteness, independence and higher self-esteem. Being expected to carry an adult role early on may lead to a positive self-concept, and feeling responsible like an adult.

CONCLUSION

This chapter has discussed two routes to bilingualism: simultaneous and sequential. The former route occurs up to the age of three when two languages are acquired consecutively. The latter route, sequential bilingualism, may be through formal educational avenues or informal paths (e.g. street, neighborhood and nursery schools). Language learning in classes and courses and 'street' acquisition allow individuals of all ages to become bilingual and multilingual.

In the home, in the street, at a nursery school, fast and efficient progress is made in an unconscious, natural manner. A particularly efficient route is the 'one parent, one language' approach. Here, each parent speaks a different language to the child. In simultaneous bilingual acquisition, the 'one person, one language' principle and the 'one context, one language' idea help encourage language boundaries to be set. Mixing languages is often an initial stage, with increasing separation with age and experience.

However, in some communities, mixing is normal and relatively stable. Codeswitching is a frequent behavior among bilinguals with a variety of valuable purposes and benefits. Interpreting is a similarly frequent expectation of bilinguals — including young children in in-migrant families.

Another route to bilingualism is via formal second language learning in school, or using a second language in school as the medium of learning. Bilingualism can also be reached by avenues outside of school. The vehicles of voluntary classes and adult courses provide the opportunity for a second or foreign language to be learnt and developed. The street and screen can also be vehicles to childhood bilingualism. Having introduced simultaneous and sequential bilingualism, the next chapter takes a global look at some of the key issues and current ideas in second language acquisition.

SUGGESTED FURTHER READING

BAKER, C., 1995, *A Parents' and Teachers' Guide to Bilingualism*. Clevedon: Multilingual Matters.
HAKUTA, K., 1986, *Mirror of Language. The Debate on Bilingualism*. New York: Basic Books.
ROMAINE, S., 1995, *Bilingualism* (2nd edn). Oxford: Basil Blackwell.

REVIEW AND STUDY QUESTIONS

(1) Write short revision notes on the following:
     (i)   The difference between language acquisition and language learning.
     (ii)   Different methods of simultaneous childhood bilingual acquisition.
     (iii)   The advantages and problems of children acting as interpreters.
(2) What are the main differences between simultaneous and sequential bilingualism?
(3) How influential do you think age is in learning a second language?
(4) Give examples of the ten purposes of codeswitching. Are there any other purposes you can think of or have observed?
(5) Examine between three and six of the 117 'questions about bilingualism most asked by parents' in Baker (1995b). Does the advice given in the answers (a) match your experience and (b) seem relevant. Write your own advice to any one question selected from that book.

STUDY ACTIVITIES

(1) Create a case study of one person's bilingual development. This may be yourself or someone you know. By interviewing that person, or self reflection, make a cassette tape or a video or a written case study of the factors which seem personally important to that person in their bilingual development. This may be developed as a project. A project may include the following stages. First, look in the library for case studies of bilinguals. Books by Arnberg (1987), Fantini (1985), Harding & Riley (1987), de Jong (1986), Saunders (1988), Lyon (1996) and Döpke (1992) provide examples. Second, prepare an interview guide. Write down (as an aide memoire) the topics and

kinds of questions you would like to ask in an interview. Third, try to use a tape recorder, or write down when the respondent is talking to record the interview. If you make a tape, transcribe the key quotes or all of the interview. Fourth, write out a case study of the bilingual development of that person. Are there particular stages or periods in the development? Or was the development more smooth with gradual changes?

(2) Interview a mother or father who is learning a second language at the same time as their child. Ask about the progress each is making. What differences are there? Ask about why there are qualitative and quantitative differences in progress? What attitudes and motivations do the language learners have? If there are differences of attitude, try to work out an explanation.

(3) By observation or tape-recording, gather samples of codeswitching. Try to find illustrations of different purposes of codeswitching. Ask the people in your sample (after completing the observation/recording) how conscious they are of codeswitching. What are their explanations for codeswitching? What particular purposes for codeswitching were most found in your samples? How regular was codeswitching in the conversation? What was the personal history of those you observed or recorded that helps explain such codeswitching?

CHAPTER 6

Second Language Acquisition

CHAPTER 6

Second Language Acquisition

INTRODUCTION

This chapter examines the foundations of second language acquisition research and theory. The topic is a broad one, and is an important part of the question 'How do you become bilingual?' This chapter on second language acquisition focuses on key summarizing frameworks and theories. These include theories of a psychological, socio-psychological and a pedagogic nature that attempt to describe holistically major features of language learning in an interactive and inter-connected model. Such theories provide an overview of a wide variety of research from different perspectives, and make a relatively comprehensive statement of the current state of understanding of second language acquisition.

THE CENTRAL QUESTION

The important issues surrounding second language acquisition can be summarized in one question: '**Who learns how much of what language under what conditions?**' Spolsky (1989c: 3). Answers to this question form the substance of this chapter.

The '**who learns**' question raises a debate about individual differences. Who learns a second language more easily, more quickly and with better retention? What part do general ability, aptitude for learning a language, attitudes to a language, motives and personality play in second language learning? What is the size of each factor's contribution? How do these factors inter-relate in a 'successful' second language acquisition equation? The word **learns** accents the idea of a process, constantly changing. The factors listed above need to be seen as parts in a moving film and not a static snapshot.

The '**how much of what language**' part of the question focuses on what is being learnt: oral skills, written skills, fluency for everyday communication, grammar for test and examination purposes? What is the yardstick for successful learning? What dialect of language has been learnt? Has another culture been acquired as part of language acquisition?

95

The '**under what conditions**' phrase in the question highlights situation and context. What effect do different learning environments have on the acquisition of a second language: a formal teacher directed classroom, flexible individual learning, adult classes (e.g. an Ulpan), acquisition in the street and community, correspondence courses, different forms of bilingual education (e.g. immersion and submersion — see Chapters 10 and 11)? What teaching strategies are more or less effective? The topic of second language learning in school is considered in Chapter 14 of this book.

Simple, clear guidelines for effective second language acquisition that suits all learners would be much welcomed. In the second language shop window, there are many alternative theories, many different teaching methods. Choosing the 'best' theory or the 'best' teaching method is as dangerous as choosing one garment for all occasions. The **complexity** of language acquisition makes the wearing of the same cloth unwise. Different learners, different environments, different teachers, different props (e.g. computer assisted language learning) make theories and teaching methods contain 'part-truths'.

Such 'part-truths' will be a resource for teachers, and not a source that solely determines teaching; having implications rather than direct application; providing propositions rather than prescriptions; insights rather than edicts. In this spirit, the chapter proceeds by highlighting some important ideas in second language acquisition.

DISTINCTIONS AND DEFINITIONS

Ellis (1985) makes a distinction between three parts to the development of a second language. First, there is the **sequence** in second language learning. This refers to the general stages through which children and adults move in learning a second language. Ellis (1985) argues that, irrespective of the language and irrespective of whether that language is acquired naturally or formally in the classroom, there is a natural and almost invariant sequence of development. Moving from simple vocabulary to basic syntax, to the structure and shape of simple sentences, to complex sentences is a fairly universal sequence in language acquisition. Second, the **order** in which a language is learnt may be different from the sequence. The term 'order' in this respect refers to specific, detailed features of a language. For example, the order in which specific grammatical features or situation-specific vocabularies of a language are acquired may differ from person to person, classroom to classroom. Third, there is the **rate of development** of the second language and the level of proficiency achieved. While the sequence of second language development may be invariant, and while minor variations in the order of development may occur, there may be major variations in the speed in which a second language is acquired and in the level of final proficiency achieved.

Ellis (1985) suggests that **situational factors** (who is talking to whom, about what, where and when) considerably affect the rate of development of the second language. However, situational or contextual factors '*do not influence the sequence of development, and affect the order of development only in minor and temporary ways*' (p. 278). Similarly differences in **attitude, motivation, learning strategy and personality** may affect the rate at which the second language is acquired and the level of final proficiency, but do not influence sequence nor the order of the development of the second language. The sequence of development is also not affected by the learner's **first language**. The first language, particularly concerning the degree to which it has developed (see Cummins' interdependence theory in Chapter 9) is likely to affect the order of development, the rate of development and the level of final proficiency.

In becoming functionally bilingual in the classroom and in the community, Cummins' **interdependence** theory suggests that second language acquisition is influenced considerably by the extent to which the first language has developed. When a first language has developed sufficiently well to cope with decontextualized classroom learning (see Chapter 9), a second language may be relatively easily acquired. When the first language is less well developed, or where there is attempted replacement of the first language by the second language (e.g. in the classroom), the development of the second language may be relatively impeded

ELLIS' (1985) FRAMEWORK

Ellis' (1985) summarizing framework of second language acquisition provides an overview of research and theory. Ellis (1985) suggests that there are five inter-related factors that govern the acquisition of a second language: situational factors, input, learner differences, learner processes and linguistic output. The relationship between these is illustrated in the diagram below (adapted from Ellis, 1985):

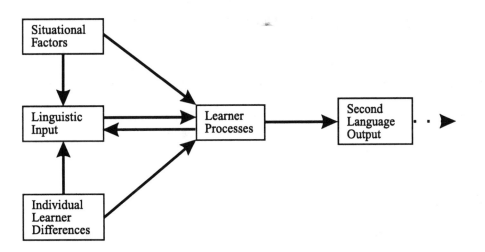

Situational Factors

Situational factors have been mentioned already in consideration of sequence, order and rate of second language acquisition. Situational factors will be considered in more detail later in the chapter when examining the theories of Krashen, Byrne & Giles and Gardner. Situational factors refer to who is talking to whom, the environment of the interaction, whether it is in a classroom, formal situation or in a naturalistic setting (e.g. a basketball game) and the topic of the conversation. Previous chapters of this book have suggested that situation has an important effect on language production.

Linguistic Input

Linguistic input concerns the type of second language input received when listening or reading in a second language. For example, how do teachers or native speakers adjust their language to the level of second language learners to make it comprehensible? What kind of differences are there in the input from natural settings compared with formal classroom settings? In a behaviorist theory of language learning, precise and tight control of input from the teacher is regarded as very important. The second language has to be presented in small, highly sequenced doses with plenty of practice and reinforcement. Individual bricks need to be carefully laid in a precise sequence to build second language skills and habits. In contrast, Chomsky's mentalist view of language acquisition regards input as merely activating the learner's **internal language acquisition device**. Input from a teacher sets the wheels in motion rather than creating the wheels of language.

Current research and theory is between the behaviorist and the Chomskyian view point. Learning a language is not simply putting bricks in place nor pressing the button to start the machine. Efficient and effective second language learning does not occur purely by the building of stimulus–response links. Nor does second language learning occur by merely exposing a child or adult to the second language. Providing input which suits the stage of development of the second language learner becomes important. Discourse analysis has shown that a second language learner and a native speaker work together to produce purposeful and efficient communication. That is, one needs to understand the interaction, particularly the negotiation of meaning to understand how input and output interact. There are strategies and tactics to make conversation appropriate and meaningful. For example, finding topics of conversation that can be mutually understood, speaking at a slow pace, repeating important phrases, stressing the key words in a sentence will help the input factor in second language acquisition. A learner will similarly give signals by verbal and non-verbal communication to indicate understanding, lack of understanding or to indicate the need to switch topics or level of language.

The **input** of language learning classrooms varies according to the type of second language learning occurring. While it is dangerous to over-generalize, the foreign language and the second language classroom may sometimes focus more on the form of the language (e.g. grammar) rather than on meaning. In contrast, in genuinely bilingual classrooms, where the second language may be a medium of teaching in the curriculum, the focus may be more on meaning than on form. While the aim in both situations is to ensure the comprehensible input of the second language, input is different from intake. The learner receives input of the second language from 'outside'. Intake refers to the inner assimilation of that second language. Input does not always result in intake; only when there is intake does second language acquisition occur.

In terms of what might comprise optimal **input in the classroom situation**, Wong Fillmore (1982) compared second language acquisition in United States kindergarten classrooms. She found that effective input differed according to the language composition of different classrooms. In classrooms where there were large numbers of second language learners, effective input comprised a teacher directed rather than an open, informal classroom organization. In contrast, where the classes comprised second language learners *and* native speaking children, open classroom organization rather than teacher direction seemed to constitute the optimal learning environment. This may be explained as follows:

(1) In classes where there were large numbers of second language learners, the teacher was most effective by herself controlling the input. In such classes where there was more open organization, students tended to talk to each other in their **first** language, thus not obtaining practice in the second language.

(2) In classes of mixed second language learners and native speaking children, the optimal environment was a more open organization where second language learners received input from the teacher and from native speaking children. In such mixed classes, where the teacher tended to control the input, this tended to be at the level of **native** speakers and did not necessarily provide comprehensible input for second language learners.

Wong Fillmore (1982) thus shows the importance in second language input of the interaction between teaching style and the peer composition of different classes.

Individual Learner Differences

An important part of Ellis' (1985) framework is **individual learner differences**. It is popularly regarded that the level of proficiency a child attains in the second language is not only a factor of exposure to various contexts and to classroom teaching methodology, it is also due to individual differences. For example, the age at which somebody learns a second language, their aptitude for learning languages, cognitive style, motivation, attitude, previous knowledge, learning style, learning strategies and personality variables such as anxiety have variously been thought to influence second language acquisition.

A distinction is important between variables on which there are individual differences (e.g. anxiety level) and universal capabilities. Universal capabilities are basic, shared features of human beings. An example is Chomsky's (1965) idea of an innate, endowed capability for developing grammar. Available to all learners, universal capabilities are a necessary condition for learning. However, they need to be viewed as a 'prior assumption' that will not explain variations in second language learning among learners.

Variations among individual language learners creates two different questions (Ellis, 1985). **First**, do individual differences in age and learning style, for example, result in children and adults following different routes in second language acquisition? **Second**, do individual differences affect the speed or rate at which second language acquisition occurs and the level of final proficiency achieved? People who research on individual differences in second language acquisition tend to emphasize the importance of individual differences (Wong Fillmore, 1979). Inbuilt into research designs is often the likelihood of finding significant differences between learners. On the other hand, second language acquisition theory and research that concentrate on situation, input and process tend to de-emphasize the role of individual differences.

While it is possible to list the factors which research has connected with more or less effective second language acquisition, what is unclear is the extent to which those factors affect both the route and the rate of second language acquisition. For example, there is some evidence to suggest that extroversion and reduced inhibition may be connected to second language acquisition. In both these cases, the research is not only methodologically weak (see Ellis, 1985) but also fails to examine, in an overall model, the relative influence of these factors against other individual differences, situational factors and language input variables.

It is possible to specify a *list* of factors that appear to be related to second language acquisition. Anxiety, self-esteem and self-concept, competitiveness in the classroom, anxiety that may be facilitative or interruptive, field independence as a cognitive style and social skills have each and all been related by research to second language acquisition. On the other hand, the separate and interacting size of influence of each of these ingredients in the overall recipe is not clear.

Learner Processes

Another part of Ellis' (1985) framework is **learner processes**. It is clearly insufficient to consider second language acquisition by external input and by second language output. The input that second language learners receive is sifted, processed and organized. Such processing cannot be easily observed; rather it has to be inferred mostly from cognitive strategies in language learning. Clarification of the processing strategies of the learner is important for the teacher to decide what comprises comprehensible input and facilitative situations. One three-fold typology of learner strategy is by Tarone (1980). **First**, there are learning strategies, that is ways in which the learner consciously and subconsciously processes second language input (e.g. memorization). **Second**, there are production strategies that comprise attempts to use second language knowledge in an efficient way. **Third**, a learner has communication strategies or the means of communicating with others in using the second language when there is a lack of linguistic proficiency available.

An alternative way of peering into the black box of the mind is that of Chomsky (1965). Chomsky tends to depart from positing general cognitive strategy devices, claiming instead that there are mental mechanisms that are specifically linguistic. Chomsky describes this as the **language acquisition device** that contains an innate blueprint for a person to acquire a language. Chomsky thus proposed that in-between language input and language production is a linguistic process that involves the activation of universal principles of grammar with which the learner is endowed.

Second Language Outputs

Another part of Ellis' (1985) framework is **second language outputs**. The language proficiency of any learner at any one point of time is best seen as:

(1) Evolutionary and not fixed. A language competence test as a measure of current language output should ideally reveal not just the current ceiling, but also the fittings and floors that need to be added and developed.
(2) Variable according to the context where the learner is placed. A learner may appear relatively fluent in a restaurant or shop situation, yet much less fluent in a business or religious context.

An important contribution to the idea of language output is by Swain (1985, 1986). Swain argues that the opportunity to engage in meaningful oral exchanges (in the classroom or in the community) is a necessary component in second language acquisition. In conveying meaning, a person learns about the structure and form of a language.

A person may understand a language (passive, receptive skills) but, through lack of meaningful practice, speak that second language less than fluently. People learn to read by reading, and learn to write by writing. To speak, and to be understood when speaking, requires meaningful and realistic conversations. We learn to speak a second language when given the opportunity to speak it. Such opportunities may be too infrequent in language classrooms.

The danger of the classroom is that students may learn to understand a second language (comprehensible input), but not to produce (**comprehensible output**). The classroom emphasis has traditionally been on written correctness and not on spoken language skills. When a student has opportunities to use their spoken language outside the classroom (e.g. in the street), language skills (e.g. grammar, syntax and communication of meaning) may be considerably enhanced (Housen & Baetens Beardsmore, 1987; Baetens Beardsmore & Swain, 1985).

SOCIO-PSYCHOLOGICAL THEORIES

Lambert's (1974) Model

Lambert's (1974) model is valuable because it combines both the individual and societal elements of bilingualism and is presented in a diagram below. It is the important societal element of the model that is emphasized in the following discussion.

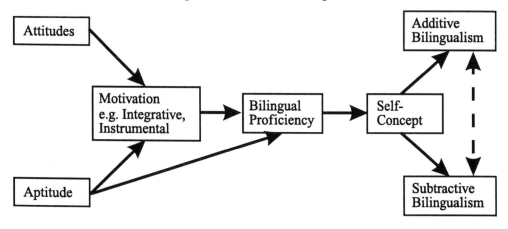

The model starts with an individual's **attitudes and aptitude** towards a language. As will be considered later, aptitude and attitude are regarded as two major and relatively separate influences on becoming bilingual. For example, aptitude in learning a second language may be an important factor in second language learning (Skehan, 1986). Similarly, the attitudes of a person towards a language may be important not only in learning that language but also in maintaining or restoring the language and avoiding attrition. The next part of Lambert's (1974) model is **motivation** — the readiness to engage in language learning or language activity. The third part of the model is a person's **bilingual proficiency**. The factor that comes after bilingual proficiency is **self concept**.

For Lambert (1974), becoming bilingual or being bilingual has effects on the **self esteem** and the ego. Having mastered a second language and being able to interact with a different language group may change one's self concept and self esteem. An English monolingual who has learnt Spanish may develop new reference groups and engage in new cultural activities that affect the self concept. This suggests that bilingualism usually involves enculturation. Someone who is bicultural or multicultural may have different aspirations, world views, values and beliefs because of being bilingual or multilingual.

Lambert's (1974) model finishes with an alternative outcome: **additive or subtractive bilingualism**. This outcome can be interpreted both in personal and societal ways. When a second language and culture have been acquired with little or no pressure to replace or reduce the first language, an additive form of bilingualism may occur. Positive self concept is likely to relate to additive bilingualism. When the second language and culture are acquired (e.g. in-migrants) with pressure to replace or demote the first language, a subtractive form of bilingualism may occur. This may relate to a less positive self concept, loss of cultural identity, with possible alienation and assimilation.

Additive and subtractive bilingualism have become important concepts in the explanation of research. Lambert's (1974) distinction between additive and subtractive bilingualism has been used in two different ways. First, additive bilingualism is used to refer to positive cognitive outcomes from being bilingual (see Chapter 8). Subtractive bilingualism hence refers to the negative affective and cognitive effects of bilingualism (e.g. where both languages are 'under developed'). Landry, Allard & Théberge (1991) suggest this first use is too narrow, with a second use of additive and subtractive bilingualism being more appropriate. This wider use of additive and subtractive bilingualism relates to the enrichment or loss of minority language, culture and ethnolinguistic identity at a **societal** level. In additive bilingualism, language minority members are proficient (or becoming proficient) in both languages, have positive attitudes to the first and second language, with ethnolinguistic vitality in the language community (Landry, Allard & Théberge, 1991).

Lambert's (1974) model contains the basic ingredients that help make up an explanation of individual and societal bilingualism. It suggests that both individual and sociocultural factors are important in the possession and passage of bilingualism. Like most models, it is static rather than dynamic. It tends to suggest that there is an easy, functional flow in relationships between the factors. What it may fail to do is to represent the dynamic, ever changing, often conflicting and politicized path of bilingualism at an individual and at a societal level.

Gardner's Socio-educational Model

Gardner and his colleagues have presented a model that has been well researched and tested. Some of its key parts will first discussed before the model is presented as a whole. We begin with **ability and aptitude for languages**, two concepts that are part of the popular 'common sense' explanation of why some learn languages quickly, some not.

Ability and Aptitude

Second language learning in the classroom has often been connected to the **general ability** of a child ('intelligence') and to a specific language ability usually termed language aptitude. While the idea of a general academic ability or 'intelligence' has been criticized (see Baker, 1988), authors such as Oller & Perkins (1978) have argued that the general factor of intelligence is allied to a general factor of language ability. At its simplest, this means that a more 'intelligent' a person is likely to learn a second language more easily. An overview would suggest that general academic ability can be substantially related to the acquisition of second language in a **formal** classroom setting. General ability may positively correlate with test scores on the formal aspects of language learning, (e.g. grammar, translation, parsing verbs).

However, as Cummins (1984b) has discussed, basic everyday language skills (see Chapter 9) may not be so related to general academic ability. That is, the skills required for 'street' conversation may be less dependent on general academic ability than the language required to operate in an academic environment — see Chapter 9). Genesee (1976) found that IQ was related to second language French reading, grammar and vocabulary but was relatively unconnected to oral skills. Naturalistic second language acquisition may be less connected to IQ than formal classroom acquisition. Also, as Ellis (1985) notes, general academic ability may affect the rate and success of classroom second language acquisition. There is 'no evidence that intelligence affects the route of acquisition' (p. 111).

In a similar way, tests of **language aptitude** have been connected with second language learning. This connection may be largely due to the similarity of aptitude test and language proficiency test items. Aptitude tests have been related to second language learning in the classroom rather than second language proficiency in naturalistic, communicative contexts. Krashen (1981), for example, argues that aptitude relates to formal language learning but not to the subconscious internal acquisition of language that occurs naturally and spontaneously. Aptitude tests measure the ability of children to discriminate sounds in a language, to connect sounds with written symbols and the rote memorization of words of an artificial language. Such items tend to relate to formal, traditional approaches to language teaching. The items tend to relate less to the modern communicative approach in language teaching.

The concept of **aptitude** tends to be a popular explanation for failing to acquire a second language. An adult finding difficulty in learning a specific second language may place the blame on a lack of aptitude for language learning in general. This tends to indicate a belief that there is something in an individual's nature that cannot be nurtured. However, the concept of aptitude has recently come under attack. It is unclear how aptitude is different from general academic ability. If there is a difference between aptitude and general ability, it is unclear as to its constituent features. If we are unsure of its definition and structure, it is difficult to know precisely what is being tested in modern language aptitude tests.

While aptitude may affect the speed of second language acquisition in the formal classroom environment, it would not seem to affect the sequence or order of second language acquisition. There is also no evidence to show that aptitude affects the route which people take in second language acquisition.

Attitudes and Motivation

Another popular explanation of failure to learn a second language (or of success in learning) is attitudes and motivation (Baker, 1992). What are the motives for learning a second language? Are the motives economic, cultural, social, vocational, integrative or for self esteem and self actualization? Reasons for learning a second (minority or majority) language tend to fall into two major groups:

Group 1: A wish to identify with or join another language group

Learners sometimes want to affiliate with a different language community. Such learners wished to join in with the minority or majority language's cultural activities, find their roots or form friendships. This is termed **integrative motivation**.

Group 2: Learning a language for useful purposes

The second reason is utilitarian in nature. Learners may acquire a second language to find a job and earn money, further career prospects, pass exams, help fulfill the demands of their job, or assist their children in bilingual schooling. This is termed **instrumental motivation**.

Considerable research on this area has been conducted by Gardner and associates (see Gardner, 1985). Gardner argues that integrative and instrumental attitudes are independent of 'intelligence' and aptitude. Integrative motivation may be particularly strong in an additive bilingual environment. This is more fully considered in the next chapter.

Much of the research in this area, but not all, links **integrative motivation** rather than **instrumental motivation** with the greater likelihood of achieving proficiency in the second language. Gardner & Lambert (1972) originally considered that integrative motivation was more powerful in language learning than instrumental motivation. The reason was that integrative motivation concerns personal relationships that may be long lasting. On the other hand, instrumental motivation may be purely self-oriented and short term. When employment has been obtained or financial gain has accrued, instrumental motivation may wane. An integrative motive was thought to be a more sustained motive than an instrumental motive due to the relative endurance of personal relationships.

Research has subsequently suggested that there may be occasions when the **instrumental motive** is stronger than the integrative motive in learning a language. Lukmani (1972) found that Bombay female school students gave instrumental rather than integrative reasons for learning English. In the research of Yatim (1988), the language motivations of student teachers in Malaysia appeared to combine instrumental and integrative motives into an integrated entity. A person's motives may be a subtle mix of instrumental and integrative motives, without clear discrimination between the two.

The research on language attitudes and motivations is summarized by Gardner (1985) and Baker (1988, 1992). Research relates such motivation not only to the desire to learn a language but also to predicting language retention and language loss in individuals over time. Another important strand in this research examines instrumental and integrative motivation within the **classroom**. One study is by Gliksman (1976, 1981). He classified 14–16 year olds by their level of integrative motivation. Gliksman (1976) also systematically observed the number of times the students:

(1) volunteered information by raising a hand;
(2) were asked by teachers without volunteering;
(3) answered correctly or incorrectly;
(4) asked questions;
(5) received positive, negative or no feedback from the teacher.

Gliksman (1976, 1981) found that students with a higher integrative motivation volunteered information more frequently, gave correct answers and received more positive feedback from the teacher than did less integratively motivated students. The two groups did not differ significantly on the number of questions they asked in class. Integratively motivated students were rated as more interested in their lessons. Gliksman found that such differences were consistent across a whole term and were not sporadic nor temporary.

The explanation lies in the functions that a second language plays in a particular society. Factors such as employment and career development can be stronger than integrative motivation. The social context will be one determinant of which kind of motivation is more powerful, and this does not preclude both motivations being equally and strongly operative in a particular context. It is clear that motivation is an important factor in second language acquisition, affecting the speed and final proficiency of the second language. It is unlikely to affect the sequence or order of acquisition.

In summary: the research of Gardner and colleagues since the early 1970s suggests that **attitudes** to the second language and **motivation** to learn a second language are crucial additional ingredients in the language learning recipe. Having the ability and aptitude without the motivation and favorable attitude would tend to result in lower achievement than having both aptitude and motivation.

To represent in an integrated fashion his own and others' research on second language learning, Gardner (1979, 1983, 1985) offers a four stage model. This is presented in the diagram on the following page.

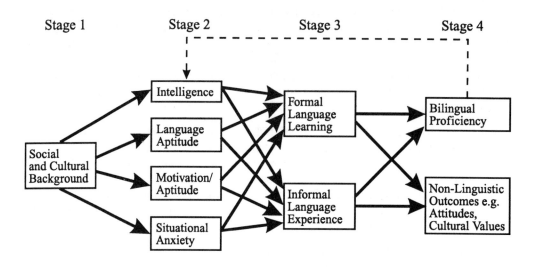

There are four stages to Gardner's (1979, 1983, 1985) model. First, the model starts with the **social and cultural background** of language learning. In this sense, Gardner starts where Lambert finishes. Children may be influenced by the beliefs, values and culture of the community in which they are placed. For many people living in England, for example, the belief is that the 'universal' English language is all that is required; bilingualism is unnecessary. In other communities of Europe, bilingualism and biculturalism reflect the values of the community. In Gardner's model, social and cultural background refers not only to the wider community but also to the influence of the home, neighbors and friends. This influence is further explored in the model of Hamers & Blanc (1982, 1983) and Siguan & Mackey (1987).

The second stage of Gardner's (1979, 1983, 1985) model is termed **individual differences**. This comprises four major variables: intelligence, language aptitude, motivation and situational anxiety. Attitudes and personality are taken to be subsumed within this section. Thus Gardner suggests that the degree of intelligence of an individual, their aptitude or talent for language learning, their instrumental and integrative motives and the anxiety they feel in language learning will all affect the outcomes of language learning.

The third stage of Gardner's (1979, 1983, 1985) model concerns the context or environment where language is acquired. He makes a distinction between **formal and informal environments** in language learning. An example of a formal context is the classroom that explicitly aims to teach a child a second language by a defined teaching method and various classroom materials and resources. A language laboratory, drill and practice, computer assisted language learning, audio visual methods and translations and grammar exercises are all examples of a formal and directed approach to language learning. An informal language learning context or experience is when language learning is more incidental, accidental or uncontrived. For example, a person watches a Spanish film not primarily to widen vocabulary, but for the entertainment value of that film. In this example, a person's Spanish vocabulary may be extended but it is an unintended outcome. Or, talking to a friend of relative in a second language may not intentionally be to practice the second language but to foster good relationships. While the person is practicing their second language skills this is an incidental outcome, not the prime reason for such conversation. There are also examples when the formal and informal experience merge. In the classroom there will be episodes where the teacher is having a friendly chat or giving simple instructions that are not primarily for language learning but have that effect.

The fourth and final stage of Gardner's model (1979, 1983, 1985) has two **outcomes**. One outcome refers to bilingual proficiency. The second outcome refers to non-linguistic outcomes such as change in attitudes, self concept, cultural values and beliefs. The placing of attitudes in the second and the fourth stage suggests that the model should be conceived as something that is not static but cyclical. Attitudes are not only ingredients in the language learning situation. Attitudes are also products or outcomes of language learning. That is, the learning of a second language and the act of becoming bilingual, may change attitudes. As the diagram above indicates by the dotted arrow from bilingual proficiency to the second stage, competence in a second language may in turn affect intelligence, motivation and situational anxiety levels.

The value of Gardner's model is that it is not only a summary of existing research in the social psychology of language learning. It also has been directly and formally tested as a complete model (Gardner, 1983; Gardner, Lalonde & Pierson, 1983; Lalonde, 1982) and found to fit collected data. This is different from most theories of bilingualism where the theory attempts to summarize previous research but is not subsequently directly and rigorously tested.

One **limitation** of Gardner's model is that it does not include the sociopolitical dimension that often surrounds routes to bilingual proficiency. As will be considered in Chapter 19, a full understanding of language acquisition, language change and bilingual education (at individual and societal levels) requires a political dimension. For example, the preference in a region for assimilation of minorities, integration or cultural pluralism, influences language policies, provision and practices surrounding bilinguals.

There are other limitations of models. Models are valuable for summarizing and providing clarity but tend to imply descriptions rather than deep explanations. They suggest a straightforward, well functioning, clearly ordered system of actions and reactions, ingredients and events. An individual's internal conflicts, the complexity of competing multiple pressures and motives, the many and varied individual recipes of success and failure, the many individual exceptions, the complexity of contexts and effects of immediate and long-standing situations are not represented in a model.

THEORIES OF SECOND LANGUAGE ACQUISITION AND LEARNING

The topics of bilingualism and second language acquisition are like brother and sister. While both have separate sets of friends and mother and father figures, they come from the same family. Becoming bilingual often involves second language acquisition, either achieved formally (e.g. in the classroom) or informally (naturally, for example, in the street and playground, via television and radio). At the same time, research into bilingualism feeds into the wide topic of second language acquisition (e.g. the Development of Bilingual Proficiency project; see Harley *et al.*, 1987, 1990).

There are multiple **theories** of second language acquisition. In major reviews, McLaughlin (1987) examines five important second language theories while Ellis (1985) considers seven second language theories. The essence of second language theories is to describe the individual and contextual conditions for efficient second language learning to occur.

The Acculturation Model of Second Language Learning

John Schumann (1978) proposes an acculturation model of second language acquisition whose essential element is the **second language learner adapting to a new culture**. The model starts with the idea that language is one aspect of culture, and the relationship between the language community of the learner and the second language community is important in second language acquisition. The basic premise of the model is 'the degree to which a learner acculturates to the target language group will control the degree to which he acquires the second language' (Schumann, 1978: 34). Schumann (1978) portrays the various factors that are important in 'good' language learning. Expressed in group rather than individual terms, these facilitating **social factors** comprise:

(1) The target language group and the second language learner group are self-perceived as relatively socially equal. The greater the equality distance (e.g. domination,subordination) the less the chance of language learning.
(2) The target language and second language learner groups both desire assimilation of the learner's social group.
(3) Both groups expect the second language group to share social facilities as operated by the target language group.
(4) The second language learner group is small, not very cohesive and can be assimilated into the target language group.
(5) The extent to which the second language learner group's culture is congruent and similar to that of the target language group thus assisting assimilation.
(6) The extent to which both groups have positive attitudes and expectations of each other; and
(7) The extent to which the second language learner group expects to stay with the target language group for a longer rather than a short period (e.g. in-migrants).

These are the social factors that for Schumann (1978) determine the probability of a second language individual or group receiving the target language group. Schumann

(1978) also lists **psychological factors** that are important in second language learning. These include: possible language confusion when using the second language (language shock); the feeling of stress, anxiety or disorientation because of the differences between the learner's culture and the target language culture (culture shock); the degree of motivation in learning a language, and the degree of inhibition or self consciousness adolescent learners particularly may have in language learning. Schumann's (1978) factors provide dimensions that may determine the amount of contact a language learner will have with the target language. The amount of contact is defined both by social, external factors and by individual factors. When social and/or psychological distances are large, the learner may fail to progress very far in learning a second language. When the social and psychological factors are positive, second language acquisition may occur relatively painlessly. When psychological and social distances are great, then, at an individual and societal level, pidginization (the development of a simplified form of a language) may occur. For Schumann (1978), pidginization is the characteristic of early second language acquisition. Also, when conditions of social and psychological distance are great, pidginization will occur at a societal level. When pidginization persists over a period, that language may decline, even die.

For Schumann (1978), language has three broad **functions**: a **communication** function, an **integrative** function and an **expressive** function. That is, language aids the transmission of information, aids affiliation and belonging to a particular social group, and allows the display of individual feelings, ideas and personality. Schumann (1978) argues that second language learners will initially use their second language for communication. Second language learners who develop in that language will then seek the use that language to affiliate to a social group. Some learners, but not all may achieve the expressive use of that second language.

Schumann's (1978) Acculturation model, extended by Andersen's (1983) Nativization model, is one way of understanding the politics and power of language in its societal contexts. It provides a valuable explanation of why some children with aptitude and ability fail to learn or use a second language. It does not specify how such language acquisition occurs via internalized learning processes. The information processing approach to second language learning is not included in this model. Absent from this account of second language learning is: the interaction between a particular defined context and the learner; the changing, variable nature of attitudes and motivation; whether attitude is a cause of language learning or an outcome of language learning, or is both a cause and an effect (Gardner, 1985); the shifting power relations and distance between groups; the role of individual and group negotiation over crucial influencing factors; and the difficulty of testing the theory. The model may also be more appropriate to learning a second language naturally rather than to formal language learning within a classroom.

Accommodation Theory

Accommodation theory derives from Giles and colleagues (e.g. Giles & Byrne, 1982). Like Schumann (1978), Giles & Byrne's theory seeks to explain **second language acquisition in a group or intergroup situation**. For Giles & Byrne (1982), the important factor is the perceived social difference between the ingroup (the language learner's social group) and the outgroup (the target language community). The **relationships between the ingroup and outgroup** are seen as both fluid and constantly negotiated. There is a tendency in Schumann's Acculturation model for social and psychological distances to be seen as static or changing relatively slowly over time. For Giles & Byrne (1982), relationships between ingroup and outgroup are dynamic and constantly changing. One way of portraying Giles & Byrne's (1982) model is to profile a person from a subordinate group who is likely to acquire the language of the dominant group.

The learner is likely to show the following characteristics (simplified from Giles & Coupland, 1991):

(1) Have a relatively weak identification with their own ethnic group. That is, such learners do not see themselves as purely a member of their minority language group separate from the dominant language group. Alternatively, their first language is not important to membership of their ethnic group.

(2) Do not regard their ethnic group as inferior to the dominant group. A good language learner makes 'quiescent' comparisons between their ethnic group and the dominant group, or is not concerned about a difference of status.

(3) Perceive their ethnic group as having low vitality compared with the dominant group. Giles & Byrne (1982) talk of a perception of ethnolinguistic vitality which includes (see Chapter 4): (1) the economic, historic, social, political and language status of the ethnic group; (2) size and distribution of an ethnic group, mixed marriages, amount of in-migration and out-migration; and (3) institutional support for the ethnic group (e.g. mass-media, education, religion, industry, services, culture and government).

(4) See their ethnic group boundaries as 'soft and open' and not 'hard and closed'.

(5) Hold adequate status within their ethnic group (e.g. in terms of employment, gender, power and religion).

Thus for Giles & Byrne (1982), a person *less* likely to acquire a second language may have: a strong identification with their own group, makes 'insecure' comparisons with the outgroup; regard their own language community as having high vitality, good institutional support, being sizable and stable and of high status; perceive the boundaries between their own and the second language group as separate and rigid, and have inadequate status within their first language group. Further factors are considered in Giles & Coupland (1991).

Like the Acculturation model, Accommodation Theory does not explain the internal mechanisms of how a child acquires a second language. It is essentially a socio-psychological model rather than a cognitive-processing model of second language acquisition. Tollefson (1991) also criticizes Accommodation Theory for its ahistorical analysis and failure to account for domination and coercion in language shift.

Glyn Williams (1992) is also **critical** in that Giles & Byrne may wrongly assume that language development is gradual and cumulative, of a consensus nature, concerned with order and cohesion with a consequent limited discussion of power, struggle and conflict.

Williams (1992: 224) argues that 'ethnolinguistic vitality is more of a typological construct than a refined concept. It suffers from a lack of integration of its constituent parts, as a consequence of which it is difficult to understand how the subjective and objective dimensions relate'. And of inter-group relationships, Williams (1992: 224) critically comments that the argument is merely 'couched in terms of individuals, rationally conditioned to behave in terms of optimization, with the quest for status and the associated positive identity being the motivating force of behavior'. This tends to play down conflict and power, thereby not expressing the anger, discrimination and frustration felt by language minority groups and their members.

One strength of the theory is that is takes into account ethnic identity in language learning, an important determining factor for many children and adults in second language acquisition.

Krashen's Monitor Model

The Monitor model of **Stephen Krashen** (1977, 1981, 1982, 1985) is probably the most widely cited of theories of second language acquisition. While there are other important theories not considered in this chapter (e.g. Discourse Theory proposed by Hatch (1978), Ellis's (1984) Variable Competence model, Chomsky's (1965) Universal Hypothesis, Wong Fillmore's (1991b) Socio-Linguistic Cognitive Theory, and the Neurofunctional Theory (e.g. Lamendella, 1979)), it is Krashen's theory that has often dominated education research and education debate in second language acquisition. Krashen's Monitor model comprises five central hypothesis plus other variables that need considering in second language acquisition. The five hypothesis are as follows.

The Acquisition Learning Hypothesis

An important initial distinction is between second language that is acquired naturally and second language that is acquired in formal situations. Thus Krashen distinguishes between acquisition and learning. Acquisition is a subconscious process that results from informal, natural communication between people where language is a means and not a focus nor an end in itself. Learning occurs in a more formal situation where the overt properties of a language are taught. Language learning has traditionally involved grammar, vocabulary learning and the teaching of other formal linguistic properties. Learning is a conscious process that enables a learner to 'know about' the second language. With second language learning, the analysis and correction of errors is formally and explicitly addressed.

Acquisition and learning are not defined by 'where' a second language occurs. Formal learning can occur in the street when a person asks questions about correct grammar, mistakes and difficulties. The key factor for Krashen is a distinction between language judgments based on rules and based on feelings. Conscious thinking about language rules is said to occur in second language learning; unconscious feelings about what is correct and appropriate occurs in language acquisition.

The **distinction between acquisition and learning** is a central idea in education theory. It is a distinction between deductive and inductive approaches, classroom and naturalistic learning, formal and informal language learning. Advocates of the communicative method in language teaching emphasize the importance of informal acquisition of authentic language inside the classroom. In educational terms, this is also referred to as a distinction between a formal training approach and apprenticeship. Formal training attempts to provide learning experiences in which languages will be learnt efficiently. Apprenticeship involves acquiring skills naturally while working on a particular task.

The Natural Order Hypothesis

This hypothesis suggests that grammatical structures are acquired in a predictable order for both children and adults, irrespective of the language being learnt. When a learner engages in natural communication, then the standard order will occur. This hypothesis has been criticized (e.g. McLaughlin, 1987). Research on morphemes and on the development of specific grammatical forms does not support a 'strong' version of the hypothesis. Variations between different people and a lack of supportive evidence suggest that only a 'weak' version of the natural order hypothesis is tenable.

The Monitor Hypothesis

The Monitor is an editing device that may operate before language performance. Utterances may be modified by being acted upon by the Monitor of learnt knowledge. Such editing may occur before the natural output of speech; it may occur after the output via a correcting device. Krashen suggests that monitoring occurs when there is sufficient time, when there is pressure to communicate correctly and not just convey meaning, and when the appropriate rules of speech are known. Examples include knowing the correct tense to use, when to use the third or first person and rules about plurals. This hypothesis has been criticized for being untestable and for a lack of supportive research evidence.

The Input Hypothesis

To explain how language acquisition occurs, Krashen proposes that when learners are exposed to grammatical features a little beyond their current level, those features are 'acquired'. Krashen emphasizes that 'acquisition' is the result of comprehensible language input and not of language production. Input is made comprehensible because of the help provided by the context. If the language student receives understandable input, language structures will be, according to Krashen, naturally acquired. For Krashen, the ability to communicate in a second language 'emerges' rather than is directly put in place by teaching. Second language is said to be caused by the process of understanding second language input.

The Affective Filter Hypothesis

An Affective Filter was proposed by Dulay & Burt (1977) with the idea that there is a filter that determines how much a person learns in a formal or informal language setting. The filter comprises affective factors such as attitudes to language, motivation, self-confidence and anxiety. Thus learners with favorable attitudes and self-confidence may have 'a low filter' with consequent efficient second language learning. Those with unfavorable attitudes and/or high anxiety have 'high filters' and so the input of second language learning may be blocked or impeded. The affective filter proposed by Krashen influences the rate of development in second language learning and the level of success in becoming bilingual.

Before considering how Krashen's Monitor model relates to classroom language learning and teaching, it is important to note various **criticisms** that have been made of this model. Apart from the possibility of the informal acquisition of language occurring in a classroom and language being learnt in informal discussion, the criticism has been that the acquisition–learning hypothesis cannot be tested empirically. Because acquisition is more subconscious and learning is relatively more conscious, it is difficult even impossible to test the hypothesis empirically and comprehensively. It may also be the case that acquisition and learning are not separate. It may be that acquired knowledge can become learnt knowledge. Once learnt knowledge is practiced it may reach a level of automatization that equates to acquired knowledge, being available in spontaneous 'unconscious' conversation. As Larsen-Freeman (1983) comments, Krashen does not explain the cognitive processes that underlie acquisition and learning. Thus the Monitor model is a 'black box' theory of language acquisition. It does not specify what goes on in cognitive processes to explain second language acquisition.

Another line of **criticism** concerns the monitoring hypothesis. In reality, is there a distinction between rule application (as in the Monitoring device) and having a subconscious feel for what is right and wrong in a communication situation? Is there an underlying critical faculty (Morrison & Low, 1983) that makes people aware of the correctness or incorrectness of their language communication? Krashen's theory also tends to fail to explain variability between individuals in language learning. Further criticisms may be found in McLaughlin (1978, 1987), Morrison & Low (1983) and Ellis (1985).

Krashen's Theory Applied to the Classroom

Krashen (1982) and Krashen & Terrell (1983) have applied the Monitor model to language teaching and classroom language learning. The classroom applications that follow from the Monitor model are as follows. **First**, Krashen & Terrell (1983) argue that the goal of language teaching must be to supply understandable input in order for the child or adult to acquire language easily. A good teacher therefore is someone who continuously delivers at a level understandable by the second language speaker. Just as father and mother talk (motherese) help the young child to acquire the first language by a simplified and comprehensible language (and non verbal language), so an effective teacher is said to facilitate second language learning by ensuring a close match between the level of delivery and the level that is understandable. **Second**, teaching must prepare the learner for real life communication situations. The classroom needs to provide conversational confidence so that, when in the outside world, the student can both linguistically cope and continue language learning.

Conversational competence also means learning strategies to get native speakers to explain their meaning when it is not initially apparent, devices for changing topics and for facilitating understandable communication with the native speaker.

Third, Krashen & Terrell (1983) suggest that teachers must ensure that learners do not become anxious or defensive in language learning. This relates to the Affective Filter hypothesis. The confidence of a language learner must be encouraged in a language acquisition process. When a learner is relaxed, confident and not anxious, then the input of the classroom situation will be more efficient and effective. If teachers insist on children conversing before they feel comfortable in doing so, or a teacher constantly corrects errors and makes negative remarks, the learner may feel inhibited in learning. **Fourth**, formal grammar teaching is of limited value because it contributes to learning rather than acquisition. Only simple rules should be learnt. Complex rules will not be used consciously or unconsciously by the language learner. Therefore, there appears little to be gained from formally teaching the rules of a second language. **Fifth**, errors should *not* be corrected when acquisition is occurring. They may be corrected when the goal is formal learning. Error correction is valuable when learning simple rules but may have negative effects in terms of anxiety and inhibition.

For Krashen & Terrell (1983), a 'Natural Approach' is required in language teaching. The **Natural Approach** is very different from traditional grammar teaching and language laboratory types of approach. Its main tenets are as follows: communicative skills should be the aim of the good language classroom; comprehension of language should precede production (listening should precede speaking); speaking and then writing will emerge when the language learner is ready and should not be forced; acquisition rather than formal learning is central in good language learning; and the affective filter needs to be kept low (that is, favorable attitudes, positive motivation and low anxiety are important in language learning).

CONCLUSION

This chapter has discussed central ideas in the acquisition of a second language. The overarching question is 'Who learns how much of what language under what conditions?' This brings into play individual differences (e.g. in ability and attitude), the skills and competences being learnt (e.g. grammatical accuracy, conversational fluency and literacy), contextual and situational factors, linguistic inputs and learner processes (e.g. code switching).

To the highways and byways of bilingualism needs to be added the geography of the journey. The journey is affected by the psychology of the individual, the environment and conditions of language travel, the political and cultural weather surrounding acquisition, fellow travelers and map makers. Becoming bilingual is a linguistic, social and a psychological event. The chapter has sought to portray the main features of different routes, while indicating that no two journeys will be the same.

A variety of theories of second language acquisition have been presented. Each provides some clues as to how a second language is more efficiently and effectively acquired or learnt. The individual and social aspects are necessarily fused; the linguistic, sociological and psychological cannot be realistically separated. General theories have been considered with Krashen's theory being directly related to classroom practice. While

Krashen's model has been criticized, it has provided teachers with a set of general guidelines grounded in second language research and theory. Whether such theories derived from psychology or linguistics have sufficient understanding of complex class-rooms and sufficient power to provide a technology of teaching is doubtful. Such theories give ideas and insights, they do not always provide answers that are translatable into comprehensive procedures or recipes for classroom practice. 'Best' or 'perfect' recipes are as unlikely in teaching as they are in cordon bleu cooking.

SUGGESTED FURTHER READING

ELLIS, R., 1985, *Understanding Second Language Acquisition.* Oxford: Oxford University Press.

GARDNER, R.C., 1985, *Social Psychology and Second Language Learning.* London: Edward Arnold.

McLAUGHLIN, B., 1987, *Theories of Second-Language Learning.* London: Edward Arnold.

SPOLSKY, B., 1989, *Conditions for Second Language Learning.* Oxford: Oxford University Press.

REVIEW AND STUDY QUESTIONS

(1) Write short revision notes on the following:
   (i) The difference between the sequence, order and rate of language acquisition.
   (ii) The nature of language aptitude and language attitude.
(2) Make a list of the factors that research and theory has located as influential in second language acquisition.
(3) Describe an idealized version of a 'good' and 'poor' second language learner from the contents of this chapter.
(4) From the various theories you have read in this chapter, make a list of those elements relevant to particular schools and classrooms known to you.
(5) Take one of the theories presented in this chapter and, by further reading, write about why you think that theory is important and valuable.

STUDY ACTIVITIES

(1) Locate a teacher or a parent or a friend who has learnt a second language in school or in adult life. Ask them about the importance of school, classroom and learning factors in their second language acquisition. Discuss with them how they see their current ability, attitudes and usage of their second language.
(2) Take Gardner's or Lambert's model and show how the model relates to one person well known to you. Show how the elements of the model are translatable into the language life of an individual of your choice.

CHAPTER 7

Bilingualism and Intelligence

Introduction

Bilingualism and 'Intelligence'
The Period of Detrimental Effects
The Period of Neutral Effects
The Period of Additive Effects

Bilingualism and the Brain

Conclusion

CHAPTER 7

Bilingualism and Intelligence

INTRODUCTION

There is one piece of advice that parents sometimes receive from well-meaning teachers, doctors, speech therapists, school psychologists and other professionals. Don't raise your child bilingually or problems will result. Predicted problems range from bilingualism as a burden on the brain, mental confusion, inhibition of the acquisition of the majority language, even split personality. Parents and teachers are sometimes advised to use only one language with individual children. When children persist in speaking two languages in school, having their mouths washed with soap and water (Isaacs, 1976) and being beaten with a cane for speaking Welsh (the Welsh 'Not') have been offered as a remedy.

A quotation from a Professor at Cambridge University portrays this deficit viewpoint:

> 'If it were possible for a child to live in two languages at once equally well, so much the worse. His intellectual and spiritual growth would not thereby be doubled, but halved. Unity of mind and character would have great difficulty in asserting itself in such circumstances'. (Laurie, 1890: 15).

The anxiety that two languages may have a negative effect on an individual's thinking skills tends to be expressed in two different ways. First, some tend to believe that the more someone learns and uses a second language, the less skill a person will have in their first language. Rather like weighing scales or a **balance**, the more one increases, the more the other decreases. This issue is addressed in Chapters 8 and 9 of this book. Second, concern is sometimes expressed that the ability to speak two languages may be at the cost of **efficiency** in thinking. The intuitive belief is sometimes that two languages residing inside the thinking quarters will mean less room to store other areas of learning. In comparison, the monolingual is pictured as having one language in residence and therefore maximal storage space for other information.

Does the ownership of two languages interfere with efficient thinking? Do monolinguals have more effective thinking quarters? Is a bilingual less intelligent than a monolingual due to a dual language system? This chapter and the next examines these typically negatively phrased questions and evaluates the evidence on bilingualism and thinking. We start by considering the relationship between intelligence and bilingualism. 'Intelligence' has been a major concept in psychology and often related to bilingualism. It is also a term used by members of the public in phrasing questions about bilingualism.

BILINGUALISM AND 'INTELLIGENCE'

The Period of Detrimental Effects

From the early nineteenth century to approximately the 1960s, the dominant belief amongst academics was that bilingualism had a detrimental effect on thinking. For example, the quote from Professor Laurie (1890) suggested that a bilingual's intellectual growth would not be doubled by being bilingual. Rather both intellectual and spiritual growth would be halved. This view of Laurie (1890) tends to parallel a view commonly held amongst the British and US populace right through the twentieth century: that bilingualism has disadvantages rather than advantages in terms of thinking.

The early research on bilingualism and cognition tended to confirm this negative viewpoint, finding that monolinguals were superior to bilinguals on mental tests (Darcy, 1953; Náñez, Padilla & Máez, 1992). Research up to the 1960s looked at this issue through one concept — 'intelligence'. A typical piece of research gave bilinguals and monolinguals an 'intelligence' test. When bilinguals and monolinguals were compared on their IQ scores, particularly on verbal IQ, the usual result was that bilinguals were behind monolinguals. An example of this early research is by a Welsh researcher, D.J. Saer (1923). He gathered a sample of 1,400 children aged seven to fourteen from bilingual and monolingual backgrounds. A 10 point difference in IQ was found between bilinguals and monolingual English speakers from the rural areas of Wales.

Saer (1923) concluded that bilinguals were mentally confused and at a disadvantage in thinking compared with monolinguals. Further research by Saer, Smith & Hughes (1924) suggested that University student monolinguals were superior to bilinguals: 'the difference in mental ability as revealed by intelligence tests is of a permanent nature since it persists in students throughout their University career' (p. 53).

While it is possible that situations exist where bilinguals will perform on such tests at a lower level than monolinguals (this is considered in Chapters 8 and 9), the early research that pointed to detrimental effects has a series of weaknesses. Such weaknesses tend to invalidate the research in terms of individual studies and cumulatively across studies. These limitations may be listed as follows.

Definition

The concept of 'intelligence' and the use of intelligence tests is controversial and hotly debated. One part of the controversy lies in the **problems of defining and measuring intelligence**. The underlying questions are: what is intelligence and who is intelligent? A thief who cracks a bank vault? A famous football coach? Someone poor who becomes a billionaire? Don Juan? A chairperson who manipulates the members of a board? Is there social intelligence, musical intelligence, military intelligence, marketing intelligence, motoring intelligence, political intelligence? Are all, or indeed any of these forms of intelligence measured by a simple pencil and paper IQ test which requires a single, acceptable, correct solution to each question? What is intelligent behavior or not requires a subjective value judgment as to the kind of behavior and the kind of person regarded as of more worth.

There are three related controversies to that of the definition of 'intelligence':

- There is a fierce debate about the relative effects of heredity and environment on the development of intelligence. A strong hereditarian viewpoint tends to argue that intelligence is relatively fixed and unlikely to be affected by becoming bilingual. An environmental view of the origins of intelligence may be more appealing to supporters of bilingualism. The environmental view holds that intelligence is not fixed or static, but modifiable by experience (e.g. family, education, culture and sub-culture). The 'extra' experience of two languages may thus contribute to the nature and growth of intelligence.
- Does intelligence comprise one unitary factor, or can intelligence be divided into a wide variety of factors or components? Is there one all-embracing general factor of intelligence (labeled 'g'), or is Guilford's (1982) 150 factor model of intelligence more valid? A multi-factor view of intelligence is more likely to reveal differences between monolinguals and bilinguals.
- IQ tests tend to relate to a middle class, white, Western view of intelligence. The cultural boundedness or relativity of IQ tests suggests that cross-cultural generalizations are dangerous and limited. The relationship between bilingualism and a non-Western view of intelligence may be fruitful and revealing.

To summarize: in the relationship between intelligence and bilingualism, the first problem is that IQ tests only measure a minute sample of everyday 'intelligence'. Therefore, whatever pattern is found between IQ tests and bilingualism refers to 'pencil and paper' intelligence. Research does not investigate the relationship between dual language ownership and all the components that might go under the wide heading of 'intelligence'. To use an analogy: we cannot fully portray a football or basketball match simply from the number of passes. Similarly, with bilingualism and intelligence, the whole game has not been studied, just one small statistic.

Language of Testing

The second problem is the language of the IQ test given to bilinguals. It is preferable to test the IQ of bilinguals in their stronger language or in both languages. In the early research, many verbal IQ tests were administered in English only. This tended to be to the disadvantage of bilinguals in that they were tested in their weaker language and thus under-performed in the IQ test.

Analysis

The early research tended to use simple averages when comparing monolingual and bilinguals groups. Statistical tests were often not performed to see whether the difference between the average scores was real or due to chance factors. Thus, for example, when

W.R. Jones (1966) re-analyzed Saer's (1923) research, he found that there was no statistically significant difference between the monolingual and bilingual groups.

Classification

As has been shown in Chapter 1, the classification of people into bilingual and monolingual groups is fraught with difficulty. It is too simplistic to place people into a monolingual or a bilingual group. We need to ask what language competences are being used for classification? Are all four basic language abilities being used? What is the degree of fluency in each language? Were bilinguals classified by their use of languages (functional bilingualism) or by their ability in language? As Chapter 1 revealed, who is or who is not bilingual is a complex issue. The earlier research on bilingualism and cognition tended to regard classification as non-problematic. This means that the research results are simplistic and ambiguous, having classified bilinguals in an insensitive and imprecise manner.

Generalization

A fifth problem concerns sampling and the generalization of research results to the population of bilinguals. With all research, the findings should be restricted to the population that the sample exactly represents. In particular, research using a non-random sample of a population, merely a convenience sample, should theoretically have no generalization beyond that sample. Much of the research on bilingualism and cognition is based on convenience samples. Thus research on 11 year olds cannot be generalized to other age groups. Findings in the US cannot be generalized to bilinguals in the rest of the world. In much of the early research on bilingualism and cognition, the sampling is both small and inadequate making generalization dangerous.

Context

The language environment of the research sample needs to be considered. This relates to the notion of subtractive and additive environments. Negative, detrimental cognitive findings may be more associated with minority language groups in subtractive environments. Subtractive environments are where the child's first language is in danger of being replaced by a more prestigious second language. Where bilingualism has high prestige in an additive environment, a different pattern of results may be more likely.

Matched Groups

The final problem is particularly important. To compare a group of bilingual children with monolinguals on IQ, or on any other measure of cognitive ability, requires that the two groups be equal in all other respects. The only difference between the two groups should be in their bilingualism and monolingualism. If such control does not occur, then the results of the research may be due to the other factor or factors on which the groups differ (rather than their monolingualism or bilingualism). Take the example of a monolingual group being mostly of higher socioeconomic status, and the bilingual group being mostly of a lower socioeconomic status. A result (e.g. showing monolinguals to be ahead of bilinguals) may be due to social class rather than, or as well as, bilingualism. The great majority of researches on bilingualism and 'intelligence' failed to match the groups on other factors that might explain the results. It is necessary to match the groups on variables such as sociocultural class, gender, age, type of school attended and urban/rural and subtractive/additive environments.

Conclusion

The period of detrimental effects research lasted from approximately the 1920s to the 1960s. While the dominant result was that bilinguals were inferior to monolinguals, particularly on verbal IQ, these early researches share many serious methodological weaknesses. Singly and cumulatively, the early research on bilingualism and IQ has so many limitations and methodological flaws that its conclusion of detrimental effects cannot be accepted. While it is possible that, in some contexts, bilinguals may have cognitive disadvantages (see Chapter 9), the early research cannot be used to support this claim. Indeed, as will be seen later in this chapter, different conclusions may better reflect the current state of research.

The Period of Neutral Effects

There are a series of researches that reported **no difference** between bilinguals and monolinguals in IQ. For example, research in the United States by Pintner & Arsenian (1937) found a zero correlation (no relationship) between verbal (and non-verbal) IQ and Yiddish-English bilingualism/monolingualism. While the number of researches with a 'no difference' conclusion is small in number, the period of neutral effects is important because it highlighted the inadequacies of the early detrimental effects research. An example is the research by W.R. Jones (1959) in Wales. Using 2,500 children aged 10 and 11, Jones (1959) initially found that bilinguals were inferior to monolinguals on IQ. A re-analysis showed that this conclusion was invalid. After taking into account the varying socioeconomic class of bilinguals and monolinguals, Jones (1959) concluded that monolinguals and bilinguals did not differ significantly in non-verbal IQ so long as parental occupation was taken into account. He also concluded that socioeconomic class largely accounts for previous research that reported the inferiority of bilinguals on non-verbal IQ. Therefore, his conclusion was that bilingualism is not necessarily a source of intellectual disadvantage.

While the period of neutral effects overlaps chronologically with the detrimental and additive periods, there was a period when (in Wales, for example) such neutral effects were taught and publicized. Such a 'neutral' conclusion was historically important as it gave a boost to parents who wished to support bilingualism in the home and in the school. As a transitional period, it both helped to question a fashionable belief of bilingualism as cerebral confusion, and became a herald for the additive effects period.

The Period of Additive Effects

A major turning point in the history of the relationship between bilingualism and cognition was reached in Canadian research by Peal & Lambert (1962). It is this piece of research that heralded in the modern approach to bilingualism and cognitive functioning. This research broke new territory in three respects, each setting the pattern for future research.

First, the research overcame many of the methodological deficiencies of the period of detrimental effects. Second, the research found evidence that bilingualism need not have detrimental or even neutral consequences. Rather, there is the possibility that bilingualism leads to **cognitive advantages** over monolingualism. Peal & Lambert's (1962) finding has been widely quoted to support a variety of bilingual policies in various educational contexts. The political implication of the study was that bilingualism within a country was not a source of national intellectual inferiority (Reynolds, 1991). Third, the research by Peal & Lambert (1962), while using IQ tests, moved research to a broader look at cognition. Other areas of mental activity apart from IQ were placed firmly on the agenda for research into bilingualism and cognitive functioning.

Peal & Lambert (1962) commenced with a sample of 364 children aged 10 years old drawn from middle-class French schools in Montreal, Canada. The original sample of 364 children was reduced to 110 children for two reasons. First, to create a group of balanced bilinguals (see Chapter 1) and a group of monolinguals. Second, to ensure that the bilingual and monolingual groups were matched on socioeconomic class.

Bilinguals performed significantly higher on 15 out of the 18 variables measuring IQ. On the other three variables, there was no difference between balanced bilinguals and monolinguals. Peal & Lambert (1962) concluded that bilingualism provides: greater mental flexibility; the ability to think more abstractly, more independently of words, providing superiority in concept formation; that a more enriched bilingual and bicultural environment benefits the development of IQ; and that there is a positive transfer between a bilingual's two languages facilitating the development of verbal IQ.

These conclusions are historically more important than the specific results concerning IQ. That is, it is analysis of the results rather than the details of the results that provided the stimulus for further research and debate.

The study of Peal & Lambert (1962), while being pivotal in research on bilingualism and cognitive functioning, has four basic methodological weaknesses that need to be briefly considered before accepting the research at its face value. **First,** the results concern 110 children of 10 years of age and of middle-class, Montreal extraction. This is not a sample that can be generalized to the population of bilinguals either in Canada or throughout the world. This is particularly so since the results concern 110 children selected from the original sample of 364. An unanswered question is how the other 254 children performed across the broad range of tests given by Peal & Lambert (1962).

Second, children in the bilingual group were 'balanced' bilinguals (see Chapter 1). While the term 'bilinguals' includes balanced bilinguals, there are many other groups of children 'less balanced'. We cannot assume that the results from this study apply to such 'less balanced' bilinguals. Are balanced bilinguals a special group with their own characteristics in terms of their motivation, aptitude for languages, cognitive abilities and attitudes? Are balanced bilinguals a special group of children who have a higher IQ that is due not only to owning two languages, but due to other factors as well (e.g. parental values and expectations)?

The **third** problem with Peal & Lambert's (1962) research is the chicken and the egg problem — which comes first? What is the cause and what is the effect? Is it bilingualism that enhances IQ? Or does a higher IQ increase the chances of becoming bilingual? When research suggests that IQ and bilingualism are positively related, we cannot conclude the order of cause and effect. It may be that bilingualism enhances IQ. It may be that those with a higher IQ are more likely to become bilingual. The relationship may also be such that one is both the cause and the effect of the other. Research by Diaz (1985) suggests that, if there is a particular direction in the relationship, it is more likely to be bilingualism positively affecting 'intelligence', rather than 'intelligence' affecting bilingualism.

The **fourth** problem concerns socioeconomic status. While Peal & Lambert (1962) tried to equate their bilingual and monolingual groups for socioeconomic class by exclusion of some children, there are residual problems. As Cummins (1976, 1984a) and MacNab (1979) have suggested, equating socioeconomic class does not control for all the differences in a child's home environment. Socioeconomic class is only a rough, simple and very partial measure of a child's home and environmental background. This is true of monolingual children. It is even more so with children who are bilingual and bicultural where there may be an even more complicated home and family background regarding sociocultural factors. Parental occupation of bilingual children is likely to summarize differences between children very inadequately.

In the following example, notice how the sociocultural element is very different, yet the socioeconomic class is the same. Take two Latino children of the same age and gender living in the same street in New York. Their fathers both have the same job — taxi drivers. One family regularly attends church services in Spanish and belongs to a Hispanic organization with cultural activities in Spanish. This taxi driver and his wife send their children to a Spanish–English dual language school. The child is bilingual. In the second family, the child speaks English only. There is no interest in sending their children to a dual-language school. Neither does the family attend a church or another organization where Spanish is spoken and valued. The Latin-American roots are neither discussed nor appreciated. While the families are matched on socioeconomic status, the sociocultural differences between them are considerable. In this example, the first child is bilingual and the second child is monolingual, with the bilingual child having a higher IQ. The child's bilingualism may not be the only explanation of a higher IQ. Rather the alternative or additional explanation may be in the different social and cultural environment of these children. Thus, with Peal & Lambert's (1962) study, socioeconomic class may have been controlled, but not sociocultural class.

This completes the examination of Peal & Lambert's (1962) important and pivotal study. Since their research, the dominant approach to bilingualism and cognitive functioning has moved away from IQ testing to a multi-component view of intelligence and cognition. Although there are researches after Peal & Lambert (1962) that examine IQ and bilingualism, most recent studies look at bilingualism in terms of a range of thinking styles, strategies and skills.

While studies since Peal & Lambert (1962) are notable for their lack of integration, their non-theoretical rationale and their lack of reference to advances in cognitive psychology, the studies mostly confirm Peal & Lambert's (1962) positive findings. These research studies are reviewed in the next chapter. Before such a review, a concept allied to IQ is considered. Just as members of the public ask basic questions about 'intelligence' and bilingualism, so questions often arise about bilinguals' brains. For example, is the storage of information different for bilinguals' and monolinguals' brains? Evidence on this topic will now be briefly considered.

BILINGUALISM AND THE BRAIN

A frequently asked question is whether a bilinguals' brain functions differently compared with that of a monolingual's brain? The issue becomes whether language is differently organized and processed in the brain of a bilingual compared with the monolingual (e.g. Gomeztortosa *et al.*, 1995). There are various researches on neurolinguistics and bilingualism. A review by Obler (1983) admits that knowledge of cellular brain structure and neurophysiological behavior as it relates to language processing is at a very rudimentary stage. The number of studies looking at bilingual aphasia, laterality and split-brain patients is not great, and Obler (1983) finds it difficult to make clear cut conclusions. An example is the research of Fromm (1970) who conducted a case study of a man who was regressed by hypnosis to the age of seven. Under hypnosis, the man spoke fluent Japanese. When he returned to his adult self, he could not speak Japanese. Yet other studies have not replicated this finding. This symbolizes the necessity of great caution, as yet, in assertions about bilinguals and the brain.

A dominant topic in the study of bilingualism and the brain is **lateralization**. In the majority of right-handed adults, the left hemisphere of the brain is dominant for language processing. The question has naturally arisen as to whether bilinguals are different from monolinguals in this left lateralization? Vaid & Hall (1991) provide a review of this topic in terms of five **propositions** derived from existing research:

(1) Balanced bilinguals will use the right hemisphere more than monolinguals for first and second language processing.
(2) Second language acquisition will involve the right hemisphere in language processing more than first language acquisition.
(3) As proficiency in a second language grows, right hemisphere involvement will decrease and left hemisphere involvement will increase. This assumes that the right hemisphere is concerned with the more immediate, pragmatic and emotive aspects of language; the left hemisphere with the more analytic aspects of language (e.g. syntax). That is, the core aspects of language processing are assumed to reside in the left hemisphere.
(4) Those who acquire a second language naturally (e.g. on the street) will use their right hemisphere more for language processing than those who learn a second language formally (e.g. in the language classroom). Learning rules about grammar, spelling and irregular verbs will result in more left hemisphere involvement in second

language learning. Picking up a language in a natural manner and using it for straightforward communication will involve more right hemisphere involvement.

(5) Late bilinguals will be more likely to use the right hemisphere than early bilinguals. This proposition states that there might be a 'predominance of a left-hemisphere 'semantic-type' strategy in early bilinguals and for a right hemisphere 'acoustic-type' strategy in late bilinguals' (Vaid & Hall, 1991: 90).

Using a quantitative procedure called **meta-analysis** to review previous research in this area, Vaid & Hall (1991) found that the left hemisphere strongly dominated language processing for both monolinguals and bilinguals. However, differences between monolinguals and bilinguals were the exception rather than the rule. Bilinguals did not seem to vary from monolinguals in neurological processes; the lateralization of language of the two groups being relatively similar:

> 'The largely negative findings from the meta-analysis must be taken seriously as reflecting a general lack of support for the five hypotheses as they have been addressed in the literature to date' (Vaid & Hall, 1991: 104).

While the relationship between the brain and bilingualism is an important area, the present state of knowledge makes a simple generalization unsafe.

A related area concerns the **mental representation** of a bilingual's two languages and the processing emanating from such representation. A principal issue has been the extent to which a bilingual's two languages function **independently or interdependently**. The early research attempted to show that early bilinguals (compound bilinguals) were more likely to show interconnections and interrelatedness in their two languages than late (coordinate) bilinguals. In the 1960s, Kolers (1963) re-defined the issue in terms of memory storage. A **separate storage** hypothesis stated that bilinguals have two independent language storage and retrieval systems with the only channel of communication being a translation process between the two separate systems. A **shared storage** hypothesis stated that the two languages are kept in a single memory store with two different language input channels and two different language output channels. Evidence exists for both independence and interdependence requiring both hypotheses to be rejected. Rather, an integrated model involving both independence and interdependence needs to be produced (Paivio, 1986, 1991; Heredia & McLaughlin, 1992; Keatley, 1992; Hummel, 1993).

Recent theories and research have therefore emphasized both the separate and connected aspects of bilingual's mental representations by integrating the topic with general cognitive processing theories (e.g. Matsumi, 1994) . For example, the bilingual dual coding systems model of Paivio & Desrochers (1980) contains:

- Two separate verbal language systems, one for each of a bilingual's two languages.
- A separate non-verbal imagery system, independent from the two language systems.
- The non-verbal imagery system functioning as a shared conceptual system for the two languages.
- Strong, direct interconnecting channels between each of these three separate systems.

- The interconnections between the two languages comprising association and translation systems; common images also being mediators. The model is given in the diagram below (adapted and simplified from Paivio & Desrochers, 1980, 1991):

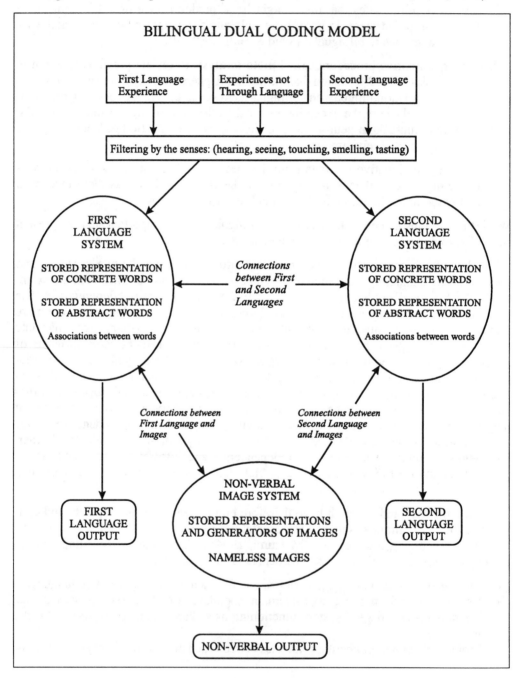

CONCLUSION

This chapter has reviewed the strong, traditional and popular expectation that bilingualism and intelligence are linked negatively. The conception is often that bilingualism leads to lower intelligence. Research from the 1920s to the 1960s supported that conception. Recent research currently regards a simple negative relationship as a misconception. The narrow view of intelligence contained in IQ tests and severe flaws in the design of early research combine with other limitations to cast doubts on this negative link.

Rather, the need is to specify the language ability levels of bilinguals (see Chapter 1) and to ensure like is compared with like. Since 1960, the indication has been that a more positive relationship between bilingualism and cognitive functioning can be expected, particularly in 'balanced' bilinguals. The next chapter examines recent research on the cognitive advantages and disadvantages of bilingualism.

SUGGESTED FURTHER READING

BAKER, C. 1988, *Key Issues in Bilingualism and Bilingual Education.* Clevedon: Multilingual Matters.
HAKUTA, K. 1986, *Mirror of Language. The Debate on Bilingualism.* New York : Basic Books.
HARRIS, R.J. (ed.) 1992, *Cognitive Processing in Bilinguals.* Amsterdam: North-Holland.

REVIEW AND STUDY QUESTIONS

(1) Write short revision notes on the following:
    (i)   The meaning of the three periods: detrimental, neutral and additive.
    (ii)   The findings and criticisms of Peal & Lambert's (1962) research.
    (iii) The difference between the separate storage and shared storage hypotheses.
(2) What were the limitations of the research in the detrimental effects period?
(3) Why is the concept of IQ a controversial one, and how does this controversy relate to bilingualism?

STUDY ACTIVITIES

(1) In a school of your choice, interview one or more teachers. Find out whether IQ tests have been used in the past and/or are currently being used. For what purposes were IQ tests used? Do teachers expect bilingual children to show a lower IQ than monolinguals? Do teachers think that IQ tests in the majority language are fair to bilingual children?
(2) Find one or more examples of an IQ test. Examine the content of the test and locate any items which you think will be unfair to bilinguals. Examine both the language and the cultural content of the IQ test. What kinds of IQ tests seem to be more or less appropriate for bilinguals? Are culture-free tests and non-verbal IQ tests more fair?

CHAPTER 8
Bilingualism and Thinking

CHAPTER 8

Bilingualism and Thinking

INTRODUCTION

Recent research tends not to compare monolingual and bilingual groups on an IQ test. Rather, the modern approach is to focus on a wider sample of products and processes of a bilingual's cognition. Do bilinguals and monolinguals differ in thinking styles? Are there differences in the processing of information? Does owning two languages create differences in thinking about language? These type of questions are examined in this chapter.

BILINGUALISM AND DIVERGENT AND CREATIVE THINKING

One problem with IQ tests is that they restrict children to finding the one correct answer to each question. This is often termed convergent thinking. Children have to converge onto the sole acceptable answer. An alternative style is called divergent thinking. A child regarded as a diverger is more creative, imaginative, elastic, open ended and free in thinking. Instead of finding the one correct answer, divergent thinkers prefer to provide a variety of answers, all of which can be valid.

Divergent thinking is investigated by asking questions such as: 'How many uses can you think of for a brick?'; 'How many interesting and unusual uses can you think of for tin cans?'; 'How many different uses can you think of for car tires?'. On this kind of question, the student has to diverge and find as many answers as possible. For example, on the 'uses of a brick' question, a convergent thinker would tend to produce a few rather obvious answers to the question: to build a house, to build a barbecue, to build a wall. The divergent thinker will tend to produce not only many different answers, but also some may be fairly original: for blocking up a rabbit hole, for propping up a wobbly table, as a foot wiper, breaking a window, making a bird bath.

In the British tradition, the term used for this area is divergent thinking (Hudson, 1966, 1968). In the North American tradition, it is more usual to talk about **Creative Thinking**. In the North American tradition, Torrance (1974a, 1974b) analyzes answers to the 'Uses of an Object' test (e.g. unusual uses of cardboard boxes, unusual uses of tin cans) by four categories. This test may be adapted into any language, with a culturally appropriate use of objects.

A person's **fluency** score in creative thinking is the number of different acceptable answers that are given. A **flexibility** score is the number of different categories (listed in the Test Manual) into which answers can be placed. **Originality** is measured by reference to the Test Manual that gives scores of 0, 1, or 2 for the originality (statistical infrequency) of each response. **Elaboration** refers to the extent of the extra detail that a person gives beyond the basic use of an object. A similar scoring system is used with divergent and creativity tests containing non-verbal questions. Sometimes called Figural Tests, a person is given a sheet of 40 circles or 40 squares and asked to draw pictures using these individual circles or squares, and subsequently place a label underneath.

The underlying hypothesis concerning creative thinking and bilingualism is that the ownership of two or more languages may increase fluency, flexibility, originality and elaboration in thinking. Bilinguals will have two or more words for a single object or idea. For example, in Welsh, the word *ysgol* not only means a school but also a ladder. Thus having the word '*ysgol*' in Welsh and 'school' in English may provide the bilingual with an added dimension — the idea of the school as a ladder. Similarly, having two or more words for folk dancing or square dancing in different languages may give a wider variety of associations than having a single word in one language.

Does having two or more words for the one object or idea allow a person more freedom and richness of thought? Research has compared bilinguals and monolinguals on a variety of measures of divergent thinking (see Baker (1988) and Ricciardelli (1992) for reviews). The research is international and cross cultural: from Ireland, Malaysia, Eastern Europe, Canada, Singapore, Mexico and the US, sampling bilinguals using English plus Chinese, Bahasa Melayu, Tamil, Polish, German, Greek, Spanish, French, Ukrainian, Yorubo, Welsh, Italian or Kannada. As Laurén (1991) notes, such research has mostly occurred in additive bilingual contexts. The research findings largely suggest that bilinguals are superior to monolinguals on divergent thinking tests. An example will illustrate.

Cummins (1975, 1977) found that balanced bilinguals were superior to 'matched' non-balanced bilinguals on the fluency and flexibility scales of verbal divergence, and marginally on originality. The 'matched' monolingual group obtained similar scores to the balanced bilingual group on verbal fluency and flexibility but scored substantially higher than the non-balanced group. On originality, monolinguals scored at a similar level to the non-balanced bilinguals and substantially lower than the balanced group. Probably due to the small numbers involved, the results did not quite attain customary levels of statistical significance. That there are differences between matched groups of balanced bilinguals and non-balanced bilinguals suggests that bilingualism and superior divergent thinking skills are not simply related. Cummins (1977) proposed that:

'there may be a threshold level of linguistic competence which a bilingual child must attain both in order to avoid cognitive deficits and allow the potentially beneficial aspects of becoming bilingual to influence his cognitive growth'. (p. 10)

The difference between balanced and non-balanced bilinguals is thus explained by a **threshold**. Once children have obtained a certain level of competence in their second language, positive cognitive consequences can result. However, competence in a second language below a certain threshold level may fail to give any cognitive benefits. Cognitive benefits may accrue when a child's second language competence is fairly similar to first language skills. This is the basic notion of the threshold theory which is examined further in Chapter 9.

The weight of the evidence suggests that balanced bilinguals have superior divergent thinking skills compared with unbalanced bilinguals and monolinguals. In a review of 24 studies, Ricciardelli (1992) found that on 20 of these bilinguals performed higher than monolinguals. Studies not supporting bilingual superiority sampled less proficient bilinguals; a result consistent with the Thresholds Theory. However, some care must be taken in too firm a conclusion. The researches on this topic have methodological limitations and deficiencies. To ensure a fair judgment, these problems need to be borne in mind.

The five major **problems** may be listed as follows: (1) Some studies fail to control adequately for differences between bilingual and monolingual groups (e.g. age and socioeconomic differences). (2) Some studies have small samples such that generalization must be very restricted or non-existent. (3) Some studies fail to define or describe the level or degree of bilingualism in their sample. As Cummins (1977) has shown, the extent of such competence is an important intermediate variable. (4) Not all studies find a positive relationship between bilingualism and divergent thinking. Cummins & Gulutsan (1974), for example, found differences on only one of their five measures of divergent thinking. Laurén (1991) found that linguistic creativity differences were found in grades three, six and nine. Older bilinguals were ahead on only one of the four measures (use of compound nouns). (5) The term 'creativity' is defined in different ways. As Laurén (1991) reveals, there is an interpretation by psychologists (e.g. cognitive flexibility, fluency, originality and elaboration; tolerance of ambiguity); by linguists (e.g. the ability to create new meanings in different contexts, complexity of sentences); child development researchers (e.g. transforming the language input of parents and teachers); and creative writing proponents. Do bilinguals show advantages on psychological rather than the purely linguistic creativity measures? (6) Human beings are ever likely to change and develop, so is it the case that bilingualism gives cognitive advantages of a permanent nature? If there are positive cognitive advantages linked with bilingualism, it is important to ask whether these are temporary, or cumulative and everlasting? Research studies tend to use children aged 4 to 17. What happens into the twenties or middle age or older age? Does bilingualism accelerate cognitive growth in the early years, with monolinguals catching up in later years? Balkan (1970) and Ben-Zeev (1977a) have suggested that such cognitive advantages are predominant in younger rather than older children. Arnberg (1981) disagrees and argues that cognitive development is additive and cumulative, and that the further the child moves towards balanced bilingualism, the more there are cognitive advantages to be gained. With cognitive style (e.g. divergent thinking) may go relatively stable and lasting effects.

BILINGUALISM AND METALINGUISTIC AWARENESS: INITIAL RESEARCH

The research on bilingualism and divergent thinking tentatively suggests that bilinguals may have some advantage over matched monolinguals. The ownership of two languages may provide some advantages in the way language relates to thinking. For many bilingual children, the size of their total vocabulary in both languages is likely to be greater than that of a monolingual child (Swain, 1972). Does a larger overall vocabulary allow a bilingual to be more free and open, more flexible and original particularly in meanings attached to words? Is a bilingual person therefore less bound by words, more elastic in thinking due to owning two languages? For example, Doyle *et al.* (1978) found that bilinguals tend to be superior in their ability to relate stories and to express concepts within those stories when compared with monolinguals.

Leopold's (1939–1949) famous case study (see Chapter 5) of the German–English development of his daughter, Hildegard, noted the looseness of the link between word and meaning — an effect apparently due to bilingualism. Favorite stories were not repeated with stereotyped wording; vocabulary substitutions were made freely in memorized songs and rhymes. Word sound and word meaning were separated. The name of an object or concept was separated from the object or concept itself.

To illustrate: imagine a kindergarten monolingual and bilingual child are taught the same nursery rhyme:

> Jack and Jill went up the hill
> To fetch a pail of water.
> Jack fell down and broke his crown
> And Jill came tumbling after.

The monolingual child may be relatively more likely to repeat the verse with little or no alteration. The focus is on the sound and the rhyme. The bilingual child may be more likely to center on the meaning than repeating the words parrot fashion. For example, the bilingual may offer the following version; the word substitutions suggesting that the nursery rhyme has been processed for meaning:

> Jack and Jill *climbed* a hill
> To fetch a *bucket* of water.
> Jack fell down and *banged* his *head*
> And Jill came *falling* after.

Hildegard is a single case and the nursery rhyme is merely an illustration based on one child. What has research revealed about samples of bilinguals?

Ianco-Worrall (1972) tested the sound and meaning separation idea on 30 Afrikaans–English bilinguals aged four to nine. The bilingual group was matched with monolinguals on IQ, age, sex, school grade and social class. In the first experiment, a typical question was: 'I have three words: CAP, CAN and HAT. Which is more like CAP, CAN or HAT?' A child who says that CAN is more like CAP would appear to be making a choice determined by the **sound** of the word. That is, CAP and CAN have two out of three letters in common. A child who chooses HAT would appear to be making a choice based on the **meaning** of the word.

That is, HAT and CAP refer to similar objects. Ianco-Worrall (1972) showed that, by seven years of age, there was no difference between bilinguals and monolinguals in their choices. Both groups chose HAT, their answer being governed by the meaning of the word. However, with 4 to 6 year olds, she found that bilinguals tended to respond to word meaning, monolinguals more to the sound of the word. This led Ianco-Worrall (1972) to conclude that bilinguals:

'reach a stage of semantic development, as measured by our test, some 2–3 years earlier than their monolingual peers'. (p. 1398).

In a further experiment, Ianco-Worrall (1972) asked the following type of question: 'Suppose you were making up names for things, could you call a cow "dog" and a dog "cow"'? Bilinguals mostly felt that names could be interchangeable. Monolinguals, in comparison, more often said that names for objects such as cow and dog could not be interchanged. Another way of describing this is to say that monolinguals tend to be bound by words, bilinguals tend to believe that language is more arbitrary. For bilinguals, names and objects are separate. This seems to be a result of owning two languages, giving the bilingual child awareness of the free, non-fixed relationship between objects and their labels.

Other research in this area, for example, by Ben-Zeev (1977a, 1977b) suggests that the ability of bilinguals to analyze and inspect their languages, stems from the necessity of avoiding 'interference' between the two languages. That is, the process of separating two languages and avoiding code-mixing, may give bilinguals superiority over monolinguals through an increased analytical orientation to language. One of Ben-Zeev's (1977a) tests, called the Symbol Substitution Test, asked children to substitute one word for another in a sentence. For example, they had to use the word 'macaroni' instead of 'I' in a sentence. The sentence to say becomes 'Macaroni am warm', thus avoiding saying 'I am warm'. Respondents have to ignore word meaning, avoid framing a correct sentence and evade the interference of word substitution in order to respond to the task correctly. Bilinguals were found by Ben-Zeev (1977a) to be superior on this kind of test, not only with regard to meaning, but also with regard to sentence construction.

Ben-Zeev (1977a), using Hebrew–English bilinguals from Israel and the United States aged 5–8, argues that bilinguals have advantages because they experience two language systems with two different sets of construction rules. Therefore bilinguals appear to be more flexible and analytical in language skills.

BILINGUALISM AND METALINGUISTIC AWARENESS: RECENT TRENDS

Much of the research on bilingualism and cognitive functioning has concentrated on cognitive style (e.g. divergent and creative thinking). The focus of research tends to be on the person and on the product. Such research has tended to focus on whether bilinguals are superior or inferior to monolinguals as people. It has attempted to locate dimensions of thinking where bilinguals perform better than monolinguals. The recent trend has been to look at the **process** of thinking rather than the **products** of thinking, working within the information processing, memorization and language processing approaches in psychology (e.g. Kardash *et al.*, 1988; Ransdell & Fischler, 1987, 1989; Bialystok, 1991; Harris, R., 1992; Keatley, 1992; Padilla & Sung, 1992; Hummel, 1993). Not all such studies are 'favorable to bilinguals' (e.g. Ellis, N. (1992) and Geary *et al.*, (1993) on the processing of numbers). However, research on memorization, language recall, reaction times and processing times tends to use bilinguals to help describe and explain cognitive processing and language processing. Comparisons with monolinguals aim to aid psychological understanding of cognitive processes rather than to focus on bilinguals *per se.*

Process research which builds cumulatively on previous research on bilingualism and cognitive functioning has focused particularly on the metalinguistic awareness of bilingual children (Galambos & Hakuta, 1988; Bialystok & Ryan, 1985; Bialystok, 1987a, 1987b; Ricciardelli, 1993; Campbell & Sais, 1995). While the topic of metalinguistic awareness is wide and ambiguous (Tunmer, Pratt & Herriman, 1984), it may loosely be defined as the ability to think about and reflect upon the nature and functions of language:

> 'As a first approximation, metalinguistic awareness may be defined as the ability to reflect upon and manipulate the structural features of spoken language, treating language itself as an object of thought, as opposed to simply using the language system to comprehend and produce sentences. To be metalinguistically aware is to begin to appreciate that the stream of speech, beginning with the acoustic signal and ending with the speaker's intended meaning, can be looked at with the mind's eye and taken apart' (Tunmer & Herriman, 1984: 12)

Such metalinguistic awareness is regarded by Donaldson (1978) as a key factor in the development of reading in young children. This hints that bilinguals may be ready slightly earlier than monolinguals in learning to read. *Early* research suggested a relationship favoring bilinguals in terms of increased metalinguistic awareness (e.g. Ianco-Worrall, 1972; Ben-Zeev, 1977a, 1977b; see Tunmer & Myhill, 1984 for a review). It appears that bilingual children develop a more analytical orientation to language through organizing their two language systems.

In research that directly engages bilingualism and metalinguistic awareness, Bialystok (1987a, 1987b) found that bilingual children were superior to monolingual children on measures of the **cognitive control of linguistic processes**. Bialystok (1987a) conducted three studies each involving around 120 children age 5–9. In the experiments, children were asked to judge or correct sentences for their syntactic acceptability irrespective of meaningfulness. Sentences could be meaningfully grammatical (e.g. why is the dog barking so loudly?); meaningful but not grammatical (e.g. why the dog is barking so loudly?); anomalous and grammatical (e.g. why is the cat barking so loudly?), or anomalous and ungrammatical (e.g. why the cat is barking so loudly?). These sentences test the level of analysis of a child's linguistic knowledge. The instructions requested that the children focus on whether a given sentence was grammatically correct or not. It did not matter that the sentence was silly or anomalous. Bialystok (1987a) found that bilingual children in all three studies consistently judged grammaticality more accurately than did monolingual children at all the ages tested.

Bialystok (1987b) also examined the difference between bilinguals and monolinguals in their processing of words and the development of the concept of a word. She found in three studies that bilingual children showed more advanced understanding of some aspects of the idea of words than did monolingual children. A procedure for testing children's awareness of 'What is a word?' is to ask children to determine the number of words in a sentence. It can be surprisingly difficult for young children to count how many words there are in a sentence. Until children are about 6–7 years of age and learning to read, they do not appear to have this processing ability.

To be able to count how many words there are in a sentence depends on two things: first, a knowledge of the boundaries of words; second, a knowledge of the relationship between word meaning and sentence meaning. At around 7 years of age, children learn that words can be isolated from the sentences in which they are contained, having their own individual meaning. Bialystok (1987b) found that bilingual children were ahead of monolingual children on counting words in sentences because: (1) they were more clear about the criteria that determined the identity of words and, (2) they were more capable of attending to the units of speech they considered relevant.

> 'Bilingual children were most notably advanced when required to separate out individual words from meaningful sentences, focus on only the form or meaning of a word under highly distracting conditions, and re-assign a familiar name to a different object.' (Bialystok, 1987b: 138).

The **conclusion** can be summarized as follows. Fully fluent bilinguals have increased metalinguistic abilities. This relates to two components (Bialystok, 1988; Ricciardelli, 1993): bilinguals' enhanced *analyzing* of their knowledge of language; and their greater *control* of internal language processing. In turn, this may facilitate earlier reading acquisition that, in turn, can lead to higher levels of academic achievement.

The research of Galambos & Hakuta (1988) provides further refinement of the reasons for differences between bilinguals and monolinguals on cognitive processes. In two studies with low income Spanish–English bilingual children in the US, Galambos & Hakuta (1988) used a series of tests that examined children's ability to spot various errors in Spanish sentences. Such errors might be in terms of gender, word order, singular and plural, verb tense and time. For example, on a grammatically oriented test item, a child had to correct the following: '*La perro es grande*'. The correction would be '*El perro es grande*'. In a content oriented test item, '*La perro es grande*' would become '*El perro es pequeno*'. In the experiment, children were read the sentences, asked to judge whether it had been said in the right way, and then correct the error.

The effect of bilingualism on the processing of the test items was found to vary depending on the level of bilingualism and the difficulty level of the items. The more bilingual the child, that is where both languages were relatively well developed, the better the performance on the test items:

> 'The information-processing approach successfully accounts for our findings that bilingualism by and large enhances the metalinguistic abilities to note errors and correct errors... The bilingual experience requires that the form of the two languages being learned be attended to on a routine basis. Experience at attending to form would be predicted to facilitate any task that required the child to focus on form upon demand.' (Galambos & Hakuta, 1988: 153)

Galambos & Hakuta (1988) concluded that metalinguistic awareness is most developed when a child's two languages are developed to their highest level. The development of two languages to their fullest, particularly the minority language, encourages metalinguistic awareness. Galambos & Hakuta (1988) agree with Cummins (1976) that a certain level of proficiency in both languages must be attained before the positive effects of bilingualism on metalinguistic awareness can occur. This is usually termed the thresholds theory and is considered in Chapter 9.

The evidence of advantages for bilinguals in terms of metalinguistic awareness seems fairly strong. What is not apparent, as yet, is the extent of these effects. For example, are these effects temporary and located with younger children? Are the effects in any way permanent? Do they give a child an initial advantage that soon disappears with growing cognitive competence? Are these early benefits for bilinguals cumulative and additive? Apart from 'balanced bilinguals', which groups of bilinguals gain such advantages?

BILINGUALISM AND COMMUNICATIVE SENSITIVITY

In Ben-Zeev's research (1977b) on the comparative performance of bilingual and monolingual children on Piagetian tests, she found that bilinguals were more responsive to hints and clues given in the experimental situation. That is, bilinguals seem more sensitive in an experimental situation, and corrected their errors faster compared to monolinguals. While Piagetian research and bilingualism is not considered in this chapter (see Baker (1988) for a review), Ben-Zeev's (1977b) research gave the first clue that bilinguals may have cognitive advantages regarding 'communicative sensitivity'.

What is '**communicative sensitivity**?' Bilinguals need to be aware of which language to speak in which situation. They need constantly to monitor what is the appropriate language in which to respond or when initiating a conversation (e.g. on the telephone, in a shop, speaking to a superior). Not only do bilinguals often attempt to avoid 'interference' between their two languages, they also have to pick up clues and cues when to switch languages. The literature suggests that this may give a bilingual increased sensitivity to the social nature and communicative functions of language.

An interesting experiment on sensitivity to communication is by Genesee, Tucker & Lambert (1975). They compared children in bilingual and monolingual education on their performance on a game. In this simple but ingenious research, students aged 5–8 were asked to explain a board and dice game to two listeners. One listener was blindfolded, the other not. The listeners were classmates and not allowed to ask any questions after the explanation. The classmates then attempted to play the game with a person giving the explanation. It was found that children in a bilingual education program (total immersion — see Chapter 10) were more sensitive to the needs of listeners. This bilingual education group gave more information to the blindfolded children than to the sighted listener compared with children in the monolingual education control group. The authors concluded that children in bilingual education 'may have been better able than the control children to take the role of others experiencing communicational difficulties, to perceive their needs, and consequently to respond appropriately to these needs' (p. 1013).

In conclusion, this implies that bilingual children may be more sensitive than monolingual children in a social situation that requires careful communication. A bilingual child may be more aware of the needs of the listener.

More research is needed to define precisely the characteristics and the extent of the sensitivity to communication that bilinguals may share. Research in this area is important because it connects cognition with interpersonal relationships. It moves from questions about skills of the bilingual mind to a bilingual's social skills.

FIELD DEPENDENCY AND INDEPENDENCY AND BILINGUALISM

One well researched dimension of cognitive style along which people vary is field dependence — field independence (Witkin *et al.*, 1971). An example from one of Witkin *et al.*'s (1971) tests helps illustrate this dimension. In the Embedded Figures Test, a child has to draw in the left hand figure over the right hand figure. Can the child recognize the cuboid in the right hand figure?

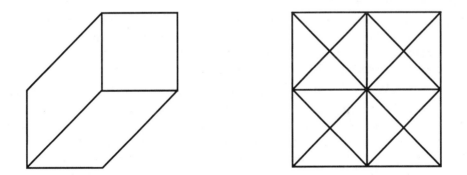

Children who are field independent will tend to see the object separate from the other lines in the right hand figure. Those field dependent will tend not to separate out the cuboid figure from the background. The simple shape is not identified in the more complex shape. Simply stated, some people tend to see in wholes, others in parts. Witkin *et al.* (1962) found that as children grow to maturity they become more field independent. While field dependence–independence may appear as a perceptual ability, Witkin and his co-workers regard it as a general ability to be aware of visual contexts, and relates particularly to problem solving ability and ease of cognitive restructuring. Field independent individuals tend to achieve higher academically than those field dependent.

One early study which examined whether bilinguals have a particular cognitive style compared with monolinguals was conducted in Switzerland by Balkan (1970). French-English balanced bilinguals aged 11 to 17 were matched with monolinguals on IQ, and compared on an adaptation of the **Embedded Figures Test**. Balkan (1970) found that bilinguals were more field independent and that those who learnt their second language before the age of four tended to be more field independent than late learners (who had learnt their second language between 4 and 8 years). In Canada, students age 12 to 13 years in a bilingual education program were superior to the control groups on the Embedded Figures Test (Bruck, Lambert & Tucker, quoted in Cummins, 1978). Although the comparison groups were different from Balkan (1970), the Canadian research provided further evidence for bilingualism being linked to greater field independence. However, Genesee & Hamayan (1980) found that those more field independent learnt a second language better. This highlights the cause-effect relationship. Does field independence cause bilingualism to occur more easily? Does bilingualism cause field independence? Or is one both the cause and the effect of the other?

Apart from the Swiss and Canadian research, one further confirmatory piece of evidence comes from English/Spanish bilinguals in the USA (Duncan & De Avila, 1979). Using the Children's Embedded Figures Test, the descending order of scores on field independence was:

(1) proficient bilinguals;
(2) partial bilinguals, monolinguals and limited bilinguals;
(3) late language learners/

The authors conclude that **proficient bilinguals** may have advantages in cognitive clarity and in analytical functioning. This theme, of more proficient bilinguals having cognitive advantages over monolinguals and less proficient bilinguals is returned to when considering the Thresholds Theory in the next chapter.

The Embedded Figures Test focuses on spatial ability. In contrast, metalinguistic awareness tests focus on linguistic domains. On the surface, they have little in common. Yet bilinguals do well on both tests compared with monolinguals. Are there any features in common between the tests that explain bilinguals cognitive advantages. Bialystok (1992) argues that there is a commonality: **selective attention** that transfers across the spatial and linguistic domains. Bilingual children can reconstruct a situation (perceptual or linguistic), focus on the key parts of a problem and select the crucial parts of a solution. They can escape from perceptual seduction and overcome cues that are irrelevant. Their 'early experience with two languages may lead them to develop more sensitive means for controlling attention to linguistic input. They are used to hearing to things referred to in two different ways, and this can alert them earlier to the arbitrariness of referential forms'

(Bialystok, 1992: 510). Bilinguals select which language to use with whom and avoid inappropriate language forms. They may need to attend to social conventions that occur in each language (e.g. different forms of politeness and deference to adults, different ways of greeting in Arabic and Spanish). Such selective attention may transfer across spatial, cognitive and linguistic domains. For Bialystok (1992), it is **selective attention** that is the explanation of bilinguals' advantages on divergent thinking, creative thinking, metal-inguistic awareness, communicative sensitivity, Piagetian tests and on the Embedded Figures Test.

EXPLANATIONS OF FINDINGS

Cummins (1976) has suggested that there are three different ways one might explain a relationship between bilingualism and cognitive advantages. The first explanation is that bilinguals may have a wider and more varied range of **experiences** than monolinguals due to their operating in two languages and probably two or more cultures. The extra range of meanings that two languages provide, the added stream of experience that two languages may give, and the extra cultural values and modes of thinking embedded in two languages may be increased for the bilingual. Cummins (1976) believed that this was a hypothesis yet to be confirmed or rejected. This remains true at the present.

The second explanation of the cognitive advantages of bilingualism concerns a **switching** mechanism. Because bilingual children switch between their two languages, they may be more flexible in their thinking. Neufeld (1974) was critical of this hypothesis, suggesting that monolinguals also switch from one register to another. That is, in different situations and contexts, monolinguals and bilinguals have to know when and how to switch between different modes of speech. This second proposition may be a part explanation only — a small component in a wider and larger whole.

The third explanation is termed the process of **objectification** (Imedadze, 1960; Cummins & Gulutsan, 1974). A bilingual may consciously and subconsciously compare and contrast their two languages. Comparing nuances of meaning, different grammatical forms, being constantly vigilant over their languages may be an intrinsic process due to being bilingual. Inspecting the two languages, resolving interference between languages may provide the bilingual with metalinguistic skills. A famous Russian psychologist, Vygotsky (1962), suggested that bilingualism enables a child 'to see his language as one particular system among many, to view its phenomena under more general categories, and this leads to awareness of his linguistic operations' (p. 110). The suggestion of Vygotsky (1962) seems the most commonly accepted single explanation for the current belief that bilinguals have cognitive advantages over monolinguals. This third explanation is backed by the recent research on the metalinguistic advantages of bilingualism (Diaz & Klingler, 1991).

While objectification may be a central component in explaining the cognitive advantages of bilingualism, it is unlikely to be a sufficient explanation. Nor does objectification relate to a complete theory of intellectual functioning. A creative attempt to fit the disparate research on bilingualism and cognition into an overarching explanation is provided by Reynolds (1991). Reynolds (1991) commences with Sternberg's (1985, 1988) three part model of intelligence. This model of intelligence has three subtheories: contextual, experiential and componential.

In the **Contextual Subtheory**, intelligent behavior is regarded as adapting to the environment in which one is placed. Going to a party and meeting new people on Saturday, next day attending church and a family get-together, then attending school and leisure activities from Monday to Friday, each and all require a person to constantly adapt to changing contexts, sometimes selecting contexts, even altering the environment to suit oneself. Reynolds (1991) argues that bilinguals may be more capable at adapting to changing environments because of their experience of separate linguistic environments and their (sometimes) wider social and cultural environments. Evidence to support this comes from studies of bilinguals' increased communicative sensitivity.

In the **Experiential Subtheory**, intelligent behavior is seen as variable, depending on how much experience a person has of a situation. Acting intelligently is through effectively adapting to new situations. Effectiveness is when behaviors become automated and habitual earlier rather than later. 'Automatization' allows cognitive resources to be more sensibly allocated to the processing of new situations and challenges. According to Reynolds (1991), bilinguals' experience of two languages and switching between languages early in life allows easier automatization in dealing with language tasks and frees resources for less familiar linguistic demands.

The **Componential Subtheory** concerns the processes that underlie intelligent behavior. Such processes firstly involve *Metacomponents* which execute, control and monitor the processing of information. Because a bilingual has to control and monitor two language systems, the metacomponent system may be more evolved and efficient.

Secondly, there are *Performance components* which administer the schemes devised by the Metacomponents. Bilinguals may have advantages with performance components:

> 'Having command of two languages leads to greater use of verbal mediation and increased use of language as a cognitive regulatory tool. Having two interlocking performance systems for linguistic codes gives double the resources for executing verbal tasks... Also there is greater use of learning strategies when learning two languages.' (Reynolds, 1991: 167)

Thirdly, Sternberg's (1985, 1988) Componential Subtheory contains *Knowledge-Acquisition* components. Such components encode new information and match old, memorized information with incoming new information to enable intelligent functioning. Reynolds (1991) considers that a bilingual's dual language system may make the reception of new information more easy and fluent. New information can be assimilated into either or both the language systems of the bilingual. A bilingual may sometimes have a double chance of acquiring new information with two vocabularies and two verbal memories available.

LIMITATIONS OF THE FINDINGS

Research in the area of bilingualism and cognitive functioning often shares methodological problems. Before conclusions are presented, it is important to bear in mind the limitations of research in this area. First, research needs to match monolingual and bilingual groups on all variables other than language. This is in order for any difference between such groups to be explained by bilingualism rather than by any other factors. While some studies do attempt to **control for alternative explanations** by matching students in pairs or by the statistical technique of analysis of co-variance, there are factors that may provide alternative explanations that are missing from such research. These factors are the motivation of the children, parental attitude, school experience and the culture of the home and community. These may be alternative explanations of many of the findings rather than, or as well as bilingualism.

A second criticism is in the nature of the bilinguals that are used in such research. Researchers who find cognitive advantages mostly focus on **balanced bilinguals**. Do balanced bilinguals represent all bilinguals? MacNab (1979) argues that bilinguals are a special, idiosyncratic group in society. Because they have learnt a second language and are often bicultural, bilinguals are different in major ways from monolinguals. For example, parents who want their children to be bicultural and bilingual may emphasize divergent thinking skills, encourage creative thinking in their children and foster metalinguistic skills. The parents of bilingual children may be the ones who want to accelerate their children's language skills. Such parents may give high priority to the development of languages within their children compared with monolingual parents. While this does not detract from the possibility that bilinguals do share some cognitive advantages, it does suggest a need to take care about a decision as to what are the determining factors. It may be that it is not only language that is important. Other non-language factors may be influential as well.

Third, the chicken and egg, **cause and effect relationship** must again be highlighted. What comes first? Most research in this area assumes that bilingualism comes first and causes cognitive benefits. It is not impossible that the causal link may run from cognitive abilities to enhanced language learning. Or it may be that language learning and cognitive development work hand in hand. One both promotes and stimulates the other. It is unlikely that a simple cause effect pattern exists. A more likely situation is the continuous process of interaction between language and cognition. However Diaz (1985), using sophisticated statistical techniques (structural equation modeling), suggests that bilingualism is more likely to be the cause of increased cognitive abilities than the reverse. From current studies, this seems a fair conclusion.

Fourth, we need to ask **which types of children have the benefits**? This concerns whether children of all abilities share the cognitive advantages of bilingualism. Do children below average in cognitive abilities also gain the advantages of bilingualism? There is certainly a tendency in research to use children from the middle classes, particularly those of above average ability. However Rueda (1983), using analytical orientation to language tests (see earlier in this chapter), found that bilingual, less able children (51–69 IQ level) tended to have cognitive advantages over 'matched' monolinguals. Rueda's (1983) research, which needs thorough replication, hints that cognitive advantages may be shared by below average ability children and not just the average and above average ability children.

Fifth, when reviewing research we need to consider the hopes and the ideologies of the researcher. Rosenthal (1966) has shown that **experimenters' expectations** can affect the outcomes and results of human and animal studies. As Hakuta (1986) suggests:

> 'a full account of the relationship between bilingualism and intelligence, of why negative effects suddenly turn in to positive effects, will have to examine the motivations of the researcher as well as more traditional considerations at the level of methodology.' (p. 43)

Have the assumptions and preferences of authors crept unintentionally into their research and affected both the results and the interpretations of the results? In the choice of psychological tests and the choice of a sample, has there been a built-in bias towards finding positive results on bilingualism and cognitive functioning?

Finally, we must ask whether the positive benefits from bilingualism in terms of thinking are **temporary or permanent**? Most research studies tend to use children of school age. There is almost no research on the cognitive functioning of bilinguals and monolinguals after the age of 17. Does bilingualism accelerate cognitive growth in the early years of childhood with monolinguals catching up in later years? Are cognitive advantages predominant in younger rather than older children? Or are the advantages additive, cumulative and long lasting? It is possible that certain advantages (e.g. sensitivity to language, separation of word sound from word meaning) may be temporary. Age and experience may eventually give bilingual and monolingual similar cognitive skills. However, with the ideas of cognitive style (e.g. divergent and creative thinking) and communicative sensitivity, may go relatively more stable and lasting effects.

CONCLUSION

A review of research on cognitive functioning and bilingualism suggests that two extreme conclusions may both be untenable. To conclude that bilingualism gives undoubted cognitive advantage fails to consider the various criticisms and limitations of research in this area. It also fails to recognize that there are studies (e.g. on memory), where bilinguals may sometimes be at a disadvantage compared with monolinguals (e.g. Ransdell & Fischler, 1987). However, to conclude that all the research is invalid, fails to acknowledge that the judgment of the clear majority of researchers tends to be that there are positive links between bilingualism and cognitive functioning. While there is insufficient evidence to satisfy the skeptic, the evidence that currently exists does lead in the direction of bilinguals having some cognitive advantages over monolinguals.

SUGGESTED FURTHER READING

BAKER, C. 1988, *Key Issues in Bilingualism and Bilingual Education*. Clevedon: Multilingual Matters.

BIALYSTOK, E. (ed.) 1991, *Language Processing in Bilingual Children*. Cambridge: Cambridge University Press.

HARRIS, R.J. (ed.) 1992, *Cognitive Processing in Bilinguals*. Amsterdam: North-Holland.

PADILLA, R.V. and BENAVIDES, A.H. (eds.) 1992, *Critical Perspectives on Bilingual Education Research*. Tempe, AZ: Bilingual Press.

REVIEW AND STUDY QUESTIONS

(1) Write short revision notes on the following:
   (i) The relationship between bilingualism and (a) divergent and creative thinking, (b) metalinguistic awareness, (c) communicative sensitivity and (d) field dependency and field independency.
   (ii) The limitations of findings that find a positive link between bilingualism and thinking.
(2) What is meant by metalinguistic awareness? Try to find in the library some recent references to metalinguistic awareness. Write down details of the variety of tests and definitions of metalinguistic awareness.
(3) What are the limitations of a conclusion that there are cognitive advantages to being bilingual? How fair do you think such a conclusion is?

STUDY ACTIVITIES

(1) Find a student or a teacher who you consider to be bilingual. Ask them to talk about the relationship between their bilingualism and thinking. Ask them if they feel it gives them any advantages and any disadvantages. Collect from them examples and illustrations.
(2) Using one of the tests or experiments mentioned in this chapter, select a student (or a group of students) and give them that test. For example, ask them how many uses they can think of for a brick or for a cardboard box. Compare the answers of those who are more and less bilingual and see if there are differences in quality and quantity of answers.

CHAPTER 9

Cognitive Theories of Bilingualism and the Curriculum

Introduction

The Balance Theory

The Iceberg Analogy

The Thresholds Theory

The Development of a Theory

Curriculum Relevance

Criticisms

Conclusion

CHAPTER 9

Cognitive Theories of Bilingualism and the Curriculum

INTRODUCTION

The previous two chapters examined the relationship between bilingualism and IQ (Chapter 7) and bilingualism and cognition (Chapter 8). These chapters were primarily based on research findings and culminated in explanations of the likely positive relationship between bilingualism and thinking processes and products. This chapter extends that discussion of explanations by firstly considering a 'naive' theory of language and cognitive functioning; then, secondly, examining the development of a major and dominating theory of bilingualism and cognition. The culmination of the chapter is a discussion of how this evolved theory has direct curriculum implications.

THE BALANCE THEORY

Previous chapters noted that initial research into bilingualism and cognitive functioning and into bilingualism and educational attainment often found bilinguals to be inferior to monolinguals. This connects with a naive theory of bilingualism which represents the two languages as existing together in a **balance**. The picture is of weighing scales, with a second language increasing at the expense of the first language. An alternative naive picture-theory attached to the early research is of **two language balloons** inside the head. The picture portrays the monolingual as having one well filled balloon. The bilingual is pictured as having two less filled or half filled balloons. As the second language balloon is pumped higher (e.g. English in the US), so the first language balloon (e.g. Spanish) diminishes in size. As one language balloon increases, the other decreases.

The balance and balloon picture theories of bilingualism and cognition appear to be held intuitively by many people. Many parents and teachers, politicians and large sections of the public appear to latently, subconsciously take the balloon picture as the one that best represents bilingual functioning. Cummins (1980a) refers to this as the **Separate**

Underlying Proficiency Model of Bilingualism. This model conceives of the two languages operating separately without transfer and with a restricted amount of 'room' for languages.

What appears logical is not always psychologically valid. While both the balance or balloon ideas are plausible, neither fits the evidence. As Chapter 8 concluded, when children become balanced bilinguals, the evidence suggests that there are cognitive advantages rather than disadvantages for being bilingual. Similarly, Chapter 11 will show that certain types of bilingual education (e.g. early total immersion and heritage language, bilingual education) appear to result in performance advantages (e.g. in two languages and in general curriculum performance) compared with submersion or monolingual education.

Research has also suggested that it is wrong to assume that the brain has only a limited amount of room for language skills, such that monolingualism is preferable. Evidence (see Chapters 5 and 8) suggests that there are enough cerebral living quarters not only for two languages, but for other languages as well. The picture of the weighing scales, of one language increasing at the expense the second language, does not fit the data. Other pictures, provided later in this chapter, better encapsulate research findings.

There is another fallacy with the balance or balloon theory. The assumption of the theory is that the first and second language are kept apart in two 'balloons' inside the head. The evidence suggests to the contrary, that language attributes are not apart in the cognitive system, but transfer readily and are interactive. For example, when school lessons are through the medium of Spanish, they do not solely feed a Spanish part of the brain. Or when other lessons are in English, they do not only feed the English part of the brain. Rather lessons learnt in one language can readily transfer into the other language. Teaching a child to multiply numbers in Spanish or use a dictionary in English easily transfers to multiplication or dictionary use in the other language. A child does not have to be re-taught to multiply numbers in English. A mathematical concept can be easily and immediately used in English or Spanish if those languages are sufficiently well developed. Such easy exchange leads to an alternative idea called **Common Underlying Proficiency** (Cummins, 1980a, 1981a).

THE ICEBERG ANALOGY

Cummins' (1980a, 1981a) **Common Underlying Proficiency model** of bilingualism can be pictorially represented in the form of two icebergs (see below). The two icebergs are separate above the surface. That is, two languages are visibly different in outward conversation. Underneath the surface, the two icebergs are fused so that the two languages do not function separately. Both languages operate through the same central processing system.

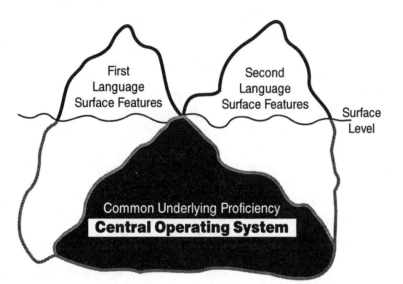

A distinction can thus been made between the **Separate Underlying Proficiency (SUP) and Common Underlying Proficiency models of bilingualism (CUP).** The former (SUP) relates to the 'two balloon' idea presented earlier in this chapter; the latter (CUP) relates to the iceberg idea. The **Common Underlying Proficiency** model of bilingualism may be summarized in six parts:

(1) Irrespective of the language in which a person is operating, the thoughts that accompany talking, reading, writing and listening come from the same central engine. When a person owns two or more languages, there is one integrated source of thought.

(2) Bilingualism and multilingualism are possible because people have the capacity to store easily two or more languages. People can also function in two or more languages with relative ease.

(3) Information processing skills and educational attainment may be developed through two languages as well as through one language. Cognitive functioning and school achievement may be fed through one monolingual channel or equally successfully through two well developed language channels. Both channels feed the same central processor.

(4) The language the child is using in the classroom needs to be sufficiently well developed to be able to process the cognitive challenges of the classroom.

(5) Speaking, listening, reading or writing in the first or the second language helps the whole cognitive system to develop. However, if children are made to operate in an insufficiently developed second language (e.g. in a 'submersion' classroom), the system will not function at its best. If children are made to operate in the classroom in a poorly developed second language, the quality and quantity of what they learn from complex curriculum materials and produce in oral and written form may be relatively weak and impoverished. This has been the experience of some Finns in Swedish schools who were forced to operate in Swedish (Skutnabb-Kangas & Toukomaa, 1976). Such children tended to perform poorly in the curriculum in both Finnish and Swedish because both languages were insufficiently developed to cope with given curriculum material.

(6) When one or both languages are not functioning fully (e.g. because of an unfavorable attitude to learning through the second language, pressure to replace the home language with the majority language) cognitive functioning and academic performance may be negatively affected.

The distinction between Separate Underlying Proficiency (SUP) and Common Underlying Proficiency models of bilingualism (CUP) does not fully sum up the findings from research on cognitive functioning and bilingualism. Therefore this chapter moves on to examining other more sophisticated theories.

THE THRESHOLDS THEORY

Several studies have suggested that the further the child moves towards balanced bilingualism, the greater the likelihood of cognitive advantages (e.g. Cummins & Mulcahy, 1978; Duncan & de Avila, 1979; Kessler & Quinn, 1982; Dawe, 1982, 1983; Clarkson, 1992). Thus the question has become 'Under what conditions does bilingualism have positive, neutral and negative effects on cognition?' How far does someone have to travel up the two language ladders to obtain cognitive advantages from bilingualism?

One theory that partially summarizes the relationship between cognition and degree of bilingualism is called the **Thresholds Theory**. This was first postulated by Toukomaa & Skutnabb-Kangas (1977) and by Cummins (1976). They suggest that the research on cognition and bilingualism is best explained by the idea of two thresholds. Each threshold is a level of language competence that has consequences for a child. The first threshold is a level for a child to reach to avoid the negative consequences of bilingualism. The second threshold is a level required to experience the possible positive benefits of bilingualism. Such a theory therefore limits which children will be likely to obtain cognitive benefits from bilingualism. It also suggests that there are children who may derive detrimental consequences from their bilingualism.

The Thresholds theory may be portrayed in terms of a house with three floors (see below). Up the sides of the house are placed two language ladders, indicating that a bilingual child will usually be moving upward and is not stationary on a floor. On the **bottom floor** of the house will be those whose current competence in both their languages is insufficiently or relatively inadequately developed, especially compared with their age group. When there is a low level of competence in both languages, there may be negative

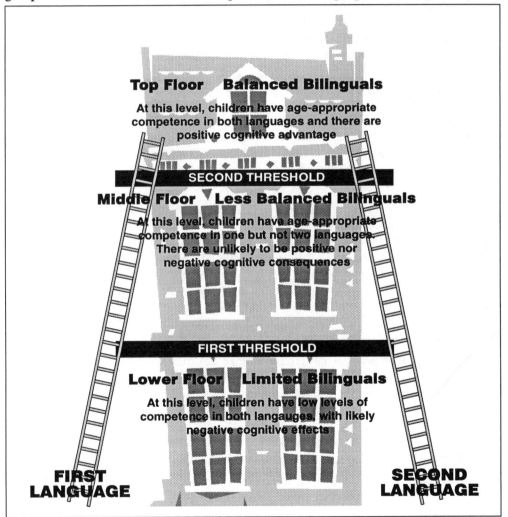

Top Floor   Balanced Bilinguals

At this level, children have age-appropriate competence in both languages and there are positive cognitive advantage

SECOND THRESHOLD

Middle Floor   Less Balanced Bilinguals

At this level, children have age-appropriate competence in one but not two languages. There are unlikely to be positive nor negative cognitive consequences

FIRST THRESHOLD

Lower Floor   Limited Bilinguals

At this level, children have low levels of competence in both langauges, with likely negative cognitive effects

FIRST LANGUAGE   SECOND LANGUAGE

or detrimental cognitive effects. For example, a child who is unable to cope in the classroom in either language may suffer when processing information. At the **middle level**, the second floor of the house, will be those with age-appropriate competence in one of their languages but not in both. For example, children who can operate in the classroom in one of their languages but not in their second language may reside in this second level. At this level, a partly-bilingual child will be little different in cognition from the monolingual child and is unlikely to have any significant positive or negative cognitive differences compared with a monolingual. At the top of the house, the **third floor**, there resides children who approximate 'balanced' bilinguals. At this level, children will have age-appropriate competence in two or more languages. For example, they can cope with curriculum material in either of their languages. It is at this level that the positive cognitive advantages of bilingualism may appear. When a child has age-appropriate ability in both their languages, they may have cognitive advantages over monolinguals.

Research support for the Thresholds Theory comes, for example, from Bialystok (1988), Clarkson & Galbraith (1992), Clarkson (1992) and Dawe (1983). Dawe's (1983) study examined bilingual Panjabi, Mirpuri and Jamaican children age 11 to 13. On tests of deductive mathematical reasoning, Dawe (1983) found evidence for both the lower and the higher threshold. As competency in two languages increased, so did deductive reasoning skills in mathematics. Limited competence in both languages appear to result in negative cognitive outcomes. Bialystok (1988) examined two parts to metalinguistic awareness (analysis of linguistic knowledge and control of linguistic processing) in six- to seven-year-old monolingual, partial bilingual and fluently French-English children. She found that 'the level of bilingualism is decisive in determining the effect it will have on development' (p. 567).

The Thresholds theory relates not only to cognition but also to education. With children in Immersion Education in Canada (see Chapters 10 and 11), there is usually a temporary lag in achievement when the curriculum is taught through the second language. Until the second language (French) has developed well enough to cope with curriculum material, a temporary delay may be expected. Once French is developed sufficiently to cope with the conceptual tasks of the classroom, Immersion Education is unlikely to have detrimental achievement consequences for children. Indeed, such an immersion experience seems to enable children to reach the third floor of the house, with resulting positive cognitive advantages.

The Thresholds theory also helps to summarize why minority language children taught through a second language (e.g. in-migrants in the US) sometimes fail to develop sufficient competency in their second language (e.g. English) and fail to benefit from 'weak' forms of bilingual education. Their low level of proficiency in English, for example, limits their ability to cope in the curriculum. Therefore Heritage Language Programs, that allow a child to operate in their more developed home language, can result in superior performance compared with submersion and transitional bilingual education.

The **problem** with the Thresholds theory is in precisely defining the level of language proficiency a child must obtain in order, firstly to avoid negative effects of bilingualism, and secondly, to obtain the positive advantages of bilingualism. At what language 'height' the ceilings become floors is not clear. Indeed, the danger may be in constructing artificial 'critical stages' or levels, when transition is gradual and smooth. This point is returned to in the following section.

THE DEVELOPMENT OF A THEORY

From out of the Thresholds theory developed a succession of more refined theories of bilingualism. The first evolution of the Thresholds theory considered the relationship between a bilingual's two languages. To this end, Cummins (1978) outlined the Developmental Interdependence hypothesis.

This hypothesis suggested that a child's second language competence is partly dependent on the level of competence already achieved in the first language. The more developed the first language, the easier it will be to develop the second language. When the first language is at a low stage of evolution, the more difficult the achievement of bilingualism will be.

Alongside this, in the 1970s, there developed a distinction between surface fluency and the more evolved language skills required to benefit from the education process. Simple communication skills (e.g. being able to hold a simple conversation with a shopkeeper) may hide a child's relative inadequacy in the language proficiency necessary to meet the cognitive and academic demands of the classroom. Cummins (1984a, 1984b) expressed this distinction in terms of **basic interpersonal communicative skills (BICS)** and **cognitive/academic language proficiency (CALP)**. BICS is said to occur when there are contextual supports and props for language delivery. Face to face '**context embedded**' situations provide, for example, non-verbal support to secure understanding. Actions with eyes and hands, instant feedback, cues and clues support verbal language. CALP, on the other hand, is said to occur in **context reduced** academic situations.

Where higher order thinking skills (e.g. analysis, synthesis, evaluation) are required in the curriculum, language is '**disembedded**' from a meaningful, supportive context. Where language is 'disembedded', the situation is often referred to as '**context reduced**'. The following example illustrates the difference at classroom level between BICS and CALP. A child is given a mathematical question such as: 'You have 20 dollars. You have 6 dollars more than me. How many dollars do I have?' At the higher CALP level, the child will conceptualize the problem correctly as 20 minus 6 equals 14. At the BICS level, the word 'more' may be taken to mean 'add-up' with the child getting the wrong answer of 26. The BICS child may think of 'more' as used in basic conversation. However, in the mathematics classroom, this illustration requires 'more' to be understood by the mathematical phrasing of the question.

The distinction between BICS and CALP has been portrayed in the image of an iceberg (see Cummins, 1984b). Above the surface are language skills such as comprehension and speaking. Underneath the surface are the skills of analysis and synthesis. Above the surface are the language skills of pronunciation, vocabulary and grammar. Below the surface are the deeper, subtle language skills of meanings and creative composition. This is illustrated on the next page.

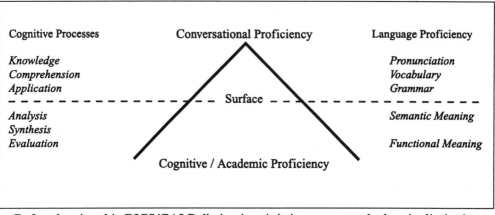

Before leaving this BICS/CALP distinction, it is important to declare its limitations.

(1) The distinction between BICS and CALP has intuitive appeal and does appear to fit the case of children who are seemingly fluent in their second language, yet cannot cope in the curriculum in that language. However, it only paints a two stage idea. The idea of a larger number of dimensions of language competences may be more exact. Children and adults may move forward on language dimensions in terms of sliding scales rather than in big jumps. Such development is like gradually increasing in language competence analogous to increasing gradually the volume on a television set. Harley *et al.*'s (1987, 1990) research suggests that a bilingual's language competencies are evolving, dynamic, interacting and intricate. They are not simple dichotomies, easily compartmentalized and static.

(2) The distinction enabled an understanding and explanation of previous research (e.g. Wong Fillmore, 1979; Snow & Hoefnagel-Höhle, 1978; Cummins, 1984b). However, the distinction between BICS and CALP lacks direct empirical support. Martin-Jones & Romaine (1986) express doubts about it being possible to test the distinction. The distinction between BICS and CALP does not indicate how the two ideas may be precisely defined and accurately tested. Thus the distinction becomes difficult to operationalize in research. For example, the abilities referred to in CALP concern culture-specific types of literacy. This may be difficult to measure validly and fully.

(3) Terms such as BICS and CALP tend to be imprecise, value-laden and become over-compartmentalized, simplified and misused. These hypothetical terms may unwittingly be regarded as real entities. The terms may over-simplify reality. Such terms may be used to label and stereotype students.

(4) The relationship between language development and cognitive development is not unequivocal or simple. It is not simply a case of one growing as a direct result of the other. Cognitive and linguistic acquisition exist in a relationship that is influenced by various other factors (e.g. motivation, school, home and community effects). Language proficiency relates to an individual's total environment, not just to cognitive skills.

The distinction between BICS and CALP helps explain the relative failure within the educational system of many minority language children. For example, in the United States, transitional bilingual education programs aim to give students English language skills sufficient for them to be able to converse with peers and teachers in mainstream education and to operate in the curriculum. Having achieved surface fluency, they may be transferred to mainstream education. The transfer is enacted because children appear to have sufficient language competence (BICS) to cope in mainstream education. Cummins' (1984a) distinction between BICS and CALP explains why such children tend to fail when mainstreamed. Their cognitive academic language proficiency is not developed enough to cope with the demands of the curriculum. What Cummins (1984a) regards as essential in the bilingual education of children is that the 'common underlying proficiency' is well developed. That is, a child's language-cognitive abilities need to be sufficiently well developed to cope with the curriculum processes of the classroom. This underlying ability could be developed in the first or the second language, but also in both languages simultaneously.

A further development of this theory proposes two dimensions (Cummins, 1981b, 1983b, 1984b). This theory is represented in the diagram below:

Both dimensions concern communicative proficiency. The **first dimension** refers to the amount of contextual support available to a student. **Context embedded communication** exists when there is a good degree of support in communication, particularly via body language (Argyle, 1975). For example, by pointing to objects, using the eyes, head nods, hand gestures and intonation, people give and receive plenty of clues and cues to help understand the content of the message.

An example of context embedded communication would be when two children who are hardly able to use each other's languages seem able to communicate quite well by gestures, non-verbal reinforcements and bodily movements. It is not infrequent to see two young children of different languages playing together without difficulty. In **context reduced communication** there will be very few cues to the meaning that is being transmitted. The words of the sentence exist almost alone in conveying the meaning. An example of context reduced communication is often the classroom where the meaning is restricted to words, with a subtlety and precision of meanings in the vocabulary of the teacher or the book.

The **second dimension** is the level of cognitive demands required in communication. **Cognitively demanding communication** may occur in a classroom where much information at a challenging level needs processing quickly. **Cognitively undemanding communication** is where a person has the mastery of language skills sufficient to enable easy communication. An example would be having a conversation in the street, shop, or stadium, where the processing of information is relatively simple and straightforward.

Surface fluency or basic interpersonal communication skills will fit into the first quadrant (see diagram). That is, BICS (basic interpersonal communication skills) is context embedded, cognitively undemanding use of a language. Language that is cognitively and academically more advanced (CALP) fits into the fourth quadrant (context reduced and cognitively demanding). Cummins (1981b) theory suggests that second language competency in the first quadrant (surface fluency) develops relatively independently of *first* language surface fluency. In comparison, context reduced, cognitively demanding communication develops inter-dependently and can be promoted by either language or by both languages in an interactive way. Thus, the theory suggests that bilingual education will be successful when children have enough first or second language proficiency to work in the context reduced, cognitively demanding situation of the classroom. For Cummins (1981b) it often takes one or two years for a child to acquire context-embedded second language fluency, but five to seven years or more to acquire context-reduced fluency. This is illustrated in the graphs below. Research by Hakuta & D'Andrea (1992) with Mexican-Americans found that 'English proficiency reaches asymptotic performance after about eight years. This corresponds quite well with the figures of five to seven years required for attainment of the full range of second language acquisition as estimated by Cummins (1984) based on a heterogeneous L1 population in Canada' (p. 96).

Children with some conversational ability in their second language may falsely appear ready to be taught through their second language in a classroom. Cummins (1981b) theory suggests that children operating at the context embedded level in the language of the classroom may fail to understand the content of the curriculum and fail to engage in the higher order cognitive processes of the classroom, such as synthesis, discussion, analysis, evaluation and interpretation.

This two dimensional model helps explain various research findings:

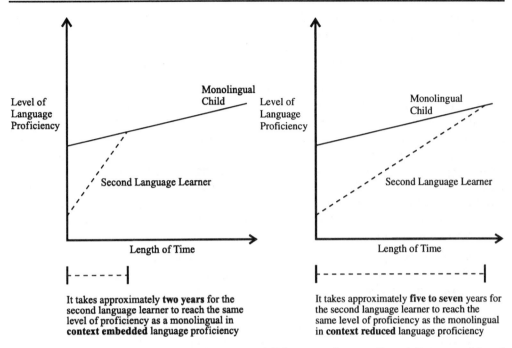

It takes approximately **two years** for the second language learner to reach the same level of proficiency as a monolingual in **context embedded** language proficiency

It takes approximately **five to seven** years for the second language learner to reach the same level of proficiency as the monolingual in **context reduced** language proficiency

(1) In the United States, minority language children may be transferred from transitional bilingual programs into English-only schooling when their conversational ability in English seems sufficient. Such students then frequently perform poorly in mainstream schooling. The theory suggests that this is due to their not having the developed ability in English (or their home language) to operate in an environment that is more cognitively and academically demanding.

(2) Immersion students in Canada tend to lag behind their monolingual peers for a short period. Once they acquire second language proficiency sufficient to operate in a cognitively demanding and context reduced environment, they usually catch up with their peers.

(3) Experiments in the United States, Canada and Europe with minority language children who are allowed to use their minority language for part or much of their elementary schooling show that such children do not experience retardation in school achievement or in majority language proficiency. Through their minority language, they develop the ability to be relatively successful in the cognitively demanding and context reduced classroom environment (Secada, 1991). This ability then transfers to the majority language when that language is well enough developed. Children learning to read in their home language, be it Welsh, Gaelic, Irish, Spanish, Frisian or whatever, are not just developing home language skills. They are also developing higher order cognitive and linguistic skills that will help with the future development of reading in the majority language as well as with general intellectual development. As Cummins (1984a) notes, 'transfer is much more likely to occur from minority to

majority language because of the greater exposure to literacy in the majority language and the strong social pressure to learn it' (p. 143).

CURRICULUM RELEVANCE

What a child brings to the classroom in terms of previous learning is a crucial starting point for the teacher. A child's reservoir of knowledge, understanding and experience can provide a meaningful context from which the teacher can build (Robson, 1995). For example, there will be occasions when a child will learn more from a story read by the teacher than listening to a language tape. When the teacher dramatizes a story by adding gestures, pictures, facial expressions and other acting skills, the story becomes more context-embedded than listening to a tape cassette. Getting a child to talk about something familiar will be cognitively less demanding than talking about something culturally or academically unfamiliar. This means that any curriculum task presented to the bilingual child needs considering for the:

- what the task requires of the child; the cognitive demands inherent in the task (as found by an individual child); the 'entry skills' that a task necessitates. This is illustrated in the table below:

The Cognitive Demands of the Classroom and Contextual Supports

Cognitively Demanding

Explaining and justifying

Solution seeking

Dramatise stories

Role play

Use simple measuring skills

Giving instructions about making a painting

Reflecting on feelings

Discuss ways that language is written; styles and conventions

Relate new information in a book to existing knowledge

Reading a book and discussing the contents

Listening to the news

Context Embedded ← → Context Reduced

Make own books based on their own spoken or written stories

Talking about the weather today

Greeting someone

Describe stories heard or seen on TV

Listening to a story or poem on cassette

Reciting nursery rhymes

Cognitively Demanding

- form of presentation to the child (degree of context embeddedness or context reduction); what form of presentation will be meaningful to the child; use of visual aids, demonstration, modeling, computers, oral and written instructions; amount of teacher assistance;
- child's language proficiencies;
- child's previous cultural and educational experience and knowledge, individual learning style and learning strategies; expectations and attitudes, confidence and initiative; the child's familiarity with the type of task;
- what is acceptable as evidence that learning has successfully occurred; what constitutes mastery or a sufficient approximation; an appropriate form of 'formative' and 'summative' assessment (see Chapter 13) that may be gestural, action (e.g. building a model), drawing, oral or written (Robson, 1995);

A simple example of using the two dimensions to produce an appropriate **teaching strategy** is now presented (see Frederickson & Cline, 1990).

A teacher wants a group to learn how to measure height and to understand the concept of height. Listed below are a few of the teaching strategies for teaching about height. Following the list is a diagram placing the four strategies on the two dimensions:

- One to one, individual teaching using various objects to measure height (1).
- A demonstration from the front of the room by the teacher using various objects (2).
- Teacher giving oral instructions without objects (3).
- Reading instructions from a work card without pictures (4).

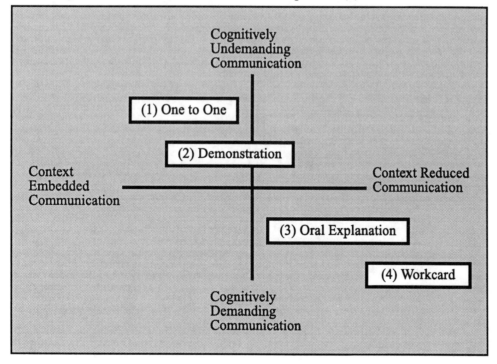

As the above diagram indicates, the example of teaching height can be analyzed in terms of the two dimensions. One to one individual teaching will fit somewhere in the context embedded, cognitively undemanding quadrant. Using work cards may be closer to the context reduced, cognitively demanding area. Demonstrations and oral explanations appear on the diagonal from 'top left' to 'bottom right', in-between individual teaching and work cards. The exact location of teaching approaches on the graph will vary according to teacher, topic, learner and lesson. The example illustrates that the two dimensions can be a valuable way of examining teaching approaches with bilingual children. The dimensions are also useful for analyzing appropriate methods of **classroom assessment**. The dimensions may help focus on task-related curriculum assessment that is more fair and appropriate to bilingual children than norm referenced testing. A teacher wanting to check progress on measuring height has a choice, for example:

- **observing** a child measure the height of a new object (1);
- asking the child to give a **commentary** while measuring a new object (2);
- asking the child to provide a **write-up** of the process (3);
- **discussing** in an abstract way the concept of height (4).

In plotting these four methods of assessment (see below), placement on the graph will vary with different kinds of tasks and testing procedures. All four quadrants can be 'filled' depending on the student, teacher, topic and test. There is also value in comparing the two graphs presented above. The teaching and learning approach taken may well influence the form of assessment. That is, if a context embedded, cognitively undemanding

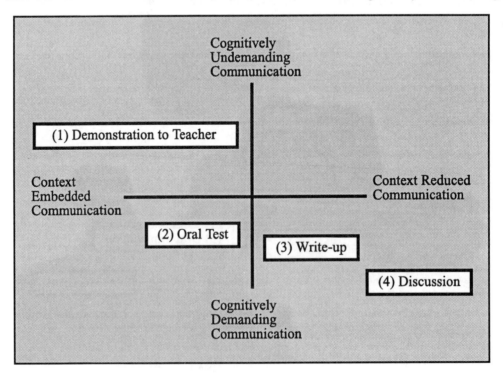

learning strategy is used with a child, assessment may be on similar lines (e.g. observation of child activity). Equally, a context reduced, cognitively demanding learning strategy suggests a 'matched' method of assessment (e.g. discussion).

CRITICISMS

There are criticisms of Cummins' (1981b) theory of the relationship between language and cognition. The main criticisms by Edelsky *et al.* (1983), Martin-Jones & Romaine (1986), Rivera (1984), Frederickson & Cline (1990) and Robson (1995) can be briefly summarized as follows:

(1) Cummins' (1981b) early theory may artificially isolate certain ingredients in a bilingual's cognitive or classroom experience. The attainment of bilingualism or the relationship between bilingual education and school achievement rests on many other factors than are presented in this theory. The early theory was essentially individual and psychological. Bilingualism and bilingual education need to consider other variables; cultural, social, political, community, teacher expectations and home factors. Each and all of these variables help explain bilingualism as an individual and societal phenomenon.

(2) Cummins (1981b) criterion of educational success tended to center on dominant, middle-class indices of achievement. Thus language skills, literacy and formal educational achievement are highlighted. Alternative outcomes of schooling such as self-esteem, social and emotional development, divergent and creative thinking, long-term attitude to learning, employment and moral development were not initially considered.

(3) The theory has been produced as a *post hoc* explanation of a variety of research findings. The theoretical framework requires direct empirical investigation and confirmation with replication across culture and country, time and educational tradition.

(4) Terms such as BICS and CALP tend to be vague, value-laden and in danger of creating an over-simplification and a stereotyping of individual functioning and classroom processes. Essentially hypothetical and abstract, the terms may be adopted as concrete and real (see earlier in this chapter).

(5) The two dimensions are not necessarily distinct, and may not best be represented by two maximally separated (90 degrees apart) axes. When applying Cummins' two dimensions to curriculum tasks, Frederickson & Cline (1990) found it... 'difficult to disentangle the 'cognitive' from the 'contextual'. In some cases, movement along the contextual dimensions has actually been represented on the model as a diagonal shift [on the diagram from top left to bottom right], as it was found in practice that making tasks or instructions more context embedded also made them somewhat less cognitively demanding. Similarly, changes in cognitive demand may result in tasks actually being presented with greater context embeddedness' (p. 26).

(6) When bilingual children appear to have learning difficulties, a teacher may decide to simplify tasks into smaller and more isolated steps. Such a strategy is part of the behavioral objectives approach or a task analysis approach to the curriculum. It may

sometimes result in a non-meaningful context to a curriculum task. By making the task context-reduced, the learning may become more difficult rather than easier, as intended.

(7) Attempting to achieve context embeddedness in any curriculum situation requires empathic understanding of a child's cultural background which itself is dynamic and ever evolving. A danger lies in the teacher developing self-defeating stereotyped assumptions about a child's ethnic experience which may transmit low expectations.

(8) The theory does not make allowances for a child's cognitive strategies in learning, nor their learning style.

CONCLUSION

Naive theories of two languages within an individual are represented by two pictures. First, two languages as a balance. Second, two languages operating as two separate balloons in the head. Such misconceptions can be replaced by pictures such as the dual iceberg and the three tiered house. Depending on language development in both languages, the cognitive functioning of an individual can be viewed as integrated, with easy transfer of concepts and knowledge between languages. Understanding and thinking will be affected by the contextual support that exists and the degree of cognitive demands in a task. Successful cognitive operations in the classroom will depend on matching curriculum tasks with language competences. Sensitivity to the need for contextual support and the cognitive demands of a classroom are important if an individual is to maximize learning in the curriculum.

SUGGESTED FURTHER READING

CUMMINS, J. 1984, *Bilingualism and Special Education: Issues in Assessment and Pedagogy.* Clevedon: Multilingual Matters.
CUMMINS, J. and SWAIN, M. 1986, *Bilingualism in Education.* New York: Longman.
RIVERA, C. (ed.) 1984, *Language Proficiency and Academic Achievement.* Clevedon: Multilingual Matters.

REVIEW AND STUDY QUESTIONS

(1) Write short revision notes on the following:
   (i) The central idea(s) of the balance theory, the iceberg analogy and the thresholds theory.
   (ii) The distinction between BICS and CALP, the value and use of these terms and criticisms of the distinction.
   (iii) The meaning of: context embedded communication, context reduced communication, cognitively demanding communication and cognitively undemanding communication.

(2) What is the curriculum relevance of theories presented in this chapter? Provide examples of relevance as in the diagrams at the end of this chapter.

(3) Define the terms used in this chapter in your own words and discuss their relevance to your own experience.

STUDY ACTIVITY

(1) Observe a classroom with bilingual children. Make a 10 minute cassette tape of the discourse between the teacher and various students, and/or between students themselves. Using the framework on pp. 143 and 144, describe and discuss the language used.

SECTION B

Bilingual Education Policies and Classroom Practices

Chapters 1 to 9 provided the definitional, psychological and sociological foundation upon which bilingual education is built. The remaining chapters focus on bilingual education and bilingual classrooms. With basic questions about language within individuals and within society having been considered in Section A, questions about bilingual education will now have more meaning and fit into a wider societal framework. Bilingual education cannot be viewed in isolation of its social, economic, cultural and political context.

This section is based around various questions about bilingual education:

- What forms of bilingual education are more successful?
- What are the aims and outcomes of different types of bilingual education?
- How important is literacy and biliteracy in bilingual education?
- What kinds of literacy are needed by language minority children?
- What are the essential features and approaches of a classroom fostering bilingualism?
- How should two languages be allocated in bilingual schooling?
- How should deaf bilinguals be educated?
- How should we approach bilingual children with special needs?
- How is a second language best learnt in a classroom setting?
- Why are there different viewpoints about language minorities and bilingual education?
- Why do some people prefer the assimilation of language minorities and others prefer linguistic diversity?
- Can schools play a role in a more multicultural and less racist society?

These questions are now examined in Section B. Chapter 10 provides a wide ranging discussion of different types of education in which bilinguals are placed. Some types of bilingual education support a child's bilingualism; others do not. Such a discussion looks at a variety of international examples. Having described types of bilingual education in

Chapter 10, the next chapter analyzes the effectiveness of different forms of such education. Research evidence is considered and differing viewpoints are encountered. These two chapters (10 and 11) may best be read as a pair.

Chapters 12 to 17 focus on different situations in bilingual education. Each moves from bilingual education systems to a consideration of classroom related issues. While Chapters 10 and 11 discuss broad bilingual education issues, Chapters 12 to 17 narrow the focus to major, practical classroom issues. Chapter 12 concerns the case of classrooms where the minority language is a major medium of instruction. It discusses the language curriculum and the way two languages need to be separated and allocated in bilingual classrooms. Chapter 13 considers the issues of the assessment of bilinguals and particularly those from language minorities; the topic of bilingual special education and analyzes causes of perceived underachievement in language minority children. Chapter 14 examines how bilingualism can be attempted through second language lessons, second language teaching and foreign language instruction. Here part of the focus is on majority language children learning a second (minority or majority) language. The chapter is also relevant to minority language children formally learning a majority language. Chapters 15 and 16 center on the important topic of literacy and biliteracy in bilingual children and multicultural societies. What kind of literacy should be transmitted in bilingual and multicultural classrooms is debated.

In Chapter 17, the well established Canadian Immersion classroom methodology is discussed. With the focus on classroom strategies, immersion classrooms provide an illustration of successful education intervention that promotes bilingualism. This area has been carefully researched and has become an internationally influential form of bilingual education

Chapter 18 is an attempt to provide two summarizing thinking tools to encapsulate Chapters 10 to 16. A model of bilingual education and a framework for language minority intervention are considered so as to gain an overall conceptualization of these chapters.

The two final chapters (19 and 20) are closely linked and form an essential conclusion to the book. Issues about bilingual education philosophy, policy, provision and practice are constantly infused with political considerations. Politics runs through much of the discourse of the book, particularly Chapters 3 and 4, and Chapters 10, 11 13, 15 and 18. The crucial sociopolitical aspect of bilingual education is addressed as a culmination of the book. Various threads from different chapters appear in these final two chapters, with an assumption that political issues are best understood once concrete examples of diglossia and bilingual education are in place. Chapters 19 and 20 discuss orientations and ideologies that connect together, and give a wide perspective and overview of the previous chapters. The key debate about assimilation and pluralism runs through these final two chapters and shows how sociological, psychological and education issues about bilingualism are fundamentally related to wider issues of personal prejudices, public perceptions and pervading politics.

CHAPTER 10

An Introduction to Bilingual Education

CHAPTER 10

An Introduction to Bilingual Education

HISTORICAL INTRODUCTION

One of the **illusions** about bilingual education is that it is a twentieth century phenomenon. In the US it may appear that bilingual education was born in the 1960s. In Ireland, bilingual education is sometimes presented as a child of the Irish Free State of 1921. The story of bilingual education in Wales often starts in 1939 with the establishment of the first Welsh-medium primary school. The Canadian bilingual education movement is often charted from an experimental kindergarten class set up in St Lambert, Montreal, in 1965. Despite these twentieth century events, the historical origins of bilingual education lie well before this century.

The illusion of bilingual education as a modern phenomenon is dangerous on two counts. **First**, it fails to recognize that bilingual education has existed in one form or another for 5000 years or more (Mackey, 1978). Bilingualism and multilingualism are 'a very early characteristic of human societies, and monolingualism a limitation induced by some forms of social change, cultural and ethnocentric developments' (E.G. Lewis, 1977: 22). Lewis (1977, 1981) sketches the history of bilingualism and bilingual education from the Ancient World through the Renaissance to the modern world.

Second, there is a danger in isolating current bilingualism and bilingual education from their **historical roots**. Bilingual education in the US, England and Sweden, for example, needs to be understood within the historical context of in-migration as well as political movements such as civil rights, equality of educational opportunity and melting pot (integrationist, assimilationist) policies. Bilingual education in Ireland and Wales can only be properly understood by the rise of nationalism and language rights movements, for example. Bilingual education, while isolated as a concept in this chapter, is one component inside a wider social, economic, cultural and political framework. As Paulston (1992b: 80) observes: 'unless we try in some way to account for the socio-historical, cultural, and economic–political factors which lead to certain forms of bilingual education, we will never understand the consequences of that education'. The political context of bilingual education is considered in Chapters 19 and 20. The history of bilingual education in the United States is now considered, with a particular emphasis on the dynamic and ever developing nature of bilingual education policy.

A SHORT HISTORY OF BILINGUAL EDUCATION IN THE UNITED STATES

Introduction

Bilingual education in the United States has moved through **four overlapping periods**: permissive, restrictive, opportunist and dismissive. These periods are not neat in their divisions and, in each period, there are variations in different States in policies and practices. There are exceptions inside these broad historical periods. However, generally, there have been changes in the perspectives of politicians, administrators, educationalists and in school practice that indicate that discernible shifts in ideology, preference and practice have occurred (Andersson & Boyer, 1971; Casanova, 1992; Casanova & Arias, 1993; Crawford, 1991; Fitzgerald, 1993; Kloss, 1977; Lyons, 1990; Malakoff & Hakuta, 1990; Perlmann, 1990; Schlossman, 1983).

The Permissive Period

Long before European in-migrants arrived in the United States, the land contained a variety of **native** (indigenous) languages. When the Italian, German, Dutch, French, Polish, Czech, Irish, Welsh and other in-migrant groups arrived, there were already around two hundred, mostly mutually unintelligible languages in the United States. The in-migrants brought with them a wide variety of languages. In the eighteenth and nineteenth centuries in the United States, up until the first World War, linguistic diversity was generally accepted and the presence of different languages was encouraged. Language variety was accepted as the norm and encouraged through religion, newspapers in different languages, and in both private and public schools.

Examples of this permissive period in bilingual education in the United States are found in German–English schools. Set up by German communities in Ohio, Pennsylvania, Missouri, Minnesota, North and South Dakota and Wisconsin, bilingual as well as monolingual German education was accepted. Norwegian and Dutch were also languages of instruction within ethnic based schools. This **openness to in-migrant languages** in the latter half of the nineteenth century was partly motivated by competition for students between public and private schools. Other factors such as benevolent (or uninterested) school administrators, the isolation of schools in rural areas, and ethnic homogeneity within an area also enabled a permissive attitude to mother tongue and bilingual education during this period. In most large cities in the latter half of the nineteenth century, English monolingual education was the pattern. However, in cities such as Cincinnati, Baltimore, Denver and San Francisco, dual language education was present. In some schools in Cincinnati for example, half the day was spent learning through German and the other half of the curriculum was delivered through English.

At the turn of the twentieth century, Italian and Jewish in-migrants were mostly placed in mainstream schools. However, examples of **bilingual education** existed and were permitted. For example, some Polish in-migrants in Chicago attended Catholic schools where a small amount of teaching was through the mother tongue. So long as policy was within the jurisdiction of local towns and districts, the language of instruction did not become an issue in educational provision.

The Restrictive Period

In the first two decades of the twentieth century, a **change** in attitude to bilingualism and bilingual education occurred in the United States. A variety of factors are linked to this change and the subsequent restriction of bilingual education.

- The **number of in-migrants** increased dramatically around the turn of the century. Public schools filled their classrooms with in-migrants. This gave rise to fears of foreigners, and the call for integration, harmonization and assimilation of in-migrants. In-migrants lack of English language and English literacy was seen as a source of social, political and economic concern. The call for Americanization was launched, with competence in English becoming associated with loyalty to the United States. The Nationality Act (1906) required in-migrants to speak English to become naturalized Americans. The call for child literacy in English rather than child labor, socialization into a unified America rather than ethnic separation, along with increased centralized control, led to a belief in a common language for compulsory schooling. By the turn of the century, California and New Mexico had 'English only' instruction laws.
- In 1919, the Americanization Department of the United States Bureau of Education adopted a resolution recommending 'all states to prescribe that all schools, private and public, be conducted in the English language and that instruction in the elementary classes of all schools be in English' (quoted in García, 1992). By 1923, thirty-four states had decreed that **English** must be the sole language of instruction in all elementary schools, public and private.
- A major influence in the movement from permissiveness to repression in bilingualism and bilingual education in the United States came with the entry of the United States into the first **World War** in 1917. Anti-German feeling in the United States spread, with a consequent extra pressure for English monolingualism and a melting pot policy achieved through monolingual education. The German language was portrayed as posing a threat to the unity of Americanization. Linguistic diversity was replaced by linguistic intolerance. Schools became the tool for the assimilation and integration of diverse languages and cultures. Socialization into being American meant the elimination of languages and cultures other than English from schools. The interest in learning foreign languages declined.
- Mandatory attendance laws in public schools were established. Such legislation made the continuation of private schools difficult. Public funding for church-affiliated schools was eliminated.

This period was not totally restrictive as García (1992c) reveals. She speaks of a **'tolerant parenthesis'** between 1923 and 1942. In 1923, the US Supreme Court declared that a Nebraska state law prohibiting the teaching of a foreign language to elementary school students was unconstitutional under the Fourteenth Amendment. This case, known as *Meyer* v. *Nebraska* concerned a case against a teacher convicted of teaching German literacy to a 10 year old child. The original Nebraska ruling was that such mother-tongue teaching cultivated ideas and affections foreign to the best interests of the country. The Supreme Court, in overturning the Nebraska ruling, found that proficiency in a foreign language was 'not injurious to the health, morals, or understanding of the ordinary child'.

Although a 'tolerant parenthesis', this **Supreme Court** finding did not support bilingualism or bilingual education. This is revealed in three ways: (1) the ruling included a requirement for English language instruction in all schools (2) it commented that the desire of a state legislature to foster a homogeneous people was 'easy to appreciate' and (3) the finding is symbolic of a shift in attitude to non-English languages (García, 1992c). No longer were such languages 'ethnic' but 'foreign'. Such languages were no longer seen as spoken by ethnolinguistic minorities in the US, but by 'foreigners' (i.e. non-US or unnaturalized citizens).

This restrictive movement continued at least until the 1960s, and has carried on being one major theme in US politics until the present. This theme is considered further in Chapter 19.

The Period of Opportunity

In 1957, the Russians launched their Sputnik into space. For United States politicians and public, a period of soul-searching led to debates about the quality of US education, US scientific creativity and US competence to compete in an increasingly international world. Doubts arose about the hitherto over-riding concern with English as the melting-pot language, and a new consciousness was aroused about the need for foreign language instruction. In 1958, the National Defense and Education Act was passed, promoting foreign language learning in elementary schools, high schools and universities. This in turn helped to create a slightly **more tolerant attitude** to languages other than English spoken among ethnic groups in the US.

In the United States in the 1960s, various other factors allowed a few opportunities to bring back bilingual education, albeit in a disparate, semi-isolated manner. The 'opportunity' movement for bilingual schools to be re-established in the United States needs to be understood in the wider perspective of the **Civil Rights movement**, the concern for the rights of African-Americans, and the need to establish equality of opportunity and equality of educational opportunity for all people, irrespective of race, color or creed. The 1964 Civil Rights Act prohibited discrimination on the basis of color, race or national origin, and led to the establishment of the Office of Civil Rights. This Act is an important marker that symbolizes the beginning of a change in a less negative attitude to ethnic groups, and possibilities for increased integration and tolerance of ethnic languages. However, the restoration of the practice of bilingual education in the US is often regarded as starting in 1963, in one school in Florida.

In 1963, **Cuban exiles** established a dual language school (Coral Way Elementary School) in Dade County in Florida. Believing they were only in exile for a short period, the educated, middle class Cubans set up this dual language (Spanish–English) bilingual school. The need to maintain their mother tongue of Spanish was aided by having highly trained professional teachers ready to service such schools, the Cubans plight as victims of a harsh Communist state, and their expected temporary stay in the United States. Their unquestioned loyalty to United States policies and democratic politics gained sympathy for the Cubans. Bilingual education in Dade County received both political support and funding. More details of this movement are found in the section on dual language schools.

While the re-establishment of bilingual schools in the US has benefited from the example and success of Coral Way Elementary School, an understanding of bilingual education in the United States requires a comprehension of legislation and lawsuits.

In 1967, a Texas Senator, Ralph Yarborough, introduced a **Bilingual Education Act** as an **amendment** of the **1965 Elementary and Secondary Education Act**. The legislation was designed to help mother tongue Spanish speakers who were seen as failing in the school system. **Enacted in 1968** as **Title VII of the Elementary and Secondary Education Act**, the Bilingual Education Act indicated that bilingual education programs were to be seen as part of federal educational policy. It authorized the use of federal funds for the education of speakers of languages other than English. It also undermined the English-only legislation still lawful in many states. However, the 1968 Bilingual Education Act allocated funds for such minority language speakers while they shifted to working through English in the classroom. The underlying aim was a transition from a minority language (e.g. Spanish) to English, rather than support for the mother tongue.

A landmark in United States' bilingual education was a lawsuit. A court-case was brought on behalf of Chinese students against the San Francisco School District in 1970. The case concerned whether or not non-English speaking students received equal educational opportunities when instructed in a language they could not understand. The failure to provide bilingual education was alleged to violate both the equal protection clause of the 14th Amendment and Title VI of the Civil Rights Act of 1964. The case, known as **Lau versus Nichols**, was rejected by the federal district court and a court of appeals, but was accepted by the Supreme Court in 1974. The verdict outlawed English submersion programs for language minority children and resulted in nationwide 'Lau remedies'. The Lau remedies acknowledged that students not proficient in English needed help. Such remedies included English as a Second Language classes, English tutoring and some form of bilingual education. The Lau remedies created some expansion in the temporary use of minority languages in schools. They rarely resulted in heritage language, enrichment or maintenance programs as the accent was still on a transitional use of the home language for English language learners. The Lau court case is symbolic of the dynamic and continuing contest to establish language rights in the US particularly through testing the law in the courtroom (Casanova, 1991; Hakuta, 1986; Lyons, 1990).

In this period of opportunity, the kind of bilingual education needed to achieve equality of educational opportunity for language minority children was not defined. However, the right to equal opportunity for language minorities was asserted. The means of achieving that right was not declared. During this period, there was a modest growth in **developmental maintenance bilingual education and ethnic community mother tongue schools**. These schools are considered in separate sections on heritage language bilingual education and dual language schools.

The Dismissive Period

While bilingual education has not disappeared in the United States in the last two decades, since the 1980s there have been both central moves against an emergence of a strong version of bilingual education, a preference for **submersion and transitional bilingual education** (see later in this chapter), and the rise of pressure groups such as English First and US English that seek to establish English monolingualism and cultural assimilation. Consideration of such political movements is found in Chapter 19.

To understand the current dismissive or repudiation period, it is helpful to examine the legislative changes with respect to bilingual education in the United States. We return to the 1968 Bilingual Education Act (Title VII and part of the Elementary and Secondary Education Act). This provided a 'poverty program' for the educationally disadvantaged among language minorities. It did not require schools to use a child's home language other than English. However, it did allow a few opportunists to bring 'home languages' into the classroom rather than exclude them. The **1974 amendments** to this **Bilingual Education Act** (see the chronology table) required schools receiving grants to include teaching in a student's home language and culture so as to allow the child to progress effectively through the educational system. Effective progress in student achievement could occur via the home language or via English. However, this gave rise to fierce debates about how much a student's native language should be used in school. Some argued that it was essential to develop a child's speaking and literacy skills in their native language before English was introduced in a major way. Others argued that educational equality of opportunity could best be realized by teaching English as early as possible and assimilating language minority children into mainstream culture.

In **1978**, the United States Congress re-authorized Transitional Bilingual Education, allowing the native language to be used only to the extent necessary for a child to achieve competence in the English language. **Title VII funds** could not be used for Maintenance Bilingual Education programs. The **1984 and 1988 amendments** allowed increasing percentages of the funds available to be allocated to programs where a students' first language was not used.

The **Reagan administration** was particularly hostile to bilingual education. In the New York Times on the 3rd March 1981, President Reagan is quoted as saying that 'It is absolutely wrong and against the American concept to have a bilingual education program that is now openly, admittedly, dedicated to preserving their native language and never getting them adequate in English so they can go out into the job market'. Reagan believed that preservation of the native language meant neglect of English language acquisition. Bilingual education programs were seen as serving to neglect English language competence in students. Reagan dismissed bilingual education in favor of submersion and transitional programs.

In 1985, **William Bennett**, the new Secretary of Education, suggested that there was no evidence that children from language minorities (whom the Bilingual Education Act had sought to help), had benefited from this Act. Some 25% of funds were made available for English monolingual, alternative instructional programs (e.g. Structured English programs; Sheltered English programs). This represented a further political dismissal of education through the minority language and a dismissal of 'strong' forms of bilingual education.

The Lau remedies were withdrawn by the Reagan government and do not have the force of law. The federal government left **local politicians** to create their own policies. Further changes in the rights to United States bilingual education are given in the table below. Legislation and litigation has often led to 'weak' forms of bilingual education (e.g. transitional bilingual education). Also, recent legislation has not tended to increase rights to a bilingual education. In the Reagan and Bush years in the United States Presidency, the accent was more on submersion and transitional bilingual education. The right to early education through a minority language failed to blossom in those years.

Conclusion

This section has suggested that bilingual education in the United States has moved through four overlapping periods: permissive, restrictive, opportunist and dismissive. These broad historical trends contain plenty of exceptions and variations within each period.

Two conclusions. First, there is common perception that educational policy is often static, always conservative and very slow to change. The history of bilingual education in the United States tends to falsify and contradict such beliefs. Such history shows that there is constant change, a constant movement in ideas, ideology and impetus. There is action and reaction, movement and contra-movement, assertion and response. One conclusion is that change will always occur in bilingual education policy and provision. Nothing is static. While there will be periods when bilingual education is criticized, forbidden and rejected, there will be reactions, with the possibility of more positive, accepting periods ahead. There is no certainty in the future history of bilingual education, only uncertainty and change. Yet uncertainty and change provide occasional opportunities for bilingual education to progress.

Second, the conclusion must *not* be that the four overlapping periods (permissive, restrictive, opportunist and dismissive) will always operate in that sequence. The history of bilingual education in Wales follows a different sequence. In Wales, the last 200 years of bilingual education have witnessed a movement through the following five approximate periods: permissive; dismissive; suppressive; opportunist and progressive. From a time when Welsh was banned in the classroom (suppressive period), there is currently a widespread acceptance, and provision of bilingual education in Wales (progressive period). No universal patterns of change can or should be deduced from either the United States or the Welsh experience. Such unpredictability provides a challenge to bilingual educators.

A summary of major events affecting the history of United States bilingual education this century is given in the table below.

Year	United States, Legislation/Litigation affecting Bilingual Education.	Implication
1906	Nationality Act passed	First legislation requiring in-migrants to speak English to become naturalized.
1923	Supreme Court in *Meyer* v. *Nebraska*	Rules that state provision requiring English language instruction is permitted by the Constitution, but proficiency in a foreign language was also constitutional.
1950	Amendments to the Nationality Act	English literacy required for naturalization.
1954	*Brown* v. *Board of Education*	Segregated education based on race made unconstitutional.
1958	National Defense and Education Act	Promotion of foreign language learning.
1965	Elementary and Secondary Education Act (ESEA)	Funds granted to meet the needs of 'educationally deprived children'.
1968	Elementary and Secondary Education Act (ESEA) amendment: The Bilingual Education Act, Title VII	Provided funding to establish bilingual programs for students who did not speak English and who were economically poor.
1974	*Lau* v. *Nichols*	Established that language programs for language minorities not proficient in English were necessary to provide equal educational opportunities.
1974	Reauthorization of Bilingual Education Act Title VII of ESEA	Grants available to include native language instruction in schools to 'effect progress' of students not proficient in English. Bilingual Education was defined as transitional (TBE).
1976	*Keyes* v. *School District no. 1*, Denver, Colorado	Established bilingual education as compatible with desegregation.
1977	National Clearinghouse for Bilingual Education is established	To provide a national information center for bilingual education.
1978	Reauthorization of Bilingual Education Act Title VII of ESEA	Reauthorized funding for bilingual programs (transitional). Poverty criterion for eligibility was removed. The term 'Limited English Proficient' (LEP) introduced.
1983	US English Movement launched	Debates about the dominant place of English in law, society and education became more prominent.

VARIETIES OF BILINGUAL EDUCATION

Introduction

So far in this chapter, the term bilingual education has been used as if its meaning is unambiguous and self-evident. The opposite is the case. Bilingual education is **'a simple label for a complex phenomenon'** (Cazden & Snow, 1990a). At the outset, a distinction needs making between education that uses and promotes two languages and education for language minority children. This is a difference between a classroom where formal instruction is to foster bilingualism and a classroom where bilingual children are present, but bilingualism is not fostered in the curriculum. The umbrella term, bilingual education, refers to both situations leaving the term ambiguous and imprecise. Precision can be attempted by specifying the major types of bilingual education.

One early and detailed classification of bilingual education is by Mackey (1970). This account of 90 different patterns of bilingual schooling considers: the languages of the home; the languages of the curriculum; the languages of the community in which the school is located and the international and regional status of the languages. A different approach to categorizing types of bilingual education is to examine the aims of such education. A frequent distinction in aims is between **transitional** and **maintenance** Bilingual Education (Fishman, 1976; Hornberger, 1991).

Transitional Bilingual Education aims to shift the child from the home, minority language to the dominant, majority language. Social and cultural **assimilation** into the language majority is the underlying aim. **Maintenance** Bilingual Education attempts to foster the minority language in the child, strengthening the child's sense of cultural identity and affirming the rights of an ethnic minority group in a nation. Otheguy & Otto (1980) make the distinction between the different aims of **static maintenance** and **developmental maintenance**. Static maintenance aims to maintain language skills at the level of the child entering a school. Developmental maintenance seeks to develop a student's home language skills to full proficiency and full biliteracy or literacy. This is sometimes referred to as **Enrichment Bilingual Education** for language minority children. (The term 'Enrichment Bilingual Education' is also used for language majority children who are adding a second language in school). Static maintenance attempts to prevent home language loss but not increase skills in that first language. Developmental maintenance has a 'goal of proficiency and literacy in the home language equal to English' (Otheguy & Otto, 1980: 351). Enrichment Bilingual Education aims to go beyond static maintenance to extending the individual and group use of minority languages, leading to **cultural pluralism** (see Chapter 20) and to the social autonomy of an ethnic group.

Ferguson, Houghton & Wells (1977) widen these distinctions and provide ten examples of varying aims of bilingual education:

(1) To assimilate individuals or groups into the mainstream of society; to socialize people for full participation in the community.
(2) To unify a multilingual society; to bring unity to a multi-ethnic, multi-tribal, or multi-national linguistically diverse state.
(3) To enable people to communicate with the outside world.
(4) To provide language skills which are marketable, aiding employment and status.
(5) To preserve ethnic and religious identity.
(6) To reconcile and mediate between different linguistic and political communities.
(7) To spread the use of a colonializing language, socializing an entire population to a colonial existence.
(8) To strengthen elite groups and preserve their position in society.

(9) To give equal status in law to languages of unequal status in daily life.
(10) To deepen understanding of language and culture.

This list shows that bilingual education does not necessarily concern the balanced use of two languages in the classroom. Behind bilingual education are varying and conflicting philosophies of what education is for. Sociocultural, political and economic issues are ever present in the debate over the provision of bilingual education. This will be addressed in Chapter 19.

The typology of education that is adopted in this chapter is presented in the table on the following page. Ten types of language education are portrayed.

The ten different types of program have **multitudinous sub-varieties**, as Mackey's (1970) 90 varieties of bilingual education indicate. One of the intrinsic limitations of typologies is that not all real-life examples will fit easily into the classification. For example, elite 'finishing schools' in Switzerland, and classrooms in Wales where first language Welsh speakers are taught alongside 'immersion' English first language speakers make classification essentially simplistic, although necessary for discussion and understanding. Thus typologies have value for conceptual clarity but they have **limitations**: (1) models suggest static systems whereas bilingual schools and classrooms constantly develop and evolve (as the short history of bilingual education in the US revealed); (2): there are wide and many variations within a model; (3) models address 'inputs' and 'outputs' of the education system, but rarely address the process (see Chapter 18); (4) models do not explain the success or failure or the relative effectiveness of bilingual education.

Each of ten broad types of program will now be briefly considered.

Submersion Education

A water metaphor is present in the idea of submersion education. The analogy is of a swimming pool. Rather than a quick dip into a second language in mainstream education, **submersion** contains the idea of a student thrown into the deep end and expected to learn to swim as quickly as possible without the help of floats or special swimming lessons. The language of the pool will be the majority language (e.g. English in the US) and not the home language of the child (e.g. Spanish). The language minority student will be taught all day in the majority language alongside fluent speakers of the majority language. Both teachers and students will be expected to use only the majority language in the classroom, not the home language. Students may either sink, struggle or swim.

Submersion Education is the label to describe education for language minority children who are placed in mainstream education. In the US, such a submersion experience is also found in 'Structured Immersion' programs. Structured Immersion programs contain only language minority children and no language majority children. As will be apparent later in this chapter, the language experience in a Structured Immersion program is submersion rather than immersion. Structured Immersion programs are thus for minority language speakers conducted in the majority language. The first language is not developed but is replaced by the majority language. **Different** from Submersion Education, the

WEAK FORMS OF EDUCATION FOR BILINGUALISM

Type of Program	Typical Type of Child	Language of the Classroom	Societal and Educational Aim	Aim in Language Outcome
SUBMERSION (Structured Immersion)	Language Minority	Majority Language	Assimilation	Monolingualism
SUBMERSION with Withdrawal Classes	Language Minority	Majority Language with 'Pull-out' L2 Lessons	Assimilation	Monolingualism
SEGREGATIONIST	Language Minority	Minority Language (forced, no choice)	Apartheid	Monolingualism
TRANSITIONAL	Language Minority	Moves from Minority to Majority Language	Assimilation	Relative Monolingualism
MAINSTREAM with Foreign Language Teaching	Language Majority	Majority Language with L2/FL Lessons	Limited Enrichment	Limited Bilingualism
SEPARATIST	Language Minority	Minority Language (out of choice)	Detachment/ Autonomy	Limited Bilingualism

STRONG FORMS OF EDUCATION FOR BILINGUALISM AND BILITERACY

Type of Program	Typical Type of Child	Language of the Classroom	Societal and Educational Aim	Aim in Language Outcome
IMMERSION	Language Majority	Bilingual with Initial Emphasis on L2	Pluralism and Enrichment	Bilingualism & Biliteracy
MAINTENANCE/ HERITAGE LANGUAGE	Language Minority	Bilingual with Emphasis on L1	Maintenance, Pluralism and Enrichment	Bilingualism & Biliteracy
TWO-WAY/DUAL LANGUAGE	Mixed Language Minority & Majority	Minority and Majority	Maintenance, Pluralism and Enrichment	Bilingualism & Biliteracy
BILINGUAL EDUCATION IN MAJORITY LANGUAGES	Language Majority	Two Majority Languages	Maintenance, Pluralism and Enrichment	Bilingualism & Biliteracy

Notes: (1) L2 = Second Language; L1 = First Language; FL = Foreign Language.
(2) Formulation of this table owes much to discussions with Professor Ofelia García.

Structured Immersion teacher will use a simplified form of the majority language, and may initially accept contributions from children in their home language (Hornberger, 1991). In the US, there are also 'Sheltered English' programs, an alternative to ESL (English as a Second Language) programs. However, since such programs can be 'pull-out' with special content and curriculum materials, they are discussed in the next section.

There are various criticisms of a submersion form of education, including its variants. In terms of the language garden analogy (see Chapter 3), one blossoming flower is displaced. The garden is re-seeded after the initial language plants have shown growth. One tender but healthy plant is simply replaced by the majority flower of the garden. The basic aim of submersion education is thus **assimilation** of language minority speakers, particularly where there has been in-migration (e.g. US, England). Also, where indigenous language minorities are perceived as working against the common good, submersion education becomes a tool of integration. The school becomes a melting pot to help create common social, political and economic ideals. As Theodore Roosevelt urged in 1917:

> 'We must have but one flag. We must have but one language. That must be the language of the Declaration of Independence, of Washington's Farewell Address, of Lincoln's Gettysburg Speech and Second Inaugural. We cannot tolerate any attempt to oppose or supplant the language and culture that has come down to us from the builders of the republic with the language and culture of any European country. The greatness of this nation depends on the swift assimilation of the aliens she welcomes to her shores. Any force which attempts to retard that assimilative process is a force hostile to the highest interests of our country' (quoted in Wagner, 1980: 32).

Language diversity has often been discouraged in the US so, it was argued, that harmony would hasten a healthy and homogeneous nation. A common language would provide, it was thought, common attitudes, aims and values. A common language and culture would cement society. A God-blest-English speaking America was preferable to the threat of Babel.

Considerable variations of language skill in a classroom may often create **problems** in teaching and class management for the teacher. With students who range from fluent majority language speakers to those who can understand little classroom talk, the burden on the teacher may be great. In such formal 'context-reduced' classrooms, there is no reason to assume that children will quickly and effortlessly acquire the majority language skills necessary to cope in the curriculum. Alongside problems of language, there are likely to be problems of social and emotional adjustment for language minority children which tend to have connections with later drop-out rates from high school. The child, the parents, the home language and culture appear to be disparaged. McKay (1988: 341) quotes from a student in a Submersion classroom:

> 'School was a nightmare. I dreaded going to school and facing my classmates and teacher. Every activity the class engaged in meant another exhibition of my

incompetence. Each activity was another incidence for my peers to laugh and ridicule me with and for my teacher to stare hopelessly disappointed at me. My self-image was a serious inferiority complex. I became frustrated at not being able to do anything right. I felt like giving up the entire mess.'

Skutnabb-Kangas (1981) indicates the **stresses** of learning through an undeveloped language as in submersion education. Listening to a new language demands high concentration, it is tiring, with a constant pressure to think about the form of the language and less time to think about curriculum content. A child has to take in information from different curriculum areas and learn a language at the same time. Stress, lack of self confidence, 'opting-out', disaffection and alienation may occur.

Submersion with Pull-Out Classes

Submersion Education may occur with or without the addition of **withdrawal classes** or **'pull-out' classes** to teach the majority language. Language minority children in mainstream schools may be withdrawn for 'compensatory' lessons in the majority language (e.g. English as a second language (**ESL**) pull-out programs in the US and England). Such **Withdrawal Classes** are provided as a way of keeping language minority children in mainstream schooling. However, 'withdrawn' children may fall behind on curriculum content delivered to others not in withdrawal classes. There may also be a stigma for absence. A withdrawal child may be seen by peers as 'remedial', 'disabled' or 'limited in English'. Other Submersion schools will have no withdrawal classes to help students develop skills in the school language. Withdrawal classes are administratively simple and require little or no additional expense. For many administrators and budget managers, Submersion creates ease of supervision and financial management.

A variation under this heading is **Sheltered English or Sheltered Content Teaching**, where minority language students are taught the curriculum with a simplified vocabulary, but also, purpose-made materials and methods (such as cooperative learning) are used — but in English only (Faltis, 1993b). In Sheltered English or Sheltered Content Teaching, content and curriculum materials are developed and pitched to match the English proficiency of the student (Faltis, 1993b). Sheltered English or Sheltered Content English is distinct from ESL (English as a Second Language), as in ESL, English is taught as a language, with a focus on learning that language.

Sheltered Content Teaching may involve temporary segregation from first language English speakers. Such segregation may produce: (1) greater opportunity for participation among students (they may be less inhibited due to no competition or comparisons with first language speakers of English); (2) greater sensitivity among teachers to the linguistic, cultural and educational needs of a homogeneous group of students; and (3) a collective identity among students in a similar situation (Faltis, 1993b). However, such language segregation removes first language role models; may produce a social isolation with overtones of stigmatization and reinforce negative stereotypes; encouraging the labeling of segregated students as linguistically and educationally inferior, deprived and in need of remedial attention; and may generate inequality in treatment (e.g. in curriculum materials and training of teachers).

Segregationist Education

A form of 'minority language only' education is segregationist language education (Skutnabb-Kangas, 1981). Monolingual education through the medium of the minority language can be for apartheid (e.g. educating the Bantus only in their native language). The ruling elite prescribes education solely in the minority language to maintain subservience and segregation. Such a language minority 'do not learn enough of the power language to be able to influence the society or, especially, to acquire a common language with the other subordinated groups, a shared medium of communication and analysis' (Skutnabb-Kangas, 1981: 128). Segregationist education **forces** a monolingual language policy on the relatively powerless.

Transitional Bilingual Education

Transitional bilingual education is the most common type of bilingual education in the United States and the form most supported by Title VII funds. The aim of transitional bilingual education is **assimilationist**. It differs from submersion education by language minority students temporarily being allowed to use their home language, and often being taught through their home language, until they are thought to be proficient enough in the majority language to cope in mainstream education. Thus, transitional education is a brief, temporary swim in one pool until the child is perceived as capable of using the four language strokes in the mainstream pool. The aim is to increase use of the majority language in the classroom while proportionately decreasing the use of the home language in the classroom.

The educational rationale is based on a question of perceived priorities: children need to function in the majority language in society. The argument used is that if competency in the majority language is not quickly established, such children may fall behind their majority language peers. Thus, arguments about equality of opportunity and maximizing student performance are used to justify such transitional programs. The extent to which such justifications are valid is considered later.

Transitional Bilingual Education (TBE) can be split into two major types: **early exit** and **late exit** (Ramirez & Merino, 1990). Early exit TBE refers to two years maximum help using the mother tongue. Late exit TBE often allows around 40% of classroom teaching in the mother tongue until the 6th grade.

While majority language monolingualism is the aim of transitional bilingual education, teachers or their assistants need to be bilingual. The temporary home language swim requires, for example, a Spanish speaking teacher who may be more sensitive and successful in teaching English to Spanish speaking children than English-only teachers. The former can switch from one language to another and be more sympathetic to the language of the children. For the government and school administrator, such bilingual teachers may become valuable allies or Trojan horses.

A **bilingual teacher** can become the unwitting promoter of transition from one language to another, and assimilation into the majority culture. Such teachers can promote the transition from home to school language from within their own cultural group. An

Anglo teacher is thus not imposed on the Hispanic language minority; the conversion job is achieved by a bilingual teacher. Similarly, in US schools with large transitional programs, there is sometimes a **hidden message** in the staffing. The people with power and prestige, such as principals and assistant principals, are often English monolinguals (García, 1993). The people with the least power and status are cooks, lunch monitors, cleaners and janitors, who, for example, speak a minority language such as Spanish. The language of formal announcements is English; the language used by those who serve may be Spanish. The language to learn is the language of power and prestige. The language to forget is the language of servitude, stigma and shame. This message is loudly proclaimed without words.

However, such Hispanic teachers may alternatively recognize the needs and wishes of their own communities. Such communities may desire their young to speak English early in schooling, but differ from administrators in wanting to preserve Spanish (García, 1991a). Hispanic teachers may continue to teach English in transitional bilingual education, but also try to preserve Spanish in the children, becoming allies of the community and not just allies of politicians and bureaucrats.

Mainstream Education (with Foreign Language Teaching)

In the US, Australasia, Canada and much of Europe, most language majority schoolchildren take their education through their home language. For example, a child whose parents are English speaking monolinguals attends school where English is the teaching medium (although some second (foreign) language teaching may occur). In Canada, this would be called a core program. In Wales and elsewhere, it is sometimes called a 'drip-feed' language program. The term 'drip-feed' highlights the kind of language element in mainstream schooling. Second (foreign) language lessons of half an hour per day may constitute the sole 'other' language diet. Drip-feeding French, German, Japanese, Russian, Spanish makes the language a subject in the curriculum similar to History, Science, Geography and Maths. This is distinct from teaching through the medium of a second language where curriculum content is the main focus rather than language learning (sometimes called embedding).

The problem in some countries (e.g. US, England) is that only a few second language flowers blossom. Too often, the tender second language shoot quickly withers and fades. Where children receive a half an hour second language lesson per day for between five and twelve years, few students become functionally fluent in the second language. LeBlanc (1992) poses the critical question. 'We all know how much our country [Canada] invests in second-language training. We are talking in terms of millions and millions of dollars... All these students are taking second-language courses and, once they have finished, should normally be able to function in the second language. But what happens in reality?' (p. 35).

The Canadians found that after 12 years of French drip-feed language teaching, many English-background students were not fluent enough to communicate in French with French Canadians. Similarly in Britain, five years of French or German or Spanish in secondary school (age 11 to 16) results in only a few growing in a second language. For the great majority, the second language quickly shrivels and dies. **Mainstream** education rarely produces fully bilingual children. A very limited form of fluency in a foreign language tends to be the typical outcome for the mass of the language majority.

This is not the only outcome of second and foreign language teaching. The learning of English in Scandinavia does not fit this pattern, with many learners becoming fluent in English. When motivation is high, when economic circumstances encourage the acquisition of a trading language, then foreign language teaching may be more fruitful.

Separatist Education

A more narrow view of language minority education would be to choose to foster monolingualism in the minority language. The aims are minority language monolingualism and monoculturalism in a context where such choice is self-determined. Schermerhorn (1970) called this a **secessionist** movement where a language minority aims to detach itself from the language majority to pursue an independent existence. As a way of trying to protect a minority language from being over-run by the language majority, or for political, religious or cultural reasons, separatist minority language education may be promoted. This type of education may be organized by the language community for its own survival and for self-protection.

It is unlikely that a school would formally state its aims in a linguistic separatist fashion. Rather, in the implicit functioning of isolationist religious schools and the political rhetoric of extreme language activists, the 'separatist' idea of such schools exists. Small in number, the importance of this category is that it highlights that language minority education is capable of moving from the goal of pluralism to separatism.

Immersion Bilingual Education

Submersion, Withdrawal Classes and Transitional approaches are often given the title of bilingual education. This is because such schemes contain bilingual children. This counts as a '**weak**' use of the term bilingual education because bilingualism is not fostered in school. Such education does not by aim, content or structure have bilingualism as a defined outcome. The next form, immersion education, has bilingualism as an intended outcome, and therefore represents a 'strong' use of the term bilingual education.

Immersion bilingual education derives from Canadian educational experiments. The immersion movement started in St Lambert, Montreal, in 1965 (Lambert & Tucker, 1972; Rebuffot, 1993). Some disgruntled English speaking, middle-class parents persuaded school district administrators to set up an experimental kindergarten class of 26 children. The aims were for students (1) to become competent to speak, read and write in French; (2) to reach normal achievement levels throughout the curriculum including the English language; (3) to appreciate the traditions and culture of French speaking Canadians as well as English speaking Canadians. In short, the aims were for children to become bilingual and bicultural without loss of achievement.

Types of Immersion Bilingual Education

Immersion education is an umbrella term. Within the concept of immersion experience are various Canadian programs differing in terms of the following:

- age at which a child commences the experience. This may be at the kindergarten or infant stage (**early** immersion); at nine to ten years old (delayed or **middle** immersion), or at secondary level (**late** immersion);
- amount of **time** spent in immersion. **Total** immersion usually commences with 100% immersion (e.g. per week) in the second language, after two or three years reducing to 80% per week for the next three or four years, finishing junior schooling with approximately 50% immersion in French per week. **Partial** immersion provides close to 50% immersion in the second language throughout infant and junior schooling.

Early Total Immersion is the most popular entry level program, followed by late and then middle immersion (Canadian Education Association, 1992). The histograms on the following pages illustrate several possibilities, with many other variations around these.

The **St Lambert experiment** suggested that the aims were met. Attitudes and achievement were not hindered by the immersion experience. Tucker & d'Anglejan (1972: 19), summarized the outcomes as follows:

> 'the experimental students appear to be able to read, write, speak, understand, and use English as well as youngsters instructed in English in the conventional manner. In addition and at no cost they can also read, write, speak and understand French in a way that English students who follow a traditional program of French as a second language never do.'

Since 1965, immersion bilingual education has spread rapidly in Canada (Rebuffot, 1993). There are currently around 300,000 English speaking Canadian children in some 2000 French immersion schools. This represents some 6% of the total school population in Canada. What are the essential features of this speedy educational growth? **First,** immersion in Canada aims at bilingualism in two prestigious, majority languages (French and English). This relates to an additive bilingual situation. Such a situation is different from the wrongly termed 'immersion' or 'structured immersion' of children from language minority backgrounds in the majority language (e.g. Spanish speakers in the US). Use of the term 'immersion' in such a subtractive, assimilationist situation is best avoided. Submersion is a more appropriate term.

Second, immersion bilingual education in Canada has been optional not compulsory. Parents choose to send their children to such schools. The convictions of parents plus the commitment of the teachers may aid the motivation of students. Immersion appears to thrive on conviction not on conformity. **Third,** children in early immersion are often allowed to use their home language for up to one and a half years for classroom communication. There is no compulsion to speak French in the playground or dining hall. The child's home language is appreciated and not belittled. **Fourth,** the teachers are

Early Total Immersion Bilingual Education

Early Partial Immersion Bilingual Education

Delayed Immersion Bilingual Education

Percentage

Second Language
French Lessons

Year/Grade in School

K = Kindergarten

◩ % of English medium lessons   ■ % of French medium lessons

Late Immersion Bilingual Education

Percentage

Also Second Language
Lessons in French

Year/Grade in School

K = Kindergarten

◩ % of English medium lessons   ■ % of French medium lessons competent bilinguals. However, they initially appear to the children as able to speak French but only understand (and not speak) English.

Classroom language communication aims to be meaningful, authentic and relevant to the child's needs; not contrived, tightly controlled or repetitive. The content of the curriculum becomes the focus for the language. Perpetual insistence on correct communication is avoided. Learning second language French in early immersion becomes incidental and unconscious, similar to the way a first language is acquired. Emphasis is placed on understanding French before speaking French. Later on, formal instruction may occur (see Chapter 17).

Fifth, the students start immersion education with a similar lack of experience of the second language. Most are monolingual. Students commencing schooling with relatively homogeneous language skills not only simplifies the teacher's task, it also means that students' self esteem and classroom motivation is not at risk due to some students being linguistically more expert. **Sixth**, students in immersion education experience the same curriculum as mainstream 'core' students.

With over a 1000 research studies, Canadian immersion bilingual education has been an educational experiment of unusual success and growth. It has influenced bilingual education in Europe and beyond. For example, with variations to suit regional and national contexts, the **Catalans and Basques** (Artigal, 1991, 1993, 1995; Bel, 1993) **Finnish** (Laurén, 1994; Manzer, 1993), **Japanese** (Oka, 1994), **Australians** (Berthold, 1992, 1995; Caldwell & Berthold, 1995), the Gaelic speakers in **Scotland** (MacNeil, 1994), **Swiss** (Stotz & Andres, 1990) and the **Welsh and Irish** (Baker, 1988, 1993) have emulated the experiment with similar success. In Catalonia, research indicates that Spanish speaking children who follow an immersion program not only become fluent in Catalan, but also their Spanish does not suffer. Throughout the curriculum, such Catalan immersion children 'perform as well and sometimes better than their Hispanophone peers who do not' [follow an immersion program] (Artigal, 1993: 40–41). Similarly, the EIFE studies in the Basque Country show that their Model B immersion program (50% Basque and 50% Spanish) has successful outcomes in bilingual proficiency (Sierra & Olaziregi, 1989).

Developmental Maintenance and Heritage Language Bilingual Education

Alongside immersion education, there is another form of bilingual education that merits a '**strong**' use of the term. This occurs where language minority children use their native, ethnic, home or heritage language in the school as a medium of instruction and the goal is full bilingualism. Examples include education through, or more often partly through, the medium of Navajo and Spanish in the US, Catalan in Spain, Ukrainian in Canada, Gaelic in Scotland, Finnish in Sweden and Welsh in Wales. The child's native language is protected and developed alongside development in the majority language. In New Zealand, the Maori language has increasingly been promoted in schools (Spolsky, 1989a) with some indications of positive outcomes in achievement (Jacques & Hamlin, 1992). A similar promotion of Aboriginal languages is occurring in heritage language education in Australia (Caldwell & Berthold, 1995). In Ireland, Irish medium education is often available for children from Irish language backgrounds. While the overall language garden will contain English and Irish and possibly other European languages, the indigenous language flower of Ireland is protected in school lest it wither and die amongst the pervading growth of English, and lately of other European majority languages.

In the US, there are schools that may be termed '**ethnic community mother tongue schools**' (Fishman, 1989). Numbering over 5000 and located in every State of the US, the list includes schools using the mother tongue of the following varied communities: Arabs, Africans, Asians, French, German, Greek, Haitian, Jewish, Russian, Polish, Japanese, Latin American, Armenian, Dutch, Bulgarian, Irish, Rumanian, Serbian and Turkish. Maintained by communities who have lost or are losing their 'native' language, the schools mostly teach that native language and use it as a medium of instruction. Other schools are supported by foreign governments and religious organizations. 'These schools must be recognized as filling an important identity-forming and identity-providing function for millions of Americans' (Fishman, 1989: 454).

Since they are fee paying, private schools, the students tend to come from middle class or the relatively more affluent working class backgrounds and achieve biliteracy and biculturalism with some success (García, 1988). For example, there are around 130 Hebrew day schools in New York alone, 'successful in teaching children to read and write English, Hebrew, and many times Yiddish' (García, 1988: 22).

The 'public school' US example is called **Maintenance Bilingual Education** or **Developmental Maintenance Bilingual Education**. These are relatively few in number with Navajo education being one major example (Holm & Holm, 1990). In Canada, the term used to describe such education is **Heritage Language Education**. However, in Canada, there is a distinction between Heritage Language lessons and Heritage Language Bilingual Education. (1) Heritage Language Programs give around two and a half hours per week language teaching, currently in more than 60 languages to about 100,000 students. These lessons often occur during dinner-hours, after school and at weekends. (2) In provinces such as Manitoba, British Columbia, Saskatchewan and Alberta, there are Heritage Language Bilingual Education Programs (e.g. see Benyon & Toohey (1991) on programs in British Columbia). The heritage language is the **medium of instruction** for about 50% of the day (e.g. Ukrainian, Italian, German, Hebrew, Yiddish, Mandarin Chinese, Arabic and Polish; see Cummins, 1992).

In essence, heritage or maintenance language education refers to the education of **language minority** children through their minority and majority language. In most cases, the majority language will be present in the curriculum, ranging from second language lessons to a varying proportion of the curriculum being taught the majority language.

The term 'heritage language' may also be called 'native language', 'ethnic language', 'minority language', 'ancestral language', aboriginal language, or, in French, 'langues d'origine'. The **danger** of the term 'heritage' is that it points to the past and not the future, to traditions rather than the contemporary. Partly for this reason, the British term tends to be 'community language' or 'where English is an additional language'. The heritage language may or may not be an indigenous language. Both Navajo and Spanish can be perceived as heritage languages in the US depending on an *individual's* perception of what constitutes their heritage language.

Developmental Maintenance programs in the US (also Heritage language programs in Canada and other countries) vary in structure and content. Some of the likely features are as follows:

(1) Most, but not necessarily all of the children will come from language minority **homes**. At the same time, the minority language may be the majority language of a local community. In certain areas of the US, Spanish speakers are in a majority in their neighborhood or community. In Gwynedd, North Wales, where the minority language (Welsh) is often the majority language of the community, heritage language programs are prevalent. The children will be joined in most programs by a number of majority language children (e.g. English monolinguals in Wales taking their education through Welsh).

(2) **Parents** will often have the choice of sending their children to mainstream schools or to heritage language education. Ukrainian, Jewish and Mohawkian heritage language programs in Canada, for example, gave parents freedom of choice in selecting schools.

(3) The language minority student's home language will often be used for approximately half or more of **curriculum time**. The Ukrainian programs in Alberta and Manitoba allotted half the time to Ukrainian, half to English. Mathematics and science, for example, were taught in English; music, art and social studies in Ukrainian. There is a tendency to teach technological, scientific studies through the majority language.

(4) Where a minority language is used for a majority of classroom time (e.g. 80% to almost 100% in Wales), the justification is usually that children easily transfer ideas, concepts, skills and knowledge into the majority language. Having taught a child multiplication in Spanish, this mathematical concept does not have to be re-taught in English. Classroom teaching **transfers** relatively easily between languages when such languages are sufficiently developed to cope with concepts, content and curriculum materials.

(5) The **justification** given for heritage language education is also that a minority language is easily lost, a majority language is easily gained. Children tend to be surrounded by the majority language. Television and train advertisements, shops and signs, videos and visits often provide or induce bilingual proficiency in an incidental way by accenting a majority language. Thus bilingualism is achieved by a concentration on the minority language at school.

(6) Heritage language **schools** are mostly elementary schools. This need not be the case. In Wales, for example, such schools are available to the end of secondary education and the heritage language can be used as a medium of study at College and University.

Two Way/Dual Language Bilingual Education

Two Way or Dual Language Bilingual Education occurs when approximately equal numbers of language minority and language majority students are in the same classroom. Or sometimes in the US, the program will contain approximately 50% of students who are English language learners (e.g. Haitian Creole speakers); the remaining students are language minority students relatively fluent in English.

Mostly to be found in the US at elementary school level, two languages are used in the classroom. For example, around half the children may be from Spanish speaking homes; the other half from English monolingual homes and they work together in the classroom in harmony. Since both languages are used for instruction and learning, the aim is to produce relatively balanced bilinguals (Lindholm, 1991; Morison, 1990). Biliteracy is as much an aim as full bilingualism, with literacy being acquired in both languages either simultaneously or with an initial emphasis on native language literacy (see Chapters 15 and 16).

There are a variety of **terms** used to describe such schools: Two Way Schools, Two Way Immersion, Two Way Bilingual Education, Developmental Bilingual Education, Dual Language Education, Bilingual Immersion, Double Immersion and Interlocking Education.

Christian (1994) and Lindholm (1987) note the **growth** of such programs since 1983 with the oldest dating back to 1963 in Dade County, Florida, and developed by a US Cuban community (see García & Otheguy, 1985, 1988). For Lindholm (1987), Two Way programs have four characteristics:

(1) A non-English language (i.e. the minority language) is used for at least 50% of instruction.
(2) In each period of instruction, only one language is used.
(3) Both English and non-English speakers are present in preferably balanced numbers.
(4) The English and non-English speakers are integrated in all lessons.

Two Way bilingual classrooms contain a mixture of language majority and language minority **students**. For example, half the children may come from Spanish speaking homes; the other half from English language backgrounds. A **language balance** close to 50%–50% is attempted. If one language becomes dominant (e.g. due to much larger numbers of one language group), the aim of bilingualism and biliteracy may be at risk. The reality of such schools is often different, with an imbalance towards larger numbers of language minority students being more common.

An **imbalance** in the two languages among students may result in one language being used to the exclusion of the other (e.g. Spanish speaking children having to switch to English to work cooperatively). Alternatively, one language group may become sidelined (e.g. Spanish speakers become excluded from English speaking groups). Segregation rather than integration may occur. In the creation of a dual language school or classroom, careful student selection decisions have to be made to ensure a **language balance**.

When an **imbalance** does exist, it may be preferable to have slightly more language minority children. Where there is a preponderance of language majority children, the tendency is for language minority children to switch to the higher status, majority language. In most (but not all) language contexts, the majority language is well represented outside school (e.g. in the media and for employment). Therefore, the balance towards the majority language outside school can be complemented by a slight balance towards the minority language in school (among student in-take and in curriculum delivery). However, if the school contains a particularly high number of language minority children, the prestige of the school will sometimes suffer (both among language majority and language minority parents).

In Two Way bilingual Magnet schools in the US, **students** may be drawn from a wide catchment area. For example, if a Magnet school focuses on Environmental Arts and Sciences, parents throughout a district may be eager to gain a place for their children. Ensuring a language balance in each classroom then becomes a key **selection** feature.

There are situations where **attracting language majority students** to a Two Way bilingual school is difficult. Where the monolingual mainstream school is as (or more) attractive to prospective parents, recruitment to Two Way bilingual schools may be a challenge. For parents, allocation of their children to such Dual Language Bilingual Programs will be voluntary and not enforced. Hence, the good **reputation**, perceived effectiveness and curriculum success of such Two Way bilingual schools becomes crucial to their continuation. Evidence from the US suggests that language minority parents may be supportive of such a program (e.g. Hornberger, 1991). Majority language parents may need more persuading. Community backing and involvement in the school may also be important in long-term success.

The **development** of Two Way bilingual schools often starts with the creation of a dual language kindergarten class rather than an implementation throughout a school. As the kindergarten students move through the grades, a new dual language class is created each year. Apart from Elementary Two Way bilingual schools, there is also Dual Language secondary education in the US and, with different names, in many other countries of the world (e.g. Wales, Spain, India). A Two Way bilingual school may be a whole school in itself. Also, there may be dual language classrooms within a 'mainstream' school. For example, there may be one dual language classroom in each grade.

Dolson & Meyer (1992) list seven major **goals** in Two Way bilingual programs: (1) students should develop high levels of proficiency in their first language; (2) students should achieve high levels of proficiency in their second language (e.g. English); (3) academic performance should eventually be at or above grade level in both languages (e.g. by Grade 6); (4) students should demonstrate positive cross-cultural attitudes and behaviors; (5) students should show evidence of high levels of personal and social competence; (6) schools should have programs of academic excellence for language majority and language minority students, and (7) communities and society at large should benefit from having citizens who are bilingual and biliterate, who are more positive towards people of different cultural backgrounds, and, who can meet national needs for language competence and a more peaceful coexistence with peoples of other nations.

The **aim** of a Two Way bilingual schools is thus not just to produce bilingual and biliterate children. To gain status and to flourish, such a school needs to show success throughout the curriculum. On standardized tests, on attainment compared with other schools in the locality, and in specialisms (e.g. music, sport, science), a Two Way bilingual school will strive to show relative success. A narrow focus on proficiency in two languages will be insufficient in aim.

The **mission** of Two Way bilingual schools may be couched in terms such as 'equality of educational opportunity for children from different language backgrounds', 'child-centered education building on the child's existing language competence', 'a positive self-image for each child', 'a community dedicated to the integration of all its children', 'enrichment not compensatory education', 'a family-like experience to produce multicultural children', and 'supporting Bilingual Proficiency not Limited English Proficiency'.

One of the special aims of Two Way bilingual schools (e.g. compared with mainstream schools) is to produce **bilingual, biliterate and multicultural children**. Language minority students are expected to become literate in their native language as well as in the majority language. Language majority students are expected to develop language and literacy skills in a second language. At the same time, majority language students must make normal progress in their first language. To achieve these aims, a variety of practices are implemented in Two Way bilingual schools.

(1) The two **languages** of the school (e.g. Spanish and English, Chinese and English, Haitian Creole and English) have **equal status**. Both languages will be used as a medium of instruction. Math, Science and Social Studies, for example, may be taught in both languages. However, care has to be taken not to be repetitive, not to teach the same content in both languages. Strategies of separating, allocating and integrating two languages in the classroom are considered in Chapter 12.

(2) The **school ethos** will be bilingual. Such an ethos is created by classroom and corridor displays, notice boards, curriculum resources, cultural events, dinner-time and extra curricula activity using both languages in a relatively balanced way. Announcements across the school address system will be bilingual. Letters to parents will also be in two languages. While playground conversations and student to student talk in the classroom is difficult to influence or manipulate, the school environment aims to be transparently bilingual.

(3) In some Two Way bilingual schools, the two **languages** are **taught** as languages (sometimes called Language Arts instruction). Here, aspects of spelling, grammar, metaphors and communicative skills may be directly taught. In other Two Way bilingual schools, use of both languages as media of instruction is regarded as sufficient to ensure bilingual development. In such schools, children are expected to **acquire proficiency** in language informally throughout the curriculum and through interaction with children who are effective first language role models. In both cases, reading and writing in both languages are likely to receive direct attention in the curriculum. Biliteracy is as much an aim as full bilingualism. Literacy will be acquired in both languages either simultaneously or with an initial emphasis on native language literacy.

(4) **Staff** in the dual language classrooms are often bilingual. Such **teachers** use both languages on different occasions with their students. Where this is difficult (e.g. due to teacher supply or selection), teachers may be paired and work together closely as

a team. A teacher's aide, paraprofessionals, secretaries, custodial staff, parents offering or invited to help the teacher may also be bilingual. Language minority **parents** can be valuable 'teacher auxiliaries' in the classroom. For example, when a wide variety of Spanish cultures from many regions is brought to the classroom, parents and grandparents may describe and provide the most authentic stories, dances, recipes, folklore and festivals. This underlines the importance of the cultural heritage of language minorities being shared in the classroom to create an additive bilingual and multicultural environment.

(5) The **length of the Two Way bilingual program** needs to be longer rather than shorter. Such a program for two or three grades is insufficient. A minimum of four years extending through the grades as far as possible is more defensible. Length of experience of a Two Way bilingual program is important to ensure a fuller and deeper development of language skills, and biliteracy in particular. Where a US Two Way bilingual program exists across more years, there is a tendency for the curriculum to be increasingly taught in the majority language — English. In some schools, the curriculum is initially taught for around 90% of time through the minority language. In later grades in the elementary school, this percentage is decreased until it reaches approximately 50%. In these programs, majority language students have an immersion experience in a second language (e.g. Spanish), while minority language students initially receive most of their education in their home language

A central idea in Two Way bilingual schools is **language separation and compartmentalization**. In each period of instruction, only one language is used. **Language boundaries** are established in terms of time, curriculum content and teaching. These will each be briefly considered, and then extended in Chapter 12.

First, a decision is made about **when** to teach through each language. One frequent preference is for each language to be used on **alternate days**. On the door of the classroom may be a message about which language is to be used that day. For example, Spanish is used one day, English the next, in a strict sequence. Alternately, **different lessons** may use **different languages** with a regular change over to ensure both languages are used in all curricula areas. For example, Spanish may be used to teach Mathematics on Monday and Wednesday and Friday; English to teach Mathematics on Tuesday and Thursday. During the next week, the languages are reversed, with Mathematics taught in Spanish on Tuesday and Thursday. There are other possibilities. The division of time may be in half days, alternate weeks, alternate half semesters. The essential element is the distribution of time to achieve bilingual and biliterate students.

The amount of **time** spent learning through each language varies from school to school. Often, a 50%–50% balance in use of languages is attempted in early and later grades. In other classrooms, the minority language will be given more time (60%, 75%, 80% and 90% is not uncommon), especially in the first two or three years. In the middle and secondary years of schooling, there is sometimes a preference for a 50%–50% balance, or more accent on the majority language (e.g. 70% through English; 30% through Spanish).

Whatever the division of time, instruction in a Two Way bilingual school will keep **boundaries** between the languages. Switching languages within a lesson is not considered helpful. If language mixing by the teacher occurs, students may wait until there is delivery in their stronger language, and become uninvolved at other times. When there is clear separation, the Spanish speakers, for example, may help the English-speakers on Spanish days, and the English speakers help the Spanish speakers on English days. Interdependence may stimulate cooperation and friendship, as well as learning and achievement. The potential problems of segregation and racial hostility may thus be considerably reduced.

However, the two languages will sometimes be **switched** or mixed in the classroom (e.g. in private conversations, in further explanations by a teacher, and internal use of the dominant language). Use of languages by children, especially when young, is not usually consciously controlled. Switching language can be as natural as smiling and using a particular accent.

Second, **bilingual teachers** ensure they do not switch languages. Children hear them using one language (during a lesson period or during a whole day) and are expected to respond in that same language. When, as in many forms of 'strong' bilingual education, there is a shortage of bilingual teachers, a pairing of teachers may ensure language separation. A teacher using Spanish only will work in close association with a teacher who only uses English with the same class. Such teamwork requires teachers to be committed to bilingualism and multiculturalism as important educational aims.

Third, language boundaries may be established in the **curriculum**. This may occur according to which 'language day' it is. Alternatively, in some schools, different parts of the curriculum are taught in different languages. For example, Social Studies and Environmental Studies may be taught in Spanish, Science and Math in English. Such a policy establishes separate occasions where each language is to be used, and keeps the two languages apart. However, one danger is that the majority language becomes aligned with modern technology and science, while the minority language becomes associated with tradition and culture. This may affect the status of the language in the eyes of the child, parents and society. The relationship of languages to employment prospects, economic advantage and power thus need to be considered.

Such Two Way bilingual schools differ from **Transitional Bilingual Education** and **Submersion/Mainstream/ESL** approaches. US Transitional Bilingual education essentially aims to move children into English-only instruction within two or more years. In contrast, Two Way bilingual schools aim to enable the child to achieve increasing proficiency in two languages (e.g. Spanish and English in the US). Two Way bilingual schools differ from Canadian **Immersion Bilingual Education** in the language backgrounds of the students. Immersion schools usually contain only language majority children learning much or part of the curriculum through a second language (e.g. English speaking children learning through the medium of French in Canadian schools). Two Way bilingual schools aim to contain a balanced mixture of children from two (or more) different language backgrounds (e.g. from Spanish speaking and English speaking homes in the US). Two Way bilingual schools differ from **Developmental Maintenance**

(Heritage Language) schools in aiming for more of a balance of majority and minority language children, with slightly more emphasis on bilingual and multicultural outcomes. Developmental Maintenance education is comparatively more concerned with preservation of the ethnic language, ethnic culture, and in many cases, has a preponderance of language minority children. The type of school possible in a neighborhood is often determined by the sociolinguistic character of the school population (e.g. the size of one or more language minority groups, the presence of recent or more established in-migrants, the numbers of majority language speakers).

Two Way bilingual schools in the US appear to date from 1963 in Dade County, Florida, and were developed by the US Cuban community in that area (see Lindholm 1987; García & Otheguy, 1985, 1988). In September 1963, the **Coral Way Elementary School** started a bilingual program that embraced both Spanish and English speaking students. During the 1960s, another 14 such bilingual schools were set up in Dade County. This is related to the fact that many Cubans expected to return to Cuba, believing the Castro regime wouldn't survive. Local people supported the maintenance of Spanish among the soon-to-leave Cubans. Local English speaking children from middle class families were enrolled in the school. This reflected a wish among parents for foreign language instruction following Russia's initial triumph over the US in the space race. (In 1958, the Russian Sputnik was launched.)

Since that era, there has been a steady **rise** in the number of Two Way bilingual schools in the US, particularly since 1989 — as the graph illustrates using data in Donna Christian (1994). Approximately a third of such schools are located in California and another third in New York. Of around 170 schools in the United States, sixteen other states have Two Way bilingual schools (e.g. Arizona, Massachusetts, Texas and Virginia). The languages of instruction in Two Way Bilingual Programs in the US are predominantly Spanish/English (over 90% of such schools) but with the following combinations also represented: Cantonese/English; Portuguese/English; Haitian Creole/English; Korean/English;

The Rise of Dual Language Schools

Russian/English; Japanese/English and French/English. Around 85% of all these schools operate from kindergarten to the 6th Grade.

Evaluations of the **effectiveness** of Dual Language schools indicate relative success (Cazabon, Lambert & Hall, 1993; Lambert & Cazabon, 1994; Lindholm, 1991; Lindholm & Aclan, 1991; Lindholm, 1994; Lindholm, 1995; Thomas, Collier & Abbott, 1993). As Christian (1994, overview page) suggests: 'Emerging results of studies of Two Way bilingual programs point to their effectiveness in educating non-native English speaking students, their promise of expanding our nation's language resources by conserving the native language skills of minority students and developing second language skills in English speaking students, and their hope of improving relationships between majority and minority groups by enhancing cross-cultural understanding and appreciation.'

One **example** of a Two Way bilingual school is the James F. Oyster Bilingual Elementary School in Washington DC which has a two way program that commenced in 1971. The initiative was taken by the local community (by parents and local politicians) to produce a school that crossed language, cultural, ethnic and social class lines. Parents are very active in the running of the school. With students from kindergarten to 6th Grade, there is a ethnic mix of 58% Hispanic, 26% white; 12% Black and 4% Asian (Freeman, 1995). Around two in every five children come from low-income families (e.g. are awarded a free lunch).

The James F. Oyster Bilingual Elementary School program is distinctive because it has two teachers in each classroom: one teacher speaks only Spanish to the students; the other teacher speaks only English. The students experience Spanish and English medium instruction for approximately equal amounts of time. A strong multicultural dimension pervades the curriculum, with the contributions of different children encouraged and respected. The notion of equality permeates the ethos of the school (Freeman, 1995). This is reflected in the school's mission statement: 'Oyster Bilingual School's focus is on the development of bilingualism, biliteracy, and biculturalism for every student through the mastery of academic skills, the acquisition of language and communicative fluency, the appreciation of differences in racial and ethnic backgrounds, and the building of a positive self-concept and pride in one's heritage.'

Bilingual Education in Majority Languages

Bilingual Education in Majority Languages comprises the joint use of **two** (or more) **majority languages** in a school. The aims of such schools usually include bilingualism or multilingualism, biliteracy and cultural pluralism. Such schools are in societies where much of the population is already bilingual or multilingual (e.g. Singapore, Luxembourg) or where there are significant numbers of natives or expatriates wanting to become bilingual (e.g. learning through English and Japanese in Japan). **Asian** examples of Bilingual Education in Majority Languages include Arabic–English, Bahasa Melayu–English, Mandarin Chinese–English and Japanese–English. In Africa and India there are also schools where a 'majority' regional language and an international language coexist as teaching medium in a school. Bilingualism in that regional language and an international language (e.g. French, English) is the aim and outcome of formal education.

Generally, such schools will contain majority language children, with variations in the language heterogeneity or language homogeneity of the classes.

In the Asian examples, a country (e.g. Brunei, Taiwan) or a region may have one dominant indigenous language with a desire to introduce a second international language such as English into the school. The international language will be used as a medium of instruction alongside the native language. The aim is for fully bilingual and biliterate students through an Enrichment bilingual education program. For example, the *Dwibahasa* (two language) school system in Brunei operates through Malay (Bahasa Melayu) and English (Jones, Martin & Ozóg, 1993). In Nigeria, bilingual education is present, particularly at the secondary school level, in English plus one of the national languages of Nigeria: Hausa, Ibo or Yoruba (Afolayan, 1995). In Singapore, English plus Mandarin, Malay or Tamil (the four official languages of the country) create bilingual education (Pakir, 1994). In Germany, German is paired with French, English, Spanish and Dutch to create a 'German model' of European multicultural and bilingual education (Mäsch, 1994). Under the umbrella heading of Bilingual Education in Majority Languages are different societal situations (e.g. a country already bilingual; a country wishing to become more bilingual) as the above discussion has revealed.

Two special examples of Bilingual Education in Majority Languages will now be considered, commencing with the International School Movement and continuing with the European School Movement.

International Schools

International Schools are a diverse collection of schools throughout the world. Numbering over 850 schools, they are found in over 80 countries of the world, mostly in large cities. Mainly for the affluent, parents pay fees for mostly **private, selective, independent education**. Children in these schools often have parents in the diplomatic service, multinational organizations, or in international businesses and who are geographically and vocationally mobile. Other children in an International school come from the locality, whose parents want their children to have an internationally flavored education. One **language** of the school is ordinarily English. International schools that have English as the sole medium of transmitting the curriculum could not be included under the heading of Bilingual Education in Majority Languages. Such schools become bilingual when a national or international language is incorporated in the curriculum. Sometimes the second language taught (for up to 12 years) is only taught as a language. In other schools, the second language is used as a medium to teach part of the curriculum. Some schools enable their students to acquire third and fourth languages. Generally, the languages of International schools are majority languages with international prestige. Minority languages are rarely found in such schools.

The primary and secondary **curriculum** of **International Schools** tends to reflect United States, British as well as the local curriculum tradition. The teachers are from various countries, usually with a plentiful supply of British and American trained staff. Sometimes preparing children for the International Baccalaureate, United States tests or British examinations, most prepare their clientele for Universities in Europe and North

America. Baker & Prys Jones (1997) and Ochs (1993) provide illustrations and further discussion of the International Schools Movement. Three illustrations of such schools follow.

One example is the **Nishimachi International School** in Tokyo. The age range of the students is from five to 15 and the school caters for over 400 students from around 30 nationalities. The fifty or so teachers in the school come from 12 nationalities. The school is a dedicated center for bilingualism in English and Japanese and for multicultural studies. The student composition is 20% Japanese; 35% United States; 20% one parent Japanese — the other parent from another nationality; and 25% other nationalities (ECIS, 1994). Another example is the **John F. Kennedy School** in Berlin. With students aged five to 19, the school comprises around 1300 students from over 20 nationalities, with German and US students being in the majority. Fifty per cent of teachers are from the United States; 50% from Germany. The school is bilingual, binational and bicultural in German and English, with instruction in both languages. Tuition is free (ECIS, 1994). The **Bayan Bilingual School** in Kuwait enrolls students aged three to 17 and contains around 900 students from 14 nationalities. Teachers come from 15 nationalities. It is a bilingual school stressing Arab culture, traditions, heritage and identity while preparing its graduates for college and university placement throughout the world. The languages of instruction are Arabic and English (ECIS, 1994).

European Schools Movement

Another European example of Bilingual Education in Majority Languages is the **European Schools movement** (Baetens Beardsmore, 1993; Housen & Baetens Beardsmore, 1987; Baetens Beardsmore & Swain, 1985; Tosi, 1991; Baker & Prys Jones, 1997). Mostly for the relatively elite workers of the European Community (EC), such schools are multilingual and cater for some 15,000 children of different EC nations. Started officially in 1958 in Luxembourg, with schools sited in Belgium, Italy, Germany, the Netherlands and England, such European Schools have up to 11 different language sections reflecting the first language of the students (and this may increase as other countries join the European Community). Younger children use their native language as the medium of learning but also receive second language instruction (English, French, or German) in the primary school years. Older children take part of their schooling in their native language and part through the medium of a '**vehicular**' or 'working' language. The 'vehicular' language will usually be a 'majority' second language for the child selected from English, French or German. This language will be taught by native speakers. Native student speakers of that language will also be present in the school as language models. The **vehicular language** is used to teach mixed language groups of students history, geography and economics from the third year of secondary education. In addition, students are taught a **third language** for a minimum of 360 hours.

The outcome of such schooling tends to be functionally bilingual and often multilingual students with a sense of cultural pluralism, European multiculturalism and European identity. Integration and harmonization of students from different nationalities is formally achieved in the '**European Hours**' lessons using the vehicular language. 'European Hours' are an important curriculum component from Grade 3 in Primary education. In classes of 20 to 25 students for three lessons a week, children from different language backgrounds work cooperatively together. A small group project with a realistic, attainable goal (e.g. making puppets) provides the focus for a context embedded and cognitively undemanding 'European Hour'. Deliberately and explicitly, students are encouraged to respect each person's native language. Games and physical education are also occasions for a cooperative mixing of students from the different language sections. Students are linguistically mixed to avoid stereotypes and prejudices, and to build a supranational European identity (Baetens Beardsmore, 1993).

A major difference between the European schools movement and the Canadian immersion programs is that the second language is taught as a subject before being used as a medium of instruction. That second language also continues to be taught as a subject, leading to a high level of grammatical accuracy (Baetens Beardsmore, 1993).

According to Housen & Baetens Beardsmore's (1987) **research** in one European School: 'This strong language commitment has no detrimental effects on academic achievement as can be gauged from results on the final European Baccalaureate examination, on which 90% of students have been successful' (p. 85). However, bilingualism, biliteracy and multiculturalism is not only due to the effects of schooling. The parents may also be bilingual or multilingual, and the children are more likely to come from literacy-oriented, middle class bureaucrat homes, with a positive view of bilingualism. Playgrounds are multilingual, satellite TV in Europe is multilingual and the growing notion of Europeanization creates privileged European schoolchildren who are 'educated bilinguals, equally at ease with two languages, with their own national culture and the supranational European identity' (Tosi, 1991: 33). The Stated **Objectives** of the European Schools Movement are (adapted from information from the Central Office of the Representative of the Board of Governors of the European Schools):

- to give students confidence in their own cultural identity — the bedrock for their development as European citizens;
- to give a sound education, based on a broad range of subjects, from nursery level to university-entrance;
- to develop high standards in speaking and writing both the mother tongue and two or more foreign languages;
- to develop mathematical and scientific skills throughout the whole period of schooling;
- to encourage a European and global perspective in the study of history and geography, rather than a narrower, nationalistic one;
- to encourage creativity in music and the plastic arts and an appreciation of all that is best in a common European artistic heritage;
- to develop physical skills and instill in students an appreciation of the need for healthy living through participation in sporting and recreational activities;
- to offer students professional guidance in their choice of subjects and in career/university decisions in the later years of the secondary school;
- to foster tolerance, co-operation, communication and concern for others throughout the school community;

- to provide high-quality teaching through the recruitment of well qualified and experienced staff by the respective countries' Ministries of Education.

In **Europe**, there are other schools (apart from the European School Movement) that use two or more prestigious languages in the curriculum (Baetens Beardsmore, 1993). For example, in **Luxembourg**, children who speak Luxemburger after birth become trilingual (Luxemburger, French and German) through education (Lebrun & Baetens Beardsmore, 1993). Children start their education at age five through the medium of Luxemburger (a variety of Low German). German is initially a subject in the curriculum, then introduced as the main teaching medium. By the end of Grade 6, children function in much of the curriculum in German. French is introduced as a subject in Grade 2, and is increasingly used as a teaching medium in secondary education. Most students have a working knowledge of three languages by the conclusion of schooling (Lebrun & Baetens Beardsmore, 1993). Through emphasis on the home tongue in the early years, emphasis on German in the primary school and emphasis on French in the secondary school, children become trilingual and biliterate (French and German literacy).

CONCLUSION

Having considered ten types of bilingual education, the natural question to ask is whether one type is more effective than another. For Spanish speaking children in the US, is it better for them to be placed in Submersion, Transitional, Maintenance or Two Way schooling? For a monolingual English speaker, is it detrimental to enter immersion schooling compared with mainstream schooling? Such questions will now be examined in the next chapter by 'effectiveness' research.

SUGGESTED FURTHER READING

BAETENS BEARDSMORE, H. (ed.) 1993, *European Models of Bilingual Education.* Clevedon: Multilingual Matters.

CAZDEN, C.B. and SNOW, C.E. 1990, *English Plus: Issues in Bilingual Education.* (*The Annals of the American Academy of Political and Social Science 508, March 1990*). London: Sage.

CRAWFORD, J. 1991, *Bilingual Education: History, Politics, Theory and Practice* (2nd edn). Los Angeles: Bilingual Education Services.

CUMMINS, J. and DANESI, M. 1990, *Heritage Languages. The Development and Denial of Canada's Linguistic Resources.* Toronto: Our Schools/Ourselves Education Foundation & Garamond Press.

DANESI, M., McLEOD, K. and MORRIS, S. 1993, *Heritage Languages and Education: The Canadian Experience.* Oakville, Ontario: Mosaic Press.

GARCÍA, O. and BAKER, C. (eds) 1995, *Policy and Practice in Bilingual Education: A Reader Extending the Foundations.* Clevedon: Multilingual Matters. (Sections 1 & 2).

REVIEW AND STUDY QUESTIONS

(1) Write short revision notes on the following:
    (i)   List the important developments in the history of bilingual education in the US or any other country of your choice.
    (ii)   What is the difference between 'weak' and 'strong' types of bilingual education.
    (iii) What are the important characteristics of the ten types of bilingual education.
    (iv) State the difference(s) between submersion and transitional bilingual education. Also, consider the differences between variations within submersion and transitional bilingual education.
    (v)   State the difference(s) between two way bilingual education, heritage language/developmental maintenance education, Canadian immersion and bilingual education in majority languages.

(2) Research the history of bilingual education in your country or area (e.g. at state level). What have been the major changes? What seems to be the causes of such major changes?

(3) What is the distinction between 'weak' and 'strong' forms of bilingual education?

(4) In what types of bilingual education may the distinction between 'strong' and 'weak' forms of bilingual education become blurred?

(5) Describe in detail one of the types of bilingual education with which you are most familiar. What are the important characteristics of that form of bilingual education, particularly those characteristics not focused on in the chapter?

STUDY ACTIVITIES

(1) Write a personal account of one type of bilingual education which you have experienced or with which you are most familiar. Describe your experience of the language dimensions of this form of education. Present this in a small group seminar to find out differences and similarities of experience.

(2) Visit a school, and by interview and observation decide the extent to which that school fits one or more of the types of bilingual education in this chapter.

(3) Visit one or more schools and ask about the history of a bilingual education program or language program within that school. What have been the aims of the school with regard to languages? Have these aims changed over the last 10 or 20 years? How do the teachers perceive the first and second language of children being ignored or used over the last decade or more?

(4) By using documents, interviews, visits to schools and visits to administrators, try to sketch the history of language and bilingual education within a specific community. Also observe what signs and symbols there are of language within the community. For example, on posters, in newspapers, mass media and community activity, is there more than one language in use?

(5) Imagine you are a parent or teacher and were required to make a public speech about changing a school from a 'weak' form of bilingual education to a 'strong' form. Prepare, and then deliver in front of the class, a speech of about five minutes to persuade the administration.

CHAPTER 11

The Effectiveness of Bilingual Education

Introduction

Research Studies

Reviews and Overviews of Research
Canadian Immersion Bilingual Education
Heritage Language Education/
Developmental Maintenance Education
The US Debate

Advancing the Effectiveness of
Bilingual Education

Conclusion

CHAPTER 11

The Effectiveness of Bilingual Education

INTRODUCTION

Having considered ten types of bilingual education, this chapter turns to considering research on the major types of bilingual education. How effective are these major models for which types of children? What are the recorded successes and limitations? What makes a bilingual school more or less effective? These are the issues considered in this chapter.

RESEARCH STUDIES

From early research in the 1920s in Wales (Saer, 1922) and Malherbe's (1946) evaluation of bilingual education in South Africa, there has been a flood of **evaluations** of bilingual projects and experiments, programs and experiences. The research is international; for example, Ireland (e.g. Harris, 1984) and England (e.g. Fitzpatrick, 1987); US (e.g. Danoff *et al.*, 1977, 1978) and Canada (e.g. Swain & Lapkin, 1982); Peru (e.g. Hornberger, 1988, 1990a); Hong Kong (e.g. Boyle, 1990); Wales (e.g. Eurwen Price, 1985; Baker, 1995) and Spain (e.g. Sierra & Olaziregi, EIFE2, 1989; Artigal, 1995; Bel, 1993). A report from the World Bank (1982) provided one of the few comparative international studies, covering bilingual education in the Philippines, Ireland, Canada, Mexico, Nigeria, Sweden and the United States.

It is possible to find **support** for most of the different forms of bilingual education by selecting and emphasizing a particular study. Some examples will illustrate. Criticism of Irish immersion education for children from English speaking homes was given by Macnamara (1966). He found such immersion children to be 11 months behind mainstream children on mechanical arithmetic. He suggested that it is 'probable that the use of Irish in teaching problem arithmetic hinders the progress of English speaking children' (MacNamara, 1966: 103). In comparison, support for immersion education comes from the Canadian research studies (e.g. Swain & Lapkin, 1982). Danoff *et al.* (1977, 1978) found submersion to be superior to transitional bilingual education with a large US sample of almost 9000 children. McConnell (1980) found US transitional bilingual education to be better than submersion, while Matthews (1979), also in the US, found no difference between these two 'weak' forms of bilingual education.

Heritage language education has been evaluated as successful in Canada by Keyser & Brown (1981) and in England by Fitzpatrick (1987). In contrast, early research in Wales (e.g. Smith, 1923) questioned educational outcomes from heritage language programs for Welsh bilinguals.

Whether research finds a consensus in favor of one or some of the types of bilingual education is examined later in this chapter. For the moment, it is important to outline some reasons why studies vary in their findings.

The Sample of Children

The results of one study are limited to that sample of children at the time of the study. If there is some form of probability sampling (e.g. a random sample of a defined population is chosen), then these results may generalize to that specific population. Such **sampling** rarely occurs in bilingual education evaluations where instead, many studies have small and unrepresentative samples. It is usually ethically questionable and practically impossible to allocate children randomly into experimental and control groups that contain perfect mirrors of a large population of schoolchildren.

Given the wide variety of samples of children used in bilingual education effectiveness research, it is not surprising that differences in findings emerge. Samples of children include urban and rural schools, various social class backgrounds, different ages and varying levels of motivation. The international research includes a mixture of bilingual groups: indigenous language minority groups, in-migrants, and majority language children in minority language education. **Generalization** of results from one group to another is not valid. Such children may be in a subtractive or additive environment at home, school, community and nation.

Unlike the physical world, simple laws of behavior that govern large groups of people are not likely. The immense variety of individual differences and environment differences makes clear cut, simple research results intrinsically elusive. Such results also say something about what has been, not what will always be. They do not guarantee that results will be stable across time.

Interacting Factors

Various factors, other than the sample of children, may have a variable effect on bilingual education. Parental interest, parental involvement in their children's education and parental co-operation with teachers is one intervening factor. Another factor is likely to be the enthusiasm and commitment of teachers to the education program. With a novel experiment in bilingual education, there may be extra enthusiasm and interest. The level of material support (e.g. books, curriculum guidelines, computers, science equipment) may also produce variable outcomes.

There is likely to be as much **variation** in outcomes (e.g. achievement in different curriculum areas) inside a particular bilingual education program (e.g. transitional, immersion or heritage language) as between different types of program. As Berliner (1988: 289) suggests of intervention programs, 'One of the major findings from studies of Follow-through programs, where competing theories and programs of early childhood education were purposefully funded, was that the variation across sites within the same program (whether it was behavioral, cognitive, requiring parent involvement, technology oriented, or whatever) was equal to the variation across the sites between the different programs.'

The crucial point is this. The language policy and language practice in schooling are only one element amongst many that make a school more or less successful. A recipe for success is unlikely to result from one ingredient (e.g. the language of the classroom). A great variety of factors act and interact to determine whether bilingual education is successful or not. As will be considered at the end of the chapter, it makes more sense to consider the wide variety of conditions which make bilingual education more or less successful. We need to specify all the ingredients in different recipes to fully understand the success or failure of forms of bilingual education. Bilingual education, whatever type or model, is no guarantee of effective schooling.

Measures of Success

An important question is: 'What tests or other sources of evidence are used to determine whether a form of bilingual education is successful?' Should the sole **outcomes** be competence in one or two languages? What aspects of language should be assessed? Should science and social studies be included? Should the measure of success be performance across the whole curriculum? Whose version of the curriculum should be used (e.g. computational versus conceptual emphasis in Mathematics; religious knowledge versus moral development)? How important is it to include non-cognitive outcomes such as self-esteem, moral development, school attendance, social and emotional adjustment, integration into society and gaining employment? What are the long term effects of bilingual schooling (e.g. students later becoming parents who raise their children in the minority language)? The questions indicate there will be debates and disputes over what are the valuable outcomes of schooling. Research on the effectiveness of bilingual education has varied in the choice of measures of outcome, as is illustrated later in the chapter.

A particular problem is that measures of success tend to be restricted to what is **measurable**. Quantitative outcomes (e.g. test scores) are used; qualitative evidence is rarely gathered. Can a play be judged only on an applause meter reading? Do a drama critic's notes add a vigorous, insightful interpretation to the performance? While critics will differ in their evaluations, they may add flesh and life to the statistical skeleton of educational tests.

The Researchers

As Fishman (1977) and Edwards (1981) have indicated, research on bilingual education is rarely neutral. Often the researchers have hypotheses which hide their **expectations**. No educational research can be totally value-free, neutral or objective. The questions asked, the methodological tools chosen, decisions in analysis and manner of reporting usually reveal ideological preferences. Many researchers will be supporters of bilingual education, ethnic diversity, minority language rights and cultural pluralism. This is not to argue that all evaluation research on bilingual education is invalid. Rather, it cannot be assumed that results are not affected by researchers, their beliefs, opinions and preferences.

Some of the research on bilingual education is committed, prescriptive in nature, with interests, idealism and ideology mixed with investigation and intelligent discussion. 'Bilingual education is not merely a disinterested exercise in the application of theory and research to real-life situations. It is also an exercise in social policy and ideology' (Edwards, 1981: 27).

REVIEWS AND OVERVIEWS OF RESEARCH

After a substantial number of different studies on bilingual education had accumulated, various reviews and overviews appeared. A reviewer will assemble as many individual studies as possible and attempt to find a systematic pattern and an orderliness in the findings. Is there a **consensus** in the findings? Is it possible to make some generalizations about the effectiveness of different forms of bilingual education? Rarely, if ever, will all the evaluations agree. Therefore the reviewer's task is to detect reasons for variations. For example, different age groups, different social class backgrounds and varying types of measurement device may explain variations in results.

The **early reviews** of bilingual education effectiveness were published in the late 1970s. Zappert & Cruz (1977), Troike (1978) and Dulay & Burt (1978, 1979) each concluded that bilingual education in the US effectively promoted bilingualism with language minority children and was preferable to monolingual English programs. That is, language minority students became skilled in both the majority and minority language. Since the late 1970s, many individual studies have been added and more recent reviews have emerged (e.g. Collier, 1989; Collier, 1992; Lam, 1992). This section now examines recent reviews in three parts: (1) reviews of Canadian immersion education; (2) a review of Heritage Language education; (3) and major, influential and controversial reviews in the US. Each has a relatively large collection of literature allowing some depth of treatment. (In comparison, there are relatively few evaluations of other types of bilingual education (e.g. Mainstream Bilingual Education, Two Way Bilingual Education) preventing consideration here.)

Canadian Immersion Bilingual Education

The various reviews of Canadian immersion tend to paint a relatively uniform picture. The overviews of Swain & Lapkin (1982), the California State Department of Education

(1984), and Genesee (1983, 1984, 1987) highlight four major outcomes of Canadian immersion bilingual education.

Second Language (French) Learning

It is easy to predict that immersion students will surpass those in mainstream (core) programs given 'drip-feed' French lessons for 30 minutes a day. Most students in **early total immersion** programs approach native-like performance in French around 11 years old in receptive language skills (listening and reading). Such levels are not so well attained in the productive skills of speaking and writing (Lapkin, Swain & Shapson, 1990).

The reviews confirm that one kind of bilingualism can be educationally engineered. Immersion students mostly succeed in gaining competence in two languages. However, as Chapter 1 revealed, bilingual ability is not the same as being functionally bilingual. One of the **limitations** of immersion bilingual education is that for many students, French can become a school-only phenomenon. Outside the school walls, immersion students tend not to use French more than 'drip feed' students (Genesee, 1978). Such students are competent in French, but tend not to communicate in French in the community. Potential does not necessarily lead to production; skill does not ensure street speech. Lack of spontaneous or contrived French language opportunity and a dearth of French cultural occasions to actively and purposefully use the second language may partly be the explanation. Other explanations will be considered later. Stern (1984) argued that the immersion programs were strong on language, but weak on widening students' cultural horizons and weak on sensitizing them to francophone culture and values.

First Language (English) Learning

If immersion education provides the route to near-native fluency in a second language, is it at the cost of attainment in the first language? Does bilingualism result in lesser achievement in English compared with 'mainstream' students? Like a balance, as one goes up, does the other go down?

For the first four years of **early total immersion**, students tend not to progress in English as do monolingual English students in mainstream classes. Reading, spelling and punctuation, for example, are not so developed. Since such children are usually not given English language instruction for one, two or three years after starting school, these results are to be expected. However, the initial pattern does not last. After approximately six years of schooling, early total immersion children have caught up with their monolingual peers in English language skills. By the end of elementary schooling, the early total immersion experience has generally not affected first language speaking and writing development. Parents of these children believe the same as the attainment tests reveal.

Indeed, when differences in English language achievement between immersion and mainstream children have been located by research, it is often in favor of immersion students (Swain & Lapkin, 1982, 1991a). This finding links with Chapter 9 that discussed the possible cognitive advantages consequential from bilingualism. If bilingualism permits increased linguistic awareness, more flexibility in thought, more internal inspection of language, such cognitive advantages may help to explain the favorable English progress of early immersion students.

Early partial immersion students also tend to lag behind for three or four years in their English language skills. Their performance is little different from that of total early immersion students, which is surprising since early partial immersion education has more English language content. By the end of elementary schooling, partial early immersion children catch up with mainstream peers in English language attainment. Unlike early total immersion students, partial immersion children do not tend to surpass mainstream comparison groups in English language achievement. Similarly, **late immersion** has no detrimental effect on English language skills (Genesee, 1983).

The evidence suggests that immersion children learn French at no cost to their English. Indeed, not only is there the gain of a second language, there is also evidence to suggest that immersion results in possible extra benefits in English proficiency. Rather than acting like a weighing balance, early total immersion, in particular, seems more analogous to cooking. The ingredients, when mixed and baked, react together in additive ways. The product becomes more than the sum of its parts.

Other Curriculum Areas

If immersion education results in children becoming bilingual in French and English, the question is whether this is at the cost of achievement in other curriculum areas. Compared with children in mainstream education how do immersion children progress in curriculum areas such as mathematics and science, history and geography? The reviews of research suggest that **early total immersion** students generally perform as well in these subjects as do mainstream children. That is, achievement in the curriculum is typically not adversely affected by early total immersion bilingual education.

The evaluations of **early partial immersion education** are not quite so positive. When children in early partial immersion learn mathematics and science through the medium of French, they tend to lag behind comparable mainstream children, at least initially. This may be because their French skills are insufficiently developed to be able to think mathematically and scientifically in their second language.

The results for **late immersion** are similar. The important factor appears to be whether second language skills (French) are sufficiently developed to cope with fairly complex curriculum material. Johnson & Swain (1994) argue that there is a gap in second language proficiency that needs bridging when students move from learning a language as a subject to learning through that second language. The more demanding the curriculum area, the higher the level of learning expected, and the later the switch to learning through a second language, the more important it is to provide 'bridging' programs. Such 'bridging programs' ease the discrepancy between second language proficiency and the language proficiency required to understand the curriculum. A 'bridging program' may require a language teacher and a content teacher (e.g. of mathematics) to operate together.

The results overall suggest that bilingual education by an immersion experience need not have negative effects on curriculum performance, particularly in early total immersion programs. Indeed, most children **gain** a second language without cost to their performance in the curriculum. However, the key factor seems to be whether their language skills have evolved sufficiently in order to work in the curriculum in their second language (see Chapter 9).

Attitudes and Social Adjustment

Apart from performance throughout the curriculum, evaluations of immersion education have examined whether immersion has positive or negative effects on students' motivation, attitude and study skills. The most positive results in this area have been found with **early total immersion students**. Parents of such students tend to express satisfaction with their offspring's learning as well as their personal and social behavior. Early immersion students also tend to have more positive attitudes towards themselves, their education and to French Canadians in comparison, for example, with late immersion students. However the danger here is attributing the positive attitudes to schooling. The cause may alternatively be parental values and beliefs, home culture and environment. This is further discussed in the next section.

Problems and Limitations

Various authors have recently highlighted possible limitations in immersion education that were not present in the early evaluations (e.g. Hammerly, 1988; reply by Allen *et al.*, 1989). **First**, Selinker, Swain & Dumas (1975) suggested that immersion students do not always become grammatically accurate in their French. Immersion students also tend to lack the social and stylistic sense of appropriate language use which the native speaker possesses. For example, the restricted use of verb tenses other than the present, and the sometimes incorrect use of 'tu' and 'vous', appear to be related to the functionally restricted language of the classroom. Certain forms of language do not naturally nor regularly occur in the classroom (e.g. because of the 'present' focus of learning and adult–student relationships). One solution is to investigate problematic areas of vocabulary and grammar, provide increased opportunities for receptive and particularly productive language in such weak areas, integrate a focus on the form of language used with meaningful content teaching, and give systematic and consistent feedback on language development to the student. Increasing group and collaborative learning is also seen as important in developing the productive language proficiency of students towards the standards of native French-Canadian speakers (Swain, 1993).

Second, surveys of graduates of immersion programs tend to find that relatively few students make much use of French after leaving school (Harley, 1994; Wesche, 1993). This partly reflects opportunity, partly a lack of confidence in their competence in speaking French, and partly a preference for English use. Also, immersion students do not tend to interact significantly more with francophones than students in mainstream (core) programs. Ability in French is not frequently translated into use of French outside the school gates, except, for example, where employment and personal economics become a focus.

Third, there is difficulty in pinpointing the crucial interacting factors that create an effective immersion experience. There are, for example, intervening variables such as teaching techniques that may change the pattern of results. Genesee (1983) argued that individualized, activity based teaching techniques may be more effective than traditional whole class techniques. Genesee (1983) also argued that the intensity of language learning, for example, how many hours per day, is likely to be more important than the length of language learning (e.g. the number of years of second language learning). This is connected with the finding that older students tend to learn a second language more quickly than younger learners. Is it immersion as a system that leads to relatively successful outcomes or, or as well as, factors such as 'student motivation, teachers' preparation, home culture, parental attitude, ethnolinguistic vitality, amount of time studying different curricula' (Carey, 1991: 953).

Fourth, immersion programs can have effects on mainstream schools. For example, effects may include: a redistribution of classroom teachers and leaders, a change in the linguistic and ability profile of mainstream classes, discrepancies in class size with increasing numbers of mixed aged classes.

Fifth, Heller (1994) has argued that immersion schools provide anglophones with the linguistic and cultural capital for increased social and economic mobility and for political power. Immersion education is thus, in this perspective, about ulterior motives and vested interests. Such education is about gaining advantages in Canadian society: educational, cultural, linguistic, social, power, wealth and dominance advantages. Hence, immersion education may produce conflict with the minority francophone community (e.g. in Ontario) rather than the harmonious unity and 'bridge building' that bilingualism aims to achieve in Canadian society. This issue is considered further in Chapter 19.

Sixth, there is a danger in generalizing from the Canadian experience to elsewhere in the world. In Canada, immersion concerns two major high status international languages: French and English. In many countries where bilingualism is present or fostered, the situation is different. Often the context is one of a majority and a minority language (or languages) co-existing. This links with additive and subtractive bilingual situations. Canada is regarded as an additive bilingual context. Many countries across the five continents contain subtractive bilingual contexts.

If immersion education is thought worthy of **generalizing to other countries**, there are certain conditions which need to be kept in mind:

(1) Immersion bilingual education as practiced in Canada is optional not enforced. The convictions of teachers and parents and of the children themselves effect the ethos of the school and the motivation and achievement of the children. Immersion education will work best when there is conviction and not enforced conformity.

(2) Immersion education in Canada starts with children who are at a similar level in their language skills. Such a homogeneous grouping of children may make the language classroom more efficient. Where there are wide variations in ability in a second

language, teachers may have problems in providing an efficient and well-structured curriculum with equality of provision and opportunity.

(3) The Canadian immersion experience ensures there is respect for the child's home language and culture. This relates to the additive bilingual situation. Parents have generally been seen as partners in the immersion movement and some dialogue has existed with administrators, teachers and researchers.

(4) Immersion teachers in Canada tend to be committed to such immersion education. Research in Wales has pointed to the crucial importance of teacher commitment to bilingual education in effecting achievement in school (Roberts, 1985).

(5) It is important not to view immersion education in Canada in purely educational terms. Behind immersion education is political, social and cultural ideology. Immersion education is not just immersion in a second language (French). Such bilingual education has aims and assumptions, beliefs and values that sometimes differ from, other times are additional to, mainstream education. It is important to see immersion education not just as a means to promote bilingualism, but also as a move to a different kind of society (see Chapter 19). By promoting bilingualism in English speakers, immersion education in Canada may support French language communities, increase the opportunities for francophones outside Quebec and help promote bilingualism in the public sector (and debatably in the private sector). However, immersion education is seen as a Trojan horse of further English assimilation by some francophones. 'Francophones question whether an increase in bilingual anglophones will simply act to deprive them of their historical advantage in occupying bilingual jobs' (Lapkin, Swain & Shapson, 1990: 649). This is linked to the finding that children from higher socioeconomic backgrounds tend to be over-represented in immersion programs. Thus immersion education may act to reproduce elite groups, giving anglophone children with bilingual abilities an advantage in the jobs market (Heller, 1994).

Heritage Language Education/Developmental Maintenance Education

Major **reviews** of heritage language education are provided by Cummins (1983a, 1993) and Cummins & Danesi (1990). Apart from looking at individual international educational interventions, the reviews also look at the pattern that can be found in the results of evaluations of heritage language education, thus attempting to derive international generalizations.

The results of such evaluations, particularly in Canada, suggest that heritage language programs can be effective in four different ways. First, the students maintain their **home language**. This is especially in comparison with language minority children who are placed in mainstream or transitional education. Such mainstreamed children tend partly to lose and sometimes avoid using their heritage language. Second, such children tend to perform as well as comparable mainstream children in curriculum areas such as mathematics, science, history and geography. That is, there is no loss in **curriculum performance** for such children taking their education in their home language. Indeed the evaluations suggest that they perform better than comparable children in mainstream education. To illustrate: take two 'equal' children from a language minority background.

One attends a mainstream program, the other attends heritage language education. The chances are that the child in heritage language education will achieve more highly, all other factors being equal. One 'cognitive' explanation is that heritage language education commences at the level of linguistic–cognitive competence reached on entry to school. (The cognitive reasons for this increased performance are considered in Chapter 9). In comparison, mainstreaming such language minority students has negative cognitive implications. It seemingly rejects a child's level of cognitive competence. It entails re-developing sufficient language capability in order for them to cope with the curriculum. If the analogy will stand, it is like someone with a basic level of skill in salmon fishing (with a fishing rod) who is made to learn big game sea fishing instead. The instructor ignores skills already attained with a rod. The student is made to practice casting on dry land, instead of building on existing skills with the fishing rod.

Third, studies suggest that children's **attitudes** are positive when placed in heritage language education. When the home language is used in school, there is the possibility that a child's self-esteem and self concept will be enhanced. The child may perceive that the home language, the home and community culture, parents and relations are accepted by the school when the home language is used. In comparison, a language minority child who is mainstreamed is vulnerable to a loss of self esteem and status. The home language and culture may seem disparaged. The school system and the teachers may seem latently or manifestly to be rejecting the child's home language and values. This may affect the child's motivation and interest in school work and thereby affect performance. A student whose skills are recognized and encouraged may feel encouraged and motivated; a student whose skills are ignored may feel discouraged and rejected.

The fourth finding of heritage language evaluations is perhaps the most unexpected. Indeed, it tends to go against 'common sense'. When testing children's **English language performance** (or whatever the second language is for that child), performance is generally comparable with mainstreamed children. To explain this, take the previous example of two children from identical heritage language backgrounds with the same 'intelligence', socioeconomic class and age. One is placed in heritage language education, the other in mainstream schooling. It might be expected that the child placed in main-stream English language education would perform far better in English language tests than the child in a heritage language education program. The prediction might be that the greater the exposure to English in mainstream education, the higher the English language test performance. Evaluations of heritage language education suggest something different. The child in heritage language education is likely to perform at least as well as the child in mainstream education. The explanation seems to lie in self esteem being enhanced, and language and intellectual skills better promoted by education in the home language. Such skills appear to transfer easily into second language (majority language) areas.

While evaluations of heritage language education are positive, the Canadian population are divided on the issue. For some, empowerment of heritage language groups is perceived as a major societal challenge — a challenge to existing power and political arrangements

(Taylor, Crago & McAlpine, 1993). Official Canadian policy has been supportive of multiculturalism, especially of the two 'solitudes' — French language and English language cultures. Extending multiculturalism to other 'heritage' languages has been more contentious (Cummins, 1992). Ethnocultural Communities (e.g. Ukrainian, German, Hebrew, Yiddish, Mandarin Chinese, Arabic and Polish) tend to support heritage language education. Anglophone and francophone Canadians tend to have a tolerance and goodwill towards such communities. Lukewarm support for heritage language communities tends to stop short if public monies are to be used to support heritage language education. The **anxieties** of sections of public opinion and of government include: the disruption of mainstream schools (e.g. falling rolls), problems of staffing, minimal communication between heritage language teachers and mainstream teachers, segregation of school communities, financial burdens of the absorption of in-migrants into the education system, loss of time for core curriculum subjects, social tensions, and effects on the integration and stability of Canadian society (Cummins & Danesi, 1990; Cummins, 1992; Edwards & Redfern, 1992).

Such **anxieties** have increased with the high levels of Canadian in-migrants since the mid 1980s onwards. Due to low birth rates and a rapidly ageing population in Canada, the population has been increased by in-migration policies. Hence language diversity in Canada has increased. In Toronto and Vancouver, for example, more than half the school population comes from a non-English speaking background (Cummins, 1992). With increased in-migration and hence increased linguistic and cultural diversity, how does a government respond? What is the consensus of public opinion in Canada about fostering language diversity and multiculturalism?

Cummins (1992: 285) portrays the **debate** about the nature of Canadian identity, the debate about multiculturalism and the self-interest of public opinion thus:

> 'While the dominant anglophone and francophone groups generally are strongly in favor of learning the other official language, they see few benefits to promoting heritage languages for themselves, for Canadian society as a whole, or for children from ethnocultural backgrounds. The educational focus for such children should be on acquiring English and becoming Canadian rather than on erecting linguistic and cultural barriers between them and their Canadian peers. In short, whereas advocates of heritage language teaching stress the value of bilingual and multilingual skills for the individual and society as a whole, opponents see heritage languages as socially divisive, excessively costly, and educationally retrograde in view of minority children's need to succeed academically in the school language.'

If the focus switches from public political opinion to the educational opinion of teachers, parents and students, there is general satisfaction with Canadian Heritage Language programs. While such programs may present administrative challenges (e.g. shortage of teachers, availability of pre-service and in-service teacher education and a lack of curriculum materials), the **advantages** may be summarized as follows (Canadian Education Association, 1991):

- positive self concept and pride in one's background;
- better integration of child into school and society;
- more tolerance of other people and different cultures;
- increased cognitive, social and emotional development;
- ease in learning of new languages;
- increased probability of employment;
- fostering stronger relationships between home and school;
- responding to the needs and wishes of community.

The overall **conclusions** from Cummins' (1983a, 1993) and Cummins & Danesi's (1990) review of heritage language education is that such education is not likely to have detrimental effects on a child's performance throughout the curriculum. Indeed, the indication from research is that language minority children tend to prosper more in such education than when placed in mainstream education. They maintain and enrich their home language and culture. Their performance throughout the curriculum does not suffer. This notably includes performance in the second language (majority language). Cognitive enhancement can also occur (Cummins, 1993; Danesi, 1991).

The US Debate

The Baker and de Kanter Review of Bilingual Education (1983)

At the beginning of the 1980s, the United States Federal Government commissioned a **major review** of transitional bilingual education by Keith Baker and Adriana de Kanter (1983). While in the 1960s and 1970s bilingual education slowly evolved in the United States, in the late 1970s, 1980s and 1990s public support for bilingual education tended not to favor such evolution. One branch of public opinion in the United States saw bilingual education as failing to foster integration. Rather, such opinion saw bilingual education as leading to social and economic divisions in society along language grounds. Minority language groups were sometimes portrayed as using bilingual education for political and economic self interest, even separatism. Thus the Baker & de Kanter (1983) review needs viewing in its political context (see Chapter 19).

Baker & de Kanter (1983) posed two questions to focus their review. These two questions were:

(1) Does Transitional Bilingual Education lead to better performance in English?
(2) Does Transitional Bilingual Education lead to better performance in non-language subject areas?

The review looked at bilingual education through 'transitional' eyes. It did not start from a neutral, comprehensive look at the various different forms of bilingual education. Notice also the **narrow range of expected outcomes** of bilingual education in the questions. Only English language and non-language subject areas were regarded as the desirable outcome of schooling. Other outcomes such as self esteem, employment, preservation of minority languages, the value of different cultures were not considered. Nor were areas such as moral development, social adjustment and personality development considered.

At the outset of their investigation, Baker & de Kanter (1981, 1983) located 300 pieces of research from North America and the rest of the bilingual world. Of these 300, they rejected 261 studies. The 39 they considered in their review of bilingual education had to conform to six criteria. These may be listed as:

(1) English and non-language subject area performance must have been measured in the research.

(2) Comparisons between bilingual education and, for example, mainstream children must have ensured the groups were relatively matched at the commencement. This means that initial differences between the two comparison groups must have been taken into account. If not, the results may be explained by such initial differences (e.g. different socioeconomic grouping) rather than the form of education in which children were placed.

(3) Baker & de Kanter (1983) required the studies to be statistically valid. For example, appropriate statistical tests needed to have been performed.

(4) Some studies were rejected because they compared the rate of progress of a bilingual education sample with national averages for a particular subject area. Such a comparison is invalid as the comparison would be between bilinguals and monolingual English speakers, rather than two different groups of bilinguals in different forms of schooling.

(5) It was insufficient for chosen studies to show that a group of students had progressed over the year. Rather 'gain scores' needed to involve comparisons between different forms of schooling. That is, relative gain (one form of bilingual education program compared with another) rather than absolute gain (how much progress made in a specified time) was required.

(6) Studies were rejected which solely used grade equivalent scores. There are problems of comparability and compatibility between students, schools and states when US grade scores are used.

The **conclusion** of Baker & de Kanter's (1983) review is that no particular education program should be legislated for or preferred by the US Federal Government:

> 'The common sense observation that children should be taught in a language they understand does not necessarily lead to the conclusion they should be taught in their home language. They can be taught successfully in a second language if the teaching is done right. The key to successful teaching in the second language seems to be to ensure that the second language and subject matter are taught simultaneously so that subject content never gets ahead of language. Given the American setting, where the language minority child must ultimately function in an English speaking society, carefully conducted second language instruction in all subjects may well be preferable to bilingual methods'. (p. 51).

The review therefore came out in support of the dominant government preference for English-only and transitional bilingual education. Functioning in the English language rather than bilingually was preferred. Assimilation and integration appear as the social and political preference that underlies the conclusions.

There has been considerable **criticism** of the Baker & de Kanter (1983) review (e.g. Willig, 1981/82; American Psychological Association, 1982). The main criticisms may be summarized as follows: a narrow range of outcome measures was considered, although this is often the fault of the original research rather than the review; focusing on transitional bilingual education implicitly valued assimilation and integration and devalued aims such as the preservation of a child's home language and culture; and the criteria used for selecting only 39 out of 300 studies was narrow and rigid.

While the studies included may be relatively more sophisticated, this still left studies with technical deficiencies (e.g. studies with small samples) included in the review. It also excluded well-known and oft-quoted studies such as the Rock Point Navajo research (Rosier & Holm, 1980; see also Holm & Holm, 1990). The review therefore concentrated on a selective sample of technically superior research. It failed to look at patterns across the broadest range of research. This is an issue returned to later in this chapter.

A further criticism of the Baker & de Kanter (1983) study provides a bridge with the next section. We have suggested that single studies seldom provide a definitive answer. Therefore an overview strategy attempts to integrate the findings of a variety of studies. Baker & de Kanter's (1983) approach is **narrative integration**. This is essentially an intuitive process, and the methods of procedure tend to be variable from reviewer to reviewer. A comparison of the reviews of Baker & de Kanter (1983) with the earlier reviews by Zappert & Cruz (1977); Troike (1978) and Dulay & Burt (1978, 1979), shows that reviews of similar studies can result in differing conclusions. That is, different reviewers use the same research reports to support contrary conclusions.

An alternative and more rule-bound strategy is to use **meta-analysis**. This is a methodological technique which quantitatively integrates empirical research studies. The technique mathematically examines the amount of effect or differences in the research studies (Glass, McGaw & Smith, 1981; Hunter, Schmidt & Jackson, 1982). For example, how much difference is there in outcome between transitional and immersion bilingual education? There is no need to exclude studies from the meta-analysis which the reviewer finds marginal or doubtful in terms of methodology. The quality of the evaluations is something that is examined in the meta-analysis and can be allowed for statistically. Meta-analysis may show consistency of finding where narrative reviewers tend to highlight variation and disagreement in findings (McGaw, 1988).

Willig's (1985) Meta-analysis

Willig's (1985) adopted a statistical meta-analysis approach to **reviewing bilingual education**. She selected 23 studies from the Baker & de Kanter (1981, 1983) review. All of her 23 studies concerned United States bilingual education evaluations and deliberately excluded Canadian immersion education evaluations. As a result of the meta-analysis, Willig (1985) concluded that bilingual education programs that supported the minority language were consistently superior in various outcomes. Bilingual education programs tend to produce higher performance in tests of achievement throughout the curriculum. Small to moderate advantages were found for bilingual education students in reading, language skills, mathematics and overall achievement when the tests were in the students' second language (English). Similar advantages were found for these curriculum areas and for writing, listening, social studies and self concept when non-English language tests were used.

Willig's (1985) analysis also portrays the variety of bilingual education programs in existence that makes simple generalization difficult and dangerous. For example, the social and cultural ethos surrounding such programs is one major variation. Another variation is the nature of students in such programs and the variety of language intake within such programs. For example, some bilingual education programs start with children at a similar level of language skills. In other classrooms, there are various language and second language abilities, rendering classroom teaching more difficult.

A **criticism** of Willig's (1985) meta-analysis is that it only included 23 studies. An international review of the bilingual educational effectiveness studies could have included many more studies and provided more generalizable conclusions. Further criticisms of Willig (1985) are given in a response by Keith Baker (1987); this includes a discussion of the relationship of meta-analysis to government policy regarding bilingual education. While there are disagreements about the various reviews of US evaluation studies of bilingual education, there is a consensus that more technically sophisticated and policy related research is required to make more rational decisions of educational policy, provision and practice for language minority children in the United States and beyond. One example follows:

Recent Research

Some major US research is now described to exemplify the problems of limited focus evaluations of bilingual education, as well as to exemplify some recent trends in research findings. An eight year, congressionally mandated, four and a half million dollar **longitudinal study of bilingual education** in the US compared Structured English 'Immersion', Early Exit and Late Exit Bilingual Education Programs (Ramirez, Yuen & Ramey, 1991; Ramirez, 1992). (The term 'Immersion' is not used in the original Canadian sense — English Submersion is more accurate.) Dual-Language or other forms of 'strong' bilingual education were not evaluated. The focus was only on 'weak' forms of bilingual education. The programs compared 'have the same instructional goals, the acquisition of English language skills so that the language-minority child can succeed in an English only mainstream classroom' (Ramirez, Yuen & Ramey, 1991: 1).

Over 2300 Spanish speaking students from 554 kindergarten to sixth grade classrooms in New York, New Jersey, Florida, Texas and California were studied. Ramirez & Merino (1990) examined the **processes** of bilingual education classrooms. The language of the classrooms were radically different in Grades 1 and 2:

- 'Structured Immersion' (Submersion) contained almost 100% English language.
- Early Exit Transitional Bilingual Education contained around two-thirds English and one third Spanish.
- Late Exit Transitional Bilingual Education moved from three quarters Spanish in Grade 1 to a little over half Spanish in Grade 2.

As a generalization, the outcomes were different for the three types of bilingual education. By the end of the third grade, Mathematics, Language and English reading skills were not particularly different between the three programs. By the sixth grade, **Late Exit Transitional Bilingual Education** students were performing higher at Mathematics, English Language and English reading than other programs. Parental involvement appears to be greatest in the late exit transitional programs. Although Spanish language achievement was measured in the research, these results were not included in the final statistical analyses.

One **conclusion** reached by Ramirez, Yuen & Ramey (1991) was that Spanish speaking students 'can be provided with substantial amounts of primary language instruction without impeding their acquisition of English language and reading skills' (p. 39). When language minority students are given instruction in their home language, this 'does not interfere with or delay their acquisition of English language skills, but helps them to 'catch-up' to their English speaking peers in English language arts, English reading and math. In contrast, providing LEP students with almost exclusive instruction in English does not accelerate their acquisition of English language arts, reading or math, i.e., they do not appear to be 'catching-up.' The data suggest that by Grade 6, students provided with English-only instruction may actually fall further behind their English speaking peers. Data also document that learning a second language will take six or more years' (Ramirez, 1992: 1).

This is evidence to support 'strong' forms of bilingual education and support for the use of the native language as a teaching medium. The results also showed little difference between early exit and the English Immersion (Submersion) students. Opponents of bilingual education have used this result to argue for the relative administrative ease and less expensive mainstreaming (Submersion) of language minority students and for the over-riding desirability of Transitional Bilingual education (e.g. Baker, K., 1992). Cziko (1992: 12) neatly sums up the **ambiguity** of the conclusions, suggesting that the research: 'provides evidence both for and against bilingual education, or rather, *against* what bilingual education normally *is* and *for* what it could be'.

A series of reviews and **criticisms** of the Ramirez, Yuen & Ramey (1991) research followed (e.g. Cazden, 1992; Meyer & Fienberg, 1992; Thomas, 1992) with particular emphasis on the following:

- The benefits of 'strong' forms of bilingual education programs are not considered (e.g. Two Way bilingual education; Heritage Language education). This makes statements about bilingual education based on an incomplete range of possibilities (Cummins, 1992b). Mainstream classrooms with English Second Language (ESL) pull-out (withdrawal) classes — widely implemented in the US — were also not included in the study (Rossell, 1992).
- The range of variables used to measure 'success' is narrow. For example, language minority parents may expect attitudinal, self esteem, cultural and ethnic heritage goals to be examined as a measure of successful outcomes (Dolson & Meyer, 1992).

- The considerable differences that exist within bilingual education programs (let alone comparing differing types of bilingual education program) makes comparisons and conclusions most difficult (Meyer & Fienberg, 1992). Also, the complexity of organization within a school, the ethos and varying classroom practices makes categorization of schools into watertight bilingual education programs formidable (Willig & Ramírez, 1993).
- The National Academy of Sciences reviewed this (and other) studies and concluded that the design of the study was ill-suited to answer key policy questions (Meyer & Fienberg, 1992; US Department of Education, 1992). More clarity in the aims and goals of bilingual education in the US is needed before research can be appropriately focused. Currently, the goals for bilingual education in the US are implicit and not defined.
- There is a lack of data to support the long term benefits of late exit transitional programs over other programs (Baker, K., 1992).

Expert Overviews of the Effectiveness of Bilingual Education

One inadequacy in bilingual education research is the relative absence of **public opinion** surveys. We lack the evidence for the amount of parental and public support that exists for different forms of bilingual education in various countries where bilingual education is a political and educational issue. Parents and children are rarely asked about their degree of satisfaction with bilingual education during or after the experience. There is a paucity of information about the democratic wishes of language minorities in the US. What does the US public think about bilingual education? What are the varieties of opinion and viewpoint expressed? How do different forms of bilingual education in the eyes of clients and consumers satisfy their wants and wishes? Is the debate only between politicians and liberal academics? Are there Hispanics who prefer assimilation via bilingual education and are there US academics who have a reasoned argument against bilingual education? There is a danger that we deal with bilingual education controversies without fairly or fully representing the varied viewpoints of public, politicians and policy makers. Rarely have the present or future clientele or the general public been asked their opinions on the aims and nature of bilingual education.

An exception is Huddy & Sears (1990) who 'telephone' interviewed a US national sample of 1170 in 1983. They found that while the majority tended to be favorable towards bilingual education, a substantial minority (around a quarter of respondents, depending on the specific question) who included well-informed respondents, opposed bilingual education particularly on the integration issue.

While public opinion surveys are infrequent, **expert opinion** is more likely to be privately or publicly sought. Following the various narrative reviews of research on bilingual education and Willig's (1985) meta-analysis, there followed an expert overview in the US. The United States Committee on Education and Labor asked the General Accounting Office (1987) to conduct a study on whether or not the research evidence on bilingual education supported the current government preference for assimilationist, transitional bilingual education. The General Accounting Office (1987) therefore decided to conduct a survey of experts on bilingual education. Ten experts were assembled, mostly professors of education, selected from prestigious institutions throughout the United States. Each expert was provided with a set of questions to answer in written form. The experts were asked to compare research findings with central political statements made about such research. The purpose was to verify the veracity of official statements.

In terms of learning English, eight out of ten experts favored using the native or heritage language in the classroom. They believed that progress in the native language aided children in learning English because it strengthened literacy skills which easily transferred to operating in the second language. With the learning of other subjects in the curriculum, six experts supported the use of heritage languages in such teaching. However, it was suggested that learning English is important in making academic progress (General Accounting Office, 1987).

That all the experts did not agree was to be expected. The group of ten had diverse research backgrounds and perspectives. Eight were knowledgeable about language learning and schooling for language minority children. Two were expert on social science accumulation and synthesis (meta-analysis). These ten people were also sent ten literary reviews to examine with the detailed questionnaire. The experts worked individually; they were not brought together for an overall discussion to produce a consensus opinion. When the experts had submitted their written report, they were given an opportunity to clarify and correct the General Accounting Office's Report to Congress of their views. Also, an outside evaluation expert reviewed the written responses of the experts, as well as the draft text, to check on the accuracy of the representation of the experts' views.

The key question is whether a different group or groups of ten experts would produce different conclusions. Experts tend to disagree amongst themselves. This tends to reflect the developing nature of research in this area and the complexity and political nature of what makes a particular school or program work successfully or not. One problem is the effect of interacting factors with different types of bilingual education. For example, the characteristics of the student, their parents and the community each serve to make a program, school or child more or less successful. The degree of parental interest and involvement in bilingual education is sometimes seen as an important intervening variable. Also, the status of the heritage language in the community and the country may affect the success of a bilingual education program. If the analogy may stand, there are multitudinous ingredients that go in the educational recipe. Focusing purely on the language part of schooling (e.g. bilingual or monolingual education) only examines a narrow range of ingredients in the recipe. Complex reactions between ingredients mean that making simple statements about what works successfully or not is difficult.

One area on which seven out of the ten experts agreed was that evidence did not exist on the long term effects of various forms of bilingual education. Seven out of the ten firmly rejected the idea that there was support for connecting bilingual education, either positively or negatively, to long-term outcomes. This reveals that research on the effectiveness of bilingual education is still low down in the evolutionary process. In the experts' survey, four out of ten experts agreed that the literature on language learning did not allow generalizations to be drawn at this stage.

Having considered overviews of research on bilingual education, it is important to note one basic factor. There is likely to be a divergence of opinion about the aims of education and bilingual education. This difference of viewpoint will exist in both the academic and the non-academic outcomes of schooling. Some may emphasize English language skills, some attainment throughout the curriculum, some the importance of second and even third language learning. Others may focus on the non-academic outcomes of education such as moral and social skills, employment, drop-out rates, absenteeism and self-esteem. At societal level, there will also be a variety of aims. For some pluralism, biculturalism and multilingualism are a **desirable outcome**. For others the assimilation of minority languages, the integration of minorities within overall society are the important outcomes. This suggests that a definitive statement that bilingual education is more or less successful than, for example, mainstream education is impossible due to the variety of underlying values and beliefs that different interest groups have about education and the kind of future society desired.

Trueba (1989: 104) sums up the use of effectiveness studies by different interest groups for their own ends. 'It is unfortunate that bilingual education and other educational programs for minority students have become part of a political struggle between opposing groups. Educators and parents have been forced into political camps, and campaigned for or against these programs, without a thorough understanding of their instructional attributes and characteristics. Perhaps it would be easier to reach a consensus regarding the nature of sound pedagogical principles and practices rather than to continue to debate such politically loaded issues'.

ADVANCING THE EFFECTIVENESS OF BILINGUAL EDUCATION

Articles by Carter & Chatfield (1986), Lucas, Henze & Donato (1990), Baker (1990) and Cziko (1992) have suggested that the effectiveness of bilingual education question can be addressed from a different perspective. Bilingual education research can look at effectiveness at four different levels. First, there is the effectiveness at the level of the **individual child**. Within the same classroom, children may respond and perform differently. Second, there is effectiveness at the **classroom** level. Within the same school and type of bilingual education program, classrooms may vary considerably. It is important to analyze the factors connected with varying effectiveness at classroom level. Third, effectiveness is often analyzed at the **school** level. What makes some schools more effective than others even within the same **type of bilingual education program** and with similar student characteristics? Fourth, beyond the school level there can be aggregations of schools into different types of **programs** (e.g. transitional compared with heritage language programs) or into different geographical regions.

It is possible to look at effective bilingual education at each and all of these levels, and at the inter-relationship between these four levels. For example, at the individual level we need to know how bilingual education can best be effective for different social classes, and for children of different levels of 'intelligence' or ability. How do children with learning difficulties and specific language disorders fare in bilingual education (Cummins, 1984a)? At the classroom level, we need to know what teaching methods and classroom characteristics create optimally effective bilingual education. At the school level, the characteristics of staffing, the size of groups and the language composition of the school all need to be taken into account to find out where and when bilingual education is more and less successful.

Apart from individual classroom and school characteristics, the effectiveness of bilingual education can take into account the **social, political and cultural context** in which such education is placed. For example, the differences between being in a subtractive or additive context may affect the outcomes of bilingual education. The willingness of teachers to involve parents, and good relationships between the school and its community may be important in effective bilingual education. These different facets are included in the input-context–process-output model of bilingual education (see Chapter 18).

It is also important in bilingual education effectiveness research to examine a wide variety of **outcomes** from such education. Such variety may include examination results, tests of basic skills (e.g. oracy, literacy, numeracy), the broadest range of curriculum areas (e.g. science and technology, humanities, mathematics, languages, arts, physical, practical and theoretical pursuits, skills as well as knowledge). Non-cognitive outcomes are also important to include in an assessment of effectiveness. Such non-cognitive outcomes may include: attendance at school, attitudes, self concept and self esteem, social and emotional adjustment, employment and moral development.

The point behind such a comprehensive consideration of bilingual education is that effective bilingual education is not a simple or automatic consequence of using a child's home language in school (as in heritage language education) or a second language (as in immersion bilingual education). Various home and parental, community, teacher, school and society effects may act and interact to make bilingual education more or less effective. The relative importance of different ingredients and processes in various school and cultural contexts needs investigating to build a comprehensive and wide ranging theory of when, where, how and why bilingual education can be effective.

This approach to studying effectiveness of bilingual education not only considers the infrastructure of such education. It can also use the important studies from Britain and North America on **what makes a school effective** (Hallinger & Murphey, 1986; Mortimer *et al.*, 1988; Purkey & Smith, 1983; Reynolds, 1985; Smith & Tomlinson, 1989). For example, Mortimer *et al.* (1988) found that 12 factors were important in making a school effective. These may be listed as: purposeful leadership by the head teacher, involvement of the deputy head teacher, the degree of involvement of the teachers, consistency amongst teachers, having structured classroom sessions, providing intellectually challenging teaching, a work centered environment, a limited focus within sessions, maximum communication between teachers and students, good record keeping, plenty of parental involvement and a positive classroom atmosphere.

When the focus changes from school to **teacher effectiveness** when dealing with language minority students, certain elements appear important (Tikunoff, 1983; E. García, 1988, 1991). These include:

(1) Teachers having high expectations of their students. Teachers being committed to the educational success of their students and serving as student advocates.
(2) Teachers displaying a sense of confidence in their ability to be successful with language minority students.
(3) Teachers communicating directions clearly, pacing lessons appropriately, involving students in decisions, monitoring students' progress and providing immediate feedback.
(4) Teachers using students' native language for instruction; alternating between languages in a compartmentalized way to ensure clarity and understanding but without translating.
(5) Teachers integrating aspects of a student's home culture and values into classroom activity to build trust and self-esteem as well as promoting cultural diversity and cultural pluralism. Teachers involving parents in their student's learning and activities in the classroom.
(6) Teachers promoting a curriculum that has coherence, balance, breadth, relevance, progression and continuity.
(7) Teachers organizing instruction to utilize collaborative instructional techniques. Students interacting with students in clearly explained, focused and meaningful activities.
(8) Teachers placing no undue pressure on students to proceed from literacy in the home to the second language (e.g. Spanish to English literacy).

An example of research into **bilingual education effectiveness** is a case study by Lucas, Henze & Donato (1990) in six schools in California and Arizona. This research revealed eight features seemingly important in promoting the success of language minority students.

(1) **Value and status were given to the language minority students language and culture**. While English literacy was a major goal, native language skills were celebrated, encouraged inside and outside the formal curriculum and flagged as an advantage rather than a liability.
(2) **High expectations of language minority students were prevalent**. Apart from strategies to motivate students and recognize their achievement, individualized support of language minority students was available. The provision of counseling, co-operation with parents and the hiring of language minority staff in leadership positions to act as role models were some of the ploys to raise expectations of success at school.
(3) **School leaders gave the education of language minority students a relatively high priority**. This included good awareness of curriculum approaches to language minority children and communicating this to the staff. Strong leadership, the will-

ingness to hire bilingual teachers and high expectations of such students were also part of the repertoire of such leaders.

(4) **Staff development was designed to help all the staff effectively serve language minority students**. For example, the teachers were provided with staff development programs which sensitized them to students' language and cultural background, increased their knowledge of second language acquisition and of effective curriculum approaches in teaching language minority students.

(5) **A variety of courses for language minority students was offered**. Such courses included English as a second language and first language courses. Small class sizes (e.g. 20–25) were created to maximize interaction.

(6) **A Counseling program was available**. Counselors were able to speak the students' home language, could give post-secondary opportunity advice and monitored the success of the language minority students.

(7) **Parents of language minority children were encouraged to become involved in their children's education**. This included parents' meetings, contact with teachers and counselors, telephone contact and neighborhood meetings.

(8) **School staff were committed to the empowerment of language minority students through education**. Such commitment was realized through extra curricula activities, participation in community activities, interest in developing their pedagogic skills and interest in the political process of improving the lot of language minority students.

CONCLUSION

This chapter has examined the development of studies which have investigated whether bilingual education is more or less effective than monolingual education. It has also examined studies which look at the relative effectiveness of different forms of bilingual education. Having considered the historical origins and the nature of different forms of bilingual education, the chapter has sought to portray how questions about the effectiveness of bilingual education have evolved. The initial studies examined individual programs and schools. A wide variety of different outcomes and conclusions resulted. Following this first stage, the second stage reviewed the voluminous research. This stage continues to the present. Reviews of Canadian immersion education, heritage language education throughout the world, reviews of United States research by government officials and by meta-analysis produced differing conclusions.

If there is a tentative overall pattern to the research, it would seem to be supportive of early total immersion education for children whose first language is a majority language. The tentative conclusion also is that maintenance or heritage language education has advantages for language minority children. Public opinion on such matters tends to be divided about the effectiveness of bilingual education. This reveals the political undertones of discussion about different forms of bilingual education.

However, one of the conclusions that comes from this chapter may be that simple questions give simplistic answers. We cannot expect a simple answer to the question of whether or not bilingual education is more or less effective than mainstream education. The question itself needs to become more refined. It needs to look at the different conditions under which different forms of bilingual education become more or less successful. This means departing from simple studies and simple results to broad investigations that include a wide variety of different conditions and situations. The scales of justice of bilingual education cannot give a simple verdict. The evidence is wide and complex; witnesses have complex accounts and arguments. There is no simple right or wrong, good and bad; no simple orthodoxy of approach that can be guaranteed to give success.

It has been suggested that the effectiveness of bilingual education needs to consider children, teachers, the community, the school itself and type of program. One particular factor cannot be isolated from another. We need to consider a whole variety of ingredients at the same time, all of which make for a more or less successful recipe. Children have a wide variety of characteristics which need investigating. Children cannot be isolated from the classroom characteristics within which they work. Within the classroom there are a variety of factors which may make for a more or less effective education. Outside the classroom the different attributes of schools may in their turn interact with children and their classrooms to make education for language minority children more or less effective. Outside the school is the important effect of community. The social, cultural milieu and political environment in which a school works will affect the education of language minority children at all levels.

The key issue becomes 'what are the optimal conditions for children who are either bilingual, becoming bilingual or wish to be bilingual?' Answers about optimal condition questions may involve a complex set of conditions. Rather than a simple black and white sketch, a complex multicolored canvas may need to be painted.

SUGGESTED FURTHER READING

ARIAS, M. and CASANOVA, U. (eds) 1993, *Bilingual Education: Politics, Practice, Research*. Chicago: National Society for the Study of Education/University of Chicago Press.

BAETENS BEARDSMORE, H. (ed.) 1993, *European Models of Bilingual Education*. Clevedon: Multilingual Matters.

CAZDEN, C.B. and SNOW, C.E. 1990, *English Plus: Issues in Bilingual Education. (The Annals of the American Academy of Political and Social Science 508, March 1990)*. London: Sage.

CUMMINS, J. and DANESI, M. 1990, *Heritage Languages. The Development and Denial of Canada's Linguistic Resources*. Toronto: Our Schools/Ourselves Education Foundation & Garamond Press.

HELLER, M. 1994, *Crosswords: Language, Education and Ethnicity in French*. Ontario & New York: Mouton de Gruyter.

GARCÍA, O. and BAKER, C. (eds) 1995, *Policy and Practice in Bilingual Education: A Reader Extending the Foundations*. Clevedon: Multilingual Matters. (Sections 1 & 2).

SWAIN, M. and LAPKIN, S. 1982, *Evaluating Bilingual Education: A Canadian Case Study*. Clevedon: Multilingual Matters.

REVIEW AND STUDY QUESTIONS

(1) Write short revision notes on the following:
  (i) The reasons why individual researches vary in their findings.
  (ii) What are the main findings from (a) Canadian Immersion research studies, (b) Heritage Language/Developmental Maintenance, (c) Baker and de Kanter's review, and (d) Ramirez, Yuen & Ramey's (1991) research.
(2) What are the differences between Canadian and United States contexts in the study of bilingual education effectiveness? Are there similarities in their research results? Explain why there are differences.
(3) List those factors which seem to make bilingual education more or less effective. Using a rating scale (e.g. very important to very unimportant), rate the importance to unimportance of these different factors.
(4) How do different approaches to bilingual education reflect different values among various groups of people?

STUDY ACTIVITIES

(1) Read the Lucas *et al.* (1990) article in the *Harvard Educational Review*. Write a summary in approximately 600 words of that article. List those effectiveness factors which you think are part of any form of education, and list separately those which you think are solely concerned with the language part of bilingual education. Are there other factors which you think are important in effectiveness not mentioned in this article? Discuss in a group what are the priorities in producing bilingual children through formal education.
(2) Make a list of 'effectiveness factors' from your reading. Following observation in one or more classrooms, consider the effectiveness of these classrooms against this list. What factors seem, as the result of your classroom observation, to be more and less important?
(3) Using the same list of 'effectiveness factors', study one program in your area (e.g. transitional bilingual education). What features of that program are effective and less than effective due to the aims and nature of that program?
(4) Collect together newspaper clippings about language in schools within your area. Try to find different attitudes in these clippings. Different newspapers may report the same story in different ways. Collect together these different interpretations and try to give an explanation of the variation.
(5) Sit with the group of children or in a formal class of children, and attempt to time how much children and the teacher spend using each language in the classroom. Try to work out over two or three sessions how much time is spent in either language. When recording, try to locate which language is being used for what purpose. For example, what language is used for classroom instructions, classroom management, discipline, questions, on-task and off-task talk among children, greetings, rewards and reinforcement.

(6) With a partner or in a small group, prepare a two minute television interview sequence on bilingual education. Locate questions which are important and likely to be of concern to the public. Prepare short punchy answers to these questions.

(7) Arrange a debate among students where two people support 'weak' forms of bilingual education, two support 'strong' forms. Present the arguments for two major kinds of bilingual education, highlighting those which are most important in your region. Allow other students to ask questions of the four presenters.

CHAPTER 12

Language Development and Language Allocation in Bilingual Education Settings

Introduction

Language Development at School

Language Allocation in Bilingual Classrooms

Bilingualism, Deaf and
Hearing Impaired People

Conclusion

CHAPTER 12

Language Development and Language Allocation in Bilingual Education Settings

INTRODUCTION

This chapter begins by examining the aims and goals of schools in the first language development of bilinguals. Schools often play a major role in the maintenance and development of home language oracy, literacy and cultural awareness. When two languages are used in the school, boundaries between the majority and minority language may be necessary. The chapter therefore examines strategies for the separation of two languages in a school. It also discusses dual language integration in the curriculum.

The chapter finishes with a special group of bilinguals who form their own language minority: deaf people. Often a neglected language minority, it will be demonstrated that many of the attributes of hearing bilinguals are shared by deaf bilinguals. Different views about deaf bilinguals are presented, followed by the debate about the kind of bilingual education valuable for deaf students.

LANGUAGE DEVELOPMENT AT SCHOOL

For bilingual children, the **school** is usually an **essential agent** in developing the home, native, heritage language. When a child enters kindergarten or elementary school, first language development needs to be formally addressed, irrespective of whether that child has age-appropriate competency or not in the home language. While first language development throughout schooling is important for majority and minority language children, the minority context places extra reasons for careful nurturance of a minority language.

Two quotes from a historically influential and important report by **UNESCO** (1953) entitled *'The Use of Vernacular Languages in Education'* provide the basis for the use of the home language in school, where possible:

> 'It is axiomatic that the best medium for teaching a child is his mother tongue. Psychologically, it is the system of meaningful signs that in his mind works automatically for expression and understanding. Sociologically, it is a means of identification among the members of the community to which he belongs. Educationally, he learns more quickly through it than through an unfamiliar linguistic medium. But as was said earlier, it is not always possible to use the mother tongue in school and, even when possible, some factors may impede or condition its use.' (p. 11)

> 'It is important that every effort should be made to provide education in the mother tongue... On educational grounds we recommend that the use of the mother tongue be extended to as late a stage in education as possible. In particular, pupils should begin their schooling through the medium of the mother tongue, because they understand it best and because to begin their school life in the mother tongue will make the break between home and school as small as possible.' (pp. 47–48)

The relative status, nationally and internationally, of the minority language, the Anglophone nature of most mass media, and the dominance of 'common denominator' majority languages outside the school requires special **attention** to the continual evolution and progression of the minority language in school. Language minority children sometimes start school speaking a different form of their heritage language compared with monolinguals. For example, Greek and Bengali speaking five year old children in London will not tend to speak the same form of Greek and Bengali as those from Greece and Bangladesh. Nor do they usually speak English in the same way as English monolingual Londoners. In the US, many Latino children speak Spanish unlike their monolingual counterparts, and speak English unlike those from English monolingual homes.

To preserve and reproduce the minority language in the young, a 'strong' form of bilingual education (that supports the heritage language) needs to include a 'first language' program with explicit language aims and goals. Such a program may involve lessons devoted to that language (e.g. Spanish listening, speaking, writing and reading development). It may also valuably involve a strategy for heritage **language development across the curriculum** (Corson, 1990a). Where children take lessons (e.g. Social Studies, Science) through the medium of their home language, language development in those curriculum areas can be overtly and consciously fostered. A child's home language develops when it is cultivated, encouraged and promoted in a purposeful way in all curriculum areas.

The benefits for a well developed home (minority) language spread to the learning of a second or third language. As Swain & Lapkin (1991a) found in research, those students **literate in their heritage language** progressed significantly more in written and oral French than those without such skills. First language heritage language literacy, in particular, enables relative ease of learning (and learning through) a second language by the transfer of knowledge, language abilities (e.g. literacy strategies, communication skills) and learning processes.

With respect to **learning a third language**, there is belief that bilinguals are relatively better at learning a new language than monolinguals, and the few studies that exist tend (although not unequivocally) to support this assertion (Bild & Swain, 1989; Cenoz & Valencia, 1994; Genesee & Lambert, 1983; Hurd, 1993; Mägiste, 1984; Ringbom, 1985; Saif & Sheldon, 1969; Swain, Lapkin, Rowen & Hart, 1990; Thomas, 1988). Cenoz & Valencia's (1994) conducted a study in the Basque country of 320 seventeen to nineteen year old students. They found that the English language achievement of bilingual students (Spanish and Basque) was higher than monolingual Spanish speakers. This result was found when other influential factors (intelligence, motivation, age and length of exposure to English) were taken into account. Bilingualism, in and by itself, appears to give an advantage in learning a third language. One explanation for this result is the greater metalinguistic awareness of bilinguals and their possible greater sensitivity to communication (see Chapter 8). Another explanation may be in the transfer between languages of phonological (sound system) and pragmatic (communication) abilities (Verhoeven, 1994). This is predicted in Cummins' (1986b) interdependence hypothesis that suggests such a transfer between languages.

Speaking and Listening

What areas of first language development need to be cultivated in language minority children? One set of teaching and learning targets for language minority children (whose first language is Welsh) comes from the National Curriculum in Wales (Department of Education and Science and the Welsh Office, 1990). These targets or language goals are somewhere in between wide and general **curriculum aims** and not so specific and fragmented as behavioral objectives. The attainment targets are illustrated in summarized form below.

The Attainment of Skills, Knowledge and Understanding in Speaking and Listening

LEVEL 1 (Approximate Age 4 & 5)

- Participate as a speaker and listener in group activities including imaginative play, (e.g. play the role of shopkeeper or a customer in a class shop).
- Listen attentively and respond to stories and poems, (e.g. re-tell a story, enact a poem, or draw a picture to illustrate a story or poem).
- Respond appropriately to simple instructions given by a teacher (e.g. follow two consecutive instructions, or choose two flowers from the tray and draw pictures of them).

LEVEL 2 (Approximate Age 6 & 7)

- Participate as a speaker and listener in a group engaged in a given task, (e.g. compose a story in a group).
- Describe a real or imagined event to the teacher or another pupil (e.g. tell the listener about something which happened at home).

- Listen attentively to stories and poems, and talk about them (e.g. state likes and dislikes about a story or poem).
- Talk with the teacher, listen, ask and answer questions (e.g. talk to the teacher about events in or out of school).
- Respond appropriately to complex instructions by the teacher, and give simple instructions (e.g. follow three consecutive actions such as: list three places where a flower will grow best in the classroom; find out the views of others in the classroom, and reach a consensus viewpoint).

LEVEL 3 (Approximate Age 8 & 9)

- Relate real or imaginary events in a connected narrative which convey meaning to a group of pupils, or the teacher or another known adult (e.g. tell a story with a beginning, middle and an ending).
- Convey accurately a simple message (e.g. relay a simple telephone message).
- Listen with an increased span of concentration to other children and adults, asking and responding to questions and commenting on what is being said (e.g. listen to a new topic and discuss).
- Give, receive and follow accurately precise instructions when pursuing a task as an individual or as a member of a group (e.g. plan a wall display or arrange an outing together).

LEVEL 4 (Approximate Age 10 & 11)

- Give a detailed oral account of an event, or something that has been learned in the classroom, or explain with reasons why a particular course of action has been taken (e.g. report orally on a scientific investigation).
- Ask and respond to questions in a range of situations with increasing confidence (e.g. conduct an interview on radio devised with other pupils).
- Take part as a speaker and listener in a group discussion or activity, expressing a personal view and commenting constructively on what is being discussed or experienced (e.g. contribute to the planning and implementation of a group activity).
- Participate in a presentation (e.g. co-operate in describing the outcome of a group activity).

Level 5 (approximate age 11 to 13), Level 6 (approximate age 12 to 14) and Levels 7 to 10 (approximate age 14 to 16) also contain attainment targets that highlight: participating in and listening attentively to group discussion; arguing and persuading by reasoning; effective oral presentation; expressing both opinions and counter-opinions in a well organized way; leading a group discussion; summarizing a discussion in a balanced manner; discussion of vocabulary (e.g. borrowings from English); regional variations; personal research using the minority language (e.g. conducting an interview survey on the street).

In addition to listening and speaking attainment targets, the National Curriculum specifies **reading and writing targets** for Welsh first language speakers. However, the inter-relationship and merger between the four language skills (listening, speaking, reading and writing) may be prominent in a successful 'language' classroom. Integration rather than separation of the four language skills is more customary and advantageous. A flavor of these reading and writing targets is now presented, illustrated from the Welsh (as a first language) National Curriculum (Department of Education and Science and The Welsh Office, 1990).

Reading

At **Level 1** (age approximately 4 & 5), students should be able to appreciate that print conveys meaning, begin to recognize the alphabet and a few words (e.g. their own and friends' names), enjoy picking up a book, looking at the pictures and pretending to read a book sequentially.

At **Level 2** (age approximately 6 & 7), students develop sight-reading skills, initially using pictures to help understanding and anticipation, begin to read semi-independently, recognize words in different contexts, talk about the stories and poems they have read (e.g. relate a story, guess what comes next in a story) to show understanding.

At **Level 3** (age approximately 8 & 9), students are expected to read in an independent and self-motivated manner, to read to a group of friends with suitable colorful expression, talk in detail about the plot, characters, context and ideas of a book.

At **Level 4** (age approximately 10 & 11), students should be reading a variety of books, including fiction, non-fiction and poetry, being openly aware of their favorite type of books, find information in encyclopedias, indexes, content lists, databases, catalogs, dictionaries, describing and analyzing a relatively complex plot and show awareness of rhyme and rhythm.

Language targets at **Levels 5 to 10** (age approximately 11 to 16) include differentiating between fact and opinion, cause and effect in a novel; reading a variety of print (e.g. magazines, reference works, archive material) to form a synthesis; responding personally and creatively to stories, drama and poetry; discuss the language register, dialect, imagery, atmosphere and style of different texts; recognizing devices to indoctrinate and persuade (e.g. advertising); analyzing the relationship between print and graphics, and evaluating critically.

Writing

At **Level 1** (age approximately 4 & 5), students should start distinguishing between pictures and handwriting, numbers and letters; start to associate written letters with sounds, and write their own names and simple words.

At **Level 2** (age approximately 6 & 7), students will write short passages, often referring to personal experiences, in their own words. Sentencing will begin to evolve as will sense of sequencing. Written vocabulary will develop alongside spelling and punctuation.

At **Level 3** (age approximately 8 & 9), students are expected to write passages that convey feelings, are more expressive, use more characterization, punctuate correctly (e.g.

capital letters, full stops, question marks), plus use a word-processor to draft and re-draft work to edit out mistakes and improve content.

At **Level 4** (age approximately 10 & 11), students should write in different forms (e.g. diary, letter, report, story, poetry), express opinions and thoughts in print, begin to summarize information, write with different readers and audiences in mind, paragraph correctly, discuss their writing with peers and re-draft to improve content and communication, and use correct tenses consistently.

At **Levels 5 to 10** (age approximately 11 to 16), the development in writing skills is expected to include: writing small plays conveying tension and conflict; writing dramatic and descriptive poetry; developing a logical, well reasoned sequence of points and defending a viewpoint; writing clear instructions and explaining a process in detail; describing unfamiliar and imaginary situations in authentic detail; avoiding stilted, uniform writing, using variety in simple, compound and complex sentences; using metaphors and similes; conveying opinions clearly on controversial topics and writing persuasive prose; integration of narrative and conversation; awareness of writing for different social contexts: writing announcements and questionnaires, writing for a community newspaper, a report on a TV program, or a football or basketball game, writing up a project, reporting to the police on a road accident; an awareness of regional language variations and dialects; developing a recognizable personal style of writing.

Cultural Awareness

While the four basic language skills are important in first language development, a language taught without its attendant culture is like presenting a body without a heart. Language and culture are entwined in the healthy functioning of a body. Therefore, **developing heritage cultural awareness** and multiculturalism alongside first language teaching is an important element in language minority education.

Classroom activities to foster minority culture awareness can include: performing social conventions; cultural rituals and traditions using authentic visual and written materials; discussing cultural variations (e.g. the colorful kaleidoscope of Latin American dances, festivals, customs and traditions); identifying the varying experiences and perspectives of the particular language variety (e.g. of French Canadians, of the French majority in France, of bilinguals in France (e.g. Bretons, Provencal); classroom visits by native speakers of the language for 'question and answer' sessions.

In Wales, **developing a cultural awareness** about Wales is contained in the concept of the '*Curriculum Cymreig*' that endeavors to reflect the whole range of historical, social, cultural, political and environmental influences that have shaped contemporary Wales. This involves giving students a sense of place and heritage, of belonging to the local and a wider community with its own traditions, access to the literature of Wales, differences and traditions in use of the Welsh and English languages, the distinctive nature of Welsh music, arts, crafts, technology, religious beliefs and practices (ACAC, 1993). There is a clear emphasis on developing heritage cultural awareness in Mathematics, Science and Technology and not just in Humanities and Aesthetic areas. For example, students study

William Jones (1675–1749), a mathematician from Llanfihangel Tre'r' Beirdd who first used the 'pi (π) symbol and Robert Recorde (died 1558) a mathematician from Tenby who devised the 'equals' (=) symbol. In Science, children discuss local soil samples and how they connect with local farming and agriculture, coal and slate mining that have been important to the Welsh economy, local small industries, and working from home via computer and communication networks. Some of this involves cross-curricular activity.

It is sometimes argued that a minority language must be fostered to **preserve the attendant culture**. The opposite is also tenable. The attendant culture must be fostered in the classroom to preserve the minority language. While separation of culture and language is false, minority language culture can be weakly or strongly represented in the classroom and in the whole ethos of the school. Such culture may be incidentally taught with little intent or rationale. Alternatively, such culture may be consciously included in language teaching and the overall physical and psychological environment of the school. This is particularly valuable to encourage participation by children in their heritage culture. Language skills in the minority language are no guarantee of continued use of that language into teens and adulthood. Enculturation therefore becomes essential if that language is to be useful and used.

To foster a minority language in school without fostering its attendant culture may be to fund a costly life-support machine attached to a dying organism. To promote the attendant culture alongside minority language teaching may be to give a life-preserving injection to that language and culture.

When the minority language and culture is fostered in the school, the majority language is also usually developed. This raises an important question. How should these two languages be allocated in the curriculum? Can both languages be used to transmit content? What boundaries are needed between languages? These questions about bilingual methodology are now considered.

LANGUAGE ALLOCATION IN BILINGUAL CLASSROOMS

Introduction

Apart from teaching the curriculum in the first language or, as in submersion education, solely in the second language, there are a wide variety of possibilities in using two languages in the curriculum. One example is the immersion strategy, for example in Canada, where majority language children are educated through the medium of their second language, but where their first language is gradually used in the curriculum. Immersion education is considered in detail in Chapter 17.

The purpose of this section is to look at different dimensions of 'how and when' two languages can be (1) separated and (2) integrated in bilingual classrooms. The initial focus will be the **separation** of languages within the curriculum. For example, when two languages are assigned to different areas of the curriculum, the intention is usually to establish clear **boundaries** between the use of those languages in the curriculum. In the second part of this section, an examination will be made of the more integrated or concurrent use of two languages. For example, a teacher may repeat an explanation in a different language. The concluding part of this section will examine the problems and limitations of the concurrent use of two languages in the classroom.

There are different reasons for separating or sometimes integrating languages in bilingual classrooms. **First**, if the purpose of bilingual education is to obtain language shift towards the majority language (e.g. transitional bilingual education), integrating languages may be preferable to separation. When there is integration and no strong boundaries between languages, the majority language is expected to develop as the minority language diminishes. **Second**, if the purpose of bilingual education is to maintain and develop the minority language, separation may be important. Classroom activity needs to create a distinct space and time for minority language usage across much of the curriculum. Clear boundaries for using the minority language, and separately using the majority language, need establishing. Without boundaries and separation, the majority language may be increasingly used to the cost of the minority language.

However, **thirdly**, if a strategic integration of languages in a class (e.g. where students are competent in both languages) gives higher student performance in science, mathematics, humanities and the arts than language separation, a concurrent use of two languages may be valued. For example, if a strategy of the teacher transmitting a concept in Spanish followed by a written activity in English reinforced and better assimilated that concept, concurrent use of languages may be desirable.

An example of a school situation where a decision about language methodology is necessary or desirable is a **mixed language classroom**. Where there is a mixture of, for example, Spanish first language speakers and English first language speakers in two way education, a clear policy and practice in language allocation is required. Where children in linguistically mixed classrooms have different levels of ability in two languages, as well as different levels of ability in tackling the curriculum, a bilingual methodology may be essential. In Wales, a class may contain children who are relative beginners in Welsh (e.g. recent in-migrants), those with some second language Welsh fluency, and native Welsh speakers. Some native Welsh speakers will be fluent in English, others may have more competence in Welsh than English. A school that aims to achieve a high standard of ability in both languages will need to consider the use and allocation of languages in classrooms and across the curriculum.

Language Separation

In the allocation of two languages in the classroom and in the curriculum, the need for **distinct separation and clear boundaries** between two languages has often been advocated. First, such separation has support from the sociolinguists who argue that, for a minority language to survive, it must have separate and distinct uses in society. In the discussion of diglossia, maintaining a relatively stable societal arrangement for the separate use of two languages was presented as important in minority language survival. Therefore, the argument has been in schools that, for a minority language to have purpose and strength, it must have a distinct language allocation in transmitting the curriculum.

Second, from child development research with bilinguals, it has often been argued that the 'one parent, one language' situation is one of the most effective patterns enabling childhood bilingualism to occur. If the mother speaks one language and the father another language, there is a distinct separation of languages. The child will therefore learn to speak one language to one parent, another language to the other parent. Such separation tends to result in the successful development of both languages within the very young child because there are distinct boundaries between the languages and a separate reception and production of language. Thus, an argument is that effective bilingual schools should find ways of mirroring language separation in such 'one parent, one language' homes by establishing **boundaries between languages**. What can constitute boundaries will be examined in detail later.

Third, a constant problem in many minority language situations is the development of an **unstable codemixing** among adults as well as children. Derogatory terms such as 'Spanglish' (for a mixture of Spanish and English) and 'Wenglish' (for a mixture of Welsh and English) highlight the concern of minority language preservationists about codemixing. The random mixing of languages within sentences and across sentences can be a half-way house, indicating a movement away from a minority language towards the majority language. Therefore, educationists have often argued for the importance of separation of languages within the school. This is particularly to strengthen and maintain the purity and integrity of a minority language.

Having established three bases for language separation in the classroom and curriculum, we will now consider **how** languages can be separated. There are eight non-independent dimensions along which the separation of languages can occur in school settings. These will now be considered in turn:

Subject or Topic

In elementary schools and high schools, different curriculum areas may be taught in different languages. For example, Language, Arts, Social Studies, Religious Education, Art, Music and Physical Education may be taught through the minority language (e.g. Spanish in the US; Filipino in the Philippines). Math, Science, Technology and Computer Studies may be taught through the majority language (e.g. English). Certain curriculum areas are reserved for one language, other curriculum areas for the second language. In kindergartens and elementary schools, the allocation may be by topic rather than subject. For example, a project on 'Conservation' may be through the minority language, a project on 'weather' through the majority language.

The examples given so far reveal 'content sensitive' issues. That is, there is sometimes a call for arts and humanities culture to be relayed through the minority language, with Science and Technology relayed in an international majority language. Curriculum areas such as History and Geography are often regarded as best reflecting the heritage and culture of a language group. In contrast, Science and Technology may be seen as international, and dominated by the English language. The **danger** is that the minority language becomes associated with tradition and history rather than with technology and science. The minority language is thereby allocated a lower status and seen as much less relevant to modern existence. The danger may be that the minority language will be seen as irrelevant in computer communications, with a view that Science is white, western and mostly English in language.

Person

The use of two languages in a school may be separated according to person. Just as in some homes there is the 'one parent, one language' system, so different school staff may be identified with different languages. For example, there may be two teachers working in a team teaching situation. One teacher communicates with the children through the majority language, the other teacher through the children's minority language. There is a clear language boundary established by person. Alternatively, teachers' assistants, parents helping in the classroom, auxiliaries and paraprofessionals may function in the classroom as an alternative but separate language source for the children.

Time

A frequently used strategy in language allocation in schools is for classes to operate at different times in different languages. For example, in some dual language schools, one day may be through Spanish, the next day through English. Other schools alternate by half days. The morning may be in Spanish, the afternoon in English, the next day reversing that situation. A third alternative is for different lessons to be allocated to different languages. This overlaps with the idea of separation by subject and topic.

The separation of time need not be solely in terms of days, half-days or lessons. It may be also in terms of whole weeks or whole months or whole semesters. It also may valuably include a policy that varies by grade and age. For example, children may be taught through the minority language for the first two or three years of elementary education for 100% of time. Over Grades 3 to 7, an increasing amount of time may be allocated to the majority language inside the school.

Place

A lesser used means of language separation in the classroom is via different physical locations for different languages. For example, if there are two Science laboratories in the school, one may be labeled as a Spanish speaking laboratory, the other the English speaking laboratory. In Canadian immersion schools, students may have different classrooms for French and English lessons, imitating the principle of territorial diglossia. The children are expected to speak the language of that laboratory when entering it. The assumption is that a physical location provides enough cues and clues to prompt the child to adhere to different languages in different places. In reality, the teacher and other students may be more crucial in influencing the choice of language. Location is however, a valuable 'extra' in encouraging language segregation.

A consideration of 'place' in language allocation needs to include all areas of the school. During morning and afternoon breaks, lunch-breaks, religious services and announcements, music and drama events, games and sports, the language balance of the school is affected. Sometimes teachers can allocate languages (e.g. in drama); other times, students have a dominant influence (e.g. in the playground). However, all informal events in the school create a language atmosphere, a language balance, and are summed to create the overall language experience of the school.

Medium of Activity

Another form of separation focuses on distinguishing between listening, speaking, reading and writing in the classroom. For example, the teacher may give an oral explanation of a concept in one language, with a follow-up discussion with the class in that same language. Then the teacher may ask the children to complete their written work in a second language. This sequence may be deliberately reversed in a second lesson. Another example would be when children read material through one language, and are then invited to write about it in the second language.

The aim of such a teaching strategy is to reinforce and strengthen learning by children. What is initially assimilated in one language is transferred and reinterpreted in a second language. By re-processing the information in a different language, greater understanding may be achieved. However, this example shows that language separation soon links with a strategy to use both languages in the learning process. This idea of a rational, structured and sequenced use of two languages in learning is considered later — when the concurrent use of languages is examined.

One **danger** of 'different medium' separation is that one language may be used for oracy and another language for literacy. Where a minority language does not have a written script this may be a necessary boundary. Where a minority language has written materials, the danger is that the minority language will be identified with oracy and the majority language with literacy. This has a potential effect of giving higher status and more functions to the majority language and its associated literacy. Hence, where this kind of 'medium separation tactic' is used, it is important for reversal to occur. For example, if oral explanations are given in one language with reading/writing in a different language, on the next day or next lesson, that situation can be reversed.

Curriculum Material

There are a variety of ways in which written, audio-visual and information technology curriculum material can be delivered in two languages, ensuring clear separation and non-duplication. Textbooks and course materials may only be allocated in one language with the oral teaching in another language. For example, in Wales, the equivalent of some three million US dollars is allocated for producing curriculum material in Welsh for all ages and all ability levels. This is separation 'across' curriculum material; there is also separation possible 'within' such material. For example, in elementary schools, dual language books (e.g. with English one side of the page and Spanish on the other, sharing the same pictures) may be useful in the early stages of biliteracy. Consideration of dual language books is given later in this section.

In high schools, reading material in History or Science may be as allocated by the teacher in both languages. However, duplication of information and ideas is not necessarily present. Rather, there can be a continuation and progression in themes and content. For example, a new topic may be introduced in one language by the student reading selected material. When a major sub-topic occurs, the teacher may require students to conduct their reading in a different language. Use of both languages helps understanding of the content while separation is occurring. The child does not have the choice of reading the English or the Spanish text, but needs to read both to gain a full comprehension of the topic. Again, it will be seen that language separation does not necessarily mean using two languages in isolation (or repeating the same content). A concern for separation can involves policy and practice that includes more or less use of **both** languages. The outcome is a classroom paradox; languages that are separated by function but are connected in an overall, holistic language and educational development policy.

Such a 'curriculum material separation' strategy tends to be used when, and only when both the child's languages are relatively secure, competent and well-developed. When this has occurred, the argument is that a child has to think more deeply about the material when moving between languages, comparing and contrasting, developing the theme of the material, assimilating and accommodating, transferring and sometimes translating in order to secure a concept and understanding.

Function

In schools and classes where there are bilingual children, there is often teaching in the majority language while the management of the classroom occurs in the minority language. For example, in US 'transitional bilingual education' schools with many Spanish speakers, the teacher may transmit the 'formal' subject matter in English, while conducting 'informal' episodes in Spanish. In this example, the stipulated curriculum is relayed in the majority language. However, when the teacher is organizing students, disciplining, in informal talks with individual students or small groups, in short 'extra-explanation' episodes, a switch to the minority language is made.

Student

The previous seven dimensions have suggested that a school or a teacher may develop a policy about language allocation in a bilingual classroom. However, there is the real situation where students themselves help define the language that is being used in a classroom. For example, if a student addresses the teacher, it may not be in the language that the teacher has used to deliver the curriculum. To explain something with clarity, and for ease of communication, the student may switch to his or her preferred language. Students influence when and where languages are used, and affect boundary making. Thus separate dual language use can occur in the classroom by varying circumstance, student influence, and the formality or informality of particular events (e.g. students may feel at ease talking to teachers in their minority language in private or in classroom conversations).

Concurrent Uses of Languages in a Lesson

In many bilingual classrooms, the frequent **switching** between two or more languages is customary. The concurrent use of two languages in a bilingual classroom tends to be regular in practice, but rare as a predetermined teaching and learning strategy. Jacobson (1990) has argued that, on occasions, the integrated use of both languages rather than language separation can be of value in a lesson. Such a purposeful and structured use of both languages inside a lesson has certain problems that will be considered later. Four concurrent uses will now be considered (Jacobson, 1990):

Randomly Switching Languages

Bilingual children may switch languages both within sentences and across sentences. In many minority language groups, this is frequent both in the home and street as it is in the school. It is relatively rare for such switching to be stable across time. More often it is a half-way house, a sign of movement towards the majority language. For minority languages to survive as relatively distinct and standardized languages, few would argue for such a random practice to be encouraged in a bilingual classroom.

Translating

In some bilingual classrooms, teachers will repeat what they have previously said in another language. For example, the teacher may explain a concept in Spanish, and then repeat the same explanation in English. Everything is said twice for the benefit of children who are dominant in different languages. The danger is that the student will opt-out of listening when the teacher is transmitting in the weaker language. The student knows that the same content will be given in their preferred language and waits for that to occur. Such duplication appears to result in less efficiency, less language maintenance value and less likely achievement in the curriculum.

Previewing and Reviewing

One strategy in the concurrent use of languages in a classroom is to give the preview in the minority language and then the fuller review in the majority language. That is, a topic is introduced in the child's minority language, for example, to give an initial understanding. Then, the subject matter is considered in depth in the majority language. This may be reversed. While there is an extension and reinforcement of ideas occurs by moving from one language to another, there is sometimes also unnecessary duplication and a slow momentum.

Purposeful Concurrent Usage

In a variety of publications, Jacobson proposed the purposeful concurrent use of two languages (see Jacobson, 1990). The properties of what Jacobson calls the 'New Concurrent Approach' is that equal amounts of time are allocated to two languages, and teachers consciously initiate movement from one language to another. Such language movement inside a lesson occurs where there are discrete events and episodes with distinct goals for each language There must be a conscious and planned movement from one language to another in a regular and rational manner. Jacobson (1990) proposes this to strengthen and develop both languages, and to reinforce taught concepts by being considered and processed in both languages. A use of both languages, it is suggested, contributes to a deeper understanding of the subject matter being studied.

Jacobson (1990) suggests a variety of **cues** that can trigger a switch from one language to another. Examples of such cues include:

- reinforcement of concepts;
- reviewing;
- capturing (and re-capturing) student attention;
- praising and reprimanding students;
- change of topic;
- change in the stimulus material;
- change from formality to informality;
- to gain rapport;
- when there is fatigue.

The **amount of time** allocated to each language in the curriculum is important. Some kind of balance (e.g. 50%/50%; or 75%/25%) between languages is needed, but more important is the purpose, manner and method in which the two languages are used. All four language abilities may need fostering in both languages. To emphasize oracy in one language and literacy in another language may result in lopsided bilingualism.

As is discussed in the limitations given below, there are potential problems in the complexity of managing, allocating and organizing such a purposeful use of two languages. However, the value of the idea is that the teacher plans the **strategic use** of two languages, thinks consciously about use of two languages in the classroom, reflects and reviews what is happening, and attempts to cognitively stimulate students by a 'language provocative' and 'language diversified' lesson.

Issues and Limitations

In decisions about language separation and language allocation in a bilingual classroom, there are other ingredients and contexts that need taking into account before an effective dual language policy can be formulated.

First, the **aims of the school** in terms of language preservation and second language competence need to be examined carefully. School teachers are language planners, even if sub-consciously. Where a minority language is to be preserved in the children, then separation may be a central part of the policy. Where teachers are more enthusiastic about competence in the majority language (a second language), then different practices and outcomes in terms of language allocation will be desired. Less language boundaries may be desired. There may be a deliberate loosening of boundaries to ensure the development of the majority language.

Second, the **nature of the students** must be taken into account in any policy with regard to language boundaries and concurrent use. Different policies and practices may be required according to the age and grade level of the children. If the children's language development is still at an early evolutionary stage, boundary setting will be more important. With older children, whose languages are relatively well developed, the concurrent use of two languages may be more viable and desirable. Older children may have more stability and separation in their language abilities.

Third, this suggests that a static policy with regard to boundaries and concurrent use within the school is less justifiable than a **progressive policy** that examines different uses across years and across grade levels. Early separation may be very important, later on in high school more concurrent use may be more defensible to enable conceptual clarity, depth of understanding and possibly to accelerate cognitive development.

Fourth, different dimensions of the school need different discussions about the separation and integration of languages (e.g. curriculum, whole school policies, classrooms, lessons). At what **level of organization** should separation occur? The discussion of language separation by curriculum material and medium of curriculum delivery showed how language separation is not a distinct issue from rational concurrent use. Language separation merges into a consideration of integrated use.

Fifth, the **language balance of the class** is often an important factor in a language separation decision. If all the children speak a minority or majority language, there may be ease in determining a language allocation. However, classes may be mixed, with differing balances of majority and minority language children. Who dominates numerically, linguistically and psychologically in the classroom? When the balance is tilted against language minority children, a clear separation with the curriculum balance towards the minority language may be desirable. Whether the children in a school are language minority children in a subtractive or additive situation will also impact on language allocation policies.

Sixth, where language minority children are in the numerical majority, a **slow change** rather than a sharp shift from language separation to concurrent use may be advisable.

Seventh, a school policy needs to take into account '**out of school exposure**' to the first and second language. Sometimes, an equal amount of time is advocated for two languages in the school, with half the curriculum in one language, the other half in a different language. If the child is surrounded by the majority language outside the school (e.g. street, screen and shop), then the balance may need to be more towards the minority language in school.

Eighth, the **replication and duplication** of content is a danger in bilingual classroom methodology. Where the same subject matter is repeated in a different language, some students will not concentrate or go 'off task'. Yet in many situations, where there is a mixture of different home and preferred languages in the classroom, for the sake of comprehension, a teacher may need to repeat. There are some multilingual classrooms (e.g. in New York, Toronto and London), with a considerable variety of languages represented among the children. This makes debates about concurrent use and language boundaries all the more difficult. One solution is the possibility of individualized learning via small groups (as occurs in progressive British and North American primary school practice). This may allow some language boundaries to be established, with different children addressed (e.g. by teachers aides) in their preferred language.

Ninth, the use of bilingual materials, particularly when they are built in a non-repetitive, non-parallel, but incremental and well sequenced and structured manner, can be valuable, particularly in high schools. However, the production and availability of materials in many minority languages is difficult to achieve. Funding may be difficult to secure for such separate minority language materials.

Tenth, in a concurrent and purposeful use of two languages in the classroom as advocated by Jacobson (1990), there is a danger of a unnatural, artificial, and highly complex language situation demanded of teachers. Where teachers are expected to manage the concurrent use of two languages in a classroom, it assumes a very high level of management skill, monitoring and reflection by such teachers. In reality, classrooms are busy, very fluid, often unpredictable places. Teachers have to react to the moment, to individual students who don't understand, with many situations being unplanable and unpredictable. Students themselves have an important influence on language use in the classroom, needing to communicate their understanding or lack of understanding in the most appropriate way. Classroom management of learning and behavior needs to be fluent, accepted by students and not abrupt and too unpredictable. Thus, language allocation in the classroom must fit naturally, predictably, fluently and flexibly into the complex management of the curriculum.

This completes a consideration of the concurrent use and separation of languages in the classroom. The chapter now moves on to focus on bilingual deaf people and issues in their schooling.

BILINGUALISM, DEAF AND HEARING IMPAIRED PEOPLE

Introduction

There is a growing awareness that those who are deaf or have partial hearing are already, or can become, bilinguals. There is a also a current campaign for the deaf to become bilingual through learning to sign first of all, followed by literacy in the language of the non-deaf (e.g. English in the United States, French in France). The aim of this section is to examine the relationship between bilingualism and the deaf and partial hearing (College for Continuing Education, 1992; Miller-Nomeland, 1993). We will find that there are many similarities between hearing bilinguals and current interests in the languages of the deaf.

Deaf Bilinguals

Deaf individuals can become bilingual through learning to sign first of all, followed by literacy in a language of the non-deaf. There are other forms of deaf bilingualism: for example, those who learn to speak from hearing parents, followed by learning to sign. Others learn to sign first and then learn an oral form of the hearing language. Others learn to communicate by different means, by signs, speaking and writing — a Total Communication approach. Some deaf people sign when in face-to-face communication, and use a written form (e.g. English) to communicate to members of the deaf community via fax, textphone and letters. The path from signing to majority language literacy is discussed later in this section.

For the moment, it is important to recognize that the deaf (like many hearing bilinguals) form relatively **disadvantaged language minorities** and have certain things in common with hearing, language minority individuals and groups. Deaf people often have their own deaf language **community**. The deaf will usually wish to identify with the deaf cultural community. Sometimes, they have been required to attempt to assimilate into the hearing community. Those with a hearing loss vary in their identification, sometimes identifying with deaf people, other times with hearing people, with many possible variations. Like most hearing bilinguals, the deaf may use their two languages for **different functions and purposes**. For example, signing may be used to communicate with the deaf community, while a spoken language or literacy in a majority language is used to communicate with the hearing community. The deaf have too often been placed in **deficit types of education** that submerge them in the language and culture of hearers rather than an enrichment model where signing is allowed as the primary language.

Two Viewpoints about the Deaf

The **first viewpoint** is the **medical view** of deafness. Here deafness is defined as a defect or a handicap that distinguishes 'abnormal' deaf people from 'normal' hearing persons. Deafness is seen as a condition that needs to be remedied or cured as much as possible. Viewed as a disability, hearing aids and other devices that enhance hearing or the understanding of speech are recommended. Deaf people are expected to become as 'normal' as possible by avoiding purely visual methods of communication such as sign language, and learning spoken language as much as is viable.

Sign language is perceived as a primitive, rudimentary, simple picture language whereas the spoken language is seen as the natural language for all in the community, including the deaf. A central aim of education for the deaf deriving from this viewpoint therefore becomes a mastery of spoken and eventually written language. Such education, and social pressures within the community, aim for the integration or **assimilation** of deaf people with hearing people. Deaf people existing in separate communities, miming to each other, using sign-speech or having a deaf culture is not entertained as wholesome or desirable. Thus such educators, professionals and policy makers see themselves as helping the deaf to overcome their 'handicap' and to live in the hearing world.

A **second viewpoint** is more in line with that increasingly expressed about hearing bilinguals: one of bilingualism, vitality as a linguistic and cultural minority community, and the need for an enriching dual language education. Such a viewpoint commences with the assertion that deaf people can do everything except hear. While there are differences between deaf and hearing people, these are natural cultural differences, not deviations from a hearing norm. Thomas Gallaudet, the founder of the first deaf school in the United States, argued that deaf children cannot learn to speak or 'speech-read' well enough to use it as their primary means of communication. Signing for the deaf is natural. As Veditz expressed in 1913, sign language is God's noblest gift to deaf people (quoted in Miller-Nomeland, 1993).

Thus, in this second viewpoint, deafness is regarded as a difference, a characteristic which distinguishes 'normal' deaf people from 'normal' hearing people. Deaf people are regarded as owning sign language which is a full language in itself, grammatically complex and capable of expressing as much as any spoken language. Deaf people are regarded as a linguistic and cultural minority that needs preservation, enrichment and celebration.

Instead of emphasizing the deficiencies of deaf people, their **abilities are emphasized**. A strong emphasis is placed on the use of vision as a positive, efficient and full communicative alternative to audible speaking and hearing. Sign language is thus used not only as equal to spoken language, but also as the most natural language for people who are born deaf.

In deaf **education**, the focus is increasingly on language development through signing, and later on bilingualism through literacy in the majority language. It is felt important that maximal language development occurs early on through signing. Early signing enables a focus on the subject matter of the curriculum (rather than learning to speak a majority language). Early use of signing in the classroom can enable deaf people to perform relatively well in the curriculum. While there are currently few teachers fluent in sign, ideas about the importance of signing in education are gradually evolving.

In this viewpoint, the deaf should form, where possible, a **cultural community** of their own. The deaf have a common language in signing, a culture and a set of needs that are distinct from the hearing community. The deaf community is seen as an important vehicle for the socialization of deaf and partially hearing people. Deaf adults can provide important role models for deaf children, either as teachers or in the community. Thus, this second viewpoint supports bilingualism, a deaf culture and the bilingual education of deaf people.

Differences in Bilingual Goals

It is important to recognize that, among the deaf and the hearing, there are not only different sub-groupings but also differences of opinion about the appropriate language of the deaf, the education of the deaf and their integration into mainstream speaking society. Such differences will now be briefly represented.

Hagemeyer (1992) suggests that there are **nine sub-populations among the deaf** in the United States. Such sub-dimensions refer to deaf culture and not to whether a person is also a member of Hispanic, native American, Asian or any other ethnic group that exists alongside being deaf. The nine groupings are as follows:

(1) Those who use sign language (e.g. American Sign Language — often represented as ASL) as their primary language.
(2) Those who can communicate both in ASL and English.
(3) Those mostly from the hearing impaired group who can communicate primarily through speech.
(4) Adults who became deaf later in life, who were not born deaf and may have acquired speech before deafness. Such people have the experience of hearing normally for a shorter or a longer period and may have speech patterns relatively well embedded before deafness occurred.
(5) The elderly who became hearing impaired or deaf later in life as the result of the aging process.

(6) Those who do not know either ASL nor English, but communicate through gestures, mime and their own signing system. Such people may have been denied access to a deaf culture, to ASL and to education at an early age.

(7) Those who have residual hearing, perhaps describing themselves as hard of hearing, and who can hear with the use of various aids.

(8) Those people who are deaf and blind. An example is Helen Keller.

(9) Those people who have normal hearing, but because their parents, children, or other members of the family are deaf, they understand signing, or are fully conversant with deaf culture and integrate with the deaf community.

Sign Language

Sign language is a fully developed, real language with a full ability to communicate the same, complete meaning as in spoken language. Sign language is not gesturing. Gesturing is relatively unsystematic, and is used in an *ad hoc* way to express a small number of basic expressions. We all use non-verbal communication to add emphasis to our speech. In contrast, signing is a very comprehensive, structurally complex, rule bound, full means of communication. Sign language can perform the same range of functions as a spoken language.

There is a **variety of sign languages** in existence throughout the world. American sign language, British sign language. Chinese sign language, Danish sign language, French sign language and Russian sign language are a few examples.

The Education of Deaf Students

There are a wide variety of approaches to the education of deaf students and those who are hearing impaired. These approaches range from minimal help to specially designed programs. At its worst, in mainstream 'hearing' education, the deaf may be regarded as having a serious mental as well as an auditory 'defect' and classified as remedial. In the history of schooling in most countries, there are plentiful examples of such an insensitive and uncivilized treatment.

In contrast, there are Special Schools and Units for the deaf where, for example, the children are taught to thoroughly learn signing first of all, are given a full curriculum mostly through signing, and develop written and/or oral skills in the majority spoken language. Strong (1995) provides a review of nine programs in North America that use American Sign Language (ASL) and English in the classroom, and aim to promote a 'strong' version of bilingualism and biculturalism among the deaf. English is usually taught as a second language (ESL) with varying emphasis on oracy and literacy in English.

There is considerable discussion, debate and development occurring in deaf education. There is not total agreement as to preferred methods of approach: for example, using signing and literacy in the spoken language, a Total Communication approach, using Sign Supported English or Signed Exact English, the kind of sign language to use, whether to develop oral and/or written skills in the spoken majority language, policies of integration with hearing children and the development of relatively segregated deaf communities.

One traditional approach has been to develop any residual hearing with the assistance of hearing aids and to develop speech reading skills and speech production among the deaf and the hearing impaired. For most of this century until the 1970s, this was the approach that dominated the education of deaf in North America and Europe. Such an approach was based on a belief:

- that deaf children should integrate into mainstream society;
- that the curriculum could not be taught through sign language but required majority language proficiency;
- that signing as a language was insufficient for full intellectual development;
- that sign language was only a temporary crutch for those for whom the majority spoken language was essential;
- that achievement in the curriculum requires oracy and literacy in the majority language (e.g. English).

A **second approach** developed since the 1970s has been based on the philosophy of Total Communication. All modes of communication are regarded as appropriate for those who are deaf or partially hearing. Simultaneous communication is used that combines auditory input plus visual information, for example, via the use of signed English. However, a Total Communication approach is often assimilationist, aiming to enable deaf people to communicate with hearing people.

A **third approach** concerns bilingualism for deaf children through bilingual education. This recent initiative is contained in twelve suggestions that are mirrored in spoken bilingual education:

(1) That sign language should be the first language of all deaf children and be regarded as their primary language.
(2) That sign language should be used to teach curriculum subjects such as science, humanities, social studies and mathematics.
(3) Sign language can be used to teach English or another majority language as a second language. Usually this will be to teach reading and writing skills in English rather than English oracy.
(4) The culture and language of the deaf community are recognized and validated, with children learning that they belong to the culture of the deaf. This approach tends to be favored by most but not all the deaf community, but has not been favored by many politicians and education professionals who formulate policy and provision.
(5) Such bilingual education for the deaf is partly based on the research and arguments for an enrichment form of bilingual education for hearing children:
  - bilingual education builds on a child's existing linguistic and intellectual resources;
  - concepts and knowledge developed in the first language transfer easily to the second language;
  - use of a children's heritage language gives pride and confidence in their culture and community;

- a child's self-esteem and self-identity are boosted and not threatened by use of their first language;
- school performance and curriculum attainment is raised when the first language is celebrated rather than devalued;
- the lower achievement of minority language students and deaf students needs to be addressed by enrichment forms (or 'strong forms') of bilingual education.

(6) Deaf children cannot acquire a spoken language easily or quickly because they have limited hearing abilities. If the curriculum is transmitted in the spoken language, they are being expected to learn the content of the curriculum using a level of language not yet acquired. This is analogous to minority language children being expected to operate in submersion education in the language of the majority they have yet to master.

(7) English or another majority language is developed through sign language. Often native sign language teachers will be employed in schools, where possible, to teach and to act as role models.

(8) The acquisition of a sign language should begin as early as possible, ideally soon after birth. Since 90% of deaf children are born to hearing parents, this is often difficult, but with such parents being increasingly willing to sign and learn signing, the first language of such deaf children can be sign language. Current thinking among the deaf tends to suggest that early signing is preferable in most cases. Parents of deaf children need to be aware of deaf communities, of bilingual education for deaf children, and to enhance their child's curriculum achievement, to expect signing as the medium of curriculum delivery plus literacy in the majority language.

(9) It is important to avoid language-delay in deaf children, as has been found to occur when using auditory approaches and sometimes the Total Communication approach. Curriculum achievement will suffer if there is language delay.

(10) The supply of trained personnel in deaf bilingual education, staff pre-service education programs, in-service education and certification and funding are often current challenges that are being faced by deaf educators. These are practical problems to be overcome rather than problems of principles that are insurmountable.

(11) The parents of deaf children need considerable emotional support, information and guidance to help their children become bilingual. In order for cognitive, linguistic, social and emotional development to occur among deaf children, there needs to be a partnership between school and parents, and between school and community. While there is a considerable debate about the integration of deaf children into a hearing society, (and their first loyalty being to the deaf community), hearing parents of deaf children need considerable support and sensitivity.

(12) The teaching situation in a bilingual deaf education system may involve team teaching. The deaf teacher may be a natural model for the acquisition of sign language with a hearing teacher acting as a model for the acquisition of proficiency in a majority language such as English or French. Ideally, both teachers should be bilingual models, being able to communicate in both sign language and the 'hearing' language. Also, both teachers in the team should have a knowledge of deaf culture, deaf differences and all the possibilities for deaf children and adults.

In conclusion, this section on deaf bilinguals has shown that there are **many similarities between hearing bilinguals and deaf bilinguals**. Many of the justifications for retaining a minority language child's first language and for a 'strong' form of bilingual education for such children also hold for deaf children. The argument that children from language minorities should become bicultural and culturally pluralistic also tends to hold for deaf bilinguals. Language minorities are often the poor, low status, low power relations of majority language speakers. Even more so the deaf. Deaf bilinguals are often the poor relations of language minority bilinguals. A spoken minority language is often disdained and derided. Even more so sign language. Achievement and status among deaf children and adults are often only recognized and granted when speech monolingualism occurs.

When the deaf come from language minority communities they form a minority of a minority. The examples of a Latino deaf person in the US, a deaf Turk in Germany and a deaf Bengali in England all represent individuals who are a minority within a minority. They are often the doubly underprivileged and the doubly despised. Where being a member of a language minority is joined by being deaf, disempowerment, low status, discrimination and low self esteem may be compounded. If many groups of bilinguals are underprivileged, even more so are deaf bilinguals.

CONCLUSION

This chapter has highlighted some of the key elements in the schooling of bilinguals. The importance of developing the home language in its oral and literate form was initially stressed. Bilingual schooling appears an essential, but not by itself, a sufficient condition for the reproduction of the minority language in students. Such language development needs to occur across the curriculum, in Science as well as Language Arts, in Math and Technology as well as History and Geography. Language development needs to be joined by cultural development. Throughout the curriculum, in all areas and cross-curricula topics, the culture surrounding the minority language needs transmitting to give that language purpose, meaning and vitality.

The minority language is also secured in students if there are clear boundaries between it and the majority language in school. Separate functions for the two languages, and a clear demarcation in the classroom and curriculum are particularly important for younger children in the elementary school. Later on, when students' two languages are both well developed, the integration and concurrent use of two languages in the classroom may be considered as a means of reinforcement and reconceptualizing curriculum material.

The chapter ended by portraying the many parallels between deaf bilinguals and hearing bilinguals. Views about deaf people vary, with the medical view and a 'competent bilingual' view contrasted in this chapter. Both views link to different beliefs about the education of the deaf. The discussion of different forms of bilingual education for the deaf highlight this topic as an important area for discussion and debate.

SUGGESTED FURTHER READING

CUMMINS, J. and SWAIN, M. 1986, *Bilingualism in Education*. New York: Longman.
GARCÍA, O. and BAKER, C. (eds.) 1995, *Policy and Practice in Bilingual Education: A Reader Extending the Foundations*. Clevedon: Multilingual Matters. (Section 3).
JACOBSON, R. 1990, Allocating two languages as a key feature of a bilingual methodology. In R. JACOBSON and C. FALTIS *Language Distribution Issues in Bilingual Schooling*. Clevedon: Multilingual Matters.
KYLE, J.G. (ed.) 1987, *Sign and School*. Clevedon: Multilingual Matters.
KYLE, J.G. 1988, *Sign Language: The Study of Deaf People and their Language*. Cambridge: Cambridge University Press.
MASHIE, S.N. 1995, *Educating Deaf Children Bilingually*. Washington, DC: Gallaudet University.
McCRACKEN, W. 1991, *Deaf-Ability Not Disability*. Clevedon: Multilingual Matters.
OVANDO, C.J. and COLLIER, V.P. 1987, *Bilingual and ESL Classrooms: Teaching in Multicultural Contexts*. New York: McGraw Hill.
WONG FILLMORE, L. and VALADEZ, C. 1986, Teaching bilingual learners. In M.C. WITTROCK (ed.) *Handbook of Research on Teaching* (3rd edn). New York: Macmillan.

REVIEW AND STUDY QUESTIONS

(1) Write short revision notes on the following:
    (i) The eight different ways languages can be separated in a classroom.
    (ii) Examples of the concurrent use of two languages in a classroom, especially purposeful concurrent use.
    (iii) The ten factors that affect decisions and strategies of language separation and concurrent use.
    (iv) Two viewpoints about deaf people.
    (v) Different approaches to the education of deaf students.
(2) What goals appear particularly important in the development of native language skills in school for one age group of your choice?
(3) What are the reasons for language separation in a class? On what occasions might a concurrent use of two languages be justified in a class?
(4) In a table or essay, show the similarities and differences between hearing bilinguals and deaf bilinguals.
(5) Read the article by Michael Strong (1995) 'A Review of Bilingual/Bicultural Programs for Deaf Children in North America' in *American Annals of the Deaf* 140 (2), 84–94 (or a similar article for your region nominated by your teacher). Compare and contrast the schools using the following headings: (1) Aims of the school and mission (2) Use of languages (ASL, English) in the school (3) Staff (4) Parents (5) Other particular features.

STUDY ACTIVITIES

(1) Interview some parents about bilingual education (preferably gathering a variety of different viewpoints). Ask them what their preferences are for the use of the home language in school. Ask the parents if they want their children to be bilingual as a result of schooling. Ask parents what value and use they see in languages being taught or two languages being used as a medium of learning in school.

(2) Interview an administrator, a parent, a teacher and a principal about their attitudes to children's home languages in school. Find out what differences and what similarities there are between these different people. Try to explain the origins and the causes of the differences. Are there different majority and minority viewpoints? Can there be any integration of these varying viewpoints?

(3) Use one or more of the attitude scales in Appendix 1 with a classroom of children. In words and in simple percentages, show the differences between students in attitude. If there are differences between groups (e.g. gender, age groups, different language backgrounds), try to provide interpretations and explanations.

(4) Visit a school where there is a policy about the allocation of languages in the classroom. Try to locate a written school policy about language allocation and compare it with what you observe in one or more classrooms. Discuss your findings with a teacher. Chart the results of your observation and discussion with a teacher on a poster to display to a small group. Compare your results with other members of the group.

(5) Visit a family with a deaf student and/or a school where there are deaf students. What are the goals in language development? What form of bilingualism exists? What are the attitudes and aspirations of the student and parents/teachers regarding language.

CHAPTER 13

Bilingual Schooling Issues

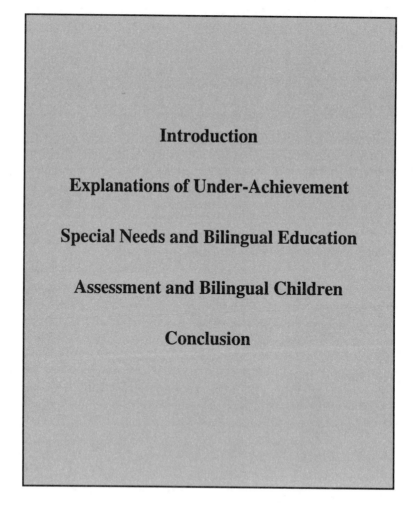

Introduction

Explanations of Under-Achievement

Special Needs and Bilingual Education

Assessment and Bilingual Children

Conclusion

CHAPTER 13

Bilingual Schooling Issues

INTRODUCTION

This chapter begins by examining some key themes in the education of bilinguals. Under-achievement is often found among language minorities, both in leaving school relatively early and in lower performance in the curriculum. The chapter examines the varying explanations for this, particularly whether bilingualism is a cause of such under-achievement. This discussion extends into children with special needs, and the purpose and effectiveness of bilingual special education. The role of assessment in the identification, and particularly the mis-identification of bilingual children follows.

EXPLANATIONS OF UNDER-ACHIEVEMENT

There are frequent occasions when language minorities are found to under-achieve. Sometimes this is reported in research as differences between ethnic groups (e.g. Department of Education and Science, 1985; Figueroa, 1984; Tomlinson, 1986). It is also discussed by teachers, educational psychologists, speech therapists, parents and students themselves in 'single individual' terms.

When language minority children appear to exhibit under-achievement in the classroom, what may be the **explanation**? When first, second or third generation in-migrant children appear to fail in the classroom, where is the 'blame' popularly placed? When guest workers' children, indigenous minorities and distinct ethnic groups are shown statistically to leave school earlier, achieve less in examinations and tests or receive lower grades and averages, what is the cause?

First, the attributed blame may be on the child **being bilingual**. Bilingualism itself is often popularly seen as causing cognitive confusion. The explanation given is a picture of the bilingual brain with two engines working at half throttle, while the monolingual has one well tuned engine at full throttle. As Chapter 9 revealed, such an explanation is usually incorrect. Where two languages are well developed, then bilingualism is more likely to lead to cognitive advantages than disadvantages (see the three level house diagram in Chapter 9). Only when a child's two languages are both poorly developed can 'blame' be attributed to bilingualism itself. Even then, the blame should not go to the victim, but to the societal circumstances that create under-developed languages.

Second, where under-achievement exists, the reason may be given as **lack of exposure to the majority language**. In the US and England, a typical explanation for the under-achievement of certain language minorities is insufficient exposure to English. Failure or below average performance is attributed to students having insufficiently developed English language competence to cope with the curriculum. Those who use Spanish or Bengali at home and in the neighborhood are perceived to struggle at school due to a lack of competence in the dominant, mainstream language. Thus submersion and transitional forms of bilingual education attempt to ensure a fast conversion to the majority language (Cummins, 1980b).

A fast conversion to the majority language stands the chance of doing more harm than good. It denies the child's skills in the home language, even denies the identity and self-respect of the child itself. Instead of using existing language skills, the 'sink or swim' approach attempts to replace those skills. The level of English used in the curriculum may also cause the child to show under-achievement, with consequent demands for more of the same medicine (more English language lessons).

Under-achievement in majority language education (e.g. submersion and transitional bilingual education) may be combated by providing education through the medium of the minority language (e.g. Two-Way, Developmental Maintenance, Heritage Language Programs). When the language minority child is allowed to operate in their heritage language in the curriculum, the evidence (see Chapter 11) suggests that success rather than failure results. Such success includes becoming fluent in the majority language (e.g. English). Thus lack of exposure to English is a popular but improper explanation of under-achievement. This explanation fails to note the advantages of education in the minority language for achievement. It inappropriately seeks an answer in increased majority language tuition rather than increased minority language education.

Third, when bilingual children exhibit under-achievement, the attributed reason is sometimes a **mismatch between home and school**. Such a mismatch is seen as not just about language differences but also about dissimilarities in culture, values and beliefs (Delgado-Gaitan & Trueba, 1991). As an extreme, this tends to reflect a majority viewpoint that is assimilationist, imperialist and even oppressive. The child and family is expected to adjust to the system, not the system to be pluralist and incorporate variety. For such an assimilationist viewpoint, the solution is in the home adjusting to mainstream language and culture to prepare the child for school. Past advice by some educational psychologists and speech therapists has been for language minority parents to raise their children in the majority, school language.

The alternative view is that, where practicable, the school system should be flexible enough to incorporate the home language and culture. A mismatch between home and school can be positively addressed by 'strong' forms of bilingual education for language minorities. By Two-Way, Developmental Maintenance and Heritage Language Programs, through the inclusion of parents in the running of the school, by involving parents as partners and participants in their child's education (e.g. paired reading schemes), the mismatch can become a merger.

Fourth, under-achievement may be attributed to **socioeconomic factors** that surround a language minority group. Some typical circumstances are described by Trueba (1991). 'Many immigrant and refugee children have a life of poverty and rural isolation in crowded dwellings where they lack privacy, toilet and shower facilities, comfort, and basic medical attention. In some cases migrant life for children means abuse, malnutrition, poor health, ignorance and neglect. Uprooting a child from his/her land can lead to a life of stigma and low status.' (Trueba, 1991: 53).

Socioeconomic status is a broad umbrella term that rightly points to a definite cause of language minority under-achievement. It provides an example of the importance of not blaming the victim, but analyzing societal features that contribute to under-achievement. Such features may be economic deprivation, material circumstances and living conditions as well as psychological and social features as discrimination, racial prejudice, pessimism and immobilizing inferiority.

While **socioeconomic factors** are a proper partial explanation of language minority underachievement, two cautions must be sounded. Socioeconomic status does not explain why different language minorities of similar socioeconomic status may perform differently at school. In Chapter 19 we discuss the different ideologies or orientations that may vary between ethnic groups. Sociocultural factors within and between ethnic groups and not simply socioeconomic status are needed to begin to work out the equation of language minority achievement and under-achievement.

This raises another issue. Under-achievement cannot be simply related to one of several causes. The equation of under-achievement is going to be complex, involving a number of factors. Those factors will **interact** together and not be simple 'standalone' effects. For example, umbrella labels such as socioeconomic status need decomposing into more definable predictors of under-achievement (e.g. parents' attitude to education). Home factors will then interact with school factors providing an enormous number of different routes that may lead to varying school success and failure. The recipes of success and failure are many, with varying ingredients that interact together in complex ways. However, socioeconomic and sociocultural features are important ingredients in most equations of under-achievement.

Fifth, part of the language minority achievement and under-achievement equation is the **type of school** a child attends. This chapter and Chapter 11 highlight the different outcomes for language minority children in 'strong' compared with 'weak' forms of bilingual education. The same child will tend to attain more if placed in programs that use the heritage language as a medium of instruction than in programs which seek to replace the home language as quickly as possible. Therefore, when under-achievement occurs in a language minority child or within a language minority group, the system of schooling needs scrutiny. A system that suppresses the home language is likely to be part of the explanation of individual and ethnic group under-achievement where such problems exist.

Sixth, type of school is a broad heading under which there can exist superior and inferior submersion schools, outstanding and mediocre Dual Language and Heritage Language schools. Where under-achievement exists, it is sometimes too simple to blame the type of school rather than digging deeper and locating more specific causes. Baker (1988, 1993), Cummins (1984a) and Hornberger (1991) have listed some of the attributes that need examining to establish the **quality of education** for language minority children (e.g. the supply, ethnic origins and bilingualism of teachers, balance of language minority and language majority students in the classroom, use and sequencing of the two languages across the curriculum over different grades, reward systems for enriching the minority language and culture).

Seventh, under-achievement may be due to **real learning difficulties** and the need for some form of special education. It is important to make a distinction between real and apparent learning difficulties. Too often, bilingual children are labeled as having learning difficulties which are attributed to their bilingualism. As we have discussed in this section, the causes of apparent learning problems may be much less in the child and much more in the school or in the education system. The child is perceived as having learning difficulties when the problem may lie in the subtractive, assimilative system which itself creates negative attitudes and low motivation. In the 'sink or swim' approach, 'sinking' can be attributed to an unsympathetic system and to insensitive teaching methods rather than individual learning problems. Apart from system-generated and school-generated learning problems, there will genuinely be those who are bilingual and have learning difficulties (Cummins, 1984a). The essential beginning is to distinguish between real, genuine individual learning difficulties and problems which are caused by factors outside the individual.

Such a **distinction between the real and the apparent**, the system-generated and the remediable problems of the individual, highlights the alternatives. When under-achievement exists, do we blame the victim, blame the teacher and the school, or blame the system? When assessment, tests and examinations occur and show relatively low performance of language minority individuals and groups, will prejudices about bilingual children and ethnic groups be confirmed? Or can we use such assessment to reveal deficiencies in the architecture of the school system and the design of the curriculum rather than blame the child? As this section has revealed, under-achievement tends to be blamed on the child and the language minority group. Often the explanation lies in factors outside of the individual. This discussion is now extended by examining bilinguals with special needs and Bilingual Special Education.

SPECIAL NEEDS AND BILINGUAL EDUCATION

It is initially important to define who are the children with special needs who may need Special Education provision. **Categories of special need** vary from country to country but are likely to include the following areas: visual impairment, hearing impairment, communication disorders, learning disabilities (e.g. dyslexia and developmental aphasia), severe subnormality in cognitive development, behavioral problems and physical handicaps. Special needs can also include those with exceptional abilities (e.g. high IQ, outstanding musical or mathematical aptitude). Some bilingual children will have special needs, and this includes children from 'elite' bilingual families (e.g. English–German) as well as from language minorities. In the United States, the Office of Special Education has estimated that nearly one million children from language minority backgrounds are in need of some form of special education. This immediately raises questions as to why language minority children may need special education.

(1) Do bilingual children experience special needs more frequently than other children due to their bilingualism and their communicative differences from monolingual children?
(2) Are bilingual children more likely to experience any specific 'problems' due to their bilingualism (e.g. stammering, language delay)?
(3) Are bilingual children often wrongly assessed and categorized as having a 'disability' and, as such, incorrectly placed in special education?
(4) Are children of language minorities regarded as having special needs due to problems resulting from their ethnic culture, community or family character? What are alternative causes of special needs and learning difficulties in children?

These four questions will now be considered in turn.

Do Bilingual Children Experience Special Needs More Frequently Than Other Children Due to Their Bilingualism and Their Communicative Differences from Monolingual Children?

It seems very unlikely that **bilingualism** is a direct cause of, or linked to the following main categories of special need, namely visual impairment, hearing impairment, learning disabilities (e.g. dyslexia and developmental aphasia), severe subnormality in cognitive development, behavioral problems and physical handicaps. Being a member of a language minority may co-exist with such conditions, but is **not connected**.

There is some evidence in the United States (on a state by state analysis) that **bilingual children are over-represented** among those in need of special education (Harry, 1992; Gersten & Woodward, 1994). Harry (1992) also suggests that the rate of placement of Latinos in Special Education rises as the number of these students in the school system increases. Any over-representation in the categories listed above is very unlikely to be a result of bilingualism by itself. The causes of over-representation are considered later.

But what about language and communication disorders (e.g. language delay and stammering)? Are these connected to bilingualism? This raises the second question.

Are Bilingual Children More Likely to Experience Any Specific 'Problems' Due to Their Bilingualism (e.g. Stammering, Language Delay)?

The communicative **differences** of bilingual children must be **distinguished from** communicative **disorders**. The failure to make this important distinction partly occurs because basic mistakes in assessment and categorization are made. The child is often assessed in a weaker, second language, thereby inaccurately measuring both language development and general cognitive development. For example, in Britain and the United States, in-migrant children are sometimes still assessed through the medium of English and on their English proficiency. Their level of language competence in Spanish, Bengali, Cantonese, Turkish, Italian or Panjabi, for example, is ignored.

The result is that such children are sometimes classed as having a 'language disability' and perhaps a 'learning disability'. Instead of being seen as developing bilinguals (i.e. children with a good command of their first language who are in the process of acquiring a second, majority language), they may be classed as of 'limited English proficiency' (LEP in the United States), or even as having general difficulties with learning. Their below average test scores in the second language (e.g. English) are wrongly defined as a 'deficit' or 'disability' that can be remedied by some form of special education.

Two particular language conditions require specific discussion: language delay and stuttering (stammering).

Language Delay

A particular language condition in children that illustrates an often wrongly attributed link between bilingualism and developmental problems is 'language delay'. Language delay occurs when a child is very late in beginning to talk, or lags well behind peers in language development. Estimates of young children experiencing language delay vary from 1 in 20 to 1 in 5 of the child population. Such varying estimates partly reflect that some delays are brief and hardly noticeable. Others are more severe.

Language delay has a **variety of causes** (e.g. autism, severe subnormality, cerebral palsy, physical problems (e.g. cleft palate), psychological disturbance, emotional difficulties). However, in approximately two-thirds of all cases, the precise reason for language delay is not known. Children who are medically normal, with no hearing loss, of normal IQ and memory, who are not socially deprived or emotionally disturbed, can be delayed in starting to speak, slow in development or have problems in expressing themselves well. In such cases, specialist, professional help needs to be sought. Speech therapists, clinical psychologists, educational psychologists, counselors or doctors may be able to give an expert diagnosis and suggest possible treatment of the problem. It is important that such professionals have an understanding of the nature of bilingualism in the clients they advise and treat.

Occasionally, well-meaning professionals make the diagnosis that bilingualism is the cause of language delay. If the causes are unknown, bilingualism might seem a likely cause. Raising children bilingually is widely believed to produce language delayed children. The evidence does not tend to support this belief.

For the teacher, psychologist, speech therapist, counselor and parent, a practical decision has to be made in respect of language delayed bilingual children. Will the removal of one language improve, worsen or have no affect on such a child's language development? Given that the cause of the problem may be partially unknown, intuition and guesswork rather than 'science' often occurs as research in this area is still developing.

Let us assume the professional advice is to move from bilingualism to monolingualism. One issue immediately becomes **which language** to concentrate on if there is major diagnosed language delay. The danger is that parents, teachers and other professionals will want to accent the perceived importance of the majority language. In the United States, the advice is often that the child should have a solid diet of English (at home and particularly at school). The perceived language of school and success, employment and opportunity is the majority language. The advice often given is that the home, minority language should be replaced by the majority language.

Even when professionals accept that bilingualism is not the cause of a child's problem, moving from bilingualism to monolingualism is seen by some as a way to help improve the problem. The reasoning is usually that the 'extra demands' of bilingualism, if removed, will lighten the burden for the child. For example, if the child has an emotional problem or a language delay condition, for whatever cause, simplifying the language demands on the child may be seen as one way of solving or reducing the problem. The apparent complexity of a two language life is relieved by monolingualism. Is this the rational and suitable solution?

There are many occasions when changing from bilingualism to monolingualism will have no effect on language delay. For example, if the child seems slow to speak without an obvious cause, or seems low in self esteem, dropping one language is unlikely to have any effect. On the contrary, the sudden change in schooling or family life may exacerbate the problem. The child may be further confused, even upset, if there is a dramatic change in the language of the school or family. If someone who has loved, cared for, or educated the child in one language (e.g. a minority language) suddenly only uses another language (e.g. the majority language), the emotional well-being of the child may well be negatively affected. The language used to express love and caring disappears. Simultaneously, and by association, the child may feel that the love and care is also not as before. Such an overnight switch may well have painful outcomes for the language delayed child. The mother tongue is denied, the language of the family is implicitly derided, and the communicative medium of the community is disparaged. The child may feel as if thrown from a secure boat into strange waters. **The solution in itself may exacerbate the problem**.

An alternative is that the **anchor language** is retained. The home language gives a sense of assurance and security amid stormy seas. Even if the child is slow in sailing in that language, with progress delayed, it is the boat known to the child. Being forced to switch to the majority language will not make the journey faster or less problematic. It is more important to learn to sail in a familiar boat (the home language) in minority language situations. Thus, in most cases, it is inappropriate to move from bilingualism to monolingualism.

However, it is dangerous to make this suggestion absolute and unequivocal. When there is language delay, there may be a few situations where maximal experience in one language is preferable. For example, where one language of a child is much securer and more well developed than another, it may be sensible to concentrate on developing the stronger language.

This does not mean that the chance of bilingualism is lost forever. If, or when, language delay disappears, the other language can be **reintroduced**. If a child with emotional problems and language delay really detests using (or even being spoken to) in a particular language, as part of a solution, the family may sensibly decide to accede to the child's preference. Again, once behavioral and language problems have been resolved, the 'dropped' language can be reintroduced, so long as it is immediately associated with pleasurable experiences.

Any temporary move from bilingualism to monolingualism should not be seen as the only solution needed. A focus on such a language change as the sole remedy to the child's problem is naive and dangerous. For example, emotional problems causing language delay may require other rearrangements in the school or family's pattern of behavior. Language delay may require visits to a speech therapist for advice about language interaction between the child and significant adults. Temporary monolingualism should only be seen as one component in a package of attempted changes to solve the child's language problem. However, it is important to reiterate that, in the majority of cases, language delay will not be affected by retaining a bilingual approach.

Stuttering

For a short period, many children stutter (stammer). This includes repeating sounds or words (e.g. p-p-p-play with m-m-me; I've got to - got to - got to go now); lengthening sounds (e.g. ffffish); time gaps between words (e.g. I'm going ... ... home now); and unfinished words or phrases. Around three and four years of age, such stuttering is particularly common. Many older children and adults, when under pressure, lose fluency. In addressing a large audience, a speaker may be so tense as to lose customary smoothness in presentation.

The causes of stuttering are still not well understood and seem varied. Some **neuro-physiological** theories locate the problem in brain activity, others in a feedback problem between the ear and the brain. Further theories attempt a **psychological** explanation in terms of personality traits, and particularly anxiety (e.g. caused by impatient, over-corrective parents). None of these theories can explain all cases of stuttering.

One **linguistic** theory sees the cause as a difference between the language that is available in the brain (potential) and control over speech apparatus (production). Another linguistic theory sees 'cognitive overload' as the cause (e.g. the child is experiencing a difficulty in producing required complex sentences; the child's capacity for fluency does not equal the demands placed on the child). Such linguistic theories may have implications for a few young bilinguals.

It has been argued in one case study that coping with two languages around the age of two to four may cause a few children 'cognitive overload' (Karniol, 1992). The resulting argument was that bilingualism causes a few children to require additional processing time (i.e. increasing the difference between 'potential' and 'production'). This case study may be rather atypical and idiosyncratic, and requires replication many times before the argument is supported. However, it does reflect the assumption made about bilinguals who stutter by some doctors, teachers, and other professionals. Overall, the evidence available indicates that bilinguals appear no more likely to stutter than monolinguals (Saunders, 1988). Bilingual and multilingual countries do not appear to have a greater incidence of stuttering than monolingual countries. The current conclusion seems to be that stuttering is **very rarely related to bilingualism**.

The Israeli case study referred to above suggests that any problems due to 'cognitive overload' are **temporary** in bilingual children. As language competence in the two languages increases, stammering usually disappears. It is also not clear from such research whether the causes were purely cognitive. Emotional problems (e.g. anxiety) may have been a prime cause; such anxiety derived from sources other than bilingualism.

Methods of **treatment** of stuttering also hint that bilingualism is rarely a cause. Developing a stutterer's breath control, learning to speak more slowly, tension reduction and relaxation techniques are examples of treatments. If potential causes of stuttering are more about specific anxieties, nervousness, worries about speaking, or more general worries and fears in the child's life, the remedy appears to be in those areas and not in bilingualism. For example, teachers who criticize a child for stuttering, or parents who exhibit anxiety when their child stutters, only increase the child's nervousness and frequency of stuttering. If the sources of tension and anxiety in the child can be located, reduced or swept away, stuttering is quite likely to be a temporary problem. For a very small number of children, however, stuttering will be a continuous characteristic, and parents or teachers can do little about treatment (e.g. when stuttering is related to brain activity).

When stuttering first occurs, it may not be necessary to seek immediate psychological or clinical advice. The sheer act of highlighting the problem may exacerbate the problem itself. Showing anxiety, indicating to the child that a problem exists, correcting the child and being impatient may only make the condition worse. Stuttering is frequent in many young children, both monolinguals and bilinguals. It is usually temporary, and reappears when a child (or adult) is particularly agitated and excited. If stuttering continues for a longer period, it may be wise to seek advice from experts in child development or clinical psychology.

Stopping children speaking one of their languages will usually be counter productive. It will not change the stuttering. Rather such an act will focus on language. This may **increase children's anxiety** about their language production. If it is genuinely felt that stuttering is caused by the child's 'potential with language' not matching 'ability in production' or by 'cognitive overload' (see the linguistic theories mentioned above), teachers and parents can attempt to:

(1) relax the level of their questions and language demands on the child;
(2) ensure that language expectations are not unrealistic — in both languages;
(3) be extra encouraging and patient when listening to the child, and
(4) in extreme cases, if felt strongly desirable, move to monolingualism for a temporary period.

Are Bilingual Children Often Wrongly Assessed and Categorized as Having a 'Disability' and, as such, Incorrectly Placed in Special Education?

When bilingual children are assessed, it is important to keep three different aspects of their development distinct: (1) first language proficiency, (2) second language proficiency, and (3) the existence (or not) of a physical, learning or behavioral difficulty. This three-fold distinction enables a more accurate and fair assessment to be made with regard to special education. The child's level of functioning in a second language must not be seen as representing the child's level of language development. The child's development in the **first language** needs to be assessed (e.g. by observation if psychological and educational tests are not available) so as to paint a picture of proficiency rather than deficiency. The child's language proficiency is different from potential problems in an individual's capacities that require specialist treatment (e.g. hearing impairment, severely subnormal in 'IQ'). Neither the language and culture of the home, nor socioeconomic and ethnic differences should be considered as handicapping conditions in themselves. Social, cultural, family, educational and personal information needs to be collected to make a valid and reliable assessment and to make an accurate placement of the child in mainstream or special education. This is considered separately in the following section on the assessment of bilingual children.

The Example of the United States

In the United States, Public Law (94-142) gives the **right** to assessment that is not culturally discriminatory, to tests in the child's native language, to multi-dimensional 'all areas' assessment for all 'handicapped' students. The misdiagnosis of bilingual students for special education has led to court cases (e.g. *Diana* v. *The California State Board of Education* — see later in this chapter). Such court cases revealed how bilingual students were wrongly assessed as in need of special education (Maldonado, 1994). In some cases, teachers were unsure how to cope with a child whose English was relatively 'weak'. On this basis only, the teacher wanted special education for the 'Limited English Proficient' child.

Such litigation has showed the importance of separating bilinguals with real learning difficulties from those bilinguals whose second language (e.g. English) proficiency is below 'native' average. The latter group should not be assessed as having learning difficulties and therefore in need of special education (Figueroa, 1989; Mercer, 1973; Gersten & Woodward, 1994). The litigation also showed the wrongs done to bilingual students: **misidentification**, misplacement, misuse of tests and failure when allocated to special education.

Unfortunately, the fear of litigation by school districts can lead to an **over-referral** of bilingual students with a real need of special education. In the early 1980s, the trend was (in California, for example) to assume that too many language minority students were in need of special education. When students did not appear to be benefiting from instruction in 'regular' classrooms, special education classes became the easy answer. Or, if teachers were unsure how to deal with a behavioral or learning problem, transfer to special education provision became an instant solution.

Towards the end of the 1980s, this had been reversed. The tendency moved to **underestimating** the special needs of language minority children (Gersten & Woodward, 1994). Wrongful placement of children in special education (over-referral) made various administrators cautious of special education placement. A fear of legal action by parents and a realization that assessment devices often had low validity led administrators to be hesitant to place bilingual children in Special Education.

The see-saw between over-estimation and under-referral of special education need makes accurate assessment very important. The section on the assessment of bilingual children raises the important issues about valid assessment of special need. However, accurate assessment and placement in different schools is not enough. The development of **effective instruction strategies** and an appropriate curriculum is crucial. So is the need to train teachers for bilingual students in special education. Educating the parents of special needs children is also a high priority.

Assessment will sometimes locate those who are bilingual *and* have a physical, neurological, learning, emotional, cognitive or behavioral difficulty. Such children may need some kind of special education or intervention. One estimate in the United States is that 1 in 8 (approximately 12%) of language minority students will fit into this category. Similar figures are quoted in other countries. What form of Special Education should such children receive? Should such education be in their home language, where feasible, or in the majority language of the region? Or should such children be provided with education that uses both home and majority languages?

Bilingual Special Education

Special Education bilingual children can be served by a **variety** of institutional arrangements (Cloud, 1994). These include: Special Education schools (resident and non-resident), hospital-based education, residential homes, Special Education Units attached to mainstream schools, specially resourced classes in mainstream schools, withdrawal and pull-out programs (e.g. for extra speech and language help, behavioral management) and special help given by teachers, paraprofessionals or support staff in 'regular' classes. The extent to which such provision will be bilingual or monolingual will vary within and across such institutional arrangements. Such bilingual or monolingual provision will also depend on availability of provision (material and human), the type and degree of special education need or condition, proficiency in both languages, learning capacity, age, social and emotional maturity, degree of success in any previous education placements, and not least, the wishes of the parents and child.

When bilingual or language minority children have been assessed as having special needs, many educators will argue that education solely in the dominant, majority language is needed. In the United States, the advice is sometimes given that Latino and other language minority children with special needs should be educated in monolingual, English language special schools. The argument is that such children are going to live in an English speaking society. When there is serious mental retardation, it seems sensible that a child should be educated monolingually, in the minority or majority language. Such a child develops very slowly in one language.

Many special needs children will benefit considerably from **bilingual special education** rather than monolingual special education (Baca & Cervantes, 1989; Carrasquillo, 1990). One example is the recently arrived in-migrant, special needs child. Placing such a child in a class where he or she doesn't speak the language of the classroom (e.g. English in the United States) will only increase failure and lower self-esteem. To be educated, the child preferably needs initial instruction mostly in the first language, with the chance to become as bilingual as possible. Most children with special needs are capable of developing in two languages. Many do not reach levels of proficiency in either language compared with peers in mainstream classrooms. Nevertheless, they reach satisfactory levels of proficiency in two languages according to their abilities. Becoming bilingual does not detract from achievement in other areas of the curriculum (e.g. mathematics and the creative arts). Canadian research tends to show that less able bilingual children share some of the cognitive advantages of bilingualism (Rueda, 1983). Just as their mathematical ability, literacy and scientific development may occur at a slower pace, so the two languages will develop with less speed. The size of vocabulary and accuracy of grammar may be less in both languages than the average bilingual child. Nevertheless, such children acquiring two languages early, will usually be able to communicate in both languages, often as well as they would communicate in one language.

The movement of a bilingual student into special education often occurs after a conclusion is reached that the child's needs cannot be met by integration in a regular (i.e. non-special) school. This holds for those currently in bilingual education who may need special bilingual education because generally, **integration** is regarded as preferable to segregation. If children are placed in bilingual special education, it is important that they gain the benefits of those in other forms of bilingual education: dual language competence, biculturalism and multiculturalism, and other educational, cultural, self-identity and self-esteem benefits. These benefits have been discussed previously in this book.

One example not discussed so far is when a child is **failing** in a mainstream school due to his or her language proficiency not being sufficient to operate in the curriculum. For example, in the United States, some Spanish speaking children are in mainstream schools (a 'submersion' experience) and, although of normal ability, fail in the system (e.g. drop out of school, repeat grades, leave High school without a diploma) because their English proficiency is insufficiently developed to comprehend the increasingly complex curriculum.

This situation creates an apparent dilemma. By being placed in some form of **special education**, the child is possibly stigmatized as having a 'deficiency' and a 'language deficit'. Such special education may be a separate school (or a special unit within a larger school) that provides special ('remedial') education for bilingual children. Such schools and units may not foster bilingualism. Often, they will emphasize children becoming competent in the majority language (e.g. English in the United States). Such segregation may allow more attention to the second language but result in ghettoization of language minorities. While giving some sanctuary from sinking in second language submersion in a mainstream school, special education can be a retreat, marginalizing the child. Will children in such special education realize their potential across the curriculum? Will they have increased access to employment? Will their apparent failure be accepted and validated because they are associated with a remedial institution? Will there be decreased opportunities for success in school achievement, employment and self-enhancement?

The ideal for children in this dilemma may be neither mainstreaming nor special education. It is education which allows them to start and continue learning in their first language. The second language is nurtured as well — to ensure the development of bilinguals who can operate in mainstream society. In such schools, both languages are developed and used in the curriculum. Such schools avoid the 'remedial' or 'compensatory' associations of special education. Such schools celebrate the cultural and linguistic diversity of their students.

Yet such bilingual education is sometimes in **danger** of being seen as a form of special education. Even when the 'language delayed' are separated from those who are in the early stages of learning the majority language (e.g. English in the United States), the danger is that the latter will still be assessed as in need of compensatory, remedial special education, including being allocated to bilingual education.

Are Children of Language Minorities Regarded as Having Special Needs Due to Problems Resulting From Their Ethnic Culture, Community or Family Character? What Are Alternative Causes of Special Needs and Learning Difficulties in Children?

The discussion of Special Education for bilingual children has suggested that one unfair assumption made about bilingual children who show learning difficulties is that bilingualism is the cause of those difficulties. Bilingualism is rarely a cause of learning difficulties. Learning difficulties are caused by a variety of possibilities, almost none of them aligned to bilingualism. Six examples of **causes outside the child** and his or her bilingualism follow. This list, which is not exhaustive or comprehensive, will indicate that bilingualism has nothing directly to do with many learning problems, either as a secondary or a primary cause.

(1) Poverty and deprivation, child neglect and abuse, feelings of helplessness and desperation in the home, extended family and community may create personality, attitudinal and learning conditions that make assessment of learning difficulties more probable. Sometimes, such assessment will reflect prejudice, misjudgements and misperceptions about the child's home experiences. The learning problem may thus be in a **mismatch** between the culture, attitudes, expectations about education and values of the home and school. In Chapters 15 and 16 on literacy and biliteracy, this

variation is examined with regard to local literacy and variations in ethnic group and social class uses of literacy. Different beliefs, culture, knowledge and cognitive approaches may be devalued with the child immediately labeled as of inferior intelligence, academically incompetent and of low potential.

(2) The problem may be in the **standard of education**. A child may be struggling in the classroom due to poor teaching methods, a non-motivating, even hostile, classroom environment, a dearth of suitable teaching materials, or clashes with the teacher.

(3) The school may be inhibiting or obstructing learning progress. If a child is being taught in a second language and the home language is ignored, then failure and perceived learning difficulties may result. One example is that of some Spanish speaking children in the United States. Such children are often placed in English only classrooms on entry to school. They must sink or swim in English. Some swim; others sink and may be deemed to have a deficiency. By being assessed in their weaker second language (English) — rather than in their stronger home language (Spanish), such children are labeled as in need of special or remedial education. Thus the monolingual school system is itself responsible for learning failure. A school that promoted bilingualism would probably ensure learning success for the same child.

(4) Another set of causes of learning difficulties are a lack of self confidence, **low self esteem**, a fear of failure and high anxiety in the classroom.

(5) A fifth possibility is failure caused partly by interactions among children in the classroom. For example, where a group of children encourage each other to fool around, have a low motivation to succeed, or where there is bullying, hostility, social division, rather than cohesion among children in a classroom, the learning ethos may hinder the child's development.

(6) Another case is where the child is a slow learner, where there is a mismatch between the **gradient of learning** expected and the ability level of the child. Some children learn to read more slowly than others, still learning to read well, but after a longer period of time. Less able children can learn two languages within the (unknowable) limits of their ability. Other children experience specific learning difficulties (for example, dyslexia, neurological dysfunction, 'short-term memory' problems, poor physical co-ordination, problems in attention span or motivation). None of these specific learning difficulties or other language disorders are caused by bilingualism. At the same time, bilingual children will not escape from being included in this group. Bilingual families are no less likely to be affected than other families.

Almost the only occasion when a learning difficulty of a bilingual child is attached to bilingualism is when a child enters the classroom with neither language sufficiently developed to cope with the higher order language skills demanded by the curriculum. In the rare cases where a child has simple conversational skills in two languages but cannot cope in the curriculum in either language, language may be related to learning difficulties. In this case, the problem is not really with bilingualism but with insufficient language practice in the home, in the nursery school or in the outside world. Here we are talking not about bilingual deprivation, but about deprivation in any language.

ASSESSMENT AND BILINGUAL CHILDREN

The allocation of bilinguals to Special Education and the attribution of learning difficulties usually depends on some form of assessment. It is essential for any psychological and educational assessment of bilingual children to be fair, accurate and broad. Too often, tests given to bilingual children only serve to suggest their 'disabilities', supposed 'deficits' or lack of proficiency in a second language. Assessment can too easily legitimize the disabling of language minority students. Such students may come to be stigmatized by such tests, for example, because tests locate apparent weaknesses in the majority language and use monolingual scores as points of comparison. English language tests and IQ tests administered in the second language to US children are particular examples.

In the United States, there is **legislation** to govern appropriate processes of assessment of those for whom English is an additional language. For example, the 1973 Californian case of *Diana* v. *The California State Board of Education* was based on nine Mexican-American parents who protested that their children (who were dominant in Spanish) were given an English language IQ test. The IQ test revealed 'normal' non-verbal IQ scores, but very low verbal IQ scores (as low as 30 for one child). As a result of this linguistically and culturally inappropriate IQ test, the Mexican-American children were placed in classes for the 'mentally retarded'. This case never went to court, but it established that testing should be conducted in a child's native language (and in English), and that non-verbal IQ tests were usually a fairer measurement of IQ than verbal tests (Valdés & Figueroa, 1994). As a result of this case, the collection of broader data on language minority children was required (rather than simple test data) to justify placement of such children in Special Education.

In 1975, Public Law 94-142, the Education for All Handicapped Children Act, federally mandated that all testing and assessment procedures should be non-discriminatory. 'Non-discriminatory' means using tests that are culturally and linguistically appropriate. Such testing procedures were only to be used by trained members of a **multidisciplinary** team. Apart from tests, teacher recommendations, observations of a child and other relevant information should create a multi-source file of evidence (Barona & Barona, 1992).

Yet for all the advice in legislation, all the discussions in academic literature and in research, bilinguals tend in many countries to be discriminated against in testing and assessment. Therefore, it is important to review the components of such bias, and more constructively, to suggest desirable practice. Ten overlapping and interacting issues in the assessment of bilingual children are now considered.

(1) The **temporary difficulties** faced by bilinguals must be distinguished from relatively more permanent difficulties that impede everyday functioning and learning. Brief language delays, temporary adjustment problems of in-migrants and short-term stammering (stuttering) are examples of transient difficulties (Baker, 1995). Dyslexia, hearing loss and neuroticism are examples where longer term problems may need treatment. This simple distinction hides different and complex dimensions. The means of distinguishing temporary and longer term problems follows below.

(2) Diagnosis needs to go beyond a few, simple tests and engage a wide diversity of measurement and observation devices. Diagnosis needs to be extended over a time period and to avoid an instant conclusion and instantaneous remedy. **Observing** the child in different contexts (and not just in the classroom) will provide a more valid profile (language and behavior) of that child. The family and educational history of the child needs assembling. Parents and teachers need consulting, sometimes doctors, counselors, speech therapists and social workers as well. Samples of a child's natural communication need gathering, with the child in different roles and different situations (Hernandez, 1994).

An awareness or basic knowledge of a child's ethnic, cultural and linguistic background is important in fair assessment, but it may not be enough. To interpret test scores and classifications meaningfully and wisely, and in particular, to make decisions on the basis of assessment, requires a highly sensitive and sympathetic **understanding of a child's community, culture, family life and individual characteristics**. Children come to school with very differing home experiences, where different kinds of ability are cultivated and stressed. Such abilities prized by parents may be different from the abilities learned at school (Chamberlain & Medinos-Landurand, 1991).

For example, discovery learning and learning through play is not a part of all cultures. An investigative, questioning mode of thinking may not be encouraged within a culture. As reflected in parent–child relationships, adults provide authoritative knowledge that must be accepted and enacted by the child. Parents may teach literacy in a similar style, where the child is expected to memorize much or all of the holy book and repeat it without comprehension. Such family and community socialization practices have implications (1) for the type of assessment that reveals the strengths and weaknesses of the child, (2) for the importance of acquiring evidence about the culture of the child, and (3) for the process of assessment by the teacher, psychologist, speech therapist, counselor or other professional.

Test scores (e.g. on educational and psychometric tests) tend to be decontextualized and attenuated (Resnick & Resnick,1992). An analogy helps to illustrate this important point. Test scores are like latitude and longitude. They provide points of reference on a map of human characteristics. As a standard measurement usable on all maps, they provide initial, rapid and instantly comparable information. But imagine the most beautiful place you know (e.g. a flower-enfolded, azure-colored lake set amid tall, green-sloped, ice-capped mountains). Does the expression of the latitude and longitude of that scene do justice to characterizing the personality and distinctiveness of that location? The attempted precision of the sextant needs to be joined by the full empathic exploration and evaluation of the character and qualities of the child.

Authentic language and behavior needs assessing rather than decomposed and decontextualized language skills. The levels of thinking and understanding of a child through both languages need assessing rather than superficial comprehension gleaned from a superficially 'scientific' test (e.g. with high test–retest reliability, and high correlations with similar tests). 'Inauthentic language' tests relate too often to a transmission style curriculum where obtaining the correct answer and 'teaching to the test' dominates teacher thinking and classroom activity. Such tests do not capture the communication abilities of the child, as for example, occur in the playground, on the street, at the family meal-table and in internal conversations when alone.

(3) The choice of **assessors** for the child will affect the assessment. Whether the assessors are perceived to be from the same language group as the child will affect the child's performance (and possibly the diagnosis). The perceived age, social class, powerfulness and gender of the assessor(s) will affect how the child responds and possibly the assessment outcomes. The assessment process is not neutral. Who assesses, using what devices, under what conditions, all contribute to the judgment being made. An inappropriate assessor creates an increased risk of making two common, opposite judgmental errors concerning bilingual children: (1) generating a 'false positive', that is, diagnosing a problem when none is present; (2) generating a 'false negative', that is, failing to locate a problem when one exists.

(4) Children need assessing in their **stronger language**. Ideally children need assessing as bilinguals — in both their languages. The tests and assessment devices applied, and the language of communication used in assessment, should ideally be in the child's stronger language. An assessment based on tests of (and in) the child's weaker language may lead to a misdiagnosis, a false impression of the abilities of the child and a very partial and biased picture of the child. This sometimes occurs in the United Kingdom and the United States where bilingual children are tested in English, partly because of the availability of well regarded psychometric tests.

(5) Parents and educators need to make sure the **language used** in the test is **appropriate** to the child. For example, a translation of the test (e.g. from English to Spanish) may produce inappropriate, stilted language. Also, the different varieties of Spanish, for example, may not that be used by the student. Chicano Spanish speaking parents will want the tests in Chicano or at least Mexican Spanish rather than the Cuban, Puerto Rican or Castilian variety of Spanish. Once Spanish speaking children have been in the United States for a time, their Spanish changes. English influences their way of speaking Spanish. So a test in 'standard' Spanish is inappropriate. A Spanish test may accept only one right answer, penalizing children for their bilingualism and their United States Spanish. A monolingual standard of Spanish is inappropriate to such bilingual children.

Since there are language problems with tests (as outlined above and continued below), it is important to distinguish between a child's language profile and **performance profile** (Cummins, 1984a). The performance profile is more important as it attempts to portray a child's underlying cognitive abilities rather than just language abilities. A performance profile seeks to understand the overall potential of the child, not just their language proficiency.

Cummins (1984a) has shown how this **distinction between a language profile and a performance** profile on one frequently used IQ test in individual assessment — the Wechsler Intelligence Scale for Children: Revised (WISC-R). Bilingual children tend to score significantly higher on the Performance than the Verbal subtests. As Cummins (1984a: 30) suggests: 'The analysis of student performance on this test suggested that the majority of Verbal subtests were tapping ESL students' knowledge of the English language and North American culture in addition to, or instead of, verbal cognitive/academic ability'.

(6) There are times when a test or assessment device cannot be given in the child's stronger language. For example, appropriate bilingual professionals may not be available to join the assessment team, tests may not be available in the child's home language, and **translations** of tests may make those tests invalid and unreliable. **Interpreters** are sometimes necessary. Interpreters do have a valuable function. If trained in the linguistic, professional and rapport-making competences needed, they can make assessment more fair and accurate. Interpreters can also bring a possible bias into the assessment (i.e. 'heightening' or 'lowering' the assessment results through the interpretation they provide).

(7) There is a danger of focusing the assessment solely on the child. If the child is tested, the assumption is that the 'problem' lies within the child. At the same time, and sometimes instead, the **focus** needs to shift to **causes outside the child**. Is the problem in the school? Is the school failing the child by denying abilities in the first language and focusing on failures in the second (school) language? Is the school system denying a child's culture and ethnic character, thereby affecting the child's academic success and self-esteem? Is the curriculum delivered at a level that is beyond the child's comprehension or is culturally strange to the child? The remedy may be in a change to the school system and not to the child.

(8) The danger of assessment is that it will lead to the disablement rather than the **empowerment** of bilingual children (Cummins, 1984a, 1986b). If the assessment separates children from powerful, dominant, mainstream groups in society, the child may become disabled. The assessment may lead to categorization in an inferior group of society and marginalization. Instead, assessment should work in the best, long-term interests of the child. Best interests doesn't only mean short-term educational remedies, but also long term employment and wealth sharing opportunities. The assessment should initiate advocating for the child, and not against the child.

(9) It is important to use the understanding of a child's **teachers** who have observed that child in a variety of learning environments over time. What do the child's teachers think is the root problem? What solutions and interventions do teachers suggest? Have the child's teachers a plan of action? A team of teachers, meeting regularly to discuss children with problems, is a valuable first attempt to assess and treat the child. Such a team can also be the school decision-maker for referral to other professionals (e.g. speech therapist, psychologist, counselor).

(10) Norm referenced **tests** are often used to assess the child (e.g. for entry into, or exit from a bilingual program). This means that the assessor can compare the child with other so called 'normal' children. The assessor can indicate how different the child is from the average. Many such tests are based on scores from 'native' language majority children. Thus, comparisons can be unfair for bilingual children. For example, tests of English language proficiency may have 'norms' (averages, and scores around the average) based on native speakers of English. This makes them

biased against bilinguals and leads to the stereotyping of particular language and ethnic groups.

The **testing of bilinguals** has developed from the practice of testing **monolinguals**. Bilinguals are not the simple sum of two monolinguals but are a unique combination and integration of languages. The language configuration of bilinguals means that, for example, a bilingual's English language performance should not be compared with a monolingual's English language competence. A decathlete should not be compared with a 100 metre sprinter solely for speed of running. Monolingual norms are simply inappropriate for bilinguals (Grosjean, 1985). One example helps illustrate this point. Bilinguals use their languages in different contexts (domains). Thus they may have linguistic competence in varying curriculum areas, on different curriculum topics and on different language functions. Equal language facility in both languages is rare. Comparison on monolingual norms assumes such equal language facility across all domains, language functions and curriculum areas. This is unfair and inequitable.

Such norm referenced tests are often written by white, middle class Anglo test producers. The test items often reflect their language style and **culture**. For example, the words used such as 'tennis racquet', 'snowman' and 'credit cards' may be unfamiliar to some in-migrants who have never seen a snowman, played or watched tennis, or know about the culture of plastic money. Assessment items that reflect the unique learning experiences of language minority children will be excluded from a test for majority language or mainstream children. Such items will be highlighted by item analysis of an early draft of the test as 'unconnected' with the majority of the test items.

Such norm referenced tests are often 'pencil and paper' tests, sometimes involving multiple choice answers (one answer is chosen from a set of given answers). Such tests do not measure all the different aspects of language, of 'intelligence' or any curriculum subject. Spoken, conversational language and financial intelligence, for example, cannot be adequately measured by a simple pencil and paper test.

Some norm referenced tests report the results in **percentiles** (especially in the United States). Percentiles refer to the percentage of children below (and above) the child being tested. For example, being in the 40th percentile means that 39% of children score lower than the child being tested. Sixty percent of children of an age group score above the 40th percentile child. The child is in the 40th group from the bottom, all children being assumed to be divided into 100 equally sized groups. Percentiles are often used for entry and exit of students into bilingual programs in the US. For example, a student may need to reach the 40th percentile on an English language test to be exited to a mainstream class. What 'percentile threshold' (e.g. 40th percentile) is used for entry or exit is essentially arbitrary, and liable to political rather than educationally derived decisions.

Norm referenced tests essentially compare one person against others. Is this important? Isn't the more important measurement about what a bilingual child can and cannot do in each curriculum subject? To say a child is in the 40th percentile in English doesn't tell the parent or the teacher what are a child's strengths and weaknesses, capabilities and needs in English. The alternative is assessment related directly to progress in each curriculum area.

Curriculum based assessment is called **criterion referenced testing**, and seeks to establish the relative mastery of a child in a curriculum area (Baker, 1994b). It seeks to establish what a child can do, and what is the next area of a curriculum (e.g. reading) where progress can be made. A diagnosis may also be made, not necessarily of a fundamental psychological or learning problem, but of weaknesses that need remedial treatment to enable conceptual understanding (e.g. if a child has a problem in reading certain consonantal blends). Such criterion referenced assessment of bilingual students gives parents and teachers more usable and important information. It profiles for parents and teachers what a child can do in a subject (e.g. mathematics) and where development, or accelerated learning, should occur next. Such assessment enables an individualized program to be set for the child.

However, the sequences of learning that underpin a criterion referenced test may still reflect a **cultural mismatch** for the child. Criterion referenced assessment (usually, but not necessarily) assumes there is a relatively linear, step-by-step progression in a curriculum area (e.g. in learning to read, in number skills, in science). Such a progression may be culturally relative and culturally determined. As Cline (1993: 63) noted 'because of their different prior experiences, their learning hierarchy for a particular task may follow different steps or a different sequence (e.g. in relation to phonology and orthography in learning to read)'. Therefore, it is important to use curriculum assessment contexts and processes that are appropriate, comprehensible and meaningful to the bilingual child.

Solutions

Three solutions to the problems of testing bilinguals are provided by Valdés & Figueroa (1994). Their **first** solution is to attempt to minimize the potential harm of existing tests when given to bilingual individuals, by applying some of the guidelines given above. Their **second** solution is, temporarily, to ban all testing of bilinguals until more valid tests can be produced for bilingual populations. Their **third** alternative is that alternative approaches to testing and development be developed. This third option may be the one most favored by many teachers, educationists and parents. It would, for example, bring in bilingual norms, more curriculum based assessment and portfolio type assessment, and a greater cultural and linguistic awareness of bilinguals.

However, this third solution is probably a new beginning but is not enough. A **more radical solution** places change in assessment within (and not separate from) a change in expectations about the nature and behavior of bilingual students. This entails a shift in the politics and policy dimensions of the assessment of bilinguals. Merely changing tests may alleviate the symptoms of a problem, but not change the root cause. The root cause tends to be a bias against language minorities that is endemic in many societies and is substantiated by tests. By being biased against bilinguals in a cultural and linguistic form, and by a failure to incorporate an understanding of the cognitive constitution of bilinguals, assessment confirms and perpetuates various discriminatory perceptions about language minority children.

Assessment thus sometimes serves by its nature and purpose, its form, use and outcomes, to provide the evidence for **discrimination** and **prejudice** against language minorities (e.g. in the US and Britain) to be perpetuated. Assessment results serve to marginalize and demotivate, to reveal under-achievement and lower performance in language minority children. These results are often a reflection of the low status, inequitable treatment and poverty found among many language minorities. Assessment provides the data to make expectations about language minority students self-fulfilling and self-perpetuating. Changing assessment does not necessarily break into that cycle, unless it is a component of a wider reform movement.

Assessment must not in itself be blamed for bias against bilinguals. It is a conveyer and not a root cause of language minority discrimination and bias. Until there is authentic and genuine acceptance of cultural pluralism in a nation, a more widespread assent for multiculturalism, a minimizing of racism and prejudice against ethnic minorities, minor modifications in the assessment of bilinguals stand the chance of merely confirming the lower status and perceived 'deficiencies' of language minority children.

Too often the focus in assessing bilinguals is on their language competence (or on their 'limited proficiencies' as in the test-designated 'Limited English Proficient' students in the United States via tests such as the English Language Assessment Battery (LAB)). Rarely does the assessment of bilinguals in the education system focus on other important competences of a bilingual.

In the US, the 1991 Secretary's Commission on Achieving Necessary Skills (SCANS) recommended that attention be given in high schools to work-related **competences**. For example, performance standards were called for in: interpersonal skills (e.g. working in a team, negotiating, working well with people from culturally diverse backgrounds), interpreting and communicating information, thinking creatively, taking responsibility, sociability, self-management and integrity. These important 'life-skills' are regarded as 'essential accomplishments' for employment, self-respect and building a better world.

On some of these attributes, there is evidence to suggest that bilinguals may have advantages over monolinguals (e.g. negotiating, working well with people from culturally diverse backgrounds, interpreting and communicating information, thinking creatively). If the assessment of bilinguals focused more on these 'outside world' attributes and less on classroom linguistic skills in the majority language, a more affirmative and favorable, productive and constructive view of bilinguals might be promoted.

CONCLUSION

The chapter has attempted to indicate that under-achievement and placement in special education is not a cause of bilingualism. The reasons for under-achievement tend to reside in factors that surround bilinguals (e.g. their social and economic conditions) and are not an inevitable component of bilingualism. Traditional assessment in education often serves to misplace and misdiagnose bilinguals. Apparent rather than real difficulties are identified, with a depreciation of bilinguals' language and potential curriculum performance.

SUGGESTED FURTHER READING

BAKER, C. 1995, Bilingual education and assessment. In B.M. JONES and P. GHUMAN (eds) *Bilingualism, Education and Identity*. Cardiff: University of Wales Press.

CLINE, T. and FREDERICKSON, N. 1995, *Progress in Curriculum Related Assessment with Bilingual Pupils*. Clevedon: Multilingual Matters.

CUMMINS, J. 1984, *Bilingualism and Special Education: Issues in Assessment and Pedagogy*. Clevedon: Multilingual Matters.

GARCÍA, O. and BAKER, C. (eds) 1995, *Policy and Practice in Bilingual Education: A Reader Extending the Foundations*. Clevedon: Multilingual Matters.

HAMAYAN, E.V. and DAMICO, J.S. (eds) 1991, *Limiting Bias in the Assessment of Bilingual Students*. Austin, TX: Pro-ed.

HARRY, B. 1992, *Cultural Diversity, Families and the Special Education System*. New York: Teachers College Press.

KEEL, P. (ed.) 1994, *Assessment in the Multi-Ethnic Primary Classroom*. Stoke on Trent (UK): Trentham Books Limited.

VALDÉS, G. and FIGUEROA, R.A. 1994, *Bilingualism and Testing: A Special Case of Bias*. Norwood, NJ: Ablex Publishing Corporation.

REVIEW AND STUDY QUESTIONS

(1) Write short revision notes on the following:
   (i) The seven explanations of under-achievement in bilinguals.
   (ii) Language delay, stuttering and bilingual special education.
   (iii) The assessment of bilingual children with special needs.
(2) What explanations are given for under-achievement of language minority groups? In what circumstances can such under-achievement be reversed?
(3) Why are children with special needs sometimes wrongly allocated to special education?
(4) Describe the nature of Bilingual Special Education? For what types of students is such education particularly valuable?
(5) Describe the kinds of assessment procedures that are potentially unfair to bilingual children? What may be the most fair and appropriate methods of assessment?

STUDY ACTIVITIES

(1) Interview some parents or teachers with a bilingual student who has special needs (preferably gathering a variety of different viewpoints). Define the exact nature of those special needs. Find out the history of that student's education. Ask the parents or teachers what their preferences are for the use of languages in school and if they want their children to be bilingual as a result of schooling. Inquire about the value and use they see in languages for special needs children.
(2) Locate two students who are considered to have 'special needs'. Write a case study of each student, with contrasts and comparisons, to show the history of assessment

and school placement. Evaluate the decisions made, indicating particular issues of practical importance.

(3) Find out about assessment practices in schools in your neighborhood. What practices exist at district and school level? What tests are used? How do assessment practices impact on bilingual students?

(4) Researching on two or three bilingual students, administer one or more assessment tests, tasks or other devices as allocated by your instructor. Analyze the results and profile the students (a) purely in terms of the test results, then (b) relating the test results to other qualitative information available on the students (e.g. interview the students).

CHAPTER 14

Second Language Learning

CHAPTER 14

Second Language Learning

INTRODUCTION: REASONS FOR SECOND LANGUAGE LEARNING

While there is much in common in second language learning for majority and minority language children, it is important initially to locate the differences. This can be achieved by examining the different reasons for second language learning.

An analysis of language teaching and learning commences from the implicit or explicit aims, assumptions and 'philosophy of practice' of the educationalist. Beneath observable second language teaching will be varying aims in second language teaching, different views of the value of second languages and foreign languages in the local and wider society, as well as varying ideas about learning and teaching in classrooms. The various overlapping reasons why children or adults learn a second or a third language may be clustered under three headings: **ideological, international and individual.**

Ideological Reasons

Examining the societal and political reasons for second language learning highlights the difference between language majority and language minority children. For language minority children, the aim of second language learning may be **assimilationist**. For example, the teaching of English as a second language in the United States and in England often aims at rapidly integrating minority language groups into mainstream society. Assimilationist ideology tends to work for the dominance of the second language, even the repression of the home, minority language. In contrast, when children learn a minority language as their second language, maintenance and **preservation** of that minority language may be the societal aim. For example, when English speaking children are taught in school language lessons to speak Irish in Ireland or Maori in New Zealand, the aim is to preserve and strengthen the indigenous minority language. Such maintenance may not only exist in indigenous language 'territory'. Where first language English children in the US learn to speak Spanish as a second language, there may be an attempt to preserve the language community within a particular area. This provides an additive situation: a second language is added at no cost to the first language.

275

A different societal reason for second language learning other than assimilationist or preservationist, is to obtain increased **harmony** between language groups through bilingualism. In Canada, French speaking children learning English, and English speaking children learning French seek to produce a dual language, integrated Canadian society. For example, the promotional video by the Canadian Official Languages Board entitled *'One Country Two Languages'* enthusiastically conveys the idea that integration into Canadian society is best achieved through widespread bilingualism and biculturalism.

The assimilationist, preservationist, additive and harmony viewpoints all argue for the importance of a second language for careers, access to higher education, access to the information explosion and for travel. However, it is important to distinguish whether the second language is to replace the first language or add to that first language. Rather than multiplying experience, second language teaching may be for divisive reasons, impoverishing the language minority child.

While teachers may be relatively powerless to change the basic aims and reasons in second language teaching, understanding the role they play in such teaching is important. Second language teaching does not exist in a political vacuum. Nor is language teaching a neutral, value-free activity. Therefore, second language teachers need to be aware of their goals at a conscious level.

International Reasons

Apart from the political and social reasons for language learning, there are international reasons given by second language educationists for second language learning. Second and third language learning is often encouraged or enforced for **economic and trade** reasons. Given notions such as common markets, open access to trade, the free market economy, the importance of international trade to developing nations, then facility with languages is seen as opening doors to economic activity. Selling cars and computers to the Japanese, for example, may be almost impossible through English or German. Speaking Japanese and having a sympathetic understanding of Japanese culture, manners, values and thinking may be the essential foundation for economic activity. Helmut Schmidt, former Chancellor of the old Federal Republic of Germany once said: 'If you wish to buy from us, you can talk any language you like, for we shall try to understand you. If you want to sell to us, then you must speak our language'.

There is a growing realization that speaking foreign languages is important in increasingly competitive international **trade**. The Californian State Department Education's (1989) 'Foreign Language Framework' suggests that, 'On a pragmatic level, schools in California as well as in other states need to develop more individuals with strong skills in a second language as a matter of long-range economic self-interest' (p. 4). The Report notes that two-thirds of translating jobs in the US Department of State are filled by foreign-born individuals because there are so few US students and adults who are proficient in the second languages required for such posts.

Second and third language learning is also encouraged for its value in **travel** across continents. For many mainland Europeans, for example, to speak two or three or four languages is not uncommon. Such language facility enables holidays to be spent in neighboring European countries or in North, Central or South America. In the attempted unification of Europe, traveling across frontiers is becoming more common, encouraging a person to acquire a repertoire of languages.

Third, languages provide access to **information**. In the information society of the twentieth century, access to information is often access to power. Whether the information is in technical journals, on large computer databases, on satellite television or in international faxing, a repertoire of languages gives wider access to social, cultural, political, economic and educational information. For the business person and the bureaucrat, for the scholar and the sports person, access to multilingual international information opens doors to new knowledge, new skills and new understanding.

Individual Reasons

There are four reasons frequently given why the individual child or adult should learn a second or third language. One reason is for **cultural awareness**. To break down national ethnic and language stereotypes, one motive in second language learning has become intercultural sensitivity and awareness. The Californian State Department Education's (1989) *Foreign Language Framework* regards one second language learning aim as being the civic and cultural benefits of foreign language teaching. Second language learning is important because 'the power language has to foster improved understanding between peoples of various cultural backgrounds. Culture is embedded in language' (p. 5). Increasing cultural sensitivity is seen as important as the world becomes more international, more of a global village, with more sharing of experience.

Cultural awareness in the classroom may be achieved by discussing ethnic variations in eating and drinking, rituals of birth, death and marriage, comparing the greetings of New Zealand Maori, Arabs and Jews, or comparing shopping rituals in Malaysian markets, San Francisco superstores or all-purpose village stores in Venezuela. Such activity widens human understanding and attempts to encourage sensitivity towards other cultures and creeds. While cultural awareness may be conveyed in the first language, the inseparability of culture and language means that such awareness may best be achieved through simultaneous language learning.

The second 'individual' reason for second language learning has traditionally been for **cognitive training**. The learning of foreign languages has been for general educational and academic value. Just as history and geography, physics and chemistry, mathematics and music have traditionally been taught to increase intellectual fitness and stamina, so modern language learning has been defended as a way of sharpening the mind and developing the intellect. Given the memorization, analysis (e.g. of grammar and sentence structure) and the need to negotiate in communication, language learning has been regarded as a valuable academic activity particularly after elementary schooling.

The third reason for an individual to learn a language is for social, emotional and moral development, self-awareness, self-confidence, and social and ethical values (van Ek, 1986). Such **affective** goals include the possibility of incipient bilinguals being able to create more, and more effective relationships with target language speakers. Bilinguals can potentially build social bridges with those who speak the second language. Self-confidence and enhanced self-esteem may result from being able to operate socially or vocationally with those who speak the second language. The addition of a second language skill can boost an individual's self-concept as a learner, a liaisor and a linguist.

The fourth 'individual' reason for learning a language is for **careers and employment**. For language minority and language majority children, being able to speak a second or third or fourth language may mean escaping unemployment, opening up possibilities of a wider variety of careers or gaining promotion in a career. Potential careers include becoming translators and interpreters, buying and selling goods and services, exchanging information with local, regional, national and international organizations, migrating across national frontiers to find work, gaining promotion in neighboring countries, becoming part of an international team or company, as well as working from home or from the local village and using multilingual telecommunications to spread a product.

TEN DIMENSIONS OF CLASSROOM LANGUAGE LEARNING

We continue by examining some of the basic variations in second language learning and teaching strategies. In second language lessons, language is the subject matter being taught and is also the means of transmitting the subject matter. In second language classrooms, the second language is often also used for classroom management. This makes second language teaching different from other curriculum areas where the language of control is separate from the subject matter taught. History and Science are different from second language lessons because the content is separate from the language of transmission and organization. That apart, what are the major variations in second language learning?

There are considerable variations in the **amount of time** in different courses and syllabuses for second language learning. There are short-course introductions to second languages that last only two weeks of a total of thirty hours duration. In stark comparison, school second language learning from kindergarten to high school may be scheduled for as long as 5,000 hours. Separate from the total amount of time in second language lessons is the distribution or concentration of that time. There are 'drip feed' lessons of about half an hour per day or per week over elementary schooling that result in a low degree of concentration. At the other end is Canadian immersion education with its high concentration, intensive second language learning.

There are a variety of labels for different second language learning and teaching methods and approaches: grammar–translation method, the direct method, the reading method, the Audiolingual approach, the audiovisual approach, situational language teaching, the total physical response method, the silent way, community language learning, the natural approach, Suggestopedia, the functional–notional approach, the information communicative approach and the social communicative approach (Stern, 1983a; Richards & Rodgers, 1986; Cook, 1991). Analysis of these approaches suggests that there are ten basic issues around which the different language teaching methods and approaches are based. These ten overlapping and interlinked issues are first reviewed, and then, for exemplification, three major variations in approach will be outlined.

(1) Explicitly, or more likely implicitly, a language teacher will have a **theory of what constitutes a second language** and what is its purpose. For some teachers, language is essentially about vocabulary, correct grammar and correct sentence structure. Such a view of language is of a rule governed structure or a linguistic system which needs to be conveyed to the student. For other teachers, language concerns communication. Such a utilitarian and sociological view of language highlights that language is for functional communication, for communicating ideas, meaning and information. For some teachers, the implicit theory or purpose of language is 'to share information'. For others, language is ultimately about creating personal relationships, about transactions between people and the successful negotiation of meaning between those conversing. For such teachers, language needs to be learnt for its ability to foster social interaction.

(2) Teachers are also likely, implicitly rather than explicitly, to hold a **theory of how children and adults best learn a language**. Is a second language best learnt through memorizing vocabulary, constantly practicing correct grammar and sentence structure, and forming correct habits? Is language best taught by constant drills and practice, constant correcting of mistakes to achieve as perfect secondary language fluency as possible? Or is language best taught as a means rather than as an end? Should the focus be on meaning and not on language forms? Should language practice be on meaningful tasks involving real communication to acquire the skills of effective communication? Many teachers believe that language has to be learnt, particularly vocabulary and grammar. Gaarder (1977) gives the opposite view. 'Never try to teach language *per se*; rather, teach life (joy, sorrow, work, play, relationships, concepts, differentiation, self-awareness of others, etc.) by involving the children in situations and activities that are highly significant to them'. (p. 78)

(3) From an implicit theory of language and a theory of language learning, there should naturally follow classroom procedures and processes, roles and relationships. Thus, some teachers will define **second language classroom goals** as the accurate control of the four language abilities, of comprehension, (e.g. listening) before production (e.g. speaking), of conscious second language learning and successful academic examination outcomes. For such teachers, the important goal is mastery over the second language to achieve skills that approach those of the native speaker. For other teachers, language for communication purposes is acquired subconsciously. The goal becomes social communication or communicating information, equipping the child with functional skills to communicate in an uninhibited and as intelligible way as possible (but not necessarily correctly).

(4) Goals in language learning have implications for a **language syllabus**. Some teachers will move through a tightly controlled and carefully sequenced set of lessons. New vocabulary will be introduced slowly in a carefully sequenced manner. The difficulty level of grammar and sentence structure will be slowly increased on a precise ladder of progress. Other teachers will have a list of functions and tasks

which are introduced to guide second language acquisition (e.g. greetings, taking leave, thanking, apologizing, giving instructions, relaying intentions).

(5) The preferred syllabus will lead to **classroom activities** that may vary from drill and practice, repetition and substitution, translation and memorization, to activities such as working in a small group on a set task (e.g. moving around a street map from shop to shop), roleplay (for example, going into a cafe ordering coffee and being introduced to a new friend) and pair work.

(6) Such classroom activities have direct consequences for the **role taken by the teacher**. When classroom activities center around drill and practice, the teacher will usually control and orchestrate the lesson. The teacher drills, corrects and tests progress. In this situation, the teacher is authoritatively working from the front of the class and directing operations. When students are working in small groups or in pairs, the teacher may take on a more informal role, being both the facilitator and a participant. The different cogs in the classroom machine are separately oiled and their motion separately monitored.

(7) The role taken by the teacher will determine the **role taken by the learner**. When teachers are controlling, students will be dependent and reactive. The student answers, imitates and hopefully internalizes. When the teacher is the facilitator rather than the director, then students may be more proactive, negotiating with teachers and their peers the route through the task. Being more independent may encourage more language improvisation by students and flexibility in the direction and format of the lesson.

(8) The role taken by the teacher and the student will relate to the **materials and facilities** that exist in and outside the classroom. A more structured, linguistic approach will tend to co-exist with graded text books, visual aids, graded exercises, language laboratories and computer assisted language learning programs. Curriculum materials will be tightly organized and carefully structured. The language laboratory or the computer assisted language learning program will give experience in carefully graded drills and practice. This may result in contrived patterns such as:

Teacher : Do you like the weather today?

Student : No, I do not like the weather today. It is raining today.

Teacher : What kind of weather do you like?

Student : The kind of weather I like is sunshine.

This is termed non-authentic language. It is correct, exact language. However, it is not usually how people speak in a conversation. A more communicative approach will not be so concerned with perfectly correct language, but more on whether the meaning has been conveyed to the listener. Attempting authentic communication will tend to connect with the use of small group work and pairwork, improvised acting and dialogue in the classroom, rather than to tightly controlled, graded lessons. Under this broad heading may be placed out-of-classroom planned experiences (e.g. short term visits to the target language community, study abroad, student exchanges, pen-pal correspondence via letter, video or cassette tape and electronic mail, intensive language learning weekend 'camps', cultural visits and local contacts with 'native' speakers of the second language.

(9)   Different methods and different approaches will relate to different **forms of assessment** of the outcomes of second language learning. For some language teachers, the outcomes should be academic examination success, often accenting literacy as much as, or more than, oracy. For example, the ability to translate from one language to another, spot deliberate mistakes, fill in missing words or phrases in a text, write a free story in the second language will often be judged as the appropriate outcomes of structured language teaching. For other second language teachers, assessment should be the child's ability to understand authentic materials (e.g. reading shop and roadsigns to travel around a town or city). For others, assessment is best achieved through an oral examination where the child's ability to convey and negotiate meaning with the examiner is the important outcome. In such assessment, interlanguage (the language abilities of a child in-between first lessons and fluency) and code switching (e.g. using first language words when negotiating meaning) are both allowable. For some, where language learning is self-controlled, self-planned and self-responsible, then assessment can be self-evaluatory.

(10)   Another variation tends to be the **contexts of second language learning**. The first issue under the context heading is the place of **culture** in language teaching. It is possible to teach a second or foreign language with little or no reference to the attendant culture. A student may become fluent in the Chinese or German language without being at all fluent in Chinese or German culture. The language learnt becomes the language of the classroom and no more. No affiliation, understanding, empathy or identification is felt with the language community. Alternatively, the language and culture may be taught in an integrated way. The way of life of different Chinese groups may be presented to, and experienced by the language learner. The second issue concerning context is the **ethos of the classroom**. Sometimes language learning goes on in classrooms without bright and colorful wall displays that create a suitable atmosphere for learning French or learning Spanish. When the same classroom serves as a science laboratory, a history room, a social studies area and a second language classroom, language learning may be more removed from a cultural context and a cultural ethos. Other second language classrooms tend to surround the student with appropriate language and cultural artifacts: posters and pictures, videos and computer assisted language learning programs, objects (e.g. costumes and food packets) and tourist relics. The student is provided with an appropriate atmosphere for learning the target language. When second language learning occurs in the Mosque, Temple, Synagogue, Church Hall or Language Community Center, the context may engender a feeling of becoming and belonging.

Having considered ten basic issues around which language teaching and language learning vary, we will now consider three major, broadly different approaches. The **Structural Approach** is an umbrella title under which comes the Grammar–Translation method, the traditional North American Audiolingual approach and the Direct Method. Second, the **Functional Approach**, sometimes called the Notional–Functional approach, will be considered. This particularly has been the method encouraged by the Council of Europe in its 'Language and Teaching Modern Languages for Communication' project and is sometimes termed the Information Communicative Approach. The third method will be termed the **Interactional Approach** and is sometimes labeled the Social Communicative approach.

THE STRUCTURAL APPROACH

The structural approach asserts that there is a language system to be mastered. The historically dominant method of second language acquisition in school has been the **grammar–translation approach**. Students were expected to memorize vocabulary lessons, learn verb declensions, learn rules of grammar and their exceptions, take dictation and translate written passages. While tests and examinations were passed and paper qualifications issued, students mostly did not become functionally bilingual. Second language learning started and stayed in school.

A new approach to language teaching, called **audiolingualism** developed, much allied to **behaviorist psychology**. According to audiolingualism, second language learning is possible by the acquisition of a distinct set of speech habits. A habit is the ability to make a sound or say a word or use grammar correctly in an automatic, unconscious fashion. In behaviorist terms, language learning comprises the linking of a particular response to a particular stimulus. The teacher provides specific, well defined stimuli. The learner responds and is reinforced or corrected. Through repetition and drills it is hoped that the student will be able to use a second language automatically.

In the **Audiolingual approach**, the system to be memorized is structure-based dialogues. Language learning becomes the learning of structures, sounds and words to attempt to achieve native speaker-like pronunciation. Such a structural view sees language as a linguistic system, with the aim being to instill linguistic competence in the student. For the grammar translation method, the accent is on literacy rather than oracy skills. The opposite is the case for the Audiolingual approach where listening and speaking are given priority. Because language teaching is based on linguistic structure, lessons should be carefully sequenced and graded. The sequencing is to be determined wholly by linguistic complexity (e.g. moving from simple grammar rules to more complex rules with their exceptions; practicing simple speaking patterns followed by ever increasing width of vocabulary and difficulty in sentence structure).

In the Audiolingual method, the focus is constantly on correct language. To achieve this, there is repetition of vocabulary phrases and sentences, imitative mimicry and memorization of short dialogues. The aim is for the learner to avoid making linguistic mistakes in sentence construction and gain an automatic, accurate control of basic sentence structures. Mastery of basic vocabulary and structures is required, by overlearning if necessary.

Part of the theory of **audiolingualism** is that the learner's first language interferes with the acquisition of the second language. Such interference occurs because the learner is ensnared by the habits of the first language. Therefore, teachers are encouraged to focus on areas of difficulty posed by negative transfer from the first to the second language (e.g. Lado, 1964). A procedure called Contrastive Analysis was developed to show the areas of difficulty in transfer from first language to second language. Such analysis resulted in a list of features of the second language, different from the first language, which posed potential problems for the teacher.

The **origins of audiolingualism** are found in the Army method of American Language Programs during World War II. Just as drill and practice are the essentials in basic training on the parade square, so drilling is the central technique in a structural approach. In the late 1960s and 1970s, the assumptions of the audiolingual method were shown to be doubtful. When the Contrastive Analysis hypothesis was researched (e.g. Dulay & Burt, 1973, 1974), grammatical errors were found that could not be explained by negative transfer from the first to the second language. The Chomskyian revolution in linguistics also cast doubts on the behaviorist view of second language learning. Chomsky (1965) suggested that human beings have an inbuilt cognitive readiness for language. Instead of language being a series of surface patterns and habits, Chomsky emphasized the abstract, mentalist and universal nature of rules that underlie an individual's language competence. A child is endowed with a **language-acquisition** device that comprises innate knowledge of grammatical principles.

Purity in second language is demanded in the **structural approach**. Therefore, students are not allowed to use their first language in conveying meaning. The model for correct language is provided by the teacher, or via prepared tapes in the language laboratory or more recently through computer assisted language learning programs. While such structural viewpoints have tended to be criticized by language learning researchers and advisors, such a formal, teacher orchestrated style is to be found as a major component in many teachers' classroom repertoire.

THE FUNCTIONAL APPROACH

In the 1970s, there developed a major alternative approach to language teaching. Instead of regarding language as a linguistic system to be conveyed to the student, an alternative viewpoint was that language is essentially about conveying meaning. The focus since the 1970s has tended to shift partly away from teaching the formal nature of a language to socially appropriate forms of communication. For example, the sociolinguist Hymes (1972a) argued that language was essentially about communication, essentially about being able to use a language for a purpose. Language is a means rather than a structural end. Effective language does not mean grammatical accuracy nor articulate fluency, but the **competence to communicate** meaning effectively.

Criticisms of the audiolingual method have led to a current emphasis on a more **communicative approach** in second language learning. What is the *language* basis of the communicative approach?

- Second language learning is controlled by the learner rather than by the teacher. Whereas in audiolingualism the teacher was regarded as crucial, the recent focus has changed to a selection and organization of second language input partly by the learner.
- Human beings possess an innate capacity and natural propensity for learning a second language. Whereas in audiolingualism the first language was thought to interfere with the learning of a second language, current thinking is that a second language can be acquired in a similar way to the first language.
- It is not necessary to attend to the form of language to acquire a second language. The systematic learning of grammar becomes of much less importance. Since first language learning occurs successfully without formal grammar teaching, considerably less emphasis could be placed on grammatical form, more on informal acquisition.
- Language errors and 'interference' or transfer are a natural part of the learning process. Children spontaneously produce unique utterances and do not just imitate adult language as behaviorists would claim. For example, a child who says 'all finish food' (I've completely finished my food) reflects the use of some underlying implicit rules. The early incorrect production of sentences does not prevent a child from going on to produce correct, well formed sentences later. Corder (1967) suggested that second language learners need to discover their own errors rather than to be continuously corrected by the teacher. Therefore, the problem of interference becomes a problem of ignorance. The avoidance of interference between languages cannot be taught in the classroom; rather the avoidance of interference comes via observation of one's own language. Language development can thus be seen as the process of implicit rule formation rather than explicit habit formation.

Van Ek (1986, 1987) outlines six different forms of **language competence** to be acquired for communication purposes: linguistic, sociolinguistic, discourse, strategic social–cultural and social competence. This essentially is a belief that there is something more than linguistic competence as fostered by the structural approach that needs to be acquired by the student.

There exists **sociolinguistic competence** in a language that concerns the ability to communicate accurately in different contexts, with different people, and when there are different intentions in the communication. Sociolinguistic competence is the awareness of the language form required in different situations. Such competence arises when natural interaction occurs between students, without prompting by the teacher. **Discourse competence** is the ability to use appropriate strategies in constructing and interpreting different texts, the ability to contribute to the construction of a spoken discourse in communication. For example, discourse competence is found in the ability to use pronouns, transition words and insert progression into communication.

Strategic competence is the ability to use verbal and nonverbal communication strategies to compensate for gaps in the language user's knowledge. Strategic competence concerns the ability to use body language (gesturing, head nods, eye contact) to give meaning when verbal language is not at a level of competence to convey meaning. **Sociocultural competence** is the 'awareness of the sociocultural context in which the language concerned is used by native speakers and the ways in which this context affects the choice and the communicative effect of particular language forms' (van Ek, 1987: 8). Finally, **social competence** is the ability to use particular social strategies to achieve communicative goals. For example, social competence includes the ability to take the initiative in a conversation, to know when to interrupt someone else speaking without being ill-mannered. Social competence involves understanding the social conventions that govern communication within a culture.

Based on the work of Wilkins (1976), Widdowson (1978), the Council of Europe in van Ek (1986, 1987) and in Girard (1988), the **notional–functional syllabus** developed for second language teaching. The notional categories to be taught include time, quantity, space, motion, sequence and location, as well as the communicative functions such as persuasion, inquiry, relaying emotions and establishing personal relationships. A Council of Europe initiative resulted in a list of topic areas to be covered against a list of language functions (van Ek, 1987: 17). The 21 different topic areas can be considered in combination with language functions (e.g. forms of greeting and taking leave need considering in the different contexts of: home, school, extended family, work, leisure, at a supermarket check-out, when happy, angry, sad and when meeting someone for the first time):

Topic Areas	**Language Functions**
Self	Being polite and sociable
Family and daily routine	Attracting attention
School	Introducing someone
Work	Expressing good wishes
Leisure	Thanking
Holiday and travel	Apologizing
Environment, places and facilities	Agreeing and disagreeing
Food and drink	Refusing and accepting
Goods and services	Approving and disapproving
Accidents and emergencies	Coping with language problems
Interesting events in the past, present and future	Asking for information Stating facts
Clothes and fashion	Opinions and feelings
People	Likes and dislikes
Personal belongings, pets and money	Reasons
Places	Needs, requests and wishes
Immediate plans	Instructions and commands
Times and dates	Intentions
The weather	Permission
Emotional state (e.g. happy, bored)	Inviting

Topic Areas	**Language Functions**
Physical state (hungry, ill)	Suggesting
	Offering

An example would be learning forms of greeting and taking leave. Appropriate vocabulary and examples of simple structures is introduced by the teacher, or video or Computer Assisted Language Learning. For instance, in French, vocabulary introduced might include: *bonjour, bonsoir, salut, au revoir, à demain, bonne fête, bon voyage, bon anniversaire, bonnes vacances, bon appétit, bonne année, Joyeux Noël, Madame, Mademoiselle* and *excusez-moi*.

Cultural variations are discussed in the classroom (e.g. shaking hands, signs of peace, conventions about kissing, use of body language such as distance from the other person, eye contact, smiles, head nods and posture). Different situations will also be explored for necessary variations (e.g. greeting older compared with younger people, different conventions in shops, with peers compared with their parents). After pair or group work to practice greetings and 'goodbyes', appropriate linguistic and social-cultural behavior may have been learnt (Girard, 1988; Sheils, 1988).

A functional view of language is language for real life activity. The language acquired in language lessons is for use in the second language community or for travel abroad. Such language learning is based on an analysis of what a student **needs to communicate** with the second language community. Thus, the emphasis is less on correct grammar and perfect sentence structuring, more on the ability to communicate meaningful information. An awareness of the context (e.g. supermarket, booking an air ticket) and of the comprehension level of the listener is regarded as important. The sequencing of the lessons is determined by a careful consideration of an order of difficulty in content and function rather than of the linguistic attributes of the second language. Using task based materials (e.g. finding the way to the supermarket, obtaining a reservation on a plane), language is learnt through trial and error, with accuracy judged in terms of context and meaningfulness rather than purely in linguistic terms. Using small group work, pair work and task based, authentic individual activity, students are encouraged to gain confidence in using the second language even in the most rudimentary form, to communicate information successfully. Thus a second language may be learnt in an unconscious, informal way rather than explicitly and directly.

THE INTERACTIONAL APPROACH

From the beginning of the 1970s, a slow shift towards teaching methods that emphasized communication has been visible. The functional approach tended to redefine what the student had to learn to be competent in communication rather than competent in linguistic structures. Knowing how to use language appropriately in particular situations has been emphasized more than knowledge of grammatical rules only in second language learning.

The accent recently has been slightly away from language functions and notions to communication for its social, transactional, personal relationship goals. In the functional approach to second language teaching, it is possible that the teacher is controlling and the students responding. Learning how to ask directions or how to greet someone can still be taught in a formal, drill and repetition style of teaching. A task such as finding the way to the cafe and ordering a snack can still result in exercises that make the student substitute words, fill in blanks in sentences and write down short phrases. While the activities of cafe visiting and ticket booking may be authentic and meaningful, the language being used may be artificial, and abstracted from the real social interaction of authentic dialogue.

In the interactional view of second language learning, the **communicative approach** requires a classroom where real interpersonal communication regularly takes place and where social and personal transactions between people actively occur. Moving away from a teacher based, teacher controlled, responsive, information communicative style, the interactional view emphasizes maximal active social communication in the classroom, between students in pairs and in groups. The teacher becomes a facilitator rather than a drill sergeant. In the interactional approach to second language teaching, the following type of exercise may be given.

A **pair** of students work together. One person has a simple map of Barcelona, the other person has a list of supermarkets with street names. Each only has partial information. Working together as best they can in the second language, they ask each other questions to find a route to particular supermarkets. The students are given basic vocabulary on the map with a sample question-and-answer sequence. The pair have to improvise a dialogue to solve their communicative tasks. Another example is when students engage in **roleplay**. One student has to engage in a telephone conversation booking a ticket for herself and her son on the plane from Barcelona to New York, Tuesday morning next week. The conversation includes problems of diet and complications about the cost. A cassette or video may be collaboratively created.

In these two examples, the essential nature of the tasks is **social communication** between people. Inter-relationships and information combine rather than the processing of information being the sole focus. In such an interactional approach to second language teaching, language is about methods of talking to people. Such a method aims to give students both the competence and the confidence to engage in real conversations with people. Errors in speech become relatively unimportant compared with finding strategies for successful communication. While the teacher may provide some feedback and correction, the essential element is to encourage students to make attempts at social communication, however grammatically flawed and limited in vocabulary. Such an approach rests on intrinsic motivation among students and a willingness to forego authoritative control by teachers. Some teachers and students find such roles difficult to accept. For some, such roles are culturally inappropriate. The expectation is teaching by formal, traditional methods of second language teaching. The teacher is transmitting, the student is receiving. The student centered rather than teacher centered approach can seem very foreign to foreign language teaching.

THE MULTIDIMENSIONAL LANGUAGE CURRICULUM

Most language classrooms and language teachers tend to be eclectic in approach, combining in different ways and in a different balance the structural, functional and interactional methods. In real classrooms, there is often a combination of drills and pairwork, task based activity and teacher directed transmission, correct habit formation and improvised dialogue between students with interlanguage allowed. At its worst, eclecticism is unselective, directionless, with constantly shifting ground. At its best, eclecticism may lead to rational integration of 'classroom-wise' approaches.

An attempt at integrating the different aims and goals of a second or foreign language approach stems particularly from the Boston Paper on Curriculum Materials (Lange, 1980). A group of second language learning experts proposed the idea of a **multidimensional curriculum**. This would comprise four types of syllabuses: (1) Linguistic, (2) Cultural, (3) Communicative, and (4) General Language Education. The Boston Paper argued that current syllabuses were too ambitious in their **linguistic** features. Too much time was spent in language classrooms in learning word lists and grammar. Too little time was spent on generating communicative competence in children. The Boston Paper suggested that a linguistic syllabus was important but it should be joined by a **cultural** syllabus that would accent the content of modern languages rather than just the form of the language. Children require an understanding of the cultural attributes of the language being learnt and this should be thoroughly integrated with the linguistic elements. Such a cultural syllabus needs to be assessed and examined in order to raise its status.

The Boston Paper (Lange, 1980) argued that a multidimensional curriculum would also involve a **communicative** syllabus. Here the focus would be on efficient communication rather than on accurate language. Language errors would be tolerated so that the accent could be on effective transmission of meaning. Authentic language needed to be encouraged. While simulation and role playing may lead to a limited degree of communicative ability, contact with foreign language speakers, preferably in natural situations, was much to be desired. Encouragement should be given to students spending time in the homes and communities of second language speakers. Alongside immersion experience in the second language community, language camps, festivals, visits to language communities and the use of native speakers within the classroom is encouraged.

The final part of the Boston Paper (Lange, 1980) suggested that a multidimensional language curriculum include a **general language education** syllabus. In the syllabus, students would come to understand more about the nature and functions of language. Topics such as learning how to learn a language, language varieties, and language and culture would be considered.

The theoretical basis of a multidimensional foreign language curriculum was subsequently expanded on and refined by Stern (1983b, 1992), by trial materials (Tremblay et al., 1989) and was furthered by the Canadian National Core French Study (LeBlanc, 1990). A national study in Canada has suggested major developments in the teaching and learning of French as a second language in mainstream, core programs.

Canadian Core French programs have hitherto taught French for between 20 and 50 minutes a day. Sometimes starting at Grade 1, often at Grade 4, or later at Grade 7, a child may receive (e.g. in Ontario) around 1200 hours of instruction in French, with a target active vocabulary of 3000 to 5000 words and around 100 basic sentence patterns (Lapkin, Harley & Taylor, 1993). The suggested development of this Core program is through four integrated syllabuses:

- **A language teaching syllabus** which is structural and functional in approach. Both the form, the functions and the context of language learning are addressed. Grammatical 'consciousness raising' and an analytical approach to language learning is to be partnered by an experiential approach. Thus, communicative competence in a second language needs to be integrated with grammatical knowledge.
- **A communicative activities/experiential syllabus** is designed to give the second language learner authentic experiences in communication and usable communication skills. Curriculum themes are to be motivating, interesting, relevant, and to enrich experience as well as give communicative competence.
- **A cultural syllabus** presents the French culture as something to be observed and analyzed as well as experienced. It aims to develop sociocultural awareness and integrate French language learning with French culture. Focusing on contemporary culture, the syllabus is principally concerned with enabling students to communicate effectively first and foremost with French-Canadians, but with other francophones as well. Stern's (1992) vision extends the cultural syllabus to increased contact with the target language community, if possible. While cultural competence is essential for successful communicative skills, the cultural syllabus underlines the essential relationship between language and culture. The one stimulates and enriches the other in second language learning. The learning of a language gathers meaning and purpose when there is simultaneous enculturation. For example, French lessons may cover different areas of cultural experience: everyday activities, (e.g. food and drink), personal and social life (e.g. relationships with friends and family), the world around (e.g. home region compared with region abroad), the world of education, training and work (e.g. tourism), the world of communications (e.g. international electronic mail and satellite TV), the international world (e.g. travel and holidays) and the world of imagination and creativity (e.g. the making of a video or magazine).
- **A general language education syllabus** explores languages and communication as intrinsically important topics. This aims to increase students' awareness of language and of the process of language learning via a three pronged attack: language awareness, cultural awareness and strategic awareness. Topics might include: dialects and registers, languages across the world, the origins of languages, the language development of children, language prejudice, and correspondence (including across distance by electronic mail).

A mathematically imaginative answer is given to the question of how much time to allot to these four strands. 'An ideal distribution of time in the core French program might be: 75% communicative/experiential, 40% linguistic syllabus, 15% general language, and 25% culture. While this may seem to add up to 155%, in reality it adds up to an effective and efficient core French program. Providing that French is *the* language of communication in the classroom, and providing that teachers and students focus on learning a living second-language for use in real life, each syllabus will compliment the others and be realized simultaneously. That is, integration will occur almost naturally and the time allocations will truly overlap' (LeBlanc & Courtel, 1990: 91). The **integration** of the four syllabuses is crucial. Limited time for second language learning, and too demanding a schedule within available time makes integration a challenge for language educators.

CONCLUSION

This chapter has considered the route to bilingualism via second language learning in school. While the route has a long history in education, recent movements away from a structural to a communicative approach, highlight classroom variations in aim, approach, strategy and style. Such variations indicate different kinds of bilingualism that may be fostered in school. One variation is linguistic bilingualism, another is functional bilingualism, another, bilingualism dedicated to human interaction. Variations in approach have recently been integrated into the concept of a multidimensional language curriculum. Culture and communication, linguistics and general language education may be combined in an attempt to harmonize varied aims and approaches, strategies and styles.

SUGGESTED FURTHER READING

CALIFORNIAN STATE DEPARTMENT OF EDUCATION, 1989, *Foreign Language Framework*. Sacramento, CA: California State Department of Education.
RICHARDS, J.C. and ROGERS, T.S. 1986, *Approaches and Methods in Language Teaching*. Cambridge: Cambridge University Press.
STERN, H.H. 1992, *Issues and Options in Language Teaching*. Oxford: Oxford University Press.

REVIEW AND STUDY QUESTIONS

(1) Write short revision notes on the following:
    (i)   Ideological, international and individual reasons for second language learning.
    (ii)   The multidimensional language curriculum.
(2) What are the important dimensions of second language learning? How do approaches to second language learning differ in their aims and differ in their classroom activities?
(3) With a form of language learning with which you are most familiar, use the 10 dimensions of classroom language learning to expand on a particular style of teaching and learning.

STUDY ACTIVITIES

(1) In a small group of students, discuss different experiences of learning a second language at school. Use the 10 dimensions of classroom language learning to record the differences between the group. From the experiences of the group, which of these

dimensions seem most important? Which approaches in the classroom seem from the personal experiences of the group to be most effective?

(2) Visit a school where students are learning a foreign language. By interviewing the teachers and observing classroom sessions, describe in terms of the 10 dimensions, the approach or approaches being used. Ask the teachers and the students their purposes in learning a foreign language. If there are differences in aim between teachers and students, examine whether you think these can be made compatible or are in conflict.

(3) Observe a classroom in which a foreign language is being taught to the majority, and one in which a second language is being taught to a minority. Describe and explain the differences in approach.

(4) Imagine you are in a classroom 20 years hence. In that futuristic classroom, describe how language learning might be taking place. What kind of technology might be in use? Will there be more or less emphasis on learning minority and majority languages? What motivations might the students have in the futuristic classroom? For what purposes are languages being learnt? What forms of assessment are being used?

CHAPTER 15

Literacy in a Multicultural Society

Introduction

The Uses of Literacy in Bilingual and Multicultural Societies

Definitions of Literacy

Approaches to Literacy
The Skills Approach
The Whole Language Approach
The Construction of Meaning Approach
The Socio-Cultural Literacy Approach
The Critical Literacy Approach

Conclusion

CHAPTER 15

Literacy in a Multicultural Society

INTRODUCTION

In education systems throughout the world, reading and writing are usually regarded as central in the curriculum. In developed and developing countries, literacy is often associated with progress, civilization, social mobility and economic advancement. A classic, if disputed claim, is by Anderson (1966) who suggests that any society requires a 40% literacy rate for economic 'take off', a belief which is embedded in many literacy programs. But, as this chapter will show, what precisely is meant by literacy is neither simple nor uncontroversial.

In today's highly literate or less literate multilingual and multicultural societies, the ability to read and write is often regarded as essential for personal survival, security and status. Literacy impacts on people's daily lives in innumerable ways. Where language minority members are relatively powerless and underprivileged, literacy is often regarded as a major key to self advancement as well as empowerment. If this is so, it is important to consider the **needs or uses for literacy** in students and adults in bilingual and multicultural societies.

In considering such needs and uses, it is important to note that literacy education for language minority students is often in a majority language (e.g. English language literacy in the United Kingdom and the United States; English in parts of Africa as an 'official' or international language). However, where language minorities have access to bilingual education, literacy may be introduced in the home/minority language. In that case, literacy in the majority language (and hence biliteracy) will be developed later in the elementary school. This issue is considered in the next chapter. For the moment, the consideration of uses of literacy refers to literacy introduced in either the minority or majority language (or both languages developed in parallel).

THE USES OF LITERACY IN BILINGUAL AND MULTICULTURAL SOCIETIES

Literacy is Needed for Survival

There are basic day to day uses of literacy. For example, a motorist needs to read road signs, a shopper needs to read instructions and labels on food packaging, the traveler needs to understand signs at bus stations, train stations and airports.

Literacy is Needed for Learning

Students need to be able to read text books, story books, laboratory manuals, examination sheets and tests for learning to take place.

Literacy is Needed for Citizenship and Political Empowerment

To complete bureaucratic forms, participate in local or regional government, read local and national newspapers, read information that comes through the post or is on billboards, citizens need basic reading skills. To respond, react, complain and assert democratic rights, reading and writing are often valuable allies to speaking skills.

Literacy is Needed for Personal Relationships

Writing letters to friends and relatives who are no longer local, and sending seasonal greeting cards, are each aided by literacy.

Literacy is Needed for Personal Pleasure and Creativity

Being able to read gives students and adults access to magazines, novels, comics, story books and non-fiction to be enjoyed in leisure time. Literacy enables the imagination to be stimulated, and creative instincts to be expressed.

Literacy is Needed for Employment

Many higher status and higher paid jobs require reading and writing skills.

Literacy is Needed to Empower the Mind

Wells & Chang-Wells (1992) suggest that literate thinking is 'the building up, metaphorically speaking, of a set of mental muscles that enable one effectively to tackle intellectual tasks that would otherwise be beyond one's powers' (p. 122). Literacy is seen as a mode of thinking, as a means of **reasoning**, reflecting and interacting with oneself. This links with the idea of the empowerment of individuals, and having a public voice.

The importance and usefulness of literacy for language minorities is revealed in public perceptions of those who are **illiterate**. Being unable to read and write is often regarded as shameful, embarrassing, a symbol of low or marginal status, and in need of remediation in school or in adult classes. Reducing illiteracy is regarded as a key priority in UNESCO's aims, irrespective of country, continent, culture or caste.

Whether language minority children should first become literate in the majority language or in their minority language will be discussed later in this chapter. Also considered later will be whether majority language monoliteracy or biliteracy should be attempted. Before engaging such discussions, it is important to explore the kind of literacy that language minority students and adults require. We start by considering three contrasting definitions of literacy. This provides an instant flavor of the keen debate about the nature and value of different kinds of literacy. The debate has important implications for bilingual students, as will be revealed.

DEFINITIONS OF LITERACY

The list of needs for literacy given above has already hinted that literacy plays different roles for different people. Compare two definitions of literacy. The first is a functional **definition** of, and skills approach to, literacy by UNESCO dating from 1962.

A literate person is someone who 'has acquired the essential knowledge and skills which enable him to engage in all those activities in which literacy is required for effective functioning in his group and community and whose attainments in reading, writing and arithmetic make it possible for him to continue to use these skills towards his own and the community's developments' (cited in Oxenham, 1980: 87).

In comparison, Hudelson (1994: 130) defines reading as 'a language process in which an individual constructs meaning through a transaction with written text that has been created by symbols that represent language. The transaction involves the reader's acting upon or interpreting the text, and the interpretation is influenced by the reader's past experiences, language background, and cultural framework, as well as the reader's purpose for reading'. This is a definition that concentrates on reading as the construction of meaning, rather than on the skills of reading. While this definition only refers to reading, the idea extends to literacy in general.

The third **definition** derives from Wells & Chang-Wells (1992) who argue that 'To be literate is to have the disposition to engage appropriately with texts of different types in order to empower action, thinking, and feeling in the context of purposeful social activity' (p. 147). This definition deliberately allows for the possibility that different language minority communities attach a different value to different types of literacy.

Cultures differ from each other in their uses and purposes for literacy. For some cultures literacy is about promoting abstract thought, rationality, critical thinking, balanced and detached awareness, empathy and sensitivity. For other cultures literacy is about memorization, transmission of life stories revealing their heritage, values and morality, and centrally in certain religions, for the transmission of rules of religious and moral behavior. A Moslem for example, will be expected to read aloud from the Qu'ran. Many Moslems are not expected to understand what they read, this being provided in their mother tongue. In some cultures, the mother is expected to read to her children and help them develop literacy skills, but is not expected to read national newspapers or complete bureaucratic forms herself. The concept of literacy is therefore not single but plural, relative to a culture and not universal.

These three definitions (skills, the construction of meaning, and sociocultural) will now be extended and explored by examining different educational approaches to literacy. These approaches, like the above definitions, are not necessarily discrete but overlap and can be combined in literacy learning. However, their emphases are different in ways that they impact on students.

APPROACHES TO LITERACY

The Skills Approach

The concept of **functional literacy**, as in the UNESCO definition, appears to assume that literacy is the simple act of reading and writing. 'Acquiring essential knowledge and skills' refers to the ability to decode symbols on a page into sounds, followed by making meaning from those sounds. Reading is about saying the words on the page and writing about being able to spell correctly, and write in correct grammatical sentences. In both reading and writing, a literate person is able to understand and comprehend the printed word.

The assumption of this approach is that literacy is primarily a **technical skill**, neutral in its aims and universal across languages. The skills of reading and writing can be decomposed into vocabulary, grammar and composition. Teaching sounds and letters, phonics and standard language may be the important focus. Errors in reading and writing will also incur keen attention, alongside a concern with achieving scores on tests of reading and writing. Such tests tend to assess decomposed and decontextualized language skills, eliciting superficial comprehension rather than deeper language thinking and understanding. These reliable but 'inauthentic' tests tend to be used as templates for instruction. Measurement-led instruction promotes 'teaching to the test' and possibly drives out opportunities for developing higher order language skills.

Underneath the skills approach to literacy tends to be a belief that children need functional or 'useful' literacy only. Effective functioning implies that the student or adult will contribute in a collaborative, constructive and non-critical manner to the smooth running of the local community. **Functional literacy** is perceived as recognizing the status quo, understanding and accepting one's place in society, and being a 'good citizen'. This view is extended later in the book when the relationship between bilingualism and politics is considered.

While there are various types of literacy, it is important not to forget the amount of illiteracy and low levels of literacy in many countries. Functional literacy does not mean reading print in 'quality' newspapers and books. Functional literacy is at a lower level: being able to read labels on tins and road signs, finding a number in a telephone directory. Among those who seem to be functionally literate, there will be those who are aliterate (who can read but don't), and those who manage to hide their illiteracy, as it is socially undesirable to be illiterate. Functional literacy may not be enough in advanced, techno-logical societies. The populace constantly faces bureaucratic forms and written instructions which demand more advanced literacy skills. Functional literacy is unlikely to be enough to cope with such complex tasks.

The Whole Language Approach

The Whole Language Approach to literacy is diametrically opposed to reading and writing as decoding and a series of separate skills. The whole language approach emphasizes learning to read and write naturally, for a **purpose**, for meaningful communication and for inherent pleasure (Whitmore & Crowell, 1994).

Generally, the Whole Language Approach supports an holistic and integrated learning of reading, writing, spelling and oracy. The language used must have relevance and meaning to the child. The use of language for communication is stressed; the operation rather than the form of language. The Whole Language Approach is against basal readers and phonics in learning to read. Basal readers are reading books that use simplified vocabulary. There is often a set order in reading these books, moving from simple to more complex text in a gradually increasing gradient of difficulty. (This is considered in more detail later in this section). In a whole language approach, writing must be for **real purposes**. A child writes for somebody in a particular situation and for a defined reason. Writing means reflecting on one's ideas and sharing meaning with others. Writing can be in partnership with others, involving drafting and redrafting.

A child learns to write when they are writing for somebody with a meaning and a message. Efficient writing means making it comprehensible for an audience. Constantly highlighting grammatical and spelling errors is soul destroying for the child. Corrections concentrate on form and not function, on the medium and not the message. Conveying meaning is important in learning to write well. Learning to read is also learning to write. A child learns to spell when learning to read. The more children read, the more their writing improves.

Reading and writing need to be fun experiences in the Whole Language Approach. This occurs when reading and writing involve real and natural events, not artificial stories, artificial sequences, rules of grammar and spelling, or stories that are not relevant to the child's experience. Reading and writing need to be interesting, relevant to the child, belonging to the child's experience, allowing choice by the learner, giving children power and understanding of their world. Reading taught for its own sake is not fun. Going through a book of writing exercises following reading is not usually interesting or relevant to the child.

Children learn to read and write when there is a need to understand the **meaning** of a story, to chant a rhyme, to share the humor of a book. Writing is fun when it is **communication**. Part of a Whole Language Approach is to stimulate the **creative imagination** and sheer enjoyment in reading. Much of what children and adults read is for leisure and pleasure, and while not politically neutral or morally objective, novels, magazines, comics and some poetry are designed to satisfy and stir the imagination. Literacy in the Whole Language Approach is thus to develop aesthetic appreciation and interpersonal sensitivity.

When reading and writing are contrived, when the form of words is put before their function, neither reading nor writing are encouraged. Reading and writing need to provide opportunities for shared language and shared meaning. A series of books that is based on how often words occur in a language, that tries very exactly to grade difficulty, moving from one level to another level slowly, might seem logical and sensible. Yet such books tend to have artificial stories, artificial language constructions and do not match nor cultivate the child's experience.

Children need imaginative, vivid, interesting books that both relate to, and increase their experience, which make them laugh and stir their **imagination**. They need to feel that books are interesting, unstuffy, relevant to their world and their way of thinking. Children don't just need books on the shelf. Magazines and newspapers, directories and posters, signs in the street, packages and labels are all reading material. Children writing to each other or to their grandparents in another country is each a form of reading and writing centered round an authentic task. The rules of reading and writing are latently being taught.

Reading books, sometimes called **basal readers**, or graded reading books, are written primarily to teach reading. They aim to provide instruction in the skills of reading and writing, being tightly sequenced and written so that vocabulary and grammar is tightly controlled in a theoretically ever increasing incline of difficulty. The learning of technical skills of reading are the prime aim of these books. Such graded series of readers fit the transmission model, entailing a movement of smaller to larger skill elements, and a carefully controlled sequence of learning. The skills in a basal reading series exist not because this is how children learn to read, but partly because of the logistics of developing a series of lessons that can be taught sequentially, day after day, week after week, year after year. Students are typically tested for their ability to master each small component of the reading scheme, often before they are allowed to move on to the next component.

Such basal reading books tend to promote the ability to recognize rather than to comprehend. The child may be able to read out loud to the teacher yet not understand the meaning and inner meanings of the stories. Basal reading series typically tell teachers exactly what they should do and say while giving a lesson, seemingly giving a technology of teaching reading that is easily implemented in classrooms.

One alternative is the reading of '**real books**'. 'Real books' is a term used to describe books that entertain, sometimes inform, often have a point and an aim that is much more than purely 'reading skills improvement' in children. While reading books are written primarily to teach reading, 'real books' will be written by people who describe themselves as authors. While too often these books in secondary and high schools are subverted for purposes similar to those that typify the use of basal readers, emphasizing comprehension and the drawing of inferences, such books are originally intended for **recreation**, enjoyment and to stir the imagination.

One important function of 'real books' is that they attempt to avoid the overwhelming white, middle class, male perspectives that are manifestly and latently present in so much of children's literature. Boys are often given the leading roles, with girls the more passive supporting roles.

> 'Robert climbed the tree and looked down the valley. "Let's go down the valley and search for gold" said Robert, while Ruth stood in the shade of the tree and agreed. Robert bravely led the way and Ruth followed in his tracks'.

Books need to challenge stereotyped gender roles, challenge traditional roles ascribed to mums and dads, and challenge the subservient portrayal of linguistic and cultural minorities. While reality has to be portrayed, understood and criticized by children, children also need informing about alternatives. Reading needs to reflect and challenge contemporary reality, and pose different life styles and values. Ethnic minorities need to be presented, not in a restricted stereotyped social context, but outside their stereotype so as to challenge the status quo.

A Whole Language Approach and attention to the skills of literacy are combined eclectically by many practicing teachers. There is an analogy with a musician. It is the overall musical performance that is important. Sometimes there is a need to practice scales (octaves), arpeggios, or trills as separate skills to improve the overall standard of musicianship. Accurately playing scales is not a musical performance. More important is the overall combination of accurate playing, interpretation of a musical score, creating an ambience with a piece of music and communicating with the listener. Similarly with reading and writing. Sometimes a teacher will concentrate on specific skills (e.g. irregular words, punctuation, spelling, grammar). Specific skills are not reading or writing. The overall activity needs to be the central focus.

The Whole Language Approach also has features that **overlap** with functional literacy. The child can be viewed by the Whole Language Approach as a relatively non-critical, monocultural, assimilated being. Literacy can be about socialization into customary, normative values and beliefs. In such an approach to literacy, the meaning of text can be decoded because it has a definite, autonomous meaning. Reading therefore is detecting the meaning of the author; writing is conveying meaning to readers. Thus, the Whole Language Approach can still result in an uncritical, accepting attitude by the child. For language minority children, in stigmatized, racist and prejudiced contexts, this may not be empowering.

The Construction of Meaning Approach

A recent consideration of literacy (partly connected to the Whole Language Approach) emphasizes that readers bring their own meanings to text, that reading and writing is essentially a **construction and reconstruction of meaning**. Part of this consideration is that the meaning individuals give to a text depends on their culture, personal experiences and histories, personal understandings of the themes and tone of text, and the particular social context where reading occurs. As will be revealed later, this idea has implications for language minority children and adults.

Readers bring **meaning** with them to texts. They make sense of a text from previously acquired knowledge. Without relevant background knowledge, readers may fail to construct any meaning at all. To help construct meaning, we need to know what kind of text it is, is it a folk story or a real event, is it an advertisement that seeks to persuade, or a balanced report. It helps to know who has written the text, what is their background and persuasion. A reader's current knowledge, family background, social and economic lifestyle, and political orientation will all affect how the reader constructs meaning from the text.

Different students of varying backgrounds will make **different meaning** from the text. When there is a mismatch between the reader's knowledge and that which is assumed by the writer, the construction of meaning will be difficult. This is the 'vicious circle' situation faced by many illiterate adults. They are denied access to certain kinds of knowledge and understanding of the world because they cannot read. Because they do not understand what is being taken for granted by writers of adult material, becoming literate as an adult is made difficult. Language minority groups in particular can be caught in this 'vicious circle' situation. Trying to make sense out of texts from a different culture, with different cultural assumptions, makes predicting the storyline and understanding the text more difficult.

One role for teachers therefore is to **mediate** in the construction of meaning by learners who are becoming literate, helping them to construct meaning from text. A central idea in constructing meaning derives from the Russian psychologist, **Vygotsky** (1962). During the decade 1924–1934, he outlined the ways that teachers can intervene and arrange effective learning, by challenging and extending the child's current state of development. Meaning is constructed by the teacher moving from the present level of understanding of a child to a further level that is within the child's capability. This 'stretching' of the child is by locating the **zone of proximal development**. Vygotsky (1962) saw the zone of proximal development as the distance between a student's level of development as revealed when problem solving without adult help, and the level of potential development as determined by a student problem solving in collaboration with peers or teachers. The zone of proximal development is where new understandings are possible through collaborative interaction and inquiry.

To help children construct meaning from text, teachers need to be aware that literacy in classrooms exists in a **social context**, guided by culturally-bound ways of thinking. Bloome (1985) suggested that:

> 'when students are asked to read a story, they must do so in socially appropriate ways: silently or orally, individually, competitively, or co-operatively with other students, in a round-robin manner, etc. Students who read orally without error or who appropriately answer teacher questions may gain social status within the classroom. Students who read with error, give inappropriate answers, or who sit quietly, may be viewed as outcasts or non participants.' (p. 135)

In classrooms, there are adult and educational criteria of relevant and appropriate ways of responding, reading and writing. Students have to learn about the rules of behavior for the different literacy events that teachers create. A typical teacher–student interaction is an initiation by the teacher, response by the student, followed by evaluation by the teacher. This signals expectancies and rules not only of classroom behavior, but also of literacy. There are rights and wrongs, authoritative knowledge and culturally inappropriate responses. The power relationships of the classroom shape language and literacy use. The social roles of students and teachers are taught and embedded in literacy events of the classroom. As will be argued later in the chapter, to promote literacy, teachers need to expand rather than limit students' roles so that literacy needs can be fully met. Children need to be empowered through celebrating the different uses of literacy, including critical literacy.

Reading and writing (and speaking and listening) are not mutual, independent activities. Reading and writing occur in a particular context that considerably influences the process of learning to be literate. Reading and writing is often for someone or to someone. Even when reading silently to oneself there is an inner, reflective conversation where meaning is being created. The words that readers know, and the experience related to the words being read combine to form a context. This context allows students to guess the meaning of words they do not know, and meanings that may be partly hidden.

The further reading and writing develops, the more text becomes socially and culturally embedded. The reading process within is shaped by the social forces from without. Dyson (1989) and Graves (1983) have shown how young writers develop and change in the midst of social influences from peers, teachers and influences from outside school such as the local community, political movements and ideological forces.

Similarly, writing is not just a technical process of putting words down on paper with correct spellings and correct grammatical structure. Writing is **sharing meaning**. When students and adults write, they have an interpersonal purpose. They write in order to be read by an audience, to inform, persuade, influence or purely delight readers. In writing, there is an anticipation of a response or reaction from the audience. We write with some kind of understanding of the background, knowledge and culture of our readers. We use language in different ways to meet particular purposes. Newspaper editorials sometimes try to persuade. Cookery books try to inform and explain. Poets try to give deeper and fresh meanings. The effectiveness of writing depends on the writer being familiar with the conventions expected by readers. This all suggests that literacy is a social event and not a private, personal event. We often discuss our reading and writing with other people, making the social dimension of literacy even more prominent.

This leads to an argument that literacy is not just about information gathering and giving. It is also about developing thinking that is appropriate within a culture. Thus Wells & Chang-Wells (1992) conceive of literacy as 'a mode of thinking that deliberately makes use of language, whether spoken or written, as an instrument for its own development' (p. 123).

The Socio-Cultural Literacy Approach

A related and overlapping approach to the Construction of Meaning approach spotlights the **enculturation** aspect of literacy. For example, a language minority literacy program may be enthusiastic to ensure the child is fully socialized and enlightened in the heritage culture.

Socio-cultural literacy is the ability to construct appropriate cultural meaning when reading. In theory, a person can be functionally literate but culturally illiterate (e.g. reading without meaning). In reading and writing, we bring not only previous experience, but also our values and beliefs enabling us to create meaning from what we read and insert understanding into what we write. Reading and writing is an act of construction by the individual. The **cultural heritage** is discovered and internalized in reading. While reading and writing have certain overt, testable skills, there is also a more hidden information processing activity ensuring enculturation. Beyond the observable skills of reading and writing is cultural literacy. For some people, such cultural literacy may lead to assimilation and integration (e.g. accepting the values embedded in English classics). Assimilationists may argue for a common literacy, transmitting the majority language culture to ensure assimilation of minority groups within the wider society.

A well known example of a majority assimilationist approach to cultural literacy is Hirsch's book (1988) *Cultural Literacy: What Every American Needs to Know*. In the Appendix to the book, Hirsch (1988) provides a list of 5000 items of what 'literate Americans know', or should know by the end of High School. The text box below lists the letter 'j' entries to provide a flavor of the entries. Such a list is intended as a 'reliable index of American literate culture' for 'effective national communication' and to 'insure domestic tranquility' (pp. xi and xii). Yet, it mainly reflects North American, white, middle class, Christian and classical culture. It is the culture of those in power and fails to represent adequately Latino, Asian or native Indian culture.

Jack and Jill (rhyme), Jack and the Beanstalk (title), Jack be Nimble (text), Jack Frost, jack-of-all-trades – master of none, Andrew Jackson, Jesse Jackson, Stonewall Jackson, Jacksonian democracy, Jacksonville, Jack Sprat (text), Jacob and Esau, Jacobin, Jacob's Ladder (song,) Jakarta, Jamaica, Henry James, Jesse James, William James, Jamestown settlement, Janus, jargon, Jason and the Golden Fleece, Java, jazz, Thomas Jefferson, Jehovah, Jehovah's Witnesses, Dr. Jekyll and Mr. Hyde (title), *je ne sais quoi,* Jeremiah, Battle of Jericho, Jersey City, Jerusalem, Jesuits, Jesus Christ, jet stream, Jew, Jezebel, *jihad,* Jim Crow, jingoism, Joan of Arc, The Book of Job, Johannesburg, Gospel according to Saint John, John Birch Society, John Brown's Body (song), John Bull, John Doe, John Henry (song), Pope John Paul II, Andrew Johnson, Lyndon B. Johnson, Samuel Johnson, John the Baptist, Pope John XXIII, *joie de vivre,* Joint Chiefs of Staff, joint resolution, Jolly Roger, Jonah and the whale, John Paul Jones, Scott Joplin, Jordan, River Jordan, Joseph and his brothers, Chief Joseph, Saint Joseph, Joshua, Joshua Fit the Battle of Jericho (song,) journeyman, James Joyce, Judaism, Judas Iscariot, Judge not that ye be not judged, Judgment Day, Judgment of Paris, judicial branch, judicial review, Julius Caesar (title), Carl Jung, Juno (Hera), junta, Jupiter (planet), Jupiter (Zeus), justification by faith, justify the ways of God to men, juvenilia.

Adapted from Hirsch (1988: 180–182)

In contrast, a cultural pluralist viewpoint will argue that national unity is not sacrificed by cultural literacy in the minority language or multicultural literacy. Multicultural literacy is likely to give a wider view of the world, a more colorful view of human history and custom, and a less narrow view of science and society.

Discussion of the **social and cultural context of literacy** raises the importance of **literacy in the mother tongue**. While the educational feasibility of this is discussed later, for the moment the educational argument is that literacy is most easily and most effectively learnt in the home language. The cultural argument is that mother tongue literacy gives access to the wealth of local and ethnic heritage contained in the literature. However, mother tongue literacy, while often culturally advantageous, is sometimes not without practical problems and objections. Some native languages lack a grammar or an alphabet, have few educational materials for teaching purposes, a shortage of teachers and teacher training. Political objections include native language literacy being an impediment to national unity and in-migrant assimilation and the cost of maintaining a variety of indigenous and 'in-migrant' languages in a region. Preservationists may wish to preserve literacy in the mother tongue to resist change, leaving that literacy to fossilize as if in a zoo.

Where there is much variety of language cultures within a region, support for local literacies may be found. Street (1984, 1994) regards **local literacies** as literacy practices identified with local and regional cultures (as different from national culture). Such local literacies may be forgotten by international and national literacy campaigns (Hornberger, 1994) or there may be tensions between local and national/international literacy practice (Street, 1994). Local literacies (for examples, see Street, 1994), avoid the impoverishment of uniformity in literacy that is created by the dominance of English. They make literacy relevant to people's lives, their local culture and community relationships.

The social and cultural context of literacy importantly includes the relationship between an **ethnic community** and literacy acquisition. What counts as reading differs between cultures, sub-cultures and ethnic groups. As Gregory (1993, 1994) demonstrates in a study of British Bangladeshi and Chinese families, the purposes of reading, the resources provided by the home and the process of parents helping their children to read may vary with the purposes, resources and processes for literacy in the school. Indeed, the varying expectations of home and school may produce a mismatch or a conflict that leads to uncertainty in the child, low achievement and even failure. She contrasts the school and language minority parents' differing viewpoints and practices. The school teaches reading for recreation and enjoyment; the family wants literacy for utilitarian purposes (e.g. avoiding unemployment and poverty, for trading and business trans-actions). The school literacy policy aims for a child-centered, individualized approach, with teacher as facilitator, partner and guide, allowing a wide choice of colorful attractive books. An ethnic group may, in contrast, provide literacy classes in Saturday schools, at the Mosque or Temple, sometimes with large numbers being tutored in the same class. The teacher may act as an authority and director. Learning the will of Allah, for example, may be the valued outcome. A treasured Bible, the Qu'ran or other holy or highly valued book may be the focus of reading.

Gregory (1993, 1994) further compares the style of literacy teaching. In school, the child is socialized gently into the 'literary club' via 'playing' with books in a relaxed atmosphere with little correction of mistakes. In ethnic Saturday schools, for example, children learn by rote, repeating letters, syllables and phrases until perfect. There is continuous practice, testing and correction of mistakes in a fairly strict and disciplined regime. Children may be given books only after they have proved their reading skills are worthy of such esteemed treasures. 'To have immediate access to books devalues both the book and the principle of hard work. Children must work their way towards knowledge slowly and the book is a reward for a child's conscious achievements. A love of books, therefore, comes after reading is learned and not as a necessary prerequisite for it' (Gregory, 1993: 57).

The **mismatch of school and ethnic group** literacy expectations and practices may be tragic for the child. The child is caught between two literacy worlds, two versions of appropriate literacy behavior, and in the middle of a clash between home and school concepts of literacy. Despondency, learning paralysis, low motivation and disaffection with school may result for the child.

Research from the United States from Shirley Brice Heath (1986) showed how Chinese-United States families, for example tend towards parent controlled conversations that closely mirror the type of language behavior expected in many traditional classrooms. The parents asked children factual questions, evaluated their language, gave verbal correction, and elaboration. Thus a certain form of literacy behavior and literacy use was established. Chinese-United States families saw their role as complementing that of the school in literacy. Such parents saw themselves as active agents in their children's literacy development.

In contrast, Mexican-United States parents often expected the extended family to share some of the responsibility for child-rearing. Such parents seldom expected conversations with their children while the parents were working. They relatively rarely asked questions of the children to assess their knowledge, understanding or attitudes. Older children within such families were expected to entertain the younger children. Younger children rarely interacted with just one adult, often being surrounded by a larger number of adults and children. However, young children grew up in a rich language environment, and although little conversation was directed specifically to them, they experienced the constant flow of language between adults, and between adults and other children. Children were taught to be respectful of adults, and usually not to initiate social conversations with adults. This cultural behavior is directly related to literacy expectations and uses. That is, literacy is not a separate cultural event, but mirrors in its form and function general **socialization** practices.

This tends to vary from the **expectations of school language** use where interaction with the teacher in traditional classrooms is expected. In such traditional classrooms, it is not expected that children should interact only with other children. Thus a mismatch may occur between patterns of language and literacy in the home and that expected in schools. For different cultural and ethnic groups, this may make school a more frightening, difficult and strange experience. The transition from the language and literacy of home to school may be more difficult for some language communities than for others. The differences between language minorities, as well as between such minorities and the language majority may affect the acquisition of literacy in school.

Heath (1986) identifies six genres of language use that are typically important for success in school.

(1) Adults engage in language activities with children that require children to label items, or adults frequently give the names of objects and ideas.

(2) Adults interpret what children have been saying, ask for explanations of what the child means or intends, and interpret classroom behavior.

(3) Children are expected to re-tell experiences or provide information that is known to adults. The listener may question the child so as to structure and 'scaffold' that information in particular ways.

(4) Children are expected to give performances to adults and their peers. The performance involves providing information or experiences that are new to the listener, or providing new interpretations of information that the listener already knows.

(5) Children provide a running narrative of events that are currently taking place or forecast what will occur in the future.

(6) Children recount stories that are familiar to them, that involve their imagination, some animation and a sequence of events towards a goal.

Heath (1986) refers to these six events as: label quests, meaning quests, recounts, accounts, event casts and stories.

While most of these patterns occur in the homes of children from all social classes and all ethnolinguistic groups, there are **differences between homes** in the frequency with which these dimensions occur. The effect is that children come to school with different degrees of familiarity with literacy linked behaviors. Some children are more literacy-ready than others and therefore have a greater potential for achievement.

In Shirley Brice Heath's (1982) research, certain preschool children gained experience of books with their parents in a manner which paralleled that of interaction with teachers in elementary schools. The initiation–reply–evaluation sequence so often used by teachers was used by a particular group of parents. Such children were therefore prepared for the literacy culture of teachers in classrooms. Such children had also learnt to build book knowledge on to their own experience of the world and use it to frame and express that experience. Such children had implicitly learnt that literacy provides new dimensions of experience.

Such 'school-prepared' children had also been taught by their parents to 'listen and wait'. They had grown accustomed to listening to adults reading stories and waiting to the end before asking questions. Thus such children became used to using books in a way that they would experience for most of their schooling.

Shirley Brice Heath (1982, 1983) also described two **communities** in the United States who had **different literacy practices**, important in themselves, but which did not match school-oriented literacy practices. Roadville children were members of working class, committed Christian parents who used literacy for Biblical and moral instruction. Fictional writing was rejected in favor of reading about real events that contained a moral message. The reading of a book in this community was a performance, rather than an interactive event. Books were used to inform and instruct a passive audience. 'Roadville adults do not extend either the context or the habits of literacy events beyond book reading. They do not, upon seeing an item or event in the real world, remind children of a similar event in a book and launch a running commentary on similarities and differences' (Shirley Brice Heath, 1982: 61).

Thus Roadville children regarded a story as a real event containing accurate facts and read or told as a lesson about being a good Christian. Fictional accounts of real events were regarded as lying. Reality and the truth was needed, not fiction. Thus Roadville children were socialized into a particular world view, a particular series of norms and beliefs, and specific beliefs about the uses (and 'to be avoided' uses) of literacy. Roadville children were encouraged and rewarded for telling stories that derived a moral message from real experience. While some may see such family training as failing to prepare the children for the literacy events of the school, another view is that the school fails to respond to the preferred literacy style of this type of community. A third view is that all children need to be exposed to the widest variety of 'cultures of literacy' and know what alternative functions exist for literacy.

Shirley Brice Heath (1982) concludes that literacy can only be understood and interpreted 'in relation to the larger sociocultural patterns which they may exemplify or reflect. For example, ethnography must describe literacy events in their sociocultural context, so we may come to understand how such patterns as time and space usage, care giving roles, and age and sex segregation are interdependent with the types and features of literacy events a community develops' (p. 74).

The Critical Literacy Approach

Literacy can work to **maintain the status quo,** to ensure that those with power and dominance in society influence, even control what the masses read and think. Propaganda, political pamphlets and newspapers and books can all be used to attempt to control the thinking and minds of the masses. Literacy can be conceived as an attempt through schooling and other formal and informal means of education to produce **hegemony** in society. Thus, those in power maintain control over those who could be subversive to social order, or democratically challenge their power base. Literacy can be used to instill certain preferred attitudes, beliefs and thoughts. Similarly, some religious traditions deliberately use literacy to ensure that their members are, at the least, influenced by writings, at the worst, brainwashed. Careful selection by religious leaders and parents over what their children read, is an attempt to use literacy to control and contain the mind.

Graff (1979) has shown that in nineteenth century Canada, literacy was used for normative, **controlling purposes.** Illiterates were conceived as dangerous to the social stability, as alien to the dominant culture, representing a threat to the established order. Thus, an effort to increase literacy was a political move to maintain and further the position of the ruling elite. Since the elite realized that literacy could also lead to radical beliefs and ideas antagonistic to those in power, the teaching of literacy was carefully controlled.

Graff (1979) also attempted to show that literacy did not necessarily improve a person's chances of acquiring employment, wealth or power. Certain ethnic groups were disadvantaged, whatever their literacy rates, while others disproportionately obtained employment despite their relatively high illiteracy rates. For example, Irish Catholics in Canada did badly irrespective of being literate or illiterate. In comparison, English Protestants fared relatively better. Similarly, literate black people did relatively less well than other literate people. Whether literacy was an advantage or disadvantage depended on ethnicity. Being unemployed or in the worst paid jobs was a function more of ethnic background than of illiteracy.

The style of literacy education that aims to control and contain tends to put **emphasis on reading skills** rather than comprehension, on being able to say the words and copy down words from a blackboard, with less emphasis on meaning and understanding. Students are not allowed to ask questions. Rather they are expected to read aloud large chunks of text that are subsequently corrected for pronunciation, stress and fluency.

Those with power and dominance in society also maintain their position by their view of what is '**correct language**'. Ethnic minorities with little political and economic power are often taught that their very patterns of speech and writing are inferior, and are connected with their economic social and cultural deprivation. Such groups are expected to adopt standard majority language use (e.g. to speak 'proper' or 'correct' English).

This restricted form of literacy is still present in many schools in all continents of the world. The functional view of literacy, as evidenced in the UNESCO definition given earlier, often involves a kind of restricted literacy that, at its worst, can maintain oppression, a distance between elites and the subservient, and not focus on the empowering and 'critical consciousness' possibilities of literacy.

Some forms of literacy education in schools and adult classes pose literacy as a **technical skill**. This reveals that literacy education always has ideological roots (Street, 1984). Literacy can be used to maintain the status quo, a stable political structure, to avert subversion or activism among the masses. National literacy may promote integration of the masses and different ethnic groups. National literacy may attempt to promote unification and standardization of both language and culture.

In colonization and 'missionary' movements, a different kind of cultural standardization was sometimes attempted. For example, when literacy was brought by the missionaries to non-Christian areas of the world in the nineteenth century, the aim was to spread the Christian gospel, control the thinking, and affect the moral behavior of those who were assumed to be primitive and heathen. In literacy projects in developing countries in the twentieth century, literacy has often been promoted for economic development. A literate workforce was considered essential for economic growth. Yet such programs were also used, consciously or subconsciously, to shore up the **established order** in a social system founded on injustice and inequality. Literacy in such programs has sometimes been used to condition the masses, to consolidate existing divisions of labor.

There is an alternative to using literacy as a way of showing people how to work co-operatively within a system from the perspective of people in power. Literacy can be a tool of oppression; it can also be a **liberator** (Hornberger, 1994). It can be bar to opportunity; or a means of opening a door to empowerment. One way of attempting to **empower** people is through critical literacy. **Freire** (1970, 1973, 1985) and Freire & Macedo (1987) have argued for a literacy that makes oppressed communities socially and politically conscious about their subservient role and lowly status in society. The argument is that literacy must go well beyond the skills of reading and writing. It must make people aware of their sociocultural context and their political environment. This may occur through mother tongue literacy, multilingual literacy (and local/national/international **'multiple' literacies** of value in differing contexts) and local literacies (Street, 1984).

For language minority speakers, literacy for empowerment can be about literacy stimulating language activism, the demand for language rights, self determination and an equitable share of power. Freire's literacy education in Brazil's peasant communities and with other oppressed groups around the world first teaches such people that they must become conscious about their subordinate role and inferior position in their community and society. People afterwards become empowered to change their own lives, situations and communities.

Through literacy, one can understand political power and activity, leading to collectively working together to change society, operating appropriately, able to challenge and complain, to assert natural rights, and to demand equality of access, opportunity and treatment. Through **critical reflection** on texts, information and propaganda, people will have a growing consciousness, an influence over their own lives and the institutions which serve them, and strive for more equal status in society.

Freire argued that people acquiring literacy must have their **consciousness raised**, enabling them to analyze the historical and social conditions which gave rise to their particular status, position and low power-base in society. Thus literacy teaching can become a direct political challenge to the hegemony of ruling capitalist states. Many adult literacy programs have been influenced by this 'critical literacy' ideology (Street, 1984).

In radical adult literacy programs, students create their own learning material rather than passively reading information and books that propagate a centralist, dominant perspective. Through creating their own books, (and the binding and distributing of them — for example poetry books), what it is to be literate is radically changed. Rather than reading becoming a passive exercise, literacy is seen as a production of ideas that need to be spread into the community. Students who had previously believed themselves a failure in learning to read and write may come to recognize that it was the system that had failed them. Their illiteracy is then seen not as a personal problem but as a condition imposed or allowed by those in power.

Such a radical viewpoint about literacy needs to be seen in contrast to the celebrated modern idea of the whole language approach in literacy development. Delpit (1988) argues that books within the whole language approach can be an uncritical celebration of stories and a transmission of accepted information. As such, the whole language movement may neglect issues of **power and social justice**, and maintain the status quo. What alternative is posed by the critical literacy movement?

At school level, the critical literacy approach is that learners should not just be invited to retell a story. They should be encouraged to offer their **own interpretation of text**. From the beginning, children should be encouraged to interpret and evaluate: Who is the writer? What is their perspective and bias? What kind of moral interpretation is made? What alternative interpretations and viewpoints are possible? Children will be encouraged not just to find the right answer to such questions, but to look critically at multiple viewpoints. Multicultural and multilingual children may be given diverse pieces of writing that reflect different cultural knowledge and attitudes. Differences in interpretation, and differences in experience and knowledge children bring to the text can be contrasted and compared.

This involves a change in teacher and student roles in the classroom. Teachers become **facilitators** rather than transmitters of authoritative knowledge. Literacy development becomes a joint developmental and co-operative event rather than duplicating the dominant–subservient relationship that often occurs in classrooms and which mirrors political domination and subservience.

For example, rather than children being solely taught that Columbus discovered America and that Columbus was a hero whose arrival brought civilization and salvation to the indigenous population, teachers may broaden out and invite students to search out other views about Columbus. Having read that Columbus initiated the slave trade, cut off the hands of any indigenous people who failed to bring him gold, and that the indigenous population suffered when Spanish rule was established, students would be asked to write their own critical versions of not only the life and contribution of Columbus, but also the way that Columbus is treated in many historical texts. Students will be encouraged by discovery methods to find that historical facts about Columbus have been selectively treated and interpreted by historians. More than one viewpoint is possible. One single viewpoint is both dangerous and biased, even if it is politically desirable and comfortable.

Flor Ada (1988a, 1988b) presents a critical literacy approach for classrooms based on Paulo Freire. She distinguishes four phases in the creative reading act.

The Descriptive Phase

In the descriptive phase, teachers will ask questions about text such as: What happened in a story? Who did what and why? This kind of phase exists in many classrooms, but in critical literacy, it must be extended beyond this stage. If reading stays at this phase, it tends to be passive, receptive and domesticating.

The Personal Interpretive Phase

Children will be asked if they have ever seen or experienced something like that portrayed in the story. What did you feel when you read the story? Did you like it? What kinds of emotion did you have? Does your family and community have similar experiences or stories? Ada points out that this process of personalization of stories may raise children's self esteem. They are made to feel that their experiences and feelings are valued by the teacher and other students. It also enables children to learn that 'true learning occurs only when the information received is analyzed in the light of one's own experiences and emotions' (Ada 1988a: 104).

The Critical Analysis Phase

The text is used to bring out broader social issues and generalizations. Students are asked is the text valid? What kind of experience or person is promoted by the story? Are there other ways in which the story could have been constructed? How and why would people of different cultures, social classes and gender have acted differently in the story? Students are invited to analyze, reflect and expand on the experiences of the story. Social implications are engaged and analyzed.

Creative Action Phase

Students are then challenged as to how their learning can be used to improve their lives or resolve issues and problems they face. Here the critical approach is transformed into constructive action. For example, students may decide to write letters to political figures, to those in their locality who have power status and authority, or create a poster to try to persuade. Students may compile a class newsletter or booklet that is given to other students in their school, or other schools, to sensitize people to the issues. They may write and circulate a petition in a neighborhood, write a play, or create poetry that tries to both analyze, and inform others, leading ultimately to empowerment and raised consciousness among language minorities.

Finally, in this consideration of critical literacy, it is valuable to contrast in more depth two relatively opposite approaches to highlight the classroom style of a critical literacy approach. The functional and critical approaches will now be compared for their representation in the classroom and the different ideology of each approach.

The functional view of literacy compared with the critical view of literacy is paralleled by two stereotypes of **literacy classrooms**. In one style, there is a lot of teacher talk, much student listening, closed and factual questions rather than open and stimulating questions, with silence and control very evident. The hidden curriculum is that teachers are implicitly teaching dependence upon authority, correct and convergent thinking, social control, passive involvement, neutral thinking and passive learning. Knowledge is posed as static, correct and inert, to be internalized and reproduced when necessary. The critical literacy concept is that children should learn to search out differing authorities often with differing viewpoints, to depend on their own judgement, to think divergently and creatively, to work co-operatively and sociably, to avoid accepting knowledge and to question its source and motive, to be actively involved in learning, and, if necessary, to be critical of social, economic and political issues in their own and their community's lives. Knowledge is seen as dynamic, ever changing, always relative, a catalyst for further inquiry and a catalyst for action. Cummins (1994) sums this up as follows:

- **In a Transmission Style**: Language is decomposed; knowledge is inert; learning is hierarchical, by internalization, moving from the simple to the complex. This may be connected to a **social control orientation** where curriculum topics are neutralized in respect to societal power relations and students are expected to be compliant and uncritical.
- **In a Critical Approach**: Language is meaningful; knowledge is catalytic, and there is a joint interactive construction of knowledge through critical enquiry within a student's zone of proximal development. This may be connected to a **social transformation orientation** where curriculum topics are focused on issues of relevant power relationships and students are enabled to become critical and empowered.

The literacy that is developed in classrooms varies considerably in reality and escapes neat classification into transmission and critical literacy orientations. However, the stereotyped positing of two opposites, while simple and sometimes extreme, reflects a key debate in literacy development in language minority children. The table on the following page lists some of the practical characteristics of the transmission and critical classrooms.

CONCLUSION

This chapter has revealed that literacy in bilingual and multicultural societies is neither a simple nor a straightforward concept. While reading and writing initially seem easily understandable events, the different uses and definitions of literacy immediately spotlight complexity and controversy. The five different approaches to literacy discussed in this chapter highlight variations and contrasts to literacy education. Each approach has different expectations about bilingual children that pervade literacy policies, provision and practices. One recent contrast is literacy in a majority language (e.g. English) or an accent on local, regional literacies perhaps leading to 'multiple literacies' with different uses of literacy in different contexts.

One expectation is that children should have skills so they can function as 'good citizens' in a stable society. A contrasting expectation is that children should become empowered, even politically activated by becoming literate. Language minority children, for example, should be able to read, for example, to understand propaganda, and write to defend their community's interests or protest about injustice, discrimination and racism. A different view is that reading and writing are for sheer pleasure and enjoyment, to celebrate, create and self-cultivate. Biliteracy may be particularly valuable for both empowerment and enjoyment approaches.

The importance of the five approaches lies in their varying proposals for the role, status and self-enhancement of bilingual children and adults. Does literacy produce cogs who aid the smooth running of a well oiled system? Does literacy produce students who are activated into asserting their rights to equality of power, purse and opportunity? The fundamental issue of literacy and biliteracy is thus political. When clarity is achieved in defining the intended uses of literacy for bilingual students, educational considerations such as approaches, methods and strategies become more rational.

Functional Literacy/Transmission Classrooms

(1) Literacy is getting the correct answers on worksheets, filling in blanks, circling appropriate answers.
(2) Literacy is answering closed questions having read a story.
(3) Literacy is reading words, sometimes without understanding their meaning.
(4) Literacy is reading aloud to the teacher and the rest of the class, being perfect in pronunciation, intonation and accent.
(5) Literacy is spelling words correctly, and writing in correct grammar.
(6) Literacy is mechanically going through exercises, practicing skills, and giving correct answers on tests.
(7) Literacy is learning to do but not necessarily to think.

Critical Literacy Classrooms

(1) Literacy is seeing oneself as an active reader and writer.
(2) Literacy involves enjoying reading, developing independent thoughts and judgments about reading and writing.
(3) Literacy is sharing ideas, reflections, experiences and reactions with others in the classroom, both peers and teachers.
(4) Literacy is gaining insights into oneself, one's life in the family and the community, into social and political control, the use of print and other mass media to inform, persuade and influence so as to maintain the status quo.
(5) Literacy is about understanding the power relationships that lie behind reading and writing.
(6) Literacy is about constructing and reconstructing meaning, critically examining the range of meanings in the story and outside the story.
(7) Literacy is active writing for various purposes and audiences, often to influence and assert.
(8) Literacy is about developing consciousness, increased self reflection, increased reflection about status, power, wealth and privilege in society.
(9) Literacy is about developing critical thinking habits, creative imagination, and posing alternatives, some of which may be radical.
(10) Literacy is about learning and interpreting the world, explaining, analyzing, arguing about and acting upon the world in which a person lives.

SUGGESTED FURTHER READING

GARCÍA, O. and BAKER, C. (eds) 1995, *Policy and Practice in Bilingual Education: A Reader Extending the Foundations*. Clevedon: Multilingual Matters. (Section 3).
HEATH, S.B. 1983, *Ways with Words: Language, Life and Work in Communities and Classrooms*. Cambridge: Cambridge University Press.
HORNBERGER, N.H. 1994, Literacy and language planning. *Language and Education* 8 (1&2), 75–86.
WELLS, G. and CHANG-WELLS, G.L. 1992, *Constructing Knowledge Together*. Portsmouth, NH: Heinemann.

WHITMORE, K.F. and CROWELL, C.C. 1994, *Inventing a Classroom. Life in a Bilingual Whole Language Community.* York, ME: Stenhouse.

REVIEW AND STUDY QUESTIONS

(1) Write short revision notes on the following:
  (i)   The seven uses of (or needs for) literacy.
  (ii) The difference(s) between the three given definitions of literacy (skills, the construction of meaning, and sociocultural).
(2) Create a table to summarize the five approaches to literacy. Show the similarities and differences between these approaches in the table.

STUDY ACTIVITIES

(1) Observe two classrooms with different literacy programs for language minority children. How do the classrooms differ? What are the different beliefs and assumptions about literacy in the two classrooms?
(2) Design a short program to illustrate how critical literacy could be introduced to language minority students in Grades 5, 6 or 7.

CHAPTER 16

Literacy and Biliteracy in the Classroom

CHAPTER 16

Literacy and Biliteracy in the Classroom

INTRODUCTION

This chapter focuses on the more practical aspects of literacy and biliteracy in bilingual and multicultural schools. Teachers often adopt a varied and eclectic approach to literacy. Hence different classroom strategies are examined. A strategic approach by a teacher includes decisions about the grouping of children, resources to aid literacy development and the key nature of home and school relationships. A second part of the chapter examines biliteracy and strategies that promote biliteracy in the classroom. One resource used in biliteracy is dual language books. The debate about their value is portrayed as an ending to the chapter.

CLASSROOM PROCESSES TOWARDS LITERACY IN BILINGUAL AND MULTICULTURAL SCHOOLS

Many teachers use a broad, comprehensive and inclusive approach to literacy development. They do not solely focus on functional literacy nor on critical literacy, but attempt to develop the different kinds of literacy that were listed in the preceding chapter. Many teachers try to facilitate a **varied** use of reading and writing in their children, to develop independent readers and writers who are both skilled in language usage (this includes correct spelling and grammar) and who can also write creatively, critically, imaginatively, reflectively and for enjoyment. The multiple purposes of reading and writing are encouraged in many classrooms.

Literacy Strategies

A broad, balanced and practical approach to the literacy development of second language children is given by Hudelson (1994). In discussing strategies for second language literacy development, Hudelson lists various dimensions that are important. These will be considered under three headings: general, reading and writing.

General

(1) **Create a literate classroom environment**. Hudelson (1994) argues for a print-rich environment in the classroom to demonstrate the multiple functions of literacy. In the classroom, there could be charts, a content study area, attendance lists, menus, calendars, words of favorite songs, a classroom library containing books of varied genres and reading levels, information books to cover science, social studies and all other areas of the curriculum, a reading corner with comfortable chairs or pillows, a writing center or area containing a variety of sizes of paper and writing implements, and a display of children's original writing and published works. In all, an environment where print is seen as varied, valuable and containing great vitality.

(2) **Encourage collaborative learning**. Hudelson (1994) suggests that teachers should encourage children to learn with, and from, each other as well as to learn from the teacher. Children need to see each other as resources with a classroom as a workshop where learners work co-operatively together and independently on projects. Children need to be able to work on literacy events independently and interdependently, with the teacher attending to small groups and individuals to provide attention where it is needed.

(3) **Include literacy development as part of the content of other areas of the curriculum**. Literacy is established throughout the curriculum and through inter-disciplinary project work. For example engaging one of the key crucial issues of the day may lend a critical perspective to literacy development. The study of racism, prejudice and supremacist attitudes may be studied in the critical literacy tradition. The aim is to make people more aware, more responsible and active citizens. Hudelson (1994) lists exemplar issues such as air pollution, water use, the destruction of the deserts, and the destruction of forests as typical areas for critical study. Such projects make learners active participants in their own literacy development, integrate oral with reading and writing development, promote interaction with others as central to literacy development, allow risk taking and initiative, requiring topics that are linguistically stimulating, intellectually challenging, rigorous and demanding so as to enable full literacy development.

Reading

(4) **Utilize predictable books**. One example of such books are the Big Books which contain relatively predictable stories in enlarged text that enable a larger group of children to read the text and see the pictures with the teacher. Hudelson (1994) provides an illustration of the way Big Books may be used with second language children to encourage literacy development, particularly focusing on the construction of meaning. Not necessarily in the sequence given below, teachers may use the following strategies with Big Books:

A. The teacher reads the Big Book to the child once or twice.

B. The teacher may read the story to the child moving her hand to show the movement of the text.

C. The children will be encouraged to read along as they see the words and hear the teacher pronounce the words.

D. A teacher may stop at a predictable part of the story, close the book and ask the children what occurs next in the story. This focuses on the meaning of the story and encourages children to think of as many words as they can to make sense of the context of the overall story.

E. The teacher may cover certain words or phrases in the text and ask children to guess what comes next. This prediction of missing words is important as 'good' readers tend to be good guessers when they cannot read a word.

F. Teachers may cover up part of a word so that learners concentrate on partial clues within a word to guess what that word is, and then uncover its meaning.

G. The teacher may focus the learner's attention on features of the text such as full stops, capital letters, other punctuation marks and particular groupings of letters (e.g. 'spr' as a consonantal blend).

(5) **Read aloud to children daily**. Children need experience of listening to fluent models of language production. Also reading aloud to children daily shares the literary heritage of varied cultures and simultaneously teaches that literature is one important way of understanding the world and making sense of everyday experience.

(6) **Organize responses of children to the literature they read**. Hudelson (1994) argues that children need time to respond to what they read, 'to construct meaning, to relate a story to their own lives, to comment on emotions and ideas that a piece has evoked' (p. 147). Such an activity recognizes that learners bring prior experiences with them to the books that they read and that they use those experiences to understand the meaning and to generalize from text. Such an activity teaches that learning is social and that reading is not a purely individual event but can be shared with others to engage multiple interpretations and varied meanings.

(7) **Include opportunities for self-selected reading**. Children need time to select their own reading material for pure enjoyment so as to learn that reading is not only a classroom and highly formal structured activity, but has value in itself.

Writing

(8) **Utilize all written personal narratives**. Learners and teachers can share their own personal stories, own experiences, own cultural events and their own constructs of the world. We all have stories we want to share with others which enables others to understand and appreciate us more, to come to terms with differences between students as well as similarities. It is valuable for students to write stories on real events in their lives, with drafting, small and large group conferences to enable co-operation and participation, further editing with the help of the group and the teacher to produce a polished final document, and where the process is as important as the product. Children will learn to take into account others' understandings of their experiences, and different meanings that need to be accommodated in understanding an issue. Children will also learn that they have to write for an audience, so that the audience understands the text and not to produce a purely egocentric piece.

(9) **Utilize dialogic writing**. The use of dialogue journals is now customary in many classrooms. Teachers and learners have written conversations with each other, often focusing on personal matters. No correction of the learner's language is necessarily

made, except that, when reading the teacher's response, the child will see a model of appropriate writing. Such a dialogue journal can also work between pairs of children. One child may be more fluent, the other child being lower down the developmental scale. Finding authentic reasons for writing a journal and carrying out a genuine dialogue will be essential to maintain interest and motivation.

(10) **Successful classrooms engage a variety of different purposes for writing.** Children may be asked to write to persuade, inform, query and question, to establish contact in relationships with other people, to express individuality and personal experience, to explore, to clarify and organize thinking, to reflect and raise consciousness, to exercise the imagination, to communicate information, to evaluate and appraise, to entertain, to provide a record of events, to give recipes and lists, to be poetic and humorous. As Willig (1990: 25) states:

> 'Writing is a key element in the search for meaning because it allows us to reflect on and to order our encounters with the world and the impact they make upon us. Equally important, we write to share thoughts and feelings with others through communications ranging from hastily written notes to formal, carefully argued essays on complex issues'.

Further Views about Writing

Smith (1982) argues that writing can be an extension and reflection of efforts to develop and express ourselves in the world around us, to make sense of the world and to impose order upon it. Writing can **communicate** with large numbers of people over an extended period of time. It can be **retrieved** by the author and the audience long after the message was created and can allow communication to take place without the presence of an audience.

For Wells & Chang-Wells (1992), the most important form of writing is when text is treated, not as a final representation of meaning that is given and self evident, but as a tentative and provisional attempt to **capture current understanding**. This can provoke further attempts at understanding as the writer or some other reader interact with the text to interpret and reinterpret its meaning. Novels and philosophy, poetry and scientific reports, books about history and legal argument can all be engaged in this manner.

The writer and subsequent readers are constantly asking whether the text makes sense in relation to their own experience. In writing, one assesses what one knows already, what one needs to find out more about, what is unknown, what needs to be selected as relevant and pertinent, how to organize and express ideas in a form that is most appropriate for understanding by the intended audience. For Wells & Chang-Wells (1992), such a process in writing is **empowering**. It enables advances in intellectual, moral and affective understanding.

To be empowering, writing needs to be developed in a variety of types and uses. For example:

(1) **Instrumental uses in writing.** Writing for practical needs to manage and organize everyday life.

(2) **Social and interpersonal writing**. Writing to establish, build and maintain relationships with family, friends, neighbors and acquaintances far away.

(3) **Recreational writing**. Writing during leisure time for the pure enjoyment of being creative and imaginative.

(4) **Educational uses of writing**. Writing to educate oneself, writing essays and assignments to fulfill the requirements of courses in schools, colleges and universities.

(5) **Financial**. Writing to record numbers, often concerning money, salaries, expenditure and banking.

(6) **Environmental**. Writing for public consumption. Writing notices, posters and information that needs to be read by members of the public.

(7) **Sending messages** when oral communication is not possible or when a written message (e.g. for legal purposes) is preferred.

(8) As an **aid to memory**. Writing down ideas, information and thoughts to preserve (for oneself and others) important information and ideas.

(9) **Autobiographical**. Writing a record of one's daily life as in self-reflective diaries so as to understand, order and organize oneself and one's experiences.

(10) **Creative**. Writing as a means of self expression and imaginative contemplation.

Grouping and Assessment

A classroom approach using a broad and comprehensive strategy, may also use diverse grouping strategies in the development of literacy. Whole classwork, pair work, small group work, co-operative learning can all be used to good effect (Johnson, 1994). A diverse approach also means avoiding narrow standardized tests that purely reflect a skills approach to literacy (Edelsky, 1991). As Genesee & Hamayan (1994) have argued, classroom based assessment needs to go much further than tests of inauthentic, decomposed language skills. Student portfolios, for example, are one important way that a teacher may gather up information about the performance of their children in a classroom that may give a much fuller understanding of the strengths and weaknesses, and therefore the diagnostic attention needed to improve and develop a child's literacy.

Resources

As far as possible, the language resources of the classroom need to be **multilingual** partly to reflect the mother tongues of the children in the classroom, but also for the multilingual awareness of all children. Sometimes it is difficult to find the quantity, quality and variety of reading materials in the mother tongues of children in bilingual classrooms. There are often problems importing books from other countries and problems in purchasing expensive books. Yet some schools do manage to collect excellent libraries of books in different languages (and multicultural books) via help from language communities, parents of children in the school and using minority language organizations who have contacts and a commitment to literacy development in children's mother tongues.

HOME AND SCHOOL RELATIONSHIPS

'Parents as partners' is as possible in the writing process as in reading. For example, parents may help compose books in their heritage language for use in the classroom.

Children, teachers and parents may collaborate together to produce a multilingual book (e.g. starting school in different countries and cultures). Personal meaning, home and community culture, and classroom activity are joined in the promotion of biliteracy. As Hornberger (1990b) has shown, there can be different effective classroom strategies to make literacy tasks congruent with the community culture and values of the children. Use of first and second language texts, using students' community-based prior knowledge enables 'connect and transfer' to promote literacy and biliteracy.

A danger occurs when the school naively imposes its literacy practices on the home. With the best of intentions in promoting school-type reading practices in the home, the worst of outcomes may result, as the research of Gregory (1993, 1994), considered in the preceding chapter, illustrates. Parents may be educated by the school about 'good reading habits' in their children, mirroring school literacy practices and school culture. This **assumes a deficit** in family literacy practices that may be unwarranted. As Auerbach (1989) has shown, marginalized language minority parents may be highly motivated towards literacy in their children. Literacy may be highly valued as a key to vocational and economic mobility. Plenty of books may be present in the home with plenty of encouragement and help given by parents within the traditions of their culture.

Delgado-Gaitan (1990) argues that there is a great need for parents to become involved in their children's literacy development. She reports **three models of parental involvement** in children's education.

The first, the **Family Influence Model** involves families attempting to provide the type of home learning environment most suited to cognitive and emotional development. Such parents believe that there is a body of information that children need to acquire for life skills. Teachers know this and teach it, and therefore parents need also to be partners in such imparting of knowledge. Parents assume that there is a correct and right way to rear children (including literacy development) that can be learnt from books or child psychology experts, and that parents who apply this information will be successful as parents. Turning the situation round, the Family Influence Model also contains the idea of the school attempting to influence and change family life so that it fits the values and strategies of learning used by the school. The family is seen as a direct recipient of the school's influence, and the school–family collaboration establishes maximally effective environments for learning.

The **School Reform Model** operates where parents take more than an interest in the schooling of their children. Parents within this model try to change schools and make them more responsive to parents. Parents may place pressure on the schools to ensure that their values and standards are transmitted by the schools. Such parents know how to pressure and interact with schools, getting schools to change to be more responsive to student needs as perceived by parents. The assumption is that the school will accommodate parents' suggestions and influence. Such parents will attempt to become part of the power structure of the school by being on advisory committees, school governing committees or parent–teacher committees.

The **Cooperative Systems Model** moves one step further. Rather than collaboration as in the first model, and influence as in the second model, parents within the third model attempt to participate directly in school activities. For example parents may attend workshops in the school, help the teachers in the classroom, and become like paraprofessionals. Such parents see the home, school and community as interrelated and functioning as a whole. Parents play the roles of volunteer, paid employee, teacher at home, adult learner and helper.

Further explication of processes in teacher-parent relationships is given by Moll (1992). Luis Moll and his colleagues at the University of Arizona have used ethnographic studies of student communities to identify skills, knowledge, expertise and interests that Mexican **households** own that can be used for the benefit of all in the classroom. For many language minority children and their families, the relationship between school and parents is limited and often non existent. Moll shows how parents and other community members have much to give children in Latino classrooms. Such people can supplement the teacher, providing what Moll calls '**funds of knowledge**' that are 'cultural practices and bodies of knowledge and information that households use to survive, to get ahead or to thrive' (Moll, 1992: 21). Examples of funds of knowledge that could be used by schools include information about flowers, plants and trees, seeds, agriculture, water distribution and management, animal care and veterinary medicine, ranch economy, car and bike mechanics, carpentry, masonry, electrical wiring and appliances, fencing, folk remedies, herbal cures and natural medicines, midwifery, archaeology, biology and mathematics.

There are a variety of possible reasons for some parent–teacher relationships showing non-cooperation, a lack of understanding, a distance and even an antagonism between home and school cultures. Understanding such reasons helps explain why many language minority children fail in the system, have high drop-out rates and exhibit relatively low achievement.

Such language minority families may be socially and educationally isolated from the school. There is a knowledge gap between such families and the school that needs bridging. If language minority parents are unable to speak the majority language of the teachers in the school, there may be an increased sense of helplessness and isolation. Such parents are reluctant or unable to discuss their children's progress with the teacher, unable or unwilling to go to parent–teacher meetings and other school events. While such parents may discuss problems about their children's schooling with one another, the issues and worries do not become resolved because there is a chasm between school and the home. Some parents may be intimidated by high status schools or feel that schools know best and should act unilaterally in dealing with their children.

In a case study of what can constructively be accomplished to empower such parents and resolve this problem, Delgado-Gaitan (1990) explains via an ethnographic study how parents were encouraged to organize themselves into a leadership group, and socialize each other about how to communicate with schools. Through building awareness, followed by mobilization, motivation, and commitment, the attitudes and actions of a group of parents were changed. Over time, **parents** became convinced that they had the right, responsibility and power to deal with their children's academic and social concerns, and to foster strong relationships with the school for their children's greater achievement. Individual parents also began to realize that they had something to offer other parents, their children and the school. As parents became more involved, they felt more in control of their lives. They became empowered. 'Feelings of incompetence create isolation for parents. Those feelings must be replaced with a recognition of the ability to collaborate with others before active participation can occur' (Delgado-Gaitan, 1990: 158).

In this research study, the preschool teacher included Mexican family activities in the classroom, and taught parents to be more conscious of their own interactions with their children. This teacher organized a parent committee that involved parents in decision making activities in the kindergarten. She also incorporated the students' culture into the daily school curriculum. Therefore, she produced a culturally and educationally congruent education experience between the home and the school. Such a teacher became an important advocate of the power of parent–teacher co-operation.

However, there are occasions when parents are a highly conservative, even a reactionary voice. For example some parents may narrowly insist on skills achievement in the core curriculum and wish to ignore the advances of progressive education in the twentieth century. It is also important for conflicts between parents and teachers to be avoided, and co-operation sought for the benefit of the children. Teachers' professionalism and expertise need to be respected, as do parents' rights and interests in their children's socialization.

BILITERACY

In Chapters 3 and 4, we briefly discussed the importance of minority language literacy in the survival, reversal or enhancement of that language. At both the individual and the group level, minority language literacy gives that language increased functions and usage. A minority language has a greater chance of survival when bureaucracy and books, newspapers and magazines, adverts and signposts are in that language. This may help to avoid the colonial situation where the majority language is used for all literacy purposes and the vernacular language is used purely for oral communication. Where oral communication is in the minority language and literacy is in the majority language, that minority language may have less chance of survival.

More positively, literacy in the minority language enables the attendant traditions and the culture to be accessed and reproduced. Reading literature in the minority language may be both for education and recreation, for instruction and for enjoyment. Whether literature is regarded as aiding moral teaching, of value as an art form, or as a form of vicarious experience, literacy is both an emancipator and an educator. As the UK Bullock Report (1975) stated:

'Literature brings the child into an encounter with language in its most complex and varied forms. Through these complexities are presented the thoughts, experiences, and feelings of people who exist outside and beyond the reader's awareness... It provides imaginative insights into what another person is feeling; it allows the contemplation of possible human experiences which the reader himself has not met.' (p. 125)

This quotation illustrates that literacy in the minority language is of value because it recreates the past in the present. It may both reinforce and extend the oral transmission of a minority culture. Minority language oracy without literacy can disempower the student. Literacy in the minority language not only provides a greater chance of survival at an individual and group level for that language. It also may encourage rootedness, self-esteem, the vision and world-view of one's heritage culture, self-identity and intellectual empathy.

Literacy enables access to language minority stories that not only shape and develop thinking. Children develop concepts through stories (oral and written). Stories are a strong means of making sense of the world and hence affect the structure of human cognition (Wells, 1986). Biliteracy gives access to different and varied social and cultural worlds. Does this in turn lead to more diversified cognitive abilities, an increased ability to process and manipulate ideas and symbols? The research of Swain & Lapkin (1991a) points to first language literacy and then biliteracy as a strong source of cognitive and curriculum advantage for bilinguals.

The Development of Biliteracy

Given that literacy emancipates, enculturates, educates and can be an inherently enjoyable activity, there seems to be a strong argument for biliteracy. Pragmatically, most students from a minority language need to **function in the minority and majority language society**. This requires biliteracy rather than literacy only in the minority language. For those in the Canadian immersion situation, for example, biliteracy in French and English is encouraged and enabled.

In different minority language situations, the same question is often asked by parents and teachers. Is it better to be thoroughly literate in one language rather than attempt to be literate (or semi-literate) in two languages? Does literacy in one language interfere with becoming literate in a second language? Questions typically tend to be phrased in this negative way. The positive questions must also be asked. Does literacy in one language aid rather than impede literacy in a second language? Do the skills learnt in reading and writing one language transfer to reading and writing in a second language?

From recent **reviews** (Hornberger, 1989; Williams & Snipper, 1990) and **research** (e.g. Lanauze & Snow, 1989; Torres, 1991; Hornberger, 1990b; Calero-Breckheimer & Goetz, 1993), the evidence tends to reflect the positive rather than the negative questions. Research has suggested that academic and linguistic skills in a minority language **transfer** relatively easily to the second language. Simply stated, a child who learns to read in Spanish at home or in school, does not have to start from the beginning when learning to read in English. Both in learning to read and in learning to write, 'language skills acquired in a first language can, at least if developed beyond a certain point in L1, be recruited at relatively early stages of L2 acquisition for relatively skilled performance in L2, thus shortcutting the normal developmental progression in L2' (Lanauze & Snow, 1989: 337).

When biliteracy is encouraged in minority language children, literacy skills and strategies from the first language appear to **transfer** to the second language (if using a similar writing system). While the vocabulary, grammar and orthography may be different, generalizable skills in decoding and reading strategies may easily transfer from first language literacy to second language literacy. Concepts and strategies (e.g. scanning, skimming, contextual guessing of words, skipping unknown words, tolerating ambiguity, reading for meaning, making inferences, monitoring, recognizing the structure of text, using previous learning, and using background knowledge about the text) readily and easily transfer from first to second language literacy (Calero-Breckheimer & Goetz, 1993; Jiménez, García & Pearson, 1995). This is the idea found in the Common Underlying Proficiency or Dual Iceberg idea of Cummins and his Interdependence principle (see Chapter 9).

Reading ability in a second language is partly promoted by the degree of proficiency in that second language. However, the view that reading ability in a second language is mainly a function of proficiency in that second language is not generally supported by research (Calero-Breckheimer & Goetz, 1993). While the sounds of letters and decoding of words have a **separation** in learning to read in each language, the higher cognitive abilities and strategies required in making meaning from text are common to both languages. Overall reading competence in two languages thus does not operate separately.

This 'transfer' rather than 'separation' viewpoint has implications for the teaching of reading among language minority students. A '**separation**' view is that reading in the second language (e.g. English for language minority students in the United States) depends on the level of proficiency in the second language and not on first language reading ability. Therefore, students should be swiftly moved to education through the second language; maximal exposure is needed to literacy in the second (majority) language. Time spent reading in the minority language is time lost in learning to read in the majority language. In contrast, a '**transfer**' view argues for initial mastery of literacy in the minority language so that the cognitive skills and strategies needed for reading can be fully developed. Once well developed, these literacy skills and strategies transfer easily and readily to the second language.

Teachers need to be concerned that classroom strategies to develop literacy in two languages are not separate, independent or unconnected. For example, there is little point introducing the use of metaphors in English lessons and then repeating the same subject matter in Spanish lessons. **Coordination**, integration and synchronization are needed to ensure learning is cumulative and not repetitive.

An important intermediate factor is the **context** in which such language and literacy acquisition occurs. In Canadian immersion programs, for example, the context is additive. That is, the child's home language of English is not being replaced but is being added to by the acquisition of French. Evaluations of immersion programs (see Chapter 11) show that literacy in French is acquired at no cost to literacy in English. In this additive, majority language context, a child may acquire literacy through the second language at no cost to literacy in the first language. In contrast, in a **subtractive environment**, the transfer of literacy skills between the two languages may be impeded. In such subtractive situations, literacy may more efficiently be acquired through the home, heritage, minority language. Literacy can be built up via the higher level of language skills in the home language rather than through the weaker majority language of English. When literacy is attempted through the second, majority language, the child's oracy skills in English may be insufficiently developed for such literacy acquisition to occur.

For teachers, this leaves the question of when to encourage biliteracy, given that there is some degree of literacy in one language. One model will be the **simultaneous** acquisition of biliteracy as well as bilingualism. Some bilingual children simultaneously learn to read and write in both languages. Other children will learn to read in their second language **before** they learn to read in their first (majority) language. An example is immersion education in Canada, where children learn to read in French before learning to read in English. Both these approaches will tend to result in successful biliteracy.

The third approach is where children acquire literacy in their first language, a minority language, and then **later** develop literacy skills in the majority language. This may, in some circumstances lead to monoliteracy in the majority language and not biliteracy. In a subtractive situation, minority (first) language literacy may become neglected. In Transitional Bilingual Education, for example, majority language literacy is promoted at the cost of minority language literacy. However, in Maintenance, Two-Way/Dual Language and Heritage Language education, this third approach tends to be additive, promoting literacy in both languages.

Simple answers about when to promote literacy in the second language are made difficult by other factors such as the educational and societal context and the age and ability of the child. Contrast the six year old just beginning to acquire pre-reading and pre-writing skills in the first language with an 18 year old student, fluent in a first language. In the first case, biliteracy may best be delayed. In the latter case, oracy and literacy in the second language may be mutually reinforcing. Contexts will also vary. When a language minority child is constantly bombarded with majority language written material, from adverts to comics, computers to supermarkets, biliteracy may occur relatively easily. The accent in school can be on minority language literacy, but not exclusively. The opportunity for extending majority language literacy is often well served outside school. The preference with younger children may be to ensure first language literacy is relatively well established before introducing literacy in a second language. Such introduction may come in the middle years of elementary schooling (e.g. from seven years of age to 12 years of age depending on the level of literacy achieved in the first language). The introduction to second language literacy may be helped by the use of dual language books. Such books are now briefly discussed.

Dual Language Books

Dual language books contain a story, folk tale, myth or information in two languages. Such languages may have a similar script (as in French and English, or Spanish and English) or different scripts (for example Chinese and English, Urdu and English, Bengali and English). Often the two languages are on the same page or on opposite sides of the page, sharing the same pictures.

The **origins** of dual language books are many. (1) Some books have resulted from funded projects. (2) Other dual language books have been created by 'smaller' publishers (e.g. ethnic minority presses). Professionally produced and published books usually have high quality text and colorful illustrations. Locally produced materials may be in black and white, sometimes word processed or occasionally hand written. (3) When teachers work with children to produce dual language texts, it is often the children themselves or their parents who produce the story lines. The final books are handwritten or word processed with group produced collages or the children's own drawings. (4) Monolingual teachers who do not want to use books in children's home languages that they themselves did not understand also instigated the production of dual language books. In this respect, dual language books offered a valuable alternative, giving teachers and learners some equality of access to understanding the storyline.

There are a variety of different **aims** in dual language books.

(1) One aim is to simply make all children, both bilinguals and monolinguals, aware that other languages exist and have the same value and functions. Such books can be a valuable part of a multicultural approach in the curriculum. As Feuerverger (1994: 136) suggests:
> 'Students learn to admire and respect those who come from other backgrounds and languages, rather than to be prejudiced against them. I believe that this is such an important part of multicultural teaching'.

(2) For children whose first language is not the majority language of the country, dual language books may serve as a bridge to literacy in the majority language. Such children will read the story in, for example, Greek or Turkish, Bengali or Urdu first of all. Subsequently, they may read the other language (e.g. English version) and, having already understood the storyline, be able to make sense of English words.

(3) Dual language books act as an important bridge between parents and children, and between the home and the school. Parents and other members of the extended family may be able to read to their children in their home language. At the same time, the child will be able to read a book in the majority language of the school, such as English.

(4) Dual language books can enable small groups or pairs of children to work collaboratively on the book. If one child can read in Bengali and the other in English, they can work together, discuss the story and complete activities set by the teacher around that story.

(5) Teachers may use such books with smaller or larger groups of children. For example, the story may be read by the teacher in one language first, and then in the other language. The teacher may be able to point out similarities and differences in script, in the use of language, and in the meaning of words in the different languages.

Dual language books are not without **controversy**. Firstly, some teachers and parents argue that children only read one language in the book, and ignore the other. Having understood the story in one language, it may be tiresome and pointless reading the story in another language. Children may thus concentrate on just one half of the book.

Secondly, teachers and children sometimes observe that the presence of the majority language such as English tends to remove the desire to read in the home, minority language. The different status of the two languages may mean that the child will only wish to read in the higher status language.

In a detailed and balanced discussion of dual language books by Viv Edwards (The Multilingual Resources for Children Project, 1995), further **problems** of dual language texts are analyzed. In the typography, one script often takes precedence, or has higher status than the other. For example, in the size of the print, the spacing between lines and the boldness of the print, there may be difference between the two languages. One script may be of higher quality than the other, this particularly occurring when a Latin and a non-Latin alphabet are used — indicating that equal status is not given to the two languages. The way the two languages are placed on a page, whether one is printed and the other typewritten or handwritten, and the order in which the languages appear, may each reflect different status accorded to the two languages.

There is also sometimes a practical problem in translation. Not only does the storyline have to be authentically conveyed in both languages, but also the style of language, the difficulty level of the text and the culturally relevant use of vocabulary may each affect the status accorded to each language. It is also important that the cultural 'message' is not lost in translation, this being very much a part of the multicultural aim of dual language books.

CONCLUSION

This chapter has examined the various classroom strategies that may be valuable in classrooms where there is an accent on multiculturalism, biliteracy in majority and minority language children, and the empowerment of language minority students and their families. There are no 'best recipes' of approach; no 'right answers' to classroom processes towards literacy and biliteracy. Different aims and goals in schooling, and different political and educational demands, make the choice partly about 'how', but also about 'why' and 'for what purpose'.

Chapters 15 and 16 are founded on the importance of literacy and biliteracy in the empowerment of bilingual students and their communities. Taken together, these chapters have sought to show that classroom practicalities are not divorced from educational and political policies; that education provision cannot be separated from issues of power that affect the lives of bilinguals.

SUGGESTED FURTHER READING

DELGADO-GAITAN, C. 1990, *Literacy for Empowerment: The Role of Parents in Children's Education*. New York: Falmer Press.

HORNBERGER, N.H. 1990, Creating successful learning contexts for bilingual literacy. *Teachers College Record* 92 (2) 212–29.

HUDELSON, S. 1994, Literacy development of second language children. In F. GENESEE (ed.) *Educating Second Language Children*. Cambridge: Cambridge University Press.

MULTILINGUAL RESOURCES FOR CHILDREN PROJECT, 1995, *Building Bridges: Multilingual Resources for Children*. Clevedon: Multilingual Matters.

PÉREZ, B. and TORRES-GUZMÁN, M.E. 1995, *Learning in Two Worlds: An Integrated Spanish/English Biliteracy Approach* (2nd edn). New York: Longman.

REVIEW AND STUDY QUESTIONS

(1) Write short revision notes on the following:
   (i) The differences between the family influence, school reform and cooperative systems models of home and school relationships.
   (ii) The advantages and disadvantages of dual language books.
   (iii) A list of practical advice (e.g. from Hudelson, 1994) for teaching literacy in bilingual and multicultural classrooms.
(2) What is the importance of biliteracy in language minority maintenance?
(3) Research the differences between basal reading books and real books. Indicate how such differences may affect the education of language minority children. Choose two passages from each type of book to illustrate some of these differences and their potential impact on language minority children.
(4) Read the article entitled 'Reading Strategies of Biliterate Children for English and Spanish Texts' by A. Calero-Breckheimer and E.T. Goetz (1993) in the journal *Reading Psychology: An International Quarterly* 14, 177–204. What are the views of the 'two main camps' (p. 178) on reading development in the second language? Summarize the research reported in the article. What are the conclusions? Do you have any criticisms of the research or the conclusions?

STUDY ACTIVITIES

(1) Visit a school where there is some attention to biliteracy. Make a case study (or a written or oral report) of one or more of the following:
   (i) Discuss with the teacher the aims of such biliteracy. Does the teacher feel that biliteracy is possible or that literacy in one language is more important?
   (ii) What provision of reading matter in two languages is available in the classroom? How many books are there in different languages? Do any of the books have two or more languages within them? What is the style and content (e.g. type of stories) of the books? Are there differences (e.g. color, datedness, level of language) between books in the two languages?

     (iii)   Observe and record how much time is spent on reading in classrooms in a school. How much time is allotted to each language?

     (iv)   Ask teachers at what stage and ages reading in each language is introduced in their classrooms? What variations are there between teachers? To what level does oral and reading achievement in one language need to develop before the introduction of biliteracy? Does a child's interest and attitude have an influence on literacy and biliteracy?

     (v)   Ask a number of students their views on being able to read in two languages. Ask the students how much reading they do after school, and in what language or languages? What are their favorite books and what language is preferred?

     (vii)   By interviewing, find examples of parent–teacher collaboration in the reading process. What kind of collaboration exists? How well do you feel it works? What improvements might be made? How are literacy practices different and similar in the home and school?

(2) Examine some dual language books (e.g. Spanish on one page, English on the opposite page). Ask some teachers and students their opinions about such books. Make a list of the pros and cons. Provide your own reasoned conclusion.

CHAPTER 17

Canadian Immersion
Classrooms

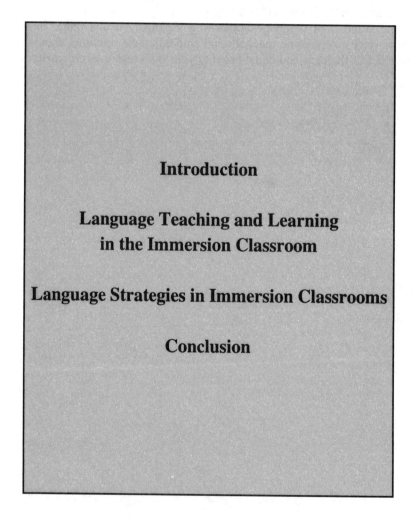

Introduction

**Language Teaching and Learning
in the Immersion Classroom**

Language Strategies in Immersion Classrooms

Conclusion

CHAPTER 17

Canadian Immersion Classrooms

INTRODUCTION

This chapter considers the approach to language learning often taken in the immersion education programs. Two introductory points. First, it is important to repeat the distinction between teaching a language and teaching through a language. Language acquisition in the Canadian immersion programs is mostly through the second language being used as a medium of instruction in 50% to 100% of the curriculum (see Chapter 10). Chapter 14 considered the teaching of language in language lessons as different from the second language as a medium of instruction.

Second, allied to the idea of language as a medium of instruction is the idea of **language across the curriculum** (Corson, 1990a). This is a view that language plays a central role across the curriculum. In all curriculum areas, students learn skills, knowledge, concepts and attitudes mostly through language. Thus, every curriculum area develops language competence. All subject areas, from Music to Mathematics, Science to Sport, contribute to the growth of a child's language. At the same time, mastery of a particular curriculum area is partly dependent on mastery of the language of that area. Obtaining fluency in the language of chemistry, psychology or mathematics, for example, is essential to understanding that subject.

LANGUAGE TEACHING AND LEARNING IN THE IMMERSION CLASSROOM

What are the main classroom features of successful immersion programs in Canada and elsewhere (e.g. Finland, Wales)? First, the minimum time the second language needs to be used as a medium to ensure 'receptive' (listening and reading) second language proficiency, is regarded as a minimum of four to six years. Around the end of elementary schooling, immersion students show equal or higher performance in the curriculum compared with their mainstream peers. Second, the curriculum tends to be the same for immersion children as for their mainstream peers. Thus, immersion children can easily be compared with mainstream children for levels of achievement. Immersion students compared with Core French Second Language students are neither more advantaged nor more disadvantaged by studying a common curriculum.

While French immersion attempts to cultivate empathy for **French culture**, the immersion curriculum has hitherto tended not to have major distinct components in it, different from mainstream education, to develop such empathy and participation. The danger is then that French becomes the language of school, and English the language of the playground, street and vocational success. The anglophone North American cultural influence is often so strong and persuasive that French immersion children are in danger of becoming passive rather than active bilinguals outside the school gates.

Third, studies of bilingual education indicate that it may be preferable to **separate languages in instruction** rather than to mix them during a single lesson (see Chapter 12). It tends to be regarded as preferable that one language is used for one set of subjects; the other language for a separate set. When there is language mixing inside a lesson, students may wait for the explanation in their stronger language. Such students may simply switch off when transmission is in their weaker language. Sustained periods of monolingual instruction will require students to attend to the language of instruction, thus both improving their language competences and acquiring subject matter simultaneously.

One residual problem is, in which language are particular subjects taught? For example, if mathematics and science, technology and computing are taught in the English language, will the hidden message be that English is of more value for scientific communication, for industrial and scientific vocations? Will English latently receive a special, reserved status? If the minority or second language is used for humanities, social studies, sport and art, is the hidden message that minority languages are only of value in such human and aesthetic pursuits? The choice of language medium for particular subjects may relegate or promote both the functions and the status of minority languages.

This raises the fourth issue. How much **time** should be devoted to the two languages within the curriculum? The typical recommendation is that a minimum of 50% of instruction should be in the second language. Thus, in French immersion, French medium teaching and learning may occur from 50% to 100% of the school week. As the graphs of Chapter 10 showed, the amount of instruction in the English language may increase as children become older. One factor in such a decision can be the amount of exposure to English a child receives outside school. Where a child's environment, home and street, media and community are English medium, such saturation may imply that a smaller proportion of time needs to be spent on English in the school. At the same time, the public will usually require bilingual schools to show that children's majority language competences, particularly literacy, are not affected by bilingual education. Bilingual schools need to ensure that, through school instruction and school learning experiences, majority language proficiency and literacy is monitored and promoted (Rebuffot, 1993). Such majority language instruction may range from a minimum of 10% for seven year olds and older, to 70% or more for those in examination classes at secondary level schooling.

Fifth, immersion education has been built around the twin towers of teacher enthusiasm and parental commitment. French immersion **parents** tend to be middle class, involved in school–teacher–parent committees, and take a sustained interest in their children's progress. Immersion education in Canada has, from its beginnings in Montreal in 1965 to the present, been powerfully promoted by parents. The first immersion classroom in 1965 owed much to parent initiation. Since then, the Canadian Parents for French organization has been a powerful pressure group for the recognition and dissemination, evolution and dispersion of immersion education. Parents have also been powerful advocates at the grass roots level for other 'strong' forms of bilingual education (e.g. Wales). Through localized pressure groups, schools which give native language medium teaching have successfully developed.

Teachers in Canadian immersion classrooms tend to have native or native-like proficiency in both French and English. Such teachers are able to understand children speaking in their home language but speak to the children almost entirely in French. Teachers are thus important language models through their status and power role, identifying French with something of value. Immersion teachers also provide the child with a model of acceptable French pronunciation and style. The teacher is a language model for the child, providing a variety of language experiences and models of different language usage.

Most **immersion teachers** are particularly committed to bilingual education, enthusiastic about bilingualism in society, acting as language missionaries. Research in Wales by Roberts (1985) suggests the important nature of teacher commitment in minority language medium education. This commitment exists beyond teachers' interest in the education of children. In the equation of a successful bilingual school, such enthusiasm and commitment by headteachers and principals, teachers and auxiliary workers, may be an important and often underestimated factor in success. There is a danger of seeing success in bilingual education as due to the system (e.g. immersion) and use of two languages in school. The commitment of bilingual teachers, and the special skills that a bilingual teacher uses beyond those required of a monolingual teacher, may be underestimated in the equation of successful bilingual schooling.

Sixth, the French immersion approach allows a relatively **homogeneous language classroom**. For example, in early total immersion, children will start from the same point. All are beginners without French proficiency. This makes the task of the teacher relatively easy. Children can grow in the French language under a shared teaching and learning approach. Initially, there will be no disparity of status due to some children being more proficient than others in French.

On a comparative education note, the term 'Immersion' is used in Finland, Australia, Wales and Ireland. In these Celtic situations, there is often a classroom mixture of those who are fluent and those who are less fluent in the classroom language. For example, in an Irish immersion school, the classroom may be composed both of children whose home language is Irish and those whose home language is English but whose parents are keen for their children to be taught through the medium of Irish. The Irish and Welsh experience tend to suggest that most children whose home language is English will cope successfully in minority language immersion classrooms. For such children, the language context is additive rather than subtractive. The danger is that the majority language of English, being the common denominator, will be the language used between students in the classroom, in the playground and certainly out of school. According to Lindholm (1990) 'To maintain an environment of educational and linguistic equity in the classroom, and to promote interactions among native and non-native English speakers, the most desirable ratio is 50% English speakers to 50% non-native English speakers' (p. 100). However, Lindholm (1990) admits that little research has been conducted to determine the optimal classroom composition for successful bilingual education. A balance towards a greater proportion of minority language speakers may help to ensure that the 'common denominator' majority language does not always dominate in informal classroom and playground talk.

Seventh, immersion provides an **additive bilingual environment**. Students acquire French at no cost to their home language and culture. Such enrichment may be contrasted to subtractive bilingual environments where the home language is replaced by the second language. For example, where the home language is Spanish and the submersion approach is to replace Spanish by English, negative rather than positive effects may occur in school performance and self-esteem. This underlines that the term immersion education is best reserved for additive rather than subtractive environments. The term 'immersion education' is appropriate only when the home language is a majority language and the school is adding a second minority or majority language.

Eighth, most immersion teachers have to 'wear two hats': promoting achievement throughout the curriculum and ensuring second language proficiency. Such a dual task requires **immersion teacher training** (Bernhardt & Schrier, 1992). This tends to be a weakness in countries using the immersion approach or a version of it. Both at the pre-service and in-service levels of education of teachers, the special needs of immersion teachers need addressing. Methods in immersion classroom require induction into skills and techniques beyond those required in ordinary mainstream classrooms. Immersion teaching (and teacher training) methods are still developing and are at a relatively early stage.

LANGUAGE STRATEGIES IN IMMERSION CLASSROOMS

Immersion education is based on the idea that a first language is acquired relatively unconsciously. Children are unaware that they are learning a language in the home. Immersion attempts to replicate this process in the early years of schooling. The focus is on the content and not the form of the language. It is the task at hand that is central, not conscious language learning. In the early stages, there are no formal language learning classes, although simple elements of grammar such as verb endings may be taught informally. In the latter years of elementary schooling, formal consideration may be given to the rules of the language (e.g. grammar and syntax). The early stages of immersion tend to mirror the unconscious acquisition of learning of the first language. Only later will a child be made conscious of language as a system, to reinforce and promote communication.

Immersion also tends to assume that the earlier a language is taught the better. While teenagers and adults may learn a second language fluently and proficiently (see Chapter 5), research evidence tends to suggest that young children acquire authentic pronunciation better than adults (Brown, 1980). A young child is more plastic and malleable, with uncommitted areas in the left hemisphere of the brain. The argument for immersion schooling tends to be, 'the earlier the better'.

In the first stages in Early French immersion classrooms, the teacher concentrates on listening comprehension skills. 'Oral skills are given more importance in kindergarten to Grade 3; reading and writing skills, even though started as early as Grade 1, are stressed in Grades 4 to 6' (Canadian Education Association, 1992). Students are not made to speak French with their teacher or with their peers in the initial stages. Children will initially speak English to each other and to their teacher, without any penalty. Immersion teachers do not force children to use French until they are naturally willing to do so. Early insistence on French may inhibit children and develop negative attitudes to the French language and to education in general. Over the first two years, immersion children develop an understanding of French and then begin to speak French, particularly to the teacher.

The most frequent grade in which English becomes part of the formal curriculum in Early Total French Immersion is Grade 3. Other practices include introducing English at an earlier grade or kindergarten and at Grade 4 (Canadian Education Association, 1992). While initially students will lag behind mainstream 'English' students in English language achievement, by Grade 5 or 6, Early Immersion students catch up and perform as well (Rebuffot, 1993).

In these early stages of Early French Immersion, it is crucial that the teacher is comprehensible to the children. The teacher needs to be sympathetically aware of the level of a child's vocabulary and grammar, to deliver in French at a level the child can understand, and simultaneously, be constantly pushing forward a child's competence in French. The teacher will be aiming to push back the frontiers of a child's French by ensuring that messages are both comprehensible and are slightly ahead of the learner's current level of mastery of the language.

The language used to communicate with the child at these early stages is often called **caretaker speech**. For the first year or two in French immersion, the vocabulary will be deliberately limited. There will be a simplified presentation of grammar and syntax. The teacher may be repetitive in the words used and the ideas presented, with the same idea presented in two or more different ways. The teacher will deliberately speak slowly, giving the child more time to process the language input and understand the meaning. This tends to parallel the talk of mother to child (**motherese**) and **foreigner talk** (a person deliberately simplifying and slowing the language so a foreigner can understand). During this caretaker stage, the teacher may be constantly questioning the child to ensure that understanding has occurred.

A teacher may also present the language to be used before a lesson topic is presented. When new words and new concepts are being introduced into a lesson, the teacher may spend some time in introducing the words and clarifying the concepts so that the language learner is prepared. Such teachers may also be sensitive to **non-verbal feedback** from students: questioning looks, losing concentration and glazed attention. A student may be encouraged to question the teacher for clarification and simplification when understanding has not occurred. These strategies cover two different areas: the importance of comprehensible input and the importance of negotiating meaning. The worst case is when neither the teacher nor the student is aware that misunderstanding (or no understanding) has taken place. A more effective classroom is when students and teachers are negotiating meaning, ensuring that mutual understanding has occurred. Not only is the negotiation of meaning important in language development and in maximizing achievement throughout the curriculum, it is also important in aiding motivation of children within the classroom. Patronizing such children and oversimplifying are two of the dangers in this process. Therefore, constantly presenting students with ever challenging and advancing learning situations is important in classroom achievement.

Such immersion classrooms need to have a particular view about **language errors**. Language errors are a usual and important part of the language learning process. Errors are not a symptom of failure. They are a natural part of learning. Errors are not permanent knots that spoil the wood. With time and practice, these knots can be removed. Therefore, immersion teachers are discouraged from over-correcting children's attempts to speak French. Just as parents are more likely to correct children's factual errors than their first language errors, the immersion teacher will tend to avoid constant correction of errors. Constant error correction may be self-defeating, negatively reinforcing language acquisition. Language accuracy tends to develop over time and with experience. Constant correction of error disrupts communication and content learning in the classroom. When a child or several children constantly make the same errors, then appropriate and positive intervention may be of value.

In the early stages of immersion, there will be a natural **interlanguage** among children. A child may change round the correct order in a sentence yet produce a perfectly comprehensible message. For example, faulty syntax may occur due to the influence of the first language on the second language. A child may put the pronoun or a preposition in the wrong order: as in 'go you and get it'. Interlanguage is not to be seen as error. Rather it indicates the linguistic creativity of students who are using their latent understanding of the first language to construct meaningful communication in the second language. Interlanguage is thus an intermediate, approximate system. It is a worthwhile attempt to communicate and therefore needs encouragement. Seen as a halfway stage in-between monolingualism and being proficient in a second language, interlanguage becomes part of the journey and not a permanent rest point.

For the immersion teacher, an assumption is that proficiency in the first language will contribute to proficiency in the second language. Concepts attached to words in the first language will easily be **transferred** into the second language. The acquisition of literacy skills in the first language tends to facilitate the acquisition of literacy skills in the second language. However, not all aspects of a language will transfer. Rules of syntax and spelling may not lend themselves to transfer. The closer a language structure is to the second language structure, the greater the transfer there is likely to be between the two languages. For example, the transfer between English and Spanish is likely to be more than Arabic to English due to differences in syntax, symbols and direction of writing. However, the system of meanings, the conceptual map and skills that a person owns, may be readily transferable between languages.

The focus of immersion classrooms is very much on **tasks, curriculum content** and creative processes (e.g. Bernhardt, 1992; Dicks, 1992; Hall, 1993). However, as Harley (1991) has indicated, there is also a place for an analytical approach to the second and the first language in the classroom. An immersion classroom will not just enable children to acquire the second language in an unconscious, almost incidental manner. Towards the end of elementary education, the experiential approach may be joined by a meaning based focus on the form of language. A child may at this point be encouraged to analyze their vocabulary and grammar. At this later stage, some lessons may have progress in the second language as their sole aim. After early sheltering with language, the development of vocabulary and grammar may be dealt with in a direct and systematic manner.

Snow (1990) provides a list of ten specific techniques that tend to be used by experienced and effective immersion teachers. This is a valuable summary of the discussion in this section.

(1) Providing plenty of contextual support for the language being used (e.g. by body language — plenty of gestures, facial expressions and acting).
(2) Deliberately giving more classroom directions and organizational advice to immersion students. For example, signaling the start and the end of different routines, more explicit directions with homework and assignments.
(3) Understanding where a child is at, thereby connecting the unfamiliar with the familiar, the known with the unknown. New material is linked directly and explicitly with the child's present knowledge and understanding.
(4) Extensive use of visual material. Using concrete objects to illustrate lessons, using pictures and audio-visual aids, giving the child plenty of hands-on manipulative activities to ensure all senses are used in the educational experience.
(5) Obtaining constant feedback as to the level of a student's understanding. Diagnosing the level of a student's language.
(6) Using plenty of repetition, summaries, restatement to ensure that students understand the directions of the teacher.
(7) The teacher being a role model for language emulation by the student.
(8) Indirect error correction rather than constantly faulting students. Teachers ensure that the corrections are built in to their language to make a quick and immediate impact.
(9) Using plenty of variety in both general learning tasks and in language learning tasks.
(10) Using frequent and varied methods to check the understanding level of the children.

CONCLUSION

Previous chapters have examined the different kinds of bilingual classroom. An integrated overview will now be presented. First and second languages are developed in school by different methods and for different reasons. For language minorities, the reasons include the survival and maintenance of the language and attendant culture. Chapter 12 started by stressing the importance of the classroom in deliberately and formally cultivating the child's home language, heritage culture, minority language literacy and biliteracy. For language minority children, growth in their home language requires nurturing classrooms to ensure tender plants blossom to maturity.

There tend to be overlapping and different reasons for second language learning. Whether for economic trade or cognitive growth, for cultural awareness or for travel abroad, there has been a growth in the call for more sowing and nurturing of second and foreign language seeds. How to nurture those seeds has been debated. Under umbrella headings of the structural approach, the functional approach and the interactional approach, fall different ideas of language growth in the classroom. Classroom language gardeners often use a variety of styles, accenting both grammar and communication, repetition and roleplay, drills and drama, correcting errors and encouraging spontaneity.

In many international contexts, second language lessons are customary and compulsory. For some, such lessons are to replace the first language; for others, such lessons are to multiply language abilities. For some, such lessons are to assimilate, to produce a subtractive language situation. For others, such lessons are to produce an additive language context. For yet others, second language learning occurs across the curriculum, as in the Canadian immersion programs. Growth in the second language is faster and greater in such privileged gardens.

Previous chapters have suggested that a colorful language garden is enriched considerably when there is literacy in both languages. Much stronger and taller language flowers will blossom when biliteracy is present in individuals and language minority groups. In the language garden of the 21st century, bilingual education may need to ensure that biliteracy co-exists with bilingualism. Otherwise, the colorful multilingualism of the world's language garden may wither and fade.

SUGGESTED FURTHER READING

BERNHARDT, E.B. (ed), 1992, *Life in Language Immersion Classrooms*. Clevedon: Multilingual Matters.

CALIFORNIA STATE DEPARTMENT OF EDUCATION, 1984, *Studies on Immersion Education. A Collection for United States Educators*. Sacramento, CA: California State Department of Education.

GENESEE, F. 1987, *Learning Through Two Languages*. Cambridge, MA: Newbury House.

HELLER, M. 1994, *Crosswords: Language, Education and Ethnicity in French Ontario*. New York: Mouton de Gruyter.

REVIEW AND STUDY QUESTIONS

(1) Write short revision notes on the following:
    (i)   A list of the main features of immersion classrooms.
    (ii)   A list of language strategies in immersion classrooms.
(2) What are the characteristics of immersion classrooms? Which of these characteristics may be generalizable to other 'strong' forms of bilingual education?
(3) Find out the different uses of the term immersion (e.g. structured immersion in the US compared with early total immersion in Canada). What are the essential differences?

STUDY ACTIVITIES

(1) By reading, a visit to an immersion school, or looking at a video tape of immersion education (e.g. from the Ontario Institute of Studies in Education), write out a plan of a typical immersion classroom lesson. The plan should be in sufficient detail for a group of students to perform a dramatic sketch simulating the classroom sequence.
(2) Visit a 'bilingual' classroom, and by diagrams, pictures or photographs, portray the bilingual displays of the classroom. Capture in picture form the wall displays, project work, activity corners, and other forms of display which attempt to provide a bilingual classroom.

CHAPTER 18

A Model and a Framework of Bilingual Education

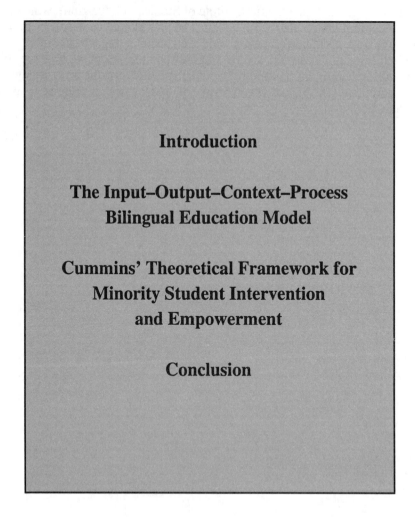

Introduction

The Input–Output–Context–Process
Bilingual Education Model

Cummins' Theoretical Framework for
Minority Student Intervention
and Empowerment

Conclusion

CHAPTER 18

A Model and a Framework of Bilingual Education

INTRODUCTION

Chapters 10 to 17 discussed bilingual education at two levels: as systems and as classrooms. It is important to integrate these and attempt an overview of the whole. Two different structures are presented to help integrate and harmonize. First, a model of bilingual education is presented, followed by a framework for intervention and empowerment through bilingual education.

THE INPUT–OUTPUT–CONTEXT–PROCESS BILINGUAL EDUCATION MODEL

In the language garden there are different seeds, different flowers which form the **inputs** into the garden. There is then the **process** of growth of those seeds and plants with **outcomes** in terms of individual flowers and individual gardens. The nature of the soil, the weather conditions and additives to the soil form the **context** of growth in the garden. Final outcomes in the language garden cannot be properly judged except by reference to the initial seeds and the contextual climate. The teacher as a language gardener has to meet the challenge of 'given' plants and climatic conditions. The same seeds sown in different soil, or in differing climates will show different growth; sometimes flourishing, sometimes not growing to their potential size and beauty. This analogy suggests that, to understand bilingual education, we need to relate and integrate the inputs, contexts, processes and outputs in any example of bilingual education. The language garden can be understood by defining and integrating four different parts: ingredients, environments, the growth process and outcomes.

A four part model gives an organizing framework for thinking about bilingual education (Baker, 1985, 1988; Stern, 1983a). Bilingual education has inputs, outputs, contexts

341

and process over and above that of 'mainstream' schooling as detailed by Dunkin & Biddle (1974). First, we will consider in an overview, the nature of the whole model.

There are **inputs** or human ingredients into the classroom which are varying student (and teacher) characteristics. Research examines how different inputs (e.g. teacher qualities, student language ability, motivation) influence outputs. **Outputs** or outcomes may be short term (e.g. test attainment) or longer term (e.g. attitude to language learning). The relationship between inputs and outputs can be modified by the **context** or environment in which schooling occurs. At a macro level, context could be, for example, ethnic group or local community effects on education. Context could also refer to the wider societal and governmental level. At a micro level, context may refer to the classroom environment (e.g. a classroom poor or rich in dual language resource material). The final part of the model is **process**, where the second by second life of actual classroom practice may be examined. The model is illustrated on the following page and then explained in more detail.

The linguistic and cultural knowledge of bilingual teachers, their competency to operate in two languages and transmit two or more cultures are examples of **teacher inputs**. **Student inputs** include aptitude and skill in the two languages, their attitudes and motivations. **Outputs** could be many and are likely to be contentious, but are likely to include proficiency in the two languages, biliteracy, attitudes towards the languages and cultures, initial and subsequent integration into linguistically and culturally different groups and self esteem.

Five overlapping categories of **context** can be defined:

(1) The nature of the wider **society**, particularly political aims and ideologies. Assimilationist and integrationist, pluralist and separatist viewpoints may variously affect language minorities. The relationship between the dominant and the dominated, the empowered and the powerless, the enabled and the 'disabled' is crucial in understanding the nature, aims and outcomes of bilingual education, in whatever form.

(2) The nature of the **community**; the extent to which a community is bilingual, bicultural, positive, negative or ambivalent towards bilingual education and bilingualism.

(3) The nature of the **school**; e.g. immersion, transitional bilingual, a bilingual unit within a mainstream school, a school using a minority language within a majority language area.

(4) The nature of the **classroom**; e.g. the language balance of the classroom (e.g. early immersion where students are at the same level in the second language, compared with some United States 'submersion' schools where minority language children are expected to learn English alongside English first language speakers).

(5) The nature of the **curriculum material**; the kind of curriculum resources used to achieve progress in bilingualism and biculturalism, the use of audio visual techniques, formal grammar lessons, technological aids (e.g. Computer Assisted Language Learning on microcomputers) and creative activity.

PROCESS VARIABLES

a) PUPIL-TEACHER
   INTERACTION
   (e.g. % use of two languages)

b) PUPIL-PUPIL INTERACTION

c) USE OF CURRICULUM
   MATERIALS
   (e.g. interpretation in the use
   of materials by teachers and
   pupils)

INPUT VARIABLES

a) TEACHER CHARACTERISTICS
   - Proficiency in Languages
   - Linguistic Knowledge
   - Cultural Knowledge
   - Teacher Competences and Attitudes
b) PUPIL CHARACTERISTICS
   - Language Abilities
   - Aptitude, Attitude and Motivation
     for Languages
   - Language and Cultural Background

OUTPUT VARIABLES

a) ATTAINMENT IN LANGUAGES
b) ATTITUDE TO LANGUAGES
c) SOCIAL & CULTURAL INTEGRATION
d) SELF-ESTEEM
e) LONG TERM EFFECTS (e.g. employment,
   cultural participation, language of the family)
f) ACHIEVEMENT THROUGHOUT THE
   CURRICULUM

CONTEXT VARIABLES

a) NATURE OF THE LANGUAGE AIMS OF
   SOCIETY
b) NATURE AND AIMS OF THE LOCAL
   COMMUNITY REGARDING
   LANGUAGE AND CULTURE
c) NATURE AND AIMS OF THE SCHOOL
d) NATURE AND AIMS OF THE
   CLASSROOM
   (e.g. language balance among pupils)
e) NATURE OF THE CURRICULUM

Note: 1. The model may be extended to include attributes not specific to bilingual education by reference to
         Dunkin & Biddle (1974).
      2. The arrows show the most typical connections made by research in relating the elements of the model.

Here, contexts are portrayed as environments. However, teachers are sometimes regarded as 'human contexts' with students the inputs. Student inputs are then connected to final outcomes. This suggests that what constitutes inputs and contexts may be debated. Classification into the four parts of the model may vary due to the focus of the research or theory.

Finally, the **process** concerns inspection and analysis of topics such as: teacher's reinforcement and reward systems when students use their first and second language; criticism for using the first language; teacher's explaining systems when using either language; language error correction; language lesson patterns and structures; language teaching styles; students' work involvement rate in their two languages, and teacher's use of two languages, in a qualitative and quantitative sense, in the classroom.

Such an 'organizing' bilingual education model pinpoints some important issues:

(1) **Generalization** of a research finding to a variety of contexts can be dangerous. Immersion education appears to work well in Canada. This does not mean it can be exported elsewhere without changes. As contexts, student characteristics and teacher attributes change, so may the success of immersion education. Different ingredients produce different meals. The nature and quality of the ingredients may vary, affecting outcomes — as all cooks will testify. Occasionally the change of just one ingredient can change the taste of the whole product. Recipes for success need testing in a variety of contexts to assess their generalization potential. Research on bilingual education needs to be replicated in as many different social and educational contexts as possible, both across and inside countries. Such research also needs replication with the inputs varied. For example, using different socioeconomic groups of children, or schools where teachers have varying levels of commitment to bilingual education. Recipes for success are likely to be varied, complex and not necessarily stable over time.

(2) Outputs from bilingual education need to be thought of in a relative, contentious and pluralistic manner. Different interest groups expect different outcomes from bilingual schooling. Some research has narrowly focused on traditional skills which can be quantitatively measured by achievement tests. There may be **alternative outcomes** of bilingual education, sometimes debated, difficult to define and measure, which need investigating (e.g. self esteem, open mindedness, responsibility, independence, initiative, tolerance, curiosity, originality, perseverance, honesty, reliability, vocational success and social adjustment). Paulston (1992b) suggests that employment rates for school leavers, drug addiction and alcoholism statistics, suicide rates, personality disorders and drop-out rates are more important indicators of the success of bilingual education than standardized test scores. Bilingual education needs to be evaluated in terms of social justice and not just school scores. Has too much emphasis been placed on end of year, end of school outcomes? Are the more important effects of bilingual schooling longer term? For example, attitude to both languages and cultures after schooling, commitment and participation in the two languages and cultures, raising children in the minority language or not, and

sending such children to bilingual schools are all researchable long term effects. Does bilingual education have a short term effect that dies after leaving school? Does bilingual schooling have long term, cumulative effects that are beneficial or otherwise to society?

(3) The **process issues** are most important in successful bilingual education. The way teachers and students behave and interact, think, feel, talk, write, move and relate to one another are vital issues for teachers, parents and school administrators. Bilingual classrooms are different from mainstream classrooms and therefore particularly need research on classroom processes (e.g. Hornberger, 1990a, 1990b).

There are endemic problems with models if used uncritically. (1) Models can lead to static descriptions of classrooms, schools and education systems. Research that focuses on inputs, outputs and contexts and ignores processes is particularly prone to such an accusation. Snap shots are less real than a moving film of processes, change and development. Classrooms, schools and systems constantly evolve. (2) Models can reduce the complex to the simple, the diverse and intricate to the smooth and basic. (3) There are often wide variations inside classrooms, schools and systems. There are usually variations across time, with many exceptions to the model proposed. (4) Models do not always provide deep explanations. They paint pictures, but don't always provide penetrating analyses to explain, criticize and inform. (5) The model does not represent the views, understanding, reasons and explanations of those acting in the drama. It is an outsiders view, and not the discourse of those involved.

CUMMINS' THEORETICAL FRAMEWORK FOR MINORITY STUDENT INTERVENTION AND EMPOWERMENT

Cummins' (1986b) theoretical framework concerns language minority students. There are three fundamental statements to Cummins' (1986b) theory. The first two ideas have been discussed in this book already. First, 'language minority students instructed through the minority language (for example, Spanish) for all or part of the school day perform as well in English academic skills as comparable students instructed totally through English' (p. 20). Teaching children through a second or minority language usually leads to the satisfactory development of English academic skills.

The second statement is the **'interdependence hypothesis'**. This proposed that 'to the extent that instruction through a minority language is effective in developing academic proficiency in the minority language, transfer of this proficiency to the majority language will occur given adequate exposure and motivation to learn the language' (Cummins, 1986b: 20). Research by Verhoeven (1994) suggests that there was positive transfer between languages in literacy skills, sound systems (phonology) and communication skills (pragmatics). As may be expected, there was little transfer in lexicon (vocabulary) and syntax (e.g. grammar). Underlying the surface characteristics of both languages is one common core of developed ability or 'academic proficiency'. Beneath two protrusions on the water lies the one iceberg.

The third statement concerns context. Community and school liaison, power and status relationships all need to be considered in a proper bilingual education theory.

Cummins' (1986b) theory suggests that minority language students are **'empowered' or 'disabled'** by four major characteristics of schools.

(1) **The extent to which minority language students' home language and culture are incorporated into the school curriculum**. If a minority language child's home language and culture are excluded, minimized or quickly reduced in school, the likelihood is there of that child becoming academically 'disabled'. Where the school incorporates, encourages and gives status to the minority language, the chances of empowerment are increased. Apart from potential positive and negative cognitive effects, the inclusion of minority language and culture into the curriculum may have effects on personality (e.g. self esteem), attitudes, social and emotional well being. This point is important because it raises a question about why bilingual education which emphasizes the minority language is successful. Is it due to such education fostering cognitive and academic proficiency, as the interdependence hypothesis suggests? Or is it also due, or more due to students' cultural identity being secured and reinforced, thus enhancing self confidence and self esteem? Cummins (1986b) sees the incorporation of minority students' language and culture existing on an **additive–subtractive dimension**. 'Educators who see their role as adding a second language and cultural affiliation to their students' repertoire are likely to empower students more than those who see their role as replacing or subtracting students' primary language and culture.' (p. 25)

(2) **The extent to which minority communities are encouraged to participate in their children's education**. Where parents are given power and status in the partial determination of their children's schooling, the empowerment of minority communities and children may result. When such communities and parents are kept relatively powerless, inferiority and lack of school progress may result. The growth of paired reading schemes is evidence of the power of a parent–teacher partnership. Parents listening to their children reading on a systematic basis tend to be effective agents of increased literacy. As an illustration of the importance of community participation, Cummins (1986b) cites the Haringey Project in London. Parental involvement in children's reading, even when parents were non-English speaking and non-literate, had an important effect on children's reading progress. Teachers are seen as being locatable on a dimension ranging from the **collaborative to the exclusionary**. Teachers at the collaborative end encourage parents of minority languages to participate in their children's academic progress through home activities or the involvement of parents in the classroom. Teachers at the exclusionary end maintain tight boundaries between themselves and parents. Collaboration with parents may be seen as irrelevant, unnecessary, unprofessional, even detrimental to children's progress.

(3) **The extent to which education promotes the inner desire for children to become active seekers of knowledge and not just passive receptacles.** Learning can be active, independent, internally motivated or passive, dependent and requiring external pulls and pushes. The **transmission** model of teaching views children as buckets into which knowledge is willingly or unwillingly poured. The teacher controls the nature of the fluid being poured and the speed of pouring. The hidden curriculum of the transmission model may reinforce and symbolize the powerlessness of language minority students. There are those in control and those controlled. The alternative model, **reciprocal interaction,**

> 'requires a genuine dialogue between student and teacher in both oral and written modalities, guidance and facilitation rather than control of student learning by the teacher, and the encouragement of student/student talk in a collaborative learning context. This model emphasizes the development of higher level cognitive skills rather than just factual recall, and meaningful language use by students rather than the correction of surface forms. Language use and development are consciously integrated with all curricular content rather than taught as isolated subjects, and tasks are presented to students in ways that generate intrinsic rather than extrinsic motivation.' (Cummins, 1986b: 28)

If the transmission model is allied to the **disablement** of minority language students, then the reciprocal interaction model is related to the **empowerment** of students. This latter model aims to give students more control over their own learning, with consequent potential positive effects for self esteem, co-operation and motivation.

(4) **The extent to which the assessment of minority language students avoids locating problems in the student and seeks to find the root of the problem in the social and educational system or curriculum wherever possible.** Psychological and educational tests tend by their very nature to locate problems in the individual student (e.g. low IQ, low motivation, backwardness in reading). At worst, educational psychologists and teachers may test and observe a child until a problem can be found in that child to explain poor academic attainment. Such a testing ideology and procedure may fail to locate the root of the problem in the social, economic or educational system. The subtractive nature of transitional bilingual education, the transmission model used in the curriculum, the exclusionary orientation of the teacher towards parents and the community and the relative economic deprivation of minority children could each or jointly be the real origin of a minority language child's problem. Therefore assessment and diagnostic activity need to be **Advocacy rather than Legitimization oriented.** Advocacy means the assessor or diagnostician advocating for the child, by critically inspecting the social and educational context in which the child operates. This may involve comments about the power and status relationships between the dominant and dominated groups, at national, community, school and classroom level.

The theoretical framework can be summarized as follows:

	Empowered Minority Language Children	Disabled Minority Language Children
Dimension 1:	Additive: Incorporation of Home Language and Culture in the School.	Subtractive: Home Language and Culture Excluded from the School.
Dimension 2:	Collaborative Community Participation.	Exclusionary Community Non-participation.
Dimension 3:	Reciprocal Interaction Curriculum.	Transmission Oriented Curriculum.
Dimension 4:	Advocacy Oriented Assessment and Diagnosis.	Legitimization Oriented Assessment and Diagnosis.

Empowerment thus becomes an important concept in transforming the situations of many language minorities. 'Empowerment means the process of acquiring power, or the process of transition from lack of control to the acquisition of control over one's life and immediate environment' (Delgado-Gaitan & Trueba, 1991: 138). Empowerment can be furthered by education, but also needs to be realized in legal, social, cultural and particularly economic and political events. Delgado-Gaitan & Trueba (1991) thus add the necessary sociocultural and political dimensions of empowerment to the possibilities of empowerment through education.

Empowerment and Pedagogy

When the focus is on the language minority group, and particularly when the focus is on the experience of individual bilinguals, differences in prosperity and economic opportunity, in power and pedagogic opportunity are evident. As a generalization, language minorities have less power and less chance of acquiring political power compared with language majorities. Such minorities are subservient to the majority who reproduce their dominance in particular classroom process (see below). This powerlessness is enacted, transmitted and reproduced in the **classroom** by the authority relationship of, for example, a majority language teacher and a submissive language minority student (Delpit, 1988). If classrooms transmit and reinforce power relations and powerlessness, is this reversible? Is language minority powerlessness reproduced inside 'weak' forms of bilingual education? Can this be reversed by 'strong' forms of bilingual education? It is important to ask 'how' and 'why' language minority children are at a disadvantage in the classroom. Can there be **attempted reversal and empowerment**? Delpit (1988) analysis is by exploring the 'Culture of Power' in classrooms.

(1) The 'Culture of Power' is enacted in the classroom by:
   • teachers having power and dominance over students;
   • the curriculum (e.g. via text books) determining a legitimate world view; the curriculum taught may be restricted to a majority language viewpoint (e.g. white, US, English language) and taught as supreme, incontestable and 'correct';

- majority language educators define narrowly what constitutes approved forms of intelligent behavior; what is regarded as 'intelligent behavior' is formulated by the language majority; this is imposed on students from a language minority whose own forms of intelligent behavior are ignored;
- school leading to employment (or unemployment) and hence to economic status (or a lack of status).

(2) The 'Culture of Power' is embedded in ways of talking and writing, ways of dressing, manners and ways of interacting (e.g. compare 'upper', 'middle' and 'lower' or 'working' class children).

(3) Success in school and employment often requires acquiring or mimicking the culture of those in power. This is essentially upper and middle class culture. 'Children from other kinds of families operate within perfectly wonderful and viable cultures but not cultures that carry the codes or rules of power' (Delpit, 1988: 283). Language minority families have their own valid, well developed and valuable cultures already in place.

(4) Those outside of the 'Culture of Power' should be taught explicitly the rules and nature of that culture in order to become empowered. If styles of interaction, discourse patterns, manners and forms of dress, for example, are explained to a child, does this lead to the language minority child being empowered, or does this move such a child towards cultural separation?

CONCLUSION

Cummins' (1986b) theoretical framework incorporates psychological functioning and educational attainment, and includes a focus on the social, economic and political background that is so often crucial to fully understanding bilingualism and bilingual education. The theory covers research on cognitive functioning, motivation, educational success or failure in different forms of bilingual education, and includes the context of education in terms of power relationships, culture, community and parental involvement. The four part bilingual education model is an attempt to organize macro level thinking about bilingual schools. Useful in planning research and understanding research findings, it also seeks to provide a way of putting pieces of a large jig-saw puzzle together to form one picture. Its limitation is that bilingual education is more like a film than a picture — constant movement and change.

SUGGESTED FURTHER READING

BAKER, C. 1988, *Key Issues in Bilingualism and Bilingual Education*. Clevedon: Multilingual Matters.

CUMMINS, J. 1986, Empowering minority students: A framework for intervention. *Harvard Educational Review* 56 (1), 18–36.

DELPIT, L.D. 1988, The silenced dialogue: Power and pedagogy in educating other people's children. *Harvard Educational Review* 58 (3), 280–298.

GARCÍA, O. and BAKER, C. (eds) 1995, *Policy and Practice in Bilingual Education: A Reader Extending the Foundations*. Clevedon: Multilingual Matters. (Sections 1 and 2).

350 FOUNDATIONS OF BILINGUAL EDUCATION

REVIEW AND STUDY QUESTIONS

(1) Write short revision notes on the following:
    (i)   The nature (and examples of) inputs, contexts, processes and outputs in bilingual education.
    (ii)   The four dimensions of Cummins' Theoretical Framework.
(2) What is meant by input, process, context and output in the bilingual education model?
(3) Discuss the variety of outputs there could be from bilingual education. Highlight those which tend to be most preferred by administrators, parents, teachers, principals, the students themselves, language minority groups, politicians and militant language activists. Why are there differences in preferred outputs of these varied interest groups?
(4) What part of Cummins' framework do you feel are the most important in bilingual education?

STUDY ACTIVITY

(1) In terms of a school you have visited, make a diagram of the inputs, outputs, contexts and processes which you particularly observed in that one school. Prepare this as a diagram to be displayed (alongside other students' diagrams) so that different schools reveal different characteristics. Discuss in a small group or with a partner what similarities or differences there are between the diagrams when they are displayed.

CHAPTER 19

The Politics of Bilingualism

CHAPTER 19

The Politics of Bilingualism

INTRODUCTION

Bilingualism not only exists within individuals, within their cognitive systems, in the family and in the local community. Bilingualism is also directly and indirectly interwoven into the politics of a nation. Bilingualism is not only studied linguistically, psychologically and sociologically, it is also studied in relationship to **power structures** and **political systems** in society. The basis of this chapter is that bilingualism and bilingual education, whatever form it takes, cannot be properly understood unless connected to basic philosophies and politics in society. The activity of a bilingual classroom, and decisions about how to teach minority language children, are not based purely on educational preferences. Bilingual education does not just reflect curriculum decisions. Rather, bilingual education is surrounded and underpinned by basic beliefs about minority languages, minority cultures, in-migrants, equality of opportunity, empowerment, affirmative action, the rights of individuals and the rights of language minority groups, assimilation and integration, desegregation and discrimination, pluralism and multiculturalism, diversity and discord, equality of recognition for minority groups and social cohesion. Education has been conceived as part of the solution and part of the problem of achieving unity in diversity.

It is important for students, teachers and educational policy makers to be aware of how their present and future activity not only concerns children in classrooms, but also fits into the overall **language policy** of a state or a nation. Teachers and education administrators are not only affected by political decisions and processes, they also deliver and implement those decisions and processes. Teachers are part of language paradoxes that are daily enacted and temporarily resolved in the classroom: to ensure equality of opportunity for all while celebrating distinctiveness; ensuring diversity does not become discord; having a common purpose while encouraging colorful variety; developing the dignity of ethnicity and aiding national stability; making a student's life safe for and from ethnicity.

THREE PERSPECTIVES ON LANGUAGES

We begin by considering different assumptions and varying perspectives that are at the root of the politics of bilingualism and bilingual education. Ruiz (1984) suggests that there are three basic orientations or perspectives about language around which people and groups vary: **language as a problem, language as a right and language as a resource**. These three different dispositions towards language planning are not necessary at the conscious level. They may be embedded in the unconscious assumptions of planners and politicians. Such orientations are regarded as fundamental and related to a basic philosophy or ideology held by an individual.

Language as a Problem

Public discussion of bilingual education and languages in society often commences with the idea of language as causing complications and difficulties. This is well illustrated in discussions about the supposed **cognitive problems** of operating in two languages (see Chapters 7 to 9). Perceived problems are not limited to thinking. **Personality and social problems** such as split-identity, cultural dislocation, a poor self image and anomie are also sometimes attributed to bilinguals. At a group rather than an individual level, bilingualism is sometimes connected with national or regional disunity and inter-group conflict. Language is thus also viewed as a **political problem**.

Part of the 'language-as-problem' orientation is that perpetuating language minorities and language diversity may cause less integration, less cohesiveness, more antagonism and more conflict in society. The perceived complication of minority languages is to be **solved by assimilation** into the majority language. Such an argument holds that the majority language (e.g. English) unifies the diversity. The ability of every citizen to communicate with ease in the nation's majority language is regarded as the common leveler. A strong nation is regarded as a unified nation. Unity within a nation is seen as synonymous with uniformity and similarity. The opposing argument is that it is possible to have national unity without uniformity. Diversity of languages and national unity can co-exist (e.g. Singapore, Luxembourg, Switzerland).

The co-existence of two or more languages is rarely a cause of tension, disunity, conflict or strife. The history of war suggests that economic, political and religious differences are prominent as causes. **Language is seldom the cause of conflict**. Religious crusades and *jihads*, rivalries between different religions, rivalries between different political parties and economic aggression tend to be the instigators of strife. Language, in and by itself, is rarely a cause of unrest (Otheguy, 1982). In a research study on causes of civil strife, Fishman (1989) found that language was not a cause. 'The widespread journalistic and popular political wisdom that linguistic heterogeneity *per se* is necessarily conducive to civil strife, has been shown, by our analysis, to be more myth than reality' (Fishman, 1989: 622). Rather, the causes of strife were found to be deprivation, authoritarian regimes and modernization.

A minority language is often connected with the **problems** of poverty, underachievement in school, minimal social and vocational mobility and with a lack of integration into the majority culture. In this perspective, the minority language is perceived as a partial cause of social, economic and educational problems, rather than an effect of such problems. This 'language is an obstacle' attitude is summed up in the phrase, 'If only they would speak English, their problems would be solved'. The minority language is thus seen as a handicap to be overcome by the school system. One resolution of the problem is regarded as the increased teaching of a majority language (e.g. English) at the expense of the home language. Developing bilingualism is an irrelevant or a secondary and less important aim of schooling. Thus submersion and transitional bilingual education aim to develop competent English language skills in minority language children as quickly as possible so they are on a par with English first language speakers in the mainstream classroom.

A **language problem** is sometimes perceived as **caused** by 'strong' forms of **bilingual education**. Such education, it is sometimes argued, will cause social unrest or disintegration in society. Fostering the minority language and ethnic differences might provoke group conflict and disharmony. The response is generally that 'strong' forms of bilingual education will lead to better integration, harmony and social peace. As Otheguy (1982: 314) comments of the US: 'Critics of bilingual education with a concern for civil order and social disharmony should also concern themselves with issues of poverty, unemployment, and racial discrimination rather than concentrate on the use of Spanish in schools. In pledges of allegiance, it is liberty and justice — not English — for all, that is to keep us indivisible'.

'Strong' forms of bilingual education should not be connected with the language problem orientation. Rather, the evidence suggests that developing bilingualism and biliteracy within a 'strong' bilingual education situation is educationally feasible and can lead to:

- higher achievement across the curriculum for minority language children;
- maintaining the home language and culture;
- fostering self-esteem, self-identity and a more positive attitude to schooling.

Such higher achievement may enable better usage of human resources in a country's economy and less wastage of talent. Higher self esteem may also relate to increased social harmony and peace.

Within this 'problem' orientation, there not only exists the desire to remove differences between groups to achieve a common culture. There can be the desire for **intervention** to improve the position of language minorities. 'Whether the orientation is represented by malicious attitudes resolving to eradicate, invalidate, quarantine or inoculate, or comparatively benign ones concerned with remediation and "improvement", the central activity remains that of problem-solving' (Ruiz, 1984: 21).

Language as a Right

A different orientation to that of 'language as a problem' is thinking of language as a **basic, human right**. Just as there are individual rights in choice of religion, so it is argued, there should be an individual right to choice of language. Just as there are attempts to eradicate discrimination based on color and creed, so people within this orientation will argue that language prejudice and discrimination need to be eradicated in a democratic society (Skutnabb-Kangas & Phillipson, 1994).

Such language rights may be derived from **personal**, legal and constitutional rights. Personal language rights will draw on the right to freedom of individual expression. It may also be argued that there are certain natural or moral language rights in **group** rather than individual terms. The rights of language groups may be expressed in terms of the importance of preservation of heritage language and culture communities and expressed as 'rights to protection' and 'rights to participation'. This includes welfare rights and rights to liberty and self-determination.

A further level of language rights may be **international**, derived from pronouncements from organizations such as the United Nations, UNESCO, the Council of Europe and the European Community. Each of these four organizations has declared that minority language groups have the right to maintain their language. In the European community, a directive (25th July 1977: 77/486/EEC) stated that Member States should promote the teaching of the mother tongue and the culture of the country of origin in the education of migrant workers' children. However, individual countries have generally ignored such international declarations. Particular international examples (e.g. Sámi in Norway, Kurds in Turkey, and Gikuyu speakers in Kenya) are portrayed in Skutnabb-Kangas & Phillipson (1994). The kind of rights, apart from language rights, that ethnic groups may claim include: protection, membership of their ethnic group and separate existence, non-discrimination and equal treatment, education and information in their ethnic language, freedom to worship, freedom of belief, freedom of movement, employment, peaceful assembly and association, political representation and involvement and administrative autonomy.

In the US, the rights of the individual are a major part of democracy. As Trueba (1989: 103) suggests, 'American democracy has traditionally attached a very high value to the right to disagree and debate, and to enjoy individual and group cultural and linguistic freedom without jeopardizing the rights of others or our national unity'. In the United States, questions about language rights are not only discussed in college classrooms and language communities, and debated in government and federal legislatures. Language rights have a history of being tested in US courtrooms. This is significantly different from European experience where language rights have rarely been tried in law. From the early 1920s to the present, there has been a continuous debate in **US courts of law** regarding the legal status of language minority rights. To gain short term protection and a medium term guarantee for minority languages, legal challenges have become an important part of the language rights movement in the United States. The legal battles are not just couched in minority language versus majority language contests. The test cases also concern children versus schools, parents versus school boards, state versus the federal authority (Ruiz, 1984). Whereas minority language activists among the Basques in Spain and the Welsh in Britain have been taken to court by the central government for their actions, US minority language activists have taken the central and regional government to court. One example will illustrate.

A landmark in United States' bilingual education was a lawsuit. A court-case was brought on behalf of Chinese students against the San Francisco School District in 1970. The case concerned whether or not non-English speaking students received equal educational opportunity when instructed in a language they could not understand. The failure to provide bilingual education was alleged to violate both the equal protection clause of the 14th Amendment and Title VI of the Civil Rights Act of 1964. The case, known as **Lau versus Nichols**, was rejected by the federal district court and a court of appeals, but was accepted by the Supreme Court in 1974. The verdict outlawed English submersion programs and resulted in nationwide 'Lau remedies'. Such remedies reflected a broadening of the goals of bilingual education to include the possible maintenance of minority language and culture. The Lau remedies created some expansion in the use of minority languages in schools, although they rarely resulted in true heritage language, enrichment or maintenance programs. For the purposes of this chapter, the Lau court case is symbolic of the dynamic and continuing contest to establish language rights in the US particularly through testing the law in the courtroom (Casanova, 1991; Hakuta, 1986; Lyons, 1990).

Language rights are not only expressed in legal confrontations with the chance of being established in law. Language rights are often expressed at the **grass roots level** by protests and pressure groups, by local action and argument. For example, the *Kohanga Reo* (language nests) movement in New Zealand provides a grass roots instituted immersion preschool experience for the Maori people. Beginning in 1982, these language nests offer a 'preschool all-Maori language and culture environment for children from birth to school age, aimed at fostering complete development and growth within a context where only the Maori language is spoken and heard' (Corson, 1990a: 154). One example of grass roots expression of 'language as a right' is the recent Celtic (Ireland, Scotland and Wales) experience. In these countries, 'grass-roots' created preschool playgroups, 'mother and toddler' groups and adult language learning classes have been established so that the heritage languages can be preserved in both adult social interaction and especially in the young. Stronger activism and more insistent demands have led to the establishment of heritage language elementary schools, particularly in urban, mostly English speaking areas. Not without struggle, opposition and antagonistic bureaucracy, parents have obtained the right for education in the indigenous tongue. Such pressure groups have contained parents who speak the indigenous language, and those who speak only English, yet wish their children to be taught in the heritage language of the area.

A specific example is the growth of Designated Bilingual Schools in South Wales (UK). The growth in such State-funded bilingual schools owes much to parents insisting on the natural **right** to have their children educated in the home language. Through the activity of 'Parents for Welsh Medium Education' and through informal networks of local parents and language activists, Local Education Authorities (often as a reaction to sustained pressure and persuasion) have responded to market preferences. Such parental groups have naturally contained Welsh speaking parents who wish the language to be reproduced in their children with the essential help of formal education. However, the pressure for bilingual schooling has also come from non-Welsh speaking parents. Merfyn Griffiths, headteacher of such a Designated Bilingual school commented that, in 1986, 'there are Welsh medium schools, at both primary and secondary levels, where over 90% of the pupils come from homes where the language is not spoken. By now it is non-Welsh speaking parents and learners who are often the most ardent advocates of Welsh medium education and who apply most pressure on local education authorities to establish more Welsh medium schools. Without their support, faith and enthusiasm, further progress will not be possible.' (p. 5)

In North American and British society, no formal recognition is usually made in politics or the legal system to categories or groups of people based on their culture, language or race. Rather the focus is on **individual rights**. The accent is on individual equality of opportunity, individual rewards based on individual merit. Policies of nondiscrimination, for example, tend to be based on individual rather than group rights. Language minority groups will nevertheless argue for rewards and justice based on their existence as a definable group in society. Sometimes based on territorial rights, often based on ethnic identity, such groups may argue for rewards in proportion to their representation in society. **Group based rights** are often regarded as a way of redressing injustices to language minorities. This may be a temporary step on the way to full individual rights. Alternatively, language minorities may claim the right to some independent power, some measure of decision making and some guarantee of self-determination.

A note of **caution** about language rights needs sounding. Liberal words about individual rights can hide preferences for coercion and conformity (Skutnabb-Kangas, 1991). Stubbs (1991) talks of the experience in England with language minorities where government reports 'use a rhetoric of language entitlement and language rights, and of freedom and democracy... [which] makes the correct moral noises, but it has no legislative basis, and is therefore empty. There is talk of entitlement, but not of the discrimination which many children face; and talk of equality of opportunity, but not of equality of outcome' (pp. 220–221).

Trueba (1991: 44) sounds a further caution: 'Language rights of ethnolinguistic minorities are not detachable from their basic human rights, their right to their culture and their civil rights'. Social, economic and political participation rights should not be jeopardized by retaining language cultural differences.

Language as a Resource

An alternative orientation to 'language as a problem' and 'language as a right', is the idea of language as a **personal and national resource**. The recent movement in Britain and North America for increased second and foreign language fluency (e.g. in French) fits into this orientation. Under the general heading of language as a resource also comes regarding minority and lesser used languages as a cultural and social resource. While languages may be viewed in terms of their economic bridge building potential, languages may also be supported for their ability to build social bridges across different groups, bridges for cross fertilization between cultures.

The recent trend in Europe and North America, for example, has been to expand **foreign language education**. Second language study is increasingly viewed as an essential resource to promote foreign trade and world influence. Thus, the paradox is that while bilingual education to support minority languages has tended to be depreciated in the United States, the current trend is to appreciate English speakers who learn a second language to ensure a continued major role for the US in world politics and the world economy. There is a tendency to value the acquisition of languages while devaluing the language minorities who have them. While integration and assimilation is still the dominant ideology in US internal politics, external politics increasingly demand bilingual citizens (Kjolseth, 1983). Ovando (1990) describes US language policy as schizophrenic. 'On the one hand we encourage and promote the study of foreign languages for English monolinguals, at great cost and with great inefficiency. At the same time we destroy the linguistic gifts that children from non-English language backgrounds bring to our schools' (Ovando, 1990: 354).

In the United States, the idea of language as a resource not only refers to the development of a second language in monolingual speakers. It also refers to the **preservation of languages** other than English. For example, children whose home language is Spanish or German, Italian or Chinese, Greek or Japanese, Portuguese or French have a home language that can be utilized as a resource. One case is the Spanish speakers in the US who together make the US the fourth largest Spanish speaking country in the world. Just as water in the reservoir and oil in the oil field are preserved as basic resources and commodities, so a language such as Spanish, despite being difficult to measure and define as a resource, may be preserved for the common economic, social and cultural good. Suppression of language minorities, particularly by the school system, may be seen as economic, social and cultural wastage. Instead, such languages are a **natural resource** that can be exploited for cultural, spiritual and educational growth as well as for economic, commercial and political gain.

Within the 'language as a resource' orientation, there tends to be the assumption that linguistic diversity does not cause separation nor less integration in society. Rather, it is possible that **national unity and linguistic diversity can co-exist**. Unity and diversity are not necessarily incompatible. Tolerance and cooperation between groups may be as possible *with* linguistic diversity as they would be *unlikely* when such linguistic diversity is repressed.

A frequent debate concerns **which languages** are a resource? The favored languages tend to be those that are both international and particularly valuable in international trade. A lower place is given in the status rankings to minority languages that are small, regional and of less perceived value in the international marketplace. For example, in England, French has traditionally been placed in schools at the top of the first division. German, Spanish, Danish, Dutch, Modern Greek, Italian and Portuguese are the major European languages placed into the second division. Despite large numbers of mother tongue Bengali, Panjabi, Urdu, Gujerati, Hindi and Turkish speakers, the politics of English education relegates these languages to an almost non-existent position in the school curriculum. In the British National Curriculum, the listed languages (Arabic, Bengali, Chinese (Cantonese or Mandarin), Gujerati, Modern Hebrew, Hindi, Japanese, Panjabi, Russian, Turkish and Urdu) are only allowed in secondary schools (for 11 to 18 year olds) if a higher division language (e.g. French) is taught first. Thus a caste system of languages is created in England. The caste system is Eurocentric, culturally discriminatory and economically shortsighted, 'allowing languages already spoken in the home and community to be eroded, whilst starting from scratch to teach other languages in schools and colleges' (Stubbs, 1991: 225).

To **conclude**: while the three orientations have differences, they also share certain common aims: of national unity, of individual's rights, of fluency in the majority language (e.g. English) being important to economic opportunities. The basic difference tends to be whether monolingualism in the majority language or full bilingualism should be encouraged as a means to achieving those ends. All three orientations connect language with politics, economics, society and culture. Each orientation recognizes that language is not simply a means of communication but is also connected with socialization into the local and wider society, as well as a powerful symbol of heritage and identity. The differences between the three orientations lie in the socialization and identity to be fostered: assimilation or pluralism, integration or separatism, monoculturalism or multiculturalism.

US LANGUAGE ORIENTATIONS

That the three orientations have common aims as well as vital differences is illustrated in the case of the United States. The US has long been a willing receptacle of peoples of many languages: German, French, Polish, Italian, Greek, Welsh, Arabic, Chinese, Japanese and Spanish to name a few examples. Bull, Fruehling & Chattergy (1992) portray the situation as follows:

> 'Cultural and linguistic differences have been a source of strength and controversy in the United States since its founding. Indeed, this country's founding and much subsequent US history can be seen as a continuing search for unity in diversity, for *e pluribus unum*, especially among its residents of European extraction. What could unite the New York Dutch, the Pennsylvania German, and the Virginia English; the Massachusetts Puritan, the Pennsylvania Quaker, the Maryland Catholic, and the Virginia Anglican; the Yankee trader, the northern farmer, and the southern plantation owner? How could the United States assimilate and capitalize upon its Norwegian, Irish, Russian, Italian, Polish, and Jewish immigrants? And more recently, what relationship could white Anglo majorities establish with formerly disenfranchised and economically marginalized African-American, Chinese, Japanese, Native American, and Latino minorities?' (Bull, Fruehling & Chattergy, 1992: 1)

The receptacle of in-migration was transformed into a **melting pot** to assimilate and unify. The dream became an integrated United States with shared social, political and economic ideals. Quotes from two US Presidents illustrate this 'melting pot' attitude.

Roosevelt in 1917 urged all immigrants to adopt the English language:

'It would be not merely a misfortune but a crime to perpetuate differences of language in this country... We should provide for every immigrant by day schools for the young, and night schools for the adult, the chance to learn English; and if after say five years he has not learned English, he should be sent back to the land from whence he came.' (quoted in Gonzalez, 1979)

President Reagan views in the late 1980s were that it is 'absolutely wrong and against American concepts to have a bilingual education program that is now openly, admittedly dedicated to preserving their native language and never getting them adequate in English so they can go out into the job market and participate' (quoted in Crawford, 1989; from Democrat Chronicle, Rochester, March 3, 1981: 2a). This melting pot attitude has continued with the English-only movement.

Within the United States, basic differences in 'language orientation' are exemplified in the contest between the **'English-only' movement** and the counter punching by various academics (see Crawford, 1992a; Crawford, 1992b; Cazden & Snow, 1990; McGroarty, 1992; Padilla, 1991). The 'English-only' movement in the US (which includes the 'US English' and the 'English First' organizations), requests that the English language become the sole official language of the United States. Imoff (1990) describes the US English movement as a public interest organization. Its principles are that the

'government should foster the similarities that unite us rather than the differences that separate us... The study of foreign languages should be strongly encouraged, both as an academic discipline and for practical, economic and foreign-policy considerations. ...All candidates for US citizenship should be required to demonstrate the ability to understand, speak, read and write simple English and demonstrate basic understanding of our system of Government.' (p. 49)

Thus, the preferred US in-migrant in the **'English-only'** view is someone who learns English quickly as well as acquiring US customs and culture, acquires skills that are useful in the economic prosperity of the country, works hard and achieves the US dream. For Imoff (1990), bilingual education only serves to destroy rather than deliver that dream.

While the debate about integration and pluralism will be examined later in this book, there is little disagreement about certain desirable outcomes between the positions of the English-only group and the **'English-plus'** pro-bilingual response in the United States (e.g. children becoming fluent in English). The difference is in the route to its achievement. For the English-only group, English language skills are best acquired through English monolingual education. For the English-plus group, skills in the English language can be successfully fostered through 'strong' forms of bilingual education. Both groups appear to acknowledge that full English proficiency is important in opening doors to higher education, business, commerce and the occupational market. Full proficiency in the majority language will usually be equated to equality of educational and vocational opportunity.

As Chapter 11 showed, the evidence exists for support of 'strong' versions of bilingual education and hence for the 'English plus' position. Such evidence supports the use of the home minority language in the classroom at least until the end of elementary education and probably further. Achievement across the curriculum, achievement in subjects as diverse as science and history, mathematics and geography would not seem to suffer but be enhanced by 'strong' forms of bilingual education. Such achievement includes English (second) language competence. Research on the cognitive effects of bilingualism seems to support the ownership of two languages to enhance rather than impoverish intellectual functioning.

The **place of English** in the US and much of the world is strong and becoming stronger. As a result of the emergence of the US as the major economic power of the 20th century, and due to British colonization before the 20th century, the world status of English is not in doubt. Some 320 million people in the world speak English as a first language. With English based Creoles and Pidgins, this rises to around 377 million speakers (Crystal, 1995). The number of English second or foreign language speakers is more contentious, with figures between 100 million and 400 million often quoted. (The variations are due to guesses or estimates being required in many countries, and to the criteria for inclusion as a second language speaker (see Chapter 1) being variable — see Crystal, 1995).

Numbers of speakers is less important than the **prestigious domains and functions** that English dominates. 'English has a dominant position in science, technology, medicine, and computers; in research, books, periodicals, and software; in transnational business, trade, shipping, and aviation; in diplomacy and international organizations; in mass media entertainment, news agencies, and journalism; in youth culture and sport; in education systems, as the most widely learnt foreign language' (Phillipson, 1992: 6). Such a widespread use of English means that Anglo culture, Anglo institutions, and Anglo ways of thinking and communicating are spread. English then tends to displace the functions of other languages and even displace them. In technology, communications and entertainment, English has become the **imperialistic language** (Phillipson, 1992). It takes over some of the internal functions of other languages in a country (e.g. in business, mass media) and becomes the means of the external link in, for example, politics, commerce, science, tourism and entertainment.

Thus Gandhi (1927) accused **English** of being an intoxicating language, denationalizing a country such as India, and bring mental slavery to Anglo forms of thinking and culture. He argued that English is used in some multilingual societies to internally colonize, and to preserve the power of ruling elites. English imposes linguistic uniformity that is culturally, intellectually, spiritually and emotional restricting. Other languages are then portrayed as confining, ethnocentric, divisive, alienating and anti-nationalistic. Yet it is not the language that is dominating but the people who use it. A language is not intrinsically dominating. No language is more suited to oppression or domination or imperialistic than another. It is the speakers of that language who are the oppressors, dominators and imperialists.

THE LANGUAGE ORIENTATIONS OF DIFFERENT MINORITY GROUPS

Alongside the in-migrant languages in the US is the existence of indigenous, native languages (e.g. Navajo — see Holm & Holm, 1990). Are there important differences between in-migrant and indigenous language minorities, or differences between different in-migrant minorities (e.g. the Chinese and the Mexican Americans) in language orientation? Ogbu (1978, 1983) makes a distinction between 'castelike', 'immigrant' and 'autonomous' minority groups. (A minority group being defined in this book in terms of 'a minority of power' and not just by relative numerical size (Haberland, 1991)).

'**Autonomous**' minorities are not subordinate to the dominant majority group and have distinct separate identities. For example, some Jews in the US often have a distinct racial, ethnic, religious, linguistic or cultural identity and are generally not politically or economically subordinate. Such autonomous minorities are unlikely to be characterized by disproportionate or persistent failure in school.

'**Castelike**' minorities tend to fill the least well paid jobs, are often given poor quality education, and are regarded as inferior by the dominant majority who sometimes negatively label them as 'culturally deprived', with 'limited English proficiency', with 'low innate intelligence' or pejoratively as 'bilinguals'. Ogbu (1978) classes Black Americans, Puerto Ricans, Mexican Americans, indigenous Indians and many Hispanic groups in the US as 'castelike' minorities. The 'outcastes' of India and some of the Caribbean in-migrants in England also share these characteristics. Such minorities may see themselves as relatively powerless, immobile in status and confined to subservience and domination. Most have been permanently and often involuntarily incorporated into the 'host' society. Such a group experience disproportionate failure at school. Failure at school confirms the low expectations they have of themselves and the negative attributions of majority groups. A sense of inferiority is joined by low levels of motivation to succeed in the wider society.

In the main, Ogbu's (1978) '**immigrant**' minorities have moved relatively willingly to the US and may be relatively more motivated to succeed at school and seek prosperity. Cubans, Filipinos, Japanese and Koreans in the US were included in this group (Ogbu, 1978). Another example is the Chinese in-migrants who, as a generalization, are keen to succeed, positive about the opportunities in schooling and are relatively optimistic about improving their lot. Some 'immigrant' language minority individuals may arrive having been educated in the home country, and are literate and motivated to achieve.

'**Immigrant**' minorities tend to lack power, status and will often be low down on the occupational ladder. However, they do not necessarily perceive themselves in the same way as their dominant 'hosts'. 'As strangers, they can operate psychologically outside established definitions of social status and relations' (Ogbu, 1983: 169). Such 'immigrant' minorities may still suffer racial discrimination and hostility, yet are less intimidated and paralyzed by dominating majorities compared with 'castelike' minorities. Parents may have relatively strong aspirations for the success of their children in school and also expect vocational and social mobility in their offspring. Pride in ethnic identity is not lost but preserved by the parents, who see their reference group as back in the homeland or in the in-migrant neighborhood.

One example of the influence of parents and the language community is given by Corson (1985, 1992). In Australia, 'Italian, Portuguese and Macedonian children from low-income backgrounds who had learned their English in school as a second language, out-performed their Anglo-Australian classmates from similar low-income backgrounds on a battery of language instruments and in school examinations, even though the latter spoke English as their mother tongue and were matched in non-verbal reasoning ability with the former' (Corson, 1992: 59). The example is important as it underlines the danger of simple statements about the expected performance of language minority children in mainstream education. The culture of the language community and the attitudes to schooling of parents may be examples of powerful influences on children's motivation to succeed in school. There are many other factors contributing to the success of children than their type of minority group, including many 'success stories' from 'castelike minorities' (Erickson, 1987; Trueba, 1988).

Ogbu's (1978) distinction between 'autonomous, castelike and immigrant' minorities does not allow easy classification of different language minorities into these three groups. The criteria for classification are not precise enough nor are they validated by research studies. There is also the **danger** of stereotyping different language groups when there is much variability within such groups; sometimes more than the variability between the groups. However, the differences between 'castelike' and 'immigrant' minorities help explain why equally disadvantaged groups facing discrimination from the dominant majority, perform differently at school. Poverty, poor quality schooling and powerlessness do not fully explain language minority failure in education. Beyond socioeconomic class and language differences, academic and economic success or failure may, in part, be due to cultural differences among language minorities. Castelike minorities seem locked into a system that perpetuates inequalities and discrimination. Other minorities attempt to escape the subtractive system which confines their participation in society and confirms their powerlessness. 'Immigrant' and autonomous minorities may show relatively less failure at school, partly explained by their different orientation to language. Language minority education ('strong' forms of bilingual education) therefore become highly important for castelike minorities to attempt to counteract the discrimination of the dominant minority and counteract the acceptance and internalization of that discrimination and economic deprivation.

The call for increased provision of 'strong' forms of bilingual education for 'castelike' and 'immigrant' minorities may not be welcomed by the dominant majority. Those with power and wealth may see such 'strong' forms of bilingual education as upsetting the status quo and usurping the power structure (Cummins, 1991a). The worry for the dominant majority may be that the 'castelike', the unemployed and those in poorly paid manual labor will be **empowered** by such education. The dominated may then begin to contest and threaten differences of rank, reward and rule. 'As the minority group is empowered through jobs, preferred status, professionalization, the majority becomes frightened. In an effort to regain control, it enforces monolingualism not only as an educational goal, but also as the most valuable educational approach' (O. García, 1991a: 5). When there is prosperity and liberal politics (e.g. the Civil Rights era), some empowerment of language minorities may be granted through 'strong' forms of bilingual education'.

When there is economic recession, less liberal politics and language minority self-assertiveness, 'strong' forms of bilingual education will be less preferred. Dominant majorities at such times may wish to control access to the more prestigious jobs, preserve their power and wealth. This may result in hostility to 'strong' forms of bilingual education which threaten to give language minorities an increased share of power, wealth and status (O. García, 1991a).

The dominant majority often see minority language education as creating national disunity rather than unity, disintegration rather than integration. The frequent **criticism of bilingual education** is that it serves to promote differences rather than similarities, to separate rather than integrate. In England and in the US, the majority public viewpoint tends to be for unity, integration and assimilation of in-migrant, language minority communities. Indeed, the strongest arguments for bilingual education on cognitive and educational grounds may well fail unless a strong argument can be advanced for linguistic and cultural pluralism. Does bilingual education lead to greater or lesser tolerance, a common or a separate identity, a sense of anomie or an ability to belong to two cultures simultaneously? Are language minority children taught (rightly or wrongly) to be in conflict or at peace with the majority? Is bilingual education the arena for a power struggle between majority and minority? These questions are now tackled through examining the debate on assimilation and pluralism.

ASSIMILATION

The social and political questions surrounding bilingual education tend to revolve around two contrasting ideological positions. 'At one extreme is **assimilation**, the belief that cultural groups should give up their "heritage" cultures and take on the host society's way of life. At the opposite pole is **multiculturalism**, the view that these groups should maintain their heritage cultures as much as possible' (Taylor, 1991: 1). The assimilationist viewpoint is pictured in the idea of a melting pot. Zangwill's play '*The Melting Pot*' (1914) introduced the idea of diverse in-migrant elements being merged to make a new homogenized whole. 'Into the Crucible with you all! God is making the American'. The idea of the melting pot immediately throws up two different perspectives.

First, there is the idea that the final product, for example the US American, is made up by a contribution of all the cultural groups that enter the pot. The cultural groups melt together until the final product is a unique combination. No one ingredient dominates. Each cultural group makes its own contribution to the final taste. However, this is not the usual view associated with the melting pot. So second, the melting pot often means cultural groups giving up their heritage culture and adopting that of the host culture. In this second melting pot picture, cultural groups are expected to conform to the dominant national culture.

The rationale for this assimilationist perspective is that equality of opportunity, meritocracy and the **individual** having a chance of economic prosperity due to personal effort are each incompatible with the separate existence of different racial and cultural groups. When the emphasis is on individuality in terms of rights, freedom, effort and affluence, the argument for assimilation is that language **groups** should not have separate privileges and rights from the rest of society. Advantage and disadvantage associated with language minority groups is to be avoided so individual equality of opportunity can reign.

Assimilationist ideology is an umbrella term under which a variety of types of assimilation may occur: cultural, structural, marital, identificational, attitudinal, behavioral, social and civic (Gordon, 1964). An important distinction is between **economic-structural** assimilation and **cultural** assimilation (Skutnabb-Kangas, 1977). Some in-migrant and minority group members may wish to assimilate culturally into the mainstream society. Cultural assimilation refers to giving up a distinct cultural identity, adopting mainstream language and culture. In general, language minorities will usually wish to avoid such cultural assimilation. However, economic-structural assimilation may be sought by language minorities. Such assimilation refers to equality of access, opportunities and treatment (Paulston, 1992b). For example, equal access to jobs, goods and services, equality in voting rights and privileges, equal opportunities and treatment in education, health care and social security, law and protection, may be desired by language minorities. Therefore, structural incorporation tends to be more desired and cultural assimilation more resisted (Schermerhorn, 1970; Paulston, 1992b).

Assimilation may be explicit, implied or concealed (Tosi, 1988). For example, **explicit assimilation** occurs when language minority children are required to take monolingual education solely in the majority language (e.g. submersion education in the US). **Implied assimilation** is when such children are diagnosed as having 'special needs' and are offered compensatory forms of education (e.g. Sheltered English and Transitional Bilingual Education in the US). **Concealed assimilation** may be found, for example, in some types of multicultural education program (see the next chapter) where language minorities may be instructed in racial harmony, national unity, and individual achievement using majority language criteria to gauge success. Such a program is designed to achieve hegemony and ethnic harmony (Tosi, 1988).

Since there are a **variety of forms of assimilation**, measuring the extent to which assimilation has occurred is going to be difficult. Is assimilation measured by segregation and integration in terms of housing of in-migrants, for example, by their positions within the economic order, by the extent of intermarriage between different cultural groups or by the attitudes they exhibit? Assimilation is thus multidimensional and complex (Skutnabb-Kangas, 1991). Assimilation is neither easily defined nor easily quantified. Assimilationists may have mildly differing views. One example will illustrate.

A few assimilationists may accept that school students should maintain their home language and culture. However, they would argue that this is the **responsibility of the home** and not the school (Porter, 1990). However, most assimilationists will argue that, if economic resources are scarce and school budgets are stretched, bilingual programs should not be supported, particularly if the costs are greater than regular mainstream programs (Secada, 1993).

With the increased accent on **ethnicity** since the 1960s, the assumptions of assimilation were challenged and the 'new ethnicity' born. Ideologies that surround the terms **'integration'**, **'ethnic diversity'**, **'pluralism'** and **'multiculturalism'** (discussed in the next chapter) challenged the assimilationist philosophy. The picture of the melting pot has been contrasted with alternative images: the patchwork quilt, the tossed salad, the linguistic mosaic and the language garden.

Integration concerns equality of opportunity for all, accompanied by cultural diversity in an atmosphere of mutual understanding and tolerance. One popular metaphor is the salad bowl, with each ingredient separate and distinguishable, but contributing in a valuable and unique way to the whole. A different 'integration' metaphor, favored in Canada, is the linguistic mosaic, with different pieces joined together in one holistic arrangement.

More recently, the **debate** over assimilation and pluralism has sharpened (Edwards, 1995; Takaki, 1993). A re-emphasis on personal endeavor, individual striving for success, a lessening of reliance on welfare and collectives (e.g. positive discrimination for ethnic groups) has been joined by ethnic conflicts (e.g. in Bosnia, Croatia, Serbia and Russia). This has led to increased arguments and disputes about the merits of assimilation and pluralism (Takaki, 1993).

ASSIMILATION AND IN-MIGRANTS

The **expectation** was that in-migrants into the US, Canada and England, for example, would be pleased to have escaped political oppression or economic disadvantage and be jubilant to embrace equality of opportunity and personal freedom. The expectation was that an individual would be pleased to give up their past identity and make a commitment to a new national identity. Yet heritage culture and cultural identity have persisted, resisted and insisted. Assimilation has often not occurred. Is this deliberate or difficult, desired or not desired?

Assimilation may be sought by in-migrants. Many wish to assimilate, but come to reside in segregated neighborhoods and segregated schools. Thus assimilation can be **prevented** by social and economic factors outside the wishes of the in-migrants. Some groups of in-migrants may wish to be categorized as US citizens, but are categorized and treated by mainstream society as different, separate and non-US. The conditions under which in-migrants live may create the negative labels and social barriers that enforce non-integration. As Otheguy (1982: 312) remarks of the US: 'Because of their experience with racism in this country, many Hispanics have long ago given up hope of disappearing as a distinct group'. The result may be the prevention of assimilation and integration with a consequent need to embrace some form of multiculturalism for survival, security, status and self-enhancement.

MAINTAINING ETHNIC IDENTITY

A different situation is where a language minority prefers not to assimilate culturally. Where an ethnic group wishes to maintain its cultural identity and a degree of enclosure (Schermerhorn, 1976), **boundaries** between it and the dominant majority may be essential to continued ethnic identity (Barth, 1966). Boundaries between the language minority group and the dominant group will aid the preservation of ethnic identity and help maintain the vitality of the heritage language. Establishing boundaries and ethnic identity rest on several criteria (Allardt, 1979; Allardt & Starck, 1981) :

(1) Self categorization as a distinct ethnic group.
(2) Common descent and ancestry, be it real or imagined.
(3) Owning specific cultural traits or exhibiting distinctive cultural patterns, of which language may be the strongest example.
(4) Well established social organization patterns for interacting within the group and separately with 'outsiders'.

Some of the members of an ethnic group will fulfill all these four criteria; every member must fulfill at least one of the four criteria to be a member of that ethnic group. These criteria highlight the difference between **self-categorization** and **categorization by others**, particularly categorization by the dominant group. Barth (1966) argued that such categorizations essentially define an ethnic group. 'The existence of an ethnic group always presupposes categorization, either self-categorization or categorization by others' (Allardt, 1979: 30).

Such categorizations are rarely stable and tend to change over time. Allardt (1979) argued that:

> 'Previously, it was majorities who mainly performed the categorization and labeling of minorities. The principal aim of categorization was exclusion: majorities acted in order to safeguard their material privileges or else to persecute minorities. The results were often severe patterns of discrimination. Of course, minorities also often defended themselves by defining their own criteria for inclusion and belonging. There has occurred a definite change in the present ethnic revival. It is now mainly the minority who categorizes... The problems in the fields of ethnic relations have, as it were, changed from problems of discrimination to problems of recognition.' (Allardt, 1979: 68)

Categorization by others will often use cultural and geographical criteria. Some categorizations are imposed upon a language minority (e.g. as having 'limited language proficiency') and at other times attributed less openly to that minority. Such categorizations from outside the group include negative remarks about non-assimilation and non-integration. Self-categorization may re-phrase outsider remarks as self-identity, ethnic awareness and self-recognition.

Ethnic identity can thus be created by imposed categorization from without, or by invoked categorization from within. Self-categorization can be achieved through promoting ethnic social institutions (e.g. law, mass media, religious units, entertainment, sport and cultural associations working in the heritage language). Ethnic community schools (heritage language education) plus the careful planning of the ethnic language in the curriculum may be major component in self-categorization (García, 1983). Mobilizing ethnic group members to agitate for language legitimacy and reform, working towards a defined idealized vision of the status of the language may also aid self-categorization (C.H. Williams, 1991b). This raises a fundamental debate of how to achieve ethnic identity and language rights: persuasion or agitation; reform or revolt? This debate is now considered.

Can minority language groups always be in a co-operative functional relationship with the majority language. Does non-violent conflict sometimes need to be present to achieve rights for a language community? The achievements of the Basques and the Welsh would both seem to suggest that **conflict** with the majority is one mechanism of achieving language rights. Such a conflict viewpoint will place more emphasis on group rights than on individual rights. To be Basque may conflict with being Spanish. To be Welsh can conflict with being British. To be Quebecois may conflict with being Canadian. In these circumstances, cultural pluralism may not always lead to order and the maintenance of majority language rules in society. Should language minority groups pursue equilibrium or conflict?

EQUILIBRIUM OR CONFLICT?

Paulston (1980, 1992b) presents two major paradigms to theoretically interpret bilingual education. In the **equilibrium paradigm**, the different wheels that create the clockwork mechanism of society interact relatively harmoniously. The school, the economic order, social mobility and social processes interlock and work relatively harmoniously together. Change in society occurs by gradual, slow and smooth evolution. Conflict and disharmony are to be avoided because they lead to a breakdown in the clockwork mechanism. Radically new components will cause the system to stop functioning smoothly. Individual components in the mechanism are relatively unimportant in themselves. It is the overall clockwork mechanism that is important.

When the clock goes wrong, the fault is not within the **system** itself. One or more components must be a problem and will need to be adjusted. With language minority groups and bilingual education, any apparent failure will not be due to the system, but will be due to those components themselves. That is, the problems lie with the minority language groups and within the form of the bilingual education system. The problem will not be the system as a whole nor the overall educational system. Any failure in language minority students may be put down to their poor English proficiency rather than to the educational system. Individuals will be blamed not the system. Since the system works through English language instruction, more English language is required by the language minorities. In turn, any disadvantage or poverty that exists in such groups can be solved by improving their achievement at school via greater competence in the majority language. Since the oil of the clockwork mechanism is English language proficiency, once this is in place, language minority students will have equality of opportunity in the educational and economic systems. Bilingual education must maintain equilibrium in society.

Genesee (1987) analyses the **Canadian immersion programs** through this equilibrium approach. Such immersion programs are regarded as giving the majority group in society — the English speaking Canadian children — the bilingual proficiency to maintain their socioeconomic dominance in Canada. Set against the protests from French Quebec about the status of the French language in Canada, immersion education may be seen as aiding the stability of the bilingual situation in Canada. More French–English bilinguals created by the immersion schools seems to answer some of the protests of the Quebec people. (Although this is not necessarily the view of Quebec people who sometimes believe that their right to French speaking jobs is threatened by such immersion students.) Thus Canadian immersion programs are seen to produce equilibrium in the Canadian language situation.

A different viewpoint to the 'clockwork mechanism' equilibrium perspective is the **conflict paradigm** (Paulston, 1980, 1992b). Such a paradigm holds that conflict is a natural and expected part of the relationship between unequal power groups in a complex society. Given differences in culture, values, the unequal allocation of resources and variations in power within society, then conflict, radical views and disruption can be expected. Such a viewpoint often argues that real change occurs more by conflict, protest, non-violent and sometimes violent action, and less through the mending of minor problems within a system. Formal education tends to reproduce the dominance of the ruling elite over the masses, reproduces economic, social and political inequalities, inequality of opportunity and inequality of outcome in society.

The picture of a clockwork mechanism is replaced by a picture of an operation on an unhealthy body. The removal of an organ, a painful injection, the replacement or addition of tissue by grafting or plastic **surgery** may be radical and initially disruptive, but perceived as important if the health of the whole body is to improve. Minority language groups may be allotted too little power, too few rewards, and be disadvantaged in resources and rights. Since schools may perpetuate that disadvantage and subordinate power position, such linguistic, cultural and educational discrimination will need radical surgery.

'Weak' forms of bilingual education tend to perpetuate inequalities experienced by language minorities. In consequence, within the conflict perspective, **bilingual education** should attempt to right such inequality and injustice by positive discrimination. Bilingual education should be interventionist, even conflicting with dominant viewpoints. Bilingual education can serve to encourage social, economic and educational change and cultural pluralism (Rippberger, 1993). 'Strong' bilingual education can aid the status of minority languages and cultures, reduce the pulls and pushes towards assimilation, and aid the empowerment of minorities. Yet the Canadian immersion program, a 'strong' form of bilingual education, can be analyzed in a different way.

The Canadian immersion programs have been analyzed through a conflict perspective and not just through the equilibrium approach (e.g. Heller, 1994). There are many language tensions and conflicts in Canada. For example, many French first language speakers feel threatened by those bilinguals for whom French is a second language. Bilingual anglophones are seen to be accessing power, prestige and privilege that have hitherto been the preserve of bilingual francophones (e.g. by gaining positions in high status professions). With immersion schools, anglophones can gain the linguistic and cultural capital for increased social and economic mobility and for political power. 'Education is currently a major site of the struggle waged between anglophones and francophones, and within each group as well, over whether or not bilingualism should be valuable; and if so, whose property it should be. As such, it represents a struggle over the distribution of wealth and power' (Heller, 1994: 7). Bilingual education is thus not about unity or integration, in this perspective, nor is it neutral. Bilingual education is about gaining advantages, cultural, linguistic and social wealth, and dominance in Canadian society. As such, it produces conflict with the minority francophone community (e.g. in Ontario).

In the conflict paradigm, the problems exist within society as a whole, not simply in terms of 'individual deficiency' or 'educational provision'. The causes and determinants of minority language problems are **within society**, and not simply due to the characteristics of minority language children. Radical surgery is sometimes defended for the survival and stability of a healthy body. Long term health sometimes requires the short term pain of radical surgery.

Teachers and education administrators, researchers and college professors may sometimes be faced with a choice: oil the wheels of the system or be radical and attempt to change the system. Often, compromises are made by professionals: seeking evolution within relative stability; development within dominant perspectives. Within an overall desire for equilibrium, small conflicts about policy and provision among school staff, for example, may regularly occur. Thus there can be a pattern of small conflict within overall equilibrium.

There is also another combination: those for whom conflict is, and must be, perpetual. For particular types of language activists (e.g. in Wales and the Basque region), conflict becomes the norm. An equilibrium of conflict. One form of conflict politics may be language minority militancy (Schermerhorn, 1970). Language militants may attempt to gain control over the dominant majority and gain some form of ascendancy.

How can schools contribute to oiling and developing the clockwork machine, or changing the sick body by interventions into the core curriculum? The part to be played by schools comes partly through cultural and language awareness courses (see Chapter 20) and mostly in attempts to introduce multiculturalism and antiracism into a part or throughout the curriculum. The next chapter explores these latter possibilities.

CONCLUSION

Underlying language planning and language shift lie, at a latent and manifest level, political beliefs and decisions. Landscaping the language garden is frequently more politically than educationally based. Underneath 'weak' and 'strong' forms of bilingual education lie different **views** about language communities, ethnic minorities and language itself. When language is viewed as a problem, there is often a call for assimilation and integration. Assimilationists will usually stress the majority language as the common leveler. When language is viewed as a right, the accent may vary between individual rights and language group rights. Such rights may be contested in law and expressed by political and grass-roots movements.

Language may also be seen as a resource, a cultural and economic benefit, with a desire to maintain cultural and linguistic diversity. The political debate is often thus reduced to assimilation versus pluralism, integration versus multiculturalism. This debate relates directly to types of schooling: for example, submersion or heritage language; transitional bilingual education or dual-language education. 'Strong' forms of bilingual education may be seen as a form of reversing the powerlessness of those language minorities living within an assimilative and discriminatory political orientation. For language majorities, sensitization to language minorities may come through multicultural awareness. It is to multiculturalism we now turn.

SUGGESTED FURTHER READING

CAZDEN, C.B. and SNOW, C.E. (eds) 1990, *English Plus: Issues in Bilingual Education.* (*The Annals of the American Academy of Political and Social Science* 508, March 1990). London: Sage.

CRAWFORD, J. 1991, *Bilingual Education: History, Politics, Theory and Practice* (2nd edn). Los Angeles: Bilingual Education Services.

CRAWFORD, J. 1992, *Hold Your Tongue: Bilingualism and the Politics of 'English Only'.* Reading, MA: Addison-Wesley.

CRAWFORD, J. 1992, *Language Loyalties: A Source Book on the Official English Controversy.* Chicago: University of Chicago Press.

GARCÍA, O. (ed.) 1991b, *Bilingual Education: Focusschrift in Honor of Joshua A. Fishman (Volume 1).* Amsterdam/Philadelphia: John Benjamins.

GARCÍA, O. and BAKER, C. (eds) 1995, *Policy and Practice in Bilingual Education: A Reader Extending the Foundations.* Clevedon: Multilingual Matters. (Sections 1 and 4).

McKAY, S.L. and WONG, S.C. (eds) 1988, *Language Diversity: Problem or Resource?* New York: Newbury House.

SKUTNABB-KANGAS, T. and CUMMINS, J. (eds) 1988, *Minority Education: From Shame to Struggle.* Clevedon: Multilingual Matters.

SKUTNABB-KANGAS, T. and PHILLIPSON, R. (eds) 1994, *Linguistic Human Rights.* New York: Mouton de Gruyter.

REVIEW AND STUDY QUESTIONS

(1) Write short revision notes on the following:
  (i)   The nature of language as a problem, language as a right and language as a resource.
  (ii)   The views of the 'English-only' movement in the US and criticisms of these views.
  (iii) The differences between castelike, immigrant and autonomous minorities; followed by criticisms of this three-fold typology.
  (iv)   The meaning of assimilation and its differences from cultural pluralism.
  (v)   Different ways of establishing boundaries between ethnic groups.
  (vi)   The differences between the equilibrium and conflict paradigms.
(2) On what dimensions do people tend to differ in their political viewpoints about bilingual education?
(3) What is Ogbu's main argument and how does he explain differences in performance in the school system by different minority groups? What criticisms do you have of Ogbu's typology?

STUDY ACTIVITIES

(1) Among student groups, teachers in schools or in language communities, find out about different political viewpoints on language. Are there differences between different groups? Or are there more differences within those groups than between those groups?
(2) Interview two local politicians with differing viewpoints on bilingual education. Attempt to locate on what dimensions there are differences and similarities between these two politicians. Try to explain why there are differences.
(3) Follow a political controversy in current or previous newspapers. This controversy may concern languages in school or bilingual education or language minorities. Portray in words the varying political dimensions of the controversy. Does the controversy fit neatly into a two-way split (e.g. left wing compared with right wing viewpoints)? Or does the controversy have a number of different sides to it? Do you feel there are aspects of the controversy that are implicit rather than explicit?
(4) Follow one particular event regarding language in education. If possible, examine how that event is treated in two different languages (e.g. a Spanish newspaper and in an English language newspaper). What differences are there of interpretation and perception?
(5) Within a specific community, locate different interest groups and different sociocultural or socioeconomic groups of people. For example, compare working class and middle class viewpoints on bilingual education. How much do you think these varying viewpoints, if they exist, relate to home, social, economic, political and educational differences between the groups? Where are there similarities as well as differences?

CHAPTER 20

Multiculturalism and Anti-Racism

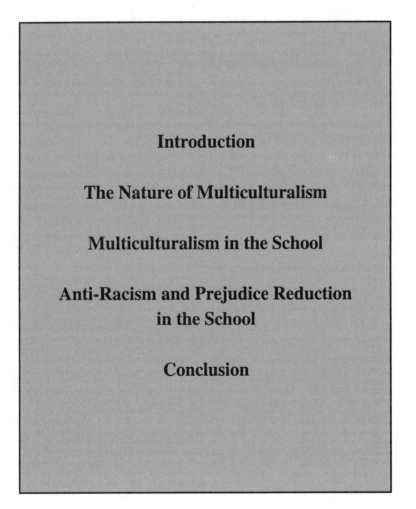

Introduction

The Nature of Multiculturalism

Multiculturalism in the School

Anti-Racism and Prejudice Reduction
in the School

Conclusion

CHAPTER 20

Multiculturalism and Anti-Racism

INTRODUCTION

Bilingualism and diglossia co-exist with biculturalism and multiculturalism. Languages connected within an individual, and languages in contact in society, become fused with multiculturalism as a personal possession and as a focus in school. This chapter explores the idea of multiculturalism, and then the role that education can play in multiculturalism. The chapter rests on the notion that 'strong' bilingual education is usually multicultural by its students, staff and curriculum.

Multiculturalism has, as one foundation, the ideal of equal, harmonious, mutually tolerant existence of different and diverse languages, and of religious, cultural and ethnic groups in a pluralist society. A multicultural viewpoint is partly based on the idea that an individual can successfully hold two or more **cultural identities**. It is possible to be Ukrainian and Canadian, Chinese and Malaysian, Cuban or Puerto Rican or Mexican and North American. In a different sense, it is possible to be a Ukrainian Canadian, a Chinese Malaysian or a Cuban North American. In this sense, identities are merged; the parts become a new whole. A redefined ethnicity creates a person who is not a replica of a Cuban in Cuba, Puerto Rican in Puerto Rico, Mexican in Mexico, nor a stereotypical white North American. Rather that person becomes a more or less integrated combination of parts of both.

Lynch (1992) suggests that there has been an historical **development of identity** from (1) the family group or tribe, through (2) the age of the city-state and single-state nationalism to (3) the present age of global rights and responsibilities and the internationalization of the lives of all inhabitants of this planet. He argues that 'we do not have to choose between local and ethnic loyalties, national citizenship and global community…and we are well on the way to recognizing three major levels of group affiliation: **local community membership**, by which is meant familial, ethnic, community or other cultural and social local groupings, including language, religion and ethnicity but not necessarily linked in the same geographic place at the same time; **national membership**, determined by birth or choice, but which may not be an exclusive membership; and **international membership**, which draws on the overlapping constellations which members of the world community have in common, regardless of the other two levels.' (p. 16–17) The concept of international citizenship is part of the aims of multicultural education, considered later.

In England and the United States, movements towards multiculturalism have not tended to receive an official blessing nor encouragement. Rather, the assimilationist viewpoint has continued. In contrast, in parts of Canada, Scandinavia and New Zealand for example, a relatively more multicultural approach has been taken, but with much **dispute and debate**. What is multiculturalism? The term tends to be used in a wide and ambiguous manner. What are the basic ideas of multiculturalism?

THE NATURE OF MULTICULTURALISM

The **basic beliefs of multiculturalists** include the following. Two languages and two cultures enable a person to have dual or multiple perspectives on society. Those who speak more than one language and own more than one culture are more sensitive and sympathetic, more likely to build bridges than barricades and boundaries. Rather than being subtractive as in assimilation, multiculturalism bequeaths an additive person and process. As an ideal, a person who is multicultural has more respect for other people and other cultures than the monocultural person who is stereotypically more insular and more culturally introspective. At its worst, assimilation leads to a positive attitude to the host culture and a negative attitude to one's heritage culture. Pluralism and multiculturalism may lead to a positive attitude, not only to the host and heritage culture, but to the equal validity of all cultures. With multiculturalism at its best, out goes prejudice and racism; in comes empathy and sensitivity.

Research by Donald Taylor and his associates has found in both the United States and in Canada that different **public groups support multiculturalism** more than assimilation. For example, the research of Lambert & Taylor (1990) showed that nine different US groups all preferred multiculturalism to assimilation. The basic research question poses two alternatives:

> **Alternative A:** Cultural and racial minority groups should *give up* their traditional ways of life and take on the American way of life. (**Assimilationist**)

> **Alternative B:** Cultural and racial minority groups should *maintain* their ways of life as much as possible when they come to America. (**Multiculturalist**)

The debate is more complex than these two statements, with other alternatives and compromise positions being possible. (There is also the insensitive use of the word 'American'. Meant to imply US, it may be denigrating to those from South and Central America). Respondents are invited to respond by marking one number on the following 7-point scale:

1_____2_____3_____4_____5_____6_____7
Agree Strongly   Neutral   Agree Strongly
    with A   with B

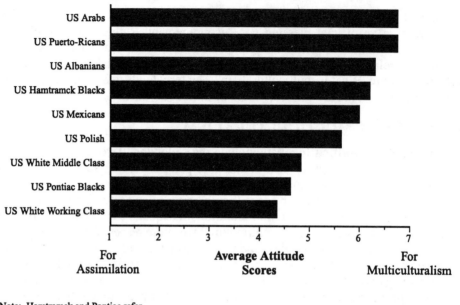

Attitudes to Assimilation and Multiculturism in US Ethnic Groups

For Assimilation — Average Attitude Scores — For Multiculturalism

Note: Hamtramck and Pontiac refer to two different areas in Detroit, Michigan

(Adapted from Lambert & Taylor, 1990: page 136)

Support for multiculturalism is generally high among Arabs, Puerto-Ricans, Blacks, Mexicans, Albanians and Polish US citizens as the above graph reveals. Both white working class and white middle class US citizens favor multiculturalism more than assimilation, though less so than most other groups.

Thus Taylor (1991) is able to conclude over a series of studies that 'there is a strong endorsement for multiculturalism and an apparent rejection of assimilation' (p. 8). However, we need to ask whether such endorsement is a latent attitude or whether it results in positive action and behavior? Is the population saying it permits multi-culturalism without being committed to it? Are there positive public attitudes but private skepticism? Is there interest in multiculturalism so long as it doesn't lead to involvement? Are such attitudes dormant as cognitive representations but not related to personal action? We must also ask along which dimensions people's attitude to multiculturalism and assimilation differ? Is there a difference between nostalgic allegiance to heritage culture compared with regarding the heritage culture as something of instrumental value?

A note of **caution** is also sounded by Huddy & Sears (1990). A large scale US public survey found a majority in favor of bilingual education. However, the authors found that 'opposition is greater among the well informed, suggesting that opposition may increase further as the issue attains greater national visibility. Opposition is also likely to increase if bilingual education is presented as promoting linguistic and cultural maintenance among language-minority students rather than as a mechanism for teaching English.' (Huddy & Sears, 1990: 119)

Research is unlikely to solve debates over assimilation and multiculturalism. While research may inform and refine opinions, the two positions of assimilation and pluralism differ in such fundamental, ideological ways, that simple solutions and resolutions are impossible. When evidence for the maintenance of heritage languages and cultures is produced, assimilationists are likely to argue that attitudes and behavior are still in the change process. That is, assimilationists will argue that, over time, people will move away from heritage cultural maintenance and prefer majority language and culture. Assimilationists tend to believe that bilingualism and biculturalism are temporary and transient, and lead to a preferable unifying monolingualism. When evidence favors assimilation having taken place in society (e.g. by the second or third generation after in-migration), multiculturalists will tend to argue in two different ways. First, that the change towards assimilation has only occurred on certain dimensions (e.g. language rather than economic assimilation). Second, that sometimes the wheel turns full circle. Revival and resurrection in future generations may occur in response to repression and renouncement by previous generations.

The **difference between assimilationists and multiculturalists** is rooted in basic human needs and motives. The movement towards assimilation or heritage cultural maintenance is likely to be affected by the **economic reward system**. Both assimilation and heritage cultural maintenance can be promoted by the need to earn a living and the desire to acquire or increase affluence. Assimilation may be chosen to secure a job, to be vocationally successful and to achieve affluence. The minority language and culture may be left behind in order to prosper in the majority language community. At the same time, language planning can be used to ensure that there are jobs and promotion within the minority language community, as discussed in Chapter 4.

The dominant group in society may at times prefer heritage cultural maintenance to assimilation. Minority groups may not be permitted to assimilate, thus keeping their members in poorly paid employment. Such a minority group is then exploited by the dominant group. The economic interests of the majority group can be served by **internal colonialism** rather than assimilation. Such economic motives and decisions may occur without reference to heritage language and culture.

Often, being fluent in the majority language is an economic necessity, and this can promote assimilation. To obtain employment and compete with members of the majority group, a person has to function in the majority language. Bilinguals may also perceive that they can function economically both in their minority group and with the dominant group. That is, they have the ability to be economically viable in either language community and form a bridge between those two communities. However, as Chapter 4 revealed, becoming bilingual by learning the majority language is no guarantee of economic improvement. Otheguy (1982: 306) provides a salutary warning from the US experience. 'English monolingualism has meant little in terms of economic advantages to most blacks and to the masses of poor descendants of poor European immigrants. Hispanics who now speak only English can often be found in as poor a state as when they first came. English monolingualism among immigrants tends to follow economic integration rather than cause it'.

Two opposing views, assimilation and pluralism have so far been discussed. Edwards (1985) indicates that **middle positions** are possible. It is possible to participate in mainstream society and maintain one's heritage language and culture. For many individuals, there will be both a degree of assimilation and a degree of preservation of one's heritage. Total assimilation and total isolation are less likely than some accommodation of the majority ideology within an overall ideology of pluralism; cultural maintenance within partial assimilation. Within multiculturalism and pluralism, an aggressive, militant pluralism may be seen as a threat to the social harmony of society. Instead, a more liberal pluralistic viewpoint may allow both belonging to the wider community and an identification with the heritage cultural community.

MULTICULTURALISM IN THE SCHOOL

Language minority groups are often the dominated in society. Those who have the power to make decisions about bilingual education usually come from the dominant group. The use of submersion and transitional forms of bilingual education has the tendency to perpetuate rather than alleviate the distance in power between the dominated and the dominating. Apart from requiring education through the dominant English language, such educational programs seek to assimilate language minority groups. Not only is the language of such classrooms English, the majority culture will be transmitted. This may make minority language children feel less confident of their cultural background, their language community, their home values and beliefs, even less confident of themselves. Such an analysis provides one context for a discussion of multiculturalism in the classroom: a raising of **awareness of relationships** between different ethnic groups, and awareness of diverse cultures.

A second context for multicultural and anti-racist teaching is the response to in-migration, refugees, migrant workers, and the ever frequent crossing of national boundaries. If ethnically diverse populations are to co-exist peacefully within a nation, one educational activity is to promote **awareness of cultural diversity**. A classroom response has been to develop various programs to develop sensitivity and sympathy, understanding and awareness of diverse cultural groups. Such classroom programs are given different names with different emphases: multicultural education, multiracial education, multi-ethnic education and intercultural education.

The aims of multicultural education are underpinned by political and ideological aims. The **assumptions of multicultural education** therefore include the following:

(1) There is a fundamental equality of all individuals and all minority groups irrespective of language and culture.

(2) In a democracy, there should be equality of opportunity irrespective of ethnic, cultural or linguistic origin.

(3) Any manifest or latent form of discrimination by the dominant power group against minorities requires elimination.

(4) A culturally diverse society should avoid racism and ethnocentrism.

(5) While generalizations about cultural behavior may be a natural part of humans making sense of their world, cultural stereotypes are to be avoided.

(6) Minority cultural groups in particular need awareness of their culture as a precondition and foundation for building on intercultural awareness.

(7) In mainstream monocultural education, language minority parents tend to be excluded from participation in their children's education. In multicultural education, parents should become partners.

(8) A pluralist integration is established by interaction and not a mosaic, by intermingling and a discovery of others to improve mutual understanding, break down stereotypes and prejudice, while increasing self-knowledge and self-esteem.

In its 'weak' sense, multicultural education focuses on the different beliefs, values, eating habits, cultural activities, dress and gestures (e.g. greetings and non-verbal reward systems) of varying ethnic groups. This form of 'cultural artifact' multicultural education attempts to extend the cultural vocabulary and cultural grammar of the individual child. The danger of such an approach is that it divorces language from culture. A 'weak' form of multicultural education pays little or no attention to the home language of minority children. Since language and culture are inseparable, and since merely using a language is to impart its culture, a stronger form of multicultural education requires attention to the minority language that is part of the minority culture. This is sometimes attempted through language awareness programs (Hawkins, 1987; Baker & Prys Jones, 1997). **Language Awareness programs** attempt to increase understanding, consciousness and sensitivity to the nature of language in everyday life. A program may include the following goals (Donmall, 1985):

(1) To make explicit a student's implicit knowledge of their first language or first languages.

(2) To develop skills in studying languages.

(3) To develop a perception and understanding of the nature and functions of language.

(4) To increase effectiveness in communication in the first, second and/or foreign languages.

(5) To give insights into the language learning process and thereby to aid the learning of the first language, second language and foreign languages.

(6) To develop an understanding among students of the richness of language variety within the class, school, community, region, nation and world. This may include discussing the variety of spoken and written forms of, for example, Spanish, Chinese, French, English, German throughout the world. This is to mitigate feelings of

inferiority amongst those who speak a variety of a language (e.g. English as a second or third language).

(7) To foster better relations between ethnic groups by arousing students' awareness of the origins and characteristics of their own language and its place in the world.

(8) To help students overcome any feeling of dislocation between the language of the home, the language of the school, of text books and employment.

(9) To impart an understanding of the value of language as a crucial part of human life.

(10) To develop an understanding of bilingualism and biculturalism in the world.

Such a Language Awareness course is as important for majority language speakers as for language minorities.

The language aspects of multicultural education may be attempted by vicarious experience of minority languages through videos, tape recordings and live performances where the language and the culture are both presented in an authentic, inseparable way. Just as there is a **danger** of teaching about cultural diversity with sparse or no reference to the attendant language, so there is a danger of teaching a second language without an immersion in the attendant culture.

In **Europe**, another variety or constituent of multicultural education is referred to as citizenship education. Citizenship education in Europe sometimes has much in common with the aims of multicultural and anti-racist education. However, it can also have assimilation aims and be linked with the education of in-migrants (e.g. to take a citizenship examination).

Lynch (1992: 42 & 43)) devised a set of working goals to guide **citizenship education** under the headings of: understandings, values and attitudes, skills and behaviors.

Understandings

- Understandings of the similarities and differences of human beings, their values, locations and styles of social and political life and the influence of these on individuals, groups, societies and the world community.
- Understandings of economic and environmental interdependence at local, national and international levels.
- Understandings of the varying ways in which pluralist democracies work.
- Understandings of the major human rights and responsibilities at the three levels and in social, cultural, economic and environmental spheres.
- Understandings of the varying ways in which pluralist democracies function.

Values and Attitudes

- Commitment to the values of human rights and pluralist democracy.
- Reciprocity, empathy and mutuality in all human affairs, whether cultural, social, economic, political or environmental.
- Willingness to participate in civic life at appropriate levels.
- Attitudes of openness to the cultures and ideas of others and mutuality in human relations.

- A strong commitment to gender and racial equality and willingness to fight socially and politically for them.
- A commitment to persuasion and dialogue as the major means to achieve social justice and change.
- Awareness of gender, cultural and national stereotyping and bias in their own culture and language and commitment to overcome them.

Skills and Behaviors

- Autonomous but socially responsible moral judgement and integrity, based on reflective and clarified values.
- Ability to accept the provisionality of human social and moral knowledge and the uncertainty which this implies.
- Responsible consumer and producer skills, responsive to the human and environmental rights of others.
- Engagement for human rights, justice and dignity.
- Ability to evaluate the economic, social, political and environmental decisions of others objectively.
- Interpersonal competence and the ability to make and maintain good human relationships.
- Ability to sustain dialogue within and across cultures.
- Communicative competence across a range of media and registers of language.
- Political literacy including the capacity for creative dissent, problem-solving, advocacy and creative conflict resolution.
- Decision-making, participatory and collaborative competences.
- Capacity for the development of satisfying and interactive human relations in different cultural contexts and across professional, personal and civic domains.

The aims of a 'stronger' form of **multicultural education**, as is revealed in Lynch's (1992) list above, have their basis partly in arousing awareness of, and sensitivity to, cultural diversity (Sleeter & Grant, 1987). The educational basis of a relatively 'strong' form of multicultural education is that all cultures are attempts to discover meaning. No one culture (including the umbrella idea of Western culture) has the monopoly of understanding. The **Postmodernist** view is that there is little or no transcendent truth, no ultimate reality outside of culture, no unalterable or fundamental qualities of women, ethnic groups or art. All meaning is socially constructed, with identities (and sense of identities) being socially constructed. In Postmodernism, all meanings are unstable, and none are neutral. Given the temporary and constructed nature of all beliefs, there is value in the sharing of different meanings across cultures. There is value in the meanings of those in a subordinate position (e.g. language minorities). The voices of the poor are as meaningful as the privileged; the understandings of the oppressed becomes as valid as the oppressor. Out of Postmodernist skepticism and uncertainty can develop new constructed meanings about language rights.

Yet when the educational basis of multicultural education is discussed, **politics** is not very far away. In the US, some 'liberals' have criticized multicultural education for being governed and manipulated from within a conservative education profession and by textbook companies and local and state education authorities (Olneck, 1993). As such, multicultural education was contained and controlled by those in power and posed little threat to the academic, cultural or bureaucratic establishments. Political **activists** in the US have regarded multiculturalism as a key battleground for a reordering of politic relationships and power structures. Multiculturalism has therefore, sometimes become a call for the mobilization of those who wish to challenge ethnic inequalities and the established order. For **conservatives**, multiculturalism symbolizes contests about whose values and ideology should be dominant in the curriculum, whose traditions and perspectives should be transmitted in the enculturation of students. For such conservatives, the hidden agenda of multiculturalism is sometimes perceived as self determination and autonomy rather than unity, the destabilization and undermining of society rather than equality, tribalization and separation rather than plurality.

Attempts to provide **multicultural education** vary widely. The term 'multicultural education' is very broad, ambiguous and diverse. It ranges from awareness programs for majority language children to the sharing of cultural experiences within a classroom containing a variety of ethnic groups. Multicultural education extends from the transmission of formal knowledge within a classroom, to the formal, hidden and pastoral curriculum each working towards mutual understanding, and to fighting against prejudice and racism. The range is from a timetabled, one lesson a week program to a radical reconstruction of both the whole curriculum and of relationships between schools and their communities (Davidman & Davidman, 1994; Nieto, 1992). Multicultural education ranges at one end from scarce, token multicultural lessons to a political movement to secure equality of opportunity, combating under-achievement, a political awareness of rights, debates about the reconstruction of society and a redress for current domination. Multicultural education can be about points of difference — dress and diet, language and religion. It may include lip-service to cultural diversity by a superficial 'saris, samosas, and steel bands' approach. This may simply accent the differences, the colorful variations and the bizarre. The hidden message may then become the superiority of the dominant culture. At its worst, multicultural education may serve to reinforce and extend differences, often accidentally.

Multicultural education may require a reappraisal of the **whole curriculum** with an analysis of how seemingly neutral subjects like science and mathematics often solely use and perpetuate majority, dominant culture. In the pictures of textbooks and the prose of the teacher, in the 'real life' problems to be tackled, the majority dominant culture may be represented and minority cultures ignored.

While more subtle differences may exist in mathematics, science and technology, the more common and obvious examples of monoculturalism appear in the teaching of history and geography, literature and art, music and home economics (e.g. cookery), social studies and health education.

For example, Welsh children have been taught the **history** of England and Europe more than the history of Wales and the Celts. Mexican American children are taught US history, but not the history of Mexico, the annexation of Mexican territory or the role of Mexican Americans in US history. Not only do many Mexicans in the US not know the history of their country of origin, they are often not taught how their ethnic group has contributed to the development of the US. The aim becomes assimilation rather than awareness; dominance rather than diversity. The fear and ignorance that tend to breed racism may unintentionally be perpetrated. Rather than celebrating ethnic identity and cultural diversity, a view of cultural inequality may latently be conveyed. As Olneck (1993: 248) states: 'marginalized and subordinated groups are represented as voiceless objects, defined by their 'apartness' and difference from, or by their inferior relationship to, those more central. In curricular representations, it is alleged, the perspectives from which history and experience occur, the actors deemed central, and the experiences, cultural expressions, and projects deemed valid and valuable are all those of dominant groups'.

One approach to multiculturalism in the curriculum is through content, showing that rationality is not the monopoly of any one culture, and that understanding requires an interdependence of peoples. The 'discovery' of North America can be taught from the perspective of native, indigenous peoples as well as the invaders; the Crusades from a Muslim and Christian perspective; and heresies from the viewpoint of heretics and 'believers'. In **curriculum** areas such as music and art, there can be a genuine celebration of diversity (e.g. African, Caribbean, Asian and different forms of Latino music; African art, Chinese and Japanese kites, Islamic and Egyptian calligraphy). In curriculum areas that systematically pursue a critical approach to understanding the world (e.g. nuclear physics), some cultures have been more fruitful than others in explaining the world. However, the methods and approaches of different cultures may all be worthwhile, as is competition between differing and opposing ideas. For example, an understanding of the complexities of the solar system have been better approximated by some cultures over the centuries. Yet an understanding of the place of the individual within the solar system may be better understood by, for example, an understanding of both eastern and western theology and philosophy.

In **Science and Social Science**, the danger is in teaching a male, white, western view of the world. Instead, the world-wide origins of scientific discoveries, for example, may be studied (e.g. paper, printing, gunpowder and the compass were discovered by the Chinese and not by Europeans as is frequently taught). Science and Technology is constructed and relative. Different cultures have used science to develop different knowledge and belief systems as Young (1987: 19) argues:

'Science is practice. There is no other science than the science that gets done. The science that exists is the record of the questions that it has occurred to scientists to ask, the proposals that get funded, the paths that get pursued and the results which lead...scientific journals and textbooks to publicize the work. ...Nature 'answers' only the questions that get asked and pursued long enough to lead to results that enter the public domain. Whether or not they get asked, how far they get pursued, are matters for a given society, its educational system, its patronage system and its funding bodies.'

Another danger in multicultural education is in stereotyping 'Third World' situations as rural and rudimentary, famished and inferior. An alternative is in profiling black scientists, learning about inventions from China and India, and discovering the rapid recent changes in horticulture and forestry, soil science and social science in Developing Countries.

Alternative perspectives should not be included as an appendix to a mainstream view, isolating different perspectives from each other, and presenting a sanitized or expurgated version of history. Instead, there is a need to present integrated multiple perspectives, with the distinctive contributions of different cultural groups fairly represented, and the interdependence of different experience faithfully told. For a school, this means avoiding the presentation of isolationist ideas in the curriculum (e.g. only a North American or Eurocentric view of the world) and avoiding cultural supremacist viewpoints (e.g. apartheid). In **religious education**, isolationism is sometimes taught. For example, a particular Christian fundamentalist or extreme Muslim viewpoint is taught with alternative viewpoints being forbidden. Similarly, supremacist viewpoints need avoiding. An example is when Christianity is sometimes latently taught as superior to other world religions. This suggests that religious fundamentalism and cultural pluralism are incompatible.

Yet religion is a key element in multiculturalism. In Europe, **religion** has re-emerged as a key social issue in relationships between different ethnic and language groups. With the relatively permanent settlement in Europe of 8 to 9 million in-migrants from West and North West Africa, the Indian sub-continent and South East Asia, the mixing of Muslim (estimated at 6.5 million adherents in Europe), Buddhist, Hindu and Sikh with different Christian denominations has made religion a key element in debates about multiculturalism and multicultural education (Perotti, 1994).

ANTI-RACISM AND PREJUDICE REDUCTION IN THE SCHOOL

The psychological roots of racial prejudice and racial hostility are separate from the philosophical basis of multicultural education. However, as will be considered later, anti-racism and prejudice reduction are often included in a 'strong' version of multicultural education. There are multicultural programs and materials that do not include a study of racism or anti-racism. To learn, for example, about other cultures and ethnic groups is not to confront the racism that exists in one's own (and other) ethnic groups. Thus such multicultural education has been accused of leaving unaltered the racist fabric of society and failing to see racism as a causal need for multicultural education. When a study of **racism and anti-racism** is absent from a multicultural program, such a program can become a tranquilizer of action against racism, diverting resistance and confrontation of racism into harmless channels. Instead a form of anti-racist multiculturalism is possible (Todd, 1991). Such a program needs to include an analysis of the structural reasons (e.g. the institutionalization of racism, social stratification, discriminatory practices by government) why racism is perpetuated, and not just viewed as an attitude of individuals. Its proponents argue that rather than just engendering sympathy for the victims of racism, some sympathy is needed for the struggle to defeat racism, even when this means confrontation and non-violent direct action.

Rarely, if ever, does language diversity, in itself, cause poor **race relations**. While color of skin, creed and language often become the symbols and badges of racism, the roots of racism tend to lie in fear and misunderstanding, and in the unequal distribution of power and economic rewards. If the school is a witting or unwitting agent in the reproduction of social and economic differences in society, then schools may be perpetrators of racism. Multicultural education in school is therefore sometimes seen as a way of raising consciousness of racism both in the aggressor and the victim.

The danger of bilingual education is focusing on two languages rather than on many cultures. Creating bilingual students may not be enough to reverse the inequalities and injustices in society. A bilingual child may still be the victim of racism and may still be confined to dominated status unless the school system as a whole works to redress rather than reproduced inequalities.

'The crucial element in reversing language minority students' school failure is not the language of instruction but the extent to which educators work to reverse — rather than perpetuate — the subtle, and often not so subtle, institutionalized racism of the society as a whole. In other words, bilingual education becomes effective only when it becomes anti-racist education. Strong promotion of students' primary language can be an important component in empowering language minority students but it is certainly not sufficient in itself.' (Cummins, 1986a: 11)

It is a debated point as to the extent of the influence of school in **combating racism and reducing prejudice**. The preconceptions and attitudes of children and teachers, of politicians and policy makers, the message of the hidden curriculum and the material of the formal curriculum may make difficult the winning of hearts and minds. So widespread, brutal and ingrained is racism in the school and street, that some argue for skill training rather than liberal education. Explicit racism may be combated in liberal education by a careful and conscious selection of teaching resources, the language of teaching, school organization and grouping in the classroom. Increased knowledge and greater understanding are sought as outcomes. For some, a more direct confrontational style with regard to racism is required. For example, through **roleplay**, white individuals may be confronted with their own racism and its consequences on others. Such roleplay will attempt to redress an inherent problem, in that some white people can never fully understand racism because they do not experience it.

A different viewpoint, pessimistic but with an element of reality, is that schools can do little to reconstruct power and racial relationships within society. This belief stems from the idea that multicultural education is a token and patronizing exercise. An alternative, radical view is that non-violent political activity is required amongst the victims of racism in school and particularly through political activity outside school. Such activity will attempt to reconstruct the power, dominance, political relationships in society and to seek to eradicate prejudice and fear, victimization and racial violence.

Such a radical view indicates that multicultural and anti-racist education can be neither value-free nor politically neutral. It aims at promoting equality of educational opportunity, the eradication of racial and cultural discrimination, and erasing racial dominance. Its danger is in being only for minorities and not for the enlightenment of majorities. In Britain, multicultural education may be provided in areas where ethnic minority children reside. It is often seen as irrelevant in all-white English-only schools.

At what point does preferring one's own language and culture become racist? If a minority language and culture, in protecting itself, wants to build strong boundaries between it and neighboring languages and cultures, is this ethnocentric and racist? Fishman (1991) argues that having security in self identity may be a necessary precondition before accepting other languages and cultures. A language minority may need security within itself before becoming multicultural. Security and status in one's own language may be a necessary foundation for accepting other neighboring cultures and languages. However, if other languages and cultures are not accepted and respected, then there is the danger of incipient racism.

This relates also to the idea that a person can belong at different levels in the community. It is possible to be Jewish and British, Hispanic and North American, Irish and European. It is possible to be international and local, a member of the local and the global village. However, there are times when belonging to two groups is seen as psychologically difficult. To be Welsh and British, Catalan and Spanish, may be difficult due to the incongruence, opposition and contested boundaries between two linked parts.

CONCLUSION

Among proponents of multicultural education, there are differences in preferred classroom style. There are those teachers who emphasize cultural folklore without the language; those who accent the superficially interesting without securing a sympathetic understanding; and those who want to provide all the colors and complexity of a multicultural world without a clear set of aims, goals, schemes, concepts and desired outcomes. Other teachers view multiculturalism as something that needs to exist throughout the curriculum, pervading every curriculum area. Through resource materials, the language of the classroom and seating and grouping arrangements, the ethos and atmosphere of the school becomes multicultural. For some, this relatively strong approach to multiculturalism will not be enough. In the widespread victimization and violence of racism, they see the mark of failure in multicultural education in school. Such an anti-racist movement requires not only direct intervention in all schools and by all teachers. It also requires changes in a society that begins with political change. In this viewpoint, monocultural fundamentalism and racism cannot be combated through education alone.

A consideration of multiculturalism and anti-racism in the classroom highlights that politics, culture and language are inter-linked. Where minority languages and cultures exist, so does personal, group, regional and national politics. The political debate around both minority languages and bilingual education tends to center on assimilation versus integration, pluralism and diversity versus uniformity and standardization. Personal resolution of the debate often reflects compromise positions. It is possible to have harmonious national unity and a measure of diversity, to assimilate partially while retaining the heritage language and culture.

A discussion of bilingual education thus inevitably includes personal orientations and political objectives. The preference at a personal or political level for the melting pot or the language garden partly determines the kind of education system preferred for language minorities. This preference separates those who see language as a problem or as a resource. It separates those who require bilingual education to dissolve language and cultural differences from those who require bilingual education to celebrate diversity. There are those who see the classroom as a recipe for the integration of problematic, diverse ingredients. For others, pedagogy is a plan for maintaining the colorful diversity of resources in the language garden.

SUGGESTED FURTHER READING

DAVIDMAN, L. and DAVIDMAN, P.T. 1994, *Teaching with a Multicultural Perspective: A Practical Guide.* New York: Longman.

DELGADO-GAITAN, C. and TRUEBA, H. 1991, *Crossing Cultural Borders: Education for Immigrant Families in America.* New York: Falmer.

GARCÍA, O. and BAKER, C. (eds) 1995, *Policy and Practice in Bilingual Education: A Reader Extending the Foundations.* Clevedon: Multilingual Matters. (Sections 1, 2 & 4).

McKAY, S.L. and WONG, S.C. (eds) 1988, *Language Diversity: Problem or Resource?* New York: Newbury House.

NIETO, S. 1992, *Affirming Diversity: The Sociopolitical Context of Multicultural Education.* New York: Longman.

TRUEBA, H.T. 1989, *Raising Silent Voices: Educating the Linguistic Minorities for the 21st Century.* New York: Newbury House.

REVIEW AND STUDY QUESTIONS

(1) Write short revision notes on the following:
   (i) The nature of language awareness, citizenship, multicultural and anti-racist/prejudice reduction programs.
   (ii) The aims of multicultural education.
(2) What is the difference, and what is the link between multiculturalism and anti-racism?
(3) Lynch (1992: 42 & 43)) proposes a set of objectives to guide citizenship education under the headings of: understandings, values and attitudes, skills and behaviors. Which of these objectives are concerned with cultural diversity, and which are more about assimilation?
(4) What are the main different curriculum approaches to multiculturalism?
(5) Examine a selection of the dualisms or dimensions presented below. These attempt to sum up some of the debates and important dimensions of thinking in this book.

Regard this as a 'summative' question that requires many other chapters of the book to be considered and integrated.

(i)   Briefly state what are the different viewpoints alluded to in those dualisms/dimensions you have chosen.

(ii) Indicate how these dualisms/dimensions relate to different views of bilingualism, bilingual education and multicultural education. What are the implications for the kind of language and cultural approach adopted in a school?

    (a)   Linguistic compared with the Sociocultural/Sociolinguistic view of bilinguals.

    (b)   Individual compared with Group analysis of bilingualism/diglossia.

    (c)   Skills compared with Competences

    (d)   Fractional compared with a Holistic view of bilinguals.

    (e)   Subtractive compared with an Additive view of bilinguals.

    (f)   Preservationists compared with Modernizers.

    (g)   The Rights (individual and group) view compared with the Empowerment view.

    (h)   Assimilationist compared with the Pluralist view.

    (i)   The Functional view compared with the Conflict view.

    (j)   The deprivation, remedial, problem, disabled view of bilinguals compared with the resource, beneficial, colorful, talent view of bilinguals.

STUDY ACTIVITIES

(1)   Visit a school with either multicultural students and/or with multicultural aims. What are the links in that school between multilingualism and multiculturalism? How is multiculturalism presented in the classroom and the school? Ask students how interested they are in learning about different cultures and different languages.

(2)   Find out how to run a simple sociometric test. For example, ask children to nominate which two children they would invite to their party or which two children they most liked working with in the classroom. By placing the choices in a table or on a diagram, analyze the relationships between children. Are there cliques of children separated by different languages? Are the clusters of children separated along ethnic or ability lines? How does language appear to play a part in the friendships of the classroom, playground and street?

(3)   As a group activity, create a collage with pictures and words as a decoration for your school or college. Using the theme of multiculturalism, present in pictures, words and symbols a theme of 'Multiculturalism For All'. Write a short explanation of the meaning of that collage.

Recommended Further Reading

AN ACCOMPANYING READER

A Reader has been produced to accompany this book. This Reader is entitled '*Policy and Practice in Bilingual Education*' and is edited by Professor Ofelia García (City College New York) and Colin Baker. It was published by Multilingual Matters Ltd in 1995. The book contains a collection of important recent articles on policy and practices in bilingual education around the world, with particular emphasis on the United States. The readings are followed by questions and activities specifically designed for the preparation of teachers. The Reader is designed to extend and develop themes in this book, for example on teaching methodology in bilingual schools and classrooms.

The readings are divided into four sections:

Section 1: Policy and Legislation on Bilingualism in Schools and Bilingual Education.
Section 2: Implementation of Bilingual Policy in Schools: Structuring Schools
Section 3: Using Bilingualism in Instruction: Structuring Classrooms
Section 4: Using the Bilingualism of the School Community: Teachers and Parents

The Reader can be used by instructors and as an interactive text for students. The book is particularly attentive to needs in teacher education, especially in the preparation of bilingual teachers. Thus, each of the readings is followed by questions and activities that engage students in reflection and practices that may transform their own thinking, as well as the schools, classrooms and communities to which they will contribute. Whenever possible, the questions and activities reflect the content of the readings, and ask students to practice among themselves processes that will enable a contribution to their own communities and schools.

NATIONAL AND REGIONAL CONTEXTS

In this book there has been an attempt to present issues that are generalizable across nations. Regional and national language situations are not usually discussed in detail due to limits of space. It is important to study such situations as an extension of this book. Sources to commence this study are given below:

(1) **World:** García (1991b), Horvath & Vaughan (1991), Paulston (1988), Paulston (1994), Spolsky & Cooper (eds, 1977).
(2) **Africa:** Adbulaziz (1991), Eiseman *et al.* (1989), Rubagumya (1990), Rubagumya (1994).
(3) **Asia:** Boyle (1990), Gaudart (1987), Jones & Ozóg (1993), Paulston (1988).
(4) **Australia:** Clyne (1988), Clyne (1991).
(5) **Britain:** Alladina & Edwards (1991), Baker (1985, 1988), Edwards & Redfern (1992), Ghuman (1995), Mills & Mills (1993), Verma, Corrigan & Firth (1995).
(6) **Canada:** Cummins & Danesi (1990), Danesi, McLeod & Morris (1993), Edwards & Redfern (1992), Genesee (1987), Genesee (1994), Heller (1994), Swain & Lapkin (1982).
(7) **Europe:** (Mainland): Allardyce (1987), Artigal (1991), Baetens Beardsmore (1993), Baetens Beardsmore & Lebrun (1991), Duff (1991), Mar-Molinero (1987), McLaughlin & Graf (1985), Novak-Lukanovic (1988), Paulston (ed., 1988), Pedersen (1992), Perotti (1994), Skutnabb-Kangas & Cummins (1988), Zondag (1991).
(8) **India:** Pattanayak (1988), Sridhar (1991).
(9) **New Zealand:** Benton, R.A. (1991), Corson (1990).
(10) **Latin America:** Albó and d'Emilio (1990), Alford (1987), Amadio (1990), Hornberger (1988), Fortune & Fortune (1987), Gurdian & Salamanca (1990), López (1990), Martínez (1990), Moya (1990), Paulston (ed., 1988), Varese (1990), Zuniga (1990).
(11) **United States:** Arias & Casanova (1993), Cazden & Snow (1990b), Crawford (1991), DeVillar, Faltis & Cummins (1994), García (1991b), García (1992a), McKay & Wong (1988), Padilla & Benavides (1992), Trueba (1989).

GENERAL SOURCES FOR EXTENDED READING

ARIAS, M. and CASANOVA, U. (eds) 1993, *Bilingual Education: Politics, Practice, Research.* Chicago: National Society for the Study of Education/University of Chicago Press.

ARTIGAL, J.M. 1991, *The Catalan Immersion Program: A European Point of View.* Norwood, NJ: Ablex.

BAETENS BEARDSMORE, H. 1986, *Bilingualism: Basic Principles.* Clevedon: Multilingual Matters.

BAETENS BEARDSMORE, H. (ed.) 1993, *European Models of Bilingual Education.* Clevedon: Multilingual Matters.

BAKER, C. 1995, *A Parents' and Teachers' Guide to Bilingualism.* Clevedon: Multilingual Matters.

CALIFORNIA STATE DEPARTMENT OF EDUCATION 1984, *Studies on Immersion Education. A Collection for United States Educators.* Sacramento, CA: California State Department of Education.

CALIFORNIA STATE DEPARTMENT OF EDUCATION 1989, *Foreign Language Framework.* Sacramento, CA: California State Department of Education.

CAZDEN, C.B. and SNOW, C.E. 1990, *English Plus: Issues in Bilingual Education* (*The Annals of the American Academy of Political and Social Science* 508, March). London: Sage.

CORSON, D. 1990, *Language Policy Across the Curriculum*. Clevedon: Multilingual Matters.

CRAWFORD, J. 1991, *Bilingual Education: History Politics, Theory and Practice* (2nd edn). Los Angeles, CA: Bilingual Education Services.

CUMMINS, J. and DANESI, M. 1990, *Heritage Languages. The Development and Denial of Canada's Linguistic Resources*. Toronto: Our Schools/Ourselves Education Foundation and Garamond Press.

CUMMINS, J. and SWAIN, M. 1986, *Bilingualism in Education*. New York: Longman.

DELGADO-GAITAN, C. and TRUEBA, H. 1991, *Crossing Cultural Borders: Education for Immigrant Families in America*. New York: Falmer.

DEVILLAR, R.A., FALTIS, C.J. and CUMMINS, J.P. (eds) 1994, *Cultural Diversity in Schools: From Rhetoric to Practice*. Albany, NY: State University of New York Press.

EDWARDS, J. 1985, *Language, Society and Identity*. Oxford: Blackwell.

EDWARDS, J. 1994, *Multilingualism*. London: Routlege.

FALTIS, C.J. 1993, *Joinfostering: Adapting Teaching Strategies for the Multilingual Classroom*. New York: Macmillan.

FISHMAN, J.A. 1989, *Language and Ethnicity in Minority Sociolinguistic Perspective*. Clevedon: Multilingual Matters.

FISHMAN, J.A. 1991, *Reversing Language Shift*. Clevedon: Multilingual Matters.

GARCÍA, O. (ed.) 1991, *Bilingual Education: Focusschrift in Honor of Joshua A. Fishman (Volume 1)*. Amsterdam/Philadelphia: John Benjamins.

GENESEE, F. 1987, *Learning Through Two Languages*. Cambridge, MA: Newbury House.

GENESEE, F. (ed.) 1994, *Educating Second Language Children*. Cambridge: Cambridge University Press.

HAKUTA, K. 1986, *Mirror of Language. The Debate on Bilingualism*. New York: Basic Books.

HOFFMANN, C. 1991, *An Introduction to Bilingualism*. London: Longman.

JACOBSON, R. and FALTIS, C. 1990, *Language Distribution Issues in Bilingual Schooling*. Clevedon: Multilingual Matters.

JONES, G.M. and OZÓG, A.C.K. (eds) 1993, *Bilingualism and National Development*. Clevedon: Multilingual Matters.

McGROARTY, M.E. and FALTIS, C. J. 1991, *Languages in School and Society: Policy and Pedagogy*. Berlin/New York: Mouton de Gruyter.

McKAY, S.L. and WONG, S.C. (eds.) 1988, *Language Diversity: Problem or Resource?* New York: Newbury House.

McLAUGHLIN, B. 1987, *Theories of Second-language Learning*. London: Edward Arnold.

MILLS, R.W. and MILLS, J. (eds) 1993, *Bilingualism in the Primary School: A Handbook for Teachers*. London: Routledge.

NIETO, S. 1992, *Affirming Diversity: The Sociopolitical Context of Multicultural Education.* New York: Longman.

OVANDO, C.J. and COLLIER, V.P. 1987, *Bilingual and ESL Classrooms: Teaching in Multicultural Contexts.* New York: McGraw-Hill.

PADILLA, R.V. and BENAVIDES, A.H. (eds) 1992, *Critical Perspectives on Bilingual Education Research.* Tempe, AZ: Bilingual Press.

PAULSTON, C.B. (ed.) 1988, *International Handbook of Bilingualism and Bilingual Education.* New York: Greenwood.

PAULSTON, C.B. 1994, *Linguistic Minorities in Multilingual Settings.* Amsterdam/Philadelphia: John Benjamins.

PÉREZ, B. and TORRES-GUZMÁN, M. 1995, *Learning in Two Worlds: An Integrated Spanish/English Biliteracy Approach* (2nd edn). New York: Longman.

REYNOLDS, A.G. (ed.) *Bilingualism, Multiculturalism and Second Language Learning.* Hillsdale, NJ: Lawrence Erlbaum.

RICHARDS, J.C. and ROGERS, T.S. 1986, *Approaches and Methods in Language Teaching.* Cambridge: Cambridge University Press

RUBAGUMYA, C.M. (ed.) 1994, *Teaching and Researching Language in African Classrooms.* Clevedon: Multilingual Matters.

SKUTNABB-KANGAS, T. 1981, *Bilingualism or Not: The Education of Minorities.* Clevedon: Multilingual Matters.

SAUNDERS, G. 1988, *Bilingual Children: From Birth to Teens.* Clevedon: Multilingual Matters.

SKUTNABB-KANGAS, T. and CUMMINS, J. (eds) 1988, *Minority Education: From Shame to Struggle.* Clevedon: Multilingual Matters.

SPOLSKY, B. 1989, *Conditions for Second Language Learning.* Oxford: Oxford University Press.

STERN, H.H. 1992, *Issues and Options in Language Teaching.* Oxford: Oxford University Press.

SWAIN, M. and LAPKIN, S. 1982, *Evaluating Bilingual Education: A Canadian Case Study.* Clevedon: Multilingual Matters.

TRUEBA, H.T. 1989, *Raising Silent Voices: Educating the Linguistic Minorities for the 21st Century.* New York: Newbury House.

WHITMORE, K.F. and CROWELL, C.C. 1994, *Inventing a Classroom. Life in a Bilingual Whole Language Community.* York, ME: Stenhouse.

Appendix 1:
Attitude to Bilingualism

Here are some statements about the English and the Spanish language. Please say whether you agree or disagree with these statements. There are no right or wrong answers. Please be as honest as possible. Answer with ONE of the following:

SA = Strongly Agree (tick SA); A= Agree (tick A); NAND = Neither Agree Nor Disagree (tick NAND); D = Disagree (tick D); SD = Strongly Disagree (tick SD)

		SA	A	NAND	D	SD
1.	It is important to be able to speak English and Spanish					
2.	To speak English is all that is needed					
3.	Knowing Spanish and English makes people cleverer					
4.	Children get confused when learning English *and* Spanish					
5.	Speaking both Spanish and English helps to get a job					
6.	Being able to write in English and Spanish is important					
7.	Schools should teach pupils to speak in two languages					
8.	School wall displays should be in English and Spanish					
9.	Speaking two languages is not difficult					
10.	Knowing both Spanish and English gives people problems					
11.	I feel sorry for people who cannot speak both English and Spanish					

		SA	A	NAND	D	SD
12.	Children should learn to read in two languages					
13.	People know more if they speak English and Spanish					
14.	People who speak Spanish and English can have more friends than those who speak one language					
15.	Speaking both English and Spanish is more for older than younger people					
16	Speaking both Spanish and English can help people get promotion in their job					
17.	Young children learn to speak Spanish and English at the same time with ease					
18.	Both English and Spanish should be important in the region where I live					
19.	People can earn more money if they speak both Spanish and English					
20.	I should not like the English language to be the only language in this area					
21.	As an adult, I would like to be considered as a speaker of English and Spanish					
22.	If I have children, I would want them to speak both English and Spanish					
23.	Both the Spanish and English languages can live together in this region					
24.	People only need to know one language					

Appendix 2: Use of Spanish

How important or unimportant do you think the Spanish language is for people to do the following? There are no right or wrong answers.

	For People To:	Important	A Little Important	A Little Unimportant	Unimportant
1.	Make friends				
2.	Earn plenty of money				
3.	Understand conversations				
4.	Read				
5.	Write				
6.	Watch TV/Videos				
7.	Get a job				
8.	Become cleverer				
9.	Be liked				
10.	Live in this region				
11.	Religious attendance				
12.	Sing (e.g. with others)				
13.	Play sport				
14.	Bring up children				
15.	Go shopping				
16.	Make phone calls				
17.	Succeed at school				
18.	Be accepted in the community				
19.	Talk to friends				
20.	Talk to teachers in school				
21.	Talk to people generally				

Appendix 3: Attitude to Spanish

Here are some statements about the Spanish language. Please say whether you agree or disagree with these statements. There are no right or wrong answers. Please be as honest as possible. Answer with ONE of the following:

SA = Strongly Agree (tick SA); A = Agree (tick A); NAND = Neither Agree Nor Disagree (tick NAND); D = Disagree (tick D); SD = Strongly Disagree (tick SD)

		SA	A	NAND	D	SD
1.	I like hearing Spanish spoken					
2.	I prefer to watch TV in English than Spanish					
3.	Spanish should be taught to most pupils in this region					
4.	Its a waste of time to keep the Spanish language alive in this region					
5.	I like speaking Spanish					
6.	Spanish is a difficult language to learn					
7.	There are more useful languages than Spanish					
8.	I'm likely to use Spanish as an adult					
9.	Spanish is a language worth learning					
10.	Spanish has no place in the modern world					
11.	Spanish will disappear in this region					
12.	Spanish is essential to take part fully in community life					
13.	We need to preserve the Spanish language					
14.	Children should be made to learn Spanish in this area					
15.	I would like Spanish to be as strong as English in this area					

		SA	A	NAND	D	SD
16.	It would be hard to study science in Spanish					
17.	You are considered a lower class person if you speak Spanish					
18.	I would prefer to be taught in Spanish					
19.	As an adult, I would like to marry a Spanish speaker					
20.	If I have children, I would like them to be Spanish speaking					

Appendix 4:
Language Use Surveys

The language background of an individual or language group needs to include many different contextual dimensions. Listed below are some of the contexts that need to be included in a language use survey:

(1) Preferred categorization of the language (e.g. minority, lesser used, community, heritage, indigenous).
(2) Geographical extent of the language.
(3) Recent history of the language; major changes in the last decade.
(4) Number of users (e.g. from a Census).
(5) Legal status of language. Existence and effect of any language legislation. Use of language in courts.
(6) Dominant language(s) of the territory.
(7) Recent migration (in and out) affecting the language.
(8) Relations with neighboring language groups and with the dominant language.
(9) (a) Use of language in education in primary and secondary education.
　　　　(i)　As a medium of instruction.
　　　　(ii)　As a subject itself.
　　　　(iii)　The history and culture surrounding the language.
　　　　(iv)　Provision of teachers, schools and curriculum materials.
　　(b) Use of language in Further, Vocational, Technical, Adult, Continuing and Higher Education.
(10) Literacy and biliteracy of the language group.
(11) Provision of language learning classes for in-migrants.
(12) Effect of retirement patterns on the language.
(13) Use of language in media (e.g. TV, radio, books, newspapers, periodicals, magazines, telephone, satellite). Subsidization.
(14) Unemployment in the language group.

(15) Types of employment among language group (e.g. socio-economic status, industri-alization, technologization). Whether language is a requirement or advantage in finding a job.

(16) Use of the language in bureaucracy, forms, with regional and local Authorities, with services (e.g. water, electricity, post office, railways, buses, police).

(17) Effect of travel on language group (e.g. road access, train systems, air travel, shipping).

(18) Effect of tourism on language group.

(19) Effect of local and central government on the language. Attitude of government to the language.

(20) Amount of language activism among the language group.

(21) Cultural vitality of the language group; institutions dedicated to supporting the language and culture; cultural festivals.

(22) Effect of urbanization and suburbanization on the language.

(23) Use of language in computing (e.g. in schools, adapted keyboards and fonts).

(24) Use of language in music: traditional, pop and rock, folk, classical.

(25) Use of language in theater, cinema.

(26) Use of translation, dubbing, subtitling of foreign language media.

(27) Promotion of translation, terminological research, standardization of language.

(28) Use of the language in advertising on TV, radio, in the press.

(29) Use of language in public speech and literacy events.

(30) Use of the language on goods labels and instructions.

(31) Use of the language in financial transactions (e.g. bills, banking).

(32) Use of the language on signposts (e.g. streets, major roads, in hospitals, schools, religious buildings, government offices).

(33) Use of the language in hospitals, care of elderly, homes and hostels.

(34) Use of the language by parents with their children.

(35) Use of the language in new and existing marriages.

(36) Use of the language in religious events and among religious leaders.

(37) Gender differences in the use of the language.

(38) Social status of the language and language speakers.

(39) Attitudes of speakers and non-speakers to the language. Optimism or pessimism surrounding the language.

(40) Promotion of research activity on the language.

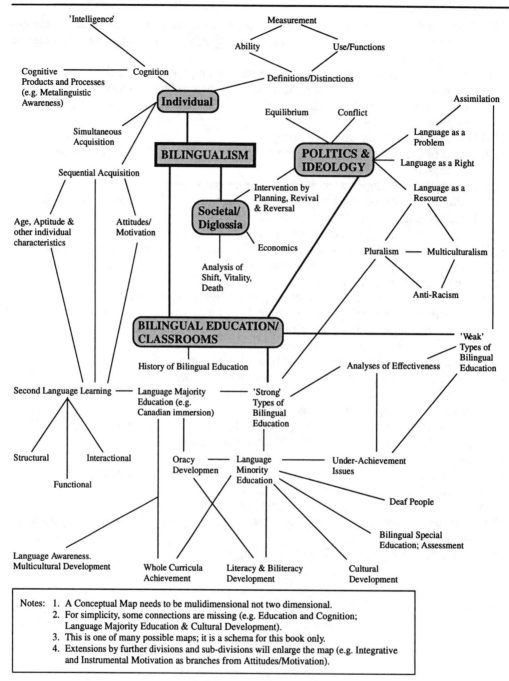

Notes: 1. A Conceptual Map needs to be mulidimensional not two dimensional.
        2. For simplicity, some connections are missing (e.g. Education and Cognition;
            Language Majority Education & Cultural Development).
        3. This is one of many possible maps; it is a schema for this book only.
        4. Extensions by further divisions and sub-divisions will enlarge the map (e.g. Integrative
            and Instrumental Motivation as branches from Attitudes/Motivation).

A Conceptual Map of the Book

Bibliography

ABDULAZIZ, M.H. 1991, Language in education: A comparative study of the situation in Tanzania, Ethiopia and Somalia. In O. GARCIA (ed.) *Bilingual Education: Focusschrift in Honor of Joshua A. Fishman*. Amsterdam/Philadelphia: John Benjamins.

ACAC (previously Curriculum Council for Wales) 1993, *Developing a Curriculum Cymreig*. Cardiff: ACAC.

ADA, F. 1988a, Creative reading: A relevant methodology for language minority children. In L.M. MALAVE (ed.) *NABE '87. Theory, Research and Application: Selected Papers*. Buffalo: State University of New York.

ADA, F. 1988b, The Pajaro Valley experience: Working with Spanish-speaking parents. In T. SKUTNABB-KANGAS and J. CUMMINS (eds) *Minority Education: From Shame to Struggle*. Clevedon: Multilingual Matters.

AFOLAYAN, A. 1995, Aspects of bilingual education in Nigeria. In B.M. JONES and P. GHUMAN (eds) *Bilingualism, Education and Identity*. Cardiff: University of Wales Press.

AITCHISON, J. 1991, *Language Change: Progress or Decay*. Cambridge: Cambridge University Press.

ALBÓ, X., and D'EMILO, L. 1990, Indigenous languages and intercultural bilingual education in Bolivia. *Prospects (UNESCO)* 20 (3), 321–330.

ALFORD, M.R. 1987, Developing facilitative reading programmes in Third World countries. *Journal of Multilingual and Multicultural Development* 8 (6), 493–511.

ALLADINA, S. and EDWARDS, V. 1991, *Multilingualism in the British Isles*. London: Longman.

ALLARDT, E. 1979, Implications of the ethnic revival in modern, industrialized society. A comparative study of the linguistic minorities in Western Europe. *Commentationes Scientiarum Socialium* 12. Helsinki: Societas Scientiarum Fennica.

ALLARDT, E. and STARCK, C. 1981, *Sprakgranser och Samhallsstruktur*. Stockholm: Almquist and Wiksell.

ALLARDYCE, R. 1987, Planned bilingualism: The Soviet case. *Journal of Russian Studies* 52, 3–16.

ALLEN, P. *et al.* 1989, Restoring the balance: A response to Hammerly. *Canadian Modern Language Review* 45 (4), 770–776.

AMADIO, M. 1990, Two decades of bilingual education in Latin America 1970–90. *Prospects (UNESCO)* 20 (3), 305–310.

AMERICAN PSYCHOLOGICAL ASSOCIATION 1982, Review of Department of Education report entitled: '*Effectiveness of Bilingual Education: A Review of Literature*', Letter to Congressional Hispanic Caucus, April 22nd.

ANDERSEN, R. 1983, Introduction: A language acquisition interpretation of pidginization and creolization. In R. ANDERSEN (ed.) *Pidginization and Creolization as Language Acquisition*. Rowley, MA: Newbury House.

ANDERSON, C.A. 1966, Literacy and schooling on the development threshold. In C.A. ANDERSON and M. BOWMAN (eds) *Education and Economic Development*. London: Frank Cass.

ANDERSON, T. and BOYER, M. 1970, *Bilingual Schooling in the United States* (2 volumes). Austin, TX: Southwest Educational Laboratory.

ANDRES, F. 1990, Language relations in multilingual Switzerland. *Multilingua* 9 (1), 11–45.

APPEL, R. and MUYSKEN, P. 1987, *Language Contact and Bilingualism*. London: Edward Arnold.

ARGYLE, M. 1975, *Bodily Communication*. London: Methuen.

ARIAS, M. and CASANOVA, U. (eds) 1993, *Bilingual Education: Politics, Practice, Research*. Chicago: National Society for the Study of Education/University of Chicago Press.

ARNBERG, L. 1981, Bilingual education of young children in England and Wales. University of Linkoping, Sweden, Department of Education.

ARNBERG, L. 1987, *Raising Children Bilingually: The Pre-School Years*. Clevedon: Multilingual Matters.

ARNBERG, L. and ARNBERG, P. 1992, Language awareness and language separation in the young bilingual child. In R.J. Harris (ed.) *Cognitive Processing in Bilinguals*. Amsterdam: North-Holland.

ARTIGAL, J.M. 1991, *The Catalan Immersion Program: A European Point of View*. Norwood, NJ: Ablex.

ARTIGAL, J.M. 1993, Catalan and Basque immersion programmes. In H. BAETENS BEARDSMORE (ed.) *European Models of Bilingual Education*. Clevedon: Multilingual Matters.

ARTIGAL, J.M. 1996, Plurilingual education in Catalonia. In R. JOHNSON and M. SWAIN (eds) *Immersion Education: International Perspectives*. Cambridge: Cambridge University Press.

AUERBACH, E.R. 1989, Toward a social-contextual approach to family literacy. *Harvard Educational Review* 59 (2), 165–181.

BACA, L.M. and CERVANTES, H.T. 1989, *The Bilingual Special Education Interface*. Columbus, OH: Merrill.

BACHI, R. 1956, A statistical analysis of the revival of Hebrew in Israel. *Scripta Hierosolymitana* 3, 179–247.

BACHMAN, L.F. 1990, *Fundamental Considerations in Language Testing*. Oxford: Oxford University Press.

BAETENS BEARDSMORE, H. 1986, *Bilingualism: Basic Principles*. Clevedon: Multilingual Matters.

BAETENS BEARDSMORE, H. 1993, The European school model. In H. BAETENS BEARDSMORE (ed.) *European Models of Bilingual Education*. Clevedon: Multilingual Matters.

BAETENS BEARDSMORE, H. (ed.) 1993, *European Models of Bilingual Education*. Clevedon: Multilingual Matters.

BAETENS BEARDSMORE H. and LeBRUN, N. 1991, Trilingual education in the Grand Duchy of Luxembourg. In O. GARCÍA (ed.) *Bilingual Education: Focusschrift in Honor of Joshua A. Fishman*. Amsterdam/Philadelphia: John Benjamins.

BAETENS BEARDSMORE, H. and SWAIN, M. 1985, Designing bilingual education: Aspects of immersion and 'European School' models. *Journal for Multilingual and Multicultural Development* 6 (1), 1–15.

BAETENS BEARDSMORE, H. and VAN BEECK, H. 1984, Multilingual television supply and language shift in Brussels. *International Journal of the Sociology of Language* 48, 65–79.

BAKER, C. 1985, *Aspects of Bilingualism in Wales*. Clevedon: Multilingual Matters.

BAKER, C. 1988, *Key Issues in Bilingualism and Bilingual Education*. Clevedon: Multilingual Matters.

BAKER, C. 1990, The effectiveness of bilingual education. *Journal of Multilingual and Multicultural Development*. 11 (4), 269–277.

BAKER, C. 1992, *Attitudes and Language*. Clevedon: Multilingual Matters.

BAKER, C. 1993, Bilingual education in Wales. In H. BAETENS BEARDSMORE (ed.) *European Typologies of Bilingual Education*. Clevedon: Multilingual Matters.

BAKER, C. 1995a, *A Parents' and Teachers' Guide to Bilingualism*. Clevedon: Multilingual Matters.

BAKER, C. 1995b, Bilingual education and assessment. In B.M. JONES and P. GHUMAN (eds) *Bilingualism, Education and Identity*. Cardiff: University of Wales Press.

BAKER C. and HINDE J. 1984, Language background classification. *Journal of Multilingual and Multicultural Development* 5 (1), 43–56.

BAKER C. and PRYS JONES, S. 1997, *An Encyclopedia of Bilingualism*. Clevedon: Multilingual Matters.

BAKER, K. 1987, Comment on Willig's 'A meta analysis of selected studies of bilingual education'. *Review of Educational Research* 57 (3), 351–362.

BAKER, K. 1992, Ramirez *et al.*: Misled by bad theory. *Bilingual Research Journal* 16 (1&2), 63–89.

BAKER, K.A. and de KANTER, A.A. 1981, *Effectiveness of Bilingual Education: A Review of Literature*. Washington, DC: Office of Planning, Budget and Evaluation, US Department of Education.

BAKER, K.A. and de KANTER, A.A. 1983, *Bilingual Education*. Lexington, MA: Lexington Books.

BALKAN, L. 1970, *Les Effets du Bilingualisme Français: Anglais sur les Aptitudes Intellectuelles*. Brussels: Aimav.

BARONA, M.S. and BARONA, A. 1992, Assessment of bilingual preschool children. In R.V. PADILLA and A.H. BENAVIDES (eds) *Critical Perspectives on Bilingual Education Research*. Tempe, AZ: Bilingual Press.

BARTH, F. 1966, *Models of Social Organization* (Occasional Paper No. 23). London: Royal Anthropological Institute.

BEL, A. 1993, Some results of the immersion programme in Catalonia. *Notícies del SEDEC/Newsletter of the Servei d'Ensenyament del Catalonia*.

BENTON, R.A. 1991, 'Tomorrow's schools' and the revitalization of Maori. In O. GARCÍA (ed.) *Bilingual Education: Focusschrift in Honor of Joshua A. Fishman*. Amsterdam/Philadelphia: John Benjamins.

BENYON, J. and TOOHEY, K. 1991, Heritage language education in British Columbia: Policy and programs. *Canadian Modern Language Review* 47 (4), 606–616.

BEN-ZEEV, S. 1977a, The influence of bilingualism on cognitive strategy and cognitive development. *Child Development* 48, 1009–1018.

BEN-ZEEV, S. 1977b, The effect of bilingualism in children from Spanish–English low economic neighborhoods on cognitive development and cognitive strategy. *Working Papers on Bilingualism* 14, 83–122.

BERLINER, D.C. 1988, Meta-comments: A discussion of critiques of L.M. Dunn's monograph '*Bilingual Hispanic Children on the US Mainland*'. *Hispanic Journal of Behavioral Sciences* 10 (3), 273–300.

BERNHARDT, E.B. (ed.) *Life in Language Immersion Classrooms*. Clevedon: Multilingual Matters.

BERNHARDT, E. and SCHRIER, L. 1992, The development of immersion teachers. In E.B. BERNHARDT (ed.) *Life in Language Immersion Classrooms*. Clevedon: Multilingual Matters.

BERTHOLD, M. 1992, An Australian experiment in French immersion. *Canadian Modern Language Review* 49 (1), 112–125.

BERTHOLD, M. 1995, *Rising to the Bilingual Challenge: Ten Years of Queensland Secondary School Immersion*. Canberra: National Languages and Literacy Unit of Australia.

BIALYSTOK, E. 1987a, Influences of bilingualism on metalinguistic development. *Second Language Research* 3 (2), 154–166.

BIALYSTOK, E. 1987b, Words as things: Development of word concept by bilingual children. *Studies in Second Language Learning* 9, 133–140.

BIALYSTOK, E. 1988, Levels of bilingualism and levels of linguistic awareness. *Developmental Psychology* 24 (4), 560–567.

BIALYSTOK, E. (ed.) 1991, *Language Processing in Bilingual Children*. Cambridge: Cambridge University Press.

BIALYSTOK, E. 1992, Selective attention in cognitive processing: The bilingual edge. In R.J. HARRIS (ed.) *Cognitive Processing in Bilinguals*. Amsterdam: North-Holland.

BIALYSTOK, E. and RYAN, E.B. 1985, Toward a definition of metalinguistic skill. *Merrill-Palmer Quarterly* 31 (3), 229–251.

BILD, E. and SWAIN, M. 1989, Minority language students in a French immersion programme: Their French proficiency. *Journal of Multilingual and Multicultural Development* 10 (3), 255–274.

BLOOME, D. 1985, Reading as a social process. *Language Arts* 62, 134–142.

BLOOMFIELD L. 1933, *Language*. New York: Holt.

BOYLE, E.R. 1990, Is there a Bilingual answer for Hong Kong? *Evaluation and Research in Education* 4 (3), 117–127.

BRAINE, M.D. 1987, Acquiring and processing first and second languages. In P. HOMEL, M. PALIJ and D. AARONSON (eds) *Childhood Bilingualism: Aspects of Linguistic, Cognitive and Social Development*. Hillsdale, NJ: Lawrence Erlbaum.

BROWN, H.D. 1980, *Principles of Language Learning and Teaching*. New Jersey: Englewood Cliffs.

BRUCK, M., LAMBERT, W.E. and TUCKER, G.R. 1976, Cognitive consequences of bilingual schooling: The St Lambert Project through Grade 6. Unpublished Manuscript. Department of Psychology, McGill University.

BULL, B.L., FRUEHLING, R.T. and CHATTERGY, V. 1992, *The Ethics of Multicultural and Bilingual Education*. New York: Teachers College Press.

BULLOCK REPORT (DEPARTMENT OF EDUCATION AND SCIENCE) 1975, *A Language for Life*. London: HMSO.

BUTTS, R.F. 1980, *The Revival of Civic Learning*. Bloomington, IN: Phi Delta Kappa.

CALDWELL, J. and BERTHOLD, M. 1995, Aspects of bilingual education in Australia. In B.M. JONES and P.S.S. GHUMAN (eds) *Bilingualism, Education and Identity*. Cardiff: University of Wales Press.

CALIFORNIA STATE DEPARTMENT OF EDUCATION 1984, *Studies on Immersion Education. A Collection for United States Educators*. Sacramento, CA: California State Department of Education.

CALIFORNIAN STATE DEPARTMENT OF EDUCATION 1989, *Foreign Language Framework*. Sacramento, CA: California State Department of Education.

CAMPBELL, R. and SAIS, E. 1995, Accelerated metalinguistic (phonological) awareness in bilingual children. *British Journal of Developmental Psychology* 13 (1), 61–68.

CANADIAN EDUCATION ASSOCIATION 1991, *Heritage Language Programs in Canadian School Boards*. Toronto: Canadian Education Association.

CANADIAN EDUCATION ASSOCIATION 1992, *French Immersion Today*. Toronto: Canadian Education Association.

CANALE, M. 1983, On some dimensions of language proficiency. In J.W. OLLER (ed.) *Issues in Language Testing Research*. Rowley, MA: Newbury House.

CANALE, M. 1984, On some theoretical frameworks for language proficiency. In C. RIVERA (ed.) *Language Proficiency and Academic Achievement*. Clevedon: Multilingual Matters.

CANALE, M. and SWAIN, M. 1980, Theoretical bases of communicative approaches to second language teaching and testing. *Applied Linguistics* 1, 1–47.

CALERO-BRECKHEIMER, A. and GOETZ, E.T. 1993, Reading strategies of biliterate children for English and Spanish texts. *Reading Psychology* 14, 177–204.

CAREY, S.T. 1991, The culture of literacy in majority and minority language schools. *Canadian Modern Language Review* 47 (5), 950–976.

CARRASQUILLO, A.L. 1990, Bilingual special education: The important connection. In A.L. CARRASQUILLO and R.E. BAECHER (eds) *Teaching the Bilingual Special Education Student*. Norwood, NJ: Ablex.

CARROLL, B. 1980, *Testing Communicative Performance*. Oxford: Pergamon Press.

CARROLL, J.B. 1968, The psychology of language testing. In A. DAVIES (ed.) *Language Testing Symposium. A Psycholinguistic Perspective*. Oxford: Oxford University Press.

CARTER, T.P. and CHATFIELD, M.L. 1986, Effective bilingual schools: Implications for policy and practice. *American Journal of Education* 95 (1), 200–232.

CASANOVA, U. 1991, Bilingual education: Politics or pedagogy? In O. GARCÍA (ed.) *Bilingual Education: Focusschrift in Honor of Joshua A. Fishman*. Amsterdam/Philadelphia: John Benjamins.

CASANOVA, U. 1992, Shifts in bilingual education policy and the knowledge base. In R.V. PADILLA and A.H. BENAVIDES (eds) *Critical Perspectives on Bilingual Education Research*. Tempe, AZ: Bilingual Press.

CASANOVA, U. and ARIAS M.B. 1993, Contextualizing bilingual education. In B. ARIAS and U. CASANOVA (eds) *Bilingual Education: Politics, Research and Practice*. Berkeley, CA: McCutchan.

CAZABON, M., LAMBERT, W. and HALL, G. 1993, *Two-Way Bilingual Education: A Progress Report on the Amigos Program*. Santa Cruz, CA: National Center for Research on Cultural Diversity and Second Language Learning.

CAZDEN, C.B. 1992, *Language Minority Education in the United States: Implications of the Ramirez Report*. Santa Cruz, CA: National Center for Research on Cultural Diversity and Second Language Learning.

CAZDEN, C.B. and SNOW, C.E. 1990a, Preface to C.B. Cazden and C.E. Snow (eds) *English Plus: Issues in Bilingual Education*. London: Sage.

CAZDEN, C.B. and SNOW, C.E. (eds) 1990b, *English Plus: Issues in Bilingual Education. (The Annals of the American Academy of Political and Social Science* Vol. 508). London: Sage.

CENOZ, J. and VALENCIA, J.F. 1994, Additive trilingualism: Evidence from the Basque Country. *Applied Linguistics* 15, 195–207.

CHAMBERLAIN, P. and MEDEIROS-LANDURAND, P. 1991, Practical considerations for the assessment of LEP students with special needs. In E.V. HAMAYAN and J.S. DAMICO (eds) *Limiting Bias in the Assessment of Bilingual Students*. Austin, TX: Pro-Ed.

CHOMSKY, N. 1965, *Aspects of the Theory of Syntax*. Cambridge, MA: MIT Press.

CHRISTIAN, D. 1994, *Two-Way Bilingual Education: Students Learning Through Two Languages*. Santa Cruz, CA: National Center for Research on Cultural Diversity and Second Language Learning.

CLARKSON, P.C. 1992, Language and mathematics: A comparison of bilingual and monolingual students of mathematics. *Educational Studies in Mathematics* 23, 417–429.

CLARKSON, P.C. and GALBRAITH, P. 1992, Bilingualism and mathematics learning: Another perspective. *Journal for Research in Mathematics Education* 23 (1), 34–44.

CLINE, T. 1993, Educational assessment of bilingual pupils: Getting the context right. *Educational and Child Psychology* 10 (4), 59–68.

CLINE, T. and FREDERICKSON, N. (eds) 1995, *Progress in Curriculum Related Assessment with Bilingual Pupils*. Clevedon: Multilingual Matters.

CLOUD, N. 1994, Special education needs of second language children. In F. GENESEE (ed.) *Educating Second Language Children*. Cambridge: Cambridge University Press.

CLYNE, M. 1988, Bilingual education: What can we learn from the past? *Australian Journal of Education* 32 (1), 95–114.

CLYNE, M. 1991, Bilingual education for all. An Australian pilot study and its implications. In O. GARCÍA (ed.) *Bilingual Education: Focusschrift in Honor of Joshua A. Fishman*. Amsterdam/Philadelphia: John Benjamins.

COLLEGE FOR CONTINUING EDUCATION 1992, *Bilingual Considerations in the Education of Deaf Students: ASL and English*. Washington, DC: Gallaudet University.

COLLIER, V.P. 1989, How long? A synthesis of research on academic achievement in a second language. *TESOL Quarterly* 23 (3), 509–531.

COLLIER, V.P. 1992, A synthesis of studies examining long-term language minority student data on academic achievement. *Bilingual Research Journal* 16 (1&2), 187–212.

CONKLIN, N. and LOURIE, M. 1983, *A Host of Tongues*. New York: The Free Press.

COOK, V. 1991, *Second Language Learning and Language Teaching*. London: Edward Arnold.

COOPER, R.L. 1989, *Language Planning and Social Change*. Cambridge: Cambridge University Press.

CORDER, S. 1967, The significance of learners' errors. *International Review of Applied Linguistics* 5, 161–170.

CORSON, D 1985, *The Lexical Bar*. Oxford: Pergamon.

CORSON, D. 1990a, *Language Policy Across the Curriculum*. Clevedon: Multilingual Matters.

CORSON, D. 1990b, Three curriculum and organizational responses to cultural pluralism in New Zealand schooling. *Language, Culture and Curriculum* 3 (3), 213–225.

CORSON, D. 1992, Bilingual education policy and social justice. *Journal of Education Policy* 7 (1), 45–69.

COULMAS, F. 1992, *Language and Economy*. Oxford: Blackwell.

CRAWFORD, J. 1989, *Bilingual Education: History, Politics, Theory and Practice* (1st edn). Trenton, NJ: Crane Publishing.

CRAWFORD, J. 1991, *Bilingual Education: History, Politics, Theory and Practice* (2nd edn). Los Angeles: Bilingual Education Services.

CRAWFORD, J. 1992a, *Hold Your Tongue: Bilingualism and the Politics of 'English Only'*. Reading, MA: Addison-Wesley.

CRAWFORD, J. (ed.) 1992b, *Language Loyalties: A Source Book on the Official English Controversy*. Chicago: University of Chicago Press.

CRYSTAL, D. 1995, *The Cambridge Encyclopedia of the English Language*. Cambridge: Cambridge University Press.

CUMMINS, J. 1975, Cognitive factors associated with intermediate levels of bilingual skills. Unpublished manuscript, Educational Research Centre, St Patrick's College, Dublin.

CUMMINS, J. 1976, The influence of bilingualism on cognitive growth: A synthesis of research findings and explanatory hypotheses. *Working Papers on Bilingualism* 9, 1–43.

CUMMINS, J. 1977, Cognitive factors associated with the attainment of intermediate levels of bilingual skills. *Modern Language Journal* 61, 3–12.

CUMMINS, J. 1978, Metalinguistic development of children in bilingual education programs: Data from Irish and Canadian Ukranian–English programs. In M. PARADIS (ed.) *Aspects of Bilingualism*. Columbia: Hornbeam Press.

CUMMINS, J. 1980a, The construct of language proficiency in bilingual education. In J.E. ALATIS (ed.) *Georgetown University Round Table on Languages and Linguistics 1980*. Washington, DC: Georgetown University Press.

CUMMINS, J. 1980b, The entry and exit fallacy in bilingual education. *NABE Journal* 4 (3), 25–59.

CUMMINS, J. 1981a, *Bilingualism and Minority Language Children*. Ontario: Ontario Institute for Studies in Education.

CUMMINS, J. 1981b, The role of primary language development in promoting educational success for language minority students. In CALIFORNIA STATE DEPARTMENT OF EDUCATION (ed.) *Schooling and Language Minority Students. A Theoretical Framework*. Los Angeles: California State Department of Education.

CUMMINS, J. 1983a, *Heritage Language Education: A Literature Review*. Ontario: Ministry of Education.

CUMMINS, J. 1983b, Language proficiency, biliteracy and French immersion. *Canadian Journal of Education* 8 (2), 117–138.

CUMMINS, J. 1984a, *Bilingualism and Special Education: Issues in Assessment and Pedagogy*. Clevedon: Multilingual Matters.

CUMMINS, J. 1984b, Wanted: A theoretical framework for relating language proficiency to academic achievement among bilingual students. In C. RIVERA (ed.) *Language Proficiency and Academic Achievement*. Clevedon: Multilingual Matters.

CUMMINS, J. 1986a, Bilingual education and anti-racist education. *Interracial Books for Children Bulletin* 17 (3&4), 9–12.

CUMMINS, J. 1986b, Empowering minority students: A framework for intervention. *Harvard Educational Review* 56 (1), 18–36.

CUMMINS, J. 1989, Language and literacy acquisition. *Journal of Multilingual and Multicultural Development* 10 (1), 17–31.

CUMMINS, J. 1991a, The politics of paranoia: Reflections on the bilingual education debate. In O. GARCÍA (ed.) *Bilingual Education: Focusschrift in Honor of Joshua A. Fishman (Volume 1)*. Amsterdam/Philadelphia: John Benjamins.

CUMMINS, J. 1991b, The development of bilingual proficiency from home to school: A longitudinal study of Portuguese-speaking children. *Journal of Education* 173 (2), 85–98.

CUMMINS, J. 1992, Heritage language teaching in Canadian schools. *Journal of Curriculum Studies* 24 (3), 281–286.

CUMMINS, J. 1992b, Bilingual education and English immersion: The Ramirez Report in theoretical perspective. *Bilingual Research Journal* 16 (1&2), 91–104.

CUMMINS, J. 1993, The research base for heritage language promotion. In M. DANESI, K. McLEOD and S. MORRIS (eds) *Heritage Languages and Education: The Canadian Experience*. Oakville: Mosaic Press.

CUMMINS, J. 1994, Knowledge, power and identity in teaching English as a second language. In F. GENESEE (ed.) *Educating Second Language Children*. Cambridge: Cambridge University Press.

CUMMINS, J. and DANESI, M. 1990, *Heritage Languages. The Development and Denial of Canada's Linguistic Resources*. Toronto: Our Schools/Ourselves Education Foundation and Garamond Press.

CUMMINS, J. and GULUTSAN, M. 1974, Some effects of bilingualism on cognitive functioning. In S. CAREY (ed.) *Bilingualism, Biculturalism and Education*. Edmonton: University of Alberta Press.

CUMMINS, J. and MULCAHY, R. 1978, Orientation to language in Ukranian–English bilingual children. *Child Development* 49, 1239–1242.

CUMMINS, J. and SWAIN, M. 1986, *Bilingualism in Education*. New York: Longman.

CZIKO, G.A. 1992, The evaluation of bilingual education: From necessity and probability to possibility. *Educational Researcher* 21 (2), 10–15.

DANESI, K., McLEOD, K. and MORRIS (eds) 1993 *Heritage Languages and Education: The Canadian Experience*. Oakville: Mosaic Press.

DANESI, M. 1991, Revisiting the research findings on heritage language learning: Three interpretive frames. *Canadian Modern Language Review* 47 (4), 650–659.

DANOFF, M.N., COLES, G.J., McLAUGHLIN, D.H. and REYNOLDS, D.J. 1977, *Evaluation of the Impact of ESEA Title VII Spanish/English Bilingual Education Programs Volume 1*. Palo Alto, CA: American Institutes for Research.

DANOFF, M.N., COLES, G.J., McLAUGHLIN, D.H. and REYNOLDS, D.J. 1978, *Evaluation of the Impact of ESEA Title VII Spanish/English Bilingual Education Programs Volume 3*. Palo Alto, CA: American Institutes for Research.

DARCY, N.T. 1953, A review of the literature on the effects of bilingualism upon the measurement of intelligence. *Journal of Genetic Psychology* 82, 21–57.

DAVIDMAN, L. and DAVIDMAN, P.T. 1994, *Teaching with a Multicultural Perspective: A Practical Guide*. New York: Longman.

DAWE, L.C., 1982, The influence of a bilingual child's first language competence on reasoning in mathematics. Unpublished PhD dissertation, University of Cambridge.

DAWE L.C. 1983, Bilingualism and mathematical reasoning in English as a second language. *Educational Studies in Mathematics* 14 (1), 325–353.

DELGADO-GAITAN, C. 1990, *Literacy for Empowerment: The Role of Parents in Children's Education*. New York: Falmer.

DELGADO-GAITAN, C. and TRUEBA, H. 1991, *Crossing Cultural Borders: Education for Immigrant Families in America*. New York: Falmer.

DELPIT, L.D. 1988, The silenced dialogue: Power and pedagogy in educating other people's children. *Harvard Educational Review* 58 (3), 280–298.

DEPARTMENT OF EDUCATION and SCIENCE 1985, *Education for All* (Swann Report). London: HMSO.

DEPARTMENT OF EDUCATION and SCIENCE AND THE WELSH OFFICE 1990, *Welsh in the National Curriculum (No. 2)*. London: HMSO.

DEVILLAR, R.A., FALTIS, C.J. and CUMMINS, J.P. (eds) 1994, *Cultural Diversity in Schools: From Rhetoric to Practice*. Albany, NY: State University of New York Press.

DIAZ, R.M. 1985, Bilingual cognitive development: Addressing three gaps in current research. *Child Development* 56, 1376–1388.

DIAZ, R.M. and KLINGER, C. 1991, Towards an explanatory model of the interaction between bilingualism and cognitive development. In E. BIALYSTOK (ed.) *Language Processing in Bilingual Children*. Cambridge: Cambridge University Press.

DICKS, J.E. 1992, Analytic and experiential features of three French immersion programs: Early, middle and late. *Canadian Modern Language Review* 49 (1), 37–60.

DIEBOLD, A.R. 1964, Incipient bilingualism. In D. HYMES *et al.* (eds) *Language in Culture and Society*. New York: Harper and Row.

DI PIETRO, R. 1977, Code-switching as a verbal strategy among bilinguals. In F. ECKMAN (ed.) *Current Themes in Linguistics*. Washington, DC: Hemisphere Publishing.

DODSON, C.J. 1981, A reappraisal of bilingual development and education: Some theoretical and practical considerations. In H. BAETENS BEARDSMORE (ed.) *Elements of Bilingual Theory*. Brussels: Vrije Universiteit Brussel.

DOLSON, D.P. and MEYER, J. 1992, Longitudinal study of three program models for language-minority students: A critical examination of reported findings. *Bilingual Research Journal* 16 (1&2), 105–157.

DONALDSON, M. 1978, *Children's Minds*. Glasgow: Fontana/Collins.

DONMALL, B.G. 1985, *Language Awareness. Report to the National Congress on Languages in Education*. London: CILT.

DÖPKE, S. 1992, *One Parent–One Language: An Interactional Approach*. Amsterdam: John Benjamins.

DORIAN, N.C. 1981, *Language Death: The Life Cycle of a Scottish Gaelic Dialect.* Philadelphia: University of Pennsylvania Press.

DORIAN, N.C. 1989 (ed.) *Investigating Obsolescence: Studies in Language Contraction and Death.* Cambridge: Cambridge University Press.

DOYLE, A., CHAMPAGNE, M. and SEGALOWITZ, N. 1978, Some issues on the assessment of linguistic consequences of early bilingualism. In M. PARADIS (ed.) *Aspects of Bilingualism.* Columbia: Hornbeam Press.

DUFF, P.A. 1991, Innovation in foreign language education: An evaluation of three Hungarian–English dual-language schools. *Journal of Multilingual and Multicultural Development* 12 (6), 459–476.

DULAY, H.C. and BURT, M.K. 1973, Should we teach children syntax? *Language Learning* 23, 245–258.

DULAY, H.C and BURT, M.K. 1974, Errors and strategies in child second language acquisition. *TESOL Quarterly* 8, 129–136.

DULAY, H.C. and BURT, M.K. 1977, Remarks on creativity in language acquisition. In M. BURT, H. DULAY and M. FINOCCHIARO (eds) *Viewpoints on English as a Second Language.* New York: Regents.

DULAY, H.C. and BURT, M.K., 1978, *Why Bilingual Education? A Summary of Research Findings* (2nd edn). San Francisco: Bloomsbury West.

DULAY, H.C. and BURT, M.K. 1979, Bilingual education: A close look at its effects. *Focus*, No. 1.

DUNCAN, S.E. and DE AVILA, E.A. 1979, Bilingualism and cognition: Some recent findings. *NABE Journal* 4 (1), 15–50.

DUNKIN, M. and BIDDLE, B.J. 1974, *The Study of Teaching.* New York: Holt, Rinehart and Winston.

DYSON, A. 1989, *The Multiple Worlds of Child Writers: A Study of Friends Learning to Write.* New York: Teachers College Press.

EASTMAN, C.M. 1983, *Language Planning: An Introduction.* San Francisco: Chandler and Sharp.

EASTMAN, C.M. 1992, Codeswitching as an urban language, contact phenomenon. *Journal of Multilingual and Multicultural Development* 13 (1&2), 1–17.

ECIS (The European Council of International Schools) 1994, *The ECIS International Schools Directory 1994–95.* London: Fieldwork Ltd.

EDELSKY, C. 1991, *With Literacy and Justice for All: Rethinking the Social in Language and Education.* London: Falmer.

EDELSKY, C. *et al.* 1983, Semilingualism and language deficit. *Applied Linguistics* 4 (1), 1–22.

EDWARDS, J. 1981, The context of bilingual education. *Journal of Multilingual and Multicultural Development* 2 (1), 25–44.

EDWARDS, J. 1985, *Language, Society and Identity.* Oxford: Blackwell.

EDWARDS, J. 1994a, *Multilingualism.* London: Routlege.

EDWARDS, J. 1994b, Parochialism and intercourse: Metaphors for mobility. *Journal of Multilingual and Multicultural Development* 15 (2&3), 171–178.

EDWARDS, V. and REDFERN, A. 1992, *The World in a Classroom: Language in Education in Britain and Canada*. Clevedon: Multilingual Matters.

EISEMAN, T.O., PROUTY, R. and SCHWILLE, J. 1989, What language should be used for teaching? Language policy and school reform in Burundi. *Journal of Multilingual and Multicultural Development* 10 (6), 473–497.

ELLIS, N. 1992, Linguistic relativity revisited: The bilingual word-length effect in working memory during counting, remembering numbers and mental calculation. In R.J. HARRIS (ed.) *Cognitive Processing in Bilinguals*. Amsterdam: North-Holland.

ELLIS, R. 1984, *Classroom Second Language Development*. Oxford: Pergamon.

ELLIS, R. 1985, *Understanding Second Language Acquisition*. Oxford: Oxford University Press.

ELLIS, R. 1990, *Instructed Second Language Acquisition*. Oxford: Basil Blackwell.

ERICKSON, F. 1987, Transformation and school success: The politics and culture of educational achievement. *Anthropology and Education Quarterly* 18 (4), 335–356.

FALTIS, C.J. 1993a, *Joinfostering: Adapting Teaching Strategies for the Multilingual Classroom*. New York: MacMillan.

FALTIS, C.J. 1993b, Critical issues in the use of sheltered content teaching in high school bilingual programs. *Peabody Journal of Education* 69 (1), 136–151.

FANTINI, A. 1985, *Language Acquisition of a Bilingual Child: A Sociolinguistic Perspective*. San Diego: College Hill Press.

FERGUSON, C. 1959, Diglossia. *Word* 15, 325–340.

FERGUSON, C.A., HOUGHTON, C. and WELLS, M.H. 1977, Bilingual education: An international perspective. In B. SPOLSKY and R. COOPER (eds) *Frontiers of Bilingual Education*. Rowley, MA: Newbury House.

FEUERVERGER, G. 1994, A multilingual literacy intervention for minority language students. *Language and Education* 8 (3), 123–146.

FIGUROA, P. 1984, Minority pupil progress. In M. CRAFT (ed.) *Education and Cultural Pluralism*. London: Falmer Press.

FISHMAN, J.A. 1965, Who speaks what language to whom and when? *La Linguistique*, 67–68.

FISHMAN, J.A. 1971, The sociology of language. In J. FISHMAN (ed.) *Advances in the Sociology of Language, Volume 1*. The Hague: Mouton.

FISHMAN, J.A. 1972, *The Sociology of Language*. Rowley, MA: Newbury House.

FISHMAN, J.A. 1976, *Bilingual Education. An International Sociological Perspective*. Rowley, MA: Newbury House.

FISHMAN, J.A. 1977, The social science perspective. In CENTER FOR APPLIED LINGUISTICS (ed.) *Bilingual Education: Current Perspectives*. Arlington, VA: CAL.

FISHMAN, J.A. 1980, Bilingualism and biculturalism as individual and as societal phenomena. *Journal of Multilingual and Multicultural Development* 1, 3–15.

FISHMAN, J.A. 1989, *Language and Ethnicity in Minority Sociolinguistic Perspective*. Clevedon: Multilingual Matters.

FISHMAN, J.A. 1990, What is reversing language shift (RLS) and how can it succeed? *Journal of Multilingual and Multicultural Development* 11 (1&2), 5–36.

FISHMAN, J.A. 1991, *Reversing Language Shift*. Clevedon: Multilingual Matters.

FISHMAN, J.A. 1993, Reversing language shift: Successes, failures, doubts and dilemmas. In E.H. JAHR (ed.) *Language Conflict and Language Planning*. New York: Mouton de Gruyter.

FITZGERALD, J. 1993, Views on bilingualism in the United States: A selective historical review. *Bilingual Research Journal* 17 (1&2), 35–56.

FITZPATRICK, F. 1987, *The Open Door: The Bradford Bilingual Project*. Clevedon: Multilingual Matters.

FORTUNE, D. and FORTUNE, G. 1987, Karaja literary acquisition and sociocultural effects on a rapidly changing culture. *Journal of Multilingual and Multicultural Development* 8 (6), 469–49.

FREDERICKSON, N. and CLINE, T. 1990, *Curriculum Related Assessment with Bilingual Children*. London: University College London.

FREEMAN, R.D. 1995, An alternative to mainstream US educational discourse: Implications for minority identity development. In *Georgetown University Round Table on Languages and Linguistics: 'Educational Linguistics, Cross-Cultural Communication and Global Independence'*. Washington, DC: Georgetown University Press.

FRIERE, P. 1970, *Pedagogy of the Oppressed*. New York: Seabury Press/Continuum.

FRIERE, P. 1973, *Education for Critical Consciousness*. New York: Continuum.

FRIERE, P. 1985, *The Politics of Education*. South Hadley, MA: Bergin and Garvey.

FRIERE, P. and MACEDO, D. 1987, *Literacy: Reading the Word and the World*. South Hadley, MA: Bergin and Garvey.

FROMM, E. 1970, Age regression with unexpected reappearance of a repressed childhood language. *International Journal of Clinical and Experimental Hypnosis* 18, 79–88.

GAARDER, A.B. 1977, *Bilingual Schooling and the Survival of Spanish in the United States*. Rowley, MA: Newbury House.

GAL, S. 1979, *Language Shift: Social Determinants of Linguistic Change in Bilingual Austria*. New York: Academic Press.

GALAMBOS, S.J. and HAKUTA, K. 1988, Subject-specific and task-specific characteristics of metalinguistic awareness in bilingual children. *Applied Psycholinguistics* 9, 141–162.

GANDHI, M. 1929 (English edition, 1949), *The Story of My Experiments with Truth*. London: Cape.

GARCÍA, E.E. 1988, Effective schooling for Hispanics. *Urban Education Review* 67 (2), 462–473.

GARCÍA, E.E. 1991, Effective instruction for language minority students: The teacher. *Journal of Education* 173 (2), 130–141.

GARCÍA, O. 1983, Sociolinguistics and language planning in bilingual education for Hispanics in the United States. *International Journal of the Sociology of Language* 44, 43–54.

GARCÍA, O. 1988, *The Education of Biliterate and Bicultural Children in Ethnic Schools in the United States. Essays by Spencer Fellows of the National Academy of Education*, Vol. 4, pp. 19–78.

GARCÍA, O. 1991a, Latinos and bilingual education in the United States: Their role as objects and subjects. *New Language Planning Newsletter* 6 (2), 3–5.

GARCÍA, O. (ed.) 1991b, *Bilingual Education: Focusschrift in Honor of Joshua A. Fishman*. Amsterdam/Philadelphia: John Benjamins.

GARCÍA, O. 1992a, Societal multilingualism in a multicultural world in transition. In H. BYRNE (ed.) *Languages for a Multicultural World in Transition*. Illinois: National Textbook Company.

GARCÍA, O. 1992b, Societal bilingualism and multilingualism (mimeo). New York: City University of New York.

GARCÍA, O. 1992c, For it is in giving that we receive: A history of language policy in the United States. Paper presented to a conference 'American Pluralism: Toward a History of the Discussion', State University of New York at Stonybrook, June 7th 1992.

GARCÍA, O. 1993, Understanding the societal role of the teacher in transitional bilingual classrooms: Lessons from sociology of language. in ZONDAG, K. (ed.) *Bilingual Education in Friesland: Facts and Prospects*. Leewarden: Gemeens Chappelijk Centrum voor Onderwijsbegeleiding in Friesland.

GARCÍA, O. 1995, Spanish language loss as a determinant of income among Latinos in the United States. In J.W. TOLLEFSON (ed.) *Power and Inequality in Language Education*. Cambridge: Cambridge University Press.

GARCÍA, O. and BAKER, C. (eds) 1995, *Policy and Practice in Bilingual Education: A Reader Extending the Foundations*. Clevedon: Multilingual Matters.

GARCÍA, O. and OTHEGUY, R. 1985, The masters of survival send their children to school: Bilingual education in the ethnic schools of Miami. *Bilingual Review* 12 (1&2), 3–19.

GARCÍA, O. and OTHEGUY, R. 1988, The language situation of Cuban Americans. In S.L. McKAY and S.C. WONG (eds) *Language Diversity: Problem or Resource?* New York: Newbury House.

GARCÍA, O. and OTHEGUY, R. 1994, The value of speaking a LOTE in US business. *Annals of the American Academy of Political and Social Science* 532, 99–122.

GARCÍA, R. and DIAZ, C.F. 1992, The status and use of Spanish and English among Hispanic youth in Dade County (Miami) Florida: A sociolinguistic study. *Language and Education* 6 (1), 13–32.

GARDNER, R.C. 1979, Social psychological aspects of second language acquisition. In H. GILES and R. ST CLAIR (eds) *Language and Social Psychology* Oxford: Blackwell.

GARDNER, R.C. 1983, Learning another language: A true social psychological experiment. *Journal of Language and Social Psychology* 2, 219–239.

GARDNER, R.C. 1985, *Social Psychology and Second Language Learning*. London: Edward Arnold.

GARDNER, R.C., LALONDE, R.N. and MACPHERSON, J. 1986, Social factors in second language attrition. *Language Learning* 35 (4), 519–540.

GARDNER, R.C., LALONDE, R.N. and PIERSON, R. 1983, The socio-educational model of second language acquisition: An investigation using LISREL causal modeling. *Journal of Language and Social Psychology* 2, 51–65.

GARDNER R.C. and LAMBERT, W.E. 1972, *Attitudes and Motivation in Second Language Learning*. Rowley, MA: Newbury House.

GAUDART, H. 1987, A typology of bilingual education in Malaysia. *Journal of Multilingual and Multicultural Development* 8 (6), 529–552.

GEARY, D., CORMIER, P., GOGGIN, J., ESTRADA, P. and LUNN, M. 1993, Mental arithmetic: A componential analysis of speed-of-processing across monolingual, weak bilingual and strong bilingual adults. *International Journal of Psychology* 28 (2), 185–201.

GENERAL ACCOUNTING OFFICE 1987, *Bilingual Education. A New Look at the Research Evidence*. Washington, DC: General Accounting Office.

GENESEE, F. 1976, The role of intelligence in second language learning. *Language Learning* 26, 267–280.

GENESEE, F. 1978, Second language learning and language attitudes. *Working Papers on Bilingualism* 16, 19–42.

GENESEE, F. 1983, Bilingual education of majority-language children: The Immersion experiments in review. *Applied Psycholinguistics* 4, 1–46.

GENESEE, F. 1984, Historical and theoretical foundations of immersion education. In CALIFORNIA STATE DEPARTMENT OF EDUCATION (eds) *Studies on Immersion Education: A Collection for United States Educators*. California: California State Department of Education.

GENESEE, F. 1987, *Learning Through Two Languages*. Cambridge, MA: Newbury House.

GENESEE, F. (ed) 1994, *Educating Second Language Children*. Cambridge: Cambridge University Press.

GENESEE, F. and HAMAYAN, E. 1980, Individual differences in young second language learners. *Applied Psycholinguistics* 1, 95–110.

GENESEE, F. and HAMAYAN, E. 1994, Classroom-based assessment. In F. GENESEE (ed.) *Educating Second Language Children*. Cambridge: Cambridge University Press.

GENESEE, F. and LAMBERT, W.E. 1983, Trilingual education for majority language children. *Child Development* 54, 105–114.

GENESEE, F., TUCKER, G.R. and LAMBERT, W.E. 1975, Communication skills in bilingual children. *Child Development* 46, 1010–1014.

GERSTEN, R. and WOODWARD, J. 1994, The language minority student and special education: Issues, trends and paradoxes. *Exceptional Children* 60 (4), 310–322.

GHUMAN, P.S. 1993, *Coping with Two Cultures*. Clevedon: Multilingual Matters.

GHUMAN, P.S. 1994, *Asian Teachers in British Schools*. Clevedon: Multilingual Matters.

GILES, H., BOURHIS, R. and TAYLOR, D. 1977, Towards a theory of language in ethnic group relations. In H. GILES (ed.) *Language, Ethnicity and Intergroup Relations.* London: Academic Press.

GILES, H. and BYRNE, J.L. 1982, An intergroup approach to second language acquisition. *Journal of Multilingual and Multicultural Development* 3 (1), 17–40.

GILES, H. and COUPLAND, N. 1991, *Language: Contexts and Consequences.* Milton Keynes: Open University Press.

GIRARD, D. 1988, *Selection and Distribution of Contents in Language Syllabuses.* Strasbourg: Council of Europe.

GLASS, G.V., McGAW, B. and SMITH, M.L. 1981, *Meta-analysis in Social Research.* Beverly Hills: Sage.

GLIKSMAN, L. 1976, Second language acquisition: The effects of student attitudes on classroom behavior. Unpublished MA thesis, University of Western Ontario.

GLIKSMAN, L. 1981, Improving the prediction of behaviours associated with second language acquisition. Unpublished PhD thesis, University of Western Ontario.

GOMEZTORTOSA, E., MARTIN, E.M., GAVIRIA, M., CHARBEL, F. and AUSMAN, J. 1995, Selective deficit of one language in a bilingual patient following surgery in the left perisylvian area. *Brain and Language* 48 (3), 320–325.

GONZALEZ, J.M. 1979, Coming of age in bilingual/bicultural education: A historical perspective. In H.T. TRUEBA and C. BARNETT-MIZRAHI (eds) *Bilingual Multicultural Education and the Professional: From Theory to Practice.* Rowley, MA: Newbury House.

GORDON, M.M. 1964, *Assimilation in American Life: The Role of Race, Religion and National Origins.* New York: Oxford University Press.

GRAFF, H.J., *The Literacy Myth: Literacy and Social Structure in the 19th Century City.* New York: Academic Press.

GRAVES, D.H. 1983, *Writing: Teachers and Children at Work.* London: Heinemann.

GREGORY, E. 1993, Sweet and sour: Learning to read in a British and Chinese school. *English in Education* 27 (3), 53–59.

GREGORY, E. 1994, Cultural assumptions and early years' pedagogy: The effect of the home culture on minority children's interpretation of reading in school. *Language, Culture and Curriculum* 7 (2), 111–124.

GRIFFITHS, M. 1986, Introduction. In M. GRIFFITHS (ed.) *The Welsh Language in Education.* Cardiff: Welsh Joint Education Council.

GROSJEAN, F. 1982, *Life with Two Languages.* Cambridge, MA: Harvard University Press.

GROSJEAN, F. 1985, The bilingual as a competent but specific speaker-hearer. *Journal of Multilingual and Multicultural Development* 6 (6), 467–477.

GUILFORD, J.P. 1982, Cognitive psychology's ambiguities: Some suggested remedies. *Psychological Review* 89, 48–59.

GURDIAN, G. and SALAMANCA, D. 1990, Bilingual education in Nicaragua. *Prospects (UNESCO)* 20 (3), 357–364.

HABERLAND, H. 1991, Reflections about minority languages in the European Community. In F. COULMAS (ed.) *A Language Policy for the European Community*. New York: Mouton de Gruyter.

HAGEMEYER, A. 1992, *The Red Notebook*. Silver Spring, MD: National Association of the Deaf.

HAKUTA, K. 1986, *Mirror of Language. The Debate on Bilingualism*. New York: Basic Books.

HAKUTA, K. and D'ANDREA, D. 1992, Some properties of bilingual maintenance and loss in Mexican background high-school students. *Applied Linguistics* 13 (1), 72–99.

HALL, K. 1993, Process writing in French immersion. *Canadian Modern Language Review* 49 (2), 255–274.

HALLIDAY, M.A.K. 1973, *Explorations in the Functions of Language*. London: Edward Arnold.

HALLINGER, P. and MURPHY, J.F. 1986, The social context of effective schools. *American Journal of Education*, May, 328–355.

HAMAYAN E.V. and DAMICO, J.S. (eds) *Limiting Bias in the Assessment of Bilingual Students*. Austin, TX: Pro-Ed.

HAMERS, J.F. and BLANC, M. 1982, Towards a social-psychological model of bilingual development. *Journal of Language and Social Psychology* 1 (1), 29–49.

HAMERS, J.F. and BLANC, M. 1983, Bilinguality in the young child: A social psychological model. In P.H. NELDE (ed.) *Theory, Methods and Models of Contact Linguistics*. Bonn: Dummler.

HAMMERLY, H. 1988, French immersion (does it work?) and the development of the bilingual proficiency report. *Canadian Modern Language Review* 45 (3), 567–578.

HANSEGÅRD, N.E. 1975, Tvåspråkighet eller halvspråkighet? *Aldus*, Series 253, Stockholm, 3rd edition.

HARDING, E. and RILEY, P. 1987, *The Bilingual Family: A Handbook for Parents*. New York: Cambridge University Press.

HARLEY, B. 1986, *Age in Second Language Acquisition*. Clevedon: Multilingual Matters.

HARLEY, B. 1991, Directions in immersion research. *Journal of Multilingual and Multicultural Development* 12 (1&2), 9–19.

HARLEY, B. 1994, After immersion: Maintaining the momentum. *Journal of Multilingual and Multicultural Development* 15 (2&3), 229–244.

HARLEY, B. et al. 1987, *The Development of Bilingual Proficiency. Final Report* (3 volumes). Toronto: Ontario Institute for Studies in Education.

HARLEY, B. et al. 1990, *The Development of Second Language Proficiency*. Cambridge: Cambridge University Press.

HARRIS, J. 1984, *Spoken Irish in Primary Schools. An Analysis of Achievement*. Dublin: Instituid Teangeolaiochta Eireann.

HARRIS, R.J. (ed.) 1992, *Cognitive Processing in Bilinguals*. Amsterdam: North-Holland.

HARRY, B. 1992, *Cultural Diversity, Families and the Special Education System: Communication and Empowerment*. New York: Teachers College Press.

HART, D., LAPKIN, S. and SWAIN, M. 1987, Communicative language tests: Perks and perils. *Evaluation and Research in Education* 1 (2), 83–94.

HATCH, E. 1978, Discourse analysis and second language acquisition. In E. HATCH (ed.) *Second Language Acquisition: A Book of Readings*. Rowley, MA: Newbury House.

HAWKINS, E. 1987, *Awareness of Language: An Introduction*. New York: Cambridge University Press.

HEATH, S.B. 1982, What no bedtime story means: Narrative skills at home and school. *Language in Society* 11, 49–78.

HEATH, S.B. 1983, *Ways with Words: Language, Life and Work in Communities and Classrooms*. Cambridge: Cambridge University Press.

HEATH, S.B. 1986, Sociocultural contexts of language development. OFFICE OF BILINGUAL AND BICULTURAL EDUCATION (eds) *Beyond Language: Social and Cultural Factors in Schooling Language Minority Students*. Los Angeles: California State University, Evaluation, Dissemination and Assessment Center.

HELLER, M. 1994, *Crosswords: Language Education and Ethnicity in French Ontario*. Berlin and New York: Mouton de Gruyter.

HEREDIA, R. and McLAUGHLIN, B. 1992, Bilingual memory revisited. In R.J. HARRIS (ed.) *Cognitive Processing in Bilinguals*. Amsterdam: North-Holland.

HERNANDEZ, R.D. 1994, Reducing bias in the assessment of culturally and linguistically diverse populations. *Journal of Educational Issues of Language Minority Students* 14, 269–300.

HERNANDEZ-CHAVEZ, E., BURT, M. and DULAY, H. 1978, Language dominance and proficiency testing: Some general considerations. *NABE Journal* 3 (1), 41–54.

HIRSCH, E.D. 1988, *Cultural Literacy: What Every American Needs to Know*. New York: Vintage Books.

HOFFMANN, C. 1991, *An Introduction to Bilingualism*. London: Longman.

HOLM, A. and HOLM, W. 1990, Rock Point, A Navajo way to go to school. In C.B. CAZDEN and C.E. SNOW (eds) *The Annals of the American Academy of Political and Social Science*, Vol. 508, 170–184.

HORNBERGER, N. 1988, *Bilingual Education and Language Maintenance: A Southern Peruvian Quechua Case*. Dordrecht, Holland: Foris.

HORNBERGER, N.H. 1989, Continua of biliteracy. *Review of Educational Research* 59 (3), 271–296.

HORNBERGER, N.H. 1990a, Teacher Quechua use in bilingual and non-bilingual classrooms of Puno, Peru. In R. JACOBSON and C. FALTIS (eds) *Language Distribution Issues in Bilingual Schooling*. Clevedon: Multilingual Matters.

HORNBERGER, N.H. 1990b, Creating successful learning contexts for bilingual literacy. *Teachers College Record* 92 (2), 212–229.

HORNBERGER, N.H. 1991, Extending enrichment bilingual education: Revisiting Typologies and redirecting policy. In O. GARCÍA (ed.) *Bilingual Education: Focusschrift in Honor of Joshua A. Fishman (Volume 1)*. Amsterdam/Philadelphia: John Benjamins.

HORNBERGER, N.H. 1994, Literacy and language planning. *Language and Education* 8 (1&2), 75–86.

HORVATH, B.M. and VAUGHAN, P. 1991, *Community Languages: A Handbook.* Clevedon: Multilingual Matters.

HOUSEN, A. and BAETENS BEARDSMORE, H. 1987, Curricular and extra-curricular factors in multilingual education. *SSLA 9*, 83–102.

HOUSTON, S.H. 1972, *A Survey of Psycholinguistics.* The Hague: Mouton.

HUDDY, L. and SEARS, D.O. 1990, Qualified public support for bilingual education: Some policy implications. In C.B. CAZDEN and C.E. SNOW (eds) *The Annals of the American Academy of Political and Social Science, Volume 508*, 119–134.

HUDELSON, S. 1994, Literacy development of second language children. In F. GENESEE (ed.) *Educating Second Language Children.* Cambridge: Cambridge University Press.

HUDSON, L. 1966, *Contrary Imaginations. A Psychological Study of the English Schoolboy.* Harmondsworth, Middlesex: Penguin.

HUDSON, L. 1968, *Frames of Mind.* Harmondsworth, Middlesex: Penguin.

HUFFINES, M. L. 1991, Pennsylvania German: 'Do they love it in their hearts?' In J. R. DOW (ed.) *Language and Ethnicity. Focusschrift in Honor of Joshua Fishman.* Amsterdam/Philadelphia: John Benjamins.

HUMMEL, K.M. 1993, Bilingual memory research: From storage to processing issues. *Applied Psycholinguistics* 14, 267–284.

HUNTER, J.E., SCHMIDT, F.L. and JACKSON, G.B. 1982, *Meta-analysis: Cumulating Research Findings Across Studies.* Beverly Hills, CA: Sage.

HURD, M. 1993, Minority language children and French immersion: Additive multilingualism or subtractive semi-lingualism. *Canadian Modern Language Review* 49 (3), 514–525.

HUSBAND, C. and KHAN, V.S. 1982, The viability of ethnolinguistic vitality: Some creative doubts. *Journal of Multilingual and Multicultural Development* 3 (3), 193–205.

HYMES, D. 1972a, On communicative competence. In J. PRIDE and J. HOLMES (eds) *Sociolinguistics.* London: Penguin.

HYMES, D. 1972b, Models of interaction of language and social life. In J. J. GUMPERZ and D. HYMES (eds) *Directions in Sociolinguistics: The Ethnography of Communication.* New York: Holt, Rinehart and Winston.

IANCO-WORRALL, A.D. 1972, Bilingualism and cognitive development. *Child Development* 43, 1390–1400.

IMEDADZE, N. 1960, On the psychological nature of early bilingualism (in Russian) *Voprosy Psikhologii* 6, 60–68.

IMOFF, G. 1990, The position of US English on bilingual education. In C.B. CAZDEN and C.E. SNOW (eds) *The Annals of the American Academy of Political and Social Science Vol. 508*, 48–61. London: Sage.

ISAACS, E. 1976, *Greek Children in Sydney.* Canberra: Australian National University Press.

JACOBSON, R. 1990, Allocating two languages as a key feature of a bilingual methodology. In R. JACOBSON, R. and C. FALTIS (eds) *Language Distribution Issues in Bilingual Schooling*. Clevedon: Multilingual Matters.

JACOBSON, R. and FALTIS, C. 1990, *Language Distribution Issues in Bilingual Schooling*. Clevedon: Multilingual Matters.

JACQUES, K. and HAMLIN, J. 1992, PAT scores of children in bilingual and monolingual New Zealand primary classrooms. *Delta (NZ)* 46, 21–30.

JIMENEZ, R.T., GARCÍA, G.E. and PEARSON, P.D. 1995, Three children, two languages and strategic reading: Case studies in bilingual/monolingual reading. *American Educational Research Journal* 32 (1), 67–97.

JOHNSON, D.M. 1994, Grouping strategies for second language learners. In F. GENESEE (ed.) *Educating Second Language Children*. Cambridge: Cambridge University Press.

JOHNSON, R.K. and SWAIN, M. 1994, From core to content: Bridging the L2 proficiency gap in late immersion. *Language and Education* 8, 211–229.

JONES, G.M. MARTIN, P.W. and OZÓG, A.C.K. 1993, Multilingualism and bilingual education in Brunei Darussalem. In G.M. JONES and A.C.K. OZÓG (eds) *Bilingualism and National Development*. Clevedon: Multilingual Matters.

JONES, G.M. and OZÓG, A.C.K. (eds) 1993, *Bilingualism and National Development*. Clevedon: Multilingual Matters.

JONES, W.R. 1959, *Bilingualism and Intelligence*. Cardiff: University of Wales Press.

JONES, W.R. 1966, *Bilingualism in Welsh Education*. Cardiff: University of Wales Press.

JONG, E. de 1986, *The Bilingual Experience: A Book for Parents*. New York: Cambridge University Press.

KARDASH, C.A. *et al.* 1988, Bilingual referents in cognitive processing. *Contemporary Educational Psychology* 13, 45–57.

KARNIOL, R. 1992, Stuttering out of bilingualism. *First Language* 12, 255–283.

KAUR, S. and MILLS, R. 1993, Children as interpreters. In R.W. MILLS and J. MILLS (eds) *Bilingualism in the Primary School*. London: Routledge.

KEATLEY, C.W. 1992, History of bilingualism research in cognitive psychology. In R.J. HARRIS (ed.) *Cognitive Processing in Bilinguals*. Amsterdam: North-Holland.

KEEL, P. (ed.) 1994, *Assessment in the Multi-Ethnic Primary Classroom*. Stoke-on-Trent (UK): Trentham.

KESSLER, C. and QUINN, M.E. 1982, Cognitive development in bilingual environments. In B. HARTFORD, A. VALDMAN and C.R. FOSTER (eds) *Issues in International Bilingual Education. The Role of the Vernacular*. New York: Plenum Press.

KEYSER, R. and BROWN, J. 1981, *Heritage Language Survey Results*. Toronto, Canada: Research Department, Metropolitan Separate School Board.

KJOLSETH, R. 1983, Cultural politics of bilingualism. *Sociolinguistics Today* 20 (4), 40–48.

KLINE, P. 1983, *Personality Measurement and Theory*. London: Hutchinson.

KLOSS, H. 1977, *The American Bilingual Tradition*. Rowley, MA: Newbury House.

KOLERS, P. 1963, Interlingual word association. *Journal of Verbal Learning and Verbal Behavior* 2, 291–300.

KOZOL, J. 1985, *Illiterate America*. New York: Doubleday.

KRASHEN, S. 1977, The monitor model for second language performance. In M. BURT, H. DULAY and M. FINOCCHIAO (eds) *Viewpoints on English as a Second Language*. New York: Regents.

KRASHEN, S. 1981, *Second Language Acquisition and Second Language Learning*. Oxford: Pergamon Press.

KRASHEN, S. 1982, *Principles and Practices of Second Language Acquisition*. Oxford: Pergamon Press.

KRASHEN, S. 1985, *The Input Hypothesis: Issues and Implications*. London: Longman.

KRASHEN, S. and TERRELL, T. 1983, *The Natural Approach: Language Acquisition in the Classroom*. Oxford: Pergamon.

KYLE, J.G. (ed.) 1987, *Sign and School*. Clevedon: Multilingual Matters.

KYLE, J.G. 1988, *Sign Language: The Study of Deaf People and their Language*. Cambridge: Cambridge University Press.

LADO, R. 1961, *Language Testing*. New York: McGraw Hill.

LADO, R. 1964, *Language Teaching: A Scientific Approach*. New York: McGraw-Hill.

LALONDE, R.N. 1982, Second language acquisition: A causal analysis. Unpublished MA thesis, University of Western Ontario.

LAM, T.C. 1992, Review of practices and problems in the evaluation of bilingual education. *Review of Educational Research* 62 (2), 181–203.

LAMBERT, W.E. 1974, Culture and language as factors in learning and education. In F.E. ABOUD and R.D. MEADE (eds) *Cultural Factors in Learning and Education*. Bellingham, Washington; 5th Western Washington Symposium on Learning.

LAMBERT, W.E. 1980, The social psychology of language. In H. GILES, W.P. ROBINSON and P.M. SMITH (eds) *Language: Social Psychological Perspectives*. Oxford: Pergamon.

LAMBERT, W. and CAZABON, M. 1994, *Students' Views of the Amigos Program*. Santa Cruz, CA: National Center for Research on Cultural Diversity and Second Language Learning.

LAMBERT, W.E. and TAYLOR, D.M. 1990, *Coping with Cultural and Racial Diversity in Urban America*. New York: Praeger.

LAMBERT, W.E. and TUCKER, R. 1972, *Bilingual Education of Children. The St Lambert Experiment*. Rowley, MA: Newbury House.

LAMENDELLA, J. 1979, The neurofunctional basis of pattern practice. *TESOL Quarterly* 13, 5–13.

LANAUZE, M. and SNOW, C. 1989, The relation between first- and second-language writing skills. *Linguistics and Education* 1, 323–339.

LANDRY, R., ALLARD, R. and THÄBERGE, R. 1991, School and family French ambiance and the bilingual development of Francophone Western Canadians. *Canadian Modern Language Review* 47 (5), 878–915.

LANGE, D.L. (ed.) 1980, *Proceedings of the National Conference on Professional Priorities, November 1980*. New York: ACTFL Materials Center.

LANZA, E. 1992, Can bilingual two-year-olds code-switch? *Journal of Child Language* 19, 633–658.

LAPKIN, S., HARLEY, B. and TAYLOR, S. 1993, Research directions for core French in Canada. *Canadian Modern Language Review* 49 (3), 476–513.

LAPKIN, S., SWAIN, M. and SHAPSON, S. 1990, French immersion research agenda for the 90s. *Canadian Modern Language Review* 46 (4), 638–674.

LARSEN-FREEMAN, D. 1983, Second language acquisition: Getting the whole picture. In K. BAILEY, M. LONG and S. PECK (eds) *Second Language Acquisition Research*. Rowley, MA: Newbury House.

LAURÉN, C. 1994, Cultural and anthropological aspects of immersion. In *Language Immersion: Teaching and Second Language Acquisition: From Canada to Europe. Second European Conference 1994, Vaasa Finland*, Issue 192, pp. 21–26.

LAURÉN, U. 1991, A creativity index for studying the free written production for bilinguals. *International Journal of Applied Linguistics* 1 (2), 198–208.

LAURIE, S.S., 1890, *Lectures on Language and Linguistic Method in School*. Cambridge: Cambridge University Press.

LEBLANC, C. and COURTEL, C. 1990, Executive summary: The culture syllabus. *Canadian Modern Language Review* 47 (1), 82–92.

LEBLANC, R. 1990, Le curriculum multidimensionnel: Une synthèse. *Canadian Modern Language Review* 47 (1), 32–42.

LEBLANC, R. 1992, Second language retention. *Language and Society* 37, 35–36.

LEBRUN, N. and BAETENS BEARDSMORE, H. 1993, Trilingual education in the Grand Duchy of Luxembourg. In H. BAETENS BEARDSMORE (ed.) *European Models of Bilingual Education*. Clevedon: Multilingual Matters.

LEMAN, J. 1993, The bicultural programmes in the Dutch-language school system in Brussels. In H. BAETENS BEARDSMORE (ed.) *European Models of Bilingual Education*. Clevedon: Multilingual Matters.

LEOPOLD, W.F. 1939–1949, *Speech Development of a Bilingual Child. A Linguists' Record* (4 volumes). Evanston, IL: Northwestern University Press.

LEVY, P. and GOLDSTEIN, H. 1984, *Tests in Education. A Book of Critical Reviews*. London: Academic Press.

LEWIS, E.G. 1977, Bilingualism and bilingual education: The ancient world of the Renaissance. In B. SPOLSKY and R.L. COOPER (eds) *Frontiers of Bilingual Education*. Rowley, MA: Newbury House.

LEWIS, E.G. 1981, *Bilingualism and Bilingual Education*. Oxford: Pergamon.

LINDHOLM, K.J. 1987, *Directory of Bilingual Education Programs* (Monograph No. 8). Los Angeles: University of Southern California, Center for Language Education and Research.

LINDHOLM, K.J. 1990, Bilingual immersion education: Criteria for program development. In A.M. PADILLA, H.H. FAIRCHILD and C.M. VALADEZ (eds) *Bilingual Education: Issues and Strategies*. London: Sage.

LINDHOLM, K.J. 1991 (also 1995), Theoretical assumptions and empirical evidence for academic achievement in two languages. *Hispanic Journal of Behavioral Sciences*

13 (1), 3–17. Also in A.M. PADILLA (ed.) 1995, *Hispanic Psychology: Critical Issues in Theory and Research*. Thousand Oaks, CA: Sage.

LINDHOLM, K.J. 1994, Promoting positive cross-cultural attitudes and perceived competence in culturally and linguistically diverse classrooms. In R.A. DEVILLAR, C. FALTIS and J. CUMMINS (eds) *Cultural Diversity in Schools: From Rhetoric to Practice*. Albany, NY: State University of New York Press.

LINDHOLM, K.J. and ACLAN, Z. 1991, Bilingual proficiency as a bridge to academic achievement: Results from bilingual/immersion programs. *Journal of Education* 173 (2), 99–113.

LINGUISTIC MINORITIES PROJECT 1985, *The Other Languages of England*. London: Routledge and Kegan Paul.

LONG, M. 1985, Input and second language acquisition theory. In S. GASS and C. MADDEN (eds) *Input in Second Language Acquisition*. Rowley, MA: Newbury House.

LÓPEZ, L.E. 1990, Development of human resources in and for intercultural bilingual education in Latin America. *Prospects (UNESCO)* 20 (3), 311–320.

LOWE, P. 1983, The oral interview: Origins, applications, pitfalls and implications. *Die Unterrichtspraxis* 16, 230–244.

LUCAS, T., HENZE, R. and DONATO, R. 1990, Promoting the success of Latino language-minority students: An exploratory study of six High Schools. *Harvard Educational Review* 60 (3), 315–340.

LUKMANI, Y.M. 1972, Motivation to learn and learning proficiency. *Language Learning* 22, 261–273.

LYNCH, J. 1992, *Education for Citizenship in a Multicultural Society*. New York: Cassell.

LYON, J. 1996, *Becoming Bilingual: Language Acquisition in a Bilingual Community*. Clevedon: Multilingual Matters.

LYONS, J.J. 1990, The past and future directions of Federal bilingual-education policy. In C.B. CAZDEN and C.E. SNOW (eds) *Annals of the American Academy of Political and Social Science*, Vol. 508, pp 119–134. London: Sage.

MACKEY, W.F. 1965, *Language Teaching Analysis*. London: Longman.

MACKEY, W.F. 1970, A typology of bilingual education. *Foreign Language Annals* 3, 596–608.

MACKEY, W.F. 1978, The importation of bilingual education models. In J. ALATIS (ed.) *Georgetown University Roundtable: International Dimensions of Education*. Washington, DC: Georgetown University Press.

MACNAB, G.L. 1979, Cognition and bilingualism: A reanalysis of studies. *Linguistics* 17, 231–255.

MACNAMARA, J. 1966, *Bilingualism and Primary Education, A Study of Irish Experience*. Edinburgh: Edinburgh University Press.

MACNAMARA, J. 1969, How can one measure the extent of a person's bilingual proficiency. In L.G. KELLY (ed.) *Description and Measurement of Bilingualism* (pp. 80–119). Toronto: University of Toronto Press.

MACNEIL, M.M. 1994, Immersion programmes employed in Gaelic-medium units in Scotland. *Journal of Multilingual and Multicultural Development* 15 (2&3), 245–252.

MÄGISTE, E. 1984, Learning a third language. *Journal of Multilingual and Multicultural Development* 5 (5), 415–421.

MALAKOFF, M. 1992, Translation ability: A natural bilingual and metalinguistic skill. In R.J. HARRIS (ed.) *Cognitive Processing in Bilinguals*. Amsterdam: North-Holland.

MALAKOFF, M. and HAKUTA, K. 1990, History of language minority education in the United States. In A.M. PADILLA, H.H. FAIRCHILD and C.M. VALADEZ (eds) *Bilingual Education Issues and Strategies*. London: Sage.

MALDONADO, J.A. 1994, Bilingual special education: Specific learning disabilities in language and reading. *Journal of Educational Issues of Language Minority Students* 14, 127–147.

MALHERBE, E.C. 1946, *The Bilingual School*. London: Longman.

MANZER, K. 1993, Canadian immersion: Alive and working well in Finland. *Language and Society* 44, 16–17.

MAR-MOLINERO, C. 1987, The teaching of Catalan in Catalonia. *Journal of Multilingual and Multicultural Development* 10 (4), 307–326.

MARTÍNEZ, P.P. 1990, Towards standardization of language for teaching in the Andean countries. *Prospects (UNESCO)* 20 (3), 377–386.

MARTIN-JONES, M. and ROMAINE, S. 1986, Semilingualism: A half baked theory of communicative competence. *Applied Linguistics* 7 (1), 26–38.

MÄSCH, N. 1994, The German model of bilingual education. In R. KHOO, U. KREHER and R. WONG (eds) *Towards Global Multilingualism: European Models and Asian Realities*. Clevedon: Multilingual Matters.

MASHIE, S.N. 1995, *Educating Deaf Children Bilingually*. Washington, DC: Gallaudet University.

MATSUMI, N. 1994, Process of words memory in second language acquisition: A test of bilingual dual coding model. *Japanese Journal of Psychology* 64 (6), 460–468.

MATTHEWS, T. 1979, *An Investigation Into the Effects of Background Characteristics and Special Language Services on the Reading Achievement and English Fluency of Bilingual Students*. Seattle, WA: Seattle Public Schools, Department of Planning.

McCONNELL, B. 1980, Effectiveness of individualized bilingual instruction for migrant students. Unpublished PhD dissertation, Washington State University.

McCRACKEN, W. 1991, *Deaf-Ability Not Disability*. Clevedon: Multilingual Matters.

McGAW, B. 1988, Meta-analysis. In J.P. KEEVES (ed.) *Educational Research, Methodology and Measurement*. New York: Pergamon.

McGROARTY, M. 1992, The societal context of bilingual education. *Educational Researcher* 21 (2), 7–9.

McGROARTY, M. and FALTIS, C. 1991, *Languages in School and Society: Policy and Pedagogy*. Berlin/New York: Mouton de Gruyter.

McKAY, S. 1988, Weighing educational alternatives. In S.L. McKAY and S.C. WONG (eds) *Language Diversity: Problem or Resource?* New York: Newbury House.

McLAREN, P. 1988, Culture or canon? Critical pedagogy and the politics of literacy. *Harvard Educational Review* 58, 211–234.

McLAUGHLIN, B. 1978, The monitor model: Some methodological considerations. *Language Learning* 28, 309–332.

McLAUGHLIN, B. 1984, *Second-language Acquisition in Childhood. Volume 1: Preschool Children.* Hillsdale, NJ: Lawrence Erlbaum.

McLAUGHLIN, B. 1985, *Second Language Acquisition in Childhood. Volume 2: School Age Children.* Hillsdale, NJ: Lawrence Erlbaum.

McLAUGHLIN, B. 1987, *Theories of Second-Language Learning.* London: Edward Arnold.

McLAUGHLIN, B. and GRAF, P. 1985, Bilingual education in West Germany: Recent developments. *Comparative Education* 21 (3), 241–255.

McMAHON, A.M. 1994, *Understanding Language Change.* Cambridge: Cambridge University Press.

MERCER, J.R. 1973, *Labeling the Mentally Retarded.* Berkeley: University of California Press.

MEYER, M.M. and FIENBERG, S.E. 1992, *Assessing Evaluation Studies: The Case of Bilingual Education Strategies.* Washington, DC: National Academy Press.

MILLER-NOMELAND, M. 1993, *Kendall Demonstration Elementary School: Deaf Studies Curriculum Guide.* Washington, DC: Gallaudet University.

MILLS, R.W. and MILLS, J. (eds) 1993, *Bilingualism in the Primary School: A Handbook for Teachers.* London: Routledge.

MOLL, L.C. 1992, Bilingual classroom studies and community analysis. *Educational Researcher* 21 (2), 20–24.

MORALES, R. and BONILLA, F. 1993, *Latinos in a Changing US Economy.* London: Sage.

MORISON, S.H. 1990, A Spanish–English dual-language program in New York City. In C.B. CAZDEN and C.E. SNOW (eds) *The Annals of the American Academy of Political and Social Science,* Vol. 508, 160–169. London: Sage.

MORRIS, D. 1992, The effects of economic changes on Gwynedd society. In L. DAFIS (ed.) *Lesser Used Languages: Assimilating Newcomers.* Carmarthen, Wales: Joint Working Party on Bilingualism in Dyfed.

MORRISON, D. and LOW, G. 1983, Monitoring and the second language learner. In J. RICHARDS and R. SCHMIDT (eds) *Language and Communication.* London: Longman.

MORTIMORE, P. *et al.* 1988, *School Matters. The Junior Years.* Wells, Somerset: Open Books.

MOYA, R. 1990, A decade of bilingual education and indigenous participation in Ecuador. *Prospects (UNESCO)* 20 (3), 331–344.

MULTILINGUAL RESOURCES FOR CHILDREN PROJECT 1995, *Building Bridges: Multilingual Resources for Children.* Clevedon: Multilingual Matters.

MYERS SCOTTON, C. 1983, The negotiation of identities in conversation: A theory of markedness and code choice. *International Journal of the Sociology of Language* 44, 115–136.

MYERS SCOTTON, C. 1991, Making ethnicity salient in codeswitching. In J.R. DOW (ed.) *Language and Ethnicity. Focusschrift in Honor of Joshua Fishman*. Amsterdam/Philadelphia: John Benjamins.

MYERS SCOTTON, C. and URY, W. 1977, Bilingual strategies: The social functions of code-switching. *Linguistics* 193, 5–20.

NÁÑEZ, J.E., PADILLA, R.V. and MÁEZ, B.L. 1992, Bilinguality, intelligence and cognitive information processing. In R.V. PADILLA and A.H. BENAVIDES (eds) *Critical Perspectives on Bilingual Education Research*. Tempe, AZ: Bilingual Press.

NEUFELD, G.G. 1974, A theoretical perspective on the relationship of bilingualism and thought: Revisited. *Working Papers on Bilingualism*, No. 2, 125–129.

NIETO, S. 1992, *Affirming Diversity: The Sociopolitical Context of Multicultural Education*. New York: Longman.

NOVAK-LUKANOVIC, S. 1988, Bilingual education in Yugoslavia. *Journal of Multilingual and Multicultural Development* 9 (1&2), 169–176.

OBLER, L. 1983, Knowledge in neurolinguistics: The case of bilingualism. *Language Learning* 33 (5), 159–191.

OCHS, T. 1993, 'Why can't we speak Tagalog?' The problematic status of multilingualism in the International School. *Journal of Multilingual and Multicultural Development* 14 (6), 447–462.

OGBU, J. 1978, *Minority Education and Caste: The American System in Cross-Cultural Perspective*. New York: Academic Press.

OGBU, J. 1983, Minority status and schooling in plural societies. *Comparative Education Review* 27 (2), 168–190.

OKA, Hideo 1994, Studies on bilingualism and their implication in Japan. In R. MICHAEL BOSTWICK (ed.) *Immersion Education International Symposium Report on Second Language Acquisition through Content Based Study: An Introduction to Immersion Education*. Numazu, Japan: Katoh Gakuen.

OLLER, J.W. 1979, *Language Tests at School*. London: Longman.

OLLER, J.W. 1982, Evaluation and testing. In B. HARTFORD, A. VALDMAN and C. FOSTER (eds) *Issues in International Bilingual Education*. New York; Plenum Press.

OLLER, J.W. and PERKINS, K. 1978, A further comment on language proficiency as a source of variance in certain affective measures. *Language Learning* 28, 417–423.

OLLER, J.W. and PERKINS, K. 1980, *Research in Language Testing*. Rowley, MA: Newbury House.

OLNECK, M.R. 1993, Terms of inclusion: Has multiculturalism redefined equality in American education? *American Journal of Education* 101 (3), 234–260.

OTHEGUY, R. 1982, Thinking about bilingual education: A critical appraisal. *Harvard Educational Review* 52 (3), 301–314.

OTHEGUY, R. and OTTO, R. 1980, The myth of static maintenance in bilingual education. *Modern Language Journal* 64 (3), 350–356.

OVANDO, C.J. 1990, Essay review: Politics and pedagogy: The case of bilingual education. *Harvard Educational Review* 60 (3), 341–356.

OVANDO, C.J. and COLLIER, V.P. 1987, *Bilingual and ESL Classrooms: Teaching in Multicultural Contexts*. New York: McGraw-Hill.

OXENHAM, J. 1980, *Literacy: Writing, Reading and Social Organization*. London: Routledge and Kegan Paul.

PADILLA, A.M. 1991, English Only vs. bilingual education: Ensuring a language-competent society. *Journal of Education* 173 (2), 38–51.

PADILLA, R.V. and BENAVIDES, A.H. (eds) 1992, *Critical Perspectives on Bilingual Education Research*. Tempe, AZ: Bilingual Press.

PADILLA, A.M. and SUNG, H. 1992, A theoretical and pedagogical framework for bilingual education based on principles from educational psychology. In R.V. PADILLA and A.H. BENAVIDES (eds) *Critical Perspectives on Bilingual Education Research*. Tempe, AZ: Bilingual Press.

PAIVIO, A. 1986, *Mental Representations: A Dual Coding Approach*. Oxford: Oxford University Press.

PAIVIO, A. 1991, Mental representations in bilinguals. In A.G. REYNOLDS (ed.) *Bilingualism, Multiculturalism and Second Language Learning*. Hillsdale, NJ: Lawrence Erlbaum.

PAIVIO, A. and DESROCHERS, A. 1980, A dual-coding approach to bilingual memory. *Canadian Journal of Psychology* 34, 390–401.

PAKIR, A. 1994, Making bilingualism work: Developments in bilingual education in ASEAN. In R. KHOO, U. KREHER and R. WONG (eds) *Towards Global Multilingualism: European Models and Asian Realities*. Clevedon: Multilingual Matters.

PATTANAYAK, D.P. 1988, Monolingual myopia and the petals of the Indian lotus. In T. SKUTNABB-KANGAS and J. CUMMINS (eds) *Minority Education: From Shame to Struggle*. Clevedon: Multilingual Matters.

PAULSTON, C.B. 1980, *Bilingual Education: Theories and Issues*. Rowley, MA: Newbury House.

PAULSTON, C.B. 1992a, *Linguistic and Communicative Competence*. Clevedon: Multilingual Matters.

PAULSTON, C.B. 1992b, *Sociolinguistic Perspectives on Bilingual Education*. Clevedon: Multilingual Matters.

PAULSTON, C.B. 1994, *Linguistic Minorities in Multilingual Settings*. Amsterdam/Philadelphia: John Benjamins.

PAULSTON, C.B. (ed.) 1988, *International Handbook of Bilingualism and Bilingual Education*. New York: Greenwood.

PAULSTON, C.B., CHEE CHIN, P. and CONNERTY, M.C. 1993, Language regenesis: A conceptual overview of language revival, revitalisation and reversal. *Journal of Multilingual and Multicultural Development* 14 (4), 275–286.

PEAL, E. and LAMBERT, W.E. 1962, The relationship of bilingualism to intelligence. *Psychological Monographs* 76 (27), 1–23.

PEDERSEN, R.N. 1992, *One Europe: 100 Nations*. Clevedon: Channel View Books.

PÉREZ, B. and TORRES-GUZMÁN, M. 1995, *Learning in Two Worlds: An Integrated Spanish/English Biliteracy Approach* (2nd edn). New York: Longman.

PERLMANN, J. 1990, Historical legacies: 1840–1920. In C.B. CAZDEN and C.E. SNOW (eds) *English Plus: Issues in Bilingual Education.* London: Sage.

PEROTTI, A. 1994, *The Case for Intercultural Education.* Strasbourg: Council of Europe Press.

PHILLIPSON, R. 1992, *Linguistic Imperialism.* Oxford: Oxford University Press.

PINTNER, R. and ARSENIAN, S. 1937, The relation of bilingualism to verbal intelligence and school adjustment. *Journal of Educational Research* 31, 255–263.

POHL, J. 1965, Bilingualismes. *Revue Roumaine de Linguistique* 10, 343–349.

PORTER, R. 1990, *Forked Tongue: The Politics of Bilingual Education.* New York: Basic Books.

PRICE, E. 1985, Schools Council Bilingual Education Project (Primary Schools) 1968–1977: An assessment. In C.J. DODSON (ed.) *Bilingual Education: Evaluation, Assessment and Methodology.* Cardiff: University of Wales Press.

PURKEY, S.C. and SMITH, M.S. 1983, Effective schools: A review. *Elementary School Journal* 86 (4), 427–452.

RAMIREZ, A.G. 1985, *Bilingualism Through Schooling: Cross Cultural Education for Minority and Majority Students.* Albany: State University of New York Press.

RAMIREZ, J.D. 1992, Executive summary. *Bilingual Research Journal* 16, (1&2), 1–62.

RAMIREZ, J.D. and MERINO, B.J. 1990, Classroom talk in English immersion, early-exit and late-exit transitional bilingual education programs. In R. JACOBSON and C. FALTIS (eds) *Language Distribution Issues in Bilingual Schooling.* Clevedon: Multilingual Matters.

RAMIREZ, J.D., YUEN, S.D. and RAMEY, D.R. 1991, *Final Report: Longitudinal Study of Structured English Immersion Strategy, Early-exit and Late-exit Programs for Language-minority Children. Report Submitted to the US Department of Education.* San Mateo, CA: Aguirre International.

RANSDELL, S.E. and FISCHLER, I. 1987, Memory in a monolingual mode: When are bilinguals at a disadvantage. *Journal of Memory and Language* 26, 392–405.

RANSDELL, S.E. and FISCHLER, I. 1989, Effects of concreteness and task context on recall of prose among bilingual and monolingual speakers. *Journal of Memory and Language* 28, 278–291.

REBUFFOT, J. 1993, *Le Point sur L'Immersion au Canada.* Anjou, Québec: Centre Éducatif et Culturel.

REID, S. 1993, *Lament for a Nation: The Life and Death of Canada's Bilingual Dream.* Vancouver: Arsenal Pulp Press.

RESNICK, L.B. and RESNICK, D.P. 1992, Assessing the thinking curriculum: New tools for educational reform. In B.R. GIFFORD and M.C. O'CONNOR (eds) *Changing Assessments: Alternative Views of Aptitude, Achievement and Instruction.* Boston: Kluwer.

RESNICK, M.C. 1993, ESL and language planning in Puerto Rican education. *TESOL Quarterly* 27 (2), 259–275.

REYNOLDS, A.G. 1991, The cognitive consequences of bilingualism. In A.G. REYNOLDS (ed.) *Bilingualism, Multiculturalism and Second Language Learning.* Hillsdale, NJ: Lawrence Erlbaum.

REYNOLDS, D. (ed.) 1985, *Studying School Effectiveness*. Lewes, East Sussex: Falmer.

REYNOLDS, P. 1971, *A Primer in Theory Construction*. Indianapolis: Bobbs-Meirill.

RICCIARDELLI, L.A. 1992, Creativity and bilingualism. *Journal of Creative Behavior* 26 (4), 242–254.

RICHARDS, J.C. and ROGERS, T.S. 1986, *Approaches and Methods in Language Teaching*. Cambridge: Cambridge University Press.

RINGBOM, H. 1985, *Foreign Language Learning and Bilingualism*. Turku: Abo Akademi.

RIPPBERGER, S.J. 1993, Ideological shifts in bilingual education: Mexico and the United States. *Comparative Education Review* 37 (1), 50–61.

RIVERA, C. (ed.) 1984, *Language Proficiency and Academic Achievement*. Clevedon: Multilingual Matters.

ROBERTS, C. 1985, Teaching and learning commitment in bilingual schools. Unpublished PhD thesis, University of Wales.

ROBERTS, C. 1987, Political conflict over bilingual initiatives: A case study. *Journal of Multilingual and Multicultural Development* 8 (4), 311–322.

ROBERTS, G. 1994, Nurse/patient communication within a bilingual health care setting. *British Journal of Nursing* 3 (2), 60–67.

ROBSON, A. 1995, The assessment of bilingual children. In M.K. VERMA, K.P. CORRIGAN and S. FIRTH. (eds) *Working with Bilingual Children*. Clevedon: Multilingual Matters.

ROMAINE, S. 1995, *Bilingualism*. Oxford: Basil Blackwell.

RONJAT, J. 1913, *Le developpement du langage observe chez un enfant bilingue*. Paris: Champion.

ROSENTHAL, R. 1966, *Experimenter Effects in Behavioral Research*. New York: Appleton-Century-Crofts.

ROSIER, P. and HOLM, W. 1980, *The Rock Point Experience: A Longitudinal Study of a Navajo School Program*. Washington, DC: Center for Applied Linguistics.

ROSSELL, C.H. 1992, Nothing matters?: A critique of the Ramirez *et al.* longitudinal study of instructional programs for language-minority children. *Bilingual Research Journal* 16 (1&2), 159–186.

RUBAGUMYA, C.M. 1990, *Language in Education in Africa*. Clevedon: Multilingual Matters.

RUBAGUMYA, C.M. (ed.) 1994, *Teaching and Researching Language in African Classrooms*. Clevedon: Multilingual Matters.

RUBIN, J. 1977, Attitudes toward language planning. In C.C. ELERT *et al.* (eds) *Dialectology and Sociolinguistics*. UMEA: UMEA Studies in the Humanities 12.

RUEDA, R. 1983, Metalinguistic awareness in monolingual and bilingual mildly retarded children. *NABE Journal* 8, 55–68.

RUIZ, R. 1984, Orientations in language planning. *NABE Journal* 8 (2), 15–34.

SAER, D.J. 1922, An inquiry into the effect of bilingualism upon the intelligence of young children. *Journal of Experimental Pedagogy* 6, 232–240 and 266–274.

SAER, D.J. 1923, The effects of bilingualism on intelligence. *British Journal of Psychology* 14, 25–38.

SAER, D.J., SMITH, F. and HUGHES, J. 1924, *The Bilingual Problem.* Wrexham: Hughes and Son.

SAIF, P.S. and SHELDON, M.E. 1969, *An Investigation of the Experimental French Program at Bedford Park and Allenby Public Schools.* Toronto: Toronto Board of Education.

SANKOFF, G. 1972, Language use in multilingual societies. In J.B. PRIDE and J. HOLMES (eds) *Sociolinguistics: Selected Readings.* Harmondsworth: Penguin.

SAUNDERS, G. 1988, *Bilingual Children: From Birth to Teens.* Clevedon: Multilingual Matters.

SCHERMERHORN, R.A. 1970, *Comparative Ethnic Relations.* New York: Random House.

SCHINKE-LLANO, L. 1989, Early childhood bilingualism: In search of explanation. *Studies in Second Language Acquisition (SSLA)* 11 (3), 223–240.

SCHLOSSMAN, S. 1983, Is there an American tradition of bilingual education? *American Journal of Education* 91, 139–186.

SCHUMANN, J. 1978, *The Pidginization Process: A Model for Second Language Acquisition.* Rowley, MA: Newbury House.

SECADA, W.G. 1991, Degree of bilingualism and arithmetic problem solving in Hispanic First Graders. *Elementary School Journal* 92 (2), 213–231.

SECADA, W.G. 1993, The political context of bilingual education in the United States. In B. ARIAS and U. CASANOVA (eds) *Bilingual Education: Politics, Research and Practice.* Berkeley, CA: McCutchan.

SECRETARY'S COMMISSION ON ACHIEVING NECESSARY SKILLS (SCANS) 1991, *What Work Requires of Schools. A SCANS Report for America 2000.* Washington, DC: US Department of Labor.

SELINKER, L., SWAIN, M. and DUMAS, G. 1975, The interlanguage hypothesis extended to children. *Language Learning* 25, 139–152.

SHARPE, P. 1994, A study of some of the environmental features found to be conducive to the bilingual development of pre-school children in Singapore. *Early Child Development and Care* 98, 59–72.

SHEILS, J. 1988, *Communication in the Modern Languages Curriculum.* Strasbourg: Council for Cultural Cooperation, Council of Europe.

SHOHAMY, E. 1983, The stability of the oral proficiency trait on the oral interview speaking test. *Language Learning* 33, 527–540.

SIERRA, J. and OLAZIREGI, I. 1989, *EIFE 2. Influence of Factors on the Learning of Basque.* Gasteiz, Spain: Central Publications Service of the Basque Government.

SIGUAN, M. and MACKEY, W.F. 1987, *Education and Bilingualism.* London: Kogan Page.

SINGLETON, D. 1989, *Language Acquisition: The Age Factor.* Clevedon: Multilingual Matters.

SKEHAN, P. 1986, Where does language aptitude come from? In P.M. MEARA (ed.) *Spoken Language.* London: CILT.

SKEHAN, P. 1988, Language testing. *Language Teaching,* 21 (January) 1–13 and (October) 211–22.

SKUTNABB-KANGAS, T. 1977, Language in the process of cultural assimilation and structural incorporation of linguistic minorities. In C.C. ELERT *et al.* (eds) *Dialectology and Sociolinguistics.* UMEA: UMEA Studies in the Humanities.

SKUTNABB-KANGAS, T. 1981, *Bilingualism or Not: The Education of Minorities.* Clevedon: Multilingual Matters.

SKUTNABB-KANGAS, T. 1991, Swedish strategies to prevent integration and national ethnic minorities. In O. GARCÍA (ed.) *Bilingual Education: Focusschrift in Honor of Joshua A. Fishman.* Amsterdam/Philadelphia: John Benjamins.

SKUTNABB-KANGAS, T. and CUMMINS, J. (eds) 1988, *Minority Education: From Shame to Struggle.* Clevedon: Multilingual Matters.

SKUTNABB-KANGAS, T. and PHILLIPSON, R. 1989, 'Mother tongue': The theoretical and sociopolitical construction of a concept. In U. AMMON (ed.) *Status and Function of Languages and Language Variety.* New York: W. de Gruyter.

SKUTNABB-KANGAS, T. and PHILLIPSON, R. (eds) 1994, *Linguistic Human Rights: Overcoming Linguistic Discrimination.* Berlin: Mouton de Gruyter.

SKUTNABB-KANGAS, T. and TOUKOMAA, P. 1976, *Teaching Migrant Children Mother Tongue and Learning the Language of the Host Country in the Context of the Socio-Cultural Situation of the Migrant Family.* Tampere, Finland: Tukimuksia Research Reports.

SLEETER, C.E. and GRANT, C.A. 1987, An analysis of multicultural education in the United States. *Harvard Educational Review* 57 (4), 421–444.

SMITH, D.J. and TOMLINSON, S. 1989, *The School Effect.* London: Policy Studies Institute.

SMITH, F. 1923, Bilingualism and mental development. *British Journal of Psychology* 13, 271–282.

SMITH, F. 1982, *Writing and the Writer.* London: Heinemann.

SNOW, C.E. and HOEFNAGEL-HÖHLE, M. 1978, The critical period for language acquisition: Evidence from second language learning. *Child Development* 49, 1114–1128.

SNOW, M.A. 1990, Instructional methodology in immersion foreign language education. In A.M. PADILLA, H.H. FAIRCHILD and C.M. VALADEZ (eds) *Foreign Language Education: Issues and Strategies.* London: Sage.

SPOLSKY, B. 1989a, Maori bilingual education and language revitalization. *Journal of Multilingual and Multicultural Development* 10 (2), 89–106.

SPOLSKY, B. 1989b, Review of '*Key Issues in Bilingualism and Bilingual Education*'. *Applied Linguistics* 10 (4), 449–451.

SPOLSKY, B. 1989c, *Conditions for Second Language Learning.* Oxford: Oxford University Press.

SPOLSKY, B. and COOPER, R. (eds) 1977, *Frontiers of Bilingual Education.* Rowley, MA: Newbury House.

SRIDHAR, K.K. 1991, Bilingual education in India. In O. GARCÍA (ed.) *Bilingual Education: Focusschrift in Honor of Joshua A. Fishman.* Amsterdam/Philadelphia: John Benjamins.

STERN, H.H. 1983a, *Fundamental Concepts of Language Teaching*. Oxford: Oxford University Press.

STERN, H.H. 1983b, Toward a multidimensional foreign language curriculum. In R.G. MEAD (ed.) *Northeast Conference on the Teaching of Foreign Languages. Foreign Languages: Key Links in the Chain of Learning*. Middlebury, VT: Northeast Conference.

STERN, H.H. 1984, A quiet language revolution: Second language teaching in Canadian contexts: Achievements and new directions. *Canadian Modern Language Review* 40 (5), 506–524.

STERN, H.H. 1992, *Issues and Options in Language Teaching*. Oxford: Oxford University Press.

STERNBERG, R.J. 1985, *Beyond IQ: A Triarchic Theory of Human Intelligence*. Cambridge: Cambridge University Press.

STERNBERG, R.J. 1988, *The Triarchic Mind: A New Theory of Human Intelligence*. New York: Viking.

STREET, B.V. 1984, *Literacy in Theory and Practice*. Cambridge: Cambridge University Press.

STREET, B.V. 1994, What is meant by local literacies. *Language and Education* 8 (1&2), 9–17.

STOTZ, D. and ANDRES, F. 1990, Problems in developing bilingual education programs in Switzerland. *Multilingua* 9 (1), 113–136.

STRONG, M. 1995, A review of bilingual/bicultural programs for deaf children in North America. *American Annals of the Deaf* 140 (2), 84–94.

STUBBS, M. 1991, Educational language planning in England and Wales: Multicultural rhetoric and assimilationist assumptions. In F. COULMAS (ed.) *A Language Policy for the European Community*. New York: Mouton de Gruyter. Also in O. GARCÍA and C. BAKER (eds) 1995, *Policy and Practice in Bilingual Education: A Reader Extending the Foundations*. Clevedon: Multilingual Matters.

SWAIN, M. 1972, Bilingualism as a first language. Unpublished PhD dissertation, University of California, Irvine.

SWAIN, M. 1985, Communicative competence: Some roles of comprehensible input and comprehensible output in its development. In S. GASS and C. MADDEN (eds) *Input in Second Language Acquisition*. Rowley, MA: Newbury House.

SWAIN, M. 1986, Communicative competence: Some roles of comprehensible input and comprehensible output in its development. In J. CUMMINS and M. SWAIN 1986, *Bilingualism in Education*. New York: Longman.

SWAIN, M. 1993, The output hypothesis: Just speaking and writing aren't enough. *Canadian Modern Language Review* 50, 158–164.

SWAIN, M. and LAPKIN, S. 1982, *Evaluating Bilingual Education: A Canadian Case Study*. Clevedon: Multilingual Matters.

SWAIN, M. and LAPKIN, S. 1991a, Additive bilingualism and French immersion education: The roles of language proficiency and literacy. In A.G. REYNOLDS (ed.) *Bilingualism, Multiculturalism and Second Language Learning*. Hillsdale, NJ: Lawrence Erlbaum.

SWAIN, M. and LAPKIN, S. 1991b, Heritage language children in an English–French bilingual program. *Canadian Modern Languages Review* 47 (4), 635–641.

SWAIN, M., LAPKIN, S., ROWEN, N. and HART, D. 1990, The role of mother tongue literacy in third language learning. *Language, Culture and Curriculum* 3 (1), 65–81.

TAKAKI, R. 1993, Multiculturalism: Battleground or meeting ground? *Annals of the American Academy of Political and Social Science* 530, 109–121.

TANSLEY, P. and CRAFT, A. 1984, Mother tongue teaching and support: A Schools Council enquiry. *Journal of Multilingual and Multicultural Development* 5 (5), 367–384.

TARONE, E. 1980, Communication strategies, foreigner talk and repair in interlanguage. *Language Learning* 30, 417–431.

TAYLOR, D.M. 1991, The social psychology of racial and cultural diversity. In A.G. REYNOLDS (ed.) *Bilingualism, Multiculturalism and Second Language Learning.* Hillsdale, NJ: Lawrence Erlbaum.

TAYLOR, D.M., CRAGO, M.B. and McALPINE, L. 1993, Education in Aboriginal communities: Dilemmas around empowerment. *Canadian Journal of Native Education* 20 (1), 176–183.

THOMAS, J. 1988, The role played by metalinguistic awareness in second and third language learning. *Journal of Multilingual and Multicultural Development* 9, 235–247.

THOMAS, W.P. 1992, An analysis of the research methodology of the Ramirez Report. *Bilingual Research Journal* 16 (1&2), 213–245.

THOMAS, W.P., COLLIER, V.P. and ABBOTT, M. 1993, Academic achievement through Japanese, Spanish or French: The first two years of partial immersion. *Modern Language Journal* 77 (2), 170–179.

TIKUNOFF, W.J. 1983, *Compatibility of the SBIF Features With Other Research Instruction of LEP Students.* San Francisco: Far West Laboratory.

TODD, R. 1991, *Education in a Multicultural Society.* London: Cassell.

TOLLEFSON, J.W. 1991, *Planning Language, Planning Inequality.* London: Longman.

TOLLEFSON, J.W. (ed.) 1995, *Power and Inequality in Language Education.* Cambridge: Cambridge University Press.

TOMLINSON, S. 1986, Ethnicity and educational achievement. In S. MODGIL, G. VERMA, K. MALLICK and C. MODGIL (eds) *Multicultural Education. The Interminable Debate.* London: Falmer.

TORRANCE, E.P. 1974a, *Torrance Tests of Creative Thinking: Directions Manual and Scoring Guide.* Lexington, MA: Ginn.

TORRANCE, E.P. 1974b, *Torrance Tests of Creative Thinking: Norms-Technical Manual.* Lexington, MA: Ginn.

TORRES, G. 1991, Active teaching and learning in the bilingual classroom: The child as an active subject in learning to write. In O. GARCÍA (ed.) *Bilingual Education: Focusschrift in Honor of Joshua A. Fishman.* Amsterdam/Philadelphia: John Benjamins.

TOSI, A. 1983, *Immigration and Bilingual Education.* Oxford: Pergamon.

TOSI, A. 1988, The jewel in the crown of the modern prince: The new approach to bilingualism in multicultural education in England. In T. SKUTNABB-KANGAS and J. CUMMINS (eds) *Minority Education: From Shame to Struggle*. Clevedon: Multilingual Matters.

TOSI, A. 1991, High-status and low-status bilingualism in Europe. *Journal of Education* 173 (2), 21–37.

TOUKOMAA, P. and SKUTNABB-KANGAS, T. 1977, *The Intensive Teaching of the Mother Tongue to Migrant Children at Pre-school Age* (Research Report No. 26). Department of Sociology and Social Psychology, University of Tampere.

TREMBLAY, R. *et al.* 1989, *Se lancer en affaires avec un jeu*. Winnipeg: Canadian Association of Second Language Teachers.

TROIKE, R.C., 1978, Research evidence for the effectiveness of bilingual education. *NABE Journal* 3 (1), 13–24.

TRUEBA, H.T. 1988, Culturally based explanations of minority students' academic achievement. *Anthropological and Education Quarterly* 19, 270–287.

TRUEBA, H.T. 1989, *Raising Silent Voices: Educating the Linguistic Minorities for the 21st Century*. New York: Newbury House.

TRUEBA, H.T. 1991, The role of culture in bilingual instruction. In O. GARCÍA (ed.) *Bilingual Education: Focusschrift in Honor of Joshua A. Fishman (Volume 1)*. Amsterdam/Philadelphia: John Benjamins.

TUCKER, G.R. and d'ANGLEJAN, A. 1972, An approach to bilingual education: The St Lambert Experiment. In M. SWAIN (ed.) *Bilingual Schooling: Some Experiences in Canada and the United States*. Ontario: Ontario Institute for Studies in Education Symposium Series/1.

TUNMER, W.E. and HERRIMAN, M.L. 1984, The development of metalinguistic awareness: A conceptual overview. In W.E. TUNMER, C. PRATT and M.L. HERRIMAN (eds) *Metalinguistic Awareness in Children*. Berlin: Springer-Verlag.

TUNMER, W.E. and MYHILL, M.E. 1984, Metalinguistic awareness and bilingualism. In W.E. TUNMER, C. PRATT and M.L. HERRIMAN (eds) *Metalinguistic Awareness in Children*. Berlin: Springer-Verlag.

TUNMER, W.E., PRATT, C. and HARRIMAN, M.L. (eds) 1984, *Metalinguistic Awareness in Children: Theory, Research and Implications*. Berlin: Springer-Verlag.

UNITED NATIONS EDUCATIONAL, SCIENTIFIC AND CULTURAL ORGANIZATION (UNESCO) 1953, *The Use of Vernacular Languages in Education*. Paris: UNESCO.

UNITED NATIONS EDUCATIONAL, SCIENTIFIC AND CULTURAL ORGANIZATION (UNESCO) 1991, *World Education Report 1991*. Paris: UNESCO.

UNITED STATES DEPARTMENT OF EDUCATION 1992, *The Condition of Bilingual Education in the Nation: A Report to the Congress and the President*. Washington, DC: Department of Education.

VAID, J. and HALL, D.G. 1991, Neuropsychological perspectives on bilingualism: Right, left and center. In A.G. REYNOLDS (ed.) *Bilingualism, Multiculturalism and Second Language Learning*. Hillsdale, NJ: Lawrence Erlbaum.

VALDÉS, G. and FIGUEROA, R.A. 1994, *Bilingualism and Testing: A Special Case of Bias*. Norwood, NJ: Ablex.

VAN EK, J.A. 1986, *Objectives for Foreign Language Learning. Volume I: Scope*. Strasbourg: Council of Europe.

VAN EK, J.A. 1987, *Objectives for Foreign Language Learning. Volume II: Levels*. Strasbourg: Council of Europe.

VARESE, S. 1990, Challenge and prospects for Indian education in Mexico. *Prospects (UNESCO)* 20 (3), 345–356.

VERHOEVEN, L.T. 1994, Transfer in bilingual development: The linguistic interdependence hypothesis revisited. *Language Learning* 44 (3), 381–415.

VERMA, M.K., CORROGAN, K.P. and FIRTH, S. (eds) 1995, *Working With Bilingual Children*. Clevedon: Multilingual Matters.

VYGOTSKY, L.S. 1962, *Thought and Language*. Cambridge, MA: MIT Press.

WAGGONER, D. 1988, Language minorities in the United States in the 1980s. In S.L. McKAY and S.C. WONG (eds) *Language Diversity: Problem or Resource?* New York: Newbury House.

WAGNER, S.T. 1980, The historical background of bilingualism and biculturalism in the United States. In M. RIDGE (ed.) *The New Bilingualism*. Los Angeles: University of Southern California Press.

WALDMAN, I. 1994, Bilingual administrative support personnel in United States corporations. *The Modern Language Journal* 78 (3), 327–338.

WEINREICH, U. 1970, *Languages in Contact: Findings and Problems*. The Hague: Mouton.

WELLS, G. 1986, *The Meaning Makers: Children Learning Language and Using Language to Learn*. London: Heinemann.

WELLS, G. and CHANG-WELLS, G.L. 1992, *Constructing Knowledge Together: Classrooms as Centers of Inquiry and Literacy*. Portsmouth, NH: Heinemann.

WESCHE, M.B. 1993, French immersion graduates at university and beyond: What difference has it made? In J.M. ALATIS (ed.) *The Georgetown Roundtable on Languages and Linguistics 1992*. Washington, DC: Georgetown University Press.

WHITMORE, K. F. and CROWELL, C. C. 1994, *Inventing a Classroom. Life in a Bilingual Whole Language Community*. York, ME: Stenhouse.

WIDDOWSON, H. 1978, *Teaching Language as Communication*. Oxford: Oxford University Press.

WILKINS, D.A. 1976, *Notional Syllabuses*. Oxford: Oxford University Press.

WILLIAMS, C.H. 1991a, Language planning and social change: Ecological speculations. In D.F. MARSHALL (ed.) *Language Planning Volume III*. Philadelphia: John Benjamins BV.

WILLIAMS, C.H. 1991b, *The Cultural Rights of Minorities: Recognition and Implementation* (Discussion Papers in Geolinguistics No. 18). Staffordshire: Staffordshire Polytechnic.

WILLIAMS, G. 1992, *Sociolinguistics: A Sociological Critique*. London: Routledge.

WILLIAMS, J.D. and SNIPPER, G.C. 1990, *Literacy and Bilingualism*. New York: Longman.

WILLIG, A.C. 1981/82, The effectiveness of bilingual education: Review of a report. *NABE Journal* 6 (2&3), 1–19.

WILLIG, A.C. 1985, A meta-analysis of selected studies on the effectiveness of bilingual education. *Review of Educational Research* 55 (3), 269–317.

WILLIG, A.C. and RAMIREZ, J.D. 1993, The evaluation of bilingual education. In B. ARIAS and U. CASANOVA (eds) *Bilingual Education: Politics, Research and Practice.* Berkeley, CA: McCutchan.

WILLIG, C.J. 1990, *Children's Concepts and the Primary Curriculum.* London: Paul Chapman.

WITKIN, H.A. *et al.* 1962, *Psychological Differentiation.* New York: John Wiley.

WITKIN, H.A. *et al.* 1971, *A Manual for the Embedded Figures Test.* Palo Alto, CA: Consulting Psychologists Press.

WONG FILLMORE, L. 1979, Individual differences in second language acquisition. In C. FILLMORE, D. KEMPLER and W. WANG (eds) *Individual Differences in Language Ability and Language Behavior.* New York: Academic Press.

WONG FILLMORE, L. 1982, Instructional language as linguistic input: Second language learning in classrooms. In L. WILKINSON (ed.) *Communicating in the Classroom.* New York: Academic Press.

WONG FILLMORE, L. 1991a, When losing a second language means losing the first. *Early Childhood Research Quarterly* 6, 323–346.

WONG FILLMORE, L. 1991b, Second-language learning in children: A model of language learning in social context. In E. BIALYSTOK (ed.) *Language Processing in Bilingual Children.* Cambridge: Cambridge University Press.

WONG FILLMORE, L. and VALADEZ, C. 1986, Teaching bilingual learners. In M.C. WITTROCK (ed.) *Handbook of Research on Teaching* (3rd ed). New York: Macmillan.

WORLD BANK 1982, *The Use of First and Second Languages in Primary Education:* Selected Case Studies (World Bank Staff Working Paper No. 504). Washington, DC: World Bank.

YATIM, A.M. 1988, Some factors affecting bilingualism amongst trainee teachers in Malaysia. Unpublished PhD thesis, University of Wales.

YOUNG, R.M. 1987, Interpreting the production of science. In D. GILL and L. LEVIDOV (eds) *Anti-Racist Science Teaching.* London: Free Association Books.

ZAPPERT, L.T. and CRUZ, B.R. 1977, *Bilingual Education: An Appraisal of Empirical Research.* Berkeley, CA: Bay Area Bilingual Education League.

ZENTELLA, A.C. 1988, The language situation of the Puerto Ricans. In S.L. McKAY and S.C. WONG (eds) *Language Diversity: Problem or Recourse.* New York: Newbury House.

ZONDAG, K. 1991, Bilingual education in Friesland from the innovator's point of view. In O. GARCÍA (ed.) *Bilingual Education: Focusschrift in Honor of Joshua A. Fishman.* Amsterdam/Philadelphia: John Benjamins.

ZUNIGA, M. 1990, Educational policies and experiments among indigenous populations in Peru. *Prospects (UNESCO)* 20 (3), 365–376.

Author Index

Taylor, S., 288
Terrell, T., 113, 114
Théberge, R., 102
Thomas, J., 228
Thomas, W., 193, 215
Tikunoff, W., 220
Todd, R., 384
Tollefson, J., 110
Tomlinson, S., 219, 251
Toohey, K., 185, 186
Torrance, E., 129
Torres, G., 323
Torres-Guzmán, M., 328, 392
Tosi, A., 195, 196, 365
Toukomaa, P., 11, 148
Tremblay, R., 288
Troike, R., 203, 213
Trueba, H., 218, 252, 253, 348, 355, 357,
    363, 387, 390, 391, 392
Tucker, G., 136, 138, 180, 181
Tunmer, W., 134

United Nations Educational, Scientific and
    Cultural Organization (UNESCO), 27, 227
United States Department of Education, 216
Ury, W., 88

Vaid, J., 124, 125
Valadez, C., 248
Valdés, G., 25, 33, 265, 270, 272
Valencia, J., 228
van Beeck, H., 55
van Ek, J., 277, 284, 285
Varese, S., 390

Vaughan, P., 390
Verhoeven, L., 228, 345
Verma, M., 390
Vygotsky, L., 139, 300

Wagner, S., 176
Waldman, L., 61
Weinreich, U., 15
Wells, G., 294, 295, 301, 312, 318, 323
Wells, M., 173
Wesche, M., 206
Whitmore, K., 297, 312, 392
Widdowson, H., 285
Wilkins, D., 285
Williams, C., 41, 42, 368
Williams, G., 37, 73, 110
Williams, J., 323
Willig, A., 213, 214, 216
Willig, C., 318
Witkin, H., 137
Wong Fillmore, L., 80, 81, 98, 99, 111, 152,
    248
Wong, S.C., 371, 387, 390, 391
Woodward, J., 255, 260
World Bank, 200

Yatim, A., 105
Young, R., 383
Yuen, S., 214, 215, 223

Zappert, L., 203, 213
Zentella, A., 90
Zondag, K., 390
Zuniga, M., 390

Subject Index

Ability in language, 5f
Academic language competence, 10f
Accommodation theory, 109f
Acculturation model, 108f
Achievement in language, 5
Acquisition planning, 65
Additive bilingualism, 66, 101f, 334, 346
Adult language learning, 83f
Age, 84f
Aims of bilingual education, 173f
Anti-racism, 374f, 384f
Anxiety, 106, 210
Aptitude, 101f
Assessment, 260f, 265f, 281
Assimilation, 173, 176, 242, 275, 264f, 375f
Asymmetrical principle, 39
Attitudes, 41f, 89, 101f, 206, 209
Audiolingualism, 282f
Australia, 184
Autonomous minorities, 362

Balance theory, 145f
Balanced bilinguals, 8, 122, 130
Basal readers, 298f
Basques, 184
BICS, 151f
Bilingual Education Act, 169f
Biliteracy, 315f
Boundaries, 38, 48, 190f, 232f
Brain, 124f
Brunei, 193f

CALP, 151f

Canada, 180f, 203f, 289f, 331f, 369f
Caretaker speech, 335
Caste-like minorities, 362f
Catalan, 184
Census, 18, 22, 54
Civil rights, 168, 356, 364
Codeswitching, 86f, 234
Common underlying proficiency, 147f
Communicative language, 25f, 283f
Communicative sensitivity, 136f
Community, 35f, 56, 61, 73, 78, 83, 243, 305, 346
Competence in language, 5, 28, 30f
Conceptual map, 400
Concurrent language use, 237f
Conflict paradigm, 368f
Content reduced communication, 151f
Context, 23, 36, 96, 97, 219, 281, 300, 341f
Context embedded communication, 151f
Conversational fluency, 10f
Corpus planning, 65
Creative thinking, 129f
Criterion referenced tests, 27f, 270
Critical literacy, 306f
Cuban, 169, 192
Cultural pluralism, 63, 365f, 378f
Culture, 64f, 108f, 231f, 277, 289, 301f, 332

Deaf bilinguals, 241f
Developmental maintenance education, 184f, 208f
Diglossia, 36f
Divergent thinking, 129f

444